FOR REFERENCE

Do Not Take From This Room

COMPENDIUM OF THE
WORLD'S LANGUAGES

COMPENDIUM
OF THE
WORLD'S
LANGUAGES

BY

GEORGE L. CAMPBELL

ROUTLEDGE

LONDON AND NEW YORK

First published 1991
by Routledge
11 New Fetter Lane, London EC4P 4EE

Simultaneously published in the USA and Canada
by Routledge
a division of Routledge, Chapman and Hall, Inc.
29 West 35th Street, New York, NY 10001

© George Campbell 1991

Typeset by Computype Limited, Horton Parade, Horton Road,
West Drayton, Middlesex UB7 8EP

Printed in England by Clays Ltd, St Ives plc

British Library Cataloguing in Publication Data

Campbell, George L.
Compendium of the world's languages.
1. Languages. Dictionaries
I. Title
413

ISBN 0-415-02937-6 (set)
ISBN 0-415-06978-5 (Volume I)
ISBN 0-415-06979-3 (Volume II)

Library of Congress Cataloging-in-Publication Data

Campbell, George L.
Compendium of the world's languages / George L. Campbell.
p.   cm.
Includes bibliographical references.
1. Language and languages.   I. Title.
P371.C36 1990   90-35827
401'.2—dc20   CIP

CONTENTS

INTRODUCTION

'Les langues imparfaites,' complained Mallarmé, 'en cela que plusieurs, manque la suprême.' ('Languages [are] imperfect, in that there are many [of them], [but] the supreme [one] is lacking.') (*Variations sur un sujet: Crise de Vers.*) In some ways, this is a puzzling remark. Exactly what does *plusieurs* refer to? If it is to the multiplicity of natural languages, there need be no disagreement, on this point at least. Languages have indeed proliferated on the planet; the most recent and most comprehensive count (Merritt Ruhlen, 1988) records around five thousand languages which are or have been spoken, some by many millions, most by several thousands, and some by only a few hundred people. We have no way of gauging how many languages, once existent, have now vanished without trace. It seems unlikely, however, that Mallarmé had made first-hand acquaintance with all or even many of the natural languages, or had been able to assess in what degree they fell short of perfection. One might have expected him to find much to his taste in Classical Chinese or Classical Arabic poetry. Moreover, how and why could or should one natural language be 'supreme'.

The sentence begins perhaps to make more sense if we take *plusieurs* to refer to *levels* of language, particularly since Mallarmé goes on to deplore the *numéraire facile* – the 'easy currency' – of everyday speech, which is non-convertible into *la notion pure*. Given this non-convertibility, it is the poet's job to transcend natural language and communication by providing what Mallarmé calls *un complément supérieur* – a 'higher complement'. In Mallarmé's hands, this higher integration functions in a realm of autonomous verbal creativity, yielding a kind of cerebral algebra of images, hardly if at all anchored in the world of everyday experience and communication. It is a construct which we acclaim as arcane and beautiful poetry.

But the *numéraire facile* rejected by Mallarmé as 'imperfect' represents something even more mysterious and far more valuable: the original mapping of the shared human environment and shared human experience onto the plane of speech. This construct is initiated and sustained by an innate human competence, whose nature we can hardly even guess at. Key factors in the mapping are the remembered use of words, and their division into constants which can be transposed, and operators and operational codes which cannot.

The 'easy currency' has enabled man *qua* Robinson Crusoe to plot his position, catalogue his possessions, and tabulate his actions. Far from being divorced from natural experience, natural language might be defined as the audible inventory of that experience, and words are its bench-marks. In contrast, the conscious creation of alternative and idiosyncratic worlds has to do rather with a secondary mimetic mapping from the spoken to the written plane. This was perfectly clear to Mallarmé himself: 'Tout, au monde, existe pour aboutir à un livre.' (Everything, in the world, exists to end up in/as a book.) (*Variations sur un sujet: Quant au Livre.*)

The natural inventory is not, of course, entirely homogeneous. There are local nuances of modality and circumstance. This or that facet of a nominal or verbal event is stressed in one language, ignored in another. Thus, where Indo-European languages tend to use adjectival and adverbial modifiers, in many American Indian languages such information inheres in the verb stem itself. In verbal systems, some languages adopt the standpoint of temporal sequence – tense, that is – while others prefer to make an aspectual distinction between completed and uncompleted action. But these are surface variations. From the Egyptian, Sumerian, and Archaic Chinese of 3000 BC to modern Russian, German, and Arabic, from Old Norse and Sanskrit to Navajo and Quechua, there is a general consensus on the fundamental parameters of existence: the spatio-temporal matrix, and the kinetic operational paradigms which underlie the surface diversity. *Vis-à-vis* Mallarmé's *notion pure* and *complément supérieur*, the world's natural languages may indeed be askew; but they are orthogonalities for their users, and none is superfluous. As Sir Thomas Browne said: 'There are no Grotesques in Nature, not anything framed to fill up empty Cantons and unnecessary spaces.'

The construct yielded by the primary mapping is not immutable. Over long periods of time, phonological and morphological systems are subject to superficial erosion and replacement. Declensions are reduced, class and gender taxonomies are amended, verbal structures simplified. Essential linguistic profiles do not seem to be affected. The relative brevity of the written record, with a cut-off point at around the third millennium BC, limits our perspectives here; extrapolation is risky. But it is difficult to imagine that Chinese was, or ever could be, 'like' Sanskrit, or Hawaiian like Ket, though the same 'generative template' underlies all four.

Innovation where it occurs is largely a surface phenomenon, involving transposition of constants, and local differentiation. Like Mallarmé, the great Tang poet Tu Fu can score brilliant aesthetic effects by transposing semantic nuclei – in Chinese, a far more radical step than it is in French (see, for example, lines 5–6 of *Wàng yuè*, 'On a Prospect of T'ai-Shan', in David Hawkes (1967) *A Little Primer of Tu Fu*, Oxford University Press). Arabic, on the other hand, prefers to make novel, not to say unheard-of, utterances via a cerebral play upon words, and a kind of phonological mirror-imagery (see, for example, the *Maqāmāt*, the 'Assemblies', of the eleventh-century poet al-Ḥarīrī, especially Assembly 32). But essential linguistic profiles are not affected by such innovations; al-Ḥarīrī could no more insert the Arabic adjective between the article and the noun than Tu Fu could mark his verbs for gender, number, and person. If the surface diversity of languages is the main subject of this book, the underlying consensus emerges, it is hoped, as a corollary.

For reasons of space, certain other properties of language receive less than the attention due to them. For example, in a sense (not that of Mallarmé), words carry their own *complément supérieur* in the form of a mythopoeic potential or charge, which seems to be latent in them from the outset, and which is activated in literary creativity, and, most particularly, in any language which is the vehicle of a religion or taboo system. Words resonate beyond themselves into more or less adjacent semantic fields. Hugo van Hofmannsthal in his wisdom put it beautifully: 'und dennoch sagt der viel, der "Abend" sagt' ('and yet he says much, who says "evening"'; *Ballade des äuszeren Lebens*).

The first eight verses of Chapter 1 of St John's Gospel, which, where available, follow each article, serve not only to exemplify the language in question, but also to show how readily co-ordinates can be tacitly transformed, so that spatio-temporal markers that are meaningful in one frame of reference appear to remain semantically invariant, that is, meaningful, in another: '*in the* beginning', '*was the* Word', '*with* God'.

The late twentieth century has witnessed an increasing tendency for both primary and secondary mappings to cede status at least to a derivatory mapping – their instantaneous and infinite electronic multiplications, with or without visual display: 'I heard it on TV'. It is too early to assess the full implications of our reliance on images but we all know what happened to the Lady of Shalott when she was suddenly deprived of them.

The book as it now appears differs considerably from that originally planned. To begin with, publisher and compiler envisaged an alphabetical list of between five and six hundred languages, each entry to contain the relevant statistical information along with a note on genetic status and a phonological and morphological profile. It soon became apparent, however, that while this format was adequate for geographical, demographic and genetic detail, little of interest could be said, within such constraints, on precisely what it is that differentiates one language from another. Thereupon, phonological and morphological sections began to expand, full or partial paradigms were introduced; and, as the articles lengthened from two or three paragraphs to several pages, the list of entries shrank accordingly. Thus, for example, *Chontal*, *Nukuoro* and *Osage*, present on the original list, are now absent, while the Procrustean paragraph originally allotted to *Abkhaz* has grown to four, still inadequate, pages, and *Chinese* has spread from one page to twelve.

Herein, however, or such is my hope, lies any real usefulness the book may have. For, while it is not difficult for someone interested in a given language to find the relevant geographical and demographic facts concerning it, it is not always so easy to find a simple account in English of how it actually works – of its nuts and bolts. There is, of course, no shortage of books on the major languages of the West, or on the more important Oriental languages such as *Chinese*, *Japanese* and *Arabic*; and today's students are fortunate in having ready to hand such invaluable exotica as Hewitt's *Abkhaz*, Saltarelli's *Basque* and Aronson's *Georgian*, to name only three of the best examples. But the quixotically curious – those who might turn to a single reference work in the hope of finding out at one and the same time how the *Navajo* verb and the *Andi* nominal system work, why vowel harmony has been eroded in *Uzbek*, and what sort of script the

Cambodians use – are not so well catered for. It has been my hope and intention that this book should provide basic guidance in simple language, and point the reader, via the bibliography, towards the more competent and more detailed accounts, to which I gratefully acknowledge my indebtedness.

In general, the articles follow the same lay-out, sub-divided as follows:

1. *Head-word*: background note on the language, its affiliation, location and number of speakers; dialects; where relevant, some remarks on the literature of which it is the vehicle;
2. *Script*: if other than Roman, the script used by a language is described and displayed in a chart at the end of the book;
3. *Phonology*: for the most part, the phonological inventories are set out in terms of mode of utterance; that is, consonants are sub-divided into stops, affricates, fricatives, nasals, laterals, semi-vowels; vowels into oral and nasal series. In a few special cases, for example *Sanskrit*, a positional grid is used, showing the phonemes of the language in terms of labial, palatal, dental, retroflex, and velar series. This positional grid is also retained in the case of certain *Caucasian* languages, for example, which make a phonemic distinction between uvular, pharyngeal, and glottal series. Tone, if relevant, is also described here.

   Wherever possible, phonological inventories are in IPA symbols. Exceptions to this general rule are provided by languages, long dead, whose phonological values are conjectural, and by languages such as *Andamanese* or *Chimu* for which no IPA values seem to be available. Transcription is broad.
4. *Morphology and syntax*: the main sub-headings are: article; noun; adjective; pronoun; numerals; verb; pre/postpositions; word order. For reasons of space, only very general questions of syntax are taken up.
5. *Illustrative text*: verses 1 to 8 of the first chapter of St John's Gospel have been chosen as a suitable example, available in most of the languages described. Alternative biblical specimens are substituted, and identified, in cases where a translation of St John's Gospel is not available.

Selection and classification

My aim was to include all of the world's literary languages, along with certain other languages which, though lacking a written literature, were nevertheless felt to be of sufficient interest and importance to warrant inclusion. The list of 1,000 languages, given by David Crystal (1988) on pp. 436–44 of his *Encyclopaedia of Language*, served as a general base, extended where necessary by specialist works such as Bernard Comrie (1981), *The Languages of the Soviet Union*. In Crystal's list, the cut-off point for number of speakers is 10,000. I have included several languages with much smaller, even minimal tallies, e.g. certain members of the *Caucasian*, *Palaeo-Siberian* and *North American Indian* groupings.

Classification

Here again, I follow David Crystal's middle course between 'lumpers' – linguists who seek to identify genetic or at least typological relationships connecting ever wider and more numerous groups of languages – and 'splitters' – linguists who, on the contrary, sub-divide large putative groupings into smaller well-defined and demonstrably coherent units. Thus, the *Semito-Hamitic* languages are described as forming part of the *Afro-Asiatic* family, and *Bantu* as *Niger-Congo*; but *Indo-European* and *Japanese* are not classified as '*Euroasiatic*', nor are *Quechua* and *Cree* lumped together as '*Amerind*'. Nor is there, perhaps mistakenly, any mention of '*Nostratic*' or '*Austric*'.

Sources

The books which have been used in the preparation of this work are listed in the Bibliography. Examples in the text, mainly in the section on Morphology and Syntax, fall into two categories. In the case of languages with which I have worked over the years, examples are drawn partly from the standard works listed in the Bibliography, partly from other sources. In the case of languages with which I am not actively familiar, all examples are taken from the works listed. Thus, for example, all *Ainu* examples are from Refsing (1986); the *Nama* examples are from Hagman (1977); *Bambara* from Brauner (1974); *Samaritan* from Vil'sker (1974), and so on. I am especially indebted to two Russian collective works: *Jazyki Narodov SSSR* and *Jazyki Azii i Afriki*.

Permissions

The Mayan glyphs on p. 911 are reproduced from *Maya Treasures of an Ancient Civilization*, Harry N. Abrams and Albuquerque Museum, New York, 1985, redrawn by Dolona Roberts from *The Ancient Maya*, 4th edn, Sylvanus G. Morley and George W. Brainerd, revised by Robert J. Sharer, with the permission of the publishers, Stanford University Press, © 1946, 1947, 1956, 1983, by the Board of Trustees of the Leland Stanford Junior University.

Bishop Landau's Mayan alphabet in the Appendix of Scripts is reproduced from Figure 60 of *Deciphering the Maya Script*, David H. Kelley, University of Texas Press, © 1976, by permission of the publisher.

In conclusion, I wish to express my gratitude to all those who have helped to make this book possible: to Wendy Morris for initiating the project, and to Jonathan Price and his colleagues at Routledge – Mina Patria, Shan Millie, Emma Waghorn, Nigel Marsh, Susie Hilsdon, Judith Watts – for seeing it through its various stages; to Jenny Potts, for her meticulous copy-editing; to Richard Caesar, Simone Osborn, and the skilled typesetters of Computype for coping so beautifully with a most forbidding manuscript; to Monotype for their co-operation in providing characters for the Appendix of Scripts; my wife for providing the bibliography; and to Alan Jesson and Gerry Bye of Cambridge University Library, who supplied the New Testament specimen passages appended to most of the articles.

G.L.C.

ABBREVIATIONS

abl.	ablative	fam.	familiar
abs.	absolute	fem.	feminine
acc.	accusative	Fin.	Finnish
adess.	adessive	Fr.	French
adit.	aditive	fut.	future
affirm.	affirmative		
Afr.	Afrikaans	gen.	genitive
anim.	animate	Gk	Greek
Ar.	Arabic	Gm.	German
Assyr.	Assyrian		
aux.	auxiliary	hon.	honorific
Av.	Avestan		
Azer.	Azerbaydzhani	IE	Indo-European
		illat.	illative
Bel.	Belorussian	imper.	imperative
BI	Banasa Indonesian	imperf.	imperfect
BP	Brazilian Portuguese	impers.	impersonal
		inanim.	inanimate
Ch.	Chinese	incl.	inclusive
Ch.Ap.	Chiricahua Apache	Ind.	Indonesian
Chip.	Chipewyan	indef.	indefinite
cl.	class	iness.	inessive
CL	Classical Latin	instr.	instrumental
com.	comitative	It.	Italian
comp.	comparative		
conj.	conjunctive	Jap.	Japanese
D	Dutch	K	Krama (Javanese)
dat.	dative		
def.	definite	Lat.	Latin
dep.	dependent	lk	link
		loc.	locative
EArm.	Eastern Armenian		
EP	European Portuguese	masc.	masculine
erg.	ergative	ME	Middle English
ESlav.	Eastern Slavonic	MF	Middle French
excl.	exclusive	MSC	Modern Standard Chinese

N	Ngoko (Javanese)	pron.	pronoun
Nav.	Navajo	prox.	proximate
neg.	negative		
neut.	neuter	refl.	reflexive
nom.	nominative	rel.	relative
		Romy	Romany
O/obj.	object	Russ.	Russian
obl.	oblique		
obv.	obviative	S/sbj.	subject
OE	Old English	SC	Serbo-Croat
OF	Old French	sing.	singular
OI	Old Irish	Skt	Sanskrit
Old Ch.	Old Church	Sl.	Slovene
Slav.	Slavonic	Slav.	Slavonic
opt.	optative	Som.	Somali
Osc.	Oscan	Sp.	Spanish
		SSlav.	Southern Slavonic
p.	person	subj.	subjunctive
part.	partitive		
pass.	passive	trans.	transitive
perf.	perfective		
pl.	plural	Ukr.	Ukrainian
Pol.	Polynesian		
poss.	possessive	V	verb
pp.	past participle	Viet.	Vietnamese
prep.	preposition(al)	VN	verbal noun
pres.	present	voc.	vocative
pret.	preterite		
prog.	progressive	WArm.	Western Armenian

LIST OF LANGUAGES

The use of bold type or small capital letters indicates that there is an article on an individual language or language family respectively. Normal type indicates that a language is covered within an article on the cross-referenced language or language family, or is an alternative name for that language.

Abaza
Abelam *see* PAPUAN LANGUAGES
Abkhaz
ABKHAZ-ADYGE LANGUAGES
Aceh *see* **Achinese**
Achinese
Adamawa Eastern *see* NIGER-CONGO LANGUAGES
Adyge
Afrikaans
Agul
Ahom *see* **Assamese**
Ainu
Āka-Bēa-da *see* **Andamanese**
Akan
Ākar-Bālē *see* **Andamanese**
Akhvakh *see* ANDI LANGUAGES
Akkadian
Albanian
Aleut
ALTAIC LANGUAGES
Altay
Alyutor *see* **Koryak;** PALAEO-SIBERIAN LANGUAGES
Amharic
ANATOLIAN LANGUAGES

Andamanese
ANDEAN-EQUATORIAL LANGUAGES
ANDI LANGUAGES
Anglo-Saxon *see* **English**
Ao *see* NAGA LANGUAGES
Apabhraṁśa *see* **Prakrit**
Apache
Arabic
Aramaic *see* SEMITIC LANGUAGES
Arapaho
Araucarian *see* **Mapudungu**
Arawakan *see* ANDEAN-EQUATORIAL LANGUAGES
Ardhamāgadhī *see* **Prakrit**
Arin *see* **Ket**
Armenian, Classical
Armenian, Modern Standard
Aromanian *see* **Romanian**
Ashkenazi *see* **Yiddish**
Aṣkun *see* DARDIC LANGUAGES
Asmat *see* PAPUAN LANGUAGES
Assamese
Assan *see* **Ket**
Assyrian, Modern
Athabaskan
Āūkāū-Jūwōī *see* **Andamanese**
Aukštait *see* **Lithuanian**
AUSTRALIAN LANGUAGES
AUSTRO-ASIATIC LANGUAGES
AUSTRONESIAN LANGUAGES
Ava *see* PAPUAN LANGUAGES
Avar
Avestan
Aymará
Azerbaydzhani
Aztec *see* **Nahuatl**
AZTEC-TANOAN LANGUAGES

Bactrian *see* IRANIAN LANGUAGES
Bagval *see* ANDI LANGUAGES
BAHNARIC LANGUAGES
Balinese
BALTIC LANGUAGES
BALTO-FINNIC MINOR LANGUAGES
Baluchi
Bambara
Banning *see* PAPUAN LANGUAGES
BANTU LANGUAGES
Bao'an *see* MONGOLIAN LANGUAGES OF
   CHINA
Bashkir
Baśkārik *see* DARDIC LANGUAGES
Basque
Batak
Bats *see* NAKH LANGUAGES
Bella Coola *see* NORTH AMERICAN
   INDIAN ISOLATES
Belorussian
Beludzh *see* **Baluchi**
Bengali
Benue-Congo *see* NIGER-CONGO
   LANGUAGES
Berber
Bhili *see* **Gujarati;** NEW INDO-ARYAN
   LANGUAGES
Bikol
Blackfoot
Bohairic *see* **Coptic**
Bolmaç *see* **Avar**
Bongu *see* PAPUAN LANGUAGES
Botlikh *see* ANDI LANGUAGES
Brahui
Brazilian *see* **Portuguese**
Breton
Bribrí
Brythonic *see* CELTIC LANGUAGES
Buginese
Bulgarian
Bulgarian, Old *see* TURKIC
   LANGUAGES
Burmese
Burushaski
Buryat
Bushman *see* **!Kung**

Buyi *see* TAI LANGUAGES

Cambodian
Canaanite *see* SEMITIC LANGUAGES
Čače rom *see* **Romany**
Caddoan *see* MACRO-SIOUAN
   LANGUAGES
Cantonese *see* **Yue**
Carib
Carib, Island *see* ANDEAN-
   EQUATORIAL LANGUAGES
Carrier *see* NA-DENE LANGUAGES
Catalan
Catawba *see* MACRO-SIOUAN
   LANGUAGES
CAUCASIAN LANGUAGES
Cayuga *see* MACRO-SIOUAN
   LANGUAGES
Cebuano
CELTIC LANGUAGES
Chagatay *see* TURKIC LANGUAGES
Cham
Chamalal *see* ANDI LANGUAGES
Chamorro
Chari-Nile *see* NILO-SAHARAN
   LANGUAGES
Chechen
Cheremis *see* **Mari**
Cherokee
Cheyenne
Chibcha
Chickasaw *see* **Choctaw**
Chimú
Chinese
Chinese, Archaic
Chinese, Classical
Chinese, Modern Standard
Chinook *see* PENUTIAN LANGUAGES
Chipewyan
Chiricahua *see* **Apache**
Choctaw
Chrau *see* BAHNARIC LANGUAGES
Chukchi
Chulim *see* TURKIC LANGUAGES
Chuvash
Circassian *see* **Kabard-Cherkes**

Citrali *see* DARDIC LANGUAGES
Cœur d'Alene *see* NORTH AMERICAN
   INDIAN ISOLATES
Comanche *see* AZTEC-TANOAN
   LANGUAGES
Coos *see* **Penutian**
Coptic
Cornish
Cornouaille *see* **Breton**
Cree
Creek *see* MACRO-ALGONQUIAN
   LANGUAGES
Crow
Cuang *see* **Juang**
Czech

DAGESTANIAN LANGUAGES
Dagur *see* MONGOLIAN LANGUAGES OF
   CHINA
Dai *see* TAI LANGUAGES
Dakota
Danish
DARDIC LANGUAGES
Dargin *see* **Dargva**
Dargva
Delaware *see* MACRO-ALGONQUIAN
   LANGUAGES
Demeli *see* DARDIC LANGUAGES
Digor *see* **Ossetian**
Dinka
DRAVIDIAN LANGUAGES
Drindari *see* **Romany**
Dutch
Dyirbal *see* AUSTRALIAN LANGUAGES
Dyula *see* **Bambara**

Easter Island *see* POLYNESIAN
   LANGUAGES; **Rapanui**
Efik
Egyptian
Elamite *see* ANATOLIAN LANGUAGES
Ellice Islands *see* POLYNESIAN
   LANGUAGES
English
Erlides *see* **Romany**
Erzyan *see* **Mordva**

ESKIMO-ALEUT LANGUAGES
Eskimo *see* **Inuit**; ESKIMO-ALEUT
   LANGUAGES
Estonian
Ethiopic
Euskara *see* **Basque**
Even
Evenki
Ewe

Faeroese
Fijian
Finnish
Fintike roma *see* **Romany**
Flemish *see* **Dutch**
Fore *see* PAPUAN LANGUAGES
Frafra *see* **Gurenne**
French
Fulani
Fulbe *see* **Fulani**
Fulfulde *see* **Fulani**
Futunan *see* POLYNESIAN LANGUAGES

Gadsup *see* PAPUAN LANGUAGES
Gaelic *see* **Scottish Gaelic**
Gagauz
Galatian *see* CELTIC LANGUAGES
Galla *see* **Oromo**
Gan
Garo
Garwi *see* DARDIC LANGUAGES
Gawar(bati) *see* DARDIC LANGUAGES
Ge'ez *see* **Ethiopic**
Georgian
German
GERMANIC LANGUAGES
Gheg *see* **Albanian**
Gilyak *see* **Nivkh**
Goajiro *see* ANDEAN-EQUATORIAL
   LANGUAGES
Godaba *see* DRAVIDIAN LANGUAGES
Godoberi *see* ANDI LANGUAGES
Goidelic *see* CELTIC LANGUAGES
Gold *see* **Nanay**
Golden Horde *see* TURKIC LANGUAGES
Goṇḍi

Gondwana *see* DRAVIDIAN LANGUAGES
Gorontalo
Gothic
Greek, Classical
Greek, Modern Standard
Guaraní
Gujarati
Gur *see* NIGER-CONGO LANGUAGES
Gurbeti *see* **Romany**
Gurenne

Haida *see* NORTH AMERICAN INDIAN
   ISOLATES
Haitian Creole *see* PIDGINS AND
   CREOLES
Hakka
Hattic *see* ANATOLIAN LANGUAGES
Hausa
Hawaiian
Hebrew
Hidatsa *see* MACRO-SIOUAN
   LANGUAGES
Hiligaynon *see* **Cebuano**
Hindi
Hittite
Hokan *see* MACRO-SIOUAN LANGUAGES
Hopi
Hsi-Hsia *see* **Tangut**
Hungarian
Hunnic *see* TURKIC LANGUAGES
Hupa *see* NA-DENE LANGUAGES
Hurrian

Icelandic
Igbo
Ilokano
INDO-ARYAN LANGUAGES (NEW) *see*
   NEW INDO-ARYAN LANGUAGES
INDO-EUROPEAN LANGUAGES
Indonesian
Ingrian *see* BALTO-FINNIC MINOR
   LANGUAGES
Ingush *see* **Chechen**
Inuit
IRANIAN LANGUAGES

Irish
Irish, Old
Iron *see* **Ossete**
Iroquois *see* MACRO-SIOUAN
Ishkashim *see* PAMIR LANGUAGES
Italian
Itelmen
Ivrit

Jain-Mahārāṣṭrī *see* **Prakrit**
Jain-Śaureseni *see* **Prakrit**
Japanese, Classical
Japanese, Modern Standard
Javanese
Javanese, Old
Jicarilla *see* **Apache**
Juang

Kabard-Cherkes
Kabyle *see* **Berber**
Kachin
Kalāṣa *see* DARDIC LANGUAGES
Kalispel *see* NORTH AMERICAN INDIAN
   ISOLATES
Kalmyk
Kam *see* TAI LANGUAGES
Kamoro *see* PAPUAN LANGUAGES
Kannada
Karachay-Balkar
Karakalpak
Karata *see* ANDI LANGUAGES
Karelian
Karen
Karluk *see* TURKIC LANGUAGES
Kartvelian *see* **Georgian**
Kashmiri
Kashubian
Katī *see* DARDIC LANGUAGES
Kawi *see* **Old Javanese**
Kazakh
Kekavyari *see* **Romany**
Kelderari *see* **Romany**
Kerek *see* PALAEO-SIBERIAN
   LANGUAGES
Keres *see* MACRO-SIOUAN LANGUAGES

Keresan *see* AZTEC-TANOAN
  LANGUAGES
Ket
Keva *see* PAPUAN LANGUAGES
Khakas
Khalkha *see* **Mongolian, Modern**
Khandeśi *see* NEW INDO-ARYAN
  LANGUAGES
Khanty
Khari-Boli *see* **Hindi**
Khasi
Khazar *see* TURKIC LANGUAGES
Kherwari *see* **Muṇḍāri**
Khmer *see* **Cambodian**
Khotanese *see* IRANIAN LANGUAGES
Khowar *see* DARDIC LANGUAGES
Khwarezmian *see* IRANIAN
  LANGUAGES
Kiowa *see* NA-DENE LANGUAGES
Kipchak *see* TURKIC LANGUAGES
Kirgiz
Klamath-Modoc *see* PENUTIAN
  LANGUAGES
Kodagu *see* DRAVIDIAN LANGUAGES
Kol *see* AUSTRO-ASIATIC LANGUAGES
Kolami *see* DRAVIDIAN LANGUAGES
Komi
Konkani *see* **Marathi**
Korean
Koryak
Kota *see* DRAVIDIAN LANGUAGES
Kott *see* **Ket;** PALAEO-SIBERIAN
  LANGUAGES
Kpelle
Kui *see* DRAVIDIAN LANGUAGES
Kumyk
!Kung
Kurdish
Kurmandji *see* **Kurdish**
Kurukh *see* DRAVIDIAN LANGUAGES
Kuvi *see* DRAVIDIAN LANGUAGES
Kwa *see* NIGER-CONGO LANGUAGES
Kwakiutl *see* NORTH AMERICA INDIAN
  ISOLATES

Ladakhi
Lahnda
Lak
Lakota *see* **Dakota**
Lamut *see* **Even**
Langue d'Oc *see* **Occitan**
Lao
Lappish
Latin
Latvian
Laz
Leon *see* **Breton**
Lezgi
Lhota *see* NAGA LANGUAGES
Li *see* TAI LANGUAGES
Lingurari *see* **Romany**
Lithuanian
Liv *see* BALTO-FINNIC MINOR
  LANGUAGES
Lotfika roma *see* **Romany**
Lovari *see* **Romany**
Lusatian
Luvian *see* ANATOLIAN LANGUAGES
Lycian *see* ANATOLIAN LANGUAGES
Lydian *see* ANATOLIAN LANGUAGES

Maasai
Macassarese
Macedonian
MACRO-ALGONQUIAN LANGUAGES
MACRO-SIOUAN LANGUAGES
Madurese
Māgadhī *see* **Prakrit**
Mahārāṣṭrī *see* **Prakrit**
Mahl *see* **Sinhalese**
Maiduan *see* PENUTIAN LANGUAGES
Maiyã *see* DARDIC LANGUAGES
Malagasy
Malayalam
Malinke *see* **Bambara**
Maltese
Malto *see* DRAVIDIAN LANGUAGES
Mam
Manchu
Mandaean *see* SEMITIC LANGUAGES

Mandan *see* MACRO-SIOUAN
  LANGUAGES
Mandingo *see* **Bambara**
Mangarevan *see* POLYNESIAN
  LANGUAGES
Mansi
Manx
Maonan *see* TAI LANGUAGES
Maori
Mapudungu
Marathi
Margi
Mari
Marind *see* PAPUAN LANGUAGES
Marquesan *see* POLYNESIAN
  LANGUAGES
Maya
Median *see* IRANIAN LANGUAGES
Melanesian *see* AUSTRONESIAN
  LANGUAGES
Mende
Menomini
Meroitic
Mescalero *see* **Apache;** NA-DENE
  LANGUAGES
MIAO-YAO LANGUAGES
Micmac *see* MACRO-ALGONQUIAN
  LANGUAGES
Micronesian *see* AUSTRONESIAN
  LANGUAGES
Middle English *see* **English**
Middle Persian *see* **Pehlevi**
Min
Minangkabau
Mingrelian
Miskito
Miwok-Costanoan *see* PENUTIAN
  LANGUAGES
Mixtec
Mobilian *see* **Choctaw**
Mohawk *see* MACRO-SIOUAN
  LANGUAGES
Mohican *see* MACRO-ALGONQUIAN
  LANGUAGES
Mokshan *see* **Mordva**
Moldavian

Mon
Mongolian, Classical
MONGOLIAN LANGUAGES OF CHINA
Mongolian, Modern
Monguor *see* MONGOLIAN LANGUAGES
  OF CHINA
Mon-Khmer *see* AUSTRO-ASIATIC
  LANGUAGES
Mordva
Mordvinian *see* **Mordva**
Mortlockese *see* **Trukese**
Motu *see* PAPUAN LANGUAGES
Mulam *see* TAI LANGUAGES
Multani *see* **Lahnda**
Muṇḍāri
Mundži *see* PAMIR LANGUAGES
Muskogean *see* MACRO-ALGONQUIAN
  LANGUAGES
Muysca *see* **Chibcha**
Mycenaean *see* **Greek, Classical**

NA-DENE LANGUAGES
NAGA LANGUAGES
Nahuatl
Naiki *see* DRAVIDIAN LANGUAGES
NAKH LANGUAGES
Nakota *see* **Dakota**
Nama
Nanay
Nasioi *see* PAPUAN LANGUAGES
Natchez *see* MACRO-ALGONQUIAN
  LANGUAGES
Navajo
Naxi
Negidal
Nenets
Nepali
NEW INDO-ARYAN LANGUAGES
Nez Perce *see* PENUTIAN LANGUAGES
Nicobarese
NIGER-CONGO LANGUAGES
NILO-SAHARAN LANGUAGES
Niue *see* POLYNESIAN LANGUAGES
Nivkh
Nogay *see* TURKIC LANGUAGES
Norse, Old

NORTH-AMERICAN INDIAN ISOLATES
NORTH-AMERICAN INDIAN LANGUAGES
Norwegian
Nubian

Occitan
Oguz *see* TURKIC LANGUAGES
Oirat
Oirot *see* **Altay**
Ojibwa *see* MACRO-ALGONQUIAN
   LANGUAGES
Old Church Slavonic
Old English *see* **English**
Oneida *see* MACRO-SIOUAN
   LANGUAGES
Ono *see* PAPUAN LANGUAGES
Onondaga *see* MACRO-SIOUAN
   LANGUAGES
Oriya
Oroch *see* **Udege**
Orok *see* **Nanay**
Oromo
Osage *see* MACRO-SIOUAN LANGUAGES
Ossete
Ostyak *see* **Khanty**
OTOMANGUEAN LANGUAGES
Otomi *see* OTOMANGUEAN LANGUAGES

Pahari *see* NEW INDO-ARYAN
   LANGUAGES
Paiśācī *see* **Prakrit**
Paiute *see* AZTEC-TANOAN LANGUAGES
PALAEO-SIBERIAN LANGUAGES
Palaic *see* ANATOLIAN LANGUAGES
Palaung
Pali
PAMIR LANGUAGES
Panjabi
Papago *see* AZTEC-TANOAN LANGUAGES
PAPUAN LANGUAGES
Parji *see* DRAVIDIAN LANGUAGES
Parthian *see* IRANIAN LANGUAGES
Paṣai *see* DARDIC LANGUAGES
Pashto
Pawnee *see* MACRO-SIOUAN
   LANGUAGES

Pecheneg *see* TURKIC LANGUAGES
Peguan *see* **Mon**
Pehlevi
Pelasgian *see* **Greek, Classical**
PENUTIAN LANGUAGES
Permic, Old *see* **Komi**
Permyak *see* **Komi**
Persian
Pervika roma *see* **Romany**
Phalūṛa *see* DARDIC LANGUAGES
Phoenician
PIDGINS AND CREOLES
Piman *see* AZTEC-TANOAN LANGUAGES
Plaščunuya *see* **Romany**
Polish
Polovets *see* TURKIC LANGUAGES
POLYNESIAN LANGUAGES
Portuguese
Potawatomi *see* MACRO-ALGONQUIAN
   LANGUAGES
Prakrit
Prasun *see* DARDIC LANGUAGES
Provençal *see* **Occitan**
Puchikwar *see* **Andamanese**
Puluwatese *see* **Trukese**
Punic *see* **Phoenician**; SEMITIC
   LANGUAGES

Quechua
Quiché

Rajasthani *see* NEW INDO-ARYAN
   LANGUAGES
Rapanui
Raratonga *see* POLYNESIAN
   LANGUAGES
Riff *see* **Berber**
Romanian
Romany
Runa Simi *see* **Quechua**
Ruska roma *see* **Romany**
Russian
Ryu-Kyu *see* **Japanese, Modern
   Standard**

Saami *see* **Lappish**

Sabaean-Himyaritic *see* SEMITIC
   LANGUAGES
Sahaptian *see* PENUTIAN LANGUAGES
Sahidic *see* **Coptic**
Saka *see* IRANIAN LANGUAGES
Salishan *see* NORTH AMERICAN INDIAN
   ISOLATES
Samaritan
Samoan
Sango *see* NIGER-CONGO LANGUAGES
Sanskrit
Sanskrit, Buddhist Hybrid *see*
   Prakrit
Santa *see* MONGOLIAN LANGUAGES OF
   CHINA
Santali
Sarcee *see* NA-DENE LANGUAGES
Sarikoli *see* PAMIR LANGUAGES
Śauraseni *see* **Prakrit**
Scottish Gaelic
Scythian *see* IRANIAN LANGUAGES
Seljuk *see* TURKIC LANGUAGES
Seminole *see* MACRO-ALGONQUIAN
   LANGUAGES
SEMITIC LANGUAGES
Seneca
Sephardic *see* **Ivrit; Yiddish**
Serbo-Croat
Servi *see* **Romany**
Servika roma *see* **Romany**
Sgaw *see* **Karen**
Shawia *see* **Berber**
Shawnee *see* MACRO-ALGONQUIAN
   LANGUAGES
Shilluk
Shluh *see* **Berber**
Shoshonean *see* AZTEC-TANOAN
   LANGUAGES
Shughn-Roshan
Siamese *see* **Thai**
Śīṇā *see* DARDIC LANGUAGES
Sindhi
Sinhala *see* **Sinhalese**
Sinhalese
SINO-TIBETAN LANGUAGES
Sinti *see* **Romany**

Siraiki *see* **Lahnda; Sindhi**
SLAVONIC LANGUAGES
Slavonic, Old Church *see* **Old**
   Church Slavonic
Slovak
Slovene
Sogdian *see* IRANIAN LANGUAGES
Somali
Sonoran *see* AZTEC-TANOAN
   LANGUAGES
Sora *see* **Khasi**
Sorani *see* **Kurdish**
Sorbian *see* **Lusatian**
Spanish
Squamish *see* NORTH AMERICAN
   INDIAN ISOLATES
Stieng *see* BAHNARIC LANGUAGES
Sui *see* TAI LANGUAGES
Sumasti *see* DARDIC LANGUAGES
Sumerian
Sundanese
Svan
Swahili
Swedish
Syriac

Tadzhik
Tagalog
Tahitian
TAI LANGUAGES
Tairora *see* PAPUAN LANGUAGES
Takelma *see* PENUTIAN LANGUAGES
Talaing *see* **Mon**
Talysh
Tamahaq *see* **Berber**
Tamazight *see* **Berber**
Tamil
Tangut
Tanoan-Kiowa *see* AZTEC-TANOAN
   LANGUAGES
Tapanta *see* **Abaza**
Tarahumar *see* AZTEC-TANOAN
   LANGUAGES
Tasmanian
Tat
Tatar

Telefol *see* PAPUAN LANGUAGES
Telugu
Thai
Tibetan
Tigre
Tigrinya
Tindi *see* ANDI LANGUAGES
Tirakhi *see* DARDIC LANGUAGES
Tlingit
Toba *see* **Batak**
Tocharian
Toda *see* DRAVIDIAN LANGUAGES
Tokelau *see* POLYNESIAN LANGUAGES
Tongan
Tonkawa *see* MACRO-ALGONQUIAN
   LANGUAGES
Tōrwālī *see* DARDIC LANGUAGES
Tosk *see* **Albanian**
Treguier *see* **Breton**
Trukese
Trukhmen *see* TURKIC LANGUAGES
Tshimshian *see* PENUTIAN LANGUAGES
Tuamotuan *see* POLYNESIAN
   LANGUAGES
Tuareg *see* **Berber**
Tulu *see* DRAVIDIAN LANGUAGES
Tunica *see* MACRO-ALGONQUIAN
   LANGUAGES; MACRO-SIOUAN
   LANGUAGES
Tupí
TURKIC LANGUAGES
Turkish
Turkmen
Tuva *see* **Tuvinian**
Tuvinian
Twi *see* **Akan**
Tzotzil *see* **Maya**

Ubykh
Udege
Udmurt
Ugaritic
Ukrainian
Ulcha *see* **Nanay**
Ungrike roma *see* **Romany**
URALIC LANGUAGES

Urartian
Urdu
Ursari *see* **Romany**
Uto-Aztecan *see* AZTEC-TANOAN
   LANGUAGES
Uvean, East *see* POLYNESIAN
   LANGUAGES
Uygur
Uzbek

Vaigalī *see* DARDIC LANGUAGES
Vakh *see* PAMIR LANGUAGES; **Khanty**
Vannes *see* **Breton**
Vedic *see* **Sanskrit**
Veps *see* BALTO-FINNIC MINOR
   LANGUAGES
Veri *see* PAPUAN LANGUAGES
Vietnamese
Visayan *see* **Cebuano**
Vogul *see* **Mansi**
Volokhuya *see* **Romany**
Volšenenge kale *see* **Romany**
Voltaic *see* NIGER-CONGO LANGUAGES
Vot *see* BALTO-FINNIC MINOR
   LANGUAGES
Votapuri *see* DARDIC LANGUAGES
Votyak *see* **Udmurt**

Wakashan *see* NORTH AMERICAN
   INDIAN ISOLATES
Walmatjari *see* AUSTRALIAN
   LANGUAGES
Warrgamay *see* AUSTRALIAN
   LANGUAGES
Welsh
Wendish *see* **Lusatian**
Wenli *see* **Chinese, Archaic**
Weršikwar *see* **Burushaski**
West Atlantic *see* NIGER-CONGO
   LANGUAGES
Western Desert Language *see*
   AUSTRALIAN LANGUAGES
Wichita *see* MACRO-SIOUAN
   LANGUAGES
Winnebago *see* MACRO-SIOUAN
   LANGUAGES

Wintun *see* PENUTIAN LANGUAGES
Wolof
Wu

Xiang
Xibo *see* **Manchu**
!Xu *see* **!Kung**

Yagnob
Yakut
Yazgulyam *see* PAMIR LANGUAGES
Yi
Yiddish
Yidiny *see* AUSTRALIAN LANGUAGES
Yokutsan *see* PENUTIAN LANGUAGES
Yoruba

Yuchi *see* MACRO-SIOUAN LANGUAGES
Yue
Yukagir
Yuki *see* MACRO-SIOUAN LANGUAGES
Yupik *see* **Inuit**; ESKIMO-ALEUT
   LANGUAGES
Yurok *see* MACRO-ALGONQUIAN
   LANGUAGES

Zapotec
Žemait *see* **Lithuanian**
Zend/Zand *see* IRANIAN LANGUAGES
Zletari *see* **Romany**
Zuni
Zyryan *see* **Komi**

COMPENDIUM
OF THE
WORLD'S
LANGUAGES

―――

VOLUME I
ABAZA TO LUSATIAN

ABAZA

INTRODUCTION

Abaza belongs to the Abkhaz-Adyge sub-group of North-West Caucasian. There are about 25,000 speakers in the Karachaev-Cherkes Autonomous Region, and many in Turkey who migrated there after the Shamil uprising in the mid-eighteenth century. The Tapanta dialect affords the basis for the literary standard.

SCRIPT

Since 1938 a Cyrillic-based script has been used for Abaza. Since Abaza is so close, both phonologically and morphologically, to Abkhaz that some authorities consider it to be an Abkhaz dialect, a common script for the two languages might have seemed a sensible proposition. The two notations differ, however, in a very confusing way. Thus the non-Cyrillic sign *I*, widely used in Caucasian languages, appears in Abaza as the ejective marker, but is absent in Abkhaz, where the unmarked consonant graph is used to notate the ejective. For example, the labial ejective stop is notated as п in Abkhaz, as пI in Abaza; п in Abaza is the unvoiced stop, represented as ҧ in Abkhaz. Similarly, the labialized pharyngeal ejective is ҟь in Abkhaz, къь in Abaza.

Altogether, the Abaza script has over 70 graphs, including 28 digraphs and 12 trigraphs.

PHONOLOGY

The phonology of Abaza is close to that of Abkhaz, with some divergencies in the spirant and affricate alveolar series. The vocalic system reduces to a basic contrast between *a* and *ɪ*. Some authorities (e.g. Allen 1956) give Abaza only one vowel – /ə/. Lomtatidze (1967), gives /a/ and /ɪ/ as basic, with positional allophones /e, o, u/.

MORPHOLOGY AND SYNTAX

Largely as in Abkhaz. Hewitt (1981) points to Circassian influence on Abaza verb structure *vis-à-vis* Abkhaz.

ABKHAZ

INTRODUCTION

Abkhaz belongs to the North-West Caucasian or Abkhaz-Adyge sub-group of Caucasian languages. Abkhaz is very closely connected to Abaza; indeed the Abkhaz-Abaza complex can be described in terms of four dialects: Southern – Bzyb and Abžui, the latter providing the basis for the Abkhaz literary language; and Northern – Aškhar and Tapanta, on which the Abaza literary language is based.

In 1979 there were some 90,000 speakers of Abkhaz, of whom about 95 per cent claimed Abkhaz as their mother tongue. Most Abkhazians live in the Abkhaz Autonomous Soviet Socialist Republic (capital Sukhumi), with a residue in Mingrelia and in Turkey.

Abkhaz oral literary tradition possesses a version of the *Narts* saga, which is regarded as more archaic than the parallel Ossetian version. The saga combines mythological accounts of the origins of Iranian society and its culture, with records, which may be historical, of migration and warfare. The fact that the Greeks seem to have borrowed some of the material (e.g. the Prometheus motif) goes to suggest that the *Narts* saga may date from at least 1000 BC.

SCRIPT

In 1862 a Cyrillic-based script was devised by Uslar. Between 1928 and 1954 various experiments were made with Romanization and with Georgian script. The present Cyrillic-based script, in use since 1954, has the following extra characters: ҷ, ҩ, ә.

PHONOLOGY

Consonants

stops: /p, b, p'; t, d, t'; k, g, k'; q'/. The ejectives are notated as p, t, etc. The dental and velar series and /q'/ occur labialized: /t°, d°, t'°; k°; g°, k'°, q'°/. The velar series and /q'/ occur palatalized: /k', g', k''; q''/.

affricates: /ts, dz, ts'; tʃ, dʒ, dʒ'/; labialized: /ts°, dz°, ts'°/; retroflex: /tʂ, dʐ, tʂ'/ (notated as dz, ç, ç̦)

fricatives: /f, v, s, z, ʃ, ʒ, x, ɣ, x°, ɣ°, x', ɣ'/; labialized: /ʃ°, ʒ°/; retroflex: /ʂ, ʐ/; pharyngeals: /ħ, ħ°, ʕ°/y°/: Hewitt (1979) describes this latter sound as a 'radico-pharyngeal voiced pulmonic fricative labialized'.

nasals: /m, n/.

lateral and roll: /l, r/.

semi-vowels: /j, w/

2

Vowels

There are only two basic vowels: /a, ı (ə)/; /a/ is the prevalent vowel in Abkhaz. Depending on phonetic environment, /a/ and /ı/ may be realized as [e, i, o, u]; e.g. the present-tense marker -*wa*- + /j/ → [o].

MORPHOLOGY AND SYNTAX

Gender in Abkhaz, though marked in the pronoun and the verb, is not marked in the noun. There are two classes of noun, the dichotomy being between human and non-human.

Nouns

Nouns are definite or indefinite. In citation form, with an *a*- prefix, they are definite: *a.çla* 'the tree'; *a.xaça* 'the man'.

The indefinite marker is -*ḵ* suffixed to the noun which, of course, drops *a*-: *çla.ḵ* 'a tree'; *xaça.ḵ* 'some man or other'.

Plural markers for each class of noun are: -*c°a* for humans: *ačḵun.c°a* 'children'; for non-humans, -*ḵ°a*: *çla.ḵ°a.ḵ* 'some trees'.

In the absence of any sort of case inflection, syntactic relationships are expressed by affixes, supported where necessary by adverbial postpositions.

POSSESSION
Possessed object follows possessor: X's Y = X lk Y, where lk is the possessive linking particle agreeing with X (*see* Possessive Pronouns, below).

Adjective

The adjective does not differ formally from the nominal. The predicate adjective is a stative verb (see below). Attributively, the adjective usually follows its noun: *a.č̌ə bzəya* 'the good horse'; *a.č̌ə bzəya.ḵ°a* 'the good horses'.

Pronoun

Personal independent

		Singular	Plural
1		sara	hara
2	masc.	wara	š°ara
	fem.	bara	
3	masc.	yara	dara
	fem.	lara	

Note: the -*ra* may be dropped to give the short forms *sa, wa*, etc.

These are invariable, and take postpositions: *sara səla* 'by me'.

POSSESSIVE PRONOMINAL PREFIXES
These are the short forms *sa, wa*, etc.: *sə.çla* 'my tree', *ha çla* 'their tree', etc.

DEMONSTRATIVE PRONOUN
Deixis here is related to person; there are three degrees: proximate, related to first person; non-proximate, related to second person; distal, related to third person. Thus: sing. *a(b)rəy, a(b)nəy, wə(b)rəy*; pl. *(ab)art, (ab)ant, wəbart.*

INTERROGATIVE PRONOUN
darban 'who?'; *yarban* 'what'?

RELATIVE PRONOUN
None. Relative clauses are formed by means of relative prefixes *yə-, zə- (see* **Verb**, below).

Numerals

The system is vigesimal and reflects the human/non-human dichotomy. 1–10: the forms for non-human items are: *akə, y°ba, xpa, pšba, x°ba, fba, bəžba, aaba, ž°ba, ž°aba*. If humans are being counted, *-ba/pa* in these forms is replaced by *-w*. 11–19: *z°a-(y)* + unit; 20 = *y°a.ž°a* = 2 × 10; 40 = *y°ə.n y°a.ž°a* = 2 × 2 × 10. 100 = *š°kə*. The numeral follows the item enumerated: *a.la.k°a pš.ba* 'the four dogs'.

Verb

Verbs in Abkhaz are stative or dynamic, transitive or intransitive, and verbal forms are finite or non-finite. Only one finite verb may appear in a sentence. As their name suggests, stative verbs denote general or resultative state; they are monopersonal and have only two tenses, present and past. Dynamic verbs express action and process; they are polypersonal and may be transitive or intransitive ('see' is dynamic transitive, 'go' is dynamic intransitive). Subject and object markers along with modal/adverbial markers are located in a pre-radical complex. Thus, an Abkhaz verb may have only three elements, subject – stem – tense formant, e.g. *d.ce.yṭ* 'he went'; or as many as six, direct object – indirect object – pre-verb – subject – stem – formant, e.g. *yə.b.zaa.z.ge.yṭ* 'I brought it for you'.

Three sets of bound affixes serve to notate the valencies of a verbal stem:

Set 1: these occupy initial position in the pre-radical complex, and denote the subject of an intransitive, or the direct object of a transitive verb (this coupling is explained by the fact that Abkhaz is an ergative language).

Set 2: includes indirect object markers, various pre-verbs, etc.

Set 3: this slot is allocated to the subject of transitive verbs.

In all three sets, the second person singular is marked for gender; the third person singular reflects the human/non-human dichotomy. Thus for set 1:

Sing.	1 s	2 masc. w, fem. b;	3 human: d, non-human: y;
Pl.	1 h	2 common: s°	3 common: y

In sets 2 and 3, the human marker in the third person singular is further marked for gender: e.g.

yə.bə.r.to.yṭ 'they gave it to her' yə = direct obj. of trans. verb: 'it'
 bə = indirect obj. set 2: 'to her'
r = sbj. of trans. verb, set 3: 'they'
to = stem: 'to give'
yṭ = tense formant

yə.z.be.yṭ 'I (z) saw (be + yṭ) it
(yə)'
yə.rə.s.to.yṭ 'I give it to them'

Abkhaz has indicative, imperative, conditional, optative, and subjunctive moods. -ṭ is a general ending for the finite forms of dynamic verbs, -n for the past and -p for the future.

Specimen tenses of indicative finite and non-finite dynamic verb c(ə) 'to go':

	Finite		*Non-finite*	
Present	d.co.yṭ	he goes	dəš.co (that, as...)	he goes
Aorist	d.ce.yṭ	I go	dəš.ca	he went
Future	d.ca.p	he will go	dəš.ca.ra	hc will go
Future II	d.ca.š.ṭ	he will surely go	dɔš.ca.ša	he has to go
Pluperfect	d.ca.x'a.n	he had gone	dəš.ca.x'o	he had gone

Note: the *x'a* in the pluperfect tense is the perfective marker.

IMPERATIVE
Second person only. In dynamic verbs, the bare stem is used; in stative verbs, the stem preceded by the subjunctive affix.

SUBJUNCTIVE
The marker is -aayṭ: d.c.aayṭ 'he should go, let him go!' In stative verbs, -aayṭ is preceded by z-.

CAUSATIVE
In -r-: bə.l.lə.r.boyṭ 'she causes her to see you (fem. sing.)', cf. bə.l.boyṭ 'she sees you (fem. sing.)'.

BENEFACTIVE
-z-: yə.l.zə.l.go.yṭ 'she brings it for her'.

PRIVATIVE
-ç°-: yə.l.ç°.l.go.yṭ 'she deprives her of it'.

RELATIVE
y(ə) – refers to intransitive subject or direct object of transitive; z(ə) – refers to transitive subject or indirect object of transitive: e.g. yə.co 'he who goes'; yə.ca.z 'he who went'; yacə yə.ca.z a.xaça 'the man who went yesterday'.

INTERROGATIVE
The affix is -ma or -w: wə.co.ma 'are you going?'; d.ca.ma 'did he go?'.

PREVERBS

There is an intricate series or preverbs, which are (a) directional, e.g. -*aa*-indicating motion towards speaker (cf. Georgian: *mo*: *šemo*); (b) locational, specifying locus and nature of motion relative to various types of surface. These determinants are correlated with postpositions following the verbal complex.

NEGATION

The negative marker is -*m*.: *d.co.m* 'he doesn't go'.

Word order

SOV in nominal sentences. For pronominal subject/object order, *see* **Verb**, above.

---

1. Аханàȶ дѵqан Àзжа, ỳi Àзжа Анца iȇѵ дѵqан; ỳi Àзжа дѵ'-Нцàн.

2. Ỳi Àзжа Анца iȇѵ аханàȶ дѵqан.

3. Зеѓѵ Ỳi iла iqалѵèiт, Ỳi ìда акѓѵ азѵqамлѵеiт ìqалаз.

4. Ỳi абзàзара iлан, Ỳi iбзàзара ауаà рзѵ лашàран.

5. Àлашара àлашцара аȇѵ iлашѵуòiт,— àлашцара Iарà iзѵiхàмꚇеiт.

6. Дѵqан Анцà iqнѵȶ iаàшꚇvз аꙅѵ; ỳi Iоàнн iх̇зѵн.

7. Ỳi даàiт шаhàꚇvс Àлашара дѵiзѵшаhаꚇразѵ,—iарà iла зеѓѵ дхàрцаразѵ.

8. Iарà длашàрамѵзт, ахà (даàшꚇѵн) àлашара зхѵлцѵуа дѵìꚍушаhаꚇхаразѵ.

6

ABKHAZ-ADYGE LANGUAGES

INTRODUCTION

These languages fall into three groups: (a) Abkhaz and Abaza; (b) Adyge and Kabard-Cherkes; (c) Ubykh. Genetically, these languages are closely related, but the three groups are not mutually intelligible. As an isolated outlier, Ubykh (now extinct) diverges considerably from (a) and (b). The Ubykh people moved *en bloc* to Turkey in the middle of the nineteenth century. The other languages are spoken by about half a million people in the Abkhaz Autonomous Soviet Socialist Republic, in Georgia, the Karachay-Cherkes, and Adyge Autonomous Regions and the Kabard-Balkar Autonomous Soviet Socialist Republic.

SCRIPT

Ubykh was unwritten; the other four are in use as literary languages. The Cyrillic script is used, but in highly inconsistent fashion, the same Cyrillic letters being used in different languages to represent different sounds. In Abkhaz, the script is extended by three non-Cyrillic graphs.

PHONOLOGY

All of these languages are characterized by an almost unique proliferation of consonants, on the one hand, and by a very simple, rudimentary vowel system, on the other. Thus, Ubykh had a basic vocalic opposition in /ə/ – /a/ plus an inventory of some 80 consonantal phonemes. Similarly, Abaza has two vowels and 66 consonants; Abhaz has 58. Clearly, such inventories can be achieved only by means of secondary articulation – glottalization, palatalization, labialization, aspiration – and each of the languages has specific refinements on these lines. For example, two dialects of Adyge extend the normal three-term series: voiced stop – unvoiced aspirate – ejective, with a semi-ejective, unaspirated member; e.g. /b – p – p' – p̄/. In Soviet terminology, this sound is called a 'preruptive'.

For detailed inventories, *see* **Abkhaz** and **Kabard-Cherkes**.

MORPHOLOGY AND SYNTAX

Noun

The human/non-human dichotomy underlies the nominal system. Nouns are also marked for definiteness/indefiniteness, number, and the genitive relationship. Adyge, Kabard-Cherkes, and Ubykh have nominative/ergative opposition; Abkhaz and Abaza have virtually no case system. Gender is marked in second and third person forms in Abkhaz/Abaza.

Verb

Abkhaz-Adyge verbs are dynamic or stative; transitive or intransitive; monopersonal or polypersonal; and are marked for person, number, tense, mood. The verbal complex contains, if required, interrogative and negative markers. Causativity, reciprocity, potentiality, and involuntary action are also indicated by markers in complex.

In a tripersonal verbal complex the sequence of personal pronominal markers is: direct object (nominative) – oblique object (ergative) – subject (ergative). The combination of polysynthetic structure on this scale and polypersonalism leads, as might be expected, to the formation of long and complex verbal forms, in which root and markers alike often consist of a single consonant.

Kumakhov (1979:144) gives the following, admittedly somewhat extreme, example from Kabard-Cherkes:

w-a-qə-də-d-ej-z-ɣe-šə-žə-f-a-te-qəm-əj

analysed as follows:

w-	2nd p. sing. direct obj. prefix
a-	3rd p. pl. indirect obj. prefix
qə	directional marker: 'hither'
də-	comitative marker
d-	locative marker
ej-	3rd p. sing. obj. prefix
z-	1st p. sing. sbj. prefix
ɣe-	causative prefix
šə-	root of verb *še-n* 'to bring'
-žə	reflexive suffix
-f	suffix of potentiality
-a	past tense suffix
-te	temporal suffix: 'then'
-qəm	suffix of negation
-əj	modal suffix

That is, root + 8 prefixes + 6 suffixes. The whole complex means: 'So then I was not able to get him to bring you back from there along with them.' Further simpler examples showing the arrangement of subject and object markers will be found in the articles on Abkhaz and Kabard-Cherkes.

Two basic syntactic constructions are found: the nominative sentence (subject in nominative; intransitive verb) and the ergative sentence (subject in ergative; direct object in nominative; transitive verb).

ACHINESE

INTRODUCTION

Achinese belongs to the Malayo-Polynesian branch of Austronesian, and is spoken by over 2 million people in northern Sumatra. The Indonesian spelling is Aceh. The language may be related to the Cham languages in Vietnam and Campuchea (*see* **Cham**). The Achinese have been Moslems since the thirteenth/fourteenth centuries.

SCRIPT

Traditionally Arabic, now replaced by romanization with diacritics denoting vowel quality. Transcription here is broad.

PHONOLOGY

Consonants

Achinese has labial, dental, palatal, and velar series of the type: unvoiced stop – voiced stop – nasal, e.g. /p, b, m; k, g, ŋ/. Other sounds: /s/ > [θ]; /l, r, h/, glottal stop or hamza; /w, j/. /p, b, t, c, k, s, h, r/, and hamza have nasalized counterparts. Stop + /r/l/ is fairly frequent: /dr-, pl-, bl-/, etc.

Vowels

/i, ɪ, ɛ, a, ə, ɔ, o, u/. /ə/ has two values: /ə/ notated as *eu*, /ə̃/ = /ʌ/ notated as *ë*. [ɪ] and [ə̃] prolong vocalic finals in colourless off-glide. All diphthongs have [ə/ə̃] as second element. /i, ɛ, a, o/ are nasalized in contact with nasal vowels, but not necessarily nasalized in contact with the nasalized counterparts of the stops (see above).

MORPHOLOGY AND SYNTAX

Noun

No grammatical gender, no marking for case or number. Reduplication may be used to suggest vague quantities: *macam-macam* 'all sorts of ...'

POSSESSION
Possessor follows: *pinto rumoh* 'the door of the house'; *alat rumoh* 'household goods'.

Adjective

As attribute the adjective follows: *ureueng tuha* 'old man', *nanggroë Aceh* 'the Achinese country'.

Pronoun

The independent personal forms are:

	Singular	*Plural*
1	keë, ulon	incl. geutanyoë, excl. kamoë
2	kah, gata	droeneuh
3	jih, gobnyan	droeneu

Related (truncated) forms act as verbal prefixes recapitulating the overtly expressed independent form, and there is a related series of possessive enclitics: e.g. for 1st p. sing. *lampoh.lon* 'my garden'; *rumoh.ku* 'your house'; *blang.meuh* 'our (excl.) paddy field'; *sikula.teuh* 'our (incl.) school'; *meuneukat.neuh* 'your (pl.) goods'.

VERBAL PREFIXES

Si N. **ji**jak u peukan ngon ma**jih**
'N. goes to market with her mother'

Gobnyan **geu**.teuka di Jawa
'He is returning from Java'

Gobnyan **geu**.beuet basa Aceh
'He is learning Achinese'

Droeneuh bandum **neu**.teuka singoh bak teumpat nyoe
'You are all to come here (to this place) tomorrow'

DEMONSTRATIVE PRONOUN/ADJECTIVE

nyan, nyoe: *rumoh nyan* 'this house'.

INTERROGATIVE PRONOUN

soë 'who?: *Bak soë ta.kheun* 'To whom did you say that?; *Rumoh soë njan* 'Whose house is that?'

RELATIVE PRONOUN

Nyang

Ureueng nyang le ji.troh meuih pirak
'People who have lots (*le*) of gold (*meuih*) and silver (*troh* = BI *taruh* 'have in one's possession')

Ureung nyang jak baroë ka **ji**.woë
'The man who went away yesterday has come back'

Verb

Since Achinese has no verbal inflection, and since there is no overt or formal difference between transitive and intransitive verbs, the sense of a statement depends on (a) the ordered syntax of pronominal components, (b) the use of adverbials, and (c) the use of prefixes, infixes, and suffixes.

There is a broad division into verbs expressing intentional action, and verbs expressing chance or unintentional action.

As noted above, the verbal personal prefix recapitulates the personal pronoun.

TENSE MARKERS

Present unmarked, past has *ka*.
Specimen past tense: *jak* 'to go' (pronounced /ja'/):

lon ka lonjak	I went
kah ka kajak	you went
jih ka jijak	he/she went
gobnyan ka geujak	
geutanyoë ka tadjak	we (incl.) went, *etc.*

PREFIXES

e.g. *meu-/mu-* 'having, provided with': *peng* 'money', *mupeng* 'moneyed'; *lampoh* 'garden', *meulampoh* 'having a garden'. *Meu-/mu-* is also a formant for denominative verbs: *madat* 'opium', *mumadat* 'to smoke opium', and also for reciprocals: *rab* 'close', *meurab* 'to approach one another'.
Peu-/pu-

(a) causative: *beuët* 'to recite, learn', *pubeuët* 'to instruct'.
(b) forms denominative verbs: *teumon* 'sleep', *peuteumon* 'put to sleep'; *pungoh* 'crazy,' *pupungoh* 'drive crazy'.

Teu-/tu- makes passives: *pula* 'to sow', *teupula* 'to be sown'; *bloe* 'to buy', *teubloe* 'to be bought'.

INFIXES

> *-eun-*: forms nouns from verb stems: e.g. *bloe* 'to buy', *beunaloe* 'a purchase'; *bantu* 'to help', *beunantu* 'a helper'; *surat* 'to write,' *seunurat* 'a writing'.
> *-eum-/-um-*: forms verbs: *pateh* 'to obey', *pumateh* 'to be docile'.

NEGATIVE

Han(a) is a general negating particle: *lon hana peng* 'I have no money'; *aneuk lon hana dalam rumoh njan* 'my child is not in the house'.

The prohibitive particle is *bek*: *bek meunan ta.kheun* 'don't speak so!'

Prepositions

Examples:

> *bak* 'to, in, on, etc.': *ta.jak bak teungku* 'go to the tungku'.
> *keu* 'at, towards, etc.': *jih na gaseh keu lon* 'he likes me (has sympathy (*gaseh* = BI *kasih*) towards me')'.

oe 'to, etc.': *lon.jak oe peukan* 'I go to market'.

di 'from': *srot di.bubong* 'fall(en) from the roof'.

ngon 'with, than': *ngon lon rayeuk gata* 'you are bigger than I am'; *lon lonwoe ngon gobnyan* 'I come back with him'.

Word order

SVO.

---

1 Bak saboh watèë Jesus teungoh geumeudo'a disaboh teumpat.
Watèë Gobnjan geupijôh nibak meudo'a, sidroë nibak murid²geuh
djikheuën ubak Gobnjan: „Gurèë, neupeurunoëkeuh kamoë meudo'a,
lagèë njang geupeurunoë lé Jahja keu murid²geuh." 2 Djaweuëb
Jesus keu awak njan: „Meunjoë gata tameudo'a, takheuën lagèë njoe:
Ja Bapa, beuneupeusutjikeuh Nan Droëneuh; beuteukakeuh Keuradjeuën
Droëneuh. 3 Neubrikeuh keu kamoë tïëp² uroë makanan kamoe njang
tjukôb, 4 dan Neupeuampônkeuh dèsja kamoë, sabab kamoë pih peuampôn
tïëp² ureuëng njang meusalah keu kamoë; dan bèkkeuh Neuba kamoë u
dalam peutjuba'an."

(Luke 11: 1–4)

ADYGE

INTRODUCTION

Adye belongs to Abkhaz-Adyge sub-group of North-West Caucasian. There are about 100,000 speakers in the Adyge AO, plus communities in Turkey, Syria, and Jordan. The literary language is based on the Temirgoi dialect, and dates from 1918. Until 1927 an adaptation of the Arabic script was used, then replaced by Latin. Since 1938 Cyrillic + *I* which here marks the ejective series.

PHONOLOGY

See **Abkhaz-Adyge Languages**.

Consonants

Peculiar to the Shapsug and Bžedug dialects of Adyge is the 'semi-ejective' (unaspirated plosive) stop which extends the normal three-way opposition – e.g. /b, p, p'/, – to a four-way opposition: /b, p, p', p̄/. This phoneme is not found elsewhere in Caucasian.

Labialization is a marked feature of Adyge, extending even to the glottal stop: '°.

Vowels

Long /a/, short /ə/, and /ɪ/.

MORPHOLOGY AND SYNTAX

See **Kabard-Cherkes**, **Abkhaz-Adyge Languages**.

AFRIKAANS

INTRODUCTION

Afrikaans belongs to the West Germanic branch of Indo-European, and is derived from the same sixteenth-century Dutch dialect, Frankish in origin, which underlies modern Dutch. It took shape first in Cape Colony, where Jan van Riebeeck had arrived in 1652, and spread to the rest of South Africa, from the seventeenth century onwards. It has been a literary language for a little over a century. On both counts, it is the youngest of the Germanic languages. At present, it is spoken by about 4 million people.

The language was originally known as Kaaps-Hollands or Plat-Hollands. The designation 'Afrikaans' was adopted towards the end of the nineteenth century. From 1910 till 1925, Dutch and English were the joint official languages of the Union of South Africa; in 1925 Afrikaans replaced Dutch. The use of Afrikaans is mainly characteristic of the Cape Province, the Orange Free State, and the Transvaal.

SCRIPT

Roman, 26 letters as in English; c, q, x, z, are rarely used. The circumflex is used to mark the long open $ê, ô: lê = $ /lɛː/.

PHONOLOGY

Consonants

> stops: p, b, t, d, k, g, ʔ; palatalized k';
> affricates: ts, tʃ
> fricatives: f, v, s, ʃ, j, x, ɦ
> nasals: m, n, ɲ, ŋ
> lateral and flap: l, r
> /z/ occurs in a few loan-words.

[g] and [x] are allophones: cf. *berg* 'mountain', /bɛrx/, pl. *berge*, /bɛrgə/. /p, t, k/ are non-aspirate, /b, d/ in final position are unvoiced → [p, t]. Dutch /sx-/ = Afrikaans /sk-/, and Dutch final -*t* drops: e.g. *nacht* > *nag* /nax/ 'night'; *nest* > *nes*, 'nest'.

Vowels

front: i, iː, e, ɛ, ɛː, y, yː
middle: ə, əː, a, ɵ, ɪ, ɪː
back: ɑ, ɔ, ɔː, oː, u, uː, ʊ

/eː/ is realized as [e(ː)ə] or [ɪə]; /oː/ as [o(ː)ə] or [ʊə]. /a,ɛ,ɔ/ are nasalized when followed by *n* + fricative: e.g. *mense* [mɛ̃ːsə], 'people'; *aangesig* [ãːxəsɪx], 'face'.

DIPHTHONGS
Simple (short) or lengthened; all are falling.

short: əy, oʊ, œy (= Dutch /ʌy/), ɑi, ɔi, ui
long: ɑːi, oːi/ɔːi, eːu

Stress

Stress is free, associated with pitch. The main stress is normally on the root. In separate verbs, however, the stress is transferred to the prefix.

MORPHOLOGY AND SYNTAX

The division into common and neuter nouns, retained in Dutch, has been lost in Afrikaans. A single definite article – *die* – applies to all nouns, singular and plural: e.g. *die vader* 'the father' – *die moeder* 'the mother' – *die kinders* 'the children'. *'n* = [ə] is used as singular indefinite article: e.g. *'n vliegtuig* 'a plane'.

NUMBER
-e is a frequent plural marker, with phonetic adjustment, where necessary, at juncture; *-s* and *-ers* are also used: e.g. *wolf* – *wolwe*; *skip* 'ship' – *skepe*; *dag* 'day' – *dae*; *oom* 'uncle' – *ooms*; *kind* 'child' – *kinders*.

CASE
There is no inflection for case in Afrikaans; the genitive relationship is expressed periphrastically with the particle *se*: e.g. *sy vader se huis* 'his father's house'; *Pretoria se koerante* 'Pretoria's newspapers, the Pretoria papers'.

The indirect objective case of a personal noun is marked by the preposition *vir* 'for, to': *gee ... vir die arme kind* 'give the poor child ...'; *Sê vir oom, hy moet tuis kom* 'Tell uncle to come home.' The use of *vir* with a direct personal object seems to be possible. Mironov (1969) gives the example: *Jan slaan vir Piet* 'Jan strikes Piet.'

Adjective

As attribute, adjective procedes noun. After either article, *-e* is normally added to all polysyllabic and some monosyllabic adjectives: e.g. *die Nederlandse taal* 'the Dutch language'. The addition of *-e* may induce change in stem final: e.g. *Die kind is goed*; but, *Dit is 'n goeie kind* 'This/he/she is a good child.' Many adjectives remain uninflected: e.g. *Dit is 'n donker nag* 'It's a dark night.'

COMPARATIVE
Made with *-er*: phonetic change at junctures: e.g. *donker* 'dark' – *donkerder*; *doof* 'deaf' – *dower*.

Pronoun

Some vestiges of common Germanic inflection survive in the singular forms: the third person singular forms are marked for gender:

		Singular			*Plural*	
				Possessive	*Subject/*	*Possessive*
		Subject	*Object*	*adjective*	*object*	*adjective*
1		ek	my	my	ons	onse
2		jy	jou	jou	julle	julle se
		U	U	U	U	U
3	masc.	hy	hom	sy		
	fem.	sy	haar	haar	hulle	hulle se
	nt.	dit	dit	—		

The predicative possessive forms are *myne, joune, U sy'n/s'n, syne, haar se*; pl. *ons sy'n, julle sy'n, hulle sy'n*: e.g. *my boek – die boek is myne – die boek is julle s'n. U* is the polite address form.

DEMONSTRATIVE PRONOUN/ADJECTIVE
e.g. *hierdie* 'this', *daardie* 'that'.

INTERROGATIVE PRONOUN
wie 'who?'; *wat* 'what?: e.g. *In wie se naam*? 'In whose name?'

RELATIVE PRONOUN
wat is used for all referents: e.g. *die boek wat daar lê* 'the book that is lying there'; *die man/die vrou wat daar woon* 'the man/woman who lives there'.

Numerals

As in Dutch with some changes in spelling: e.g. D *vijf* 'five' = Afr. *vyf*.

Verb

Apart from the *ge-* prefix on most past participles, all verbal inflection has been lost. The verbal base is identical with the present-tense of the indicative mood: e.g. *val* 'to fall', *ek/hulle val* 'I/they fall'. Auxiliaries such as *het, is, sal, word* are used to make composite tenses. The typical Germanic past-tense forms, whether strong or weak (*see* **German**), have disappeared, leaving the composite form with *het* as the sole past-tense in Afrikaans (*cf.* **Yiddish**): e.g. *ek het geval* 'I fell/ have fallen'. If the verb begins with an inseparable prefix, e.g. *be-, er-, her-, ver-,* etc., the *ge-* of the past participle is dropped; i.e. here, the past participle coincides with the stem and the present tense.

SEPARABLE VERBS

The order of components in the tense structure of verbs with separable prefixes may be illustrated as follows, for *saambring* 'to bring along with one':

present: *ek bring my broeder saam* 'I'm bringing my brother along with me'
past: *ek het my broeder saam.ge.bring* 'I brought/I've brought ...'
future: *ek sal my broeder saam.bring* 'I shall bring ...'
split infinitive: *om saam te bring* '(so as) to bring along with one'

PASSIVE

The modal auxiliary *word* is used:

present: *die huis word gebou* 'the house is being built'
past: *die juis gebou word* 'the house was built'
past anterior: *die huis had gebou word* 'the house had been built'
future: *die huis sal gebou word* 'the house will be built'

IMPERATIVE MOOD

A simple imperative form is once again identical with stem and present tense; and, as in the present tense, a separable prefix follows: e.g. *oppas* 'to take care', *Pas op!* 'Take care!' A polite hortative form can be made with the auxiliary *moet*: e.g. *jy moet weggaan* 'you should/must go'. *Moet + nie → moenie* provides a negative imperative: e.g. *Moenie hier staan nie!* 'Don't stand here!'

NEGATIVE

The negative particle *nie* is recapitulated after the verb: e.g. *hy het nie gekom nie* 'he didn't come;' *hy het niks gedoen nie* 'he didn't do anything'.

NON-FINITE FORMS

The infinitive form is heavily eroded; e.g. *hê (< heb < hebben)* 'to have'; *sê (< seg < seggen)* 'to say'.

The present participle retains its original Germanic form: e.g. *lesende* 'reading'; *vallende* 'falling'; *Al pratende het hulle uit die kamer gestap* 'Talking, they left the room.'

Past participle: *ge-* prefix, except in verbs with an inseparable prefix; cf.

Hy het die boek gelees 'He read/has read the book'
Hy het die boek vertaal 'He translated/has translated the book'

Prepositions

Prepositions require the objective form of personal pronoun: e.g. *met haar* 'with her'; *Ek hou nie van hom nie* 'I don't like him' (lit. 'hold not with him'); *Ek wil môre graag by jou kom kuier* 'I'd like to come and visit you tomorrow' (*graag* = Gm. *gerne*)

Word order

SVO in principal clause; in subordinate clause SOV; if the subordinate clause precedes the principal clause, the word order in the latter is VSO.

> Subordinate clause, past tense: OSV aux.: e.g. *die motorkar wat ek gister gekoop het* 'the car I bought yesterday'.
>
> Subordinate clause, future tense: OS aux. V: e.g. *die brief wat ek môre sal ontvang* 'the letter which I'll get tomorrow'.
>
> If a modal auxiliary is present, the order is SO aux. modal aux. V: e.g. (*Hy het gesê dat*) *hy ons môre sou kan help* ('He said that) he would be able to help us tomorrow.'

1 IN die begin was die Woord, en die Woord was by God, en die Woord was God.

2 Hy was in die begin by God.

3 Alle dinge het deur Hom ontstaan, en sonder Hom het nie een ding ontstaan wat ontstaan het nie.

4 In Hom was lewe, en die lewe was die lig van die mense.

5 En die lig skyn in die duisternis, en die duisternis het dit nie oorweldig nie.

6 Daar was 'n man van God gestuur, wie se naam Johannes was.

7 Hy het tot 'n getuienis gekom om van die lig te getuig, sodat almal deur hom sou glo.

8 Hy was nie die lig nie, maar hy moes van die lig getuig.

AGUL

INTRODUCTION

Agul belongs to the Eastern Lezgi group of Dagestanian languages. Agul is spoken by about 12,000 people, whose villages are located in ravines high in the mountains. Communications are difficult, and the language varies often quite considerably, from one village to another. The Aguls use Lezgi in communication with their neighbours, and Lezgi is, along with Russian, the language of education. The administrative centre of the Agul region of the Dagestan ASSR is Tpig.

SCRIPT

Agul is unwritten. For pedagogic purposes, the language has been notated in Georgian script, in romanization and in Cyrillic + *I* as ejective marker. In his 1970 grammar of the language, Magometov uses romanization; his article on Agul (in *Jazyki Narodov USSR* (1966–8)) uses Cyrillic.

PHONOLOGY

Consonants

The labial, dental, and velar stops appear in four-term series: voiced plosive – voiceless unaspirated geminate – voiceless aspirate – ejective: e.g. /b – pp – p – p'/. The pharyngeal series lacks the voiced plosive: /Ø – qq – q – q'/. The affricate series are /Ø – tts – ts – tʂ/, /dʒ – ttʃ – tʃ – tʃ'/.
Fricative series: /w/v, ff, f; ʒ, ʃʃ, ʃ; z, ss, s; j, x'x', x'; ɣ, xx, x/. There are two pharyngeal ejectives: /ʕ, ħ/; and two glottals: /h, ʔ/. The /dʒ/ and /ʒ/ series have labialized values [dzº], etc. (not in all dialects). Ejectives are notated as *p*, etc.

Vowels

i, e, a, u, y

/o/ is absent, and there is no nasalization.

MORPHOLOGY AND SYNTAX

Noun

In Agul, the division of nouns into grammatical classes by class marker (*see*, for example, **Avar**) is atrophied, though petrified·class markers signalling four grammatical classes can be identified in nouns, pronouns, adjectives, and numerals.

NUMBER

The plural marker of consonantal endings is *-ar*; for vocalic endings, *-bur/wur/ yar*: e.g. *is* 'year', pl. *isar*; *gada* 'son', pl. *gadawur*.

DECLENSION

There are 28 cases: four basic (nominative, ergative, genitive, dative) + 24 locative–directional cases arranged in eight series of three terms each, specifying (a) rest in given locus; (b) motion towards speaker; (c) motion away from speaker. The nominative provides the base for the ergative, which is, in turn, the base for all the other cases. For example, the basic cases of *gaga* 'father':

Nominative	gaga
Ergative	gagadi
Genitive	gagadin
Dative	gagadis

-di is only one of many endings marking the ergative; others are *-i, -u, -a, -ni*, etc. The logical subject of a transitive verb is in the ergative, the direct object in the nominative. The subject of a verb of perception is in the dative: *zus wun agwaja* 'I see you'.

The locative–directional series: the eight locus markers are: (1) 'behind': *q*; (2) 'under': *kk*; (3) 'on': *k*; (4) 'in front of': *h*; (5) 'on': *l*; (6) 'at': *w/f*; (7) 'in': '; (8) 'between/among': γ. For example: *usttulil aldi'a kitab* 'on the table (*stul*) lies a book (*kitab*)'. These markers can be affixed to personal pronouns, and recapitulated in the verb:

za**h** kitab **h**aja	in front of me there is a book
za**f** kitab **f**aja	at me there is a book (= I am holding a book)
za**kk** kursi **kk**eja	below me there is a stool

Adjective

Independent and predicative adjectives take number marker and class marker; also case if used as nominal. As attribute, they are invariable. Thus *idžed* 'good', ergative, *idžedi*, etc. *-n, -s*; pl. *idžedar*; but *Idže∅ insandi žanawar ḳini* 'The good man killed the wolf' (subject in ergative).

Pronoun

Personal:

singular	1	zun	plural incl.	x'in; excl.	čin
	2	wun		kün	

These are declined in the four basic cases. Most dialects make no distinction between nominative and ergative, e.g. *zun* and *wun* being used for both.

The genitive form provides the possessive pronoun: *ze čuj* 'my brother'.

DEMONSTRATIVE PRONOUN
me 'this', *te* 'that'; *ge* 'that (down there)'; *le* 'that (up there)'.

INTERROGATIVE PRONOUN
fiš/fuš 'who'; declined with oblique base in *hin-*; *fi* 'what?'

RELATIVE PRONOUN
None; a participial construction is used:

kitab xuraje geda	the boy who is reading the book
kitabar zaš ruxuttar	the books which I read
xurunaje kitab	the book which was read

Numerals

1–10: *sad, qüd, x'ibud, jaqud, jüfud, jegx'id, jerid, mujid, jerḳüd, jiçud*; 11–19 are made by prefixing *çi-* to units. 20, *qqad*; 30, *x'imçur*, 40, *jaɣçur*; 100, *werš*.

Verb

Like Lezgi, Agul has lost the grammatical class system which is typical of Dagestanian languages, and has not replaced it with inflection by personal endings. Conjugation is, therefore, analytic, on the model: personal pronoun – sense-verb in non-finite form – auxiliary (marked for present/past, affirmative/negative).

The non-finite forms used in the formation of tenses are:

(a) the infinitive in *-s*, linked to stem by *-a-* or *-e-* depending on stem vowel: *ruxas* 'to read'; *liḳes* 'to write'. This is the base form for future and subjunctive.
(b) present gerund in *-di, d'*: the base for imperfective forms.
(c) past gerund in *-na*: base for perfective forms.

AUXILIARY VERB
'To be' is defective: the present is *i/e*; negative, *dawa*, past *idi*/variants; negative, *dawadi*. For example *wun idemi e* 'you are a man'; *wun idemi dawa* 'you are not a man'; *zakas idemi x'ase* 'I shall be a man' (lit. 'from-me a man will become').

Example of tense formation:

zun/zas kitab xuruna.i → xuruni	I read (past) the book
wun/was kar aquna.i → aquni	you did the work
zun/zas kitab xuras.e	I shall read the book

NEGATIVE FORMS
The infinitive is negated by prefixing *d*(V)-; *aqas* 'to do': *daqas* 'not to do'. If a pre-verb is present, the negative marker follows it: *qi.ḳas* 'to open': *qi.di.ḳas*

'not to open'. The *-tt-* infix in a verb changes that verb to its antonym: *qacas* 'to put on (clothes)': *qattacas* 'to take (clothes) off'.

VOICE

Active and passive are not formally distinguished. The participial form *xuruf*, for example (with petrified class marker *-f*), can mean, with reference to *kitab* 'book', '(he) who reads ...' or 'which was read'.

PARTICIPLE

-a- is present marker; *-u-* past. The participle takes the plural (class) marker: *aquf*, pl. *aquttar* 'doing (in past)', where *-f* and *-tt-* are class markers.

MODAL AFFIXES

e.g. *gana/hana* 'when ...': *wun adi.gana* 'when you came ...'; *zun xura.gana* 'when I was reading ...'

In addition to the indicative mood there are subjunctive, conditional, imperative, and necessitative moods, the latter formed by attaching participial endings to the genitive form of the verbal noun: *aqub.an.f* 'what has to be done (sing.)'; pl. *aqub.an.tt.ar*.

LOCATIVE–DIRECTIONAL MARKERS

(*See* **noun**, above.) These markers are prefixed to verbs as pre-verbs.

Postpositions

The case system is, in general, sufficiently rich; where necessary adverbs of place/time can be used as postpositions.

Word order

SOV is usual; SVO occurs.

AINU

INTRODUCTION

The Ainu survive, in small and decreasing numbers, in Hokkaido, and, at least until recently, in Sakhalin and the Kurile Islands. It is difficult to assess how many of them retain any knowledge of the Ainu language; but certainly none are monoglot, and the language appears to be on the verge of extinction. It is unwritten, but has a rich repertory of folk and heroic tales. Ainu has no known congeners. Similarities between it and Korean have been detected, and it has been compared with several other language families, but no consistent and convincing relationship has ever been proved. R.A. Miller (1967) identifies the Ainu with the non-Yamato aboriginals who were driven northwards by the Yamato people (*see* **Japanese, Old**).

By the twentieth century two main dialect divisions existed: Sakhalin and Hokkaido, which were not mutually intelligible. The forms set out here are those of the Shizunai dialect of Hokkaido, as described by Refsing (1986).

PHONOLOGY

Consonants

labial: p (→ [b]), m
dental: t (→ [d]), n (→[ŋ]),s (→[ʃ]), ts (→ tʃ) r (→[ɖ])
velar: k (→[g])
glottal: h (→[f])

The semi-vowels /j, w/, occur as glide sounds between vowels: /io/ = [ijo]/, /ue/ = [uwe]. /ɖ/ is notated as *ḍ*.

Vowels

i, e, a, o, u

A long/short contrast was phonemic in Sakhalin Ainu, not in Hokkaido. Realization of the vowels is close to that of Japanese. Some researchers have recorded glottal onset (hamza) to vocalic initials. Refsing (1986) records juncture sandhi and pitch accent with stress on higher syllable.

23

MORPHOLOGY AND SYNTAX

Noun

There is no grammatical gender. Nouns are mainly mono- or disyllabic: *pet* 'river'; *cise* 'house'; *upas* 'snow'; *ni* 'tree'. A plural marker *utar* exists, but number is usually unmarked (*cf.* **Japanese**).

CASE SYSTEM

By affix. The ending -(*h*)V where V is a harmonic echo of the last stem vowel (i.e. a kind of vowel harmony, *see* **Altaic Languages**) is used for a genitive or construct relationship, especially where inalienable ownership is concerned: *apa* 'relative(s)', *apaha* '...'s relatives'; *caro* 'mouth', *caroho* '...'s mouth'.

Again, as generally in Altaic, *i* is neutral: *imak* 'tooth', *imaki* '...'s tooth; *hon* 'stomach', *honi* '...'s stomach'. This possessive form is also used in a partitive sense: *cep* 'fish'; *cep rurihi* 'fish (its) broth'.

The postposition *un* acts as a link between two nouns, the first of which is the origin or locus of the second: *kim un kamuy* 'god of the mountain' (= 'bear') (*kamuy* < Japanese *kami* = 'god').

The affix *kor* 'to have' appears as alienable possession marker: *ku kor menoko* 'my wife'.

Other case postpositions:

> locative: *ta*: *sine to ta* 'in one day'.
> allative: *un*: *toon nay orun* 'into that swamp' (the directional prefixes *e-/o-* + *-un*: *erun/orun*, cf. *e.kim.un* 'to the mountain').
> ablative: (*or*)*wa*: *Kusur un kotan orwa* 'from the village of Kusur'
> comitative: *tura*: *ponnispa tura* 'along with the young gentleman'
> etc.

TOPICALIZING AFFIX

Corresponding to Japanese *wa*, the affix is *anak*: *toon poru nupur* **anak** 'that big mountain' (cf. Japanese *ano okii yama* **wa**).

Adjective

Best treated as a stative verb. When used attributively (as in the last example above) it precedes the noun.

Pronoun

Personal independent with clitic forms:

		Independent	Subject affix	Object affix
singular	1	kuani	ku-	en-
	2	eani	e-	e-
plural	1	cioka	ci-/-as	un-
	2	ecioka	eci-	eci-

Third-person forms are supplied from the demonstrative series + nominalizers: e.g. *e.un.nukar.a* 'you (sing.) are looking at us' (*-a* is durative modal affix); *eci.un.kore* 'you (pl.) gave it to us'.

The base forms are *ta* (proximate), *to* (distant): *taan pe* 'this (person, thing)', *toon pe* 'that (...)'; derogatory of persons (*pe* is a nominalizer).

The root is *ne*: *nen* 'who?', *nep* 'what?'; cf. *neyta* 'where?', *nepkusta* 'why?'

Numerals

1–10: *sine, tu, re, ine, asikne, iwan, arwan, tupesan, sinepesan, wan*. If things are being counted, *-p(e)* is added: *sinep, tup, rep*, etc. For enumerating persons, *-n/-iw* is added: *sinen, tun, ren*, etc.; *waniw* 'ten people'. 11–19: construction with *ikasma* 'more than': e.g. 12, *tu ikasma wan*. 20, *hotnen*; 30, *wan e tu hotne*; 40, *tu hotne*; 50, *wan e re hotne*, etc. 100, *asikne hotne* (5 × 20).

Verb

Refsing (1986) classifies the Ainu verb as follows:

(a) non-affixing verbs denoting natural phenomena: *aptoas* 'it's raining';
(b) intransitive verbs, incompatible with the object affix: *ahun* (pl. *ahup*) 'to enter';
(c) adjectives: *cep pirka* 'the fish is good'; *pirka cep* 'a good fish';
(d) transitive verbs, taking subject and object pronominal prefixes.

Verbs take prefixes (intensifying, moderating, etc.) and suffixes (e.g. of causality). There are no tenses: aspect (perfective, imperfective, terminative, and concomitant) is distinguished, as is modality (durative, iterative, hortative, imperative, desiderative, etc.). The verb is not conjugated for person.

The perfective aspect is marked by the presence of *isam*, linked to the verb by *wa*: *cep ku e wa isam* 'I ate the fish (and finished it)'. The imperfective aspect is marked by two particles: *an* (for sing.), *oka* (for pl.).

Both durative and iterative moods are expressed by reduplication of stem. For the imperative, the bare stem is used, without pronominal affix. For other moods various markers are in use: e.g.

necessitative: *nankor na*: *e nu.nankor.na* 'you must listen' (*nu* 'to listen').
desiderative: *rusuy*: *e e.rusuy.cik* 'if you want to eat it' (*e* 'to eat', *cik* 'if').
intentional: *kusu ki*: *e oman.kusu.ki* 'you intend to go' (*oman* 'to go').
potential: *askay* (affirmative) *aykap* (negative) preceded by summarizing particle *e*: *ku apkas.e.aykap* 'I can't walk' (*apkas* 'to walk').

Somo is a general negating particle: *somo e nu yakka* 'even if you don't listen' (*yakka* 'even though...'). In prohibitions, *iteke* is used. Some verbs have negative versions: *amkir* 'know'; *eramiskari* 'not know'; *easkay* 'be able'; *eapkay* 'be unable'.

Interrogative sentences are marked by final *ya* (cf. Japanese *ka*, Korean *kka*).

Indefinite person: *an-/a-* prefixed to transitive verbs; *-an* suffixed to intransitives: e.g. *an e rusuy* 'one feels like eating it'.

Verbal formatives are added to root to express extensions, modifications of meaning: e.g. *-kor*, which denotes possession of quality expressed in root: *tum* 'strength'; *tumkor* 'to be strong'.

Relative clauses

In attributive position to left of head word: *ekimne kusu soyene nispa* 'the man (*nispa*) who had gone out (*soyene*) to hunt (*ekimne kusu*)'.

Word order

SOV is normal; under certain conditions OSV is found.

---

1   Atpaketa anak ne Itak an, Itak anak Kamui tura
2   an, Itak anak ne Kamui ne ruwe ne. Nei Itak anak
3   ne atpaketa Kamui tura no an nisa ruwe ne. Obitta
       no an okaibe anak ne nei Itak orowa no akara,
       orowa, akarape shinep ne yakka Shinuma isama no
4   akara shomoki nisa ruwe ne Shinuma otta inotu
5   an, inotu anak ne utara pekere ne ruwe ne. Nei
       pekere kunne-i ta at, kunne-i anak ne nei ambe
6   eramushkare nisa ruwe ne. Kamui orowa no
       ateshkara ainu an, reihei anak Yoannes ne ruwe ne.
7   Nei guru paweteshu-i gusu ek, utara obitta shinuma
       gusu aeishokore kuni ne nei pekere gusu paweteshu
8   ki nisa ruwe ne na. Shinuma anak ne nei a pekere shomo
       ne, nei pekere gusu paweteshu ki kuni gusu an gun'ne.

AKAN or TWI

INTRODUCTION

This language is spoken in two major dialects, Ashanti and Fante, by up to 8 million people in Ghana. Akan belongs to the Kwa group of the Niger-Congo family. The form described here is Ashanti, the dialect spoken by the great majority of the Akan-speaking population.

The Basler Evangelische Missionsgesellschaft undertook the task of creating a Twi literary language in the 1840s, and the next 40 years saw the appearance of a Twi Bible, a definitive grammar, and a dictionary, mostly the work of J.G. Christaller. This early literary activity was based on the minor but politically and geographically accessible Akuapem dialect. Through the first half of the twentieth century, however, Ashanti began to be recognized as the proper base for a national literary language. Though certain scholars (e.g. Danquah) continued to write in Akuapem, others like Nketia and Tabi switched to Ashanti. In 1968 A.C. Denteh launched the important literary periodical *Odawuru*.

SCRIPT

Roman plus ɛ, ɔ. In 1961 the Bureau of Ghana Languages devised a common standardized script for all forms of Akan. Tone is not normally marked, nor is nasalization. The correspondence between the script and the actual sounds of Akan is rather weak.

PHONOLOGY

Consonants

stops: p, b, t, d, k, g, ɖ
affricates: tʃ, dʒ
fricatives: f, ɸ, s, ʃ (ç), h
nasals: m, n, ɲ, ŋ
trill: r

Note: all consonants tend to be palatalized before front vowels, and stops tend to affricates.

There is a labialized series: /k°, g°, h°, n°, ŋ°/; /v/ and /l/ occur in foreign words. /ɖ/ is notated as *ɖ*; /ɸ/ as *w*.

Vowels

i, ɪ, e, ɛ, æ, å, ɔ, o, ŭ, u, y

/e/ and /å/ have no nazalised counterparts; all other vowels take nasalization.

VOWEL HARMONY

lax series: ɪ, ɛ, ɑ, o, ʊˆ
tense series: i, e, a, o, u

This division is important for vowel harmony: briefly, a *lax* vowel followed by /i/, /a/, or /ʊ/ is promoted to the next-highest vowel in the *tense* series, e.g. the sequence /ɪ...ʊ/ → /i...u/.

Vowel harmony determines the vocalic structure of the possessive and subject pronouns.

Tones

Three tones, which are phonemic: high, middle, and low. The tones in Akan are characteristically 'terraced', i.e. successive highs begin on a slightly lower level. This in turn affects successive middle tones, but low pitch is not affected.

MORPHOLOGY AND SYNTAX

Noun

No grammatical gender. Nouns are uninflected, though tonal patterns vary, depending on whether the noun is isolate, in construct (e.g. preceded by possessive pronoun), or in a compound.

There are several ways of making a singular noun plural. *-nóm* is a pluralizing suffix: *ɔyére* 'wife', pl. *ɔyérenóm*.

Pluralizing prefixes:

m-: *ɔba* 'child', pl. *mma*;
a-: *ɔkérāmāñ* 'dog', pl. *akérāmāñ*;
n-: *ɛdá* 'day', pl. *nná*.

Some plurals are suppletive: *osáni* 'warrior', pl. *asáfoɔ*

POSSESSION

Marked by order: X's Y = XY – *Ghánà māñ* 'the country of Ghana'; or, a possessive pronoun may be inserted: *abofára nó nhómā* 'the child's (his) book'.

In compounds *ab*, *a* may retain its isolate tone, *b* takes possessive tonal pattern: *Asante.héne.fié* 'the king of Ashanti's palace' (*héne* 'king', *ofíe* 'house').

LOCATIVE

There is a locative marker in *-beá*, and the noun expressing agency adds *-fo*; thus from the root *yaré* 'to be ill', we get: *ayaresábèa* 'hospital'; *ɔyaresáfò* [ɔyar-esáfɔɔ], 'doctor'.

Adjective

As attribute, adjective follows noun, and is often reduplicated: *mmára fófòro pii* 'many new laws' (*mmará* 'law', *fófòro* 'new'); *búùku kétewaa tuntuḿ* 'a small black book' (*tuntuḿ* 'dark in colour').

Exceptionally, some adjectives make a plural form.

Comparative is made with *sēñ*: *eyé duru* 'it is heavy', *eyé duru sēñ búùku nó* 'It is heavier than the book.'

Pronoun

Emphatic personal independent + subject markers (here + copula)

	Singular		Plural	
	Independent	Subject marker	Independent	Subject marker
1	mē	mēyɛ	yéŋ	yɛyɛ
2	wó	wóyè	mó	móyè
3	ɔnó	ɔyɛ	wóŋ	wɔyɛ
impersonal	ɛnó	ɛyɛ	ɛnó	ɛyɛ

The objective forms: *mē, wo, nō* are reduced as verbal suffixes to *-m̀, -ẁ, -ǹ*.

DEMONSTRATIVE PRONOUN
(ɛ)*há* 'this/here'; (ɛ)*hó* 'that/there'. *Eyí* is a demonstrative adjective: *nhómā yí* 'this book'.

INTERROGATIVE PRONOUN
ɛhēna 'who?'

RELATIVE PRONOUN
nea, áà; *ɔyaresáfóɔ áà ɔ́ɔkɔ* 'the doctor who is going'.

Numerals

1–10: *baakó, mmienú, mmiensá, ɛnnáñ, enúm, ensíá, ɛnsóñ, ɛŋwɔtwé, ɛŋkoróŋ, edú.* 11, *dúbàakó*; *12, dúmìenú* ... 20, *aduonū*; 21, *aduonúbàakó* ... 30, *aduasá*, 40, *aduanáñ*. 100, *ɔhá*, 101, *ɔhá né baakó* ...

Verb

Subject markers prefixed to stem: *hu(nu)* 'to see', present tense:

singular	1	mīhu	plural	yehū
	2	wúhū		múhū
	3	ohū		wohū

Negated by low-tone nasal prefixed to stem: *mēte Twìi* 'I speak Twi'; *mēnté Twìi* 'I don't speak Twi'.

Prefixed pronominal object: *mēte asέε* 'I understand' (*asέε* 'meaning'), e.g.:

mēte **w**ásè	I understand you	ɔte **m**ase	he understands me
nasè	him	**w**ase	you
másè	you (pl.)	**w**ɔn ase	them

TENSE AND MOOD MARKERS

progressive tense: the pronominal vowel is lengthened: *mēká* 'I speak': /mēekā/ 'I'm speaking' (lengthening not notated in script).

future positive: prefix *bέ*: *wóbɛko* 'you will go' (+ tonal changes).

immediate future: with *kɔ* 'to go': (+ lengthening of vowel as in progressive): *mēekɔtɔ́ nsuomnám* 'I'm going to buy fish' (*tɔ* 'to buy').

past tense: lengthening or gemination of final vowel: *-y* is added for intransitives: *mēbaay* 'I came'.

perfect: *a-* prefix + specific tonal pattern + contractions. For example, *kɔ* 'to go':

singular	1	makɔ	plural	yɛakɔ
	2	woakɔ		moakɔ
	3	wakɔ		wɔakɔ

The *past* negative is the *perfect* affirmative + low-tone nasal before stem; the *perfect* negative is the *past* affirmative + low-tone nasal before stem: e.g. *mēŋkɔɔ* 'I haven't gone'; *mēŋkóhūù* 'I haven't gone to see it'; *minnii* 'I haven't eaten'; *onnii* 'he hasn't eaten'; *wonnii* 'they haven't eaten'.

CAUSATIVE
ma + low-tone nasal prefix on verb: *mā nō ŋkò* 'have him go!'

SUBJUNCTIVE
Low-tone nasal prefix + high tone on verb.

IMPERATIVE
Stem + low tones; the plural prefix is *mɔ́n-* + high tones: *mɔ́nkasa* 'would you please talk'.

CONSECUTIVE FORM
a- prefix; e.g. with *tumí* 'to be able', *mītumí àkɔ̀* 'I can go'.

Postpositions

Nouns are used to define spatial relationships; e.g. *ɛso* 'upper part (of sth.)', *ɔpɔ́n nɔ́ só* 'on the table('s top)'.

Word order

Any part of speech can be stressed by being promoted to initial position, and additionally stressed, if a noun, by the topicalizer *dέε*. SVO is normal.

1. Mfiase no na Asɛm no wɔ hɔ, na
Asɛm no nɛ Nyankōpoṅ na ɛwɔ hɔ, na
Asɛm no yɛ Onyame.

2 Onoara na mfiase no ɔ-nɛ Nyankōpoṅ wɔ hɔ.

3 Ɛnam no so na woyɛɛ ade nnyinā,
na woankwati no anyɛ biribiara a woyɛɛ.

4 No mu na ṅkwä wɔ, na ṅkwä no
ne nnipa hāṅ;

5 na haṅ no hyerɛṅ wɔ sūm mu, na
esûm no annye no.

6 ¶ Onipa bi wɔ hɔ a Onyankōpoṅ so-
maa no a ne diṅ de Yohane;

7 ɔno na ɔbaa adansedi sɛ orebedi
haṅ no hō adanse, sɛ nnipa nnyinā mfa
no so nnye nni.

8 Ɛnyɛ ɔno ne haṅ no, na sɛ orebedi haṅ no hō adanse.

AKKADIAN

INTRODUCTION

This north-eastern outlier of the Semito-Hamitic family is the oldest known Semitic language. For more than 2,000 years, from the middle of the third millennium BC onwards, it was in use in southern Mesopotamia, whence it spread as the language of international communication and diplomacy to most of the Near East and to Egypt. The language as we know it is not pure Semitic, being, even in its earliest stages, much influenced by Sumerian, which continued, indeed, to act as joint liturgical language of the Assyro-Babylonian Empire. About 2000 BC the language – known up to this point as Old Akkadian – split up into Babylonian (southern Mesopotamia) and Assyrian (northern Mesopotamia).

The most important example of Akkadian literature, the Assyrian version of the Sumerian epic of Gilgamesh, was found in Assurbanipal's library at Nineveh. Other works found here and at other sites such as Uruk, Nippur, and Kültepe, include the Etana myth, the *Enuma Elish*, and *Ludlul bel Nemeqi*, a specimen of Akkadian wisdom literature.

SCRIPT

Akkadian adopted the wholly unsuitable Sumerian cuneiform script (*see* **Sumerian**): not only the syllabic system but also the logographic elements, the ideograms to which Akkadian values were given. For example, when the Sumerian ideogram LUGAL 'king' occurred in an Akkadian text, it could be read as *šarrum* 'king' (Akkadian). Conversely, the Akkadian scribe wishing to write the word *šarrum* could chose either the Sumerian ideogram LUGAL or the phonetic/syllabic writing *ša-ar-ru-um*. The Sumerian use of determinatives, or generic markers, was also adopted. In transcription, determinatives are written in index position to the nominal. For example [d] (shorthand for *dingir* 'god' in Sumerian) precedes Akkadian names of gods: [d]*Marduk*. Similarly, [ki] ('place', in Sumerian) follows place-names: *Bābili*[ki] 'Babylon' (in Akkadian).

A minority of signs are phonetically single-valued, but most have many possible readings; e.g. the simple sign ▷— has at least 15 readings, ranging from V*s*/*š*/*z* to *rum*, *šup*, *dal*. Conversely, the sound /a/ has several different graphs in cuneiform.

Where more than one Akkadian reading of a Sumerian ideogram was possible, the final syllable of the required reading was added in phonetic script;

and these phonetic complements were used to distinguish cases in Akkadian. Thus:

LUGAL-ru-um read as šarrum = nominative case, 'the king'
LUGAL-**ra-am** read as šar**ram** = accusative case, 'the king'

PHONOLOGY

Consonants

labial: p, b, m, w
dental: t, d, n, s, z, l, r; emphatic dentals: ṭ, ṣ /[ts]
palatal: ç, ʃ, j
velar: k, g, ḫ
uvular: q, ', '

Note: ' is basically hamza, but also does duty for /h, ɦ/, *gh* (/ɣ/); ' = Arabic 'ain.

Vowels

Four vowels are notated in the script: common Semitic /a, i, u/ + /e/ as secondary vowel. Traces of vowel harmony may be due to Sumerian influence.

Sandhi: the language is characterized by an extensive system of environmentally induced consonant and vowel change, regressive assimilation, consonant and vowel loss, epenthetic vocalization.

MORPHOLOGY AND SYNTAX

Noun

The triliteral root is basic in the language (*see* **Semito-Hamitic Languages**). Nouns are masculine or feminine. The masculine marker is Ø, feminine is *-t*: *mār-u(m)* 'son'; *mart-u(m)* 'daughter'; *bēl-u(m)* 'lord'; *bēlt-u(m)* 'mistress'.
    Mimation was regular in the Old Akkadian period, but lost in the later Assyrian-Babylanian period.
    Many very old Akkadian feminine nouns have no *-t* marker: *ummu(m)* 'mother'; *īnu* 'eye'; *lišānu(m)* 'tongue'.

STATE
Absolute or construct. In the construct, the two items are treated as a unit, with the stress on the second: *bīt ábi(m)* 'the father's house'; or with pronoun enclitic: *harrān-ša* 'her way'. The construct case unit remains invariable for all cases: *sar mātim* 'the king of the land (nom., acc., gen., dat.)'.

NUMBER
Singular, dual, and plural. In the oldest period use of the dual was generalized, i.e. it could be used of any two referents. From Old Babylonian on, use of the dual was restricted to paired parts of the body: *īnān* 'the eyes'; *šēpān* 'the feet'.

The masculine plural is formed (a) by lengthening the final vowel; (b) by changing -*ānu* to -*āni*. Some nouns may have both forms.

Most feminine nouns take -*ātu*: *ummu* 'mother' – *ummātu; šarra* 'empress' – *šarrātu*.

In the later period, the oblique forms (see below) -*āni*/-*āti* seem to have ousted the direct forms -*ānu*/-*ātu*.

CASE

The characteristic pattern (especially in Babylonian texts) is -*u*, -*i*, -*a* in the singular, i.e. triptote, with diptote in dual and plural: -*a*/-*i*, *e*; -*u*/-*i*, *e*: e.g.

masc. sing.	nom. šarru(m),	gen.	šarri(m), acc. šarram
dual	šarrān	gen.–acc.	šarrīn
pl.	šarrū		šarrī *or* šarrānū – šarrānī

fem. bēltum – bēltim – bēltam; pl. bēlētum – bēlētim

Adjective

As attribute, the adjective follows noun and agrees with it in gender, number, and case: e.g. *nakrum* 'hostile':

masc. sing. nakrum – nakrim – nakram; pl. nakrūtum – nakrutīm;
fem. nak**art**um – nakrim – nakram; pl. nak**rāt**um – nak**rāt**im

Pronoun

The independent personal pronouns are:

				Enclitic forms		
	Singular			*Plural*	*Singular*	*Plural*
1		anāku		nīnu	-i,-ja	-ni
2	masc.	attā	masc.	attunu	-ka	-kunu
	fem.	attī	fem.	attina	-ki	-kina
3	masc.	šū	masc.	šunu	-šu	-šunu
	fem.	šī	fem.	šina	-ša	-šina

These are declined for gen.–acc. and dative: e.g. for *anāku*: gen.–acc. *jāti*, dat. (*ana*) *jāšim*.

The enclitic forms are added to nouns to act as possessive pronominal endings: *bēli* 'my lord', *bēlka* – *bēlki*, etc. These are nominative–accusative forms, and are declined for genitive: *bēlīja*, *bēlīka*, etc.

DEMONSTRATIVE

šu, fem. *ši*; pl. *šunu* – *šina*; *annu*(*m*), fem. *annītu*(*m*). The oblique forms vary very considerably; the dual is very rare.

INTERROGATIVE

mannu(*m*) 'who?'; *mīnu*(*m*) 'what?' These are not marked for person, number, or gender, but take three-fold case pattern, -*u*, -*i*, -*a*.

RELATIVE PRONOUN

šu, fem. *šat*; pl. *šūt*, *šāt*. These have genitive forms. For relative-clause formation, see below.

Numerals

1–10: *ištēn, šena, šalaš, erbe, ḫamiš, šiššu* (?), *sebe, samāne, tiše, ešer*; these are masculine forms. The feminine forms are: *ištiat, šitta, šalāšat, erbet*, etc. From 3 to 10, a masculine noun takes a feminine numeral, and vice versa (*cf.* **Arabic**). 100, *me'at*. 20 to 50: decades are the dual forms of the corresponding units: 40, *erbā*, etc.

Verb

The root is typically CCVC: **mḫur* 'to receive'. Verbs are active or stative; formally they are grouped as: (a) strong verbs (triliterals, including strengthened biliterals); (b) weak verbs; (c) verbs doubly or triply weak; (d) quadriliterals. There are finite and non-finite forms. Finite forms show gender, person, and number. The non-finite forms are treated as nouns; the infinitive has case, but is not marked for person or number. The following moods are distinguished: indicative, imperative, optative, allative, subjunctive.

Instead of the typical Semitic division into perfective and imperfective aspects, Akkadian has an idiosyncratic quadruple segmentation which corresponds broadly to a present/preterite/perfect system, with the fourth member acting as a kind of stative. This stative includes adjectival verbs: e.g. *damiq* 'he is good'.

The forms here set out are for Version I (*see* Versions, below):

Indicative
present: the formants are prefix + gemination of second radical + suffix: *imaḫḫaṣa* 'he strikes'; *tamaḫḫaṣa* 'you (pl.) strike'.
preterite: prefix + root: *imḫaṣ* 'he struck'.
perfect: prefix + root with *-ta-* infix: *imtaḫaṣ* 'he has struck'. This form is peculiar to Akkadian.
stative: root + personal suffixes: *bēl* 'he is lord'; *bēlēta* 'you (masc.) are lord'.
Imperative second person only. Formally, the second person prefix *ta-* of the preterite is dropped, and an epenthetic vowel inserted: (*taprus*, *∅prus*) *purus* 'cut!'
Optative Particle *lū/lu* + preterite: *lušpur* 'I want to write' (*ašpur* 'I wrote'); *lū salim* 'may he prosper!'
Allative Present, preterite, and stative take *-am* (consonantal final) or *-nim* (vocalic final); the form expresses benefactive mode, or motion towards speaker: *išpuram* '(from there) he wrote (to me)'. The form is often used with the indirect object: *irrubū.nim.kum → irrubūnikkum* 'they come in to you'; *ašpurakkuššu* 'I sent him to you.' (← *ašpur.am.kum.šu*).

Subjunctive Used in subordinate clauses only; the marker is *-u*: *sa... iksudu* '(that) he conquer...' (*iksud* 'he conquered').

VERSIONS

(Cf. *binyanim* in **Hebrew**; derived stems in **Arabic**):

1. base stem;
2. second radical geminated: intensifies;
3. the so-called *š*-stem: made by prefixing *š(a)*-: causative in meaning;
4. the *n*-stem: made by prefixing *n(a)*-: passive;
5. *-ta*- infix following the first radical in stems 1, 2, or 3; reciprocals;
6. *-tan(a)* infix following the first radical in stems 1 or 2, or following the first pre-radical formant in stems 3 and 4; iterative.

NEGATION

ul(a) negates the predicate in the principal clause; *lā* is used in subordinate clauses, and as the particle of prohibition.

Relative clauses

Relative clauses are genitival complements introduced by *ša*; the verb is in the subjunctive:

> ḫammurabi ša Šamaš kīnātim išruku-šum
> Hammurabi, on whom Šamaš conferred the truth ...

Ša may be omitted: *bīt ipušu* 'the house he built'.

Prepositions

Preposition and noun are in construct relationship, i.e. the noun takes the genitive ending: *ina bīti(m)* 'in the house'; *ana jāšim* 'to me'; *ana nāri(m)* 'to the river'; *eli šarrāni* 'against the emperor'; *adi ḫamšim warḫim* 'till the fifth month'.

Word order

SOV is normal, OSV is possible; relegation of the verb to final position is untypical of Semitic, and may be due to Sumerian influence.

ALBANIAN

INTRODUCTION

Generally regarded as the sole survivor of the Illyrian branch of Indo-European languages, Albanian (*gjuha shqipe*) is spoken today in two main dialects: Tosk (southern) and Gheg (northern). The boundary between the two forms is roughly marked by the river Shkumbini. The total number of speakers of both dialects within the Socialist People's Republic of Albania is about 3 million. In addition, there are some 2 million Gheg speakers in the Kosova Autonomous Region of Yugoslavia, and a few thousand speakers of a third dialect, *arbëresh*, in southern Italy and Greece. Albanian literature, mainly in Gheg, dates from the sixteenth century (1555, Buzuku's *Meshari*). Tentative steps towards the creation of a unified national language culminated first in the adoption of the Roman alphabet (1908, Congress of Manastir) and secondly in the selection of the Elbasan (central) dialect (a form of Gheg) as the most suitable base for such a language. From 1920 to the 1950s both dialects were used for literary purposes. In 1952, however, Tosk was officially declared as the base for the new standardized literary language. In Yugoslavia, Gheg continues to prosper as both spoken and literary language. Tosk and Gheg are mutually intelligible, and differ indeed only in certain points – most importantly in the rhotacism of Tosk: Gheg -V*n*V- = Tosk -V*r*V-; e.g. Gheg *zani* 'voice', Tosk *zëri*; and in the formation of the future tense (*see* Verb, below).

SCRIPT

As noted above, the Congress of Manastir (1908) provided Albanian with a standardized script based on the Roman alphabet plus *ç* and *ë*; *w* is not used. The following digraphs are used: *th* = /θ/, *dh* = /ð/, *sh* = /ʃ/, *zh* = /ʒ/, *xh* = /dʒ/, *gj* = /g'/, *nj* = /ɲ/, *ll* = /ɫ/, *rr* = /rr/.

PHONOLOGY

Consonants

    stops: p, b, t, d, k, g; k', g'
    affricates, ts, dz, tʃ, dʒ
    fricatives: f, v, θ, ð, s, z, ʃ, ʒ, j, h
    nasals: m, n, ɲ, ŋ
    laterals: l, ɫ, r, rr

Vowels

Tosk has seven vowel phonemes; Gheg has twelve, including five nasal vowels. The Tosk series:

i, e, a, ə, o, u, y
/ə/ is notated as *ë*.

Stress

Stress is frequently on the penultimate syllable.

MORPHOLOGY AND SYNTAX

Noun

Albanian has two genders, masculine and feminine, with traces of an old neuter, limited now to very few words.

There are two articles, definite and indefinite. The latter is sing. *një*, pl. *ca* or *disa*; thus, *një shok* 'a comrade', *disa shokë* 'comrades'.

The definite article is affixed to the noun and is coded for gender (*cf.* **Bulgarian** and **Romanian**):

> masculine affixes: *-i*, *-u*, *-ri/-ni*, *-a*: *mal* 'mountain', *mali* 'the mountain'; *zog* 'bird', *zogu* 'the bird'.
> feminine affix: *-a*: *shtëpi* 'house', *shtëpia* 'the house'; *motër* 'sister', *motra* 'the sister'.

PLURAL
Typical masculine plural endings are *-a*, *-e*, *-nj*, *-q(e)*, *-gj(e)*, *-ë*: e.g. *mësim* 'lesson' – *mësime*; *mal* 'mountain' – *male*; *ari* 'bear' – *arinj*; *mik* 'friend' – *miq*; *pyll* 'forest' – *pyje*; *punëtor* 'worker' – *punëtorë*.

Feminine plural: *-a*, *-e*; often no change: e.g. *lule* 'flower' – *lule*; *dhomë* 'room' – *dhoma*.

Umlaut occurs in some masculine nouns: *breg* 'coast' – *brigje*; *plak* 'old man' – *pleq*.

The plural nominative definite form ends in *-t(ë)*.

CASE
The following two paradigms show a masculine and a feminine noun declined with and without definite article, in four cases and two numbers.

Masculine: mal 'mountain'

	Singular		Plural	
	Indefinite	*Definite*	*Indefinite*	*Definite*
nom.	mal	mali	male	malet
gen.	mali	malit	malesh	malevet
dat.	mali	malit	maleve	malet
acc.	mal	malin	male	malevet

Feminine: shtëpi 'house'

	Singular		Plural	
	Indefinite	*Definite*	*Indefinite*	*Definite*
nom.	shtëpi	shtëpia	shtëpi	shtëpitë
gen.	shtëpie	shtëpisë	shtëpive	shtëpivet
dat.	shtëpie	shtëpisë	shtëpive	shtëpivet
acc.	shtëpi	shtëpinë	shtëpi	shtëpitë

Adjective

The attributive adjective follows the noun to which it is connected by the inflected article.

	Indefinite 'a good friend'		*Definite 'the good friend'*	
	Singular	*Plural*	*Singular*	*Plural*
nom.	mik i mirë	miq të mirë	miku i mirë	miqt e mirë
gen.–dat.	miku të mirë	miqve të mirë	mikut të mirë	miqvet të mirë
acc.	mik të mirë	miq të mirë	mikun e mirë	miqt e mirë

Certain adjectives, e.g. those derived from nouns or verbs, do not take the connecting article: *një shkollë fillore* 'an elementary school' (*fillore ← filloj* 'to begin').

An adjective which takes the article in attributive position keeps it in predicative position: *vendi është i bukur* 'the place is beautiful', *vendet janë të bukura* (pl.).

Pronoun

The base forms are:

	Singular		Plural	
	Subject	*Oblique*	*Subject*	*Oblique*
1	unë	më	na/ne	na
2	ti	të	ju	ju

Third-person forms are supplied by the demonstrative series (see below).

DEMONSTRATIVE PRONOUN/ADJECTIVE

The proximate series is based on *ky*, fem. *kjo*; the distal series is *ai*, fem. *ajo*.

The series *ai, ata; ajo, ato* is used for the third-person pronoun, with oblique forms *e* 'him, her', and *i* 'to him, to her'.

These forms fuse with other oblique pronouns: e.g. *më + e → ma*: *ma dha librin* 'he gave me the book'.

A noun as complement is anticipated by a pronominal copy:

Do t'**i** them edhe Abazit 'I'll tell A. as well'

E njihte mirë Dinin 'He knew D. well'

Unë **i** fola asaj vajze 'I spoke to this girl'

POSSESSIVE PRONOUNS

These follow the noun possessed; here, the singular and plural nominative forms are given for each person:

libri im	my book	librat e mi	my books	libri ynë	our book
				librat tanë	our books
libri yt	your book	librat e tu	your books	libri juaj	your (pl.) book
				librat tuaj	your (pl.) books
libri i tij	his book	librat e tij	his books	libri i tyre	their book
				librat e tyre	their books

INTERROGATIVE PRONOUN

kush 'who?', inflected for case only; *çka* 'what?'; *cili* 'which?' is inflected for gender, number, and case: *cili djal dhe cila vajzë* 'which boy and which girl?'

RELATIVE PRONOUN

që is not inflected; *i cili*, etc. is inflected; e.g.

nje ndërtesë e vogël, e cila ndryshonte fare pak nga shtëpitë e tjera
a building which differed little from the other houses
(*ndërtesë* (fem.) 'building'; *ndryshoj* 'to differ'; *tjeter*, (pl.) *tjerë* 'other')

Numerals

1–10: *një, dy, tre/tri* (the only numeral marked for gender), *katër, pesë, gjashtë, shtatë, tetë, nëndë, dhjetë*. 11, *njëmbëdhjetë*; 12, *dymbëdhjetë* ... 20, *njëzet*; 30, *tridhjetë*; 40, *dyzet*; i.e. *dyzet* is a vigesimal form; 60 and 80, however, revert to decimal form: *gjashtëdhjetë, tetëdhjetë*. 100, *(një)qind*.

Verb

The Albanian verb has two voices, active (unmarked), and medio-passive, the latter having a specific set of endings. There are six moods and eight tenses; only the indicative mood has all of these tenses, the other moods – subjunctive, conditional, optative, admirative – have present and perfect tenses, to which the subjunctive and the admirative add an imperfect and a pluperfect. The imperative mood has a present form only.

Tenses may be further sub-divided by aspect into perfective and imperfective categories. Finite forms are marked throughout for person and number.

There are two conjugations: (a) vocalic stems, e.g. *jetoj* 'I live'; and (b) consonant stems, e.g. *sjell* 'I bring'.

Tenses are primary or analytical; the latter are formed by means of the auxiliaries: *jam* 'I am', and *kam* 'I have'.

Thematic stems are affected by umlaut/ablaut, and some forms are suppletive: e.g. *shoh* 'I see'; imperfect *shihja*; aorist *pashë*.

THE AUXILIARIES
The basic forms of *jam* and *kam* are:

present:	*jam, je, është*; pl. *jemi, jeni, janë*
imperfect:	*isha, ishe*
aorist:	*qeshë, qe* ...
subjunctive:	*të jem, të jesh* ...
past participle:	*qenë*

present:	*kam, ka*; pl. *kemi, kanë*
imperfect:	*kisha, kishe*
aorist:	*pata, pate* ...
subjunctive:	*të kem, të kesh* ...
past participle:	*pasur*

MODAL VERBS
Two important modals are: *dua* 'I want' and *mund* 'I can'.

SPECIMEN CONJUGATION
Vocal stem, *kërkoj* 'I ask for, seek'.

Indicative

present:	*kërkoj, -n; -n*, pl. *kërkojmë, -ni, -jnë*
imperfect:	*kërkoja, -je, -nte*; pl. *kërkonim, -nit, -nin*
aorist:	*kërkova, -ve, -i*; pl. *kërkuam, -uat, -uan*
perfect:	*kam, ke*, etc. *kërkuar*
future:	*do të kërkoj, do të kërkosh* ... (subjunctive endings, see below).

This is the Tosk form of the future tense; the Gheg model is *kam me* + infinitive.

Subjunctive

present:	*të kërkoj, -sh, -jë*; pl. as indicative present.
imperfect:	*të* + indicative imperfect forms

Admirative

present:	*kërkuakam, kërkuake*, etc. (i.e. *kërkua* + present tense of *kam*)

Optative

present:	*kërkofsha, -fsh, -ftë*; pl. *kërkofshim, -fshi, -fshin*

Imperative:	sing. *kërko*; pl. *kërkoni*
Past participle:	*kërkuar*

Medio-passive voice: vocalic stems have the augment *-h-* in the present:

present:	*kërkohem, -hesh, -et*; pl. *kërkohemi, -heni, -hen*
imperfect:	*kërohesha, -heshe* . . .
aorist:	*u-kërkova, u-kërkove, u-kërkua*; pl. *u-kërkuam, -uat, -uan*
perfect:	*jam kërkuar* ... etc.

NEGATIVE

nuk and *s'* are general negating particles; *kemi* 'we have'; *s'kemi* 'we don't have'; *Goni nuk flet inglisht* 'Goni doesn't speak English.' *Mos* is used with the imperative: *mos pini duhan* 'don't smoke'.

Prepositions

(a) with nominative (usually in definite form): e.g. *nga* 'from', *tek* 'at', *gjer* 'until', etc.
(b) with accusative: e.g. *mbi* 'on', *me* 'with', *në*, 'in', *pa* 'without', etc.
(c) with dative (ablative): e.g. *pranë* 'near', *kundër* 'against', *mbrapa* 'after', etc.

Word formation

(a) compounding: e.g. noun + noun: *hekur* 'iron + *udhë* 'way': *hekurudhë* 'railway'.
(b) by suffix: e.g. *-im* forming abstract nouns: *kujtimi* 'memory' (cf. *kujtoj* 'remember'); *-(t)ore* denoting locus of activity: *grunore* 'wheatfield' (cf. *grüne* 'wheat').
(c) by prefixing preposition or adverb: *në(n)* 'below' + *punës* 'working': *nëpunësi* 'employee'
adverb + adjective: *jashtzakònshëm* (*jasht* 'outside' + *zakon* (Slav.) 'law, custom') 'unusual, extraordinary'
privative prefix *pa-*: *pakuptueshëm* 'incomprehensible' (cf. *kuptoj*, 'I remember'; *kuptueshëm* 'comprehensible')

Prefixes frequently used to form derived verbs are: *(sh)për-*, *mb-*, *sh-*, *c-*: e.g. from

> *shkruaj* 'to write', *përshkruaj* 'to describe'
> *jashtë* 'outside', *përjashtoj* 'to exclude'
> *lidh* 'tie, *mbledh* 'to collect'.

Word order

SVO is normal.

1   Që përpara herësë ishte Fjala, edhe Fjala
ishte me Perëndinë, edhe Fjala ishte Perëndi,
2 Këjo ishte që përpara herësë me Perëndinë.
3 Të-gjitha u bënë me anë t' asaj; edhe pa
atë nuk' ubë as ndonjë *gjë* që është bërë.
4 Nd' atë ishte jetë, edhe jeta ishte drita e
5 njerësvet. Edhe drita ndrit nd' errësirët, edhe
errësira nuk' e kupëtoj.
6   Qe *një* njeri dërguarë nga Perëndia, i-
7 cili *e kishte* emërinë Joan. Ky erdhi për dëshmim, që të apë dëshmim. Dritënë, që të be-
8 sonjënë të-gjithë me anë t' ati. Ay nuk' ishte
Drita, po *qe dërguarë* që të apë dëshmim
për Dritënë.

(Tosk dialect)

43

ALEUT

INTRODUCTION

Aleut is distantly related to the Eskimo languages: a proto-Aleut/Eskimo language seems to have been spoken in pre-historic times in the western seaboard (Bering) area of Alaska. Today, Aleut is spoken by small numbers in the Aleutian Islands, the Alaskan Peninsula, and the Commander Islands (USSR). Krauss (1979) estimated that out of 2,000 Aleuts on US territory, about 700 spoke Aleut. Pedagogic efforts to revive the language are being made at the Alaska Native Language Center in Fairbanks. There are two main dialects: Western (Attuan) and Eastern (Unalaskan). On Soviet territory the language is virtually extinct.

SCRIPT

In the 1830s the Russian scholar I.E. Veniaminov used an adaptation of Cyrillic to notate Aleut, and laid a substantial foundation for the study of the language. Cyrillic continued to be used for religious texts and instruction even after the Alaska Purchase (1867). In the twentieth-century the Roman script was adopted.

PHONOLOGY

Consonants

The consonantal inventory is notable for the absence of the labial series, apart from /w/ and /m/. The dental series includes /t/→ [θ] and /d/→[ð]: lateral /ł/. There are parallel velar and uvular series: /k/q, x/χ, g/γ./. Here, ń = /ŋ/.

Vowels

The basic vowel pattern is /a, i, u/; /i/ blends into [ɛ], /u/ into [ɔ]. Veniaminov distinguished four values of *a*: over-short, short, long, and over-long.

MORPHOLOGY AND SYNTAX

Noun

All stems are potentially nominal and verbal. Most nouns are disyllables: e.g. *tánakh* 'water'; *kannogh* 'heart'. The final *-kh/-gh* is discarded before the case endings are added: e.g. *ádakh* 'father': *áda.n* 'the fathers', *áda.m* 'of the father'.

A stem treated as nominal has three numbers: e.g. *agitudakh* 'the brother', *agituda.kek* 'the two brothers', *agituda.n* 'the brothers'.

Veniaminov's paradigms show, in addition to nominative, accusative (= nom.), and genitive (*-m*), a dative (*-man*), and a relative genitive in *-gan*, apparently used obviatively (cf. Algonquian 4th person). Cf. *-p/-ata* in **Inuit**. Example: *agôghum anále.gan tunó* 'the word of the kingdom of God'.

Other case relationships are supplied by postpositions: e.g. *ésik* 'with', *khulèn* 'for', *ko'an* 'on', take the genitive: *áda.m ésik* 'with the father'; *alèghu.m ko'an* 'on the sea'. Note that the number marker moves to the end of the postpositional phrase if the noun is in the relative genitive: e.g. *tána.gan il.kek* 'in the two lands' (*il.in* 'in', *kek* = dual marker).

Pronoun

PERSONAL
Subject and object forms with possessive enclitics:

	Singular	Possessive	Dual	Plural
1	thiň	-ň	toman	toman
2	txen	-n	txidhek	txiče
3	iňan	-n	iňakux	iňakun

There are also dative forms, e.g. for first person *noň – tumanan – tumanen*.

DEMONSTRATIVE PRONOUN/ADJECTIVE
Three grades of distancing with many sub-divisions specifying locus, modality, etc.

POSSESSIVE MARKERS
For example, *áda.ň* 'my father'; *áda.n.ň → áda.neň* 'my father's'. The third person is distinguished from the second by stress shift (vowel lengthening): e.g. *áda.n* 'thy father', *adá.n* 'his father'. The possessive-marker grid is, thus, 9×3, the middle term being a double dual: e.g. *tána.keňen* 'the two lands of us two'. All possessive forms can be declined.

INTERROGATIVE
kin 'who?'; *alhkhotakh* 'what?'

Numerals

1–5: *attákan, 'álak, khánkun, síčen, čáň*; 6–10: *attóň, ullyóň, khamčíň, sečíň, 'átkekh. Khankódhem 'áthekh* 30, where *-dhem* = 'times'. *Sísikh* 100.

Verb

The verb shows class, mood, tense, person, number, voice, and version (affirmative or negative). Examples of tense formation, indicative mood:

present: *-ku-*, e.g. *táṅa.ku.kh* 'he drinks'
past indef.: *-na-*, e.g. *táṅa.na.kh* 'he was drinking'
perfective: *-kha-*, e.g. *táṅa.kha* 'he drank'
future: *-doka.(ku)-*, e.g. *táṅa.dóka.ku.kh* 'he will drink'
semelfactive: *-kha.gan-*, e.g. *táṅa.kha.gan* 'he will drink once'
conditional: *-gu-*, e.g. *táṅa.gu.n* 'if he drinks'
imperative: markers are *-da*, *-dhek*, e.g. *táṅa.da/dhek!*

The above forms apply to the great majority of Aleut verbs; a few vary.

Negative version: three particles are used: óluk, affixed to conjugational endings, and *laka/laga* added to stem, preceding modal and tense markers. e.g. *táṅa.laka.kh* 'he doesn't drink', *táṅa.nagh.óluØ.theṅ* 'I haven't drunk'.
Prohibitive: *táṅa.laga.da/dhek! 'don't drink!'*

PERSONAL ENDINGS
There are several sets, each with specific usages: e.g.

	Singular	Dual	Plural
1	kheṅ/theṅ	1, 3 kek	neṅ
2	xtxen	xtxidhek	xtiče
3	kh		ṅen

These are used for affirmative version in present, past indefinite, and future, and for the negative version in *oluk*, etc.: e.g. *táṅa.ko.kheṅ* 'I drink', *táṅa.laka.kheṅ* 'I don't drink', *táṅa.ko.xtxen* 'you drink'.

PASSIVE
-lga-/-ghe- infixed immediately after stem: e.g. *táṅa.lga.kukh* 'it is drunk/one drinks it'; *táṅa.lga.da* (passive imperative).

FINITE VERB WITH PRONOMINAL OBJECT
The verb agrees in person with the subject, in number with the object: e.g. *thiṅ imdhek exxta.ko.kek* 'I speak to you two', where *-kek* is first person dual.

Participles marked for tense are available in both versions and all three voices, including reflexive: e.g. *táṅa.na.kh* 'who drank'; *táṅa.dóka.kh* 'having to drink, about to drink'; *táṅa.dóka.na.ghóluk* 'not having to drink'.

AUXILIARY CONJUGATION WITH *á-* INFIX
ákukh 'is/are'; *axta.kukh* (durative); *axkhakukh* 'becomes'; *aghekukh* 'has/have': e.g.

*táṅa.**ṅan**.aghe.kó.**kheṅ*** 'I'm drinking right now' (*ṅan* is first person infinitive marker)

*táṅa.**men**.aghe.kó.**xtxen*** 'you are drinking right now' (*men* is second person infinitive marker)

The periphrastic conjugation with *á-* can be used with all moods, versions, tenses. Note that the *-ghe-* infix in *aghekukh* 'he has', is the passive marker. Cf.

ádakh axtakukh → *ádaxtakukh* 'he is a father' ⎫ both forms can then
ádakh aghekukh → *ádaghekukh* 'he has a father' ⎰ be conjugated in full

That is, 'he has a father' is treated as the passive of 'he is a father'.

There is in addition a wide inventory of verbal infixes expressing many nuances: causative *-čxhi-*; terminative *-kada-*; inchoative *-kali-*; desiderative *-tu-*; potential *-masyo-*: collective *-gya-*, etc. Example: *táña.kali.gó.men* 'if you start to drink'.

Word formation

For example, agentive, *-takh/-nakh*: e.g. *tayá* 'sell', *tayánakh* 'seller'. Possessive, *-ghekh*: 'endowed with': e.g. *makha* 'riches', *makhághekh* 'wealthy'. Instrumental, *-sekh*: e.g. *mayaghá* 'to fish', *mayaghásekh* 'harpoon'. *-lukh* indicates locus: e.g. *tayá* 'sell', *tayálukh* 'market'.

Compounding occurs, but is not prolific.

ꙁ҃. Уматáликъ [1] камга-
дáчи: тꙋмáнинъ А́дакъ [z]᾽,
А́манъ акꙋ́хтхинъ и́нинъ кꙋ́-
нинъ! А сáнъ амчꙋ́гасꙋ̑даѝта [3];

і҃. А́гали́нъ а̂кáѝга; Анꙋ_
хтанáѝгхинъ малгáѝганъ и̂_
нимъ кꙋ́ганъ кáюхъ тáнамъ
кꙋ́ганъ;

а҃і. Калгáдамъ анꙋ́хтанá
ни́нъ а̂качá ꙋ̑а̂́мъ;

в҃і. Кáюхъ тꙋмáнинъ á_
дꙋ̑нъ нѝнъ игниͦда᷑, а̂мáкꙋнъ
тꙋ́манъ кáюхъ малгали́гинъ
ни́нъ адꙋ́гинанъ игнидакꙋнъ;

г҃і. Кáюхъ ѝтꙋманъ сꙋ̂глá_
тачхи̂ганахѝтхинъ; ѝа́ѝга адá_
лꙋ̑дамъ илꙋ̑нъ ѝтꙋ́манъ а̂ѝгичá.
А́галинъ᷑, Кáюнъ кáюхъ А́лгꙋ_
насꙋ̑дáꙋ́синъ аꙋ̑áнъ ꙋ́сіо̑ганъ
акꙋ́нинъ мáлникъ. А́ли́нь.

(Matt. 6: 9–15)

ALTAIC LANGUAGES

Three contiguous groups of languages – Turkic, Mongolian, and Tungusic – occupy a broad swathe of territory in Inner Asia, extending from the borders of China in the east and north to the Urals and the Mediterranean in the west. While they are mutually unintelligible, these three groups share so many common features that genetic relationship seems probable. They are accordingly united under a collective title as the 'Altaic' languages, after the mountain range which cuts diagonally through their territory, dividing Mongolian and Tungusic in the north and east from Turkic in the west. Internally, all three groups are remarkably homogeneous.

The salient common features may be listed as follows:

1. A rather simple consonantal inventory based on the series /b, p, m; d, t, n; g, k, ŋ/; + /r, l/, one or two sibilants, some palatalized consonants and velar fricatives like /x/ and /γ/. The vowel systems are well developed, usually containing rounded vowels: /œ, y/.
2. Vowel harmony is observed throughout the family, except where alien influence has been strong (e.g. in the case of Uzbek, a Turkic language affected by long contact with the Iranian language Tadzhik). In general, back vowels are followed by back, front by front, with /i/ neutral.
3. All Altaic languages are basically agglutinative; suffixation is used to the virtual exclusion of prefixation.
4. There is no grammatical gender; no articles.
5. In the 1st person plural a distinction is often made between inclusive and exclusive forms.
6. All member languages have case endings showing a basic parallelism. The number of cases in individual languages varies from about a dozen in the Tungusic languages to five or six in Turkic.
7. There is a recurrent parallelism between the personal possessive markers and the verbal personal endings.
8. Absence of verb meaning 'to have'; possession indicated by dative or postpositional constructions.
9. Absence of relative pronoun; relative clauses are turned into participial constructions.
10. Modifier precedes modified; attributive adjective precedes noun without concord (exceptions in Tungusic).
11. The singular is used with numerals.
12. No prepositions; postpositions are used throughout the family.

13. Lexicon: evidence here for a Proto-Altaic parent language rests mainly on establishing sets of regular phonological correspondences between the three families, yielding referents at least belonging to related semantic fields. In several cases it has proved possible to extend these equations to Korean and Old Japanese, and the Altaic family has been correspondingly expanded. By means of glottochronological techniques, a separation date for Korean and the Tungusic languages has been put at 3500 BC.

The thesis of a common 'Altaic' origin is not universally accepted. It has been pointed out that the common features listed above, along with others, may be due to socio-linguistic contact and mutual interaction over the millennia. Contemporary evidence of such contact in action can be seen, for example, in the mutual interaction of the Turkic language Yakut with Evenki, which is Tungusic.

The undoubted similarities between the three groups would then be typological rather than genetic, and they can be shown to be shared with other languages which are in no way connected with the Altaic question.

At present, some 40 Altaic languages are spoken by about 100 million people, more than half of this total being made up by one language – Turkish. Proof that Korean and Japanese are Altaic languages would, of course, increase the number of speakers by about 200 million.

See **Turkic Languages, Altay, Azerbaydzhani, Bashkir, Chuvash, Gagauz, Karachay-Balker, Karakalpak, Kazakh, Khakas, Kirgiz, Kumyk, Tatar, Turkish, Turkmen, Tuvinian, Uzbek; Buryat, Kalmyk, Mongolian (Classical and Modern), Mongolian Languages of China, Oirat; Even, Evenki, Manchu, Nanay, Negidal, Nenets, Udege; Korean; Japanese (Classical and Modern Standard).**

ALTAY

INTRODUCTION

Altay belongs to the Kirgiz-Kipchak group of Eastern Turkic, with about 50 to 60 thousand speakers in the Gorno-Altay Autonomous Region of the Altay Kray. Prior to Russian colonization in the eighteenth century, the Altay region, inhabited by several Turkic tribes, formed part of the Dzhungaria Khanate. In the early years of Soviet rule, the Altay peoples were collectively known as 'Oirots'. They are now officially designated as 'Altay'. Northern and southern dialects of the language differ markedly, the former tending towards the Uigur-Oguz group (in Baskakov's 1966 classification). The modern literary language is based on southern usage. Literature in Altay is almost exclusively post-1920. At least one newspaper and some periodicals appear in the language.

At least two forms of taboo language are found in Altay. The primary words for certain objects in the environment are also used as male proper names: e.g. *malta* 'axe' (Turkish, *balta*). Accordingly, if her husband's name is Malta, a woman is required to use the acceptable substitute word *keziner* for 'axe', instead of the taboo word *malta*.

Similarly, there is a specific hunter's lexicon for taboo words denoting animals; e.g. the wolf must be called *bööstoy* instead of *börÿ*.

SCRIPT

As far back as 1845, a Cyrillic script was provided by missionaries. As usual in the case of minority languages of the USSR, the 1930s saw a period of experimental romanization. The Cyrillic script now in use has the following additional letters: *j, ö, ÿ. j* = /dʒ/→[d'], *ÿ* = /y/.

PHONOLOGY

Consonants

    stops: p, b, t, d, k, g
    affricates: tʃ/ts, dʒ/d'
    fricatives: (f, v) s, z, ʃ, ʒ, x, ɣ
    lateral and trill: l/l', r
    nasals: m, n, ŋ

[x] and [ɣ] are allophones of /k/, /g/; *l* in the script represents both /l/ and /l'/.

Vowels

a, ε, o, œ, ɪ, i, y, u

All occur short or long; when long, they are written doubled: *aa*, etc. Here *ö* = /œ/, *ü* = /y/.

VOWEL HARMONY
Front (/ε, i, œ, y) followed by front; back (/a, ɪ, o, u/) by back; rounded followed by rounded, unrounded by unrounded.

Stress

Stress is on the final syllable, with secondary stresses within the word. Exceptionally for a Turkic language, the negative infix is stressed: e.g. *barbázɪm* 'I shan't go'. Stress is phonemic in homonymous forms: e.g. *algánɪm* 'I took'; *alganím* 'taken by me'.

MORPHOLOGY AND SYNTAX

(*See also* **Turkic Languages**.)

Noun

The noun has two numbers and five cases. The plural marker is *-lar*[12]. The index +[12] indicates that the combination of three possible initials with four vowels (a, e, o, œ) gives the following twelve forms: *l*-series: *-lar*, *-ler*, *-lor*, *-lör*; similarly for *d*-series and *t*-series: *dar/tar*, etc.

CASE
Basic forms, all with six to twelve variants:

genitive: *-nVŋ*: *balanɪŋ* 'of the boy'
dative: *-gV*: *balaga* 'to the boy'
accusative: *-dɪ*: *koldɪ* 'the hand (acc.)'
locative: *-dV*: *atta* 'on the horse'
ablative: *-dVŋ baladaŋ* 'from the boy'

The possessive suffixes are added to the norm, preceding case endings: sing. 1 *-Vm*; 2 *-Vŋ*; 3 *-(z)V*; pl. 1 *-(ɪ)bɪs/(i)bis*; 2 *(ɪ)gar/(i)ger*; 3 = sing.: e.g. *ada.m.naŋ* 'from my father'; *ada.bɪs.taŋ* 'from our father'.

Adjective

As attribute, adjective precedes noun, and is invariable.

Pronoun

Sing. 1 *men*, 2 *sen*, 3 *ol*; pl. 1 *bis(ter)*, 2 *sler(ler)*, 3 *olor*. These are declined in all cases; the oblique base of *ol* is *on-*.

DEMONSTRATIVE PRONOUN/ADJECTIVE
bu 'this', *ol* 'that'. The oblique base of *bu* is *mɪn-*, e.g. *mɪnɪn* (genitive).

INTERROGATIVE PRONOUN
kem 'who?'; *ne* 'what?'

RELATIVE PRONOUN
None; as in Turkic languages generally, participial forms are used in relative constructions. *See* **Verb**, below.

Numerals

1–10: *bir, eki, ÿč, tört, beš, altɪ, jeti, segis, togus, on*; 11 *on bir*; 12 *on eki*; 20 *jirme*; 30 *odus*; 40 *tört on* or *kɪrɪk*; 100 *jÿs*.

Verb

The Altay verb has voice, mood, tense, marked for number and person; the non-finite forms – participles, gerunds – play a crucial role in the syntax, as in other Turkic languages. All forms have from two to six or more allophones.

VOICE
The passive voice marker is -V*l*, with assimilation of stem final: e.g. *tök-* 'to pour': *tögÿl* 'to be poured':

  reflexive: -(V)*n*: e.g. *al-* 'to take', *alɪn-* 'to take for oneself';
  reciprocal: -(V)*š*: e.g. *ber-* 'to give', *beriš-* 'to give each other';
  causative: -*d*/*t*V*r*: e.g. *bil-* 'to know', *bildir-* 'to inform'.

MOODS
Indicative, imperative, conditional, optative, subjunctive. The imperative has a specific set of endings: sing. 1 -*ayɪn*, 2 -*gɪn*, 3 -*zɪn*; pl. 1 -*alɪk*, 2 -*ɪgar*, 3 -*zɪn*.

The participles may be listed here, as their markers reappear in the tense system:

(a) of definite past time: *dɪ*
(b) of indefinite past time: *gan*
(c) imperfective aspect: *galak*
(d) present/future time: *atan*
(e) future indefinite: V*r*
(f) conditional: *sa*
(g) optative: *gay*

The most important gerund is in -*ɪp* marking concomitant or immediately preceding action; used in compound tense formation.

TENSE FORMATION
The personal endings (*see* **Turkic Languages**) have been truncated; e.g. *mɪn* > *m*, *zɪŋ* > *ŋ*, and scarcely differ from the possessive enclitics.
  The main tenses in the indicative mood are, for root *bar-* 'to go':

past definite: *bar.dɪ.m* 'I went'; *bar.dɪ.ŋ* 'you went', etc.
past indefinite: *bar.gan.ɪm* 'I went' (at some unspecified time)
future indefinite: *bar.ar.ɪm* 'I shall go'
conditional mood: *bar.za.m* 'if I go'
optative mood: *bar.gay.ɪm* 'that I may go'

Compound tenses are made with various auxiliaries; the sense verb is typically in the *-ɪp* gerundial form: e.g. *bar.ɪp jadɪm* 'I'm going now'; *bar.ɪp turum* '(it appears that) I went'.

Relative clause

Participial constructions: e.g. *bargan* 'he/she came; he/she who came'; *barar* 'he/she will come; he/she who will come'; *ayɪl.ga kirgen* 'he/she who had gone into the village'.

Postpositions
Primary or derived:

> primary: e.g. *učun* 'for': *meniŋ učun* 'for me'; *le* 'with': *sen le* 'with you'.
> derived: e.g. *ara* 'interval': *arazɪnda* 'among, between'; *agaštɪŋ arazɪnda* 'among the trees'.

Word order

SOV.

---

1. Баш-башкыда Сöс болгон, Сöс Кудайда болгон, ол Сöс Кудай болгон.

2. Ол башкыда Кудайда болгон.

3. Ончо ончозы Анаҥ пӱткен; неле пӱткен Анаҥ пӱтпей пӱткен эмес.

4. Аныҥ Бои тӱрӱ болгон, Аныҥ тӱрӱӱ кижилерге јарык полгон.

5. Јарык карачкыда јарып, карачкаа пӱркетпеди.

6. Кудайдаҥ іилген кижи болгон, аныҥ ады Іоанн.

7. Ол, јарыкты керелеирге, керее келген, ончолор анаҥ ары пӱтсин, деп.

8. Ол бои јарык полгон эмес, јарыкты керелеирге іилгенболгон.

54

AMHARIC

INTRODUCTION

This Afro-Asiatic (Semito-Hamitic) language South Semitic in origin (*see* **Ethiopic**) but has acquired a very considerable non-Semitic element, presumably through contact with neighbouring Cushitic languages such as Oromo. The word *Amhara* is the ethnonym of the 10 to 12 million people in central and north-western Ethiopia (an area which includes the capital, Addis Abbeba) who speak *amarǝñña*. As the official language of Ethiopia, Amharic is also used as a second language by about a third of the total population of Ethiopia. The main dialects are those of Gondar, Gojjam, and Shoa.

Before the late nineteenth century little was written in Amharic. Missionary activity involving the use of written Amharic was encouraged for political reasons by the Emperors Menelik II and Haile Selassie I. The first printing press for Amharic books was established in the 1880s. Through the twentieth century there has been a gradual drift from the total religious commitment of previous Ethiopian writing, towards cautious experimentation in such Western genres as the novel and the stage play, which allow social and economic issues to be raised.

SCRIPT

The Ethiopic syllabary of 26 characters has been extended by seven letters denoting specifically Amharic sounds. Phonological reduction from Ethiopic to Amharic has resulted in some redundancy; thus, there are, for example, four graphs for /h/. A major omission in the script is the absence of a sign denoting gemination, which is very important, usually phonemic, in Amharic. Signs for the numerals up to 20 are derived from Greek. Words are separated from each other by the marker ':'.

PHONOLOGY

Consonants

stops: p, b, p', t, d, t', k, g, k' ʔ
affricates: tʃ, dʒ, tʃ'
fricatives: f, v, s, z, s', ʃ, ʒ, h
semi-vowels: j, w
nasals: m, n, ɲ, (ŋ)
lateral and flap: l, r;

The ejectives, i.e. glottalized consonants, are notated as p, t, k, s; /k'/ is often notated as q. Most consonants occur labialized. In the case of the velar series and /h/, this labialization is notated for all vowels by a specific series of graphs; in realization, however, /k°/, /g°/, /k'°/ and /h°/ precede /a/; before other vowels, the labialization tends to be lost.

Vowels

i, e, ɛ, a, ə, u, o
/ɛ/ is notated here as *ä*.

Stress

Very weak.

MORPHOLOGY AND SYNTAX

Noun

In contrast to Tigrinya and Tigre, gender is not formally marked. Nouns are treated as masculine or feminine for reasons of natural gender or by convention; thus, *färäs* 'horse', is masculine, but *baqlo* 'mule' is feminine. Inanimate objects are usually treated as masculine, but there are exceptions. Words like *ləj* 'child', can be made more specific by the addition of *wənd* 'male', or *set* 'female': *wənd ləj* 'boy'. Gender is specifically marked in the affixed definite article, the demonstratives and the second and third persons of the verb. The Semitic feminine ending *-t* reappears in certain words, e.g. *mušərrit* 'bride' (*mušərra* 'bridegroom').

The concept of gender merges in Amharic with that of dimension, giving rise to an opposition between normal size/masculine and diminutive/feminine. Thus, concord fluctuates: a noun which takes 'masculine' concord when the referent is of normal dimensions may take 'feminine' concord when departure from the norm is to be stressed; cf. *yih bet tilliq nəw* 'this house is big', but *yih bet bäṭam tinniš näč* 'this house is very small'.

Conversely, nouns like *ṣähay* 'sun', *çäräqa* 'moon', *kokäb* 'star', which normally take feminine/diminutive concord, acquire masculine status when unusual size is stressed; cf. *kokäb wəṭṭač* 'a star came out', but *talaq kokäb kä.sämay wädäqä* a great star fell from heaven' (Revelation, 8.10).

DEFINITE ARTICLE
-u/-w identifies a singular noun as masculine; the feminine affix is *-wa/-itu*: e.g. *bet* 'house'; *betu* 'the house'; *lam* 'cow', *lamwa* 'the cow'.

NUMBER
The plural affix is *-očč*, which takes the definite article: e.g. *bet.očč.u* 'the houses'. There are some traces of a broken plural. The numeral *and* 'one' can be used as an indefinite article.

CASE RELATIONS

The accusative is marked by *-n*: e.g. *innatwa.n ayyəč* 'she saw her mother'.

Genitive: the particle *yä* 'precedes the noun: e.g. *yä.Yohannəs innat* 'John's mother'; *yä.Ityopya häzb* 'the people of Ethiopia'.

Other case relationships are expressed with the help of prefixes, circumfixes, and affixes: *see* **Postpositions**, etc., below.

Adjective

The attributive adjective precedes the noun and is formally unmarked: e.g. *təlləq bet* 'big house'. If the noun is definite, the article is affixed to the adjective: e.g. *təlləqu bet* 'the big house'; and similarly for the case ending in *-n*. The adjective may take the plural marker: e.g. *addis.očč bet.očč* 'new houses'.

COMPARATIVE

kä or *tä* precedes the word compared: e.g. **kä**.*Gondar Addis Ababa təlləq näw* 'Addis Abbeba is bigger than Gondar.'

Pronoun

The independent personal pronouns with copula and enclitic markers:

		Singular		*Plural*	
1		əne näññ	-ññ	əñña nän	-n
2	masc.	antä näh	-h	ənnantä naččəhu	-ččəhu
	fem.	anči näš	-š		
3	masc.	əssu näw	-w/-t	ənnässu naččäw	-ččäw
	fem.	əsswa näčč	-t		

The enclitic markers are shown in characteristic form without the linking vowels that usually precede them. They are used as the object pronouns of transitive verbs: e.g. *Bä.gäbäya ayyu.t* 'They saw him/her at market'; and may be anticipated by a noun or the relevant pronoun in the accusative case: e.g. *əssu.n ayyu.(t)* 'they saw him'.

There are respectful forms for independent second and third persons: second *ərswo*; third *əssaččäw*.

POSSESSION

This may be expressed by the affixed personal markers: sing. 1 *-e*, 2 *-əh/š*, 3 *-u/wa*; pl. 1 *-aččən*, 2 *-aččəh*, 3 *-aččäw*: e.g. *bete* 'my house'; *betaččən* 'our house'.

The verb 'to have' is expressed by the existential verb *allä* plus a composite ending coded for person of owner and gender and number of object(s) possessed: e.g. *alläññ* 'I have' (masc. sing. obj.); *alläccəññ* 'I have' (fem. sing. obj.); *alluññ* 'I have' (pl. obj. either gender).

DEMONSTRATIVE PRONOUN/ADJECTIVE

'This': masc. *yəh*, fem. *yəčč, pl. ənnäzzih*; 'that': masc. *ya*, fem. *yačč*, pl. *ənnäzziya*.

INTERROGATIVE PRONOUN
man 'who?'; *mən(dən)* 'what?'

RELATIVE PRONOUN
See Relative Clause in **Verb**, below.

Numerals

1–10: *and, hulätt, sost, aratt, amməst, səddəst, säbatt, səmmənt, zäṭäññ, assər*; 11 *asra and*; 12 *asra hulätt*; 20 *haya*; 30 *sälasa*; 40 *arba*; 100 *mäto*.

Verb

Roots are mainly two-, three-, or four-radical, the majority being triliterals. A few verbs have five radicals, and there is one monoradical – *ša* 'to want'. The citation form is, as customary in Semitic languages, the third person masculine past tense (more accurately, perfective): e.g. *mätta* 'he came', *fällägä* 'he wanted'. A typical triliteral perfective is conjugated as follows:

> singular 3 masc. *fällägä*, fem. *fällägäčč*; 2 masc. *fällägh*; fem. *fällägš*;
> 1 *fälläghu*;
> plural 3 common, *fällägu*; 2 common, *fällägaččəhu*; 1 common, *fällägən*.

IMPERFECTIVE, OR PRESENT–FUTURE FORM
The stem is modulated by prefix and affix to provide this form, which is not predictable from the perfective form. There are two patterns, which hinge on differing treatment of the geminated second radical: that is to say, if **1**, **2**, **3** are the radicals, **1ä22ä3** may yield *yə1ä23al* or *yə1ä22ə3al* as present–future form: thus, *fällägä* yields *yəFäLLəGal*; but *säbbärä* yields *yəSäBRal*.

This is, in fact, a composite form. The *-al* component is a shortened form of the existential verb *allä*, and the pronominal object is therefore infixed between the stem and the *-al* component: cf. some examples with **FäLLäGä**:

> *əFäLLəGä.w.allähu* 'I want him/it': *-w-* is the third person masculine pronominal object, and *ə...hu* is the present–future circumfix for first person singular.
> *təFäLLəGə.n.alläh* 'you (masc. sing.) want me': *-n-* is the first person pronominal object, *tə...h* is the second person singular masculine circumfix.

The prefixes in this verbal form are the familiar Semitic series: sing. 3 *yə-/tə-*, 2 *tə-*, 1 *ə-*; pl. 3 *yə-*, 2 *tə-*, 1 *ənnə-*; and the affixes are forms of the existential verb + personal markers.

Biliterals are conjugated essentially as triliterals: e.g. *qomä* 'he stood'; *qomku* 'I stood'; *yəqomal* 'he stands'; *əqomallähu* 'I stand'.

Amharic has an imperative mood used only in the second person singular, and a jussive, used in the first and third person singular and plural and in second plural. The verbal noun takes the prefix *mä-*: e.g. *mäfalläg* 'wanting'; *mähed* 'going'. These forms can take the personal affixes: e.g. *kä.mähede bäfit* 'before I went' (for the form *kä...bäfit*, *see* **Postpositions**, etc., below).

GERUND

The base patterns are: **1***ä***23**, or **1***ä***22***ə***3**: the gerund takes personal affixes similar to the possessive series: *fälləgo...* 'wanting ... he ...'; *fälləgän* 'wanting ... we ...' e.g. *Betun šəţo yət agər məhed yəfälləgal?* 'Having sold his house, to which country does he want to go?'

DERIVED STEMS

(a) -*a* prefixed to base stem changes intransitive to transitive: e.g. *moqä* 'he was warm'; *amoqä* 'he warmed sth. up';
(b) -*tä*- passive of transitive, e.g. *anäbbäbä* 'he read': *tänabbäbä* 'it was read';
(c) *as*-: causative, e.g. *wässädä* 'he took'; *aswässäda* 'he had sth. taken'.

THE SHORT IMPERFECTIVE FORM

This is the present–future form minus the -*allä* component. It is used, e.g. in subordinate temporal and causal clauses introduced by such pre-posited relational conjunctions are *sə*-, *lə*-, *bə*-, *əndə*-, etc. (with juncture sandhi). Examples: *Almaz simäţţa wädä bet əhedallähu* 'When A. comes, I'll go home'; *Yohannəs mäşhafun sifälläg* 'when John was looking for the book'. And in negative: *baburu sa.y.mättä* 'the train not coming' = 'before the train comes'.

NEGATION

For the perfective, the circumfix *al...m* is used: e.g. *alfällägäm* 'he didn't want'; *alfälläghum* 'I didn't want'. The circumfix for the imperfective negative is: *aC...m*, where C varies: cf. *ayfälləgəm* 'he doesn't want'; *anfälləgəm* 'we don't want'. With infixed pronoun object: *alfälləgäwəm* 'I don't want it'; *ayfälləgaččəhum* 'he doesn't want you (pl.)'.

RELATIVE CLAUSES

These are treated as qualifiers preceding the head-word: *yä*- introduces a relative clause in the perfective; *yämmə*- in the imperfective. Cf. *yämäţţaw säw* 'the man (*säw*) who came'; *yämäţţut säwočč* 'the men who came'; *gänzäb yäţäffabbat säw* 'the man who lost his money'; *yämmənorəbbat bet yəhäw* 'This is the house in which I live.'

Prepositions and postpositions

Circumfix: e.g.

bä 'in': *bä.kätäma* 'in the city';
kä 'from': *Kä.yät mäţţa* 'From where has he come?';
wädä 'towards, to': *kä.gära wädä ḳäññ* 'from left to right';
kä...bəhwala 'after': *Kä.hullu bəhwala mäţţa* 'He came after all the others';
bä...mäkakäl 'among, between': *bä.säwočč mäkakäl* 'among people';
lä...silə 'for, on behalf of': *lä.ageru silə motä* 'to die for one's country'.

Also *bä...lay* 'on', *bä...wəsţ* 'inside'; *kä...bäfit* 'before', etc.

Word order

SOV; OSV is permissible.

በመጀመሪያው ቃል ነበረ ፤ ቃልም በእግዚአብሔር ፩ ፤
ዘንድ ነበረ ` ቃልም እግዚአብሔር ነበረ ። ይህ በመጀመ ፪ ፤
ሪያው በእግዚአብሔር ዘንድ ነበረ ። ሁሉ በእርሱ ሆነ ፤ ፫ ፤
ከሆነውም አንዳች ስንኳ ያለ እርሱ አልሆነም ። በእርሱ ፬ ፤
ሕይወት ነበረች ፤ ሕይወትም የሰው ብርሃን ነበረች ። ብር ፭ ፤
ሃንም በጨለማ ይበራል ፤ ጨለማም አላሸነፈውም ።

ከእግዚአብሔር የተላከ ስሙ ዮሐንስ የሚባል አንድ ፮ ፤
ሰው ነበረ ፤ ሁሉ በእርሱ በኩል እንዲያምኑ ይህ ስለ ብር ፯ ፤
ሃን ይመሰክር ዘንድ ለምስክር መጣ ። ስለ ብርሃን ሊመ ፰ ፤
ሰክር መጣ እንጂ ፤ እርሱ ብርሃን አልነበረም ።

60

ANATOLIAN LANGUAGES

From the late nineteenth-century onwards, archaeological excavation has been instrumental in bringing to light the existence of several languages which were used in Anatolia during the three millennia preceding the Christian era. Some of these were Indo-European languages – Hittite, Palaic, Luwian, Lycian, Lydian. Non-Indo-European stock is represented by such languages as Urartian, Hurrian, Hattic, and Elamite. So far, only one of these languages – Hittite – is attested in sufficient quantity, and is, because of its Indo-European nature and structure, sufficiently accessible to us, to permit of study in depth.

Here, Lydian, Hattic, and Elamite are briefly described.

See **Hittite**, **Hurrian**, **Urartian**.

LYDIAN

INTRODUCTION

This apparently Indo-European language is attested in 64 inscriptions, including a few bilinguals, mostly of a funerary and votive nature, dating from the seventh to the fourth centuries BC. The most ancient was found in Egypt. The Lydian capital was Sardis in western Anatolia.

SCRIPT

The Lydian script was probably borrowed from the Anatolian Greeks early in the seventh century BC, though an indigenous origin is possible. It runs generally from right to left. Eight vowels are notated.

PHONOLOGY

Consonants

The following consonants figure in the script:

>   stops: b, t, d, k, q
>   fricatives: f, v, s, ś
>   nasals: m, n
>   lateral and flap: l, r

/t, d, l, n/ seem to have palatalized counterparts, notated by researchers as τ, ↑, λ, ν.

Vowels

a, ā, e, ē, i, o, u

Also a vowel transliterated as *y*, which may indicate closed /ę/.

MORPHOLOGY AND SYNTAX

Noun

Lydian had two genders, common and neuter, with two numbers, singular and plural. Common nouns have a nominative ending in -*s/ś*, which also appears in Hittite, Palaic, and Luwian. Similarly, the common accusative in -*n/v* is shared with these three languages. There is a dative/locative in -*λ*; cf. *vānaś* 'tomb': acc. *vānav*, loc. *vanaλ*.

PLURAL
Nominative and accusative in -(*a*)*ś*; dative/locative in -*av*.

Pronoun

The following forms are known: sing. 1 *amu* 'I', *ēmi* 'mine'; sing. 3 *bi* 'he'; *bili* 'his'. The possessive pronoun form *ēmi* has nom. *ēmis*, acc. *ēmv*, dat./loc. *ēmλ*.

DEMONSTRATIVE PRONOUN
es 'this'; *eś.ś* – *es.v* – *es.λ*. Neuter accusative in *es.t*.

RELATIVE PRONOUN
qi, which takes the -*s*, -*v*, -*λ* endings, with a neuter nominative and accusative in -*d*: *qid*.

Verb

Certain present–future and past-tense forms have been identified; e.g. present–future: sing. 1 -*u/-v*, 2 -*s*, 3 -*d/-t* (the plural forms seem to be identical); past: sing. 1 -*v*, sing./pl. 3 -*l*.

Some Lydian bases:

bi	'to give'	da-	'to give'
bira-	'house'	e-	'to be'
borli-	'year'	ēna-	'mother'
brafr-	'brother'	istamin-	'family'
kofu-	'water'	laλe-	'speak'

Bira- 'house', may be compared with Hittite *pir*.

HATTIC

INTRODUCTION

This language is also known as Proto-Hittite, which is confusing, as the Hattic people who lived in north-west Anatolia throughout the third millennium BC were not Indo-European, and had, beyond cultural contact, nothing to do with the Indo-European-speaking Hittites who invaded their country. Hattic influence on the Hittite-Luwian peoples was particularly strong in the field of religion, and the substantial Hattic element in Hittite vocabulary bears witness to this. By the first millennium BC, Hattic was a dead language. Its existence is known primarily from a small number of tablets found in the royal archives at Hattušaš (*see* **Hittite**). Some of these are bilingual texts, from which about 150 Hattic words have been tentatively identified.

SCRIPT

Hattic was written in the Akkadian cuneiform.

PHONOLOGY

Consonants

The following consonants are identifiable:

> stops: p, t, k
> fricatives: s, z(tʃ), ʃ, ḫ
> nasals: m, n
> lateral and flap: l, r
> semi-vowels: j, w

Vowels

There were four vowels:

> i, e, a u.

MORPHOLOGY AND SYNTAX

Hattic was an agglutinative language. About twenty formants, in the shape of prefixes and suffixes have been identified. Some of these appear to be case or number markers, others have a pronominal character. Gender seems to be distinguished, in that *-el/-il* appears as a suffix associated with masculine names, *-aḫ* with feminine.

Hattic verbal complexes have been typologically reconstructed (e.g. by Kammenhuber), and display some similarity with the **Abkhaz-Adyge** model (q.v.). The formula comprises four main slots: (1) affective: desirability or otherwise of action; negation; (2) subject group; (3) object group; (4) pre-verbs and base.

While certain endings have been tentatively identified as accusative (-*šu*), genitive (-V*n*), dative (-*ja*), and ablative (-*tu*), Hattic seems to have no ergative endings.

Some markers appear to have a dual role ; e.g. -*e*-/-*ja*- is a dative ending in nouns, and an indirect object marker in the verbal complex.

ELAMITE

INTRODUCTION

This non-Indo-European language was spoken and written from the third to the middle of the first millennium BC, in a territory which covered the present-day provinces of Khuzistan and Fars. The Elamites called their country Hatamti. The best-known of the Elamite city–states were Susen and Ancan.

Elamite has been variously connected with Hurrian, Turkic, Caucasian, etc. The closest parallels, e.g. in the pronominal system, are with Dravidian. D'akonov (1979) considers it probable that Elamite and Dravidian had a common ancestor.

SCRIPT

The earliest texts are in a so far undeciphered hieroglyphic script. Through the second millennium a cuneiform of Sumero-Akkadian type was in use. In the seventh century BC the area fell to the Iranians, and thereafter Elamite was strongly influenced by Old Persian. The royal inscriptions of the Achaemenians are in three languages – Old Persian, Akkadian, and Elamite. In its late form, the script has signs for about a dozen consonants and three vowels (*i, a, u*).

MORPHOLOGY AND SYNTAX

A basic opposition in the nominal system is between the class of humans, with singular markers -(*i*)*k* and -(*i*)*r*, plural in -(*i*)*p*, and the non-human class, with an apparently optional marker (-*um*)*me*: e.g. *u šak* (N).*k.ik* 'I am the son (*šak*) of N.'; *temti napp.**ip.ir** 'ruler of the gods'.

Both qualifier and qualified may take the class marker; e.g. *ruhu.r riša.**rra** 'big man'.

Pronoun

The base forms are:

	Singular	*Plural*
1	hu/u	*incl.* ela/elu; *excl.* nuku/nika
2	nu/ni	num
3	he/e, i	ap(i)

Verb

A typical form is an agglutinative complex comprising the following slots: (1) base; (2) direct object; (3) aspect, directional marker; (4) participial marker; (5) subject marker; (6) modal marker. Certain slots are mutually exclusive; e.g. slot 2 is occupied only if -*ma*- appears in 3: e.g. *pepši.(i)r.ma.h* 'I founded it' (*ma* is imperfective aspect marker). The subject marker in slot 5 may be -*k*, -*t*, -*h*, etc.

Verbal nouns take class markers: *kušik* 'built by me (?)'; *kuši.p* 'built by me (pl.)'. D'akonov gives forms for a verbal noun of action: e.g. *kuši.kk.a* 'having built, who has built'; and a gerundive form: e.g. *kuši.n* 'requiring to be, able to be built'.

INDICATIVE MOOD

The personal endings that have been identified are:

	Singular	Plural
1	-hu	-h.h(u)
2	-(a)t(i)	-h.t
3	-ši	-h.š(i)

The negative marker was -*in*.

Postpositions

For example, -*ma* 'on, in'; -*(i)kku* 'at, on, towards'; -*(i)mar* 'from, after'.

SPECIMEN ELAMITE SENTENCE (from D'akonov 1979)

tiri.mite.š. taššu.p. appa.pet.ip. u.me.na. inni. tiri.ma.n.pi. hupi.pi. halpi.š. man.ka
'Thus I say: smite the warriors who are hostile, as they do not call themselves mine, slay them' (*tiri...man.ka* 'thus I say'; *mite.š* 'smite'; *taššu.p* 'warriors'; *app* 'who'; *pet.ip* 'hostile'; *u.me.na* 'mine'; *in.me...inni* 'they...not'; *tiri.ma.n.pi* 'as they call themselves'; *hupi.pi* 'these'; *halpi.š* 'slay!')

ANDAMANESE

INTRODUCTION

Andamanese may be an isolate like Basque or Burushaski. Recently, it has been tentatively linked with the Indo-Pacific group, which includes the Papuan languages. In 1898, M.V. Portman's *Notes on the Languages of the South Andamanese Group of Tribes* – a work forming a part of his *Record of the Andamanese*, 'undertaken for the British Museum and the Government of India' – was published in Calcutta. In his Preface, Portman, who was 'Officer in Charge of the Andamanese', describes the Andamanese race as 'almost extinct'.

The work is a very valuable and detailed study of five South Andamanese languages: Āka-Bēa-da, Ākar-Bālē, Pūchikwār, Āūkāū-Jūwōī, and Kol, with a comparative vocabulary of 2,286 words, specimens of Andamanese songs, and much anthropological information of great interest.

PHONOLOGY

Consonants

Portman gives the following inventory of consonants:

> stops: p, b, t, d, k, g
> affricates: ts, dʒ
> fricatives: s, h
> semi-vowels: j, w
> nasals: m, n, ɲ, ŋ
> lateral and flap: l, r

/dʒ/ is notated here as ǰ.

Vowels

> iː, ɪ, eː, ɛ, ə, ʌ, a, aː, ɔ, o, oː, œ, u, uː

Dipthongs: ai, aw, ow, oi
Long vowels are notated here as ī, ē, etc.

MORPHOLOGY AND SYNTAX

Roots are modulated by prefixes, which indicate physical properties of the referent – roundness, softness, length, flexibility, etc. – and by suffixes which are functional: i.e. they mark syntactical relationships in nominals, temporal/ aspectual distinctions in verbs.

Portman classifies Andamanese roots into the following:

(a) parts of the human body; roots relating to mankind in general:
(b) natural objects, animate or inanimate;
(c) functional roots;
(d) pronouns;
(e) postpositions, adverbs, conjunctions, exclamations, proper names.

Nouns

Examples of class (a) roots in Pūchikwār:

> ōte-tā-da 'head'; ōte is the prefix marking roundness, -da /də/ is the nominal marker;
> ōng-tā-da 'foot': ōng- is the prefix used to denote hands or feet.

Similarly, ēr-kawdak-da 'eye', īr-bo-da 'ear'. The prefixes function, that is to say, like class markers in Bantu languages, though the motivation for the Andamanese taxonomy is often no longer clear. For example, with root yōp.(da) 'soft':

> with prefix ōt- (round things): ōt-yōp-da 'a sponge';
> with prefix auto- (long, thin things): auto-yōp-da 'a cane';
> with prefix āka- (pointed things): āka-yōp-da 'a pencil'.

In association with class (a) nouns (parts of the body), the prefixes are construed as third person possessive pronouns, and take plural forms. Thus, number, normally ignored in Andamanese, may be shown by the third person pronominal prefixes: cf. ōt-chēta-da 'his/her/its head'; ong-kaura-tek 'by his hand(s)'; ōtōt-chēta-da 'their heads'.

Adverbial roots expressing the notion of plurality = more than one, may also be used: thus, in Āka-Bēa-da, rōko-da 'canoe': rōko l'ar-dūru-da 'lots of canoes'.

Relational affixes in Āka-Bēa-da: root chāng-da 'hut': chāng-lia 'of, belonging to a hut', chāng-len 'in a hut', chāng-lat 'to a hut', chāng-tek 'by a hut'; X-lia ērem-len 'in the land of X'.

Modifiers follow modified root, e.g. ōgar-da 'the moon'; ōgar-dērēka-da ' "baby" moon' (i.e. 'new moon'); ōgar-chao-da ' "big" moon' (i.e. 'full moon'). Cf. jūrū chao 'big sea' (i.e. 'the open sea').

Pronouns

The Pūchikwār forms are:

	Singular	Plural
1	tū-le	mū-le
2	ngū-le	ngū-wel
3	ū-le	nū-le

Have full and shortened forms:

Singular		Plural	
Full	*Short*	*Full*	*Short*
1 tiye-da	d'	mīye-da	m'
2 ngīye-da	ng'	ngīyil-da	ng'...l
3 īye-da	Ø	nīye-da	n'

A specific series of pronominal subject forms is used with verbs. The Āka-Bēa-da set is:

	Singular	Plural
1	dō	moicho
2	ngō-	ngoicho
3	dā-	ēda

For example, *dō māmi-kē* 'I sleep, shall sleep'; *dō wēliǰ-kē* 'I shall drink'; *tuk mōli-kē* 'I sleep, shall sleep' in Pūchikwār.

Numerals

The Āka-Bēa-da set 1–5 is: *ūbatūl, ik-paur, ēd-ār-ūbāī, ē-īǰi-pagi, ār-dūru*.

Verbs

Functional suffixes attached to verbals:

-*kē*	for	present–future tense
-*kā*		imperfect
-*rē*		perfect
-*ba*		negative
-*nga*		present participle

e.g. *mami-nga* 'sleeping'; *Lūratūt-la chāpa tāp-nga ōmō-rē* 'Luratut (proper name) came stealing fire' (Āka-Bēa-da language; -*la* is honorific affix; *chāpa* 'fire'; *tāp-nga* = present participle; -*rē* = perfect marker).

The personal pronouns appear to change their form in association with certain tenses; e.g. *dō-māmi-kē* 'I (shall) sleep', but **dā** *māmi-ka* 'I was sleeping'; **dā** māmi-rē 'I slept'; **dōna** *ī-dai-nga yāba-da* 'I do not understand' (*yāba-da* 'not').

Word order

SOV is usual.

ANDEAN-EQUATORIAL
LANGUAGES

This very extensive grouping of South American Indian languages stretches the full length of the continent, from Central America to Tierra del Fuego. Its four most important branches are:

1. Quechuamaran: demographically, the largest unit of American Indian languages, with about 10 million speakers in Ecuador, Peru, Bolivia, Colombia, and Argentine. Quechua itself is spoken by about 6 million in Peru, Bolivia, and Ecuador. Aymará, in Peru and Bolivia, has over 1 million speakers.
2. Tupí: Guaraní, the principal Tupian language, has semi-official status alongside Spanish in Paraguay, where it is spoken by some 3 million people. Many Tupian languages of Brazil are moribund or already extinct.
3. Arawakan: a very extensive, but deeply fragmented, branch, found in enclaves in Brazil, Venezuela, and Central America. Goajiro, spoken by about 40,000 in Colombia and Venezuela, is the main Arawakan language.
4. Island Carib is spoken by about 30,000 in Honduras, Guatemala, and some parts of the West Indies.

Some authorities regard Mapudungu as an Andean-Equatorial language (but *see* **Penutian**).

The 250 Andean-Equatorial languages are spoken by around 15 million people.

See **Aymará**, **Quechua**, **Guaraní**, **Tupí**.

ANDI LANGUAGES

INTRODUCTION

Genetically a sub-division of North-East Ibero-Caucasian, the Andi languages are spoken by about 40,000 people in the south-west corner of Dagestan. Andi itself accounts for about a quarter of the total number of speakers. The other members of the sub-group are: Botlikh, Godoberi, Karata, Akhvakh, Bagval, Tindi, and Chamalal. None are written languages. Avar (*see* **Avar**) is used as a lingua franca and as literary language throughout the Andi-speaking area.

PHONOLOGY

As in Avar, the four-term series consisting of simple stop + geminate, ejective stop + geminate is normal: e.g. /k – kk – k' – k'k'/. The ejectives are notated with subscript dots here. There are from five to seven laterals, and a rich inventory of post-velar sounds. The vocalic system is simple /i, e, a, o, u/; nasalization of vowels occurs throughout the group. Stress is weak and movable.

MORPHOLOGY AND SYNTAX

Nouns

As in Avar, nouns in the Andi languages are arranged in grammatical classes. Broadly speaking, male and female human classes are distinguished from those comprising animals, inanimate objects, and natural phenomena. Most Andi languages have three classes in the singular, two in the plural. Andi itself has five classes in both singular and plural; Chamalal has five in the singular, two in plural.

The taxonomy in Andi is as follows:

Class		Singular marker	Plural
1	human male	w-	w
2	human female	y-	y
3	all other animates	b-	y
4, 5	inanimate objects	b-	r

Taxonomies vary: e.g. classes 4 and 5 in Chamalal contain certain animals, reptiles, birds.

In contrast with Avar, where verbal and adjectival recapitulation of a given nominal class is grammatically automatic, the Andi languages have developed a

70

degree of option in the selection of classifiers. In Chamalal, for example, there may be a semantic element in the selection (Bokarev 1949). Position of classifier: usually prefix or suffix, sometimes both; rarely infix. Cf. in Chamalal:

Class 1	*weçaṭu heḵwa*	'black man'
Class 2	*yeçaṭwi yah*	'black woman'
Class 3	*beçaṭub çatw*	'black horse'
Class 4	*yeçaṭul tay*	'black foal'
Class 5	*yeçaṭwi yeła*	'black night'

Evidence for a noun's class has to be sought in material in concord with that noun. Nouns themselves do not carry class markers, though petrified class markers occur: e.g. in Chamalal, *wac* 'brother', *yac* 'sister'; here, the initials do not change in the plural form, as they would if the *w-/y-* were still construed as class markers.

DECLENSION

As in Avar, the division into basic cases (absolute, ergative, genitive, dative) + several series of locative cases, is usual. The absolute form does not provide the base for the oblique cases.

Pronoun

The singular first and second persons are true pronouns with suppletive plurals. The third person forms are supplied from the demonstrative series, and take classifiers, e.g. in Andi:

	Singular		*Plural*
1	din/den	excl.	iššil
		incl.	ikłil
2	min/men		bissil

In the first and second singular, the *din/min* forms are used by men, the *den/men* forms by women.

Verb

The verb in Andi is marked for class, number, tense, and mood. All the member languages have indicative, imperative, conditional, and subjunctive moods. There are three basic tenses: present/future, past and aorist, plus many periphrastic forms based on the past gerund.

Examples of transitive and intransitive verbs in Andi:

Transitive: *imudi çul r.u.'i* 'the father (ergative case) was cutting a stick'; *imudi çulibol r.a.'i* 'the father was cutting sticks'. The subject of a transitive verb is in the ergative, the object in the absolute.

Intransitive: *wocci w.u.lon* 'the brother went away'; *woccul w.o.lon* 'the brothers went away'; *yocci y.i.xo* 'the sister came'; *yoccibol y.o.xo* 'the sisters came'.

The verbal structure of Akhvakh exhibits both the class system (Akhvakh has three classes: I male humans; II female humans; III everything else) and personal endings (first person opposed to second/third person; singular opposed to plural). Thus:

vu.q'ado	'I (male) died'
vu.q'ari	'you (male), he died'
yi.q'ari	'you (female), she died'
ba.q'vidi	'we (human) died'
ba.q'viri	'you/they (human) died'
bi.q'vari	'it/they (non-human) died'

The above paradigm shows an intransitive stem with subject class markers. An example of a transitive stem without class markers for subject but with ending coded for class of object plus person and number of subject, follows:

qvaredo	'I killed him'
qvarede	'I killed her'
qvareri	'you/he/she killed him/her/it'
qvaridi	'I killed them (human)'
qvarede	'I killed them (non-human)'

In these examples, *q* represents the strong, *q'* the weak lateral ejective in Akhvakh.

NEGATION

Negating particles are added to affirmative verbal forms. In Andi itself the negating affix is -*ssu*, which is the negative version of the copula: *ssu* 'not to be'. The affix ç̌ is also used.

In Botlikh the negative affixes are differentiated for grammatical class: thus, -*xuč̌* for inanimates, -*ɬič̌* for animates, -*guč̌* (indeterminate).

The negative affixes are attached to the tense ending: e.g. in Godaberi: *īh.a.u.či* 'doesn't do'; *īh.i.či* 'didn't do'; *īh.e.či* 'will not do'.

APACHE

INTRODUCTION

Along with Navajo, the Apachean languages form the southernmost branch of the Athabaskan family (*see* **Athabaskan Languages**). The Western Apache languages – Chiricahua, Mescalero, Jicarilla – are very closely interrelated and have much in common with Navajo; the eastern form – Kiowa – is completely or very nearly extinct. The total number of Apache speakers is estimated at about 10,000. The form described here is Chiricahua, after Hoijer (1946). At present, the Chiricahua – in the mid-nineteenth century the most warlike of the Apache tribes – live with the Mescalero in the Mescalero Reservation in New Mexico.

PHONOLOGY

Standard Athabaskan, and very close to the Navajo system (*see* **Navajo**).

MORPHOLOGY AND SYNTAX

As in other Athabaskan languages the main division of words is into particles, nouns, and verbs. Particles are never inflected.

Noun

Nouns may be basic monosyllables, e.g. *ka̧a* 'arrow', bound stems, e.g. *bì.kèe* 'his foot', thematic nouns (i.e. stem + affix), e.g. *kòo.γ̧ǫ* 'camp', compounds, e.g. *ka̧a.béeš* 'arrow-head', nominalized verbal, e.g. *dìγì* 'it is holy' → 'ceremony', or verbal + relative marker, e.g. *ńčìɫ'xìɫ.í* 'that wind which is black' = 'tornado' (*-í* 'relative marker, *ńčì* 'wind').

The possessive markers: first person, *ši-*; second person, *ni-*; third person, *bi-*; obviative, *go-*; indefinite, *'i*; + dual and plural forms. The objective pronominal forms, infixed in verbal complex, are very similar. Affixing the possessive marker may induce phonetic change in the stem, and a vowel may be added: e.g. *béeš* 'knife'; *nì.béež.è* 'your knife'.

Verb

(For general structure, *see* **Athabaskan Languages**.)
    Hoijer analyses the pre-verbal stem complex as follows:

73

Position	Theme	Adverbial prefixes	Paradigmatic prefixes
1			indirect object
2		postposition	
3		adverbial prefix	
4	theme prefix		
5			iterative mode
6			number prefix
7			direct object
8			deictic prefix
9		adverbial prefix	
10			tense prefix
11			modal prefix
12			subject prefix
13			classifier
14	stem		

Some points with reference to the above model:

1. Stems modulate for mode/aspect/tense. In Chiricahua, three stems are usual, though five or six may occur.
2. Adverbial prefixes, here exemplified with the theme '*àa* 'to handle a round object':

    + prefix *dàh.yí* 'upon, on top': *dàh.yí...'àa* 'to put a round object on top of something';
    + prefix *céh* 'into a fire': *céh...'ǫ́* 'to have put a round object into the fire' ('*ǫ́* is perfective stem).

3. Certain components are in complementary distribution; e.g. if position 5 is occupied, 10 and 11 must be vacant.
4. Choice of subject markers: deictic prefix position (8) or pronominal position (12). The former is used for the fourth person (obviative), the indefinite subject, or a subject marking time or locus. The twelfth slot contains any pronominal marker except for third person. Where both positions 8 and 12 are empty, third person subject is understood. That is, the third person subject marker in Apachean is Ø.
5. Apart from third person, the choice of subject pronoun depends on which classifier is used in position 13: Ø, *d*, *l*, or *ł* (*see* **Athabaskan Languages**), and on which mode of the stem is being conjugated. There are two sets of subject pronoun, virtually identical except for the first person singular, which is *š-* in set (a) and *í-* in set (b). In Chiricahua, the latter set is used with the perfective stem of Ø- and *ł*-class verbs. Extensive assimilation takes place here. Thus, for the *si*-perfective of Ø- and *ł*-class verbs the first three singular personal markers are: *sí-*, *síñ-*, *sì-*; for *d*- and *l*-class verbs, the equivalent forms are: *sìš-*, *síñ-*, *sì-*.
6. Markers for other modal/temporal paradigms: progressive, *ho-*; future, *do-*; iterative, *ná-*; optative, *ho-*.

1 Dantsé godeyaadá' Yati' golį́į́ lék'e, Yati' Bik'ehgo-'ihi'nań yił nlįį, Yati'íí Bik'ehgo'ihi'nań nlįį.

2 Yati'íí dantsé godeyaadá' Bik'ehgo'ihi'nań yił nlįį.

3 Áń dawahá áyíílaa; áń doo hak'i dayúgo dawahá álzaahíí doo álzaa le'at'éé da.

4 Ihi'naahíí biyi' golį́į́; áí ihi'naahíí nnee yee daago'įį.

5 Got'iiníí godiłhiłyú idindláád; godiłhiłíí got'iiníí doo yitis nlįį da.

¶6 Bik'ehgo'ihi'nań nnee John holzéhi yides'a'.

7 Áń Begot'ínihíí nnee yił nagolni'go nyáá, bíí bee nnee dawa da'odląą doleełgo.

8 John doo Begot'iiníí nlįį da, áídá' Begot'iiníí yaa nagolni'go nyáá.

(Western Apache)

ARABIC

INTRODUCTION

Arabic belongs to the South Central Semitic branch of Semito-Hamitic family. Modern standard literary Arabic (*al-fuṣḥa*) is the official language of some 20 countries, ranging from Morocco on the Atlantic seaboard of Africa to the Persian Gulf states. As such, it is used in the press and other media, and is the language of diplomacy and official communication between Arab states. Basically, this literary standard is the language of the Qur'ān and the Hadith, lexically enriched, of course, largely from Arabic's own generative resources. Modernisms abound, but they are additions to a core structure which has hardly changed in a thousand years. Colloquial Arabic is spoken as mother tongue, in various dialect forms, by an estimated 150 million people. And again, as the canonical language of Islam, Arabic is understood up to a point by many millions of people, wherever the Qur'ān is taught – in Iran, Pakistan, Indonesia, East and West Africa, etc. Finally, one should mention the thousands of Arabic words that have been borrowed by Iranian, Turkic, Indian, and African languages, with little or no reciprocal borrowing by Arabic.

Arabic literature, one of the world's richest, dates from the sixth century AD, i.e. from the period immediately preceding the composition of the Qur'ān and the birth of Islam. The following periods may be broadly distinguished:

1. Pre-Islamic paganism (*al-jāhiliyya*, 'the period of ignorance').
2. The Qur'ān and the Hadith (to mid-seventh century).
3. The Umayyad period (to mid-eighth century).
4. The 'Abbāsid' period the 'golden age' of Arabic literature (to mid-thirteenth century).
5. The age of decadence (thirteenth to nineteenth centuries).
6. The nineteenth-century revival (*al-nahḍa*).
7. The twentieth century. Confrontation with European modes of thought and expression, and vast proliferation of literature in all genres.

SCRIPT

(*See* **Appendix of Scripts**.) There are two main forms: (a) Kufic, an angular script in general use up to the ninth century, and the ancestor of the present-day Moghrebi scripts of North-West Africa; (b) the flowing cursive character known as *nasxī* and its derivatives, *ta'līq* and *ruq'a*. The latter is much used in handwriting. The Arabic script is consonantal; vowels are not normally written except in pedagogic literature, and, of course, in the Qur'ān, texts of which are always fully vocalized.

PHONOLOGY

Consonants

> labial: b, f, m, w
> dental: t, d, n, θ, ð, s, ʃ, z, l, r
> velarized emphatic: , ƫ, ɖ, ş, ẓ
> palatal: dʒ, j
> velar: k, χ, ɣ
> uvular: q
> pharyngeal: ħ, ʕ(')
> glottal: h, ʔ(')

Emphatic /ƫ/, etc. are notated here as ṭ, etc.

ASSIMILATION

The so-called 'sun letters': the -l of the article is assimilated to a following initial dental or an emphatic, e.g., al-šamsu → [eʃ-ʃamsu] 'the sun'; al-nāru → [ɛn-nɛːru] 'the fire'; al-tājiru → [ɛt-tɛːjiru] 'the merchant'; al-ṭabīb → [ut-tɔbiːb] 'the doctor'.

Vowels

> long and short: i, a, u

Long vowels are notated as ā, etc. Initial /i, a, u/ are supported by alif in the script, and pronounced with glottal onset (hamza). /a, aː/ tend towards [ɛ, ɛː]; after the emphatic consonants, a → [ɔ]: e.g. ḍaraba → [ɖɔraba], 'he struck'. In proximity to l, /a/ → [ɛ]: malik → [mɛlik], kalb → [kɛlb].

Stress

Primary stress tends to fall on the penultimate if this is long. If the last two syllables are short; stress moves to the antepenultimate: e.g. falláhun 'a peasant'; šáriba 'he drank'.

MORPHOLOGY AND SYNTAX

Noun

The form of an Arabic word (wazn, pl. awzān) is related to its function. Thus, if we use C_1, C_2, and C_3 to denote the components of a triliteral root:

> $C_1aC_2C_2\bar{a}C_3$ denotes the practitioner of the verbal action: e.g. NaJJār(un) 'carpenter'; XuBBāZ(un) 'baker'.

$maC_1C_2aC_3$ is a noun of place: e.g. *MaDRaS(un)* 'school'; *maṬBaX(un)* 'kitchen'.

$C_1aC_2\bar{\imath}C_3(un)$ is often an adjective; may also be infinitive or broken plural (see below): e.g. *KaRīM* 'noble'; *JaMīL* 'beautiful'.

For a general note on the triliteral root, *see* **Semitic Languages**.

There are two genders, masculine and feminine, and three numbers.

ARTICLE

Indefinite status is indicated by nunation: e.g. *malik**un*** 'a king'. The definite article for all genders and numbers is prefixed *al-*: e.g. *al-maliku* 'the king'. As pointed out above, the *-l* of the article assimilates with the 'sun letters'.

GENDER

A common feminine marker is *-at*, written with tā' marbūṭa, i.e. *-h* with two dots, in the singular, but reverting to ordinary *t* in the plural: e.g. *xādimun* 'a servant': *xādimatun* 'a female servant'. Several common nouns are feminine, though not so marked, e.g. *al-'arḍu* 'the earth', *al-nāru* 'the fire', *al-šamsu* 'the sun'.

NUMBER

Singular, dual, and plural. The plural form may be sound or broken. The sound plural is in *-ūna*, oblique *-īna*; feminine, *-ātun*, oblique *-ātin*. Broken plural: the form of a broken plural is unpredictable, though there are certain recurrent patterns. Thus, with radicals $C_1C_2C_3$

$'aC_1C_2iC_3\bar{a}'u$ is a plural of $C_1aC_2\bar{\imath}C_3un$: e.g. *ṢaDīQun* 'friend', pl. *'aṢDiQā'u*;

$maC_1\bar{a}C_2iC_3u$ is a plural of $maC_1C_2aC_3un$: e.g. *maKTaBun* 'school', pl. *maKāTiBu*.

Common broken plural forms are (omitting nunation):

$C_1uC_2\bar{u}C_3$: e.g. *QaLB*, pl. *QuLūB* 'heart';
$C_1iC_2\bar{a}C_3$: e.g. *KaLB*, pl. *KiLāB* 'dog';
$C_1uC_2uC_3$: e.g. *KiTāB*, pl. *KuTuB* 'book'.

Dual: masc. *-āni*, obl. *-aini*. In the feminine *-t-* is inserted: *-tani*, obl. *-taini*. Nunation drops in construct: e.g. *bābāni* 'two doors': *bābā∅.l-bait* 'the two doors of the house'. Formally, a broken plural is a feminine singular collective noun, and therefore takes a feminine singular adjective.

CASE

Most nouns are triptotes with three cases, nominative, genitive, accusative, with characteristic vowels *-u* (nom.), *-i* (gen.), *-a* (acc.). Diptotes have nominative in *-u* and general oblique in *-a*: e.g. triptote *al-bait**u*** 'the house'; *daxala baita.ka* 'he went into your (*-ka*) house'; *fi.l-baiti* 'in the house'. In the colloquial, the endings *-u*, *-a*, *-i* tend towards ∅.

THE CONSTRUCT

(Ar. *'iḍāfa*) Noun defined by noun. In Arabic, the two nouns are put in the construct relationship, whereby the first, the defining member, necessarily loses its article: thus, with *al-baitu* 'the house'; *al-rajul* 'the man': **Ø***baitu.l-rajuli* [baitu.**r-r**ajul], 'the man's house'. Similarly, *al-šubbāku* 'the window': **Ø***šubbaku.l-baiti* 'the window of the house'. (*Cf.* **Hebrew**. In Arabic, there is no obligatory stretto of first component.)

Plural and dual in construct: *kutubu.l-mu'allimīna* 'the teachers' books'; *kitābā.r-rajuli* 'the man's two books'; *waladai.l-wazīri* 'the wazir's two sons' (acc.).

Adjective

Certain *awzān* (*see* **Noun**, above) are adjectives, e.g. $C_1\bar{a}C_2iC_3$, $C_1aC_2\bar{\imath}C_3$, $C_1aC_2\bar{u}C_3$: e.g. *ṣādiq* 'just, upright'; *kabīr* 'big'; *jahūl* 'very ignorant'. The attributive adjective follows the noun and takes the article, if definite: e.g. *al-baitu.l-kabiru* 'the big house'; *al-bintu.l-ḥasanatu* 'the beautiful girl'. As pointed out above, broken plural forms are construed as feminine singular for purposes of concord: e.g. *durūsun sa'batun* 'difficult lessons'. But broken plural adjectives may be used to qualify broken plural nouns denoting male humans: e.g. *rijālun ṭiwālun* 'tall men' (*ṭawīl* 'tall').

Adjectives denoting colours or bodily defects have the following pattern: masc. sing. *'aC_1C_2aC_3u* (i.e. no nunation), fem. $C_1C_2\bar{a}C_3'u$, pl. $C_1uC_2C_3un$: e.g. *'aḥmaru* 'red', fem. *ḥamrā'u*, pl. *ḥumrun*; *'aṭrašu* 'deaf', fem. *ṭaršā'u*, pl. *ṭuršun*. The masculine form of this pattern is used for the elative (comparative); thus from *kabir* 'big', *'akbar* 'bigger'; from *jahil* 'ignorant', *'ajhal* 'more ignorant'.

Pronoun

Independent and enclitic:

		Singular		Dual		Plural	
		Independent	Enclitic	Independent	Enclitic	Independent	Enclitic
1		'anā	-ya, -(n)ī			naḥnu	-nā
2	masc.	'anta	-ka	'antumā	-kumā	'antum	-kum
	fem.	'anti	-ki			'antunna	-kunna
3	masc.	huwa	-hu/hi	humā	-humā	hum	-hum
	fem.	hiya	-hā			hunna	-hunna

The enclitics are bound forms attached to verbs as object pronouns, and to nouns as possessive markers. They also follow prepositions. e.g. *waladuhu* 'his son'; *ḍarabtuhu* 'I struck him'; *'alaikum* 'on you (pl.)'. The following sentence ilustrates all three usages:

Ba'aθat**ni** 'ummi 'ilai**ka**

'My mother sent me to you' (*ba'aθa* 'he sent'; *'umm* 'mother'; *'ila* 'to')

DEMONSTRATIVE PRONOUN/ADJECTIVE

Masc. *hāðā*, dual, *haðāni*, pl. *hā'ulā'i*; fem. *hāðihi*, dual, *hatāni*, pl. *hā'ulā'i* 'this, these'. Masc. *ðālika*, fem. *tilka* (no plural) 'that'. The demonstrative adjective precedes the noun, which is definite: e.g. *hāðā.l-kitāb* 'this book';

tilka.l-jibāl 'those mountains'.

INTERROGATIVE PRONOUN

man 'who?'; *mā* 'what?' (or, *māðā*). The introductory interrogative particle is *hal* or *'a*: e.g.

> wa hal b'imkāni.l-bašari 'an ya'rifū.l-ḥaqīqata?
> 'and is it in the power of men to know the truth?' (Gibran Khalil Gibran)

RELATIVE CLAUSES

Where the antecedent is indefinite, no link is required: e.g.

> baṭalun wahaba ḥayātahu li.bilādihi
> 'a hero who laid down his life for his country'

> bayānun ṣadara fī London
> 'a communiqué which appeared in London'

Where antecedent is definite, the linking pronoun *allaði*, fem. *allati*, is used. This has dual, plural, and oblique forms: *al-šaix...*, *allaði zāra London 'axīran* 'Sheikh ..., who visited London recently'.

Numerals

Professor Tritton's definition of the Arabic numerals as 'the nightmare of a bankrupt financier' is celebrated.

1: this is a pronoun agreeing in gender with its referent: masc. *'aḥadun*, fem. *'iḥdā*. The form *wāḥidun*, fem. *wāḥidatun* is an adjective.

2: *'iθnāni*, fem. *'iθnatāni* (with oblique and construct forms) is a noun in concord with referent. The dual form of the noun may also be used to indicate duality: *'usbū'aini* 'two weeks'.

3–10: the Arabic equivalents for these numerals are fully declined nouns which obey the law of inverse polarity, i.e. feminine form for masculine referent, and vice versa. e.g. *θalāθatu rijālin* 'three men' (lit. 'a threesome of men'); *θalāθu marratin* 'three times'. The base forms of the numbers 3–10 are: *θalāθ-*, *'arba'-*, *xams-*, *sitt-*, *sab'a-*, *θamān-*, *tis'a-*, *'ašar-*.

11, 12: here, both components agree in gender with the referent: *'aḥada 'ašara* (masc.) 13–19: partial polarity. The ten is in concord with referent, the unit is not: e.g. *xamsa 'ašrata sanatan* 'fifteen years'. 20–99: the tens are diptotes, the units triptotes. 100 *mi'atun*; 200 *mi'atāni*, 300 *θalāθu mi'atin*.

Verb

The dictionary form is the third person masculine singular perfective: e.g. *KaTaBa* 'he wrote'. The strong verb has three radical letters; hamza, *yā*, and *wāw* are excluded. Weak verbs have hamza, *yā*, or *wāw* in initial, medial, or final position; doubly weak verbs have initial, medial, or final hamza + *yā* or *wāw*; thus, *ra'ā* 'he saw' is medial hamza + final *yā*.

Roots may have four radicals, or may be doubled verbs, i.e. geminated second radical: e.g. *ZaXRaFa* 'to adorn'; *MaRRa* 'to pass'.

Aspect rather than tense is denoted by the finite forms: perfective and imperfective. The vowel following the second radical may be *a*, *i*, or *u*, and is known as the characteristic: e.g. *KaTaBa* 'he wrote'; *ŠaRiBa* 'he drank'; *KaRuMa* 'he was noble'. The perfective is marked by suffix for person, number, and, in part, gender; the imperfective is marked by prefix and suffix for person, number, and gender (except for 1st person singular and plural): e.g.

perfective, *kataba* 'he wrote' (Arabic order of person is maintained):

		Singular	*Dual*	*Plural*
3	masc.	kataba	katabā	katabū
	fem.	katabat	katabtā	katabnā
2	masc.	katab**ta**	katab**tumā**	katab**um**
	fem.	katab**ti**		katab**tunna**
1		katab**tu**		katabnā

imperfective indicative:

		Singular	*Dual*	*Plural*
3	masc.	**yaktubu**	**yaktubāni**	**yaktubūna**
	fem.	**taktubu**	**taktubāni**	**yaktubna**
2	masc.	**taktubu**	**taktubāni**	**taktubūna**
	fem.	**taktubīna**		**taktubna**
1	common	**'aktubu**		**naktubu**

From the imperfective indicative are formed, with slight changes in final vowel, the subjunctive and the jussive.

IMPERATIVE

E.g. from *KaTaBa*: *uKTub*, pl. *uKTubū*, fem. *uktubī*, *uktubna*. The negative imperative: here the jussive is used: *lā taKTuB* 'do not write!'.

THE DERIVED STEMS

These correspond to the *binyanim* in Hebrew (*see* **Hebrew**). Servile letters are added to and/or inserted in the base form to generate extensions and modifications of the base meaning. (I is the base form; R = radical.)

Form		*Meaning*	*Example*
II:	geminate of R$_2$	intensive	*KaSaRa* 'he broke': *KaSSaRa* 'he smashed'
III:	vowel following R$_1$ lengthened	extension of meaning to involve addressee of action	*KaTaBa* 'he wrote': *Kātaba* 'he wrote to, corresponded with'
IV:	*'a* prefix	causative trans. ← intrans.	*JaLaSa* 'he sat': *'aJLasa* 'he seated'
V:	*ta-* prefixed to II	reflexive of II	*FaRRaQa* 'to separate': *taFaRRaQa* 'to be scattered'

Form		Meaning	Example
VI:	*ta-* prefixed to III	reciprocal	*ḤaRiBa* 'to be furious': *taḤāRaBa* 'to fight each other'
VII:	*n-* prefix with liaison	reflexive passive	*KaSaRa* 'he broke': *'inKaSaRa* 'it got broken'
VIII:	*-t-* inserted after R₁ + liaison	heterogeneous	*NaðaRa* 'he saw, expected': *'iNtaðaRa* 'he expected, awaited'
IX:	alif-prefix with liaison; V₁ dropped, R₃ geminated	used for colours and bodily defects	*'iḤMaRRa* 'to turn red' (cf. *ḤaMMaRa* 'to make red; *'aḤMaR* 'red': *see* **Adjective**)
X:	*sta-* prefixed with liaison	to seek, pursue, require action denoted by root	*XaLaFa* 'he remained behind': *istaXLaFa* 'he appointed a successor' (*XaLiFa* 'caliph') *akbar* 'great': *istaKBaRa* 'he regarded … as great' *ḤaSuNa* 'to be handsome': *istaḤSaNa* 'he thought well of…'

PASSIVE

The Arabic passive is made by internal flection – *-u* after first radical – e.g. from *KaTaBa*: *KuTiBa* 'it was written'; *yuKTabu* 'it is being written'. Similarly for the derived stems, e.g. in VIII: *'iNtaðaRa* 'he expected': *'uNtuðiRa* 'it was expected'. If a passive verb is used, the agent cannot be overtly specified, i.e. *ḍuriba* X 'X was struck'; but if Y, the striker, is mentioned, the sentence must be rephrased in the active voice: *ḍaraba* Y X.

NEGATIVE

Arabic has several negating particles:

lā is a general negating particle followed by a noun in the accusative or by a verb in the imperfective: e.g. *lā mahalla li.l-'ajab* 'there is no need to be surprised'; *lā yaktubu* 'he doesn't/didn't write'.

mā denies verbal sentences in either aspect: e.g. *mā kataba* 'he didn't write'; *mā yaktubu* 'he doesn't write'.

lam with the jussive = *mā* with perfective: *lam yaktub* = *mā kataba* 'he didn't write'.

lan + subjunctive denies the future: e.g. *lan yaktuba* 'he will not write'.

laisa 'is not/are not': *laisa lī 'a'dā'u* 'I have no enemies'.

PARTICIPLES

E.g. from *kataba* 'he wrote':

active: *kātib(un)* 'writing' →' writer';
passive: *maktūb(un)* 'written' (with a plural form *makātību*).

Prepositions

The noun following a preposition is in the genitive case: e.g. *fī.l-bayti* 'in the house'. The enclitic forms of the pronouns follow prepositions: e.g. *min.hum* 'of them, from them'; *fī.hā* 'in her'.

Word-formation

Originally and essentially, word-building in a 'God-given' language is reduced to the regular process of expansion of the triliteral root in accordance with the established moulds or patterns (awzān). A root capable of natural semantic expansion may have as many as 44 verbal nouns; and any root not hitherto so exploited could be used to generate new, but orthodox and therefore intelligible forms by analogy (al-qiyās). Permutation of the 28 consonants of Arabic yields over 3,000 potential bases 'theoretically existent with all their regular derivatives' (Massignon, quoted in Monteil 1960: 107). (But note phonotactic constraints on formation of roots, e.g. in neighbourhood of emphatics.) Al-qiyās was a fertile source of lexical enrichment in the Umayyad-Abbasid period.

Since the Indo-European predilection and aptitude for the formation of compound words is alien to Arabic, the problem of how best to provide the language with equivalents for modern scientific, technical, and political terms has proved a difficult one. Monteil (1960) gives an interesting account of tentative steps in this field. Many of the proposed equivalents are paraphrases rather than compounds, along the lines of, e.g., *mā fawqa.l-banafsajī* 'ultra-violet' (lit. 'what-is-beyond-violet-ness'). However, the truncated root *kahra-* (← *kahraba* 'to electrify') has been successfully used in many compound forms: e.g. *kahra-jābī* 'electro-positive'; *kahra-rākid* 'electrostatics'. Scientific and political terms with the privative prefixes *a-*, *an-*, *non-* go readily into Arabic by means of *lā-*, *γayr*, or *'adam*: e.g. *lā-iš'ā'ī* 'non-radioactive'; *γayr mustaqīm* 'non-linear'; *'adam al-i'tida* 'non-aggression'.

Word order

VSO is normal in verbal sentence, though inversions are found. SV in nominal sentence.

١ ١ فِي الْبَدْءِ كَانَ الْكَلِمَةُ وَالْكَلِمَةُ كَانَ عِنْدَ اللّٰهِ وَكَانَ

٢ الْكَلِمَةُ اللّٰهَ ٭ ٢ هٰذَا كَانَ فِي الْبَدْءِ عِنْدَ اللّٰهِ ٭ ٣ كُلُّ شَيْءٍ بِهِ

٤ كَانَ وَبِغَيْرِهِ لَمْ يَكُنْ شَيْءٌ مِمَّا كَانَ ٭ ٤ فِيهِ كَانَتِ الْحَيٰوةُ وَالْحَيٰوةُ

٥ كَانَتْ نُورَ النَّاسِ ٭ ٥ وَالنُّورُ يُضِيءُ فِي الظُّلْمَةِ وَالظُّلْمَةُ لَمْ
تُدْرِكْهُ ٭

٦ ٦ كَانَ إِنْسَانٌ مُرْسَلٌ مِنَ اللّٰهِ اسْمُهُ يُوحَنَّا ٭ ٧ هٰذَا جَاءَ

٨ لِلشَّهَادَةِ لِيَشْهَدَ لِلنُّورِ لِكَيْ يُؤْمِنَ الْكُلُّ بِوَاسِطَتِهِ ٭ ٨ لَمْ يَكُنْ هُوَ
النُّورَ بَلْ لِيَشْهَدَ لِلنُّورِ ٭

ARAPAHO

INTRODUCTION

This member of the Algonquian family is spoken by about 1,000 people in the borderlands of Oklahoma and Wyoming.

PHONOLOGY

The sparse consonantal inventory includes /b, w, t, θ, s, n, tʃ, j, k, x, h, ʔ/ + allophones. The vowels are /i, e, o, u/. High and low tones.

MORPHOLOGY AND SYNTAX

Noun

The noun may be simple or compound, dependent or independent; the latter are absolute or possessed. Examples: *néč* 'water'; *hinén* 'man'; *heebeθíinen* 'big man'. Some Arapaho stems are ambivalent, i.e. can be treated as nouns or verbs. The basic dichotomy between animate and inanimate (on non-Indo-European lines) affects concord: e.g. *hinén nonoohówoot X* 'a/the man sees X-animate'; *hinén nonoohóóto' X* 'a/the man sees X-inanimate';

Plural: animate plurals are, e.g., -*o'*, -V*n*, -*uu/ii*; inanimate -*o*, -V*n*, -V. The stem itself may be profoundly altered before the plural affixes: e.g. *henééčee* 'buffalo', pl. *henééčeen*; *wóx* 'bear', pl. *wóxuu*; *nééčee* 'chief', pl. *nééčeen*; *wóxhoox* 'horse', pl. *wóxhooxebii*; *bééte'* 'bow', pl. *béétéíi*.

Dependent nouns occur only in possessed form; the indefinite possessive marker is *b-/w-*: *bétee* '(one's) heart'; *béíčíθ* '(one's) tooth'. The 1st person singular personal possessive marker is *n-*: *nétee* 'my heart'; second person *h-*: *héíčíθ* 'your tooth'; plural of object possessed: e.g. *néíčito* 'my teeth'; plural of possessor, suffix -V́*noo* is added: *heteθebiibínoo* 'your (pl.) dogs' (*he* 'dog').

The 1st person plural distinguishes inclusive and exclusive forms.

Verb

An Arapaho verb consists of a stem plus prefixes and suffixes. Transitive verbs are inflected for agent and for object/target; intransitive verbs are inflected for agent only. In each version, the distinction between animate and inanimate categories is observed.

There are four tenses – present, future, preterite, and narrative (aorist).

85

The main verbal *prefixes* are:

interrogative marker: *koo/kuu*
narrative tense: *hee'ih*
first person pronoun singular: *ne/né*
second person pronoun singular: *he/hé*
obviative: *h*V/Ø
preterite: *nih*
future: *hoot*
negative: *-ihoowu-*; *-cii-*.

Transitive verbs have suffixed inflections specifying the subject/object pronominal relationship. Thus, for a first person singular acting upon a second person singular the ending is *-eθen* (if the object is animate). Similarly, *-ún* indicates action by second person singular on first person singular animate; *-ót* specifies action by second person singular on obviative animate (the so-called fourth person), etc. Examples:

nihnoohobéθen 'I saw you' (where *nih-* is the preterite-tense prefix)

nohoohobeθen 'I see you'

héíhoowunoohobeθébe 'I don't see you (pl.)' (*-ihoowu-* is negative prefix)

heetnéíhoowunoohobeθébe 'I shan't see you (pl.)' (*heet* = *hoot*, future marker)

koohonoohobeθ? 'do I see you (sing.)?'

nonóóhowún 'you (sing.) see me'

níhnóóhowót 'you (sing.) saw him (obv.)'

Word order

As in Navajo, the verb tends to be final.

1 Nau hethauwuu, henee, daunausuvevethahede hae-
daunanenee, hāejenedaude, hanesāhenith hethauguhā-
daune hathāhuk, Vahadāhene, jeechauhauthehāa hadne-
sevevethahee, waude Jaun jea neesechauhauthehaude
hethauguhādaunau.

2 Nau hanaāāedauwunaude, hāene nananena vanevc-
thahenā jeenanesenehena, Hāsaunaunene Nananede
hanedaude hejavaa, Vadanauha Nananene haneseede.
Nananene hanajanede hanājaunauau. Nananene hatha-
navāane hadnaasedaunee hasauau hejavaa, nau jee nuu
vedauauwuu.

3 Hejevenāa hadauchusenee hayauwusenee vethewau.

4 Nau jejaegudanauwunāa hewauchudaudenedaunau
hanau nechau nejaegudanauwunade haunauude hanesā-
de nethāesayānedanauwunāade. Nau jevaechauhāa ne-
dauvasehadee; hau haugaunayauhāa hehethee hadau
wausauau.

(Luke 11: 1–4)

ARAUCANIAN

See **Mapundungu**.

ARMENIAN, CLASSICAL

INTRODUCTION

A branch of Indo-European, Armenian seems to have reached its present location, to the south of the main range of the Caucasus, during the second millennium BC, when Indo-European-speaking invaders from the Balkans or the Pontic area (*see* **Indo-European**) overthrew the Urartian kingdom (*see* **Urartian**).

Though traces of some kinship with Hellenic are discernible, Armenian is in two senses something of an isolate within the Indo-European family: in contrast to such groupings as Indo-Iranian, Italo-Celtic, Balto-Slavonic, it has no correlative; and, secondly, its Indo-European phonological identity has been crucially modified by long sojourn in a non-Indo-European phonological environment. The close analogy between the Armenian and Georgian sound systems has been emphasized by authorities on the two languages, e.g. A. Meillet.

Specifically, the term 'Classical Armenian' denotes the language as fixed early in the fifth century AD, by Mesrop Mashtots, who provided it with an alphabet, and who initiated the translation into it of the Bible and the writings of the Church Fathers. Mesrop himself seems to have translated the New Testament into Armenian.

Thus codified, the classical language, known as *grabar* or 'book language' continued to be used as the written language of Armenia up to the nineteenth century a literary norm from which the spoken forms had by then long diverged. (Compare the Katharevousa–Demotike situation in Greek.) Grabar is still in use as the liturgical language of the Armenian Church.

SCRIPT

The 36 letters invented by Mesrop Mashtots to notate the sounds of Armenian fit the language so well that hardly any modification has proved necessary. As Emile Benveniste wrote: 'un analyste moderne n'aurait presque rien à y changer' (quoted in Minassian, 1976: 31). The letters *O* and ֆ were added in the twelfth century: *O* representing a shift in the pronunciation of -*av* to /o/, while ֆ was introduced to denote /f/, a sound alien to Armenian, found in loan-words.

PHONOLOGY

Consonants

stops: b, p, p'; d, t, t'; g, k, k'
affricates: dʒ, tʃ, tʃ'
fricatives: v, s, ʃ, ʒ, x, h
nasals: m, n
liquids: r, rr, l, ł
semi-vowels: w, j

Central to Armenian phonology is the distinction between a voiced consonant, its unvoiced aspirate, and glottalized counterpart, for labial, dental, palatal, and velar series. Glottalized sounds are notated here with subscript dots. c = /ts/.

Vowels

i, e, ə, a o, u
diphthongs: ui, ai

/ə/ occurs in consonantal clusters as an epenthetic vowel which is not notated; e.g. *marṭnčel* 'to fight' is pronounced [marṭ'ənčɛl]. /e/ is realised as [e] and [ɛ]. The digraph *ու* may be read as /u/ or /vo/: *տուն* = /ṭ'un/; *զինուոր* = /zinvor/. When Classical Armenian is being read aloud, either modern standard Oriental or Occidental pronunciation may be used.

Stress

Stress is fixed on final full syllable.

MORPHOLOGY AND SYNTAX

As an Indo-Euroean language, Armenian presumably had gender originally, but there is no trace of it in the historical record.

Article

DEFINITE

There are three forms of the definite article: -*s*, -*d*, -*n*. These are suffixed to the noun, and are associated with the three persons of the pronominal system. They are found also in the demonstrative series: cf.

ṭuns ays 'this house (near me)'
ṭunt ayd 'that house (near you)'
ṭunn ayn 'that house (yonder, near third person)' (*ṭun* 'house')

This postfixed article may also be added to a noun in apposition to a subject pronoun: e.g. *yes ṭers yev vardapeṭs* 'I, lord and master ...'

INDEFINITE

The numeral *mi* 'one', may be used as an indefinite article following the noun: e.g. *er ayr mi* 'there was a man ...' (John 3.1). The plural marker is *-k* with various link vowels; often the stem is subject to elision and umlaut, and there are many irregularities: e.g. *ṭun* 'house', pl. *ṭunk*; *kałak* 'town', pl. *kałakək*; *hayr* 'father', pl. *hark*; *gin* 'woman', pl. *ganayk*. The definite article is added to the plural marker: *geṭk.n* /get'əkn/ 'the rivers'.

Noun

DECLENSION

There are seven regular declensions depending on the vowel used to form the genitive singular. This vowel may be added to the nominative singular or inserted before the final consonant if this is *-n*, *-ł*, or *-r*.

Example of declension: *geṭ* 'river' (external flection):

	Singular		*Plural*
nom., acc	geṭ	nom.	geṭ**k**
		acc.	geṭs
gen., dat.	geṭ**uy**		geṭ**oc**
abl.	**i** geṭuy		**i** geṭoc
instr.	geṭ**ov**		geṭ**ovk**

A definite object is marked by *z-* prefixed to the accusative: e.g.

> *Hanel č.garen z.dev.n*
> 'They cannot expel the demon' (*hanel* 'to expel', *garel* 'to be able', *dev* 'demon')

Genitive: possessor may precede or follow possessed: e.g. *Voč sa e hivsann vordi?* 'Is this not the carpenter's son?' (Matthew 13.55); *luys mardkan* 'the light of men' (John 1.4).

Adjective

As attribute, adjective may precede or follow noun, and may or may not be in concord. The non-attributive adjective is declined as a noun, with plural in *-k*. There are a few irregular formations, e.g. *pokr* 'small', pl. *pokunk*.

> Irk havasṭik paṭmin 'They relate things that are certain' (concord marked, adjective follows noun)

> yev tnán noca arkanelis spiṭaks 'and they were given white robes' (Rev. 6.11) (concord in acc. pl.)

> Snoṭiθ bank en 'These are vain words' (no concord, adjective precedes noun)

Comparative: there are three ways of making a comparative:

(a) positive + *kan* + acc.: e.g. *čar kan zṭer* 'more evil than the master';
(b) adverb + positive: *aveli čar* ...;
(c) *-aguyn* added to positive: *čaraguyn* ...

Pronoun

PERSONAL

The basic independent forms are:

sing. 1 *yes*, 2 *du*, 3 *na*; pl. 1 *mek*, 2 *duk*, 3 *noka*

These are declined in all cases; e.g. for first person singular:

acc. *zis*, gen. *im*, dat. *inj*, abl. *yinen*, loc. *is*, instr. *inev*

Examples:

yev yecuyc **inj** makur geṭ 'and he shewed me a pure river' (Rev. 22.1)
porjea zis, Ṭer 'examine me, Lord' (Armenian Liturgy)

DEMONSTRATIVE PRONOUN/ADJECTIVE

Three-degree series (*see* **Article**, above): sing. *ays*, *ayd*, *ayn*; pl. *aysk*, *aydk*, *aynk*. These are fully declined in all cases. The demonstrative pronoun *na*, pl. *noka*, supplies the third person pronoun.

INTERROGATIVE PRONOUN

zi 'who? what?'; *vov* 'who?'; *inč* 'what?'.
The sign ◠ is placed over the focused word in an interrogative sentence: e.g.

Zînč čar arar? 'What evil hath he done?' (Matthew 27.23)

Aržân e mez Ḳayser harḳs ṭal te voč? 'Is it lawful for us to give tribute to Caesar, or no?' (Luke 20.22)

RELATIVE PRONOUN

Sing. *vor*, pl. *vork*. Use of plural form with singular antecedent is optional. e.g.

Zînč en ban.k.n, **zor** duk.d asek?
'What words are these that you say?'

Čarik.n, **vor** gorçin ḳamaçink en yev voč bnaḳank
'The evils which are committed are intentional, not natural'

Numerals

1–10: *mi*, *yerḳu*, *yerek*, *čork*, *hing*, *vec*, *yutn*, *ut*, *inn*, *ṭasn*. 11–19: unit + link + *ṭasan*, e.g. 18 *ut.ev.ṭasn*; 20 *ksan*; 30 *yeresun*; 40 *karrasun*; 100 *haryur*.

Mi, *yerḳu*, *yerek*, and *čork* are declined and may precede or follow noun. The other numbers up to 9 may be declined.

Verb

The infinitive ending is *-al/-el/-ul*. *-el* verbs are further sub-divided into those which retain the *-e* as characteristic vowel, and those that change it to *-i*. There are thus four basic conjugations.

The modal and tense structure is built on two aspectual bases:

the imperfective (present) = the infinitive minus *-l*;
the perfective (aorist) = the root, often extended by *-Vc*.

From the imperfective base are formed the present, the imperfect, the first future tense, and the prohibitive mood. The imperfect is often used as a subjunctive (there is no optative in Classical Armenian). The perfective aspect provides the aorist, the second future, the imperative, and the hortative. (The original distinction between 'first' and 'second' future seems to have been aspectual: 'first' is based on the present root, hence imperfective; 'second' on the aorist root, hence perfective.)

PRESENT TENSE
The endings for all verbs are *-m*, *-s*, *-y*; pl. *-mk*, *-yk*, *-n*: e.g. *lavanam*, *lavanas*, *lavanay* 'I wash, you wash, he washes'.

Passive forms are made from active present-tense verbs by change of characteristic vowel to *-i*: e.g. *sirem ayl vočʿ sirim* 'I love but am not loved'.

FIRST FUTURE
The endings are *-ycem*, *-yces*, *-yce*, etc.: e.g.

Vočʿ ḳare kałak takčel, vor i veray lerin **ḳayce**
'A city that (of such a kind) is set on a hill cannot be hid' (Matthew 5.14)

PROHIBITIVE
Negative particle *mi* + singular form in *-r*, pl. in *-ayk*. This form is used in place of the missing negative imperative: e.g.

Ṭer, **mi** hamarir toca z.ays meł.s
'Lord, lay not this sin to their charge' (Acts, 7.59)

AORIST
Two sets of endings: active and passive. The two forms are not available for all verbs. For example, in the *-el* series, while all verbs have the active forms, only four verbs have the passive. 'Passive' here includes middle voice: e.g. *zarmacay* 'I was surprised'.

The active endings are: sing. *-i*, *-er*, *-Ø*; pl. *-ak*, *-ek*, *-in*. Passive endings: sing. *-ay*, *-ar*, *-av*; pl. *-ak*, *-ayk*, *-an*. Example: *Vor inčʿ greci, greci* 'what I have written, I have written' (John 19.22).

Short aorist passive forms may take an augment *ye-*: e.g. *ṭes yeṭes* 'he saw'; *giṭ* = *yegiṭ* 'he found'.

SECOND FUTURE
This has both future and subjunctive sense. The endings are: -ic, -ces, -ce; pl. -cuk, jik, -cen. -e → -i for passive. Example: Mi xrrovescin sirṭk jer 'Let not your hearts be troubled' (John 14.1).

PARTICIPLES
The participle in -eal may be used as a noun, and is then declined as, e.g., gorçk arrakeloc 'the Acts of the Apostles' (arrakeal 'the one who is sent'). A perfect tense is made with this participle and the auxiliary yem 'I am'. The forms of yem are: sing. yem, yes, e; pl. yemk, yik, yin: e.g. ṭeseal yem 'I have seen'; ṭeseal ei 'I had seen'. Here, the logical subject can be in the genitive case with the auxiliary in third person singular: e.g. i bazum paṭerazmuns mṭeal e im 'and of me there has been a going into many wars' = 'I have been in many wars'.

Future participle: -oc is added to the infinitive: e.g. Krisṭos yayṭneloc e 'Christ will reveal himself.'

IMPERATIVE
Made from aorist root, is found in second person only, and is always positive: e.g. from havaṭal 'to believe': havaṭa!, pl. havaṭacek!

HORTATIVE
Aorist root + -jir (sing.), -jik (pl.).

NEGATION
The general verbal negator is voč (→ č- preceding verb): e.g. voč yertayk̲ = čertayk̲ 'you do not go'. The prohibitive takes the negating particle mi.

CAUSATIVE
Aorist root + -ucanel (restricted use): e.g. from čanačel 'to know', čanucanel 'to cause to know'.

Prepositions

There are six basic prepositions: arr, z-, ənd, i(y), əsṭ, c-. Each of these can be used with more than one case, and each varies accordingly in meaning. Thus, arr with the accusative means 'at, towards'; with the dative/ablative means 'because of'; with the instrumental means 'beside, at the time of'. Examples:

Mi yerḳnčir arrnul **arr kez** Mariam gin ko
'Fear not to take unto thee Mary thy wife (Matthew 1.20)

ənd with dative:
yes ənd jez em … minčev **i** k̲aṭarac ašxarhi
'and I am with you even unto the end of the world (Matthew 28.20)

Word formation

Armenian is rich in compound and derived words. A very frequent model is X-a-Y, where X is usually a noun or adjective, and Y is a noun, adjective, or verb:

e.g. *arçat.a.ser* 'silver-loving' = 'miser'; *meç.a.ṭun* '(having) a big house' = 'rich'. The link element may be assimilated after *-i* stem-final: e.g. *gin.e.ber* 'wine producing' (from *gini* 'wine').

Derivation is by prefix: e.g. the privative prefixes *an-*, *ap-*, *ṭž-*, etc.: *ṭžgoh* 'dissatisfied'; *anmardi* 'inhuman'; *apyeraxṭ* 'ungrateful'; and by suffix, of which there are many: e.g.

-anoc, *-aran*: making nouns of place, e.g. *çaḷkanoc* 'flower garden';
-ak, *-ik*: diminutives, e.g. *navak* 'small boat';
-avor: bearer of ..., e.g. *daṭavor* 'judge';
ič, *-ord*: agent, e.g. *orsord* 'hunter';
pes: formant for adverbs
-utyun: makes abstract nouns, e.g. *canḳutyun* 'desire'.

Word order

Very free.

ARMENIAN,
MODERN STANDARD

INTRODUCTION

This Indo-European language is spoken by about 5 million in the Armenian Soviet Socialist Republic, in Georgia and elsewhere in the Soviet Union; and, in a slightly different form, by about a million in several Middle Eastern countries (Turkey, Lebanon) and by emigré colonies throughout the world. This second form is known as Western Armenian; Eastern Armenian is the written and spoken language used in the Soviet Union. The two forms are mutually intelligible, indeed very close to each other. Within Eastern Armenian the sub-dialectal system is very complex: Garibian distinguishes over 50 dialects, sub-divided into seven groups, according to the method used to form the present tense.

For Old Armenian language and literature, *see* **Armenian, Classical**.

Classical Armenian continued to be used as a written language until the nineteenth century and was the medium for the notable and very important renaissance of Armenian culture initiated by the Mekhitarist Order in Venice from the early eighteenth century onwards. In Armenia itself, the first steps towards the creation and development of a new literary language, closer to the spoken norm, were taken in the early nineteenth century by Khachatur Abovian and Ghevond Alishan. The late nineteenth century produced many outstanding writers, notably the novelists Raffi and Shirvanzade, the poets Tumanian and Isahakian, and the playwright Sundukian.

SCRIPT

(*See* **Appendix of Scripts**.) Devised by Mesrop Mashtots around the year AD 400, the Armenian alphabet has survived, almost intact, to the present day. Two letters were added in the twelfth century.

PHONOLOGY

Consonants

stops: b, p, p', dt, t', g, k, k'
affricates: dz, ts, ts', dʒ, tʃ, tʃ'
fricatives: f, v, s, z, ʃ, ʒ, x, h
nasals: m, n
lateral and flap: r, rr, l, ł (→[ɣ]).
semi-vowel: j

The ejectives are notated here as dotted letters; like Ossete, Armenian seems to have taken these phonemes from the Caucasian languages which surround this small Indo-European enclave. There are thus five series (three of stops, two of affricates) consisting of voiced member – aspirate surd – voiceless ejective: e.g. /b – p – p'/. The contrast between the aspirate and the ejective is often phonemic: cf. *yerek* 'three'; *yereḳ* 'yesterday'. Final voiced consonants are unvoiced: e.g. *yerb* 'when' → [yer**p**]. In this article *c* = /ts/.

Vowels

> front: i, e ([e] and [ɛ])
> mid: a, ə
> back: o, u

The vowel /ə/, represented in the script by the letter ℓ , occurs unnotated in many consonant clusters: thus *գրել* 'to write', is pronounced [gərel]. It is more convenient, however, to transliterate such words without the epenthetic vowel, which is in any case fleeting and often close to a shwa: *grel*.

Stress

Stress is virtually always on the final syllable.

MORPHOLOGY AND SYNTAX

Noun

There is no grammatical gender. Armenian has two numbers. The definite article is affixed to the noun: -ə/-n: e.g. *ṭun* 'house', *ṭunə* 'the house'; *gini* 'wine'; *ginin* 'the wine'. In Eastern Armenian, the indefinite article is *mi* preceding the noun; in Western it follows in the form *mə*: thus, EArm. *mi mard* = WArm. *mard mə* 'a man'. The plural marker is *-er* for monosyllables, *-ner* for polysyllables: e.g. *tun.er* 'houses'; *tun.er.ə* 'the houses'; *kayak.ner* 'towns', *kayak.ner.ə* 'the towns'.

DECLENSION

There are seven cases. Various types of declension are distinguished in the singular, differing mainly in the formation of the genitive and dative cases. There are no irregularities in the plural, as all nouns take -(n)er. Specimen declensions: *banvor* 'worker'; *gari* 'barley'; *or* 'day'.

	Singular	*Singular*	*Singular*
nom.	banvor	gari	or
gen.	banvor**i**	gar**u**	or**va**
dat.	banvor**i**	gar**u**	or**va**
acc.	banvor	gari	or
abl.	banvor**ic**	gar**uc**	or**vanic**
instr.	banvor**ov**	gar**ov**	or**ov**
loc.	—	gar**um**	or**um**

Examples of anomalous genitive formation: *hayr* 'father' – *hor*; *kuyr* 'sister' – *kroč*. All nouns in *-tyun* have a genitive in *-tyan*. Very many Armenian nouns are formed from two root words linked by *-a-*: e.g. *mayr* 'mother' + *kayak* 'town': *mayrakayak* 'capital city'; *hay* 'Armenian' + *-stan* 'place': *Hayastan* 'Armenia'.

Adjective

As attribute, adjective precedes noun and is invariable: e.g. *lav barekam* 'good friend'; *lav barekam.ner.i* 'of good friends'.

COMPARATIVE
With *aveli* 'more than': e.g. *spitak* 'white': *aveli spitak* 'whiter'. The compared nominal is in the ablative: e.g. *Yerevan.ic* (*aveli*) *meç* 'bigger than Yerevan'.

Pronoun

PERSONAL
The independent forms of the personal pronouns, with accusative case:

	Singular		*Plural*	
	Nom.	*Acc.*	*Nom.*	*Acc.*
1	yes	inj	menk	mez
2	du	kez	duk	jez
3	na	nran	nrank	nranc
	ink	iren	irenk	irenc

The full declension of *yes* 'I', for example, is: *yes – im – inj – inj – injnic – injnov – injnum*: *asek inj* 'tell me'; *inj asacin, vor...* 'they told me that ...'

POSSESSIVE ADJECTIVES
These are provided by the genitive forms of the above listed personal pronouns (*im – ko – ir*, etc.) and are paralleled by a series of personal possessive affixed markers for first, second, and third person: *-s, -t, -n*. Thus, *im anunə* = *anunəs* 'my name' (in both cases, with the definite article).

DEMONSTRATIVE PRONOUN/ADJECTIVE
Three forms closely connected with the personal endings: *ays/sa* 'this' (Lat. *apud me*), *ayd/da* (Lat. *apud te*), *ayn/na* (Lat. *apud eum*). These have plural forms: *srank, drank, nrank*; as adjectives they are invariable: e.g. *ayd čašaran.ner.um* 'in these restaurants'.

INTERROGATIVE PRONOUN
vov 'who?'; *inč* 'what?'.

RELATIVE PRONOUN
Sing. *vor*, pl. *vronk*; e.g. *duk, vor uzum ek sovorel hayeren* 'you who wish to learn Armenian'. Relative clauses may also be made with participles (*see* below): e.g. *ayn gnacoy usanoy* 'the student who is walking over there' (*gnal* 'to go, walk').

Numerals

1–10: *mek̲, yerk̲u, yerek, čors, hing, vec, yot, ut, inn, t̲as*; 11 *t̲as.n.mek̲*; 12 *t̲as.n.yerk̲u*; 20 *ksan*; 30 *yeresun*; 40 *ksařasun*; 100 *haryur*.

Verb

The Armenian verb has active and passive voices and four moods: indicative, optative, conditional–subjunctive, and imperative. Only the indicative mood has a full set of tenses.

The infinitive ends in *-el/al*; as in Old Armenian, two bases are formed from the infinitive:

(a) the present base, formed by dropping the *-el/al*: e.g. *grel* 'to write': present base *gr-*; *k̲ardal* 'to read': present base *k̲ard-*; *mt̲nel* 'to go': *mt̲n-*.
(b) the aorist base: *-l→aç* or *-acaç*: *grel*: aorist base *graç*; *k̲ardal*: *k̲ardacaç*

From the present base are formed the optative, the subjunctive, the conditional, the imperfective participle in *-um*, and the future participle in *-u*. From the aorist base are formed the simple past tense and the participle in *-o*. The past participle is identical with the second base: *graç, k̲ardacaç*.

The main auxiliary used in conjugation is *yem* = I am:
present sing. 1. em, 2. es, 3. ē; pl. 1. enk, 2. ek, 3. en ; y- anlaut if neccssary.
past sing.: 1. ēi, 2, ēir, 3. ēr; pl. 1. ēink, 2. ēik, 3. ēin

Specimen conjugation: *grel* 'to write'; indicative mood (main forms):

> present: grum em, es, *etc.*
> past imperfect: grum ēi, ēir, *etc.*
> future: grelu yem, yes, *etc.*, *or with particle* k̲ə: k̲ə grem (*optative*)
> preterite: grel em, *etc.*
> pluperfect: grel ēi, *etc.*
> perfect: graç em, *etc.*
> Simple aorist: sing. greci, grecir, grec; pl. grecink, grecik, grecin
> Optative: sing. grem, gres, gri; pl. grenk, grek, gren

GERUNDS

The present gerund ends in *-um* (the form used in the present and imperfect tenses above) or in *-elis/alis*; the latter form is used to denote action upon which a second action is contingent: e.g. *Senyak̲ mt̲nelis girkəs hanum em* 'Upon entering the room, I take my book.' The future gerund is seen as a tense formant in the future: *grelu yem*, etc. It can also be used as an infinitive of purpose; e.g. *Gnaci gradaran girk k̲ardalu* 'I went to the library to read a book'; and attributively: e.g. *k̲ardalu girk* 'a book to be read'.

IMPERATIVE

Sing. *grir!* 'write!' pl. *grecek!*

HORTATIVE

Optative form preceded by *biti*: e.g. *biti grem* 'I am to/have to write'.

99

PASSIVE

The marker is -v-: e.g. *sirel* 'to love'; passive, *sirvel* 'to be loved'; *Vočnčacvec mek r̆mbak̦oc̦ič* 'One bomber was destroyed.'

CAUSATIVE

-Vcn-: e.g. *nsțel* 'to sit', *nsțecnel* 'to ask to be seated'.

NEGATIVE

The negative particle *čə* is prefixed to the auxiliary if there is one; the auxiliary then precedes the sense verb: e.g. *grum ēi* 'I was writing', *čei grum* 'I wasn't writing'; *grelu e* 'he will write': *či grelu* 'he will not write'. The negative particle for the imperative mood is *mi*.

Prepositions and postpositions

Armenian uses both.

PREPOSITIONS

With genitive case: *ar̆anc* 'without': e.g. *ar̆anc k̦ask̦aci* 'doubtless'; and with accusative case: *depi* 'towards': e.g. *gnum em depi hyusis* 'I am going northwards'.

POSTPOSITIONS

Usually follow the genitive case: e.g.

> *hamar* 'for': e.g. *hayreniki hamar* 'for the motherland';
> *masin* 'about': e.g. *Xosum enk girki masin* 'We're talking about the book';
> *heț* 'with': e.g. *nra heț gnaci* 'I went with him';
> *vra* 'on': e.g. *seɣani vra* 'on the table'.

Word order

SVO is basic; can be altered for emphasis.

1 Սկզբունն էր Բանն . եւ Բանն Աստուծոյ մօտ էր . եւ Աստուած էր

2 Բանն : Նա սկզբունն Աստուծոյ

3 մօտ էր : Ամէն ինչ նորանով ե-
ղաւ , եւ առանց նորան ոչինչ չե-

4 ղաւ , ինչ որ եղաւ : Նորանով էր
կեանք , եւ կեանքը մարդկանց լոյսն

5 էր : Եւ լոյսը խաւարումը լոյս է տու-
լիս , եւ խաւարը չիմնացաւ նորան :

6 Մի մարդ եղաւ Աստուածանից
ուղարկուած , անունը Յոհաննէս :

7 Սա վկայութեան համար եկաւ ,
որ այն Լուսոյ համար վկայ է .
որ ամէնքը նորանով հաւատան :

8 Նա չէր Լոյսն , այլ որ Լուսոյն
համար վկայէ :

ASSAMESE

INTRODUCTION

This Eastern New Indo-Aryan language derives, like Bengali and Oriya, from the Māgadhī Prakrit. It is spoken by around 9 million people in the state of Assam, which forms linguistically an enclave between Tibeto-Burman and Mon-Khmer territories. There are two dialects, Eastern (Sibsagar) and Western (Kamarupa). The literary standard is based on the former. Assamese is one of the 14 official languages recognized in the Indian constitution.

From the thirteenth to the nineteenth centuries the Tai invaders known as the Ahoms ruled the country, their power culminating in the early eighteenth century. 'Ahom' is the normal Assamese pronunciation of the word *āsām* (Indo-Aryan sibilants reduced to /h/ in Assamese, *see* **Phonology**, below).

Literature in Assamese is recorded from the fourteenth century onwards. A distinctive and specifically Assamese genre is the historical chronicle, many of which were produced anonymously during the last two centuries of the Ahom state. There is a flourishing contemporary literature in prose media, e.g. the novel.

SCRIPT

The Bengali script, introduced in the nineteenth century, is used for writing Assamese. There is an extra letter for /w/, which has no counterpart in Bengali. Also, Assamese *r* differs from Bengali *r*.

There is an extremely poor correspondence between script and sound in this language, in that 49 graphs are available for 33 phonemes.

PHONOLOGY

Consonants

> stops: p, b, t, d, k, g; with aspirates ph, bh, th, dh, kh, gh
> fricatives: s, z, x, h
> nasals: m, n, ŋ
> laterals and flap: l, r, rh
> semi-vowels: j, w

It will be noticed that, in comparison with the standard New Indo-Aryan inventory, the palatal series, *c*, *ch*, *j*, *jh*, and the retroflex, *ṭ*, *ṭh*, *ḍ*, *ḍh* are missing from the above table. In Assamese the palatals have turned into /s/, /z/, while the

IA cerebrals have merged with the dental series, and the IA sibilants are represented by /x/ and /h/.

Sandhi rules reflect both Classical Sanskrit practice (*see* **Sanskrit**) and a later series of accommodations at junctures.

Vowels

a = [ɐ], i, e, æ, a = [ɔ], o, u

These occur nasalized, and the following palatalized variants are found: [œ, y]. Diphthongs: /oi, ou/.

VOWEL HARMONY
/ɔ/, /o/ followed by /i/ → [u]: e.g. *khora* 'lame man' – fem. *khuri*; /æ/ followed by /i/, /u/ → [e]: e.g. *bæta* 'son' – *beti* 'daughter'.

Stress

In Eastern dialect stress is on the penultimate syllable.

MORPHOLOGY AND SYNTAX

Noun

The basic dichotomy is between humans (masculine and feminine) and non-human (neuter). The distinction between masculine and feminine may be reflected morphologically: thus, -(*n*)*i* is a feminine marker: e.g. *burhi* 'old woman'.

NUMBER
The plural is formed with the help of various agglutinative suffixes: *-bilak* (humans), *-bor* (animals); *-sakal* /xɔkɔl/ is an honorific suffix: e.g. *dewtasakal* 'gods'.

SPECIMEN DECLENSION
manuh 'man, human being'.

	Singular
nom./agentive	manuhe
acc.	manuhak
gen.	manuhar
instr.	manuhere, manuhar **ddara**
	(*ddara* is a postposition)
dat.	manuhak, manuh**lai**
abl.	manuh**ar para**
loc.	manuhat

The same endings are added to form plurals: e.g. *manuhbilake, manuhbilakak*. There is no article as such in Assamese, but a singular animate noun may acquire some degree of definiteness by the insertion of *-to-* between base and case ending: e.g. *manuhtok* 'to that man (already mentioned)'. This enclitic seems to be an importation from contiguous non-Indo-European linguistic stock. Non-Indo-European influence is also seen in the Assamese practice of adding personal markers to kinship terms in the singular: e.g. for *zi* 'daughter': *zi* 'my daughter'; *ziyer(a)* your daughter'; *ziyek* 'his/her daughter'.

Adjective

The adjective is not sharply distinguished from the noun, and can be declined as such. As attribute it is invariable for case, but takes fem. *-i* where necessary.

COMPARISON
A comparative form is made by means of *koi/kari* following the locative case: e.g. *Xei gharat koi ei ghar daŋar* 'This house is bigger than that house.'

Pronoun

The independent personal forms are:

		Singular	Plural
	1	mai /mɔi/	ami
	2	tai /tɔi/	tahāt
hon.	2	apuni	aponasakal

In the third person the demonstratives, *i* (masc.), *ei* (fem.); *xi/xei* (masc.) *tai* (fem.) are used, with honorary forms *eȭ* and *tēȭ*.

The base forms are declined, e.g. for *mai*: acc. *mok*, instr. *more/mor ddara*, abl. *mor para*, gen. *mor*, loc. *mot*: e.g. *mor bandhu* 'my friend'.

DEMONSTRATIVE PRONOUN
Not declined when used attributively: e.g. *ei manuhak* 'of this man'. The plural marker may be added to either the noun or the demonstrative, not both: e.g. *ei manuhbilake = eibilak manuhe* 'these people'.

INTERROGATIVE PRONOUN
kih 'who?'; *kon* 'what, which?': e.g. *kon manuh/kitap* 'which man/book?'

RELATIVE PRONOUN
yi /zi/, pl. *yibilake*. These have oblique bases: *yā-* /zaː/ for humans, *yiha-* for non-human.

Verbal participle + the particle *thaka* is also used for relative constructions: e.g. *kitap parhi thaka manuh* 'the man who is reading the book'.

Numerals

1–10: *æk, dui, tini, sāri, pās, say, xāt, āth, na, dah*; 11–19 have synthetic forms; 20 *bis*; 30 *tris*; 40 *sallis*; 100 *xa*. Formation of numerals up to 100 is not predictable.

Verb

Has active and passive voices, and the following moods: indicative, imperative, subjunctive, conditional, presumptive.

Personal endings (*see* table) are the same for both numbers; where necessary -*hāk* may be added to mark plural. Gender is nowhere specified.

Personal endings:

		Present	Past	Future
1		-ō	-(i)lō	-(i)m
2	familiar	-a	-(i)li	-(i)bi
	neutral	-ā	-(i)lā	-(i)bā
2 & 3	hon.	-e	-(i)lē	-(i)ba

The past forms are composed of the past passive participle + personal markers. The auxiliary *ach* /as/ is used with the present participle to make an analytical present tense: e.g. *mai kitap parhi achō* /asō/ 'I am reading a/the book'. Similarly with past indefinite: *mai kitap parhi achōilō* /asōilō/ 'I was reading a/the book'.

Invariable particles enter into the composition of the subjunctive, the presumptive, and the conditional. The three moods are also specifically associated with tense – the subjunctive with the past tense + *hēten*, the presumptive with the present tense + *habalā*, the conditional with the non-finite form in -*ā* + *hēten*: e.g. *mai gəlo hēten* 'I'd have gone'; *xi ahise habala* 'he must have come'.

NON-FINITE FORMS

Infinitive in -(*i*)*ba*: e.g. *buliba* 'to speak'.

Present participle in -*i*; past participle in -*a*. Perfective conjunctive in -*i*.

Negative: *na* /nɔ/ is prefixed to verb: e.g. *mai nakarō* 'I don't do'.

PASSIVE VOICE

The auxiliaries *ya* /za/ and *ha* /hɔ/ are used + transitive past participle. Where *ya* is used, the logical subject is in the instrumental, the logical object in the nominative: e.g. *mor ddara ei kamto kara zay* 'by me this work is done' = 'I do this work'.

Ha construction: the logical object is in the accusative, subject is in the instrumental + third person of *ha*: e.g. *Tar ddara tomak mara nahaba* 'You will not be beaten by him' (examples from Babakaev 1961).

CAUSATIVES

Add -*a*/-*wā* to the root: the second grade, in -*wa*, implies that an intermediary is involved in the action: e.g. *laru* 'to run', *laruwa* 'cause someone to run'; *di* 'to give', *diya* (< *di.y(w)a*) 'cause someone to give'.

Postpositions

The language has about three dozen New Indo-Aryan postpositions, plus a few drawn from Arabo-Persian.

Word order

Normally SOV.

> ১   আদিতে¹ বাক্য² আছিল, আৰু বাক্য ঈশ্বৰে সৈতে আছিল,
> ২ আৰু বাক্যেই আপুনি ঈশ্বৰ। তেওঁ আদিতে ঈশ্বৰে সৈতে আছিল।
> ৩ তেওঁৰ দ্বাৰায় সকলোৰেই হল ;³ আৰু যি যি হল, সেইবোৰৰ
> ৪ এটাও, তেওঁৰ বিনে নহল।   জীৱন তেওঁতেহ ;⁴ সেই জীৱনেই
> ৫ মানুহৰ পোহৰ।⁵ পোহৰ আন্ধাৰত প্ৰকাশিত হৈ আছে ;
> ৬ কিন্তু আন্ধাৰে তাক গ্ৰহণ* নকৰিলে। ঈশ্বৰৰ পৰা পঠোৱা যোহন⁶
> ৭ নামেৰে এজন মানুহ আছিল ; তেওঁৰ দ্বাৰায় সকলোৱে যেন
>   বিশ্বাস কৰে, এই নিমিত্তে, সেই পোহৰৰ সাক্ষ্য দিবলৈ⁷ তেওঁ
> ৮ সাক্ষ্যৰ অৰ্থে আহিছিল।   তেওঁ আপুনি সেই পোহৰ নাছিল,
>   কিন্তু পোহৰৰ সাক্ষ্য দিবলৈহে আহিছিল।

ASSYRIAN, MODERN

INTRODUCTION

This is the name given to the eastern group of modern spoken Aramaic dialects. A western form, known as Ma'lūla, is spoken in a few places in the Anti-Lebanon mountains of Syria. The eastern varieties – Modern Assyrian – are in turn split up into many dialects spoken by small communities in the area stretching from Iranian Azerbaydzhan through Turkish Kurdistan to the Mosul region of Iraq. Speakers of Modern Assyrian are also to be found in Georgia, Armenia, and in the USA. Denominationally, Assyrians are Nestorians, Monophysite Jacobites, and Uniates. Over centuries of sojourn in alien linguistic surroundings, Modern Assyrian has assimilated many Arabic, Iranian, Turkish, and Kurdish words. In the Soviet context, both Russian and Georgian have provided loan-words.

Total numbers of Modern Assyrian speakers are estimated at c. 300,000.

SCRIPT

Assyrian can be written in either Jacobite (Serto) or in Nestorian Syriac script (*see* **Syriac**).

PHONOLOGY

Consonants

stops: b, p, p', d, t, t', g, k, k', q, ʔ
affricates: ts, dz, ts'
fricatives: f, v, s, z, ʃ, ʒ, x, γ, ẖ, ħ, ʕ, h
nasals: m, n
laterals and flap: l, ł, r
semi-vowels: j, w

/ẖ/ is a voiceless velar fricative; /ħ/ is pharyngeal and /h/ is glottal, both are voiceless fricatives. Typical is the series consisting of voiced plosive, voiceless aspirate, glottalized plosive: e.g. /b – p – p'/. /dz/ is notated as ǰ; glottalized sounds as dotted letters.

Assimilation occurs, especially of /r, l, n/: cf. Syriac *karsā* 'stomach' – Mod. Assyr. *kīsä*. Palatalization of velars: e.g. *k'älbä* 'dog' (cf. Arabic *kälb*).

Vowels

a, e, i, o, u

All occur long or short, and each has three pitch variants. Thus, /a/ ranges from [ɛ] (front; notated as ä) through [a] (middle) to [å] (back). Similarly, /i – ɪ – i̯/; Tsereteli (1964) compares [i̯] to Russian ы.

VOWEL HARMONY
Three-way opposition by pitch of vowel: i.e. the vowels in a word tend to be all front, middle, or back: cf. *laħma* 'bread'; *mälkä* 'king'; *qi̯tmå* 'ashes'; *bicätünütä* 'without difficulty'; *bi̯såråsṭütå* 'truly'.

MORPHOLOGY AND SYNTAX

The basic Semitic tripartite division into nominals, verbals, and particles is observed. Adjectives are treated as nominals.

Noun

Masculine and feminine are distinguished, the feminine being marked by -*ta*/*tä*. Two numbers, with very little trace remaining of the old dual. Masculine plural in -*i*, -*ani*; e.g. *dižmin* 'enemy' – *dižmīni*; *juma* 'day' – *jumani*. Also by reduplication with invariable -*i* added: e.g. *birkä* 'knee' – *birkäki*. Feminine plural in -*äti*.

STATE
The old emphatic state – noun + determinant – is now the citation form; the absolute and construct states have virtually vanished. Old Aramaic masculine emphatic state ending -*ā* > -*a* in Modern Assyrian: e.g. *malkā* > *mälkä*.

There is no inflection; case relations are expressed by preposition or particle + citation form:

genitive: *de*/*dᵉ*: e.g. *brūna dᵉmälkä* 'son of the king';
accusative: the marker is *l*/*lᵉ*; *qa* is used in the spoken language (may be omitted);
dative: *lᵉ*.

Adjective

As attribute, adjective follows noun, and agrees in gender (if singular) and number: e.g. *ħamra smūqa* 'red wine'; *baidägi smūqi* 'red banners'.

Pronoun

PERSONAL
Independent:

		Singular	Plural
1		āna	aḥnan
2	masc.	at	aḥtun
	fem.	at	
3	masc.	aw	äniy
	fem.	ay	

Oblique suffixal series: used with nouns and prepositions:

sing. 1 -ī, 2 masc. -uḫ, fem. -aḫ, 3 masc. -u, fem. -o;
pl. 1 -an, 2 -ōḫun, 3 -ē.

Following verbs, the same series attached to oblique case marker *l-* is used: e.g. *bit yāvin.luh* 'I shall give you (masc. 2nd sing.)'.

POSSESSIVE SUFFIXES
These endings are added to the relative particle *dī*: e.g. *diyu* 'his'; *diyan* 'our'.

DEMONSTRATIVE
āha (common) 'this'; pl. *āni*; *o* (masc.), *e* (fem.) 'that'; pl. *äniy*.

INTERROGATIVE
Māniy, *man* 'who?'; *mūdiy*, *mu* 'what?'.

RELATIVE
de-/dᵉ = *genitive link (see above)*.

Numerals

1–10: *ḫa*, fem. *gda*; *tre*, *tłå*, *årpå*, *hamša*, *ištä*, *šåvå*, *tmänjä*, *içå*, *işrå*. 11–19: units in absolute state preceding -*sår*: e.g. *håṭisår*, *tᵉrịsår*. 30–90: decades are plurals of base unit: 30 *tłäy* (pl. of *tłå*; 20 conforms to this pattern: *işrị*. 100 *imä*.

Verb

The Modern Assyrian verb differs strikingly from the general Semitic pattern in two ways:

1. Finite forms are found only in the imperative; in the indicative and subjunctive moods, tenses are formed by adding pronominal suffixes to verbal nouns. These suffixes are marked for person, gender, and number. Thus, tense replaces aspect.
2. Modern Assyrian has more quadriliteral stems than any other semitic language. In part, this is because morphological formants have been treated as radicals, e.g. *måqṭil* 'to cause someone to be killed'; where *m* is non-radical (root *QTL*).

STRONG AND WEAK VERBS
Weak verbs are those containing $w, j, ', h, '$.

TENSE
Tenses are based selectively on the three verbal nouns: the active participle, the passive participle, and the infinitive.

(a) active participle: this is the base for the subjunctive and conditional moods and for four basic tenses: general present, general imperfect, future, and first preterite. The active participle is marked for masculine/feminine singular and for plural common (masculine form).
(b) passive participle: the base for four indicative tenses – second preterite, the perfect, and two pluperfect forms.
(c) infinitive: the base for the continuous (progressive) tenses.

Tense particles: e.g. *kī*, marker for general present; *bit*, future; *qam*, first preterite; *-va*, general imperfect, both pluperfects; *bi*, continuous tenses. In certain tenses, e.g. future and general present, all three persons distinguish gender in the singular, but not in the plural.

NEGATION
lē/la/lēli; *lē* and *la* are invariable, *lēli* is conjugated (*see* paradigm of *pātiḫ*, below).

PARADIGM OF REGULAR STRONG VERB
pātiḫ, 'to open':

> Second preterite: 3 masc. *ptiḫli*, fem. *ptiḫla*; 2 masc. *ptiḫluḫ*, fem. *ptiḫlaḫ*; 1 *ptiḫliy*: pl. 3 *ptiḫlun*, 2 *ptiḫlohun*, *1 ptiḫlan*. Negated by *la* preceding these forms.
> Future: 3 masc. *bit pātiḫ*, fem. *bit patḫa*; 2 masc. *bit patḫit*, fem. *bit patḫat*; 1 masc. *bit patḫin*, fem. *bit patḫan*; pl. 3 *bit patḫiy*, 2 *bit patḫītun*, 3 *bit patḫaḫ*. Negated by replacing *bit* by *lē*.
> Present: 3 masc. **biptāḫeli**, fem. **biptāḫela**; 2 masc. **biptāḫevit**, fem. **biptāḫevat**; 1. masc. **biptāḫevin**, fem. **biptāḫevan**; pl. 3 **biptāḫena**, 2 **biptāḫetun**, 1 **biptāḫevaḫ**. Negation: the form *biptāḫa* is preceded by the conjugated particle *lēli*: *lēli, lēla – lēvit, lēvat – lēvin, lēvan*: pl. *lena – lētun – lēvaḫ biptāḫa*.

There are two verbs of being: *it*, neg. *lit*; past tense: *itva*, neg. *litva*. This is the existential verb; the copula is as follows: e.g. *īli* 'he is'; *īvin* 'I am (masc.)'; past: e.g. *īvä* 'he was'; *īvinvä* 'I (masc.) was'; *ivänvä* 'I (fem.) was'.

Prepositions

Independent or bound; the bound forms are *-l, la-, k-, b-*; independent: e.g. *min* 'out of, from'; *(l)kis* 'at, *chez*'; *(t)ḫut* 'under'; *bar* 'behind'. Some of these require relative particle *d-*: e.g. *dipnä d-* 'around'; *sabab d-* 'because of'.

Word formation

Many of these are old construct formations (*see* **Semitic Languages**): e.g. *bärdimä = bär + dimä* 'son of blood', i.e. 'killer, slayer'; *braqāla = brā + qāla* 'daughter of the voice', i.e. 'echo'.

Adjectives: often with *mar/māri*: e.g. *märšimä = māri + šimä* 'owner of a name', i.e. 'famous'.

la is prefixed to a word to denote its negative or opposite: e.g. *ḥoš* 'pleasant', *laḥoš* 'unpleasant'.

Prefixes: some general Semitic formants retained, e.g. *mi-* (agent), *ti-* (abstracta).

Suffixes: e.g. *-āna*, denoting agent: e.g. *kätvänä* 'writer' (root *KTB*). *-ūna* forms diminutives. *-anāya* denotes origin: e.g. *aramnāya* 'Armenian'; or tendency towards: e.g. *smūqa* 'red', *smuqnāya* 'reddish'.

Word order

SVO is frequent, but order is fairly free.

ATHABASKAN

INTRODUCTION

In his 1929 classification of the North American Indian languages Edward Sapir placed Athabaskan as the major branch of the Na-Dene phylum, to which he also allocated Tlingit and Haida. This grouping is retained in the Voegelin classification of 1966.

Athabaskan itself falls into three major divisions:

1. Northern: about a dozen languages including Chipewyan, Dogrib, Sarsi, Carrier; a total of perhaps 10,000 speakers.
2. Californian: included Hupa and half a dozen other languages. All extinct.
3. Apachean: an internally closely related sub-group including Navajo, Western Apache, Chiricahua and Mescalero Apache, Jicarilla Apache, Kiowa (extinct). Estimated total of c. 92,000 speakers, of whom c. 80,000 are Navajo.

PHONOLOGY

In general, Athabaskan languages are marked by nasalization, glottalization, and the presence of tones. There is often extensive differentiation of the lateral and velar–uvular series; e.g. Chiricahua Apache has five laterals, Navajo has nine affricates in the dental–alveolar series. /p/ and /r/ are often absent. For inventories of Athabaskan consonants, *see* **Apache**, **Chipewyan**, **Navajo**.

Vowels

Typically, /i, e, a, o, (u)/, extended by length distinction and by nasalization.

MORPHOLOGY AND SYNTAX

Some main features:

Nominals

There is a basic common stock of monosyllabic nouns: e.g. Nav. *béésh*, Ch. Ap. *béésh*, Chip. *bes* 'knife'.

Many nouns have a dual base – absolute form and possessed form: e.g. Nav. *béésh* 'knife', *-béézh* '...'s knife'. Inalienable possession (bodily parts, kinship terms) is denoted by bound forms: e.g. Nav. *'ajaad* 'one's leg' → 'leg'.

Verbals may be nominalized: e.g. Nav. *ólta'* 'reading is done' = 'school'; Chip. *nátsər* 'he is strong' = 'strength'.

Personal pronominal possessive markers are prefixed to nouns, e.g. Nav. *shí-*, Ch. Ap. *shì-*, Chip. *sɛ-* for first person singular: Ch.Ap. *shì.dìbéhé* = Nav. *shi.dibé* 'my sheep'.

Typical pronominal markers are:

				Example
sing.	1	sh/s	Ch. Ap.	shí
	2	n		ní
3rd sing. pl.		b		bi
	4	h	Nav.	ha/ho
	1/2	nVh		nihi

Personal pronominal markers can be prefixed to postpositions: e.g. Nav. *shi.ķi* 'on me', *ni.ķi* 'on you'.

There is extensive use of directional and relational postpositive enclitics, plus non-affixed postpositions.

Verbals

The typical Athabaskan verbal paradigm comprises a verbal stem preceded by a strictly ordered sequence of prefixes. If these are numbered 1 to 10, the stem is in tenth position; the pronominal subject prefix occupies position 8, the pronominal object, if any, is in 4 (in other words, slot 4 is empty for intransitive verbs). Some positions are in complementary distribution: for example, if the iterative marker is present in slot 2, slot 7 – the position for non-iterative moods and aspects – must be vacant.

Position 9 is obligatorily occupied by the verbal classifier. The division by classifier – Ø, /d, l, ł/ – into transitive, intransitive, and passive verbal paradigms runs right through Athabaskan. In some of the languages the classifiers have merged, and may be represented by their phonetic reflexes. Together with aspect, the class of verb determines the form of the subject pronominal series in position 8. For example, in Apachean the first person singular marker is *-sh-* or *-éłí*, depending on class and aspect.

The stem itself is monoform if the verb is stative. Active verbs, however, modulate into several stems to denote different aspects and modes. A Navajo active verb, for example, modulates into progressive, imperfective, perfective, iterative, and optative modes, which will be listed in a Navajo dictionary. E.g. the stem meaning 'to handle a round, bulky object' has the following five stems:

'ááł, 'aah, 'ą́, 'ááh, 'ááł

The stems are unpredictable, as is their functional relationship to each other. Often the progressive and iterative stems are identical. In the Chiricahua Apache verb 'to copulate' four stems are identical and only the perfective varies by a change of tone from high to falling, and *ł* → *l*: 'iłł, 'iłł, 'iłl, 'iłł, 'iłł

TENSE

Future, past, present. The future tense is expressed by the progressive mode, the present by the imperfective or progressive, the past by the perfective. The objective pronoun is incorporated in the verb complex (position 4). Formal means exist for expressing passive, reciprocal, reflexive, inchoative, and other nuances, assisted by a great many sense-modulating verbal prefixes.

For a detailed description of an Athabaskan verb system, *see* **Navajo**.

AUSTRALIAN LANGUAGES

INTRODUCTION

In the late eighteenth century, when Europeans first reached Australia, round about 200 languages were spoken in the continent. At least 50 of these are now extinct, about 100 are in various stages of obsolescence, many close to extinction. Only 50 are officially 'stable', with numbers of speakers ranging from 6,000 – the Western Desert Language – to a few hundred. There is a fairly even distribution of languages over the continent, with somewhat denser incidence in Arnhem Land, Northern Queensland, and in Victoria and New South Wales. All but a handful can be shown to belong to one 'Australian' family: that is, there was a Proto-Australian language (estimated time-depth about 40,000 years ago) and there is no evidence of any connection with any other language family.

The family can be further sub-divided into genetically comparable groups, each such group having from one to ten members. The genetic relationship is often difficult to distinguish from areal typological features.

Various classifications have been put forward. Schmidt (1919) offered a roughly geographical classification between north and south. In 1956 Capell proposed a formal classification between languages which use both prefixes and suffixes, and languages which use suffixes only. Then in the 1960s Kenneth Hale made a typological distinction between the 'Pama-Nyungan' languages, covering 90 per cent of the continent, and the non-'Pama-Nyungan' languages of Arnhem Land and the north-west of Western Australia. These latter have developed complex verbal systems of the polysynthetic type.

SCRIPT

No Australian language was written. Adaptations of the English alphabet are in use for a few of the major languages; e.g. the retroflex series in Yolŋu is marked by underlining: d̲, t̲, n̲, l̲, and ' denotes the glottal stop.

PHONOLOGY

Sound systems, both consonantal and vocalic, show a surprising degree of homogeneity over the whole continent. A standard and typical inventory comprises:

Consonants

stops and fricatives: b, d, ḍ, ð, ʒ, g
associated nasals: m, n, n', ɳ, ŋ
laterals: l, ʎ, ļ
rhotics: r
semi-vowels: w, y
vowels: a, i, u

Fricatives and sibilants are almost unknown in Australian languages. Where they occur, they are due to phonological change leading to enhancement of, or subtraction from, the typical inventory. Thus, a few languages have developed greatly augmented vowel systems, up to twelve phonemes in some cases. The six standard stops have voiceless allophones; the contrast between [b] and [p], for example, is, however, not phonemic.

Areal typological factors have to be taken into account; thus, the dental/retroflex contrast is missing in most eastern languages, but is typically found throughout the central and western areas.

Typical of the whole field is the word pattern CVC(C)V(C).

MORPHOLOGY AND SYNTAX

Dixon (1980) lists these word classes: nominals (including adjectives), pronouns, verbs, adverbs, locative and temporal qualifiers, particles, interjections.

Nominals

Three numbers are usually found: singular, dual, plural. Plural number is optionally marked, often by reduplication. The numeral 'two' may accompany the dual affix.

Some northern languages, e.g. in Arnhem Land, have class systems on Bantu lines (*see* **Bantu Languages**). The noun class prefix is recapitulated in the adjective and echoed in the verb. A different kind of class system is found in Dyirbal, where gender-marked determinatives act as articles: masc. *bayi*, fem. *balan*, neuter *bala*. A fourth form, *balam*, indicates edible, but non-flesh, foodstuffs.

Widespread use is made of genetic markers, to which specific terms are added: e.g. in Dyirbal the feminine class marker will precede a nominal denoting a bird (since the Dyirbal believe that women turn into birds when they die).

CASE

In most languages five or six cases are found; coverage varies. The absolute case, usually with Ø inflection, provides the subject of an intransitive verb and the object of a transitive. The ergative case affix marks the subject of a transitive verb. The genitive affix is used for alienable possession; inalienable possession is expressed by simple apposition (*cf.* **Chinese**). Other cases are: dative, allative and ablative locatives, purposive, instrumental. Australian languages may be

unique in having an 'aversive' case, used in such contexts as 'for fear of the dog'.
A typical set of endings may be taken from Yidiny:

absolute	-Ø
ergative	-ŋgu/du
genitive	-ni
locative and instr.	-da/la/ŋga
ablative	-mu/m
dative	-nda
purposive	-gu
aversive	jida/yida

All show sandhi at junctures. Analogous endings are found in many languages, though, as noted above, the semantic boundaries of the cases are fluid.

Adjective

As attribute, the adjective follows the noun and takes its case: Dixon gives an example from Warrgamay: *ɲulmburu.ŋgu wurrbi.bajun.du* '(by) the very big woman (ergative)'.

Pronoun

There are singular, dual, and plural forms; trial and paucal also occur. The first person dual/plural is marked for inclusive/exclusive possession. This is average practice. More complicated systems take kinship degree into account. Only the forms for first and second persons are true personal pronouns; the third person forms are supplied from the demonstrative pronominal series, on a scale of relative proximity, e.g. in Western Desert Language:

ngaa- 'this'	he, she ... (close at hand)
pala- 'that'	he, she ... (further away)
nyarra- 'that'	he, she ... (remote)
palunya 'that'	he, she ... (not visible)

In some languages the personal pronouns have absolute, ergative, object, genitive forms.

Bound pronominal clitics appear in many languages. Where these are available, use of free pronouns is optional: e.g. in Western Desert, singular:

	Subject	Object
1	-rna	-rni
2	-n	-nta
3	-Ø	-lu

There are corresponding series for dual and plural. Dixon gives the following example from the Western Desert Language: *pu.ngku.rna.nta* 'I will hit you' (*pu-* = stem; *-ngku* = future marker; *-rna-* = 1st p. sbj. marker; *-nta-* = 2nd p. obj. marker).

DEMONSTRATIVE PRONOUN
See Personal pronoun above.

INTERROGATIVE PRONOUN
A widespread pattern is: *w/n – a – n'a*: e.g. Dyirbal, *wanya*, Western Desert, *ngana* 'who?'; Dyirbal, *minya*, Western Desert, *nyaa* 'what?'.

Numerals

The concepts unity, duality, triality are covered by singular, dual, and plural inflection. There are no numbers in aboriginal languages higher than three. For everyday purposes, the English numerals are used.

Verb

Roots do not occur without inflection. Most languages have anything up to half-a-dozen different conjugations, distinguished by phonetic criteria, not semantic. A comparison of five languages in Dixon 1980 shows that transitivity is in general associated with the *-l-* conjugation; intransitive verbs are generally in the *y/Ø* conjugation. Typical markers are: Ø, *ŋ*, *n*, *l*, *rr* (these taken from Walmatjari).

Derivational/modal affixes may appear. If present, they are sited between the stem and the inflection. They give reflexive, causative, inceptive, habitual, semelfactive connotation to the stem.

Almost all Australian languages have an imperative mood; the negative imperative may be a distinct form.

TENSE
Many languages have past, present, and future inflections. The precise frame of reference varies from one language to another: in some, the future is contrasted with the non-future, i.e. past and present are lumped together; in others, past is contrasted with non-past.

In typical inflection patterns the conjugation marker is followed by the tense marker; in Walmatjari the tense endings for an *-l-* conjugation verb are:

> imperative: *-nyja*
> future: *-lku*
> past: *-rni*
> customary: *-lany*
> subordinate: *-rnu*

As will be seen from the last entry in this list, there is a specific marker for the verb in a subordinate clause in Walmatjari, as there is for switch reference.

It should be pointed out that in many cases a conjugation has very few members: e.g. the *-n-* conjugation in Walmatjari has only three members: *ya.n* 'to go', *ma.n* 'to do', and *la.n* 'to pierce'.

Negation is by particle.

AUSTRO-ASIATIC
LANGUAGES

This is the designation adopted for a collocation of three typologically comparable but not necessarily genetically related groups of languages. They are:

1. Mon-Khmer languages: spoken in Vietnam, Laos, and Cambodia, with extensions into Burma and Malaysia. One member – Khasi – is in India. Estimates of the total numbers of Mon-Khmer speakers depend on whether Vietnamese is or is not regarded as a member of the family (*see* **Vietnamese**). With Vietnamese, the total comes to around 70 million; without it, to about 10 million.
2. Munda languages: also known as Kol. These languages are spoken in the Indian states of Bihar, Orissa, and Madhya Pradesh. Their original distribution must have been far wider, and their presence in the sub-continent antedates the coming of the Aryans in the third/second millennium BC. About 6 million people speak a dozen Munda languages, of which the most important by far are Santali and Muṇḍārī.
3. Nicobarese: spoken by around 18,000 in the Nicobar Islands.

See **Khmer**, **Vietnamese**, **Mon**, **Khasi**, **Palaung**, **Bahnaric Languages**, **Santali**, **Muṇḍārī**, **Nicobarese**.

AUSTRONESIAN LANGUAGES

This very extensive family of some 700 languages, spoken by about 200 million people, falls naturally into two divisions, which intersect close to the island in which the whole Austronesian family is believed to have originated – New Guinea.

The Western division centres on Indonesia and the Philippines, with outliers in Taiwan, Madagascar, and Micronesia. Ninety-eight per cent of the total number of speakers of Austronesian languages are to be found in this division.

The Eastern division has not more than 2 million speakers, who inhabit thousands of islands scattered over a vast area of the Pacific Ocean. Three main sub-divisions are distinguished: Polynesian, Melanesian, and Micronesian languages.

While the Polynesian languages form a remarkably homogeneous group, the genetic affiliation between them and the Melanesian and Micronesian groups is not obvious, and was only finally demonstrated by Otto Dempwolf in the middle of the twentieth century. Since then, progress has been made on the reconstruction, by comparative methods, of the parent language, or Proto-Austronesian.

Recent research goes to show that Proto-Austronesian split, about 4,000 years ago, into two branches which are, today, highly divergent: Formosan (small and dwindling; about 100,000 speakers in the mountains of Taiwan) and Malayo-Polynesian.

See **Polynesian Languages**, **Achinese**, **Balinese**, **Batak**, **Minangkabau**, **Indonesian**, **Javanese**, **Sundanese**, **Madurese**, **Gorontalo**, **Buginese**, **Macassarese**, **Hawaiian**, **Samoan**, **Tongan**, **Maori**, **Tagalog**, **Cebuano**, **Ilokano**, **Bikol**, **Trukese**, **Marshallese**, **Chamorro**, **Cham**, **Malagasy**, **Fijian**, **Tahitian**, **Rapanui**.

AVAR

INTRODUCTION

Avar belongs to the Avaro-Andi-Dido group of the Dagestani branch of the Ibero-Caucasian family. There is a basic split into northern and southern dialectal forms. The literary standard is based on *bolmač*, a kind of lingua franca developed on a northern variety of Avar for trade and communication purposes. The Avars form by far the largest ethnic group in the Dagestan Autonomous Soviet Socialist Republic, with an estimated number of speakers now approaching the half-million mark. The earliest record of Avar is found in bilingual inscriptions (with Georgian) dating from the tenth century AD. The Avar Khanate, which arose from the ruins of Mongol dominion in the Caucasus, reached its zenith in the seventeenth to eighteenth centuries, and the Avar literary tradition is of equivalent age. Until relatively recently, however, Arabic was the main, not to say sole, literary language. The late nineteenth century saw the emergence of creative writing in Avar (Mahmud of Kahabroso, Hamzat Tsadasa, and, in the mid-twentieth century, Rasul Hamzatov). The Avar press dates from the early Soviet period; newspapers, journals, and some books are published in the language.

Script

Arabic until 1928, followed by ten years of experimental romanization. Since 1939 Cyrillic + *I*, which is here the marker for ejective consonants.

PHONOLOGY

Consonants

There are 44 consonants, including a rich inventory of fricatives, affricates, and sibilants. A typical series is affricate – geminate – ejective affricate – geminated ejective: e.g. /tʃ, ttʃ, tʃ̣, ttʃ̣/. Here, gemination is marked by the macron and the subscript dot indicates an ejective consonant.

There are at least four laterals, here transcribed as ƙɬ, ɬ, ɬ̄, l. The velar series: /g, k, kk, k', k'k'/ is extended deeper into the throat by consonantal phonemes described as uvular (five values based on /q/), pharyngeals (/ʕ/ and /ħ/) and laryngeals (ʔ/ and /h/).

Vowels

> front: i, ε
> central: a
> back: o, u

Stress

Weak, free, usually on first or second syllable.

MORPHOLOGY

Noun

Nouns are marked for number and case, and are divided into three classes: male persons, female persons, animals, and objects. Specific markers for these classes are affixed as prefixes to verbs, and as suffixes to adjectives. Pronouns and adverbs also reflect class. Thus the class markers articulate the sentence as syntactic relay points (*cf.* **Bantu**). For class 1, male persons, the marker is *v-/-v*; for class 2, *y-/-y*, and for class 3, *b-/-b*. The plural marker for all three classes is *r-/-l* (*r-* for verbs, *-l* for adjectives). Examples:

> *emen vačana* 'the father came'
> *čužu yačana* 'the woman came'
> *ču bačana* 'the horse came'
> *vasal račana* 'the boys came'

NUMBER

Plural markers, e.g. *-zabi*, *-zal*, *-bi*, *-al*, are suffixed to noun stems: e.g. *khur* 'field', pl. *khurzal*; *ber* 'eye', pl. *beral*; *halmaγ* 'comrade'; *halmaγzabi* 'comrades'.

CASE SYSTEM

The basic cases are: nominative, ergative, genitive, dative. In addition, Avar has three series of locative cases specifying (a) rest in a place; (b) motion towards a focus; and (c) motion out of, away from a focus. Each of these series is further sub-divided into five referential frames, depending on whether the rest or motion is related to the surface of something, contiguity with something, inclusion in something, being underneath something, or, lastly, being inside something. Thus, *šaharalda* 'in the town'; this is an (a)-class locative (rest in a place) with reference to a surface: *Dos hudulasde kaγat qvana* 'He wrote a letter to a friend'; here, *hudulasde* is a class-(b) locative (motion towards something → indirect object) with reference to contiguity.

Using the ergative singular ending as criterion, we get three declensions: (1) ergative in *-s*; (2) ergative in *-ł* (3) ergative in *-ca*.

Specimen declension: first declension, *vas* 'son'; *čužu* 'woman';

	Singular	Plural	Singular	Plural
nominative	vas	vasal	čužu	ručabi
ergative	vasas	vasaz	čužuyał	ručabaca
genitive	vasasul	vasazul	čužuyałul	ručabazul
dative	vasase	vasaze	čužuyałe	ručabaze

To each paradigm 30 locative cases must be added.

Adjective

Attributively, the adjective precedes the noun and is in class concord with it, by suffixed marker: e.g. *tiriyav vas* 'lively boy'; *tiriyał vasal* 'lively boys'; *tiriyay yas* 'lively girl'. Only when used substantively is the adjective marked for case.

Pronoun

PERSONAL
The basic personal forms are: sing. 1 *dun*; 2 *mun*; plural: 1 incl. *nił*; excl. *niž*; 2 *nuž*. Demonstrative pronouns are used for the third person forms. The personal pronouns are declined in the basic cases + two locatives: e.g. for first person singular: *dun, dica, dir, die*; *dida, diq*. They do not take class markers. Possessive forms precede noun: e.g. *dir halmay* 'my comrade'.

DEMONSTRATIVE PRONOUN
A three-degree series of relative proximity is further complicated by a distinction in relative altitude, above or below speaker. Thus, *hev* suggests a class 1 (male) person in distal relationship with speaker; *hov* further identifies him as being situated lower down than the speaker. That is, the demonstratives take the class markers.

INTERROGATIVE PRONOUN
Also takes class marker: *šiv* 'who?' (class 1).

RELATIVE PRONOUN
None.

Numerals

The root forms for 1–10 are: *co, ḳi, łab, unq, šu, anł, anḳł, miḳł, ič, anç*. *-go* is added to form the cardinals. Formation of the decades may be decimal or vigesimal: 20 *qogo*; 30 *łebergo*; 40 *ḳiqogo* = 2×20; 100 *nusgo*.

Verb

Transitive and intransitive; syntactically, verbs of perception and affective verbs form specific sub-divisions.

TRANSITIVE VERBS

Logical subject in ergative case, verb in class concord with logical object in nominative (absolute) case: e.g. *Ebelał vas vačana* 'The mother brought her son'; *Ebelał yas yačana* 'The mother brought her daughter.' With certain verbs, the pronominal class marker is an infix: e.g.

> *Muslimatica vas havuna* 'Muslimat bore a son';
> *Muslimatica yas hayuna* 'Muslimat bore a daughter';
> *Muslimatica łumal haruna* 'Muslimat bore children.'

INTRANSITIVE VERBS

Subject in nominative (absolute) case: e.g. *cŭ bačana* 'the horse came'.

> Affective verbs: subject in dative: verb in class concord with logical object:
> e.g. *Muradie yas yoķļula* 'Murad loves (his) daughter.'
> Verbs of perception: subject in class-(a) locative, verb in class concord with
> logical object: e.g. *Ebelalda vas viẋana* 'The mother saw the son'; *Insuda yas yiẋana* 'The father saw the daughter.'

MOOD

There are four moods – indicative, imperative, conditional (subjunctive), and interrogative. The indicative mood has three tenses: a general/aorist tense, a past, and a future. These may be illustrated with the stem *çali(ze)* 'to read': general, *çalula*; past, *çalana*; future, *çalila*. The general tense and the future are negated by affixing *-ro*; *çalularo*. The past is negated by adding *-čo*.

A specific present is made by combining a present participial form with class-marked forms of the verb 'to be'; the participial form is also marked for class: *çaluleb bugo* 'is being read'. Similarly, *çalaleb* 'was being read'; *çalileb* 'will be being read' (+ *bugo*).

The conditional/subjunctive marker is *-ni*, negated by *čoni*. The participial forms are negated by infix: e.g. future, *çalileb*, neg. *çalilareb*. Similarly, negative past participial form, *c̄aličeb*.

Postpositions

Several of these, e.g. *žanib* 'inside', *ṭad* 'on', do little more than resume the meaning of the spatial case series. Others, like *yorł* 'between, among', *naqa* 'behind', *dande* 'against', serve to extend or amplify the spatial series:

> Poyezdalda ṭad reķana dov
> 'He boarded (onto) the train'
> Stolalda ṭad łe dir sa'at
> 'Lay my watch on the table'
> (*poyezd*, *stol* are Russian loan-words, 'train', 'table'; *sa'at* 'watch' (Arabic loan-word))

Word formation

By affixation or by compounding. Thus, -*či* and -*qan* form nouns denoting agent from verbal stems, e.g. *ħalṭuqan* 'worker' (*ħalṭize* 'to work'). Compounding: e.g. *kver* 'hand' + *bač̣*, root of the verb *bač̣ine* 'to clean'; *kverbač̣* 'handkerchief'.

Word order

SOV is normal in ergative construction, but note intransitive and imperative constructions in examples of postpositions above.

---

1. АВАЛАЛДА вукӀана Калам. Гьев вукӀана Аллагьгун, ва Гьев вукӀана Аллагъ.

2. Авалалдасаго Гьев Аллагъгун вукӀана.

3. Гьесдасахун тӀолабгояб бижизабуна; Гьев гьечӀого щибниги лъугьинчӀо.

4. Гьесулъ букӀана гӀумру, ва чагӀазе гьеб гӀумру букӀана нур.

5. Гьеб нур кенчӀола бецӀлъуда, ва бецӀлъиялда кӀвечӀо гьеб свинабизе.

6. Аллагьас витӀана, жинда ЯхӀя-ян абулев цо чи.

7. Гьес гӀадамазда нур бихьизабизе кколаан, гьелдалъун цинги киналго гьелда божизе гӀоло.

8. Гьев живго гьеб нурлъун вукӀинчӀо; гьесул тӀадкъай букӀана гӀищӀго, гьес гьеб нур бихьизаби.

AVESTAN

INTRODUCTION

Avestan belongs to the Iranian branch of Indo-European, and is one of the oldest attested Indo-European languages. Textual material in Avestan may be divided by content into (a) the religious texts of Zoroastrianism, in part dating from the middle of the first millennium BC; and (b) a poetic corpus embodying the mythology and the heroic traditions of ancient Iran; some of this material is pre-Zoroastrian. Neither sector was recorded in writing until long after Avestan had ceased to be a spoken language. Both were handed down by word of mouth until the first known codification, which took place between the fourth and sixth centuries AD, during the Sasanid period. For this purpose the Pehlevi script was available (*see* **Pehlevi**), and it was forthwith adapted and amplified so as to accommodate the richer phonological inventory of the ancient language. To this codification the name *avesta* was given, while the accompanying translation and commentary in Pehlevi were known as *zand*. It is probable that the material thus codified was far more extensive than that extant today, the losses being due in part at least to the Moslem invasions. The content as now known comprises:

(a) the Zoroastrian canon: the *Yasna*, including the *Gāthās* and the *Homyašt*: in part very old, in part rewritten.
(b) the 'little Avesta', a collection of Zoroastrian hymns, including some of the most ancient.
(c) the *Yašts*: an ancient heroic and mythological stratum reworked in the spirit of Zoroastrian homiletics by the priesthood.

SCRIPT

The 16-letter Pehlevi script was expanded to 48; some of the graphs are positional variants. There are 14 vowel signs, the rest denote consonants. Some Pehlevi ligatures were adopted.

PHONOLOGY

No one phonological inventory can be given for the different strata in the Avestan corpus; what is valid for one stratum is invalid for another. The authorities in this field – Emile Benveniste, G. Morgenstierne – have reconstructed an 'idealized' inventory, in the light of Sanskrit/Vedic congeners and the general principles of Indo-European philology. The proposed 'idealized' system comprises:

Consonants

labials: /p, b, f, v, m/;
dentals: /t, θ, d, n, s, z, r/;
alveolar–palatals: /tʃ, dʒ, j, ʃ, ʒ/;
velars: /k, g, x/;
glottal: /h/; + allophones.

The absence of /l/ is striking.

Vowels

long and short: i, a, u

There are also signs for the allophones [e, ə, əː, a, oː] (long vowels are here indicated by a macron). The basic diphthongs are: /ai, aːi, au, aːu/. Vocalic /r̥/ seems to be present, though not notated.

VOWEL GRADATION
(*See* **Sanskrit**.) Gradation is present, but not always strictly observed: /Ø – a – aː; r̥ – ar – aːr/, etc.

CONSONANT GRADATION
E.g. alternation of /k/tʃ/: e.g. root *vak* 'to speak', perfect *vavača*

Tone and stress

Internal evidence in the *Gāthās*, along with parallel evidence in the congener languages, points to the existence in the oldest Avestan period of a tonal system similar to that in Vedic (*see* **Vedic**). In later stages, tone was replaced by a stress accent on the penultimate if this was long, otherwise on the ante-penultimate.

MORPHOLOGY AND SYNTAX

Noun

The structure of Avestan is synthetic and flectional. Nominals, including nouns and adjectives, are marked for gender (masculine, feminine, neuter), number (singular, dual, plural), and case (eight cases).

The case endings are analogous to those in Sanskrit. As a specimen, here is the full set of endings for a masculine -*a* stem:

	Singular	Dual	Plural
nom.	-as → ō	-ā	-ā, -a
acc.	-m	-ā	-əŋg
gen.	-ahe	-ayā	-ānam
abl.	-āt → āθ		-aēⁱbyō
dat.	-ai	-aēibya	-aēⁱbyō
instr.	-ā		-āiš
loc.	-ōi, -e, -aya	-ayō	-aēšu
voc.	-a, -ā		

127

There are analogous paradigms for stems in *-ā*, *-i/-ī*, *u/ū*, *-āu*, and consonantal stems. Not all possible forms are actually attested, though the record is very much fuller than it is for Old Persian; e.g. the *-ant/-at* paradigm is fully attested in Avestan, whereas for Old Persian only the nominative, accusative, and genitive singular are known.

Some examples of case formation:

  -a stems:
      aspa 'horse', *aspahe* (gen.) 'of a horse';
      ahura 'lord', *ahurā* (voc.) 'Oh Lord!';
      spāda 'army', *spādā* (dual nom.) 'two armies';
      zast- 'hand', *zastōibya* (dual instr.) 'with both hands'.
  -ā stems:
      daēnā 'religion'; *daēnayā* 'of religion';
      gaēθā 'being', *gaēθanām* 'of the beings';
  -ī stem:
      xšaθrī 'woman', *xšaθrišu* 'in the women'.
  -u stem:
      pasu 'cattle', *pasvō* (acc. pl.);
      vaŋhu- 'good', *vaŋhubyō* 'to the good (ones) (dat. pl.)'.
  Consonant stems:
      sna^iθiš 'weapon', *snaiθīžbya* 'to/with/from the two weapons'.
  -n:
      urvān- 'soul', *urvānəm* (acc. sing.);
      čašman- 'eye', *čašmanat* [-aθ] 'from the eye'.

Adjective

Adjectives make a comparative in either *-yah* or *-tara*: e.g. *vahu* 'good', *vahyah* 'better'; *aka* 'bad', *aka**tara*** 'worse'.

Pronoun

PERSONAL
Full forms:

	Singular	Dual	Plural
1	ažəm	—	vaēm
2	tvəm	—	yužəm

Only two dual forms are known – the first person accusative, *əəāva*, and the second person genitive, *yavākəm*.

The pronouns are declined (not all cases are attested). The oblique base for first person is *ma-* (acc. *mam*, gen. *mana*. The third person forms are drawn from the demonstrative series, and therefore marked for gender:

	Masculine	Feminine	Neuter
singular	aēm	īm	tat (> ta)
dual	tā	—	—
plural	tē, tōi	tā	tā

Some enclitic forms – in oblique cases only – are attested.

RELATIVE PRONOUN

	Masculine	Feminine	Neuter
singular	hᵃya	hᵃyā	tᵃya
plural	tᵃyaiy	tᵃyā(iy)	tᵃyā

Numerals

1–10: *aēva-, dva-, θray-, čaθwār-, panča, xšvaš, hapta, ašta, nava, dasa/dasā*; 20 *vīsaiti*; 100 *satəm*.

Verb

Avestan has active and middle voices. Middle-voice forms are mainly character-istic of the older stratum in the language; there are four moods – indicative, imperative, subjunctive, and optative. Tense distinction is found only in the indicative mood. Tenses are marked for number and person.

There are three bases – present, aorist, perfect – each generating relevant tense forms. Personal inflections vary according to tense.

TENSE FORMS

From present base: present, imperfect. The imperative mood is also formed from this base. From aorist base: aorist. From perfect base: perfect, pluperfect. The subjunctive and optative moods are made from any base. The subjunctive marker is -a/-ā, the optative marker is -i: e.g. *kərᵊnavāne* 'that I may do' (middle voice, subj. of *kərᵊnav.* 'to do').

Example of present tense: *bara-* 'to carry, bear'. Active voice:

			cf. Sanskrit
singular	1	barāmi	bharāmi
	2	barahi	bharasi
	3	baraⁱti	bharati
plural	1	barāmahi	bharāmaḥ
	2	(barayaθā)	bharatha
	3	barənti	bharanti

In both the imperfect and the aorist the *a-* augment is optional. As in Sanskrit, there is a sigmatic aorist (IE -*s* > Av. *š/h*) and an asigmatic: e.g. (*aivi-*) *visəm* 'I saw'; *sas* 'he hindered'.

The perfect tense is formed from the perfect base by reduplication: e.g. *susruye* 'I have heard'; *yayata* 'he has moved'; *dadāθa* 'thou hast created'.

NEGATION

The general negating particle (prepositive) for the indicative tense system is *nōit → nōiθ*. The imperative is negated by *mā*. Use of either negating particle is optional in the subjunctive and the optative.

PRE-VERBS

These are mainly directional and very widely used: e.g.

> *fra-* indicating motion forwards;
> *niš-/niž-*: motion towards something;
> *para-*: motion away from something;
> *a^{i}ti-*: motion through something;
> *ava-*: motion downwards.

NON-FINITE FORMS

Each of the three bases has an active and a middle voice participle. The present active participle, for example, is in *-nt*, fem. *-ntī*, and is declined like a noun in *-nt*. There is also a passive past participle made from the Ø grade stem + *-ta*: e.g. *gatō* (masc. nom.) from root *gam-*.

Pre- and postpositions

Both prepositions and postpositions were used.

Word order

Free.

(٢٩ ·ﺮﺳﻣﺩﺳﺮﺳ ·ﺮﺳﻩﺩﺳﻣ)

(١) ·ﺮﺳﻩﻣﻩﻣﺳﺩﺭﺳ ·ﺳ(ﻣﺩﺭﺳ· (ﺮﺳﻩﻣﻩ ·ﺳﺩ)ﺩﺭﺳ

·ﺳﻩﻣﻩﻣﺳﺳ ·ﻩ ·ﻣﺳﺩﺳﺭﺳ·

·ﺳ ﻩﺳ ·ﺳﻩﻣﻩﺳﺳﻣﺳﺩﺳﺭﺳ·

·ﺳﺮﺳﺩﺳ(ﻩ(ﻩ ·ﺳﺩﻣﻩﻣﺳﻣﺳﺳﺭﺳ ·(ﺳ)ﺩﻩﻩﺩﺳﺳ·

·ﻩﺩ}ﺩﺳ ·ﺳﻩﻣﻩﺳﺳﻣﺳ ·ﺳﻣﻣﻣﺳﺳﺳﻩ ·ﺩ{ﻩﻩ

ﻩﺳﺳﺩﺳﻣﻣﺳﺳﺳﻩ ·ﻩﺳﻣ{ﻩ ·ﺳﻣﺳﺳﺳﺩﺳﺳﺳﺩ ·ﺩ{ﻩ ·ﺳﺳ}ﺳ

xšmaibyā gōuš urvā gərəždā
kahmāi mā θwarōždūm? kə̄ mā tasaθ?
ā.mā aēšəmō hazas.čā; āhišāyā dərəščā təviščā
nōiθ mōi vāstā xšmaθ anyō aθ mōi sastā vohu vāstryā

To you, the spirit of the Bull complained: to what purpose did you make
me? Who created me? Passion and tyranny, ruthlessness and brutality
threaten me: other than you there is for me no Herdsman. Grant me,
therefore, (the bounty of) your good herding.

(For vāstryā, see last paragraph of Indo-European Languages. Compare
Svetāśvataropaniṣad I).

AYMARÁ

INTRODUCTION

This language belongs to the Quechumaran group of the Andean-Equatorial family. 'Aymará' is an umbrella term for about a dozen ethnic groups, some of which, e.g. the Colla and the Lupaka, had formed independent states before the Incas came to power. The Aymará of today call themselves 'la nacionalidad qulla'. Estimates of their numbers vary from 500,000 to 1½ million. They live mainly in Bolivia and Peru, especially on the Titicaca plateau.

SCRIPT

Aymará can be written in the Roman alphabet. A standardized orthography was agreed in 1983.

PHONOLOGY

Consonants

Characteristic of Aymará is the three-term series of voiceless stops: voiceless plosive – aspirated voiceless plosive – ejective voiceless plosive: /p, ph, p'; t, th, t'; k, kh, k'; q, qh, q'/ (and so notated in script) and a similar affricate series: /tʃ, tʃh, tʃ'/ (notated as *ch*, *chh*, *ch'*). The velar and post-velar fricatives /x/ɣ/ and /χ/ʁ/ are present, along with alveolar/s/. There are three nasals: /m, n, ɲ/; two laterals: /l, ʎ/; one trill: /r/; two semi-vowels: /j, w/. The voiced plosives are missing. The velar and post-velar fricatives are denoted by *j* and *x*.

Vowels

short and long: i, u, a

Final short vowels are regularly elided unless they are sentence-final.

Stress

Stress seems to be mainly on the penultimate, as in Quechua, but may move to final, e.g. postposition *-takí*.

MORPHOLOGY AND SYNTAX

Noun

There is no grammatical gender. There are two numbers, singular and plural; the plural marker is -*naka*. Native Aymará usage requires only one member of a plural complex to be so marked (numerals, for example, take the singular) but Spanish influence is leading to reduplication. Thus *akanakax qalanakawa* 'these are stones', might now be heard instead of the more idiomatic *akanakax qala.θwa*. (In this phrase, -*x* is a subject marker, -*wa* is a confirming particle.)

CASES

Cases are formed by the addition of suffixes; in the plural, these follow the plural marker.

The genitive marker is -*n(a)*; the noun denoting the object possessed takes the appropriate possessive marker (as in Turkic): e.g. *awki.xa.n uta.pa.x* 'my father's house' (-*xa*- is 1st p. poss. marker; -*pa*- is 3rd p. poss. marker); *jila.ma.n yapu.pa.x* 'your brother's chacra' (-*ma*- is 2nd p. poss. marker).

Other case endings:

> ablative, -*ta*: *markat(a) ... alta* 'I bought ... from the market';
> comitative, -*mpi*: *awki.xa.mpi* 'with my father';
> inessive, -*n*: *utan* 'in the house';
> benefactive, -*taki* 'for': *wawa.ma.taki* 'for your son';
> terminative, -*kama*: *Marka.kama.w* 'It's as far as the market', *Q'arurukama* 'Until tomorrow!'

A personal indirect object can be marked by -*r(u)*.

The interrogative affix is -*ti*; a negative of the copula is -*kiti* preceded by jan(iw): e.g. *Uka.x anu.wa* 'That (*uka*) is a dog (*anu*); *Anuti? 'Is it a dog?'*; *Jan(iw) anukiti* 'It isn't a dog.'

Adjective

As attribute, adjective precedes the noun and is invariable: e.g. *Machaq(a) marka.ti? 'Is it a new market/village?'*; *Mirqi marka.wa* 'It is an old village.'

COMPARISON

A comparative can be made with *juk'ampi* + -*ta* case: e.g. *misk'ita juk'ampi muxsa* 'sweeter than honey'.

Pronoun

Personal independent + enclitic possessive:

	Singular	Enclitic	Plural	Enclitic
1	naya	-xa	jiwasa (incl.)	-sa
			nanaka (excl.)	

2	juma	-ma	jumanaka
3	jupa	-pa	jupanaka

Examples: *utaxax* 'my house'; *uta.naka.pa.x* 'his houses; *qawra.naka.sa.x* 'our llamas'.

DEMONSTRATIVE PRONOUN
Three degrees of relative distance: *aka – uka – khaya*.

INTERROGATIVE PRONOUN
khiti 'who?'; *kuna* 'what?' supported by -*s*(*a*), the interrogative marker: e.g. *Khitisa jupa.xa? 'Who is he?'*

RELATIVE PRONOUN
The interrogative *khiti* may be used with -*ti* added to subject, and -*k*- inserted in verb: e.g. *khiti warmi.mpi.ti jupa.x sarnak̲ke* ... 'the woman with whom he went ...'; or the relative clause may be rephrased as two principal clauses: e.g. *Jaqi.x jut.k.i uka.x jach'awa* 'The man who has come is big' (*jutaña* 'to come').

Numerals

1–10: *maya, paya, kimsa, pusi, phisqa, suxta, paqallqu, kimsaqallqu, llātunka, tunka*; 11 *tunkamayani*; 12 *tunkapayani*; 20 *pātunka*; 30 *kimsatunka*; 100 *pataka*.

Verb

All infinitives end in -*ña*: e.g. *saraña* 'to go', *munaña* 'to want'. Moods: indicative, imperative, subjunctive, optative, dubitative. Tenses: present, progressive, future, preterite, pluperfect, conditional. Verbs are conjugated for number and person; there are inclusive and exclusive forms of first person plural.

TENSES
Present tense of *saraña* 'to go':

	Singular		*Plural*
1	sarta	incl.	sarapxta
		excl.	sarapxtan
2	sarta		sarapxta
3	sari		sarapxi

Note: -*px*- is the plural infix for all tenses.

> progressive: the infix is -*sk*- in present tense: e.g. *Markar saraskiwa* 'He's going to the village.'
> future: *sarā, sarāta, sarani*; pl. *sarapxā*, etc.
> preterite: infix is -*yā*-: e.g. *sarayāt(w)a* 'I went', *sara.pxa.yā.ta(n)* 'we went'
> pluperfect: infix is -*tā*-: e.g. *sara.pxa.tā.ta* 'we had gone'
> conditional: -*tixa* (sbj. marker) + -*xa* (verbal marker): e.g. *Jumatix(a) muntaxa, naya.x jutāwa* 'If you like, I'll come.'

NEGATION

As noted above, the negative confix is *janiw/jan ... ti*. In the verb, this is supported by the negative infix *-k-*. Thus, in the present: *jan sarkti* 'I don't go', in the plural *-px- → pk*: *jan(iw) sarapkti* 'we don't go'. Future: *jan sarkāti* 'I shan't go'; pl. *janiw sarapkāti*

IMPERATIVE

Abrupt in *-m*: *saram!* 'go!'; pl. *sarapxam*. Negative: *jan saramti!* 'don't go!'

SUBJUNCTIVE

Infinitive + personal marker + *-taki* for terminative, *-layku* for causative: e.g. *manq'aña.xa.taki* 'so that I may eat'; *manq'a.pxa.ña.sa.taki* 'so that we may eat' (note pl. *-px-* infix in inifinitive).

PRONOMINAL FORMS

Specific conjugations provide forms coded for subject, indirect object, and tense. Thus, for *churaña* 'to give':

present tense:	*chursma*	'I give to you' → 'I have given to you'
	churista	'you give to me'
	churitu	'he gives to me'
future tense:	*churāma*	'I shall give to you'
	churitāta	'you will give to me'
	churitani	'he will give to me'

Similarly for other tenses. The plural forms are ambiguous; thus, *churapxāma* may mean 'I shall give ... to you (pl.)' or 'we shall give ... to you (sing.)'. Examples:

nayax qullq chursma 'I have given you money'
nayax qullq churāma 'I shall give you money'
nayax qulq churayāsma 'I gave you money'

PARTICIPLES

The past participle in *-ta* can be used adjectivally: e.g. from *usuña* 'to be/fall ill': *usuta warmi.pa.taki* 'for his sick wife'. This form may also be used as a verbal noun: e.g. *jutata.pa.kama* 'until his arrival' ('until he is having-come').

Present participle: *-sa-* is the marker if both principal and subordinate clauses have the same subject, *-ipan(a)-* otherwise: *Mark sarasaw jupar unjta* 'I saw him (when I was) going to the market'; *Pīrun mark saripanxa sarayātanwa* 'When Pedro went to the market, we went away'; *Naya mark saripanxa jumax parlta* 'While I was going to market, you were speaking.'

Where the action in the subordinate clause is the object of the principal verb, *-iri-* is used: e.g. *Pirur mark sarir/sarkirt uñjtan* 'We saw Pedro going to the market' (i.e. 'Pedro was going ...').

Examples of other affixes:

benefactive, *-rapi-*: *Yapuxa irnaqarapita* 'He works my farm for me';
causative, *-ya-*: *Chachaxar manq'ayatwa* 'I feed (make to eat) my husband' (*-r(u)* marks indirect object).

The order in which affixes are attached to stems is fixed. The main inflectional items occur in the following order: possessive marker – case endings – locative markers – *r(u)* of direction – interrogative marker.

Word order

SOV.

---

1 KALLTANJJA Arünwa, Arusti Diosampïnwa, Arusti Diosänwa.
2 Kalltanjja ucajj Diosampïnwa.
3 Take cunanacawa jupan lurata; jan jupampisti janiu cuna luratasa luratäquiti.
4 Jacañajj jupancänwa, jacañasti jakenacan khanapänwa.
5 Khanasti ch'amacanac taypinjja khaniwa; ch'amacanacasti janiu ucjja catokapquiti.

Juanan Khanañchäwipa

6 Diosan qhitanita mä jakewa utjäna, ucasti Juan sutinïnwa.
7 Ucawa khanañchañataqui juti, khanata khanañchañataqui, takeni jupa toke iyausapjjañapataqui.
8 Janiu jupajj khanäcänti, ucatsipana khanata khanañchiriu juti.

AZERBAYDZHANI

INTRODUCTION

Generally treated as a member of the Oguz-Seljuk group of Turkic, a group which also includes Osmanli Turkish and Turkmen. It is spoken by about 4 million in the Azerbaydzhan Soviet Socialist Republic, where it is joint official language (with Russian). In addition, Azerbaydzhani is spoken by at least 3½ million people in north-western Iran, and by smaller communities in Georgia, Armenia, and Dagestan. There are four main dialect divisions.

The earliest writer in Azerbaydzhani Turkish is also its greatest master – Füzuli (fl. early sixteenth century), the author of the mystical epic *Leylâ ve Mecnûn* and the *Šikâyetnâme*. Modern Azerbaydzhani literature is probably, in terms of quality and quantity, second only to Uzbek among the Turkic languages. Newspapers and periodicals have been appearing since the mid-nineteenth century.

SCRIPT

Initially Arabic. As far back as in the middle of the nineteenth century Akhundzadä proposed the introduction of the Roman alphabet, but this reform had to wait until the general period of experimental romanization in the 1920s–30s. The Cyrillic script was introduced in 1939 and variously amended over the following 20 years: e.g. я and ю were discarded in 1958 and replaced by *ja, jy*. The alphabet includes the following non-Cyrillic letters: ә, θ, γ, ҝ, ҹ, h.

PHONOLOGY

Consonants

stops: p, b, t, d, k, g; palatalized: g'
affricates: tʃ, dʒ
fricatives: f, v, s, z, ʃ, ʒ, j, x, γ, h
nasals: m, n
lateral and flap: l, r

In the flow of speech in Azerbaydzhani, two phonological processes are very important: these are unvoicing of voiced consonants before pause or consonant; and stop → related fricative in the same conditions.

Vowels

There are nine vowels:

high: i, ɪ
mid: e/ɛ, œ, y, u, o
low: ə = [ɛ], a

/œ/ is notated as *ö*; /ɛ/ is notated as *ä*.

VOWEL HARMONY

See **Turkic Languages**. The assimilation processes are normal in Azerbaydzhani, but note that /e, œ, o/ cannot appear in certain, indeed most, affixes: that is, rounding (labial harmony) is progressively cancelled. Certain very important affixes have only a two-way choice between *-a-* and *-ä-*: e.g. *bilmäk* 'to know'; *görmäk* 'to see'; *bašlamak* 'to start'.

MORPHOLOGY AND SYNTAX

(For a general conspectus of Turkic morphology, *see* **Turkic Languages**.)

Noun

In Azerbaydzhani the case endings are:

genitive: $-ɪn^4$, $-nɪn^4$ (i.e. four allomorphs: *ɪn, in, un, ün*)
dative: $-(j)a^2$
accusative: $-(n)ɪ^4$ (contrast with Bashkir: $-nɪ^{16}$)
locative: $-da^2$
ablative: $-dan^2$

The plural marker is *lar/lär*, the latter used with high and mid vowel-stems: e.g. *ev* 'house', pl. *evlär*.

The predicative and possessive suffixes:

	Predicative		Possessive	
	Singular	*Plural*	*Singular*	*Plural*
1	$-(j)am^2$	$-(j)ɪg^4$	$-m, -ɪm^4$	$-(ɪ)mɪz^4$
2	$-san^2$	$-sɪnɪz^4$	$-n, -ɪn^4$	$-(ɪ)nɪz^4$
3	$-dɪr^4$	$-(dɪr)lar^2$	$-ɪ, -sɪ^4$	$-ɪ, -sɪ^4$

Adjective

Follows general Turkic model.

Pronoun

PERSONAL INDEPENDENT

Sing. 1 *män*, 2 *sän*, 3 *o*; pl. 1 *biz*, 2 *siz*, 3 *onlar*. These are declined in all cases:

e.g. for *män*: *mänim*, *mänä*, *mäni*, *mändä*, *mändän*.

DEMONSTRATIVE PRONOUNS
bu 'this'; *o* 'that'.

INTERROGATIVE PRONOUNS
kim 'who?'; *nä* 'what?'.

Numerals

1–10: *bir*, *iki*, *üč*, *dörd*, *beš*, *altı*, *yeddi*, *säkkiz*, *dogguz*, *on*; 20 *iyirmi*; 30 *otuz*; 40 *gırx*; 100 *yüz*.

Verb

The verb in Azerbaydzhani has voice, mood, tense, and non-finite forms. Voice and mood markers are standard: passive -il^4, reciprocal -*š*, reflexive -*n/l*, conditional: sa^2, etc.

TENSE SYSTEM
The indicative mood has simple and composite tense forms: these latter for past tense only.

> present: -ir^4: *alıram* 'I take'; 2 *alırsan*, 3 *alır*; pl. *alırız*, -*sınız*, -*lar*.
> definite future: -$adžag^2$: e.g. *aladžayam* 'I shall take'.
> definite past: -$dı^4$: e.g *aldım* 'I took'.
> perfect: two forms:

> (a) -$mıš^4$: e.g. *almıšam* 'I've taken';
> (b) -$(dž)ıb^4$ + predicative affix: e.g. *o alıb.dır* 'he has taken'. No first person.

Composite tenses are formed with the auxiliary *i*- (defective): e.g. *alır idim* → *alırdım* 'I took'.

A continuous tense is made with the formant -$magda^2$- + predicative affix: e.g. *almagdayam* 'I am taking'; composite past continuous: *almagda idim* → *almagdajdım* 'I was taking'.

NEGATION
The standard Turkic negating infix -*m*(V)- follows the stem: e.g. *aldım* 'I took', *almadım*; *aladžayam* 'I shall take', *almajadžayam*.

PARTICIPLES
Present in -an^2, -$(j)ır^{12}$; past in -$mıš^4$.

Verbal nouns: there are two: -$dıg^4$, relating to present and past, and -$adžag^2$, future. They are neutral as to voice, expressing both active and passive: e.g.

> mänim (i.e. gen. case) oxuduyum kitab
> 'the book which I am/was reading'

atamɪn yazdɪɣɪ mäktub
'the letter which my father is writing/wrote'

onun yazadžaɣɪ mäktub
'the letter which he is going to write'

The gerund in -(j)ɪb⁴ is used where two finite verbs denote concomitant or consecutive actions: e.g. g'älib söjlädi 'he came and said' (lit. 'coming, he said'). There are several more gerundial endings denoting specific relationships between actions: e.g. -arag², -anda².

RELATIVE CLAUSES

The examples given above in illustration of the -dɪg form also show the normal transfer of an Indo-European right-branching clause to participial form preceding the headword. Exposure to Iranian influence, however, has led to the use in Azerbaydzhani of a relative construction with ki + right-hand branching: e.g. Adam var ki, hejvan ondan jaxšɪdɪr, lit. 'There are people who – animals are better than they'.

Postpositions

Follow several cases: e.g.

following dative: g'örä 'according to', e.g. onun dedijine g'örä 'according to what he said';
following ablative: sonra 'after', e.g. därsdän sonra 'after the lesson';
following nominative/genitive: kimi 'like, as', e.g. guš kimi učur 'flies like a bird'.

Word order

As in Turkic generally.

١ ابتداده كلمه وار ایدی وكلمه اللّهن یاننه ایدی وكلمه الله ایدی * بو ابتداده اللّهن
٢ یاننه ایدی * هر زاد اونن واسطهلغی اینن موجود اولدی و هیچ بر موجود اولمش
٣ زاد اونسز وجوده كلمدی * اونده حیات وار ایدی واو حیات آدمارن نوری ایدی*
٤ ونور ظلمته اشیخ ویرر ایدی امّا ظلمت اوزی درك ایلمر ایدی * الله طرفندن كوندرلمش
٥ بر آدم وار ایدی آدی یحیی * بو شهادت ایچون كلدیكه نورن خصوصنه شهادت
٧ ویرسون تا كه هامی اونن واسطهلغی اینن ایمان كنورسونلر* اوزی او نور دكل ایدی
٨ آنجق كلدی كه او نورن خصوصنه شهادت ویرسون *

140

AZTEC-TANOAN LANGUAGES

This grouping formed one of Edward Sapir's (1929) six superstocks of North American Indian Languages. It included Zuni. The Aztec-Tanoan phylum, included in the 1965 classification of Voegelin and Voegelin, is very much the same as Sapir's, with the exclusion, however, of Zuni. The grouping falls into two parts: Uto-Aztecan, including Nahuatl, Hopi, Piman (Sonoran), and Shoshonean (with Comanche and Paiute); and Tanoan-Kiowa. It is possible that Keresan is also an Uto-Aztecan language; in the 1965 classification it is treated as an isolate.

The most important Aztec-Tanoan language in terms of numbers is Nahuatl with about a million speakers in Mexico. Classical Nahuatl was the language of the Aztec Empire, overthrown by Cortes. Two other member languages in Mexico, Tarahumar and Papago (Pima) have, respectively, 50,000 and 20,000 speakers.

The Shoshonean languages are spoken in the southern United States.

See **Nahuatl**, **Hopi**, **Zuni**.

BAHNARIC LANGUAGES

INTRODUCTION

The Bahnaric languages form a branch of Mon-Khmer, spoken by about 750,000 people in Southern Vietnam. There are three main divisions: northern, including Bahnar itself; western, about half-a-dozen small languages; southern, including Stieng and Chrau. In all, about 20 or 22 languages.

All are unwritten, apart from translations of some parts of the Bible.

PHONOLOGY

Consonants

A typical Bahnaric consonantal inventory includes:

p, ɓ, b/v, m, w
t, ɗ, d, n, l, r, s
ts, dz, ɲ, j
k, g, ŋ
ʔ, h

/ɓ/ and /ɗ/ are implosive, e.g. in Chrau, and may show Vietnamese influence. Bahnar has aspirated consonants: /ph, th, kh/ and such initial clusters as /ml, mr, hn, br/: e.g. Bahnar *bri* 'forest', *kram* 'bamboo', *klik* 'deaf', *klan* 'python'.

Vowels

The vowel system is relatively simple in comparison with certain other branches of Mon-Khmer. The short vowels in Bahnar are /i, e, ɛ, a, œ, ə, o, ɔ, u/. In Chrau, long vowels tend towards diphthongization.

Some Northern Bahnaric languages have a rudimentary tone system.

MORPHOLOGY AND SYNTAX

The typical Bahnar root is CVC, often with a prefix: $C_1VC_2VC_3$ where C_2 may be a cluster, and C_1V- is usually a reduced syllable (Cə): e.g. *klik* 'deaf': *pəklik* 'to deafen'.

Noun

As there is no inflection of any kind, word order is crucial, and certain markers are used, e.g. in Bahnar *kœ* for dative: e.g. *an kœ iɲ* 'give (to) me'.

POSSESSION
X's Y is YX: e.g. *hnam bahnar* 'the Bahnar's house'.

NUMBER
Singularity and plurality inhere in the word; number can be made more precise by the use of numerical classifiers, e.g. *nu* for human beings: Bahnar *kədrang bar nu* 'two men' (lit. 'man – two – classifier'). Similarly, *to* is used for animals and objects in the plural, *pōm* for an animal or object in the singular: e.g. *min pōm hnam* 'one house'; *peng to hnam* 'three houses'.

Order fluctuates in both Chrau and Bahnar: numeral – classifier – noun or noun – numeral – classifier.

Adjective

Follows noun attributatively: Chrau *ca măq* 'big fish', Bahnar *ka tih*.

Pronoun

Chrau has a gender distinction in the second person singular: masc. *may*, fem. *ay*. Both Bahnar and Chrau have inclusive and exclusive forms in first person plural. Bahnar has a dual series: *ba* 'we two'; *bre* for animals: *bre rœmo* 'the two bullocks'.

Numerals

The Chrau series 1–10 is: *muôi, var, pe, puôn, prăm, prau, pŏh, pham, su'n, mât*; 20 *varjât*; 100 *rayeng*.

Verb

The stem is invariable. Markers are used for tense/mood distinctions; in Bahnar:

> present: Ø
> imperfect: *kəmlung* (cf. Thai *gamlang*)
> past: *ji, klaih*, etc.; these precede the stem
> future: *gô*, e.g. *iɲ gô an kœ e* 'I shall give it to you' (*iɲ* = Chrau *anh* /aɲ/ 'I'; *an* 'to give'; *e* 'you')

Bahnar has a participial form with the preposition *pang* 'with, by': e.g. *pang bœ ma dap hoan* 'by working with all one's strength' (*dap* 'all'; *bœ* 'to work manually').

NEGATIVE MARKER
uh (kœ).

Word formation

In Bahnar, roots with simple initial consonant make a derived form by infixing -*œ*-; usually noun from verb, but other forms of derivative occur: e.g. *dol* 'to support': *dœnol* 'pillar'; *kœl* 'head': *kœnœl* 'pillow'. Roots with initial cluster have -*œd*- infix: e.g. *krol* 'to roll down': *kœdrol* 'cascade'.

Prefixes: *pœ*- (← *pœm* 'to do, make') forms causatives: e.g. *et* 'to drink': *pœet* 'to give to drink'; *dek* 'quick': *pœdek* 'to hasten'. *Tœ*- forms reciprocals: e.g. *go* 'to wait': *tœgo* 'to await each other'; *kœ*- is a passive formant: e.g. *dap* 'to cover': *kœdap* 'to be covered'.

Word order

SVO.

BƠR PÔH TRONG. 1 - Dơng tơm, tơnŏk dei I. Kon, mă I. Kon duh oei atŭm păng B.I.. mă I. Kon duh adoi B.I.. 2 - Kơna dơng tơm xơ Di xang oei atŭm lơm B.I.. 3 - Tòm tơdrong ling dơng Di xang pơjing; uh dei kıkiơ xang dei, mă bĭ dơng Di pơjing. 4 - Lơm Di dei tơdrong erih, tơdrong erih ji Ang chră kơ kon bơngai. 5 - Ang pơrang lơm măng-mu, chŏng bơngai lơm măng-mu uh gơnăl kơ ang. 6 - Dei minh nu mă B.I. xang phai, măt di ji Joang. 7 - Di truh oă potil, ji pơtil gah ang, oă kơ tôm bôl gơh lui, gơnơm kơ di bơtho. 8 - Kơxĭ kơ di ji ang. chŏng ji oă pơtil kơ de gah ang mơnoh dik.

Bahnar

BALINESE

INTRODUCTION

A member of the Malayo-Polynesian branch of Austronesian, Balinese is spoken by 3 to 4 million people in the island of Bali and some smaller adjacent islands. It has three socio-linguistic registers:

1. basa *ketah* (K): everyday Balinese for family and friendly use;
2. basa *madia* (M): basically *ketah* with an injection of more formal words for use in situations where low *ketah* would be unacceptable;
3. basa *singgih* (S): corresponds to Javanese kråmå; a somewhat artificial construct containing many Sanskrit and Javanese words.

Many *ketah* words have no *singgih* equivalents, and have to be promoted to *singgih* status when the latter is being used. For many key concepts, however, each register has its own word; cf.

	Ketah	*Madia*	*Singgih*
'eat	naar	neda	ngadjengang
'dead'	mati	padem	séda
'live'	idup	urip	njeneng

SCRIPT

Originally Javanese. A standard romanization, based on Dutch spelling, was provided by H.J. Schwartz in Batavia in the early twentieth century.

PHONOLOGY

In the main, as in **Malay**. Final /k/ is not entirely glottalized. The vowel *a* in such prefixes as *pa-*, *ka-*, *ma-* is /ə/; final *a* tends to /œ/.

Stress

Tends to be on the penultimate syllable.

MORPHOLOGY AND SYNTAX

The definite article is affixed *-(n)é:* e.g. *batuné* 'the stone'; *guruné* 'the teacher'. Before proper nouns the article *i* is used.

NOMINAL FORMS
Simple and derived; the latter are made with such prefixes as the following:

(a) *pa-*: forms verbal noun, e.g. *rérén* 'to stop': *pa.rérén* 'the stopping'; *pa-* + ... *-an*: *pa.réré.an* 'the stopping place'.
(b) *para-/pra-*: forms collectives, e.g. *parawanita* 'women'.
(c) *ka...an*: forms abstract concepts, e.g. *ka.djegég.an* 'beauty'.

POSSESSION
Possessed – possessor: *see* **Pronoun**, below.

Adjective

Invariable; as attribute, adjective follows noun: e.g. *anaké odah ento* 'the old man' (*odah* 'old').

Pronoun

Number is not distinguished.

First person (excl.): S form is *titiang*; M form, *tiang*; K form, *itjang*.
Second person: K forms are *tjai* (masc.) and *njai* (fem.). For polite address, e.g. to strangers, *djero* can be used, at least until the caste situation has been clarified. The Malay form *tuan* is replacing the old Balinese forms. In very elevated S speech, *tjokor i ratu/tjokor i déwa* may be used, the latter to a prince.
Third person: the caste forms were *dané* for a vaiśya, *ida* for a satria or brahman, and these forms are still in use where such distinctions are called for. Omnibus forms are S *ipun* and K *ia*.

There is a general tendency to use the polite third person form when speaking of first or second person.

POSSESSION
In first and second person the personal pronoun is used: e.g. *umah tiang(é)* 'my house'. Third person: the K form is *-ne*, e.g. *limanné* 'his hand', *abian iané* 'his field' (the gemination in the first example is necessary to distinguish the form from noun + definite article, *limané* 'the hand'). S and M form: *-ipun*, e.g. *somahipun* = *rabinida* 'his wife' (*ida* is S 3rd p. pron.)

DEMONSTRATIVE PRONOUN
S *puniki* = K *ené* 'this'; S *punika* = K *ento* 'that'.

INTERROGATIVE PRONOUN
S *sira* = K *njén* 'who?'; S *punapi* = K *apa* 'what?'.

RELATIVE PRONOUN
S *sané* = K *ané*; or, *sang/kang*; e.g.

anaké ané **n**ulungin tjai 'the man who helped you'

anaké ane **tulungin** tjai 'the man who was helped by you'

mémé bapa sang sampun nguripin titiang
'my parents who gave me life' (*nguripin* 'life')

Numerals

1–10: *sa*, *dua/kalih*, *telu/tiga*, *empat*, *lima*, *enem*, *pitu*, *akutus*, *asia*, *adasa*. These have positional variants: (a) reduplicated; (b) with *-ng*: e.g. *dua – dadua – duang*. The reduplicated form is used where the numeral is treated as a nominal; the *-ng* form where the numeral immediately precedes a noun.

Verb

Stems are neutral, and become transitive or intransitive by morphophonemic change. Nearly all intransitive verbs in Balinese have a non-nasal initial: e.g. *lunga* 'to go', *urip* 'to live'. Transitive verbs may focus either on subject or on object: if on subject, the initial is a nasal: e.g. *batuné ané mara gebeg* 'the stone was polished'; *tiang né **ngebeg** batuné* 'I polished the stone'.

Stems may be made transitive by affixation of *-ang*: e.g. *takén* 'to ask', *takénang* 'to ask someone for something'. Also, transitive verbs can be intensified by addition of *-ang*: e.g. *mireng* 'to hear', *mirengang* 'to pay attention to'; *ngelah* 'to own', *ngelahang* 'to exercise rights of ownership'; or made causative: e.g. *uning* 'to know', *uningang* 'to bring something to someone's knowledge'.

-ang also makes verbs from adjectives and nouns: *utama* 'excellent', *utamaang* 'to regard something as excellent'; *soré* 'afternoon', *njoréang* 'to do something in the afternoon'; *sugih* 'rich', *njugihang* 'to get richer'.

The Balinese verb appears in four forms (plus or minus affixation): (1) the simple (weak) form; (2) the strong (nasalized) form; (3) the *ka-* form; (4) the *ma-* form.

1. The simple form: the agent follows the verb, e.g.

   Buku punika tumbas tiang di pidan adji limang rupiah
   'I bought the book formerly for 5 guilders'.

2. Some examples of the nasalized form have been given above.

3. The *ka-* form focuses on verbal action; normally + *-ang/-in* affix, though this is not used for first or second person: e.g. *katulungin baan bapanné* 'helped by his father'; *Øtulungin itjang/tjai* 'helped by me/you'.

4. The *ma-* form: if the base is intransitive, so is the *ma-* form; if the base is transitive, the *ma-* form is usually intransitive → passive, e.g. *padiné jén suba matebuk...* 'once the rice has been pounded...'; *padi ané matebuk* 'the pounded rice'.

Word order

Depends on verbal construction: SVO, VSO, OVS are possible.

1 Sadurung jagate puniki kaadakang antuk Ida Sang Hyang Widi Wasa, Sang Sabda sampun wenten. Sang Sabda punika sinarengan ring Ida Sang Hyang Widi Wasa, tur Sang Sabda punika taler maraga Widi. 2 Saking pangawit Sang Sabda punika sinarengan ring Ida Sang Hyang Widi Wasa. 3 Malantaran Sang Sabda punika Ida Sang Hyang Widi Wasa ngadakang saluiring sane wenten. Tur tan wenten sane kaadakang sane tan malantaran Sang Sabda. 4 Sang Sabda punika maraga wit urip, tur uripe punika dados galang manusane. 5 Galange punika macahya ring tengah petenge, tur petenge punika tan mrasidayang ngaonang galange punika.

6 Ida Sang Hyang Widi Wasa sampun ngutus utusan Idane, sane mapesengan Yohanes. 7 Dane rauh jaga midartayang pariindik galange punika ring i manusa, mangda manusane sami miragiang tur percaya. 8 Boya ja dane Yohanes ngaraga galange punika, nanging rauh danene buat midartayang indik galange punika.

BALTIC LANGUAGES

This branch of Indo-European is of special interest in comparative linguistics because of its retention of certain very archaic features, both phonological and morphological. Baltic is genetically close to, and seems to have been always geographically contiguous with, Slavonic and Germanic. East and West forms of Baltic are distinguished. Of several East Baltic languages known to have existed, only two survive – Lithuanian and Latvian. Evidence for the extinct congeners is entirely toponymic; thus the name of the Curonians survives in Courland (Latvian: *kurzeme*). The sole attested West Baltic language – Old Prussian – survived into the seventeenth century.

The toponymic evidence shows that Baltic was formerly spoken over an area considerably exceeding its present limitations: south-eastwards across White Russia towards the Dniepr, and southwards into what is now Poland. This original habitat shrank as Baltic stock gave ground to Slavonic and Germanic. To a lesser extent, local Finno-Ugric languages have been absorbed or ousted by Baltic (*see* **Liv**, *under* **Balto-Finnic Minor Languages**).

The oldest written records in Baltic are Old Prussian texts of the fourteenth century. Records in Lithuanian and Latvian date from the sixteenth century.

Both Lithuanian and Latvian are tonal, exhibit archaic Indo-European features, and share an extensive common vocabulary. In spite of this homogeneity, however, they are usually treated as belonging to different areal groupings. Thus, on areal criteria, Gyula Décsy classifies Lithuanian along with Polish, Ukrainian, Belorussian, and Kashubian: Latvian with Estonian, Vot, and Liv.

The total number of people speaking Baltic languages is probably about 5 million (including emigré populations).

See **Lithuanian**, **Latvian**, **Balto-Finnic Minor Languages**.

BALTO-FINNIC MINOR
LANGUAGES
(Ingrian, Liv, Veps, Vot)

INGRIAN

Ingrian, also known as Izhor, is spoken by fewer than a thousand people, all of whom are bilingual (with Russian), in the Kingisepp and Lomonosov areas, immediately to the west of Leningrad. Genetically, Ingrian is close to Karelian, and has been influenced by Vot, Estonian, Finnish, and Russian. Some attempt to write Ingrian in the Roman alphabet was made in the 1930s. The language is now unwritten.

The consonant inventory is notable for the presence of half-voiced labial, dental, and velar stops, notated in pedagogical literature as *B, D, G, Z*. Both consonant gradation and vowel harmony are present: cf. *otta* 'to take', *oDan* 'I take'; *iskiä* 'to strike', *iZen* 'I strike'.

Nouns have the usual Balto-Finnic cases, with a nominative plural in -D: e.g. *katto* 'roof', gen. *kaDon*, part. *kattoa*, pl. nom. *kaDoD*. Exceptionally for Finno-Ugric, the plural marker may be added to the possessive affix: e.g. *veneh.emme.D* 'our boats'.

Compound tenses are made with *olla*, as in Finnish, etc., and the past participle is marked for number: e.g. *olen ommelD* 'I have sewn', *olemma ommellēD* 'we have sewn'.

LIV

From a former position of dominance in Courland and Livonia (Livland), where they had been settled for about 2,000 years, the Livs are now reduced to a remnant of some 300 persons who live in fishing villages at the tip of the Courland peninsula. It is estimated that most of these people, who call themselves 'fisher folk' – *kalamiez* – still use the language in their homes; but Latvian is otherwise in general use.

Some portions of the New Testament were translated into Liv in the 1860s, and some revival of Liv writing and culture took place under the auspices of the Latvian Republic (up to 1939). Today, Liv is unwritten.

The half-voiced stops *B, D, G* are present, and palatalization is a major feature of Liv phonology. Consonant gradation has been lost, as have the vowels /œ, y/. The historical presence of *h*, now lost, is marked by a broken intonation or glottal stop: e.g. *rā'* 'money' (cf. Finnish *raha*); *lē'D* 'leaf, page' (cf. Finnish *lehti*). Consonantal clustering, unusual in Finno-Ugric languages, is tolerated in medial position.

The nominal declension includes a dative (in *-n*), unique in Balto-Finnic. The plural marker, nominative, is *-D*.

In the verbal system, the first and third person singular endings have coalesced: *ma luguB* 'I read', *ta luguB* 'he/she reads'; past: *ma lugiz* 'I read', *ta lugiz* 'he, she read'; *ma vol' lu'ggən* 'I had read', *ta vol' lu'ggən* 'he/she had read'. Similarly, *ma volks lu'ggən* 'I would have read'; *mi'nnən vol' lu'ggəm-əst* 'I had to read'; *ma lu'ggiji* '(it seems) I am reading'.

The negative conjugation is remarkable in that some forms are doubly marked:

Singular		*Plural*	
1	ma äb lu'G 'I don't read'	mēg äb lu'ggəm	
2	sa äd lu'G	tēg äd lu'ggət	
3	ta äb lu'G	ne äb lu'ggət	

(*contrast* **Finnish** and **Estonian**).

Also interesting is the presence of Liv roots with Latvian prefixes: e.g. Latv. *aiz-* + Liv *lä'də* 'to go': *aiz.lä'də* 'to go away' (= Latv. *aiziet*)

VEPS

Veps is spoken in the area to the south of the Karelian Autonomous Soviet Socialist Republic, bounded by Lakes Ladoga and Onega and the Byeloye Ozero. Estimates of numbers vary greatly. Crystal (1988) gives 6,000–7,000, Comrie (1981) 3,000.

Veps is unwritten. There was an attempt to create a literary language in the 1930s.

As in Liv, palatalization is a major feature of the phonology. Consonant gradation has been lost; and vowel harmony is observed only in the first two or three syllables of a word.

The case system can be extended by agglutinative affixes; e.g. *-nou*, indicating proximity, can be added to the genitive case ending: *laps'id'en.**nou*** 'along with the children (where they are)'. Similarly *-pai* is added to the locative case: *jarvele.**pai*** 'in the direction of the lake'.

As in Finnish, the negative marker is conjugated preceding the sense-verb in stem form marked for number: e.g. *joksen* 'I run', *en jokse* 'I don't run'; *joksemai* 'we run', *emai jokskoi* 'we don't run'.

Veps has an inceptive mood, with the marker *-škand/ška-*:

> *k'ir'jutaškanden* 'I'll begin to write'
> *k'ir'jutaškanz'in'* 'I began to write'
> *en k'ir'jutaškande* 'I shan't begin to write'

VOT

The ethnonym is *vad'd'ałain*. Décsy (1973) describes the Vots as the original inhabitants of Ingermanland, historically the province between present-day

Leningrad and the river Narva. Today, the language is virtually extinct, spoken by a few dozen people in the Kingisepp area. Vot has never been a written language.

As described by Adler in JaNSSSR (1966), Vot has standard vowel harmony and a very elaborate system of consonant gradation: according to Adler the most elaborate of any Finno-Ugric language. Such oppositions as /ttʃ–d′d′/ are found: e.g. *väittšiä* 'to call' – *väd′d′i!* 'call!' Consonant gradation extends even to the affix system.

The noun is declined in 14 cases. Plural marker is -*D* (nominative), i.e. the half-voiced plosive, as in Ingrian and Liv.

Present indicative of *tehä* 'to do':

   singular: *tēn, tēD, tēB*; pl. *tēnmä, tēttä, tetševäD;*
   negative: *en, ed, ep tē; emmä, että, eivät tē.*

Perfect: *ełen tehnü*; negative: *en ełe tehnü.*

Word order

SVO is frequent; if adverbial material introduces sentence, VSO is used.

1. *Ÿrgandõksõs voł Sõna ja Sõna voł Jumal jūs ja Jumal voł Sõna.*

2. *Ÿrgandõksõs ta voł Jumal jūs.*

3. *Amad ažad āt leb täm tiedõt ja ilm tānda äb ūo mittõ midagist tiedõt, mis um tiedõt.*

4. *Täms voł jelami ja jelami voł rovz sieldõm.*

5. *Ja sieldõm pāistiz pimdõms ja pimdõm iz võta tānda rastõ.*

6. *Ÿkš rišting, nimtõt Jāņ, sai Jumalst kaimdõt.*

7. *Ta tuł tapartõks pierast, āndam tapartõkst ył sieldõm, laz amad uskõgõd leb täm.*

8. *Ta iz ūo sieldõm, aga tämmõn roł ył sieldõm tapartõmõst.*

Liv

BALUCHI (*Beludzh*)

INTRODUCTION

Baluchi belongs to the North-West Iranian group of languages. The ethnonym is *balūč* or *balūdž*. The original habitat of the Baluchi people seems to have been near the southern shores of the Caspian Sea, whence they migrated during the first millennium AD to their present habitat in south-east Iran and south-west Pakistan. East and west Baluchi are divided from each other by the Brahui enclave (*see* **Brahui**).

Between 2 and 2½ million people speak Baluchi, of whom 1 million are in Pakistan, and well over half a million in Iran. There are about 200,000 speakers in Afghanistan, and smaller communities in India, the Arabian Peninsula, and the Soviet Union.

The Baluchi people have a rich oral tradition in folk literature, the main feature being the *daptar* – heroic ballads in stereotyped format, recounting the origins of the Baluchi, their wars, and wanderings. The twentieth century has produced several notable writers in Baluchi; newspapers and periodicals in the language appear in Quetta and Karachi. The Baluchi in the USSR use Turkmen as their literary language.

SCRIPT

Arabo-Persian. Attempts made in the 1930s to provide a Roman script for the Baluchi in the USSR were abandoned.

PHONOLOGY

Consonants

    stops: p, b, t, d, ṭ, ḍ, k, g
    affricates: tʃ, dʒ
    fricatives: s, z, ʃ, ʒ, x, γ, h
    nasals: m, n, ŋ
    lateral and flap: l, r
    semi-vowels: j, w

The eastern dialects have additional series of labial, dental, retroflex, and velar aspirates, plus the fricatives /θ, ð, f/. Stops in western dialects are often represented by fricatives in eastern; thus western *dāta* 'given' = eastern *dāθa*; *lōg* 'house' = *lōγ*; *āp* 'water' = *āf*.

The outline given here refers essentially to western Baluchi.

Vowels

    long: aː, iː, eː, uː, oː
    short: a, i, u

Baluchi preserves the Middle Persian series; and this quantitative opposition between long and short vowels links Baluchi to Middle Persian in contradistinction to other present-day Iranian languages, whose vocalic structure turns on a qualitative difference between vowels. Long vowels in Baluchi tend to be articulated clearly with a certain amount of tension; short vowels are slacker and reduced.

Stress

Stress is usually on the final syllable, excluding affixes and indefinite marker.

MORPHOLOGY AND SYNTAX

Noun

Parts of speech fall under two headings: nominals and verbals. There is no grammatical gender. A plural marker in *-ān* is, in general, optional in nominative.

CASE SYSTEM
Typical endings are:

	Singular	*Plural*
nominative	Ø	(-ān)
genitive	-a	-āni
accusative	-ā, -ārā	-ān(r)ā
prepositional	-ā	-ān

The accusative case may also denote the indirect object: e.g. *mardumār* '(to) the man'. An enclitic *-ē*, which can take case endings, is used as an indefinite article: e.g. *mard* 'man'; *mardē* = *yak mard* 'a man'; genitive: *mardēa*.

Adjective

Adjectives do not change for number or case when used attributively but take the affix *-ēn*: e.g. *šarrēn mard* 'good man'. Used predicatively, they take the ending -V*nt*[2]: e.g. *Ān mard šarrant* 'These people are good.' When used as an independent nominal, the adjective is declined for number and case, and takes the indefinite marker.

COMPARISON
A comparative is made with *-tir* + *či*: e.g. X *či* Y *šarrtir.in* 'X is better than Y.'

Pronoun

PERSONAL INDEPENDENT

Sing. 1 *man*, 2 *ta(u)*, 3 *ē*, *ēš*, *ā*; pl. 1 *(a)mā*, 2 *š(u)mā*, 3 *ē*, *ēšān*; *ā*, *āyān*. The declension of the personal pronouns is subject to much dialectal variation.

ENCLITIC FORMS

These are (sing. and pl.) 1 *un*, 2 *-it*, 3 sing. *-ī/ē*, pl. *-iš*. These are used both as possessive markers and as direct-object markers. According to Frolova (1960), they also figure in the so-called ergative construction as subject markers.

DEMONSTRATIVE PRONOUN

ē 'this', *ā(n)* 'that'; pl. *ēšān*, *āyān*. Not declined when used attributively.

INTERROGATIVE PRONOUN

kai 'who?'; *či* 'what?'.

Numerals

1–10: *yak*, *dō*, *say*, *čār*, *panč*, *šaš*, *(h)apt*, *(h)ašt*, *nō*, *dah*; 11 *yāzdah*; 12 *dwāzdah*; 20 *gīst*; 30 *sī*; 100 *sad/saθ*.

Verb

As in other Iranian languages, the Baluchi verbal system is constructed on two bases, the present and the past, each of which is used to generate a series of appropriate tenses. The past base is normally the present base plus *-(i)t*. There are several irregular formations, some suppletive:

> regular: *guš – gušt* 'say';
> irregular: *nind – ništ* 'sit';
> suppletive: *gind – dīšt* 'see'.

There are two voices, active and passive; and three moods: indicative, subjunctive, imperative. The passive is rare. The auxiliary verb *bayag* 'to be' is used. Imperative: second person only. The prefix is *b(i)-*. Subjunctive: this is represented by the aorist tense (prefix *b(i)-*) and the form expressing unreal conditions. *See* **Tense**, below.

Tense system

Two prefixes are used, *ak/a*, with phonetic variants; and *b(i)-/ak-* is used in the present/future tense and the past continuous; *b(i)-* in aorist, imperative, and unreal conditional tense.

The personal endings:

	Singular	Plural
1	-ān, -ūn etc,	-an, -in, -ēn
2	-ē, -ay	-it
3	-it, -t, -i	-ant, -en

The copula is (*h*)*ast-* + above endings for both present and past tense.

TENSES ON PRESENT BASE

Present/future: prefix *ak-* (or variant) + stem + ending. In certain phonetic conditions the *a* and *k* of the prefix are treated as separable, the *a* being attached to the preceding word, the *k* prefixed to the verb: e.g. *Laškar.a k.āyt* 'the army is coming'.

Aorist: the *b*(*i*)- prefix is attached to the present–future form; sandhi at juncture: b + surd → p, b + n → m, b + b → Ø: e.g. *mnīndit* 'so that you should sit down'; *pkanit* 'so that you should do'.

TENSES ON PAST BASE

The distinction formerly made here between transitive verbs with ergative construction appears to be unstable. Frolova (1960) gives the following examples: *bādšāhā* (i.e. oblique case in -*ā*) *ā mard* (direct case) *kuštag* 'the emperor killed that man'; *bādšāhā manārā* (accusative) *kuštag* 'the emperor killed me'.

A peculiarity of Baluchi is the use of the 'ergative' construction with certain verbs which are semantically intransitive: e.g. *bādšāhā kandita* 'the emperor began to laugh'.

SPECIMEN TENSES

> present–future: e.g. *gušun*, *gušay*, 'I/you (will) say'
> simple past: e.g. *gušt.un*, *gušt.ay*
> perfect: past participle in -*a*(*g*) + shortened copula: e.g. *guštagun*,
>   *guštagay*, *guštagØ*
> aorist: e.g. *bgušun*, *bgušay*

UNREAL CONDITIONS

The suffix -*en*- is added to the past base followed by personal endings: e.g. (*b*)*guštēnan*, (*b*)*guštēne*, (*b*)*guštēnØ* 'I, you, he/she would have spoken'.

INFINITIVE

Is in -*ag*: e.g. *guštag* 'to speak'.

PARTICIPLES

A present–future participle in -*ī* suggests intention: e.g. *šutinī* 'intending/having to go'.

NEGATION

The negating prefix is *na-* in the indicative mod, *ma-* in the subjunctive and the imperative. It is interesting that where -*a* and *k*- are separated as present–future tense markers, -*na*- is inserted between them. Frolova gives the example: *taγatt.a.na.k.ārit* '... can't stand it'.

Relative clause

Relative clauses are made with connecting particle *ki*: e.g.

> Ō manī pit, či mālā har bahar **ki** manīg bīt, manārā bidai

Father, give me each (= that) part of the property which is to be mine'
(Grierson 1921)

Prepositions

For example, *pa(r)* 'on, for'; *aš/ša/ač* 'about, from, etc.'; *gō(n)* 'with'.

There are a few postpositions, e.g. *sarā* 'on'; *lāpā* 'in'; *padā* 'after, behind'.
These are used along with prepositions: e.g. *ša mašmay **padā** kāyt* 'he comes
behind us' (*mašmay* is an inclusive 1st p. pl. pron. characteristic of USSR
Baluchi).

Word order

SOV.

---

1   Pesha awula nyama hawe KALAM ath, o hawe KALAM go HUDHA
2 de gon ath, wa HUDHA hawe KALA'M de astath. Hawesh awwula
  nyáma go HUDHA gon ath. Durust chie
  eshi márifata bithaghant, wa azh eshiya siwa hech na bitha, an chie ki
4 bitha. Eshi nyama ZINDAGHI ath, wa an ZINDAGHI an NUR in-
5 sanegh ath. Wa an NUR man thahára chimkaghe, wa thahárá anhi
6 sama na girt. Marde bitha Hudhá shashthatha eshi nám Yuhanna.
7 Hawan pha sháhidi akhtá ki NU'R phara shahidi khat, ki darnst mardán 'sh
8 eshiya iman khanant. Hamesh an NUR niyath, bale ki an NURA phara
  shahidi khat.

BAMBARA

INTRODUCTION

This member of the Mande group of the Niger-Congo family is the main language of the Republic of Mali, where it is spoken by about 2 million people. The similarity between Bambar and its sister languages Malinke and Dyula is such that the three were grouped by Delafosse as one language which he called Mandingo.

SCRIPT

In the 1960s a standardized script was adopted; this uses the Roman alphabet plus *è* = /ɛ/ and *ò* = /ɔ/.

PHONOLOGY

Consonants

    stops: p, b, t, d, k, g
    affricates: tʃ, dʒ
    nasals: m, n, ɲ, ŋ
    fricatives: f, s, z, ʃ, h
    lateral and flap: l, r
    semi-vowels: j, w

Vowels

    i, e, ɛ, a, ɔ, o, u

The contrast between /e/ and /ɛ/ is phonemic: cf. /kelel/ 'one'; /kɛlɛl/ 'war'. Nasalization is notated by vowel + nasal consonant: *dan* /dã/. The apostrophe is used to mark vowel elision.

TONES

High and low; the contrast is phonemic: cf. *sá* 'snake'; *sa* 'die, death'.

MORPHOLOGY AND SYNTAX

Noun

Natural gender can be indicated by affix: *kè* (male), *muso* (female): e.g. *denkè* 'son'; *denmuso* 'daughter'. There is no inflection. A plural marker is *-u/-Cu*, where C is, e.g. *r*: e.g. *mogo* 'man', *mogou* 'men'; *den* 'child'; *denu* = /dēu/, 'children'; *bááràkèlá* 'worker', *bááràkèláu* 'workers'.

POSSESSION

X of Y = YX: e.g. *nègè sira* 'way of iron' = 'railway'; *Mali bááràkèláu* 'the workers of Mali'.

Adjective

As attribute, adjective follows noun, and appears in doublets: XØ and X*man*: e.g. *kòrò* = *kòròman* 'old'; *misira ba* 'the big mosque'; *tasuma ble* 'the red light'.

COMPARATIVE

X *ka … ni* Y *ye* 'X is …er than Y'.

Pronoun

	Singular	Plural
1	ne	an
2	i, e	au
3	a	u

When using these as possessives, a distinction is made between material and non-material possession (often inalienable): for the former *ka* is added, e.g. *n' teri* 'my friend'; *n' fa* 'my father'; *n' ka fali* 'my donkey'; *n' ka faliu* 'my donkeys'. But see also postpositions *fè*, *la*, *na*.

DEMONSTRATIVE PRONOUN/ADJECTIVE

nin 'this'; *o* 'that'. These may precede or follow the noun; if following, they take the plural marker: e.g. *nin watiri kurau* = *watiri kurau ninu* 'these new cars'.

RELATIVE PRONOUN

min, pl. *minu*: e.g. *dunan min na.na* 'the foreigner who came'.

Numerals

1–10: *kele(n)*, *fila*, *saba*, *naani*, *duuru*, *wòoro*, *wolonfla*, *segi*, *kònòntò*, *tan*; 20 *mugan*; 30 *bi saba*; 40 *bi naani*; 100 *kèmè*.

Verb

Brauner (1974) distinguishes four predicating particles: *do* and *ye* identify; *ka* is descriptive; *bè* localizes. The infinitive marker is *ka*: e.g. *ka cike* 'to plough'.

TENSE MARKERS

> present: *bè*, negative *tè*: e.g. *m'be taga* 'I go' (/n'/ → /m'/ before /b/); *n'tè taga* 'I don't go'.
> perfect: *-ra*, *-la*, *na* depending on stem final: e.g. *ne taga.ra* 'I went'; *a yele.la* 'he laughed'.

These are negated by *ma*: *m'ma taga* 'I didn't go'.

future: *na*: e.g. *n'na taga* 'I shan't go'.

There are forms for imperfect, immediate present, and pluperfect.

IMPERATIVE
Singular expressed by bare stem; plural marked by *a ye*: e.g. *a ye ta(g)a!* 'go!'.

CONDITIONAL
tunna: e.g. *n'tunna a fò* 'I'd say it'.

SUBJUNCTIVE
Affirmative *ka*: negative *kana*: e.g. *n'ka a fò* 'that I should say'; neg. *n'kana a fò*.

VERBAL NOUN
E.g. from *mi* 'to drink': *mini* 'drinking'.

PARTICIPLES
Present -*tò*; past -*le*/-*ne* (with passive sense): e.g. *Mali tlale do yòrò saba* 'Mali was (= is) divided into three regions'; *Liwru kalanna an fè* 'The book was read by us' (*kalan* 'to read').

Postpositions

Examples:

> *bè* 'with, at': used to express possession, e.g. *so bè n'fè* 'I have a house (*so*)';
> *fè* 'by': e.g. *an fè* 'by us';
> *la, kònò* 'in, within': e.g. *so kònò* 'inside the house';
> *cè, cè la* 'among'.

Word formation

Mainly by suffixation, though prefixes and compounding are also found. Examples:

> -*ni*: forms diminutives, e.g. *den* 'child', *denni* 'small child';
> -*ya*: forms abstracts; e.g. *muso* 'woman', *musoya* 'femininity';
> -*la*/-*na*: indicates agent, e.g. *sènè* 'agriculture', *sènèla* 'peasant';
> -*bali* is privative, e.g. *balo* 'life', *balobali* 'lifeless'; *balobaliya* 'lifelessness';
> -*tò* makes qualitative adjectives, e.g. *kongo* 'hunger', *kongotò* 'hungry';
> -*ta* gives potential sense, e.g. *ye* 'see', *yeta* 'visible';
> -*lan* indicates instrument or means, e.g. *gosi* 'strike', *gosilan* 'hammer'.

Word order

SOV.

1 قُلْقُلْ كُمَرِبِيبِي . كُمَرِ بَعَرَآبِي .
كُمَرِ عَلَّلْ :.

2 وُلِبِي عَلَّ جِي قُلْقُلْ :.

3 فِنِبِي دَنْدَ عَـلِبُلْ . فِي مِنِّي بَرِدَآ .
وُوِنْبِي مَادَآ عَـلِبْكُرِ :.

4 بَلْ دَبِرِ عَـلِبُذْ . وَبَـلُّلِ مُقُلَّلْ كِبِدْ .

5 كِبِنِبِي مِنِتِي دِيبُرْ دِ يِمَا قَـلَاقْ :.

6 كَدَلْبِي عَلَّ بُلْ . عَتِتِي بُوتِتَا :.

7 وُلْتَار بِسِرِبَـلْ كُكِيَا بِسِرِبَبُو وُكَنِبِي
هَـابِي يَـادِنْكِـبِيبِي عَـجِي :.

8 عَلِتِي وُكِبِدْ . حَتِّي عَنَارِكُو عَـيَا
سِرِبَبُو وُجَـبِبِي :.

BANTU LANGUAGES

INTRODUCTION

The Bantu languages form a major component of the Benue-Congo branch of the Niger-Congo family of languages; the other branches are the Kwa group, the Voltaic or Gur group, the West Atlantic group, the Mande group and the Adamawa-Eastern group. Altogether, the Benue-Congo branch comprises about 700 languages, and 500 of these are Bantu.

Geographically, the Bantu languages cover most of sub-Saharan Africa, across which they seem to have spread, eastwards and southwards, from a West African point of origin, in the early part of the first millennium AD. As in the case of the Turkic languages, dispersal was not accompanied by any marked degree of innovation on the linguistic plane; and the features which go to identify a language as 'Bantu' remained remarkably stable as the dialectal continuum expanded over great distances and through long periods of time, so that even outliers like Zulu-Xhosa, Herero, and Makua are instantly recognizable as Bantu. Indeed, it is mainly in areas close to the original Bantu homeland in West Africa that the characteristic genetic imprint is found to be somewhat modified. This may be due either to Proto-Bantu connections with contiguous languages of the isolating type (Kwa, Kordofanian, Nilo-Saharan) or to the influence of these languages on Bantu in the historical period.

At the other extreme of the Bantu continuum, the clicks in Zulu-Xhosa represent importations from neighbouring Khoisan languages. The Zulu grid of click sounds, for example, shows a labio-velar, a dental–velar, and a lateral–velar series, each containing four phonemes – a surd, its aspirate, its voiced allophone, and its nasal, e.g. in the dental–velar series /q, qh, gq, nq/.

The earliest descriptions of Bantu languages date from the mid-seventeenth century – e.g. Giacinto Brusciotto's Latin grammar of Kongo, published in 1659. The task of providing an internal classification of the Bantu languages based on scientific criteria, was first undertaken by W.H.J. Bleek (1862–9), who coined the name *Bantu* to designate the people and their languages. The word is a plural form meaning 'people', and functions as such in many Bantu languages; cf.

	Singular	*Plural*
Rwanda	umu.ntu 'man'	aba.ntu
Kongo	mu.ntu	ba.ntu
Zulu	umu.ntu	aba.ntu
Herero	omu.ndu	ova.ndu
Swahili	m.tu	wa.tu

Lingala	mo.to	ba.to
Sotho	mō.thō	bā.thō
Shona	mu.nhu	va.nhu
Luganda	omu.ntu	aba.ntu

The Common Bantu prototype, of which these are reflexes, has been reconstructed as, sing. *mo.to*; pl. *ba.nto*.

Bleek was followed by Carl Meinhof (1901) and Sir Harry Johnston (1919). In 1948, Professor M. Guthrie published the first part of his definitive *Classification of the Bantu Languages* (complete edition, 4 vols, 1967–70). This classification lists about 700 languages (including those which Guthrie calls 'semi-Bantu') divided into 16 areal groupings, each grouping having specific phonological and morphological features.

The Bantu languages are spoken by a total of about 160 million people. Numbers for individual languages vary very considerably; between 50,000 and 100,000 is about average. Rwanda tops the list as the mother tongue of at least 10 million, followed by Swahili, Zulu-Xhosa, and Makua (in Mozambique) with 5–6 million each. The picture changes if second-language status is taken into account: Swahili, with some 50 million, then easily outstrips all its congeners.

A broad areal division, based on Guthrie's 16 zones, with the names of some of the most important representative members, is given:

1. North-West Central Africa: Duala, Fang, Buja, Lingala/Losengo;
2. West and South-West Central Africa: Kongo, Songe, Herero, Ciokwe;
3. East Central: Swahili, Sango, Bemba, Tonga, Nyanja;
4. North-East Central: Luganda, Gikuyu, Nyankole, Soga, Rundi, Rwanda, Nyamwesi;
5. South-East: Shona, Tsonga, Ronga, Makua, Yao;
6. South: Sotho, Swazi, Tswana, Zulu-Xhosa.

PHONOLOGY

Consonants

The parent Proto-Bantu language had a relatively simple inventory of stops /p, t, k/, plus /tʃ/ with their voiced, nasal, and pre-nasalized (both voiced and unvoiced) allophones: e.g.

p, b, m, ᵐp, ᵐb; t, d, n, ⁿt, ⁿd

The plural forms in the *umuntu/abantu* chart on p. 163 illustrate reflexes in modern Bantu languages of the unvoiced pre-nasalized series. In Swahili, for example, the nasal has been lost, *wa.tu*; in Herero, the unvoiced has merged with the voiced series, *ova.ndu* (cf. a.*ndu* in Thagicu); while in Shona the stop has been lost, *va.nhu* (cf. *wa.nu* in the Luguru language of Tanzania).

Common Bantu seems to have had no sibilants, while /s/ and several other fricatives – /ʃ, z, h, f, v/ – are widespread in the successor languages. In many of these, the fricatives and some sonants are reflexes of the parent voiced series.

Vowels

Proto-Bantu had seven vowels, /i, e, ɛ, a, ɔ, o, u/, an inventory which is characteristic today of two of Guthrie's areal groupings (North-East and North-West Central), and is also found (along with the five-vowel system) in seven others. The five-vowel system, /i, ɛ, a, ɔ, u/, is found in about 60 per cent of Bantu languages.

Tone

Proto-Bantu was probably a tone language, and tone is a general characteristic of present-day Bantu languages, where it is often phonemic. The curious phenomenon of tone reversal has been noted in Western Congo languages (high tone for Common Bantu low, and vice versa). Tone has been lost in Swahili.

Stress

Stress normally tends to the penultimate syllable.

MORPHOLOGY AND SYNTAX

Noun

It seems clear that Proto-Bantu was already in possession of the class prefix system which is now the most general and the most typical feature of Bantu morphology. Proto-Bantu had 19 classes, an inventory which has been retained in many of the daughter languages, and much reduced (usually by syncretic processes) in others; Sotho, for example, has only seven classes. Class 1, the class of human beings, is largely homogeneous over the whole field; the other classes are heterogeneous, though some of them are associated, at least in part, with certain semantic fields: e.g. trees are often in class 3, animals in class 9. In origin, the classes may well have been associated with an elaborate system of classifiers such as are found in South-East Asia. The class system has nothing to do with gender; nor is it, at least in origin, connected with an animate/inanimate dichotomy. The animate concord which is now a feature of Swahili and some other East Central languages is a recent development.

Class is marked in nouns by prefix which is then echoed by concordial coefficients in all associated parts of speech, thus producing a kind of semantic alliteration: e.g. Swahili

> **wa**geni **wa**zungu **wa**ngi **wa**lifika Kenya (ili) **wa**pande mlima wa Kilimanjaro; nime**wa**ona.
>
> 'Many European visitors came to Kenya to climb Mount Kilimanjaro; I have seen them.'
>
> (-*fika* 'to arrive, come'; -*geni* 'strange'; *Mzungu* 'European'; -*ingi* 'many'; -*pande* 'to climb'; *mlima* 'mountain'; -*li* = past-tense marker; -*me-* = perfect-tense marker; -*ona* 'to see')

Classes are normally paired: a class containing singular nouns is followed by the class containing the respective plurals. Classes 1 and 2, containing singular and plural nouns denoting human beings, have been illustrated above: *umu.ntu/ aba.ntu*, etc. Similarly, class 3 comprises singular nouns with a *m-/mw-/mu-* prefix; class 4, the relevant plurals with a *mi-* prefix. The semantic field in classes 3/4 is heterogeneous, basically animate, e.g.

	Class 3	Class 4 plurals
Swahili	m.ti 'tree'	mi.ti
Kongo	n.ti	mi.ti
Zulu	umu.thi	imi.ti
Shona	mu.ti	mi.ti
Lingala	mw.ete	mi.ete
Luganda	omu.ti	emi.ti
Gikuyu	mu.ti	mi.ti

It will be noticed that certain prefixes – e.g. *m-* in classes 1 and 3 – are duplicated. This can only give rise to confusion in citation form; in connected utterance, oral or written, specific concordial sequence ensures semantic discrimination.

Some classes are at least partially correlated with specific semantic fields, the obvious example being class 1/2. This is on the whole atypical, however, and not consistent. *See* **Swahili** for a specific set of classes. For comparative purposes, here is the Luganda system, which is notable for the retention of classes which have been lost in other North-East Central Bantu languages:

Class	Prefix	Class features and examples
1	omu-	class of human beings: **omu***ntu* 'man'
2	aba-	plurals of nouns in cl. 1: **aba***ntu* 'men, people'
3	omu-	plants, trees, etc.: **omu***ti* 'tree'
4	emi-	plurals of nouns in cl. 3: **emi***ti* 'trees'
5	li-/eri-	with sandhi at junctures; heterogeneous field: **e***jjinja* 'stone' (li + j- > (e)jj)
6	ama-	plurals of nouns in cl. 5: **ama***yinja* 'stones'
7	eki-	human artefacts: **eki***zimbe* 'building'; may have disparaging nuance: **eki***renzi* 'overgrown youth'
8	ebi-	plurals of cl. 7 nouns: **ebi***zimbe* 'buildings'
9	en-	heterogeneous; includes some animals: **en***jovu* 'elephant'
10	zi-	provides plural forms for nouns belonging to various classes
11	olu-/olw-	class of long and/or thin objects: **olu***tindo* 'bridge'
12	otu-	nouns denoting small quantities of something: **otu***zzi* 'drops of water'
13	aka-	heterogeneous field: **aka***mwa* 'mouth'; **aka***ntu* 'something small'; **aka***wungeezi* 'evening'
14	obu-/obw-	plurals of nouns in cl. 13: **obu***mwa* 'mouths'
15	oku-	actions: **oku***genda* 'going' (< -*genda* 'to go')
20	ogu-	augmentatives based on nouns in other classes:

		oguntu 'giant' (cf. *omuntu* 'man')
22	aga-	plurals of nouns in cl. 20: *agantu* 'giants'

It is worth pointing out here that Luganda has, in addition, a series of prefixes denoting high rank, which draw on class 1 for their concordial agreement, e.g. *sse-*, *nna-*, with plural forms *basse-*, *banna-*: e.g. *ssabasajja Kabaka* 'His Highness the Kabaka'.

Classes 16, 17, and 18, left blank in the above table, are the locational classes with prefixes *pa-*, *ku-*, *mu-* indicating, respectively, definite locus, indefinite locus, and locus within something: cf. Swahili *nyumba.ni mwa mwalimu* 'in the house of the teacher' (*-ni* is a locative suffix; *nyumba* 'house'; *mwalimu* 'teacher').

Adjective

There are very few root adjectives in Bantu. Examples are:

	'Large'		*'Bad'*
Zulu	-kulu	Zulu	-bi
Swahili	-kuu	Herero	-i
Nyanja	-kulu	Luganda	-bi
Tswana	-xolo	Kongo	-bi
		Swahili	-baya

Attributively, root adjectives follow the noun qualified, taking the proper class prefix: e.g. with root *-ema* 'good', in Swahili: *mtu mw.ema* 'a good person'; *watu wema* 'good people'; *-dogo* 'small': *wa.toto wa.dogo wa.wili* 'two small children' (*-wili* 'two') (cl. 2). Often, a relative construction is preferred, e.g. in Zulu: *umu.ntu o.na.amandhla* 'a strong man' (lit. 'a man who is strong'; relative *-a + u* → *o*).

Pronoun

The conjunctive pronouns, subjective and objective, are remarkably homogeneous over most of the Bantu area. Meinhof (1906) gives the Common Bantu forms for the subject verbal prefixes as:

	Singular	*Plural*
1	ni	ti/tî
2	γu	mî/mu
3	γa, γyu	βa

Reflexes of 1st person singular: e.g. Swahili *ni*; Zulu *ngi*; Luganda *n* (with variants); Kongo *n* (with variants); Duala *na*; Rundi *n/ndi*; Yao *ni*.

In Meinhof's table of 38 languages (1906: 88), only two – Makua and Sotho – are non-conformist, each with a *ke/ki* form for the first person singular.

DEMONSTRATIVE PRONOUNS
Three degrees of relative distance are normally distinguished; *see* **Swahili**.

RELATIVE PRONOUN

Many Bantu languages have no relative construction. Where such a construction exists it may take various forms:

(a) with demonstrative in the (*hu*) *yo* → *ye*, (*ha*)*o* form; with tense marker: e.g. *a.li.ye.soma* 'he who read'; pl. *wa.li.o.soma* (*-li-* is past-tense marker);

(b) subject prefix + stem + relative particle: e.g. (*mtu*) *a.soma.ye* '(the man) who reads';

(c) relative pronoun: e.g. in Sotho, *mōthō ea rutang* 'a person who teaches'; *bathō ba rutang* 'persons who teach';

(d) analytical construction with *amba-* (in Swahili) + relative particle: e.g. *mtu ambaye a.na.kuja* 'the man who is coming' (*-na-* is present-tense marker).

Indirect relative: the concordial object pronoun precedes the verb + suffixed relative form agreeing with object: e.g. (*kitu*) *ni.ki.taka.cho* 'the thing I want', where *kitu* is a class 7 noun, *-ki-* is the class 7 subject/object prefix, and *-cho-* is the class 7 relative pronominal form.

Verb

Most primary roots are disyllables. Derived stems are formed by suffixation, e.g. the reciprocal in *-ana*. This marker is found in many Bantu languages:

Swahili	pendana 'to love each other'
Lingala	lingana 'to love each other'
Zulu	bonana 'to see each other'
Rwanda	ku.bonana 'to see each other'
Sotho	ho.bonana 'to see each other'
Shona	onana 'to see each other'
Luganda	yombagana 'to quarrel with each other'

Similarly, with the causative ending in *-Vsha* in Swahili (e.g. *weza* 'be able to', *wezesha* 'to enable'); this ending appears as *-ithia* in Gikuyu, as *-isa* in Zulu, as *-Vsa-Vdza/-Vtsa* in Shona, as *-Vsa* in Sotho, as *-a/-e* in Luganda, as *-isa* in Lingala, and as *-itha* in Herero.

Other derived stems: passive, in *-(i)wa*, with variants: cf.

Zulu	bon.wa 'to be seen'
Gikuyu	igu.(w)o 'be heard'
Luganda	lab.wa 'be seen'
Sotho	ho rōngŏa 'be sent' (← *rōma* 'to send': /m/ → [ŋg] before /w/)
Swahili	ku.on.wa 'be seen'

The Lingala passive is in *-ema/ama*: e.g. *ekosalema* 'to be done'.

Some Bantu languages have a neutral passive of state in *-Vka(la)*, e.g. in Zulu *inkanyezi ya.bona.ka.la* 'the star was visible'; cf. *thandwa* 'to be loved', *thand.eka* 'be loving, affectionate'.

Prepositional or benefactive: e.g. -Vla/ra in Zulu, -ri/-er in Shona, depending on vowel harmony; Zulu *hlala* 'to wait', *hlal.ela* 'to wait for someone'; *hamba* 'to travel'; *hambela* 'to go to visit someone'.

Antonymous: typically -Vl/ra; e.g. Gikuyu, *hinga* 'to shut'; *hingura* 'to open'.

MOODS

Moods are generally marked by suffix. Most Bantu languages have seven moods: infinitive, indicative, imperative, subjunctive, perfect, continuative, relative.

The infinitive is a noun (Swahili *ku-* class, corresponding to *uku-* in Zulu, *hō-* in Sotho). The infinitive (or gerund), the indicative, and the direct imperative usually have *-a* final; the subjunctive has *-e*, the negative *-i*. Cf. Swahili.

> *ku.soma* 'reading, to read'
> *ni.ta.soma* 'I shall read'
> *soma!* 'read'
> *ni.some (nini)?* 'What shall I read?', 'What am I to read?'
> *si.somi* 'I do not read'

Negative tense formation provides one of the criteria by which Bantu languages may be internally classified. Negation by tone pattern occurs in some, e.g. in Fang, but the use of a negative infix is much more usual and typical. For a characteristic set of negative tenses, *see* **Swahili**. Cf. Zulu:

past affirm.	*nga hamba* 'I travelled'
neg.	*a.ngi.hamba.nga* 'I didn't travel'
pres. affirm.	*ngi hamba* 'I travel'
neg.	*a.ngi.hambi* 'I don't travel'
proximate future affirm.	*ngi.za.uku.hamba* 'I shall travel shortly'
neg.	*a.ngi.zi.uku.hamba* 'I shall not travel shortly'

In Gikuyu the negative particle *-ti-* is used to negate plural verbs in principal clauses, e.g. with stem *gwāta* 'to get, take hold of'; present habitual negative plural: first person *tuti.gwat.aga*; second person *muti.gwat.aga*; third person *mati.gwat.aga*, where *-aga* is the habitual present-tense marker.

The singular forms are negated by modification of the pronominal prefix:

1	affirm	ni.ngwat.aga
	neg.	**ndi**.gwat.aga
2	affirm.	u.gwat.aga
	neg.	**ndu**.gwat.aga

The *-ti-* negative forms of certain tenses, are used in an *interrogative* sense only: e.g. immediate past perfect, affirm. *(ni)nd.a.gwat.a* 'I did not get'; *-ti-* neg. *ndi.a.gwat.a?* 'Did I not get?' To negate such a tense, the negative of another past tense (the *-īte* perfect) must be used.

The negative particle may be reduplicated, e.g. Kongo *ke be.tonda ko* 'they do not love'; and may precede or follow the personal prefix, e.g. Nyanja *si.ndi.dziwa(i)*, Shona *ha.ndi.ziwe* 'I do not know', but Duala *na.si.loma* 'I don't read'.

In general, the negative particle tends to follow the subject pronoun in the subjunctive mood, the relative version, and the participial forms: e.g. Zulu, indicative *a.ngi.hambi* 'I do not go'; subjunctive *ngi.nga.hambi* 'I may not go'. Some negative tenses in Bantu have no affirmative correlatives.

The typical Bantu verbal complex consists of prefix (subject concord marker) – tense marker – object marker – stem – modal/voice marker (with negative particle variously sited): e.g., in affirmative version, Swahili *ni.li.ki.soma* Ø 'I read (past) it' (where *ni-* is the personal subject marker for first person singular; *-li-* is the past-tense marker; *-ki-* is a class 5 object marker, referring presumably to *kitabu* 'book'; *soma* 'to read', Ø is the null marker for the indicative mood). Similarly, *ni.ta.ku.ele.za* 'I shall explain (it) to you' (*-ta-* is the future marker; *-ku-* is the second person singular object marker; *ele.za* is the causative of *elea* 'to be clear'). Cf. Gikuyu *Ni.ma.a.tu.ona?* 'Did they see us?' (*ni-* is the interrogative marker; *ma* = third person plural subject; *-a-* is the immediate past marker; *-tu-* is first person plural object marker; *ona* 'to see'). Examples from other Bantu languages:

Zulu	*u.ya.yi.thanda*	'he loves it'
	ngi.ya.ba.thanda	'I love them'
Shona	*ndi.cha.mu.ona*	'I shall see him/her (*cha* is future marker)
Sotho	*kēa mō ruta*	'I teach him'
	oa n.thata	'she loves me' (the root is *rata* 'to love'; *rata* → *thata* following /n/)
	ba m.pona	'they see me' (**n.bona* > *m.pona*)
Lingala	*ako.li.mɔna*	'he sees it' (*-li-* is cl. 5 marker)
	bako.lo.yoka	'they hear us'

TENSE MARKERS
Considerable variation; the Swahili set is: present *-na-*; past *-li-*; future *-ta-*; perfect *-me-*; conditional *-ki-*; present indefinite *-a-*; habitual *-hu-*; narrative: *-ka-*.

Numerals

The numerals 1 to 5 inclusive are Common Bantu stock; so is the word for 10. 6, 7, 8, 9 vary very considerably from language to language; often they are missing and have to be expressed by compounds: 5 + 2, etc.

Word order

SVO is basic.

1 Yoi linaliyaaki ena limatsako, ko Yoi linaliki la Yakomba, ko Yoi linaliki Yakomba. 2 Ende ayaaki la Yakomba ena limatsako; 3 toma tohatotu tonunolamaki l'ende, efan'iyema imoko iniciki inik'ende atanunola. 4 Liiko li-yaaki eneyal'ende, ko liiko lo-yaaki fololo en'ato: 5 koko fololo eololoma ena liucu, ko liucu lit'umbak'eho. 6 Bot'omonyi am'enya, onoki Yakomba otomaka, lina linande liyaaki Yoane. 7 Ende ayaki oyalama bosumoli, lacina asumola bosimo bona fololo, lacina bato bahatu bimedya l'ende. 8 Ende atayalaki fololo eho, ende ayaki lacina asumola bosimo bona fololo.

Lingala

1 Pakutanga Shoko raivako, Shoko raiva kuna Mwari, iro Shoko raiva Mwari. 2 Irori pakutanga raiva kuna Mwari. 3 Zvinhu zvose zvakaitwa naye; kunze kwake hakuna kuitwa kunyange chinhu chimwe chete chakaitwa. 4 Maari ndimo maiva noupenyu; ihwo upenyu hwaiva chiedza chavanhu. 5 Zvino chiedza ichi chinovenekera murima, asi rima harina kuchikunda. 6 Kwakanga kuno munhu wakanga atumwa naMwari; zita rake wainzi Johane. 7 Iyeyu wakauya kuzopupura, kuti apupure zvechiedza ichi kuti vose vatende naye. 8 Iyeyu wakanga asati ari icho chiedza kwete, asi wakauya kuti azopupura zvechiedza.

Shona

1 Tshimolohong Lentswe le ne le le teng, mme Lentswe le ne le le ho Modimo, mme Lentswe e ne e le Modimo. 2 Le ne le le ho Modimo tshimolohong. 3 Dintho tsohle di bile teng ka lona, mme ha ho letho le bileng teng ha e se ka lona. 4 Bophelo bo ne bo le ka ho lona, mme bophelo e ne e le lesedi la batho; 5 lesedi le kganya lefifing, mme lefifi ha le a ka la le hlola.

Sotho

1 Ekuqaleni libeliko I-lizwi, Ilizwi libelikwano-Tixo, ne-Lizwi lalingu-Ti-xo.

2 Elo libeliko ekuqale-ni kwano-Tixo.

3 Zonke izinto zadalwa lilo ; akudalwanganto eya-dalwa lingeko lona.

4 Kulo bekuko Ubomi; nobomi bebulukanyiso lwa-bantu.

5 Ukanyiso luyakanyi-sa ebumyameni; koko ubu-mnyama abuluqondanga.

6 Kwabekuko indoda eyatunywa ivela ku-Tixo, egama libelin-gu-Yohan-nes.

7 Yona yeza ukuze i-belinqina galo Ukanyiso, ukuba bonke abantu ba-kolwe lulo.

8 Yona ibingelulo olo-kanyiso : koko yatunywa ukuze inqine golokanyiso.

Xhosa

EKUQALENI wa be e ko-na uLizwi, uLizwi wa be e noTixo, uLizwi wa be e nguTixo.

2 Yena lowo wa be e no-Tixo ekuqaleni.

3 Konke kwenziwa uye ; ngapandhle kwake a kwe-nziwanga uto olwenziwayo.

4 Kwa be ku kona ukupi-la kuye ; ukupila kwa ku ukukanya kwabantu.

5 Ukukanya kwa kanya ebumnyameni ; kepa ubu-mnyama a bu kwamkela-nga.

6 Kwa ku kona umuntu e tunyiwe uTixo, igama lake la li nguJohane.

7 Yena weza ukuqinisa, ukuba a qinise ngokuka-nya, ukuba bonke ba ko-lwe ngaye.

8 Yena wa be e nge siko lo-kukukanya, kodwa wa tu-nyelwa ukuqinisa ngoku-kanya.

Zulu

BASHKIR

INTRODUCTION

Bashkir belongs to the Kipchak group of Western Turkic (Baskakov's 1966 classification) and is at present spoken by about 900,000 people in the Bashkir Autonomous Soviet Socialist Republic. It is close to Tatar (*see* **Tatar**), towards which Bashkir gravitated till the 1930s, when a new literary norm was introduced on the basis of the eastern (mountain) dialect. In the past, Tatar had been used as a literary language by the Bashkirs, much as Avar is used by the Andi-speaking people in Dagestan. Newspapers, journals, and some books are now pubished in Bashkir.

SCRIPT

Until 1929 Arabic. Following the typical period of experimental romanization in the 1930s, a Cyrillic script was introduced, with additional letters for specifically Bashkir sounds, e.g. the dental fricatives.

PHONOLOGY

Consonants

    stops: p, b, t, d, k, g, q, ʔ; palatalized: t′
    affricates: tʃ
    fricatives: f, s, z, θ, ð, ʃ, ʒ, x/χ, γ, h
    nasals: m, n, ŋ
    lateral and flap: l, ł, r
    semi-vowels: j, w

The alveolar /ts/ occurs only in loan-words.

Vowels

    front: i, y, ə, œ, ε, e
    back: u, ɪ, o, a

Note that front vowel /i/ has no back correlate. /œ/ is notated as *ö*, /ε/ as *ä*; /y/ as *ü*.

VOWEL HARMONY
Both palatal and labial (*see* **Turkic Languages**).

Stress

Vowels in unstressed syllables tend to be reduced: e.g. *keše* → [k′šə], 'person'. Stress is on the final syllable in Turkic words (with certain constraints, e.g. never on negative or interrogative marker).

MORPHOLOGY AND SYNTAX

Noun

All case-forming affixes are affected by juncture sandhi and by the laws of vowel harmony. Thus the accusative ending has 16 allomorphs: 4 initials ($n, d, t, ð$) × 4 vowels ($ı, e = [ə], o, ö$).

Specimen declension: *bala* 'child', pl. *balalar*:

	Singular	*Plural*
genitive	balanıŋ	bala.larðıŋ
dative	balaγa	bala.lar.γa
accusative	balanı	bala.lar.ðı
locative	balala	bala.larða
ablative	balanan	bala.lar.ðan

Plural affix: *lar*[8] (i.e. 4 initials × 2 vowels: *l, t, d, ð, a/ä*): e.g. *kül* 'lake', pl. *küldär*; *taw* 'mountain', pl. *tawðar*.

THE POSSESSIVE AFFIXES
Specimen paradigm as attached to *bala* 'boy':

	Singular possessor	*Plural possessor*
1	balam	balabıð
2	balaŋ	balaγıð
3	balahı	balaları

Examples: *bašqort tele(neŋ) grammatikahı* 'a grammar of the Bashkir language' (*tele* = Turkish *dil* 'language').

Adjective

As attribute, adjective precedes noun and is invariable. When independent, behaves as nominal, taking all case affixes, the plural marker, and the possessive markers. Also used adverbially: e.g. *yaqšı bala* 'good boy'; *yaqšı uqıy* 'he reads well'.

Pronoun

PERSONAL INDEPENDENT
Sing. 1 *min*, 2 *hin*, 3 *ul*; pl. 1 *bəð*, 2 *həð*, 3 *ular*. These are declined in all cases: e.g. for *min*: *mineŋ, miŋə, mine, minən, mində*.

DEMONSTRATIVE PRONOUNS
bıl 'this'; *šul* 'that'.

INTERROGATIVE PRONOUNS
kəm 'who?'; *ni* /nəy/, 'what?'.

Numerals

1–10; *ber, ike, ös, dürt, biš, altı, ete, higeð, tuyıð, un. e* here is /ə/. Thus, *ete* is /yətə/. 20 *egerme* /yəgərmə/; 30 *utıð*; 40 *qırq*; 100 *yöð*. Numerals are followed by the singular of the noun enumerated.

Verb

JaNSSSR (vol. 2) lists five voices and six moods, with standard markers (*see* **Turkish Languages**) in their Bashkir format. Thus, e.g. the conditional marker – in Turkish *-sa-* – appears here as *-ha-*: *bar.ha.m* 'if I go'.

MOOD
Moods may be sub-divided into (a) those that take the predicative suffixes, and (b) those that take the possessive suffixes with certain changes: e.g. the ending of the first person plural is *-q* instead of *-bıð*; of third person singular $\emptyset$.

(a) The predicative suffixes are:

	Singular	Plural
1	-mVn	-bVð
2	-hVn	-hVgVð
3	-$\emptyset$	-$\emptyset$ + 1Vr (*or* -1VrðV$_2$r)

where V = *ə, ı, ö, o*, and V$_2$ = *a/ä*.

Only the intentional mood takes the predicative affixes; the marker is *-maqsı-*: *bar.maqsı.min* 'I intend to go'.

(b) Moods taking possessive affixes:

conditional: *bar.ha.m* 'if I go'
necessitative: *bar.ahım.bar* 'I have to go'
subjunctive: *barır inem* 'that I should go'

The imperative mood has $\emptyset$ in second person singular; *-gı* in second person plural.

The tenses of the indicative mood are similarly sub-divided by predicative or possessive ending:

(a) Predicative ending:

present: *bar.a.mın* 'I go'
future: *bar.a.saq.mın* 'I shall go'
reported past: *bar.yan.mın* '(it seems that) I went'

(b) Possessive suffixes:

past definite: *bar.dɪ.m* 'I went'
past habitual: *bar.a.toryanɪ.m* 'I was in the habit of going'
relative past: *bar.a.inem* 'when I went ...'

PASSIVE VOICE
The marker is *-l/n-*.

NEGATION
The general negative marker is *-ma/mä-*, unstressed, following the stem: e.g.
yaha 'to make', *yaháma* 'not to make'; *kit-* 'to go', *kitmä* 'not to go'. To negate
certain verbal forms, e.g. those with *-asaq-*, *-bar-*, the negating particles *yoq* and
tügel are used: e.g. *baryanɪm yoq* 'I didn't go (in general).'

PARTICIPIAL FORMS
-yan, *-ɪr*, *-yas* are used in the formation of compound tenses and of relative
clauses: e.g.

barɪr keše/barasaq keše 'the man who is coming/will come'
kilgänende belmänem 'I didn't know you had come'
uqɪy toryan kitap 'the book that is being read'

Postpositions

Examples:

following nominative: *menən* 'with': *ösön* 'for'; e.g. *xalɪq ösön* 'for the
  people';
following genitive of pronoun: *menən* 'with', e.g. *hineŋ menən* 'with you';
following dative: *saqlɪ* 'until', e.g. *bɪyɪya saqlɪ* 'until this year';
following ablative: *birle* 'since, from', e.g. *köððən birle* 'from autumn
  onwards'.

Such postpositions as /aθ/ 'down', /œθ/ 'up', *art* 'behind' follow dative, locative,
or ablative as required for sense (rest in a place or motion towards/from a place).

Loan-words in Bashkir

Russian and Arabic loans are illustrated in the following sentence:

Sovyet vlase yɪldarɪnda bašqort xalqɪnɪn əðəbiəte həm iskusstvohɪ ɪsɪn-
  ɪsɪndan səskə atɪuya ölgəšte.
'In the years of Soviet rule the literature and art of the Bashkir people really
  came to bloom.'

Vlase = vlast' 'power, rule' (Russian); *iskusstvo* 'art' (Russian); *sovyet* 'Soviet'
(Russian); *xalq* 'people' (Arabic); *əðəbiət* 'literature, culture' (Arabic).

Word order

As normal in Turkic.

Тäӱлä Ґӱз булган. Ґӱз Хозайза булган. Ґӱз Хозай булган. Ул тäӱлä Хозайза булган. Бар нäрсä лä Ул (Ґӱз) аркыры була баштаган; нейгенä була баштаґа ла, Анґыз була баштамаган. Андā теректек булган, теректек кешелäрзен йактыґы булган. Йакты карангылыкта йактырыб тора, караңгылык аны йеңä-алмай. Хозайзан йебäрелгäи бер кеше булган; анын исеме Іоаниъ (булган). Ул таныктык итäргä килгäи, ул аркыры барыґыла эшäнґендäр тиб, йактыны таныктарга (килгäн). Ул йактылык булмаган, ул йактылыкты таныктар öсöн йебäрелгäн.

BASQUE

INTRODUCTION

Euskara, as the Basques call their language, is an isolate, with no known congeners. Structural analogies with Caucasian languages have been pointed out, and from time to time attempts are made to connect Basque with various other languages and language families. No conclusive evidence has been adduced, however, and it seems safer to regard Basque as a relic of the prehistoric language or languages spoken in the Iberian peninsula before the arrival of Indo-European.

Basque is spoken today by over half a million people in *Euskal Herria*, the Basque country in North-Western Spain (Guipuzcoa, Vizcaya, Navarra), and by about 100,000 in the Pyrénées-Atlantiques region of France.

The language is attested in fragmentary form from c. AD 1000 onwards. The first Basque printed book appeared in 1545. Writing in Basque is now recovering from the period of proscription following the Spanish Civil War.

SCRIPT

Roman alphabet; the orthography, which is not yet stable, has been influenced by Spanish.

PHONOLOGY

Consonants

> stops: /p, b, t, d, k, g/; Saltarelli (1988) includes two palatal plosives /tj, dj/, which are notated in Basque orthography as *tt*, *dd*.
> affricates: /ts, t̯s, tʃ/: notated in the orthography as *tz*, *ts*, *tx*; /ts/ is lamino-alveolar; /t̯s/ is apico-alveolar. The difference is phonemic: cf. *atzo* 'yesterday', *atso* 'old'.
> fricatives: /f, z̦, s̩, ʃ/; the lamino-alveolar /z̦/ is notated as *z*, the apico-alveolar /s̩/ as *s*; /ʃ/ is notated as *x*. /z̦/ and /s̩/ have voiceless allophones before voiceless consonants or vowels.
> nasals: /m, n, ɲ/;
> laterals and flaps: /l, ʎ, r, rr/.

Vowels

> i, e, a, o, u

diphthongs:

au, ai, ei, oi, ui

MORPHOLOGY AND SYNTAX

Basque has no grammatical gender, though a gender distinction is made in the second person singular of the synthetic conjugation: cf. *hik daukak* 'you (fam. masc.) have', *hik daukan* 'you (fam. fem.) have'.

ARTICLES

The definite article is affixed: *-a* (sing.), *-ak* (pl.), e.g. *mendi* 'mountain', *mendia* 'the mountain', *mendiak* 'the mountains'. As indefinite article, the numeral *bat* 'one', may be used: e.g. *gizon bat* 'a man'. *Bat* may take the case endings: e.g. *mendi bat.en igaera* 'the ascent of a mountain'.

Noun

DECLENSION

Nine cases may be distinguished, but several additional endings occur. Basic cases of *gizon* 'man':

nominative	gizon	comitative	gizon**arekin**
ergative	gizon**ak**	inessive	gizon**an**
dative	gizon**ari**	aditive	gizon**ara**
genitive	gizon**ako** (of origin)	ablative	gizon**atik**
	gizon**aren** (of possession)		

The plural endings may be illustrated with *etxe* /etʃe/, 'house':

nominative	etxe**ak**	comitative	etxe**ekin**
ergative	etxe**ek**	inessive	etxe**etan**
dative	etxe**ei**	aditive	etxe**etara**
genitive	etxe**en**/etxe**etako**	ablative	etxe**etatik**

The distinction between the two genitive forms is seen in a phrase such as *Bilboko arte ederren museoa* 'the museum of (poss.) fine art of (origin) Bilbao' (*eder* 'beautiful, fine'; *-(r)en* = gen. ending). Cf. *Manuren semea* 'Manu's son'; *nere aitarekin* 'with my father'; *etxean* 'in the house'; *menditik* 'from the mountain'.

Adjective

As attribute, adjective follows noun, e.g. *asto txuri bat* 'a white donkey', and takes the definite article: e.g. *etxe𝟢 ederra* 'the beautiful house'; *gure ahuntz politak* 'our pretty goats' (*polit* 'pretty'). Case endings are also transferred to the adjective: e.g. *ardo berria za(ha)gi berrietan* 'new wine in(to) old bottles' (*ardo* 'wine'; *berri* 'new'; *za(ha)gi* 'bottle').

Pronoun

The personal forms with the present tense of *izan* 'to be', are:

	Singular	*Plural*
1	ni naiz	gu gara
2	hi haiz	zu zara; zuek zarete
3	hura da	haiek dira

The resumed characteristic (*n-* in first person singular, *g-* in first person plural, *z-* in second person plural) is found throughout the verbal system (*d-* is characteristic of third person).

The ergative forms are: *nik*, *hik*, *hark*; *guk*, *zuk/zuek*, *haiek*.

The personal pronouns may take other cases: cf. *zeuk Nigan, eta Ni zuengan* 'ye in me, I in you' (St John's gospel, 14.20), but see note on verbal system, below.

The possessive forms are: *nire*, *zure*, *bere*; *gure*, *zuen*, *beren*.

DEMONSTRATIVE PRONOUN
Three degrees of relative distance: *hau* 'this' – *hori* 'that' – *hura* 'that (yonder)'; these are postpositional: *gizon hori* /ɔri/ 'that man'.

INTERROGATIVE PRONOUN
nor 'who?, – with ergative, *nork*; *zer* 'what?'

RELATIVE PRONOUN
See **Verb**, below.

Numerals

1–10: *bat, bi, hiru, lau, bost, sei, zazpi, zortzi, bederatzi, hamar*; 11 *hamaika*; 12 *hamabi*, 13 *hamahiru*; 20 *hogei*; 30 *hogei eta hamar*; 40 *berrogei*; 60 *hirurogei*; 70 *hururogei eta hamar*; 80 *laurogei*; 100 *ahun*. That is, vigesimal system. Apart from *bat*, which follows its noun, the numerals precede the noun, which is in the singular: e.g. *bost seme* 'five sons'.

Verb

As in Georgian, a relatively simple nominal system is accompanied by a very complicated verbal system. But, whereas in Georgian the complication lies in the proliferation of permutations and combinations to which the sense-verb is subjected, in Basque the sense-verb itself usually appears in simple stem or participial form, accompanied by an enormously rich network of auxiliary forms which are deictically coded for person and regimen, and which are quasi-bound in the sense that they only acquire full meaning when associated with a sense-verb stem. For example, by itself *diot* indicates action by first person singular directed in some way at third person singular, i.e. it specifies a deictic relationship. Following the stem *eman* 'to give', plus a noun, e.g. *liburu* 'book', *liburu eman* **diot**, *diot* generates the meaning '**I** give **him** a book'. If the deixis code is changed by substituting *dizut* for *diot*, the meaning becomes 'I give **you** a book'. A quantitative change can also be introduced by changing *dizut* to *dizkizut*: this indicates that '**I** gave **you** more than one object – books'.

With this sort of deictic relational network at its disposal, Basque makes very sparing use of personal pronouns. Nouns continue to be marked: e.g. *Gizonari liburua eman dio* 'I give the book **to the** man.'

All Basque verbs can be conjugated thus analytically or periphrastically, but half a dozen crucially important auxiliaries and a few other verbs – e.g. *joan* 'to go', *etorri* 'to come', *eduki* 'to have', *jakin* 'to know', *esan* 'to say', *ikusi* 'to see' – retain a synthetic form of conjugation, which seems to have been formerly more widespread. As an example of a synthetic conjugation, here are the present and past-tenses of *etorri* 'to come':

	Present		*Past*	
	Singular	*Plural*	*Singular*	*Plural*
1	ni nator	gu gatoz	ni nentorren	gu gentozen
2	hi hator	zu zatoz	hi hentorren	zu zentozen
3	hura dator	haiek datoz	hura zetorren	haiek zetozen

THE ANALYTICAL CONJUGATION

The most important auxiliaries are (present and past forms):

da – zen: used to conjugate intransitive verbs:
du – zuen: used to conjugate transitive verbs;
zaio – zitzaion: with indirect object; subject in possessive case;
dio – zion: polypersonal (direct and indirect objects).

Altogether, these four auxiliaries produce about a thousand forms, which are:

1. Coded for person and deixis: e.g. *diot – dizut*, as shown above.
2. Coded for number:

   (a) of subject: *du – dizut*, as shown above.
   (b) of object: *diot* indicates singular object; *dizkiot* indicates plural object.

3. Tense: from *du*, *nauzu* indicates second person/first person singular in present; *ninduzun* in past.
4. Mood: e.g. *niezaioke* indicates potential action of first person singular on third person singular, involving singular object; *niezazkioke* indicates the same deixis but involving plurality of object; *zeniezazkigukeen* indicates potential action in past by second person plural on first person plural involving a plurality of objects.

SOME NOTES ON THE MAIN AUXILIARIES

Izan 'to be'; the present tense is given above (*see* **Pronoun**); the past tense is *ni nintzen, hi hintzen, hura zen; gu ginen, zu zinen/zuek zineten, haiek ziren*. The general negating particle is *ez*: e.g. *ni euskalduna naiz* 'I am a Basque'; *ni euskalduna ez naiz* 'I am not ...' In the negative, *ez* plus auxiliary precede the sense-verb: e.g. *ni etorri naiz* 'I have come', *ni ez naiz etorri* 'I haven't ...'

Future: participle in *-ko* + auxiliary: e.g. *ni etorri.ko naiz* 'I'll come'.

Du – zuen: this auxiliary is used in the conjugation of transitive verbs; the nominal/pronominal subject is in the ergative with *-k*: e.g. with *ikusi* 'see': (*zuk*) *ikusi nauzu* 'you have seen me'; (*guk*) *ikusi zaitugu* 'we have seen you', where *nauzu* encodes second person action on first person and *zaitugu* encodes first person plural action on second person. In *ekarriko zituen* 'he was going to bring them', *zituen* encodes third person singular action on third person plural. A further example: *Maite **zintudan**, baina zuk ez **ninduzun** maite* 'I loved you, but you did not love me'.

Zaio – zitzaion: this auxiliary is used with stative verbs, intransitive verbs with ethic dative, and verbs whose subject is in possessive case, and is usually translated in English as transitive verb + direct object: e.g. (*niri*) *jausi zait* 'to-me it has fallen' = 'I've dropped it'; (*niri*) *jausi zaizkit* 'to-me they have fallen' = 'I've dropped them'; *gozo zaio* 'pleasant to him' = 'he likes it'; *haurrak joan zaizkio* 'the children have gone off on-him' = 'his children have left him' (where *zaizkio* indicates indirect action on third person singular by third person plural); *liburua galdu zait* 'the book has gone lost on me' = 'I've lost my book'.

Altogether, the *zaio – zitzaion* paradigm, including present, past, conditional, resultant, potential, subjunctive, and imperative forms for all persons and both numbers, has a total of about 280 forms, not all of them in everyday use.

Dio – zion: this auxiliary is used in polypersonal verbs with direct and indirect objects, of the type 'I gave it to him', *eman nion*; cf. *eman dizkiot* 'I give him things'; *eman nizkion* 'I gave him things'; *gutun bat idatzi zion* 'he wrote him a letter'.

The *dio – zion* paradigm has a total of about 700 forms.

RELATIVE FORMS

-(e)n is added to relevant auxiliary form: *da* → *den*; *gizonari eman dioten ogia* 'the man to whom I gave the bread' (*ogi*); *ogia eman diten gizona* 'the man who gave me the bread'.

As mentioned above, in connection with *zaio – zitzaion*, the deictic grid has full conditional, subjunctive, potential, resultative, and imperative versions. Cf. *ekar **ziezagun*** 'so that he might bring us (a singular object)'; *ekar **ziezazkigun*** 'so that he might bring us (a plurality)'.

Ba- is a characteristic prefix for auxiliaries in the conditional mood: e.g. *erosi nai **ba.dituzu*** 'if you want (*nai*) to buy (*erosi*) …'

Postpositions

These may follow plain stem or case ending: e.g. *bostak aldean* 'about 5 o'clock'; *bihar arte* 'until tomorrow'. Following genitive: *euskaldunen artean* 'among the Basques'; *gerla zibilaren ondo.tik* 'since the (time of) the Civil War'; *mahai(a.ren) azpian* 'on the table'.

Word order

Free.

Asieran Itza ba-zan,
ta Itza Yainkoagan zan,
ta Itza Yainko zan.
[2] Asieran Bera Yainkoagan zan.
[3] Dana Berak egiña da,
ta Bera gabe ez da egin
egindako ezer ere.
[4] Beragan bizitza zan,
ta bizitza gizargia zan;
[5] ta argia iluntan ageri da,
ta ilunak ez zun artu.
[6] Gizon bat azaldu zan
Yainkoak bidalia;
aren izena Yon.
[7] Aitortzat au etori zan,
argiaren aitortzat,
aren bidez guziek siñesteko.
[8] Ez zan ori argia,
argiaz aitor egitekoa baño.

BATAK (Toba)

INTRODUCTION

Batak belongs to the Malayo-Polynesian branch of Austronesian, and is spoken by about 2½ to 3 million people in Northern Sumatra. The Batak have a rather rich traditional literature, consisting mainly of folk-tales in prose, orations, panegyrics, and ritual texts for use in divination and invocation. Van der Tuuk in his grammar (1864–7) describes special forms of Batak, e.g. the language of keening, the esoteric language of the 'muttered invocation', and the private language of the camphor-gatherers. There are several widely differing dialects.

SCRIPT

Based on an Indic original. Originally used on bark and bamboo.

PHONOLOGY

Consonants

    stops: p, b, t, d, k, g; palatalized: t', d'/d
    nasals: m, n, ŋ
    fricatives: s, h
    lateral and flap: l, r
    semi-vowels: w, j

There is extensive juncture sandhi, especially of nasals with homorganic stops: e.g. *t'an.pasaribu* → [t'appasaribu].

Vowels

    i, e, ɛ, a (→ [ɔ]), ɔ, o, u

Stress

Stress is a function of word class and of morphophonology.

MORPHOLOGY AND SYNTAX

Noun

Natural gender is marked by lexical means: e.g. *hoda* 'horse', *hoda tunggal* 'stallion'. Nominals are primary (e.g. *biyang* 'dog', *gadja* 'elephant') or derived. The latter form an open class, drawn regularly from transitive/intransitive verbal stems. This process is two-way, in that verbal valencies may be applied to nominal stems. Van der Tuuk relates the derived nominal to the passive form of the verb.

> the passive imperative form of a transitive verb = stem = nominal form;
> the passive imperative form of an intransitive verb = stem = nominal form
>   with stress shift.

If the verb has a *pa-* or *mar-* prefix, the nominal form = active verbal substantive: e.g. *mar.mahan: par.mahan* 'a herdsman'.

NUMBER
Not normally marked. Plurality is inherent in certain verb forms, e.g. *mar.habang.an* 'to fly' (where a flock of birds is concerned).

POSSESSION
Positional, or with linker *di*: e.g. *isi ni huta* 'the contents/inhabitants of the village'.

Adjectives

The adjectival verbs have the *ma-* prefix; the prefix is discarded to give an attributive form: e.g. *ma.rára bunga on* 'this flower is red' (verb *ma.rára* 'to be red'); *rará bunga on* 'red – this flower'. Cf. *balga biyang on* 'this dog is large'; *biyang na balga* 'a dog that is large' (*na* is relative pronoun).

Pronoun

Personal independent with enclitic forms:

	Singular		Plural	
	Independent	*Enclitic*	*Independent*	*Enclitic*
1	au	-hu	*incl.* hita, *excl.* hami	-ta, -nami
1	ho	-mu	hamu	-muna
3	ibana	-na	nasida	-nasida

DEMONSTRATIVE PRONOUN
on 'this'; *an* 'that'; *aduwi* 'that yonder'.

INTERROGATIVE PRONOUN
ise 'who?'; *aha* 'what?'.

RELATIVE PRONOUN
na.

Numerals

1–10: *sada, duwa, tolu, opat, lima, onom, pitu, uwalu, siga, sappalu*; 11 *sappulu.sada*; 12 *sappulu.duwa*; 20 *duwa pulu*; 30 *tolu pulu*; 100 *sa.ratus*.

Verb

A few simple stems are in use, e.g. *lao* 'to go', *hundul* 'to sit', but the great majority of Batak verbs are derivatory. Derivation takes place by means of (a) simple prefix, often plus suffix, e.g. *mang- – mang-....-hon*; or (b) composite prefix, again often with associated suffix, e.g. *ma.si-* stem (*-hon*). With these affixes a very extensive and subtly differentiated lexicon of verbal forms is generated, not only from primary verbal stems but also from numerals, nominals, adjectival stems, etc. The underlying stem itself may not always be attested. The forms express many shades of modality and relationship to locus and nature of action, the involvement of other persons as direct or indirect objects, beneficiaries (coded for number); nuances which cut across the simple active/passive, transitive/intransitive oppositions. The class is open.

Van der Tuuk (1864 (1971)) classifies verbs in terms of formation, version (broadly, transitive/intransitive), and meaning. The most important prefixes are:

(a) simple: *ma-, mang-, mar-, pa-, ha-*; used with zero suffix or with *-i, -hon, -an*. The infixes *-um-, -ur-/-al-/-ar-* are also found.
(b) composite: *ma.hi-, ma.si-, ma(ng).hu-, mang.si-, pa.tu-*; again, + suffixes. There is extensive use of sandhi at junctures.

Some representative examples:

ma-: qualitative and stative verbs, e.g. *ma.rara* 'to be red'; *ma.timbo* 'to be high'; *ma.bugang* 'to be wounded'.
mang- intransitive, e.g. *mambuwat boru* 'to get married';

> involuntary action, e.g. *mang.embang* 'to unfold' (as a flower);
> involuntary action on something, e.g. *maninggang* 'to fall accidentally on sth.'.

mang-....-i: transitive, e.g. *mang.a.napuran.i* 'give betel to someone' (*napuran* 'betel').
mang-....-hon: with reference to a desired or intended result, e.g. *man.angi.hon* 'to listen for something'; *mang.adop.pon* 'to turn to face someone; make use of something', e.g. *mang.ultop.pon* 'to blow (arrow) from blowpipe'.
mar-: to own object denoted by nominal, e.g. *mar.hoda* 'to own a horse'.
mar-....-hon: causal, e.g. *mar.bada.hon* 'to have a quarrel over

something'.

mar-...-an: indicates plurality in action, e.g. *mar.songgop.an* 'to roost, perch' (many birds).

-um-: involuntary action, e.g. *s.um.urut* 'to recoil involuntarily'.

pa-: reciprocity, e.g. *pa.djuppa* 'to meet each other'; plus reduplication, e.g. *pa.djuppa-djuppa* 'to meet each other often'.

pa-...-hon: cause someone to enter a certain state or condition, e.g. *pa.pande.hon* 'to make someone a labourer'; *pa.pahat.ton* 'to make an animal eat'; to express ordinal, e.g. *pa.duwa.hon* 'to be second'.

ma.si-: to acquire the object denoted by stem, e.g. *ma.si.hotang* 'to get cane'.

ma.si-...-an: plural reciprocity, e.g. *ma.si.pangan.an napuran* 'to eat each other's betel'.

mar.si...: onset of action leading to intended or desired result, e.g. *mar.si.gorgor* 'to flame up' (of funeral pyre).

TENSE

Expressed by adverbs of time (of which there are several, expressing in addition aspect) or is deduced from context. Demonstrative adverbs of place or time are made by prefixing prepositions; e.g. *i-* is a demonstrative pronoun of past time, e.g. *pidong i* 'the bird referred to' (i.e. not visible); *di s.i* 'at that time'; this can be used as a past-tense marker.

NEGATIVE

The particle is *inda(d)ong*, abbreviated to *indang*: e.g. *indang/indaong hu.boto* 'I don't know'; *indang adong* 'is not there'.

Sowada 'neither': e.g. *Sowada hu.ida sowada hu.boto* 'I haven't seen it and I don't know about it.'

PASSIVE FORMS

In place of a simple passive form available for all verbs in mechanical fashion, Batak has several passives, whose usage depends on the circumstances attending the action, and on such factors as agency, intention, accident, completion/non-completion, etc. The relationship between the passive form and the derived nominal has already been mentioned.

1. Pronominal marking for agent may be suppressed, especially in third person where *di-* is prefixed to the nominal form: e.g. *di.buwat* 'is taken by him/her'; *di.timbung ma tu aek* 'the river was jumped into by him' (*aek* 'river'; *tu* 'towards, into'; *ma* is particle of continuing action).

2. Practicability of action is expressed by the prefixes *tar-*, *ha-*: e.g. *tar.tuhor hita* 'it can be bought by us'. Chance occurrence: e.g. *tar.podom* 'falling-asleep by him' = 'he has fallen asleep'. With qualitative verbs: e.g. *tar.gorsing* 'be yellowish'.

3. Nominal form + preposition *ni*: e.g. *ni.ultopmi* 'the thing shot at by you with your blowpipe'; *pidong na ni.ultopmi* 'the bird (which is) the thing shot at ...'. Hence, many substantives are formally passives of this type: e.g. (*na*) *pinahan* 'the things that have been fed' = 'the cattle'.

Preposition

Examples: *di* 'in, at, because of', etc.': *di au* 'because of me'; *dibana* 'at his place, with him'; *tu* 'towards': *tu tonga ni uma* 'to (the place of) the field'. The preposition may not require a verb of motion: e.g. *tu aek ibana* 'he goes/has gone/will go to the river' (*aek*).

Compound words

a.b. where b qualifies a: e.g.

ari.logo 'dry weather', *ari.udan* 'wet weather' (*ari* 'day');
anak.tubu 'newly born child' (*anak* 'male child'); separable for pronominal
    enclitic, e.g. *anak**ku**.tubu i* 'my newly born child';
pande 'skilled at …', e.g. *pande.bodil* 'gunsmith' (*mamodil* 'to shoot at
    something with a gun');
gondang.dalan 'path-music' = 'music for the journey'

Word order

Basically SVO.

(Mark 3: 31-5)

188

BELORUSSIAN

INTRODUCTION

Belorussian is a member of the East Slavonic group of the Slavonic branch of Indo-European. Often regarded in the past as a dialect of Russian, it has now achieved official status as the language of the Belorussian Soviet Socialist Republic (BSSR) (capital Minsk). It derives from a complex of West Russian dialects which were spoken in the large area between the Pripet and the western Dvina, and which, from the thirteenth century onwards, coalesced towards a common norm. This process was hastened by the fact that an ecclesiastical form of West Russian was the official language of the Grand Duchy of Lithuania (thirteenth to sixteenth centuries). By the same token, Polish influence on Belorussian is due to Polish ascendancy within the Grand Duchy (Lithuanian itself was not used as a written language till the sixteenth/seventeenth centuries). Under the Russian tsars, Belorussian was proscribed. Since 1917, the language has been codified and standardized, and is now the vehicle for a considerable literature.

Belorussian means 'White Russian'. Exactly what 'white' means here is not clear. The authors (Birillo, Bulaxov, Sudnik) of the article on Belorussian in JaNSSSR, Vol. 1, 1966, interpret 'white' as meaning 'free' in contrast to the 'black' territories which were the first to succumb to the Grand Duchy in the thirteenth century.

Today, Belorussian is spoken in the BSSR and in the adjoining republics by about 9 million people. All are bilingual in Belorussian with Russian or Ukrainian.

SCRIPT

Cyrillic. The alphabet, fixed in 1933, is identical to the Russian alphabet, minus и, and plus the letters I /i/ and ў /w/. The digraphs дж and dz occur.

PHONOLOGY

Consonants

stops: p, b, t, d, k, (g)
affricates: ts, dz, tʃ, dʒ
fricatives: f, v, s, z, ʃ, ʒ, x, γ, h
nasals: m, n
lateral and flap: ł, r
semi-vowels: j, w

Followed by soft vowels, the following consonants are soft, i.e. palatalized: /p, b, f, v, m, s, z, ̇n, l, k, g (=[h]), x, γ/. /t/ and /d/ are hard only: their soft correlatives are /ts/ and /dz/.

Vowels

> hard: ɪ, e, a, o, u
> soft: i, ye, ya, yo, yu

/ɪ/ is notated as ы; /i/ as *i*; the remaining four soft vowels are notated as in Russian. The Cyrillic soft sign ь is used to mark /l, n, z, s, ts, dz/ as soft, e.g. in word-final position: e.g. *pisac'* 'to write' (-*i*-, here, being invariably soft, does not require marking). In this entry, ɪ = hard, /ɪ/; i = soft, /i/.

Some characteristics of the Belorussian phonological system:

1. *ciekannie*: Russ. *t'* = Bel. *c'*: e.g. *t'en'* 'shadow' = *c'en'*;
2. *dziekannie*: Russ. *d'* = Bel. *dz'*: e.g. *d'en* 'day' *dz'en'*;
3. initial *o* = /vo/, initial *u* = /vu/: e.g. *voka* 'eye', *vuxa* 'ear';
4. presence of voiced velar fricative: *gorad* 'town', /γorat/.
5. the shift of unstressed /o, ɛ/ to /a/ is regular in Russian, where, however, it is not notated in the orthography. In Belorussian it is notated, which complicates the inflectional system. Thus, *zólata* 'gold' – *zalatí* 'golden'.

Stress

On any syllable and movable.

MORPHOLOGY AND SYNTAX

Noun

Three genders: masculine, feminine, and neuter. Three declensions are distinguished:

1. *a*-stems: mostly feminine, e.g. *rabota* 'work', pl. *rabotɪ*;
2. *o*-stems: masculine and neuter, e.g. *stol* 'table', pl. *stalɪ*;
3. *i*-stems: feminine, *miš* 'mouse', pl. *mɪšɪ*.

A few neuter nouns can be declined either in a specific form or as (2) above: e.g. *imya* 'name' may have plural *imyonɪ* or *imi*.

Specimen declension of first declension feminine noun: *galava* 'head':

	Singular	Plural
nom.	galava	galovɪ
acc.	galavu	galovɪ
gen.	galavɪ	galow
dat.	galavye	galovam
instr.	galavoy	galovami
prep.	galavye	galovax

The nominal paradigms have a great many variants depending on phonetic environment: e.g. consonantal alternation in the prepositional case: *ruka* 'hand' – prep. *ruce*; *narod* 'people' – *narodze*; *malako* 'milk' – *malace*.

As in Russian, an animate/inanimate distinction is observed in the formation of the second declension masculine singular and the plural of all nouns: e.g. *brat* 'brother' – *brata* – *bratow* (gen. sing./pl.). For all nouns denoting inanimates, the accusative = the nominative.

Adjective

In general, as in Russian.

Pronoun

The first and second person series behave much as in Russian, with spelling differences: e.g. from *tɪ*, acc./gen. *cyabye*, but dative: *tabye*. The third person series is unique in Slavonic in that the palatalized onset of the oblique cases is also present in the nominative: *yon* – fem. *yana* – nt. *yano*; plural for all three genders: *yanɪ*.

DEMONSTRATIVE PRONOUN/ADJECTIVE
getɪ 'this'; *toy* 'that'.

INTERROGATIVE PRONOUN
xto 'who?'; *što* 'what?'

RELATIVE PRONOUN
As interrogative.

Numerals

Formally as in Russian, apart from spelling differences. As in Ukrainian, however, and in opposition to Russian, 2, 3, 4 are followed by nominative/accusative plural: e.g. *dva stalɪ* 'two tables'; *čatɪrɪ bratɪ* 'four brothers'.

Verb

The aspect/mood/tense system of Russian and Ukrainian is shared by Belorussian. Most Belorussian verbs are paired for aspect. The infinitive is in -*c'*, -*c* (-*cɪ* after velar).

ASPECT
Many perfective forms are made from imperative by prefixation.

Imperfective	Perfective
isci 'to go'	pa.isci
pisac' 'to write'	na.pisac'
magčɪ 'to be able'	z.magčɪ

The reverse process, imperfective form from perfective, may use, e.g. *-va-*: *vɪpisac'* 'to write out'; imperfective: *vɪpisvac'* 'to be writing out'.

VERBS OF MOTION
As in Russian and Ukrainian, the imperfective aspect is equipped to distinguish between a generalized concept and a particular application thereof: the latter can then be made perfective: e.g. *yezdzic'* 'to travel' (in general) – *yexac'* 'to make a specific journey': perf. *pa.yexac'*.

TENSES
There are two conjugations:

(a) verbs in *-(v)ac'*, *-yec'*, *-nuc'*, etc.;
(b) verbs in *-ic'*, *-ɪc'*, *-yec'*, etc.

Specimen present tense: conjugation (a), consonant stem: *nyesci* 'to carry' (stress on final syllable throughout):

Singular	*Plural*
nyasu	nyasyom
nyasyeš	nyesya**cyé**
nyasye	nyasuc'

It is noteworthy that the *-e-* of the second person singular ending does not change to *-o-* under stress.

Past tense: as in Russian and Ukrainian; in masculine form, *-l* → *-w*: e.g. *Čɪtaw* 'I (masc.) read'.

Future:

(a) perfective: formally, the present endings of the imperfective: e.g. *skažu* 'I shall say';
(b) imperfective: future tense of *bɪt'* + imperfective infinitive: e.g. *ya budu čɪtac'* 'I shall read/be reading'.

SUBJUNCTIVE MOOD
Past-tense + invariable particle бɪ.

IMPERATIVE
There are forms for second person singular and first and second persons plural: e.g. from *kupic'* 'to buy': *kupi*; *kupyem*, *kupicye*.

PARTICIPLES
Only the past passive participle is regularly used in spoken Belorussian: e.g. *napisanɪ* 'written'; *kuplyenɪ* 'bought'; *uzyatɪ* 'taken'.

Prepositions

Prepositions govern the oblique cases. Many prepositions can take more than one case, with corresponding changes in meaning. Usually, however, there is a preferred case, e.g. *dlya* 'for' with the genitive, *k/ka* 'to' with the dative, *ab* 'concerning' with the prepositional.

Word order

As in Russian.

> В начале было Слово, и Слово было у Бога, и Слово было Бог.
> 2. Оно было в начале у Бога.
> 3. Все чрез Него на̀чало быть, и без Него ничто не на̀чало быть, что̀ на̀чало быть.
> 4. В Нем была жизнь, и жизнь была свет человеков;
> 5. И свет во тьме светит, и тьма не объяла его.
> 6. Был человек, посланный от Бога; имя ему Иоанн.
> 7. Он пришел для свидетельства, что-бы свидетельствовать о Свете, дабы все уверовали чрез него.
> 8. Он не был свет, но *был послан*, чтобы свидетельствовать о Свете.

BELUDZH

See **Baluchi**.

BENGALI (*bāṅlā*)

INTRODUCTION

This Eastern New Indo-Aryan language is the official language of Bangladesh, where it is spoken by about 110 million people, and the official regional language for another 55 million people in the Indian state of West Bengal. There are also sizable Bengali-speaking communities in Orissa, Assam, Bihar, Tripura, and Meghalaya. Along with its close congeners, Oriya and Assamese, Bengali crystallized from the Magadhi Apabhraṁśa, roughly between AD 1000 and 1200. Texts dating from this period (e.g. the esoteric Buddhist–Tantric hymns known as *Caryāpada*) show general Magadhan areal features, but are usually described as being in Old Bengali. Middle Bengali was the vehicle for a very rich literature on traditional Indian themes, which is remarkable in view of the fact that by then Bengal was Moslem; indeed, Bengal remained part of the Mughal Empire until the eighteenth century. The British take-over in the nineteenth century added a third strand to an already composite cultural scene. Bengal now became the focal point of European cultural influence in India, and literary genres, alien to the sub-continent, began to appear: e.g. the novel, first in imitation of Scott, but soon developing to culminate in the socio-political realist novel of criticism and protest. The list of outstanding names includes Sáratcan-dra Caṭṭopādhyāy and one figure of world stature – Rabīndranāth Ṭhākur. A key role in the formation and education of a secularized and anti-traditionalist reading public was played by critical, often pro-Marxist periodicals such as *Kallol* (1923 onwards). Mention should also be made of the rich Bengali folk-literature, the songs of the Bāuls, or wandering minstrels, and the yātrās, nocturnal celebrations of Hindu gods and goddesses.

The numerous dialects are classified by most authorities on a broad east/west basis. Some are highly divergent, e.g. the Chittagong dialect. Until the twentieth century Bengali was written in a somewhat artificial, heavily Sanskritized book-language known as *sādhu-bhāṣā*. Modern writing is almost entirely in *calit-bhāṣā*, a demotic based on the Calcutta colloquial. Even here, however, the distinction between book-language and spoken language persists; that is, even modern calit-bhāṣā is, in a sense, an artificial medium. Wherever philosophical or scientific terminology is required, of course, the limitless Sanskrit reservoir is always available. In addition, it should not be forgotten that most Bengalis are Moslems, and the language now contains several thousand Arabo-Persian words.

SCRIPT

Bengali shares with Assamese a specific derivative of the Devanagari character.

PHONOLOGY

Consonants

    stops: p, b, t, d, ʈ, ḍ, k, g
    aspirated: ph, (bh > β), th, dh, ʈh, ḍh, kh, gh
    affricate: unaspirated: tʃ, dʒ
            aspirated: tʃh, dʒh
    fricatives: ʃ, s, h
    nasals: m, n, ŋ
    laterals and flaps: l, r, ɽ, ɽh

In Bengali, as typically in the Magadhan daughter languages, the three sibilants of Sanskrit (dental, retroflex, and palatal) have coalesced to give /ʃ/ > /s/. Consonant clusters are simplified in pronunciation: e.g. *laksya* is realized as /lɔkkʰo/, *anekkṣan* as /ɔnekkʰon/, *pakši* as /pokkhi/.

Vowels

    i, e, æ, a, ɔ, o, u

All occur nasalized. Difference in length is not phonemic. The inherent vowel in the base consonantal form is /ɔ/, corresponding to Sanskrit/Hindi /a/. In the section on **Morphology and Syntax** below, *a* = /aː/, *ă* = /ɔ/.

'Vowel raising', a form of vocalic assimilation, is a characteristic feature of Bengali phonology. It can be broadly summarized as follows:

/ɔ, e, o/ → [o, i, u] if the following syllable contains /i/ or /u/
/i, u, e/ → [e, o, æ] if the following syllable contains /ɔ, a, e/ or /o/
/a/ →   [e] if the preceding syllable contains /i/
/a/ →   [o] if the preceding syllable contains /u/

For example, *cali* 'I go', is pronounced [coli]: /ɔ/ raised to [o] before /i/; from *šona* 'to hear': *šuni* 'I hear': /o/ → [u] before /i/; *iccha* 'wish' → *icche* : /a/ → [e], as preceding syllable contains /i/. The /ɔ/ → [o] and /e/ → [æ] shifts affect pronunciation only; the others are notated in the script.

Stress

On first syllable in citation form, on headword of phrase in speech.

MORPHOLOGY AND SYNTAX

Noun

Bengali has lost the grammatical gender system of Indo-Aryan, and has replaced it with a natural taxonomy of animate versus non-animate categories. Animates make a plural form in -(*e*)*ra*. For non-animates, there is a variety of affixes, e.g. -*guli*/-*a*/-*o*, -*šăkăl*, -*šăb*, -*šămăšto*, etc. Some vestiges remain of the typical Indo-Aryan association of certain endings with gender, e.g. the -*a*/-*i* opposition: *buṛa* 'old man', *buṛi* 'old woman'.

CASE
Only the genitive marker -(*e*)*r* is obligatory. There follow specimen declensions of animate *manuṣ* 'man', and non-animate *nădi* 'river':

	Singular	Plural	Singular	Plural
nom.	manuṣ /maːnus/	manuṣera	nădi	nădiguli
gen.	manuṣer	manuṣder (ke)	nădir	nădigulir
dat.	manuṣke	manuṣder	nădike	nădigulike
acc.	manuṣkc	manuṣder	nădi	nădiguli
loc.	manuṣe	—	nădite	—

These endings are typical; for all cases except the genitive, however, there is a choice of ending. There is a tendency for the agglutinative plural suffixes -*šăb*, -*šăkăl*, etc. to be used with animates as well.

The enclitics -*ṭa*/*ṭi* may act as defining articles: e.g. *Năgărṭa khub băṛo* 'The town is very big.'

Adjective

As attribute the adjective is indeclinable and precedes the noun. A periphrastic comparative is made by means of *čeye* (the perfective participle of *čaoya* /tʃawa/ 'to look at') + genitive case: e.g. *Še amar čeye băṛo* 'He is older than I am.'

Pronoun

PERSONAL INDEPENDENT
In contrast to the dual base pattern found in the pronominal system of Western New Indo-Aryan, Bengali uses single bases to which endings are added agglutinatively: sing. 1 *ami*; 2 *tumi* (familiar), *apni* (polite); 3 *še* (familiar), *tini* (polite). The plural forms are: *amra*, *tomra*, *apnara*, *tăhara*/*tara*. These are declined as nouns: *ami*, *amar*, *amake*, etc.: e.g. *Tini amader kače prătidin ašten* 'He came to us every day' (the postposition *kače* 'to, at', takes genitive case).

DEMONSTRATIVE PRONOUN
Three degrees of removal are recognized: *e*, *iha*, *ini* 'this' (proximate); *o*, *uha*, *uni*, 'that' (distal); *še*, *taha*, *ta* 'that' (not visible but known).

INTERROGATIVE PRONOUN
ke 'who?'; *ki* 'what?'

RELATIVE PRONOUN
ǰe/ǰini/ǰa + correlative: e.g. *ǰe...še*; *ǰini...tini*

> **ǰe** lokṭa kal ekhane čhilo, **še** abar eseče
> 'The man who was here yesterday has come again'

> Tumi **ǰe**khane thakbe, ami.o **še**khane thakba
> 'Where you will be, there shall I be also'

Numerals

1–10: *æk*, *dui*, *tin*, *čar*, *pāč*, *čhɔě*, *šat*, *aṭ*, *nɔě*, *dɔš*. 11–19: the forms are based on the units, ending in *-o*: e.g. *ægaro*, *baro*, *tæro*, *čoddo*, *pɔnero*. 20 *biš*; 30 *triš*; 40 *čolliš*; from 20 to 99 the forms are unpredictable, though decade + 9 is always related to the following decade: e.g. 30 *triš*; 39 *unɔčolliš*; 40 *čolliš*; 49 *unɔpɔ̃čaš*; 50 *pɔ̃nčaš*. 100 /šɔto/ (the word is written as *šɔtɔ*: the second *ɔ* is raised to /o/).

Verb

Roots are mono- or disyllabic. Many derived bases are made from nouns by adding *-a*: e.g. *ghum* 'sleep': *ghumana* 'to sleep'. The rules for vowel harmony (see above) apply throughout the verbal system: e.g.

> root *čăla* 'to go': /tʃɔlo/ 'you go', /tʃoli/ 'I go';
> root *dekha* 'to see'; /dækho/ 'you see', /dekhi/ 'I see';
> root *lekha* 'to write': /lekho/ 'you write', /likhi/ 'I write'.

On the basis of such alternations, Chatterji (cited in Zograph 1982) has divided Bengali verbs into seven classes.

Aspect/tense markers are added to the stem before the personal inflections: e.g. *-čh-* for imperfective/continuative, *-b-* for future, *-l-* for past.

TENSE SYSTEM
Number is not marked. The first person has one form for both singular and plural: e.g. *jani* 'I know/we know'. The second person has three forms depending on status of addressee: familiar, everyday polite, and respectful; typical endings are *-i*, *-e*, *-en/-iš*, *-o*, *-en*. The third person has an ordinary form in *-e/-o* and a respectful in *en*. Thus, the form *janen*, for example, may mean 'you know' (sing./pl.), 'he/she knows' or 'they know'. The correct meaning can be fixed by the personal pronoun.

As an example of tense formation, here are the third person ordinary forms of the indicative mood of the root *kɔra* 'to do' (čalit-bhaṣa forms as pronounced):

simple present	kɔre 'does'
imperfective present	korče 'is doing'
perfective present	koreče 'has done'

simple past	korlo 'did'
imperfective past	korčhilo 'was doing'
perfective past	korečhilo 'had done'
habitual past	korto 'would do'
future	korbe 'will do'
imperative mood	koruk 'let him/her (etc.) do'

NON-FINITE FORMS

There are two verbal nouns: present -a/-wa/-na etc., and future in -(i)ba. Participles: imperfective in -(i)te, perfective in -iya/-e and conditional in -(i)le: e.g. *Ami kičhu kărte pari na* 'I can't do anything'; *Še kătha šune apni ki bălečhilen*? 'What did you say when you heard that?'

CAUSATIVE

The marker is -a- between stem and ending: e.g.

jana 'to know': *janana* 'to inform' (/janano/)
dekha 'to see': *dekhana* 'to show' (/dekhano/)

PASSIVE

An impersonal construction involving nominalization is preferred: e.g. the use of the verbal noun in -a, etc. plus an auxiliary, /jawa/ 'to go', or /hɔwa/ 'to be'. The auxiliary does not agree with the logical subject: e.g. *amake pawa gælo* 'to-me finding it-went' = 'I was found'; *E rasta diye jawa jay na* 'this street going-along goes not' = 'One cannot go along this street.'

NEGATIVE

The particle is *na*, with allophones [ne,ni]. It is never stressed. Example: *Tar sambandhe kičhui jani ne* 'I know nothing about it.'

Postpositions

Postpositions follow either the nominative or the genitive: e.g. *ţebiler upăr* 'on the table'; *ghărer bhităre* 'inside the house'.

The perfective participles of certain verbs, e.g. /dewa/ 'to give', /newa/ 'to take', act as postpositions: e.g. from /tʃawa/ 'to look at', /tʃeye/ has come to mean 'than' (*see* **Adjective**, above). Similarly, /theke/ from /thaka/ 'to stay', means 'from'; /diye/ from /dewa/ means 'through': *Janala diye dekhi* 'I look through the window.'

Word order

SOV is normal.

১ আদিতে বাক্য ছিলেন, এবং বাক্য ঈশ্বরের কাছে ছিলেন, এবং বাক্য ঈশ্বর ছিলেন।

২,৩ তিনি আদিতে ঈশ্বরের কাছে ছিলেন। সকলই তাঁহার দ্বারা হইয়াছিল, যাহা হইয়াছে, তাহার কিছুই

৪ তাহা ব্যাতিরেকে হয় নাই। তাঁহার মধ্যে জীবন ছিল,

৫ এবং সেই জীবন মনুষ্যগণের জ্যোতি ছিল। আর সেই জ্যোতি অন্ধকার মধ্যে দীপ্তি দিতেছে, আর অন্ধকার তাহা গ্রহণ * করিল না।

৬ এক জন মনুষ্য উপস্থিত হইলেন, তিনি ঈশ্বর হইতে

৭ প্রেরিত হইয়াছিলেন, তাঁহার নাম যোহন। তিনি সাক্ষ্যের জন্য আসিয়াছিলেন, যেন সেই জ্যোতির বিষয়ে সাক্ষ্য দেন, যেন সকলে তাঁহার দ্বারা বিশ্বাস

৮ করে। তিনি সেই জ্যোতি ছিলেন না, কিন্তু আসিলেন,

৯ যেন সেই জ্যোতির বিষয়ে সাক্ষ্য দেন

BERBER

INTRODUCTION

Berber is a member of the Afro-Asiatic (Semito-Hamitic) family. For the Greeks and Romans who colonized North Africa, the local inhabitants were βάρβαροι, *barbari*, who spoke a 'barbarous' tongue. The designation found its way into Arabic, and into English as Berber. An ethnonym for the mainstream of Berber tribes is *amažiyen*; the language is *tamažiyt*.

Berber seems to have been originally spoken in a strip of North African territory stretching from the Atlantic coast to the borders of Egypt. Over the last thousand years, Berber-speaking populations have spread beyond this original habitat, and today two or three hundred Berber dialects are spoken in about a dozen North African countries: Egypt, Libya, Tunisia, Algeria, Morocco, Mauretania, Mali, Burkina Faso, Niger, Chad. The total number of Berber speakers is put at c. 12 million. The principal dialects are: Shluh, Tamazight, and Riff in Morocco; Kabyle and Shawia in Algeria; Tamahaq (Tamashek) or Tuareg in several Saharan countries. Shluh is also known as *tašelḥait*, Shawia as *tašawit*, and Kabyle as *taqbaylit*.

SCRIPT

The oldest inscriptions in a Berber language – two diglot inscriptions found at Dugga in Tunisia – are written in Tifinag, which is still in use among the Tamahaq. This script is consonantal, written from right to left, with no way of indicating vowels. Ancient Berber inscriptions found in Libya, on the other hand, are in Roman script and are vocalized.

For administrative purposes, both Arabic and Roman scripts have been and still are used to notate Berber.

PHONOLOGY

A basic inventory includes the following phonemes:

Consonants

    stops: b, d, ḍ, t, k, g
    affricates: (in Kabyle and elsewhere: ts, dz, tʃ, dʒ)
    fricatives: f, s, z, ẓ, ʃ, ʒ, γ
    nasals: m, n
    lateral and flap: l, r
    semi-vowels: j, w

/ŧ, ḍ/ emphatics appear in Kabyle and other northern dialects. Several Arabic sounds – / ṣ, q, ʕ (= ain), ħ, ẖ/ – have been widely borrowed.

Consonants are long or short; long consonants are tense and held: C̄, not C.C. The contrast between C and C̄ is fundamental in Berber phonology.

Vowels

The basic contrast is between full grade /i, a, u/ and reduced or null grade /ə/ or Ø. Central Atlas Tamazight has the following inventory:

> front: i, ɪ, e
> central: ɛ, a, ə
> back: o, ʊ, u

All with allophones.

MORPHOLOGY AND SYNTAX

Most roots have two or three radicals; mono- and quadriliterals also occur. Common Afro-Asiatic features in Berber are: *t* as feminine marker, *k* as second person marker; the prefix/suffix conjugational paradigm; broken plural.

Nouns

There are two genders in Berber, masculine and feminine. All feminine nouns have *t-* initial, and feminine nouns with a final root consonant also take *-t* following this consonant: e.g. *agmar* 'horse', *tagmart* 'mare'; *afunas* 'bull', *tafunast* 'cow'; in Tamahaq *ekahi* 'cock', *tekahit* 'hen'. The feminine *t...t* circumfix is also used for certain natural phenomena: e.g. *tafukt* 'sun'; *takat* 'fire' (both of these are also feminine in Arabic).

NUMBER
(a) broken plural; (b) sound plural by affix:

(a) For example, (*a*)*drar* 'mountain', pl. *durar* or (*i*)*drarən*. In the broken plural, *-a-* is typical vocalization between R_2 and R_3 (R = radical): cf. *tamazirt* 'garden', pl. *timaza*r. In Tamahaq *atri* 'star', pl. *itran*; *amagur* 'old camel', pl. *imugar*.
(b) Suffixation: the characteristic ending is *-wən* (masc.), (*w*)*in* (fem.): e.g. *amɣar* 'man', pl. *imɣaren*; *tamɣart* 'woman', pl. *timɣarin*.

DECLENSION
Nouns are free or annexed; free nouns have vocalic initial (masc.) or *t-* + vowel (fem.). In the annexed state, expressing the genitival/relational link, masculine nouns take *w-*, feminine nouns do not change (i.e. = free state).

The genitival/relational construct is also expressed by the *-n-/-l-* link realized as /ən/ /nə/ /əl/ /lə/: e.g. Tamahaq *amɣar n aɣerem* 'the sheikh of the town'; *aiis wareɣ n abba* 'this horse of my father'; Central Atlas Tamazight *tamazirt l lmɣrib* 'the country of Morocco'; *ssuq l l.ḥdd* 'Sunday market'; Kabyle *aḇriḏ n ssuq* 'the road to market'.

Adjective

No specific form; a participial construction is used: e.g. Tamahaq *yulayən* 'being good' (masc.); *tulayət* (fem.); *illa yur.i aiis yulayən* 'I have a good horse' (*illa* 'there is'; *yur.i* 'to me'). Tamazight: *lāil amẓẓian* 'small boy', pl. *luašum imẓẓian*; *tarbat tamẓẓiant* 'small girl', pl. *tirbatin timẓẓiamin*.

Pronoun

Free and affixed forms. The free forms are used only for emphasis; the set is remarkable for having feminine forms for all persons and both numbers, with the sole exception of the first person singular (in Kabyle).

The Kabyle forms for emphatic free and post-prepositional affix are:

		Singular		Plural	
		Free	Affix	Free	Affix
1	masc.	nəkk	-i	nukni	-nəy
	fem.	–	–	nukə nti	-ntəy
2	masc.	kəčč	-k	kunwi	-wən
	fem.	kəm	-m	kunə mti	-nkwətt
3	masc.	nətta	-s	nutni	-nsən
	fem.	nəttaṯ	-s	nutə nti	-nsətt

For example, in Tamahaq: *akal n.nəy* 'our country'; *akal n wən* 'your (masc. pl.) country'.

There are also pronominal affix series for kinship terms and for direct and indirect object; these sets do not differ greatly from the one tabulated above. Cf. in Tamahaq:

ekfiy **ak** 'I gave you (masc.)'
ikfa ha**sen** 'he gave them (masc.)'
enniy **am** 'I told you (fem.)'
inna ha**s** 'he said to him/her'

With prepositions: Tamahaq *yur.i* 'at my home'; *dat em* 'before you (fem.)'; *gar awən* 'among/between you (masc. pl.)'

DEMONSTRATIVE PRONOUN
E.g. in Tamahaq and Kabyle: *wa* (masc.), pl. *wi*; *ta* (fem.), pl. *ti*.

INTERROGATIVE PRONOUN
ma 'who? what?'.

RELATIVE PRONOUN
The *wa* series can be used + resumptive pronoun, e.g. in Tamahaq: *ales wa as ekfiy tiraut* 'the man who to-him I gave the letter', (i.e. ... to whom ...); *araben wi*

asen ekfiɣ ehari'n azref 'the Arabs to whom I gave money'.

Numerals

The older (indigenous) numerical system is best preserved in Tamahaq and in the Tašelhayt of the High Atlas. Masculine and feminine forms are distinguished. The masculine forms, 1–10: *ya(n)*, *sin*, *kṛaḍ*, *ḳḳuẓ*, *səmmus*, *sḍis*, *sa*, *tam*, *tẓa*, *mra*; the feminine forms add *-t* to these (with some variants, e.g. the feminine of *sin* is *snat*).

This indigenous series has been largely replaced by the Arabic numerals from 3 onwards.

Verb

Three bases are distinguishable: (1) C_1C_2; (2) $C_1C_2C_2 + a$; (3) $C_1C_2 + i/a$; i.e. base 1 is unmarked for vocalization, bases 2 and 3 are marked. It is customary to designate these bases, (1) aorist–imperative, (2) strengthened aorist, (3) preterite.

Exactly how these bases are related to tense and mood – if, indeed, the categories of tense and mood can be usefully applied to the Berber verb – is a controversial question. Different researchers have distinguished an aorist and a preterite, a past tense from a present/future, a present/past from a future; some make an aspectual distinction between perfective and imperfective. Hanoteau in his grammar of Tamahaq (1896) uses the term 'aorist' for his '*mode unique*', which can refer equally to present, past, or future: this 'aorist' can be modulated by vocalization, e.g. by *-a-* between the second and third radicals: cf. *elkemeɣ* 'I follow, have followed', *elkemaɣ* 'I am now following'.

The general paradigm of personal markers, prefixal and suffixal, is:

		Singular	Plural
1		Ø R -əɣ	nə- R Ø
2		tə- R -t/-d	tə- R -əm
			tə- R -əmt
3	masc.	y/i- R Ø	Ø R -ən
	fem.	tə- R Ø	Ø R -ən(t)

DERIVED FORMS

s- causative; *t-* passive; *n-* reflexive/passive; e.g. Tamahaq forms of *əɣbər* 'to kick':

    səɣbər 'to cause to beat, kick'
    təɣbər 'to be beaten, kicked'
    nəɣbər 'to beat, kick each other'

PARTICIPLES

y/i…n is a frequent formula: e.g. in Tamahaq *ilkəm* 'follow', participle *ilkəmən*; in Kabyle, *əkšəm* 'go in', participle *ikəšmən*.

NEGATION

In Tamahaq, *ur* is a general negtator: e.g. *ur essineγ* 'I don't know'. Similarly in Tamazight, *ur d.idzi* 'he didn't come'. In Kabyle and some other dialects, /j/ acts as a negator in the past tense: e.g. *unfəγ* 'I left', *unifəγ* 'I didn't leave'.

Prefixed particles may be tense formants, e.g. *kelad* (imperfect), *ad* (future), in Tamahaq: *kelad iregeh dat.i* 'he was walking in front of me'. *-d* and *-n* are directional markers: e.g. *awi* 'to take', *awid* 'to bring', *awin* 'to take away'.

Prepositions

Examples: *dat* 'before', *deγ* 'in', *s* 'from', *γur* 'at the home of'; e.g. Tamahaq *deγ aγerem* 'in town'; *s akal ennit* 'from his country'.

Word order

VSO.

G'LIḂD̄Ā illa Aoual; Aoual illa for Rebbi, Aoual 1
illa d̂'Rebbi. Ouagi illa ġ'liḃd̄ā for Rebbi. Irkoul ⅔
elḱaouaïdj tsououqement yīs; oulach ain our-netsouou-
qem ara yīs, d̂eg irkoul ain itsououqemen. D'eg-s ai 4
thella thoud̂erth, thoud̂erth thella tsafath g-ergazen.
Thafath thechâcha ġe-ṭlam, ṭlam our ts-ifhim ara. 5

Illa íoun ourgaz, ism-is Yaḱyā, itsouchegâ-d s'for 6
Rebbi. Yousa-d ad̂-yili d̂' inígi, íouakken ad̂-ichehed̂ fef 7
thafath, íouakken ad̂-amnen irkoul fedéma en-*chehād̂a*-s.
Our ill'ara entsa s'iman-is tsafath, lamâna *itsouchegá-d* 8
íouakken ad̂-ichehed̂ fef thafath.

(Kabyle dialect)

BIKOL

INTRODUCTION

This language belongs to the Philippine group of Malayo-Polynesian languages. It forms a dialect complex sited between the Tagalog and Visayan speech areas in Southern Luzon and in the offshore islands. The standard dialect is that of Naga city. The standard language is used in local broadcasting and journalism. There are many Spanish loan-words.

SCRIPT

Romanization. Spanish loan-words are reproduced in terms of Bikol spelling.

PHONOLOGY

As in Tagalog, with addition of palatalized series: /t', d', s', n', l'/.

Stress

Stress is mobile: e.g. in the verb it shifts as tense, aspect, and modal markers are added.

MORPHOLOGY AND SYNTAX

Noun

Nouns are introduced by specific markers: *si/an* for focused items, *ki/ni/nin/kan* for non-focused items. These have plural forms, and there is a locative series in *ki/sa*: e.g. *nagpuli' si Carlos* 'Carlos went home'; *inapod ako nin maestro* 'a teacher called (*inapod*) me'; *nagbakal ako nin tinapay* 'I bought bread'; *nagbakal ako nin tinapay sa sa'od* 'I bought bread in the market.'

POSSESSION
The ending is *-ng/na*; e.g. *an mga linguahe.ng Pilipino* 'the languages of the Philippines'; or by simple apposition, e.g. *an lapis kan maestro* 'the teacher's pencil'. The word *mga* in the example above is pronounced /maŋga/ and is a plural marker: cf. *lalaki* 'boy', *mga lalaki* 'boys'.

Adjective

As attribute, adjective precedes noun, to which it is linked by *-ng/na*: e.g. *dakula* 'big', *an dakulang lapis* 'the big pencil'; *magayon* 'beautiful', *magayon na babayi*

206

'beautiful woman'. Adjectives are divided into *ma-* stems, *ha-* stems, and Ø-stems. The plural of *ma-* adjectives is made by reduplicating the first syllable after *ma-*: e.g. *magayon*, pl. *magagayon*. *ha-* stems insert *-r* with echo vowel: e.g. *halangkaw* 'tall', pl. *haralangkaw*.

COMPARATIVE

The Spanish *más* is generally used.

Pronoun

There are four sets corresponding to the marker series: in the *si* class the singular forms are: *ako*, *(i)ka*, *siya*; pl. *kami/kita*, *kamo*, *sinda*. The *ni* class has singular *ko*, *mo*, *niya*; pl. *mi/ta*, *nindo*, *ninda*. The forms for the *ki* and locative classes are identical: sing. *sakuya*, *saimo*, *saiya*: pl. *samuya'/satuya'*, *saindo*, *sainda*. The second form in the paired forms for first person plural is the inclusive form: e.g. *Ika an nagapod* 'Was it you that called?'; *Inapod ka niya* 'he called you'.

Locative class: *Nagiba siya saindo* 'Did he go with you?'; *Nagiba siya sakuya'* 'He went with me'; *Binakal ko an libro saimo* 'I bought a book from you (sing.)'; *Binakol ko an libro sainda* 'I bought a book from them.'

DEMONSTRATIVE PRONOUNS

Like the personal pronouns, these are correlated with the *si/ni/ki* locative classes: three degrees of relative distance + linker: e.g. *ini*, *iyan*, *ito*; *an libro.ng ini = ini.ng libro* 'this book'; *sa lalaki.ng iyan* 'that boy'.

INTERROGATIVE PRONOUN

Appears as *si'isay*, *ni'isay*, *ki'isay*: i.e. correlated with the pronominal and marker series.

RELATIVE PRONOUN

an can often be used: e.g. *Ano an itina'o saimo* 'What was (that which was) given you?'

Numerals

The Bikol numbers 1–10 are: *saro'*, *duwa*, *tulo*, *apat*, *lima*, *anom*, *pito*, *walo*, *siyam*, *sampulo'*. The Spanish numerals may be used for these, and are the sole forms for numbers beyond 10. They are spelled according to Bikol orthography: e.g. *katorse* 14.

Verb

INTRANSITIVE

The prefix is *mag-*, with a past-tense form in *nag-* or *pig-*. The agent is focused; if pronominal, from the *si* class: e.g. *mag.balik* 'to return', *Nag.balik ako alas kuatro* 'I came back at 4 o'clock.'

TRANSITIVE
Here, by definition, either agent or patient can be focused. If the agent is focused, the primary prefixes are *mag-/nag-* as in intransitive verbs; if patient is stressed, the prefix *i-* or the suffixes *-an/-on* are used. Subject and object pronouns cannot be from the same class. Example: *inapod ko siya* 'I called him' (*ko* – subject – is *ni* class; *siya* – object – is *si* class).

TENSE STRUCTURE
Past, progressive, and future tenses are formally distinguished.

> Past: *nag-* and *pig-* are past-tense markers. The infix *-in-* can also be used following a consonant initial: e.g. *kakan* 'to eat', past *kinakan* (or *pig.kakan/nag.kakan*: *Pig.kakan mo an ice cream na ini?* 'Have you eaten the ice-cream?').
> Future: usually by reduplication of first base syllable: e.g. *gibohon* 'to do', future *gigibohon*; *tabangan* 'to help', future *tatabangan*.
> Progressive: the future form + infix *-in-*: the final *-on* of *-on* verbs drops: *gibohon* – future *gigibohon* – prog. *ginigibo*: e.g. *Ano an ginigibo mo?* 'Where (is it that you) are (you) going?' *mag-* verbs add the prefix *nag-* to the progressive: *mag.hugas* 'to wash', progressive *nag.hu.hugas*.

POTENTIAL VERBS
Verbs denoting change or accidental happening. Three basic prefixes are used: *ma-* with focus on object; *maka-*, focus on subject; *ika-*, focus on recipient, beneficiary, etc. Examples: from verb *tumba* 'to fall': *matumba* 'to trip over something and fall'; *makatumba* 'to knock something over by accident' (onus on agent). These have tense forms: e.g. *matungtungan* 'get stepped on'; past *natungtungan*; future *matutungtungan*; progressive = past.

CAUSATIVE
The characteristic marker is *pa-*: e.g. for *mag-* verbs, *magpa-* with focus on agent, and *pa-...-on* with focus on patient. Cf. stem *basa* 'read': *pa.basa.hon* 'to have X read something'; *ipa.basa* 'to have something read by X'. These have tense forms, e.g. from *pa.basa.hon*: past *pinabasa/nagpa-/pigpa.basa*; future *papabasahon*; from *ipabasa*: past *ipinabasa*, future *ipapabasa*, prog. *ipinapabasa*.

The above is a simplifed outline of basic formulae. Additional prefixes and variant forms proliferate; e.g. the *maki-/paki-* series used in making requests, the *para-* series for reiteratives, and *magka-* series giving a terminative or perfective sense to the verb.

> *Pag-* is a formant applied to both transitive and intransitive stems to generate nominals or adverbial turns of phrase: e.g. *an pagbalik mo* 'your return'; *pagbalik mo* 'when you came back ...'. The general negating particle is *da'i*: e.g. *da'i ko aram* 'I don't know'.

Prepositions

The basic formula is *sa* + noun + article: e.g. *sa likod kan sa'od* 'at the back of the market' = 'behind the market'; *sa tahaw kan laguerta* 'in the (middle of) the orchard'.

Word order

SVO/VSO, depending on construction.

---

1 Sa caenotenote sia iyo an Verbo, asin an Verbo nasa caibahan nin Dios, asin an Verbo iyo an Dios.

2 Sia sa caenotenote nasa Dios.

3 An gabos na magña bagay guinibo nia, asin cun day sia day nin anoman na náguibo sa naguinibo.

4 Sa saiya duduman an buhay; asin an buhay iyo an ilao nin magña tauo.

5 Asin an ilao minaliuanag sa magña cadiclomán, alagad an magña cadicloman day namansayan an ilao.

6 Iguá nin saróng tauo, na sinogò nin Dios, na gñinagñaranan si Juan.

7 Ini napadigdi sa pagsacsi, ta gñaning mapatotoohan an dapit sa ilao, ta gñaning an gabos magturubod huli sa saiya.

8 Bacò sia an ilao, condi napadigdi sa pag-patotoo dapit can ilao;

BLACKFOOT

INTRODUCTION

This Algonquian language is spoken today by about 6,000 Indians, divided into two groups, one in Montana, the other in Alberta.

PHONOLOGY

Consonants

Blackfoot has no voiced stops or fricatives. The consonantal inventory is /p, t, k; c, ç, χ; s; m, n; h, ʔ/. /ç/ is notated as *x*; a notable feature of the phonology is the presence of clusters based on *k* and *x*: *xk* = /çk/, *xts* = /çc/, *ksts* = /ksc/, *xp* = /çp/ etc.

Vowels

aː, ă, ɔ, ɔː, ʌ, eː, ε, iː, oː, u

This is Uhlenbeck's list (1938). Uhlenbeck makes the point that [e, i] and [u, o] are likely to be variants of two phonemes.

There is a strong tonic accent; it is free and may be accompanied by prolongation of stressed vowel.

MORPHOLOGY

Noun

For a more detailed description of an Algonquian congener, *see* **Cree**. Blackfoot is also characterized by a fundamental dichotomy between animate and inanimate categories, a dichotomy which, from the Indo-European point of view, is not logically followed through. Thus, some trees are animate, others are not. Parts of the body are inanimate. Uhlenbeck quotes the interesting case of *motokis* 'skin, hide', which is animate but becomes inanimate after processing. Nouns denoting geographical terms are inanimate.

NUMBER

Animate nouns make a plural in *-iks(i)*: e.g. *imita* 'dog', pl. *imitaiks*; *ponoka* 'elk', pl. *ponokaiks*. An inanimate plural form is in *-ists(i)*: e.g. *nitummo* 'hill', pl. *nitummoists*. There are many variant forms, e.g. *ake* 'woman', pl. *akeks*.

CASE

There is no declension, in an Indo-European sense. Congruence in the verb determines syntactical relations.

Genitive: possessor precedes possessed: e.g. *ninna otănni* 'my father's daughter'.

Obviative: (*see* **Cree**): obviative forms are used in Blackfoot for third person singular forms topically subordinate to focused (third) person. The focused third person may be implicit, e.g. *unni* 'his father': the form *unni* is obviative because the third person form actually though covertly focused is 'son'.

Most animate nouns have a primary form in *-ua, -a* /wa/, with obviative in *-ai/-i*: e.g. for root *-nn-* 'father': *ninna* 'my father'; obv. *ninni*; *kinna* 'your father'; obv. *kinni*. The third person form *unni* (obv.) has no primary form.

Many kinship terms and designations for parts of the body are always accompanied by the indefinite personal possessive prefix *mo-*.

Adjective

A small number of independent adjectives precede or follow the noun as attributives: e.g. *ponokāmitaiks aχsiks* 'the good horses' (*aχsi* 'good'). Qualifying material is usually prefixed to the noun; there is a large number of such adjectival prefixes: e.g.

> *inak-* 'small', e.g. *aatsista* 'rabbit', *inakaatsista* 'small rabbit';
> *ino-* 'long', e.g. *inokinistsiu* 'he has long arms';
> *man-* 'new', e.g. *manokimiu* 'he has a new lodge' (*oki* 'lodge');
> *matsiu* 'good-looking', e.g. *matsoake* 'good-looking woman';
> *sik-* 'black', e.g. *siksika* 'Blackfoot tribe'.

Pronoun

Emphatic (independent) and possessive/verbal subject or object (prefixed):

	Singular				Plural	
	Emphatic	*Prefix*			*Emphatic*	*Prefix/Suffix*
1	nistoa	ni(t)-, ho-		excl.	nistunan	ni(t)-...(i)nan
				incl.	ksistunan	ki(t)-...(i)nun
2	ksistoa	ki(t)-, ko-			ksistoau	ki(t)-...oau
3	ostoi	o-, ot-			ostoauai	o-...oauai

Example of possessive declension, stem *-kos* 'child': *nokos* 'my child':

	Singular		Plural
1	nokos	excl.	nokosinan
		incl.	kokosinun
2	kokos		kokosoau
3	okos		okosoauai

DEMONSTRATIVE PRONOUN

amo 'this' ('here-being'); *oma* 'that' ('there-being'). These are declined for singular and plural, animate and inanimate, and the forms can be verbalized.

INTERROGATIVE PRONOUN

taka 'who?'; *tsa/aχsa* 'what?'. Often combined with relative pronoun (see below): e.g. *Taka annaχk ninauaxk?* 'Who is (it that is) the chief?' (*ninau* 'chief').

RELATIVE PRONOUN

anna/anni + *χka* (singular); many variants. The form is marked for number and category, animate/inanimate: e.g. *Anniχk nit.axpummaiχk napioyisk ikomaxko* 'The house which I bought is very large.'

Numerals

Three sets, simple or neutral, animate, and inanimate. The neutral series 1–10: *nitokska, natoka, niuokska, nisoo, nisito, nau, ixkitsika, naniso, pixkso, kepo.* 11–19: primary + *koputo*. 20 *natsippo*; 30 *nippo*; 40 *nisippo*; 100 *kekippo*.

Animate/inanimate series: coded endings are added to the neutral series: e.g. the rows for 7, 8, are:

animate:	ixkitsikami	inanimate:	ixkitsikaii
	nanisoyimi		nanisoyi

Numerical correlatives can also be prefixed to nouns: e.g. *Niuokskaitapiau* 'There are three people.'

Verb

The basic division is into transitive and intransitive verbs, with each of which classes a specific set of endings is associated. Whereas there is only one paradigm for most intransitive verbs, the transitive verb has two paradigms, depending on whether the object is animate or inanimate. Thus, *nit.siksipau* 'I bite him (anim.)'; *nit.sikstsixp* 'I bite it (inanim.)'. Structurally, passive forms underlie the transitive paradigms: cf. *siksipau*, which is an indefinite passive animate form 'he is bitten by somebody'. The same form *siksipau* also means 'we (incl.) bite him (indic. trans. anim.)'. To this form the personal prefixes are added: *nit.siksipau* 'I bit him' (lit. 'he is bitten by me').

The verbal paradigm is marked for two numbers, three persons, and obviative.

MOODS

The indicative is not specifically marked. There are three versions: affirmative, negative, and interrogative.

As specimen of Blackfoot conjugation: here are the singular forms of the *-siksi-* stem 'to bite', in three persons plus obviative; intransitive and transitive affirmative.

	Intransitive	*Transitive animate*	*Transitive inanimate*
1	nit.ai.sikstaki	nit.(ai).siksipau	nit.(ai).sikstsixp
2	kit.ai.sikstaki	kit.(ai).siksipau	kit.(ai).sikstsixp
3	Ø ai.sikstakiu	Ø siksipiu	Ø sikstsim
4	Ø ai.sikstakinai	Ø siksipinai	Ø sikstsiminai

The paradigm continues with forms for plural 1, 2, 3, plus forms for plural object, animate, and inanimate.

There are several other moods: e.g. the causative, formed from the intransitive stem + -ats- + transitive animate ending: e.g. *nit.ai.simi* 'I drink' (intrans); *nit.ai.simi.ats.au* 'I cause/give him to drink'. (NB -ai- in the above example and in the paradigm, is the durative marker). Similarly, the imperative, benefactive, translative, conditional, subjunctive, and optional moods have specific markers. The negative marker is -mat-.

The many hundreds of forms thus generated in the basic conjugation of the Blackfoot verb are infinitely extended by means of composition with nominal stems, and by modal prefixes of manner, locus, time, degree, etc. For example, almost any noun denoting a part of the body can be compounded with any relevant verb in any form, and with any relevant affix of manner. This leads naturally to rather long words. One example from Uhlenbeck (1938):

> osotămomaχkakaiitapisaksitokaie
> 'Then he was suddenly shot by him (obv.) in the thigh, so that there was a gap in it'

The nominal component here is *mo.apisak* 'thigh'. Uhlenbeck lists about 150 modal prefixes.

[1]Oki. Isskoohtsika itsaoma'paistotoahpi ksaahkomma
iikayissitsstsiiwa annaahkayii iihto'tsstsiiwa aamo
iihkana'paisiiyi. Annahkao'ka annaahka Jesus Christ.
Itohpoka'paitapiimiwa anniska A'pistotookiiyiska. Ki
noohkattamiwa A'pistotooki. [2]Awaanio'pa
iikayissitsstsiiwa itsaoma'paistotoahpi ksaahkomma.
Iitohpoka'paitapiimiwa anniska A'pistotookiiyiska.
[3]Kana'paisi iihtsistapitsstsiiwa ostoyi.
Matoohkitsstsiihpa aahksaohtsistapitsstsii ostoyi,
imaki'tokska. [4]Iihtsistapitsstsiiwa aissksipaitapi'ssini
ostoyi. Ki amiiksiska iihkotaiksi amohka
niipaitapi'ssinihka akohkottohtsistapohta'pawaawahkaayaawa
ksistsikoinattsii. [5]Ki amohka ksistsikoinattsiiyihka
itapsstsiiwa amiiksiska ita'pawaawahkaaiksi
isskii'nattsi. Ki amohka isskii'nattsiyihka
mataonoao'tsitsksskonata'pssatoomaatsi ksistsikoinattsi.
Ki annihkayii matakonoawaahtsaaka'siwa amiia
ksistsikoinattsiiyi.

[6]Oki. Aamayii matapiiwa, A'pistotookiwa
otssksksimo'taani aanistawa John Awaatoa'pistotakiwa.
[7]Ostoyi ota'po'takssinayi maahkitaokakianistahsi
matapiiyi. Iihtokamo'tsi'poyiwa anniska iihkokkiiyiska
aahkita'pawaawahkaao'si ksiistsikoinattsi. Ki annihkayii
otapi'ssina ayaakomai'takiiksi maahkitomai'takssi. [8]John
matamiiwaatsi anniska iihkokkiiyiska
aahkita'pawaawahkaao'si ksistsikoinattsi.

BRAHUI

INTRODUCTION

Brahui is a Dravidian outlier. The language seems to have been separated from the mainstream of Dravidian, about three or four thousand years BC, before the latter embarked on the southward migration to India. At present, Brahui is spoken in an enclave between Eastern and Western Baluchi, in Western Pakistan, by about 360,000 people, many of whom are bilingual in Brahui and Baluchi. There are also sizable Brahui communities in Hyderabad and Karachi; and nomad Brahui groups are found in Afghanistan and Iran. The language shows Iranian, specifically Baluchi, influence.

According to Andronov (1971), the -*hui* part of the ethnonym is identical with the *Kui, Kuvi*, which appears in the ethnonyms of other Dravidian peoples, and means 'mountain'. (cf. Tamil *kō*). Andronov analyses the name as *vaṛa-kō-ī* > *brā'ūī* 'northern mountain people'.

SCRIPT

Brahui is unwritten, but the Arabic script has been used to notate its folk literature.

PHONOLOGY

Consonants

> stops: p, b, t, d, ṭ, ḍ, k, g, ?
> affricates: tʃ, dʒ
> fricatives: f, v, s, z, s', z', x, γ
> nasals: m, n, ɲ, ŋ
> laterals and flaps: l, ł, r, ɽ

Retroflex consononts are notated with a dot in the following text.

Vowels

> i, iː, e, eː, a, aː, oː, u, uː

Stress

Stress is weak, tending towards beginning of word.

MORPHOLOGY AND SYNTAX

Noun

The noun has two numbers; the plural marker is -(*ā*)*k* for the nominative; -(*ā*)*t* is the base for plural oblique cases. /γ/ may figure as a link element: e.g. *urā* 'house', pl. *urāk*; *xal* 'stone', pl. *xalk*; *īr* 'sister', pl. *īrk*; *bāva* 'father', pl. *bāvayāk*; *lumma* 'mother', pl. *lummayāk*. The oblique base in -(*ā*)*t* is specific to Brahui, and is not found in other Dravidian languages. In the light of the Caldwell thesis (*see* **Dravidian Languages**) this -*t* has been compared with the -*t* plural formant in Uralic.

CASE SYSTEM
Ten case endings are added to the singular stem, to plural oblique base:

> genitive: sing. -*nā*, pl. -*ā*; e.g. *kannā īlumnā 'ullī* 'my brother's horse'
> dative: -*ki* (with link vowel); e.g. *mār* 'son', *māraki* 'to the son'
> accusative: -*e*; e.g. *māre* 'the son'
> instrumental: -*aṭ*, pl. -*eaṭ*; e.g. *māraṭ* 'by the son'; *māteaṭ* 'by the sons'
> comitative: -*tō* (with link vowel); e.g. *māratō* 'with the son'
> ablative: -*ān* (with link vowel); e.g. *mateān* 'from the sons'
> locative: -*ṭī* (with link vowel); e.g. *urāṭī* 'in the house'; *o kanā s'a'raṭī tūlik*
>   'he lives in my village'
> additive: -*āy*; e.g. *urāāy* 'into the house'
> adessive: -*isk*; e.g. *dūnisk* 'at the well'
> terminative: (*is*)*kā*; e.g. *draxt* 'tree' (Iranian loan-word), *draxtiskā* 'as far as
>   the tree'

Adjective

Qualitative adjectives have short, indefinite and definite forms: e.g. short *džuān* 'good'; indefinite *džuānō*; definite *džuanā*/-*aŋgal*/-*īkō*. The short form is used predicatively, the other two as prepositive attributes: e.g. *mary unā kasar* 'the long road'; *rāstīkō dū* 'the right hand'.

COMPARISON
A comparative is made with -*tir* (= Iranian -*tar*): e.g.

> Dā 'ullī džuān aff, asi džuān.*tir.ō* 'ullī-as 'ata
> 'This horse is no good, bring me a better one'

Pronoun

PERSONAL INDEPENDENT

	Singular	Base	Plural	Base	
1	ī	kan-	nan	nan-	
2	nī	ne-	num	num-	
3	dād	dād/dār	dāfk	daft-	proximate
	ōd	ōd/ōr	ōfk	ōft-	intermediate
	ēd	ēd/ēr	ēfk	ēft-	remote

These are declined in all cases: e.g. for first person singular: *ī*, *kanā*, *kanki*, *kane*, *kaneaṭ*, *kantō*, etc.

DEMONSTRATIVE PRONOUN
Three degrees of proximity: *dā* – *ō* – *ē*. These are invariable.

INTERROGATIVE PRONOUN
dē(r) 'who?'; *ant* 'what?'. Declined in most cases.

RELATIVE PRONOUN
The Iranian loan-word *ki* is used.

Numerals

Only the words for 1, 2, and 3 are Dravidian: *asi(ṭ)*, *iraṭ/irā*, *musi(ṭ)*. All other numerals are borrowed from Iranian.

Verb

For almost all positive forms there is a parallel set of negative forms (*see* **Dravidian Languages**; **Finnish**).

Finite forms are marked for mood, tense, number, and person; non-finite forms are participles, gerunds, and verbal noun (infinitive).

In the great majority of cases, personal and non-personal forms are made from a single base form, which is the verbal noun minus the ending -(*i*)*ŋg*: e.g. *biniŋg* 'to hear', base *bin*-; *salīng* 'to stand', base *salī*-. Some verbs have three or more bases, which may be suppletive; e.g. *'iniŋg* 'to go', has two bases, *'in* and *ka*.

INDICATIVE MOOD
The present/future tense has the endings -*iva*, *isa*-, -*ik*; -*ina*, -*ire*, -*ira*, added directly to the base, optionally preceded by *a*: e.g. (*a*)*tixiva* 'I put', (*a*)*tixik* 'he puts'. Simple past: tense markers are added to the base; -*ā*- is the most common. The personal endings for the past are: -*ṭ*, -*s* -∅; -*n*, -*re* -*r*: e.g. *maxiŋg* 'to laugh', *maxāṭ* 'I laughed'. There are similar sets of endings for past continuous, past perfective, past anterior.

NEGATIVE CONJUGATION
The markers are -*p(a)(r)*-/-*f(a)(r)*-/-*t(a)*-, to which specific sets of personal endings are added for the various tenses. For example, the endings for the present/future tense are:

	Singular	Plural
1	-ra	-na
2	-ēsa	-ēre
3	-k	-sa

Examples: *xam-pa-ra* 'I do not see'; (*a*)*tix.p.ēre* 'you do/will not put'.

PAST TENSE

The tense marker -*v*- follows the negative marker -*ta*-, and a specific set of personal endings is added: e.g. *ī urāṭī pē'i.ta.v.aṭ* 'I didn't go into the house'; *tix.ta.v.as* 'they did not put'.

POTENTIAL MOOD

No specific marker; specific set of endings: e.g. *tixe* 'he may put'.

IMPERATIVE MOOD

Singular markers are -*a*(*k*), -Ø, pl. -*bō*: e.g. *tixØ* 'put!', pl. *tixbō*. Negative: -*pa*/-*fa*: e.g. *tixpa* 'don't put!'; *bafa* 'don't come!' (*banniŋg* 'to come').

CONDITIONAL MOOD

The marker is -*ōs*-: e.g. *binōsuṭ* 'if I should hear'.

AUXILIARY VERB

anning 'to be'. The present tense is: *uṭ*, *us*, *e*; *un*, *ure*, *ō*. This verb is used with the genitive case in sense of 'to have': e.g. *kanā irā mār ō* 'I have two sons'. The negative is *affaṭ* 'I am not'; *allavaṭ* 'I wasn't': e.g. *ī brā'ūī affaṭ* 'I am not a Brahui'.

NON-FINITE FORMS

There are two participles, in -*ōk* and in -*ōī*. The former is invariable and is not related to any specific tense. The form in -*ōī*, also invariable, is linked with the future: e.g. *Ī dā kārēme karōī uṭ* 'I am the one who has to do this work.'

Preposition

Some prepositions have been borrowed from Baluchi, and there are a few postpositions, e.g. *bā*(*r*) 'like', which follows the ablative case: e.g. *'ullīām bā* 'like a horse'.

Word order

SOV.

مُستَیبِکوباب

١ موهنااۇ لیکوتِیٰي هندا کلام اس اوهندا کلام خدااتواس

٢ دخُدا هموکلام اس ٢ هموهناا ۇ لیکوتا خدا اتو اس ٣ کل

اونا معرفتت مسونو و بغیرهمور ان هیچره متوَ هند اگرااس

٤ که مسونی ٤ دالي زِنْدِگي اس وهمي زِنْدِگي مے اِنْصانْ نا

٥ نور اس ٥ وهمي نور قارِ سِٹي نودي روشنایا کیک و

قار ما لودي فِتوَکه

.

٧ نزِیِس بَے خدا اخان موتِزُروک اس دانابِن یوحنّا ٦ لوشاهِدِیٰكِيَ

٨ بله نور نایا بتت شاهِدِي ابِقِي که کُل بندغاک هندران ایمان هتن ٨

شموا ر نور آنَز یِٹے اِسے خاطِرات کله نور نا شاهِدِی ابِقِي

BRETON

INTRODUCTION

Breton belongs to the Brythonic branch of Celtic (i.e. P-Celtic; *see* **Celtic Languages**). In 1930 75 per cent of the Breton population in North-Western France, totalling about 1½ million, spoke the language; fifty years on, the percentage had dropped to just over 40 per cent. With an estimated half a million speakers, however, Breton is still outstripped only by Irish among Celtic languages. Middle Breton was used as a literary language up to the nineteenth century. The modern language is spoken in four main dialects: Léon (*leoneg*), Cornouaille (*kerneveg*), Tréguier (*tregerieg*), and the divergent dialect of Vannes (*gwenedeg*).

SCRIPT

The Roman alphabet minus q and x. The 1941 orthography known as *zedacheg* is in general use. The tilde marks nasalization. ch = /s, z/, c′h = /x, γ/, zh = /z/ (or /h/ in gwenedeg).

PHONOLOGY

Consonants

> stops: p, b, t, d, k, g; labalized k°, g°
> fricatives: f, v, s, z, ʃ, ʒ, x, γ, h
> nasals: m, n, ɲ, ŋ
> laterals: l, λ
> rolled: r
> semi-vowels: w, j

Among the stops various degrees of gemination and of fortis/lenis articulation occur, depending on position. *ñ* is not pronounced and simply represents nasalization of the preceding vowel.

Vowels

> i, e, ɛ, a, ɔ, o, œ, ø, u, y

All vowels can be long or short, and all can be nasalized, with marked variation in degree of closure. /ø/ is notated as *ö*, /y/ as *ü* in the following text.
There are several diphthongs, e.g. /ɛa, ao, ɛi, ɛ̃ɔ̃/.
Stress is movable.

Mutation

(*See also*, **Celtic Languages**). In Breton, mutation takes four main forms:

(a) Lenition: /p, t, k/ → /b, d, g/; /b, d, g/ → /v, z, x/γ/; /m/ → /v/. This mutation occurs regularly after articles (with constraints on gender, see below), certain possessive adjectives, prepositions, verbal particles, etc.: e.g. *tad* 'father': *e dad* 'his father'; *mamm* 'mother': *ar vamm* 'the mother'; *Bretoned* 'Bretons': *ar Vretoned* 'the Bretons'. Following the definite article, lenition occurs in feminine singular and masculine plural nouns only; thus, *ar vamm*; but *mor* 'sea', being masculine, does not mutate: *ar mor* 'the sea'. Example of mutation in attributive adjective: *merc'h* 'girl'; *brav* 'pretty': *ar verc'h vrav* 'the pretty girl'.

(b) Spirantization: /p, t, k/ → /f, z, x/. This mutation occurs after certain possessive adjectives, e.g. *ma* 'my', *he* 'her', *o* 'their': *ki* 'dog': *ma c'hi* 'my dog'; *penn* 'head': *ma fenn* 'my head'; *tad* 'father': *he zad* 'her father'. Since *e* 'his' and *he* 'her' are homophones, the presence or absence of mutation in the following initial is phonemic: *e vreur* 'his brother'; *he breur* 'her brother' (*breur* 'brother').

(c) Hardening: /b, d, g/ → /p, t, k/. This mutation occurs after *ho(c'h)* 'your (pl.)', *az/ez* 'your (sing.)': e.g. *dent* 'teeth': *ho tent* 'your teeth'; *daouarn* 'hands': *ho taouarn* 'your hands'.

(d) Mixed: /b, d, g/ → /v, t, x/; /g°/ → /w/; /m/ → /v/. This occurs after the verbal particles *e* and *o*: e.g. *gwelout* 'to see': *o welout* 'seeing'.

MORPHOLOGY AND SYNTAX

Noun

The presence of an indefinite article, *un/ur/ul*, is unique in Celtic. Similarly, the definite article has three forms, *an/ar/al*, depending on following initial.

GENDER
Masculine and feminine. Gender and mutation are co-related.

NUMBER
There is a wide inventory of plural terminations, some of which induce vowel change in stem. Some common endings are:

- *-ed*: e.g. *loen* 'animal', pl. *loened*;
- *-ez*: *ti* 'house', pl. *tiez*;
- *-(i)ou*: pl. form for many inanimates: e.g. *tra* 'thing', pl. *traou* (but note exceptions such as *tadou* 'fathers', *mammou* 'mothers');
- *-i* + umlaut: e.g. *bag* 'boat', pl. *bigi*; Ø ending + umlaut: *maen* 'stone', pl. *mein*.

Stress may shift in plural: e.g. *michérour*, pl. *micheróurien*.
Traces of a former dual appear in the prefix *daou-/div-*: e.g. *an daoulagad* 'the eyes'.
The ending *-enn* is added to collective plurals to make the singular: e.g. *ar*

gwez '(the) trees': *gwezenn* 'a tree'; *askol* 'thistles': *askolenn* 'a thistle'.
Plural nouns take a singular verb.

Possessor follows possessed object: e.g. *breur Yann* 'John's brother'. As in the
Semitic construct, the noun denoting the possessed object loses the article: e.g.
gouleier an ti 'the lights of the house'. However, other words can be interposed
between N$_1$ and N$_2$, which is impossible in Semitic: e.g. *Økador vras ar bugel
bihan* 'the small child's big chair' (*bras* 'big').

Adjective

As attribute, adjective follows noun, and is invariable apart from initial
mutation: e.g. *an ti kozh* 'the old house'; *un den pinwidig* 'a rich man'; *ur skol
vihan* 'a small school' (*bihan* 'small').

COMPARISON
The comparative is made with the ending *-oc'h* + *eget* 'than': e.g. *koant* 'pretty':
koantoc'h 'prettier'.

Suppletive forms: *mat* 'good': *gwelloc'h* 'better'; *drouk* 'bad': *gwashoc'h*
'worse'.

Pronoun

PERSONAL
Gender is distinguished in third singular only.

		Singular		Plural	
		Base form	Possessive	Base form	Possessive
1		me	ma	ni	hon
2		te	da	c'hwi	ho
3	masc.	en	e	int	o
	fem.	hi	he		

Used as subject or direct object, these base forms always precede the verb,
which is itself preceded by the particle *a*: e.g. *me a welit* 'you see me' (*gwelout* 'to
see').

In adjectival form, the possessive pronouns can also be used as direct object
pronouns: e.g. *Da kwelout a raimp* (*warc'hoazh*) 'We'll see you (tomorrow).'

By adding personal pronominal affixes to prepositions, the ubiquitous 'conjugated prepositional' form is obtained: e.g. with *gant* /gã/ 'by, with, for, etc'.

		Singular	Plural
1		ganin 'by (etc.) me'	ganeomp
2		ganit 'by you'	ganeoc'h
3	masc./fem.	gantan/ganti	ganto

Similarly with *da* 'to': *din*, *dit*, *dezhan/dezhi*; *dimp*, *deoc'h*, *dezho*.

The prepositions *a* 'to' and *eus* 'from', share the extended bases *ac'han-* for first and second person, *anezh-* for third, and provide direct and indirect object forms: e.g. *C'hwi a gavo ac'hanon war ar blassenn* 'You'll find me in the square.'

DEMONSTRATIVE PRONOUN

Three degrees of relative distance are marked by masc. *heman – hennezh – henhont*; fem. *houman – hounnezh – hounhont*. The plural for both genders is: *ar re-man – ar re-se – ar re-hont*.

Enclitic forms: *an ti-man* 'this house'; *an ti-se – an ti-hont*.

INTERROGATIVE PRONOUN

piv 'who?'; *petra* 'what?'. Interrogative sentences are introduced by (*daoust*) *ha(g)*: e.g. *Daoust ha brav eo am amzer?* 'Is the weather fine?' (*amzer* 'weather').

RELATIVE PRONOUN

Represented by the particle *a*: e.g. *ar paotr a welit* 'the boy whom you see'; *Setu ar paotr a zo klanv e dad* 'This is the boy whose father is ill.'

Numerals

1–10: *unan, daou, tri, pevar, pemp, c'hwec'h, seizh, eizh, nav, dek*; 11 *unnek*; 12 *daouzek*; 20 *ugent*; 21 *unan warn-ugent*; 30 *tregont*; 40 *daou-ugent*; 50 *hanter-kant*; 60 *tri-ugent*; 100 *kant*.

Verb

Breton has active and passive voices. The active voice has three moods – indicative, imperative, conditional. The indicative has past, non-past, and future tenses, and distinguishes perfective, habitual, punctual, and continuous aspects. There are three persons, singular and plural, plus an impersonal form. Tense forms may be (a) synthetic: here the verb is marked for person and number; (b) analytic: the verb is unmarked, and the personal pronoun must be present; (c) mixed, with auxiliary *bezān* 'to be', or *ober* 'to do, make'; if *bezan* is used, the verb is marked for person, and number. For example, the present tense of *labourat* 'to work', in three versions:

(a) Synthetic:

Singular	*Plural*
1 bremañ e labouran 'I work now'	bremañ e labouromp
2 bremañ e labourez	bremañ e labourit
3 bremañ e labour	bremañ e labouront
impersonal: e labourer 'one is working'	

(b) Analytic, e.g.:

1 me a labour bremañ 'I am working now'
2 te a labour bremañ

(c) Mixed, e.g.: with *bezañ* → *bez'*:

1 bez' e labouran
2 bez' e labourez
3 bez' e labour

with *ober*: base of *ober* is *gra-*, e.g:

1 labourat a ran bremañ 'I'm working now'
2 labourat a rez bremañ
3 labourat a ra bremañ

The three versions differ slightly in stress/focus.

Past:

(a) marked: e.g. *dec'h e labouren, e laboures, e laboure* (*-e-* is past discriminator)
(b) unmarked: e.g. *me a laboure, te a laboure*.

Future:

(a) marked: sing. *e labourin, e labouri, e labouro*: pl. *e labourimp, e labouroc'h, e labourint* (*-i-/-o-* discriminators)

The (c) forms for past and future, with *ober* 'to do', are:

past, e.g.: sing. *labourat a raen, a raes, a rae*; pl. *a raemp*
future, e.g.: sing. *labourat a rin, a ri, a raio*; pl. *a raimp*

The markers *a* and *e* precede the finite verb form; *a* induces lenition, *e* the mixed mutation.

a is the syntactic linker between the subject and the verb, or between the fronted object and verb. It appears in the (b) conjugation above: *Me a labour bremañ* 'I'm working now'; *Bara a zebran bremañ* 'Bread it is I'm eating now.'

e links attributive or adverbial material, or indirect object to verb: e.g. *Er gegin e tebran* 'It's in the kitchen I'm eating now' (*kegin* 'kitchen').

The auxiliary *bezañ* (which has three sets of forms expressing state, habitual action, and spatio-temporal localization) is used to make composite tenses and the passive mood, e.g. with the past participle in *-et*.

The passive may also be expressed by the impersonal form in *-r*: e.g. *Al levr a lenner* 'The book is (being) read.'

The conditional is marked by *-f-* inserted between base and past endings: e.g. *bremañ de labourfen = bez' e labourfen = labourat a rafen bremañ* 'if I worked/were working now'.

Negative

The negative is expressed by a circumfix: *ne … ket*. Only the marked conjugation can be negated; both *a* and *e* are then discarded: e.g. *ne labouran ket, ne labourez ket, ne labour ket*; etc.

Prepositions

Most are compatible with the personal endings (*see* **Pronoun**, above). Examples of prepositions without personal endings: *eus ar mor* 'from the sea'; *edan an douar* 'under the earth'; *goude ar bresel* 'after the war'; *e-kichen an ti-post* 'next to the post-office'. Some prepositions take an infixed personal marker: e.g. *war.lerc'h* 'after': *war-ma-lerc'h, war-da-lerc'h, war-e-lerc'h*, etc.

Word formation

By prefix, suffix, or compounding:

(a) Prefixation: e.g. *di-/dis-/diz-* is privative: e.g. *dizaon* 'fearless'; *dizampart* 'awkward'. *Peur-* gives a perfective sense: e.g. *peurskrivañ* 'to finish writing'. *enep-* 'contrary to': e.g. *enepriezh* 'injustice'; *hanter-* 'half-': e.g. *hanterzigor* 'half-open'.
(b) Suffixation: e.g. *-ded/-der* (masc./fem., no plural forms) make abstract nouns: e.g. *uhelded* 'nobility' (*uhel* 'high'). *-our* forms noun denoting agent, subject of action, or state: e.g. *klañvdiour* 'nurse'. *-erezh* forms abstract nouns: e.g. *bruderezh* 'publicity'.
(c) Compounding: various combinations, e.g. *bag-pesketa* 'fishing-boat'; *mont-dont* 'coming and going'; *pinwidig-mor* 'very rich'.

Word order

VSO is a basic formula, SVO frequent (*see* **Verb**, above).

1 Er gommansamant e oa ar Ger, hag ar Ger a oa gand Doue, hag ar Ger a oa Doue.

2 He-ma a oa er gommansamant gand Doue.

3 An holl draou a zo bet grëd drezan, hag hepzan n'eo bet grët netra hag a zo bet grët.

4 Ennan e oa ar vuez, hag ar vuez a oa goulou an dud.

5 Hag ar goulou a sclera en devalien, hag an devalien n'e deus ked e resevet.

6 Bez' e oe un den caset gand Doue, hanvet Ian.

7 He-ma a zeuaz da desteni, evit rei testeni diwarben ar goulou, evit ma credche an holl drezan.

8 Ne ket hen a oa ar goulou, mes *cased e oa* evit rei testeni diwarben ar goulou.

(Léon dialect)

BRIBRÍ

INTRODUCTION

Bribrí and Cabécar, spoken by a joint total of two or three thousand in Costa Rica, are very closely related members of the Talamanca group of Chibchan languages. William Gabb, writing at the end of the nineteenth century, described Bribrí as having a very deficient vocabulary of between fifteen hundred and two thousand words (Gabb 1891–6). Gabb found that while all Cabécars spoke Bribrí, the language of the dominant tribe in the region, very few Bribrís spoke Cabécar.

PHONOLOGY

Consonants

According to Arroyo (1972), Bribrí has most of the Spanish consonantal inventory, apart from /θ/, /f/, and /ʎ/. /ʃ/ and /ts/ are present. /ʃ/ is notated by Arroyo, and here, as *x*.

Vowels

i, e, a, o, u

Both oral and nasal series. Arroyo describes /o/ as tending to be raised to [ø] and /e/ to [i].

MORPHOLOGY AND SYNTAX

Noun

There is no gender; where necessary, lexical items are used, e.g. for persons *wib* 'man' and *arákr* 'woman': e.g. *yará wib* 'son', *yará arákr* 'daughter'. A plural can be made with -*pa*, e.g. *wibpa* 'men'; or *tsotséi* 'many', can be used: *kar tsotséi* 'lots of trees'. Possessive relationship by apposition: e.g. *arákr urá* 'the woman's hand'; *kar máma* 'the tree's blossom'.

Adjective

The attributive adjective follows the noun, and is often reduplicated: e.g. *wib deríri* 'strong man'; *baba* 'hot'; *sese* 'cold'.

Pronouns

PERSONAL

	Singular	Plural
1	yé	sá
2	bé	já
3	yié	yiépa

These are both subject and object forms, and have many variants.

POSSESSION

Marked by -cha: e.g. yécha 'my, mine'; beicha 'your'.

DEMONSTRATIVE

Three degrees by relative distance: jí 'this' – basé 'that' – jerkí auir 'that (yonder).' These have plural forms.

Verb

The infinitive is in -V*k*, -*k*V, -*wa*, -*ta*, etc. Tense formation is highly unpredictable and irregular. As specimen, the main parts of two verbs are given:

tsuk 'to sing'

present	tsuke	passive participle	tsé
preterite	tsí	active participle	tsúmbra
future	mike tsuk	gerund	itsúkedak
perfect	tsírure		

xege 'to eat'

present	xegegé	passive participle	xagajká
preterite	xagajká	gerund	xegegé
future	ma xege		

Word order

SOV.

1. Kéue eror Sibu ufto, ufto e tso Sibu ta eta ufto eror Sibu.

2. Ih ror kéue Sibu ta.

3. Iyir ulítane yoh ie-ror; eta ie ke kupa ema iyir tso yor-ule ke ku̱n.

4. Ieh ta sauac tso, eta sauac eror koñi-na uepa urítane e-ia.

5. Eta ko tsetse-a̱ ko̱uonin; ére ko tsetse ke en-a ia̱na.

6. Ieh ror uéb apatke Sibu to, uak kie Juan.

7. Ih débite eh biyo-ie, ko̱nin ufte amuk se-ia, o̱s se urítane to ieh bikeitso.

8. Ke ieh ror koñin; irir koñin ufte amuk se-ia̱.

BUGINESE

INTRODUCTION

A member of the Malayo-Polynesian branch of Austronesian, Buginese is spoken by about 4 million people in Southern Sulawesi (Celebes). Originally Buddhist, the Buginese were converted to Islam, along with the Macassarese, in the seventeenth century. The ethnonym is (*w*)*ugi'* or *to.ugi'* (*to* < *tau* 'man'); the language is *basa* (*w*)*ugi'*.

Buginese has a very rich traditional literature, still largely in manuscript form. The enormous cycle of mythological poems known as the *Surə' Galigoe* portrays and records an ethnic Sulawesi culture which is neither Islamic nor Hindu. There is also a rich prose literature, consisting of historical chronicles and *surə' bilang* or diaries.

SCRIPT

The Buginese–Macassarese syllabary is based on an Indian model, and retains the typically Indian method of marking vowels as super- or subscript additions to consonants.

Attempts have been made in the twentieth century to write Buginese in romanization.

PHONOLOGY

Consonants

stops: p, b, t, d, k, g, ʔ
affricatives: tʃ, dz
fricatives: ɸ, s, j
nasals: m, n, ɲ, ŋ
lateral and trill: l, r
semi-vowels: j, w

Vowels

i, e, a, ə, o, u

/e/ and /o/ have positional variants.

Stress

Tends to penultimate syllable, but may be on antepenultimate or on final, depending on structure and composition of word or complex.

230

MORPHOLOGY AND SYNTAX

Article

An enclitic article is *-e* (with allomorphs), which can be added to complex: e.g. *bola.e* 'the/a house'; *bola aruŋŋ.e* 'princely house, the chief's house'; *utti u.tanəŋŋ.e* 'the bananas which I planted'. The article also serves to substantivize such units as extended verbs: e.g. *mallopi* 'to go by ship', *mallopi.e* 'a voyage'. The personal articles *i-la* (masc.) and *i-we* (fem.) are applied to Buginese proper nouns, names of boats, weapons, etc.

Noun

Buginese nouns are primary or derivatory; the latter mainly by prefixation: *pa*C-, for example, forms nouns of agency. The suffix *-aŋ* suggests something connected with or the result of the activity denoted by the base: e.g. *daŋkaŋ* 'trade', *daŋkaŋəŋ* 'goods'. Circumfix is also used: cf. from *musu* 'war', *am.musu.r.əŋ* 'warlike actions'. There is no case system.

Adjective

Most adjectives have the form *ma* + stem: e.g. *ma.lampe* 'long'; *ma.loppo* 'big'. As attribute, adjective follows noun. As predicate, the adjective forms, along with transitive and intransitive verbs, the third class of verb.

Pronoun

There are free and bound series; three persons; a plural distinction is made only with regard to first person.

	Free series	*u- series*	*-ku series*
1	ia'	u-, ku-	-(k)ku
2	idi', iko, io	ik-, ta-, mu-	-(t)ta, -(m)mu
3	ia	na-	-(n)na

An exclusive plural first person is provided by *idikkəŋ*, *ikəŋ* in the free series. The *u-* series has exclusive first person plural *ki-*, inclusive *ta-*, and the distinction appears also in the *-ku* series, but the opposition is not strictly observed.

The *u-* series forms provide the subject pronouns for transitive verbs, e.g. *u.tarima* 'I receive'; *na.tarima* 'he receives'; and the logical object in passive constructions, e.g. *u.ri.tarima* 'and they receive me' = 'I am received' (*ri* is passive marker).

The *-ku* series forms may follow nouns or verbs. Following nouns, they denote the possessive relationship: e.g. *amak.ku* 'my father'; *lopin.na* 'his boat'. Following a verb they set up a temporal or causal relationship: e.g. *ma.bela.n.na* 'when he is far away/because he is far away'; *u.tarima.mu* 'when I received you'.

A third series of bound pronouns, the *a'* series, provides object forms for transitive verbs: e.g. *ri.tarima.i* 'he undergoes reception' = 'they receive him'. *See* **Verb**, below.

DEMONSTRATIVE PRONOUN

Three-degree series: *-e/-we* 'this', *-tu* 'that', *-ro* 'that (far away)': e.g., combined with interrogative *aga* 'what?': *aga.e.tu* 'What is that?' (where *-e-* is the article). Cf. *Maloppo.i.tu bola.e* 'That house is big.'

INTERROGATIVE PRONOUN

niga 'who?'; *aga* 'what?'

RELATIVE PRONOUN

None. Relative constructions are formed with the help of bound pronouns.

Numerals

1–10: *seua/se'di, dua, təllu, əppa, lima, ənnəŋ, pitu, arua, asera, -pulo. Səppulo* is base for 11–19: e.g. *səppulo lima* 15. 20 *dua.pulo*; *-ratu* is base for hundreds.
  Numeral can combine with noun: e.g. *pattatauŋ* 'four years'.

Verb

Transitive and intransitive. Transitive verbs can take a passive construction, and are always correlated with an object (simple or composite). This object is copied or anticipated in the verbal form by a bound pronoun or deictic marker. Sirk (1975) gives the example: *ttiwirəŋŋ.i inanre ana'na* 'to bring food to her children'. Here, the root is *tiwi* 'to bring': the stem is made transitive–benefactive by addition of *-aŋŋ/-əŋŋ*, and then means 'to bring something to or for someone'. The object of the benefactive action, *ana'na* 'her children', is anticipated in the verbal form by the pronominal affix *-i*. The gemination of the stem initial: *tt-* is an allomorph of the active voice marker, which is *mm-* before a vowel initial.
  As an example of transitive structure, Sirk (1975) gives the stem *llian* 'to sell':

> base form: *əlliaŋ* 'sell'
> active: *mməlliaŋ* 'to (proceed to) sell'
> passive: *riəlliaŋ* 'to be sold'
> personalized forms: *uəlliaŋ* 'to be sold by me' = 'I sell'; *muəlliaŋ* 'to be sold by you' = 'you sell'; *taəlliaŋ* 'to be sold by us/you' = 'we/you sell'

Negation: by proclitic *təŋ*.

Intransitive verbs are heterogeneous in structure. Many are formed from substantives by means of prefix *(m)a'*, and then mean 'to have to do with' (object denoted by stem): e.g. *galuŋ* 'rice-field', *ma'galuŋ* 'to work (in) the ricefield, cultivate ...'

CAUSATIVES

The prefix is *paC-* with allomorphs: e.g. *ita* 'to see', *p(a)ita* 'to show something to someone'. Cf. for active/passive construction and formation of relative clauses:

tomacca **mmuki'**.əŋŋ.**i** surə'.**e** 'the scholar who writes the letter'
surə' **riuki'**.**e ri**.tommaca.**e** 'the letter written by the scholar'
surə' **nauki'**.**e** 'the letter which he writes'

Preposition

ri- is an all-purpose preposition applying to spatio-temporal frames without differentiation: this is supplied by the verb, e.g. *lləttu' ri.dusuŋŋe* 'to enter the village'; *pole ri.dusuŋŋe* 'to come out of the village'.

Word order

SVO in active construction: in passive construction V is fronted.

9. ꤿꤰꤲꤰꤰꤱꤸ ꤼꤱꤸꤶ ꤰꤲꤱꤰꤶꤱ꤫꤬

10. ꤰ꤫꤬ ꤰꤰꤱꤱ ꤰꤰꤱꤲꤱ꤬

11. ꤿ꤫꤬

12. ꤸꤰ ꤰꤱ ꤰꤰꤱꤰ ꤰꤰꤱꤰꤰꤱꤱ꤬

13. ꤰꤰꤰ ꤰꤸ꤫ꤸꤰ ꤸꤰꤰꤰꤰ ꤰꤰꤱꤰꤸꤱ꤬

14. ꤰꤸꤱꤸꤰꤰꤱꤱ꤬ ꤸꤱꤸꤶ ꤰꤸꤰ꤫ꤸꤰ

15. ꤰꤰ ꤰꤱꤰꤰꤱꤰꤰ꤫꤬ ꤰꤰꤸ ꤸꤱꤸꤶ ꤰꤰꤸ

(Matt. 6: 9–15)

234

BULGARIAN

INTRODUCTION

The ancient Bulgars were a Turkic people speaking a language classified by Baskakov as Western Hunnic; its congener, still spoken today, is Chuvash (*see* **Chuvash**; **Turkic Languages**). The Bulgars enter history in the seventh century AD, when they moved westwards from the Crimea area, and settled to the south of the Danube, in the Balkan peninsula. Here, they gradually merged with the Slav population already established along the Black Sea coast, and even adopted the local Slavonic language. Of the original Bulgar(ian) language, only the name remains. The language now known as Bulgarian forms, together with Macedonian, the eastern branch of South Slavonic. It is the official language of the Republic of Bulgaria where it is spoken by over 8 million people. (For the 'Old Bulgarian' literary language, *see* **Old Church Slavonic**.) Through the Middle Bulgarian period (twelfth to fifteenth centuries) and again under Turkish suzerainty from the fifteenth century onwards, Bulgarian was a spoken language only, a kind of demotic accompanying the Church Slavonic literary language. By the eighteenth century it had deviated more than any other Slavonic tongue from the common Slavonic norm. The declension of the noun had disappeared, an affixed definite article had been introduced, and the infinitive had been replaced by a construction with the particle *da* plus a finite form of the verb (these are areal features, cf. Tosk Albanian, Romanian, Serbian, and, in part, Greek). In addition, Bulgarian has developed the *preizkazano naklonenie*, a set of inferential tenses which has no parallel in other European languages (but cf. **Turkic**).

The first Bulgarian writer of distinction is Khristo Botev (1848–76). Two years after Botev's death, Bulgaria gained its independence, and from then until the outbreak of the Second World War, a sustained and innovative output of verse and prose appeared in Bulgarian from such writers as Ivan Vazov, Pencho Slaveykov, Peyo Yavorov, Dimcho Debelyanov, Elin Pelin, Elisaveta Bagryana, and Nikolai Vaptsarov.

There is an east/west dialect division; literary Bulgarian is based on the western dialect.

SCRIPT

Cyrillic minus *ё*, *ы*, *э*. The hard sign *ъ* is used to notate the typically Bulgarian sound /ʌ/ > /ɪ/. Here, for typographical reasons, the sound will be notated as *ă*. The Cyrillic letter *щ* is /ʃt/ in Bulgarian, not /ʃtʃ/ > /ʃʃ/ as in Russian. The soft sign *ь* denotes palatalization of the preceding consonant: *синьо* = /sin'ɔ/.

PHONOLOGY

Consonants

> stops: p, b, t, d, k, g
> affricates: ts, tʃ
> fricatives: f, v, s, z, ʃ, ʒ, j, x
> nasals: m, n, ɲ
> lateral and trill: l, r

ASSIMILATION

Voiced to unvoiced and vice versa: e.g. *gradski* = /gratski/; *velikden* = /veligden/. Final voiced is unvoiced: *grad* → [grat]; *vrag* → [vrak].

Vowels

> i, ε, a, ə, ɔ, u

The script distinguishes the palatalized vowels *yu, ya*. Diphthongs: /ai, oi/.

Vowel reduction is typical of Bulgarian pronunciation of unstressed syllables: e.g. /a/ → [ə]: *kníga* → [knigə]; /ε/ → [ɪ]: *zeléno* → /zɪlenɔ/; /o/ → [u]: *polé* → [pule].

Stress

Stress is free and can fall on any syllable. Bulgarian stress often agrees with Russian, but there are many exceptions.

MORPHOLOGY AND SYNTAX

Noun

There are three genders: masculine, feminine, and neuter. The case system has disappeared. The sole remaining inflectional distinction is that between nominative and non-nominative masculine singular, where the nominative form takes the definite article (affix): e.g. *gradăt* 'the town (nom.)'; *grada* 'the town (obl.)': *v centăra na grada* 'in the middle of the town'.
Compare:

> *časăt* e devet i polovina 'the time is half past nine' (nom.)

> V kolko *časa* zaminavaš 'At what time are you going?' (obl.)

DEFINITE ARTICLE

Masc. hard: *-ăt*, soft: *-yat*; fem. *-ta*; neuter: *-to*; plural, all genders: *-te/-ta*: e.g. *gradăt* 'the town'; *borbata* 'the struggle'; *cveteto* 'the flower'; *rabotnicite* 'the workers'.

PLURAL ENDINGS

Most polysyllabic masculines take -*i* with 2nd palatalization of final consonant (*see* **Slavonic Languages**) where necessary: e.g. *rabotnik* 'workers': pl. *rabotnici*; *pedagog* 'teacher': *pedagozi*; *kožux* 'fur coat': *kožusi*.

Masculine monosyllables often take -*ove*: e.g. *plod* 'fruit', pl. *plodové*; *xlyab* 'loaf', pl. *xlyábove*; *nož* 'knife', pl. *nožóve*. Note that stress may be on stem, penultimate, or final.

The feminine plural is in -*i*; neuter: final *o* → *a*, *e* → *ya*/*eta*, *ne* → *niya*: e.g. *pero* 'pen': *perá*; *cvéte* 'flower': *cvetyá*; *momče* 'boy': *momčéta*.

The particle *na* is used to indicate both genitive and dative: e.g. *knigata na deteto* 'the child's book'; *davam knigata na deteto* 'I give the book to the child.'

Adjective

Adjectives are marked for gender and number. The attributive adjective precedes the noun, and the definite article, if present, is transferred to it, the distinction between masculine nominative and oblique being maintained: e.g.

> golem**iyat** grad∅ 'the big town (*golem* 'big', *grad* 'town')
>
> viždam golem**iya** grad∅ 'I see the big town'

Cf. *visokata kăšta* 'the tall house'; *novoto pero* 'the new pen'; *golemite prozorci* 'the big windows'.

PREDICATIVE

knigata e červena 'the book is red'; *molivăt e červen* 'the pencil is red'.

COMPARATIVE

Comparative is made by prefixing *po*-: e.g. *dobăr* 'good', *pó-dobăr*/-*dobra*/ -*dobro* 'better': e.g. *Našeto žilište e pó-xubavo ot tova* 'Our apartment is nicer than that one.'

Pronoun

The personal independent forms are:

> sing. 1 *az*, 2 *ti*, 3 *toi*, *tya*, *to*; pl. 1 *nie*, 2 *vie*, 3 *te*

That is, the third person singular forms are marked for gender.

The pronouns have full and short oblique forms; thus, for first person, direct object full form: *mene*; short: *me*; indirect object full: *na mene*, short, *mi*. Example of full form used for emphasis:

> Na tebe, ne na nego davam knigata
> 'I'm giving the book to you, not to him.'

Short forms: *viždam go* 'I see him'; *ne te viždam* 'I don't see you.' Both long and short forms may be used together: e.g. *na mene mi xaresva* 'I *do* like it.'

POSSESSIVE FORMS
Full forms:

		Singular			*Plural*		
1		moy	moya	moe	naš	naša	naše
2		tvoy	tvoya	tvoe	vaš	vaša	vaše
3	masc.	negov	negova	negovo	texen	tyaxna	tyaxno
	fem.	nein	neina	neino			

The short indirect object forms may also be used: e.g. *moyata kniga* = *knigata mi* 'my book'.

DEMONSTRATIVE PRONOUN
tozi 'this', *onya* 'that'. Both declined for gender and number.

INTERROGATIVE PRONOUN
koy 'who?'; *kakvo* 'what?'. Interrogative enclitic: *li*.

RELATIVE PRONOUN
koyto/koyato/koeto; pl. *koito*. If *koyto* refers to a male person, the oblique case is *kogoto*; otherwise, *koyto*: cf.

> čovekăt, **kogoto** viždam 'the man whom I see'

> vlakăt, **koyto** viždam 'the train which I see'

Numerals

1: *edin/edna/edno*; 2 *dva/dve*; 3–10: *tri, četiri, pet, šest, sedem, osem, devet, deset*. 11: *edinayset*; 12 *dvanayset*; 20 *dvayset*; 30 *triyset*; 100 *sto*.

Verb

Bulgarian verbs have perfective and imperfective aspects. The present perfective form (usually with a prefix, e.g. *uča* 'I learn', perfective *nauča*) cannot be used independently but only in a relative capacity; cf. *trăgvam* 'I leave, start off' (imperfective); *iskam da trăgna* 'I want to leave'.

The citation form is the first person present imperfective.

There are active and passive voices; indicative, imperative/hortative, and conditional moods. In addition, Bulgarian has the unique inferential version of all eight indicative tenses (see below). Three types of conjugation are distinguished: *-e* stems, *-i* stems, and *-a/-ya* stems. Negative particle is *ne*.

THE COPULA

> present: *săm, si, e*; pl. *sme, ste, sa*
> past: *byax, be(še), be(še)*; pl. *byaxme, byaxte, byaxa*
> past participle: *bil, bili*

Specimen conjugation: *četá* 'I read': indicative:

present: *četá, četeš, čete*; pl. *četem, četete, četat*
future: present forms preceded by particle *šte*: e.g. *šte četá*
past imperfective: *četyáx, četese, četese*; pl. *četyaxme, cĕtyaxte, četyaxa*
past perfective: *cĕtox, čete, čete*; pl. *četoxme, četoxte, četoxa*
conditional mood: with auxiliary: *bix, bi, bi čel*; pl. *bixme, bixte, bixa čeli*
imperative: the endings are *-i/-ete*: *piši, pišete* 'write!'

THE INFERENTIAL VERSION
All indicative tenses have parallel forms in the indirect tense or reported-speech system. The indirect tense forms may be preceded by some such phrase as 'It is reported that ...' (cf. Lat. *allatum est...*) but the verb form in itself is enough to stamp the utterance as reported speech. The copula is used in all inferential tenses, except in the third person, where the participial form by itself (singular or plural) is used. Thus the inferential parallel for the present tense of *četa*, given above, is:

sing. *četyal săm, četyal si, četyal Ø*; pl. *četeli sme, četeli ste, četeli Ø*

E.g.

Tuk živee i semeystvoto na Ivan 'John's family too lives here';
(Čuse,če)tukživeeloisemeystvotonaIvan
'(It is said that) John's family ...'
Stopanstvoto ima kăm 1,000 ovce
'The farm has up to 1,000 sheep' (indicative statement)
Stopanstvoto imalo kăm 1,000 ovce '(I'm told) the farm has ...'

As a further example, a passage from the novelist Elin Pelin in both versions:

Indicative	*Inferential*
Pisatelyat vse sedeše i vse pišeše.	Pisatelyat vse sedyal i vse pišel.
Toi ne znaeše počivka. Beše	Toi ne znael počivka. Bil mnogo
mnogo trudolyubiv.	trudolyubiv.

'The teacher was always sitting and writing. He never thought of taking a break. He was very much devoted to his work.'

PARTICIPLES
Use of the active past participle in *-l* has been illustrated above. The present active participle ends in *-eyki/ayki*: e.g. *pristigayki v grada ...* 'arriving in the town ...' The past passive participle is in *-n* or *-t*: e.g. *pisan* 'written'; *vzet* 'taken'. This participle can be used to make passive sentences: e.g. *Vestnikăt e četen ot všicki* 'The newspaper is read by all', which can also be expressed as a reflexive verb: *vestnikăt se čete ot všicki*.

Prepositions

For example, *v* 'in'; *sled* 'after'; *kăm* 'towards'; *izvăn* 'beyond': e.g. *Tazi rabota e izvăn silite mi* 'This job is beyond my powers.'

Word formation

Derivatives mainly by suffixation: e.g.

> *-ar*: *stol* 'chair': *stolar* 'carpenter'
> *-nik*: *rabota* 'work': *rabotnik* 'worker'
> *-stvo*: *bogat* 'rich': *bogatstvo* 'wealth'
> *-ota*: *čist* 'pure': *čistota* 'purity'
> *-ište*: *igraya* 'I play': *igrište* 'playground'

Compounding is prolific: e.g. *zelenčukproizvoditel* 'market gardener' (*zelen* 'green', *-čuk*: *zelenčuk* 'vegetable'; *-tel* suffix denoting agent; *vodya* 'I lead'; *pro-*, *iz-* are prefixes denoting 'out of', 'from').

Word order

SVO is basic.

1 Въ начало бѣ Словото; и Словото бѣше у Бога; и Словото бѣ Богъ.

2 То въ начало бѣше у Бога.

3 Всичко това чрезъ Него стана; и безъ Него не е станало нищо *отъ това*, което е станало.

4 Въ Него бѣ животътъ и животътъ бѣ свѣтлина на човѣцитѣ.

5 И свѣтлината свѣти въ тъмнината; а тъмнината я не схвана.

6 Яви се човѣкъ изпратенъ отъ Бога, на име Иоанъ.

7 Той дойде за свидетелство, да свидетелствува за свѣтлината, за да повѣрватъ всички чрезъ него.

8 Не бѣше той свѣтлината, но *дойде* да свидетелствува за свѣтлината.

BURMESE

INTRODUCTION

This language belongs to the Burmic branch of Tibeto-Burmese family. From South-West China, where its close congener, Yi, is still spoken, Burmese was carried southwards to reach its present habitat by the ninth century AD. Here it came into contact with the Mon language (*see* **Mon**) and the Pali scriptures of Buddhism. The result was an amalgam: Tibeto-Burman stock with a Mon-Khmer substratum and writing system, plus a Pali–Buddhist ideological superstructure. The earliest written records in Burmese date from the eleventh century. By the twelfth century Burmese had replaced Mon as the literary language of court.

For the study of the Pali texts, a specific genre known as *nissaya* Burmese was introduced, in which Pali words are accompanied by Burmese calques (*cf.* **Tibetan**). An interesting feature in Burmese classical verse is the so-called 'climbing rhyme', with rhymes regressing through successive four-syllable lines:

1, 2, 3, *4*, 1, 2, *3*, 4, 1, *2*, 3, *4*, 1, 2, *3*, 4 ... etc.

Burmese is the official language of the Republic of Burma, and is now spoken by about 30 million people. There are three main dialects: Central (the basis of the literary language), Arakanese, and Tavoi (Tenasserim). Over and above the dialectal division is a fundamental distinction between written and colloquial Burmese, with the latter exerting constant upward pressure on the former, as shown, for example, in the erosion of the old literary particles.

SCRIPT

Indic, derived from the Mon version of Brāhmī. There are 43 basic graphs: 11 vowels and 32 consonants. In addition, as in all Indic scripts, there are secondary forms for all vowels and for certain consonants. Eleven graphs are inherently coded for tone; for all other consonant + vowel graphs tone is indicated by subscript dot ‚ , by *visarga* ⁚ , or by the absence of either. Thus အာ = /a/ is *coded* for tone; အာ⁚ = /à/ is *marked* for tone.

PHONOLOGY

Consonants

stops: p, ph, b, t, th, d, k, kh, g, ʔ
affricatives: ʃ, tʃh, dʒ
fricatives: θ, ð, s, sh, ʃ, z, h
nasals: m, mh, n, nh, ɲ, ŋ, ŋh
lateral and flap: l, r
semi-vowels: j, w

Sixteen of the consonants can be set out in five-term series (including aspirate sonant): surd – aspirate surd – voiced stop – sonant – aspirate sonant, e.g. for labial series: /p – ph – b – m – mh. (There is no specific graph for the aspirate sonant, which is written with the secondary form of *h*: e.g. ⴱ = *ma*, ⴲ = *hma*.) Aspiration and consonant are pronounced simultaneously, and may be conventionally notated either as C*h*, or as *h*C, where C = consonant.

Most consonants can be labialized: /p°, t°, k°/, etc.; /p, b, m/ can be palatalized.

CONSONANT GRADATION
Unvoiced stop → voiced stop in intervocalic position or following a nasal: e.g. *kauŋ + kauŋ* → [kauŋgauŋ]; *θwa + tɔ* → [θwàdɔ́].

Vowels

i, e, ɛ, a, ɔ, o, u, ə

DIPHTHONGS

ei, ou, au, ai

Diphthongs are always followed by /ŋ/ or by /ʔ/, e.g. /eiŋ/ 'house'; /kauŋ/ '(to be) good'.

Syllables are *full*, i.e. with all components receiving their full phonetic value, or *reduced*, with vowels tending to /ə/. This characteristic is not typical of Tibeto-Burman, and may indicate Mon-Khmer influence.

The Burmese syllable must contain a vowel or diphthong, which may be preceded and/or followed by a consonant: $(C_1)V(C_2)$ where V = vowel or diphthong. There is a wide choice for C_1, but C_2 can only be /ŋ/ or /k, t, p/, realized as [ʔ]. C_1 may be followed by the semi-vowel /j/ or /w/ (i.e. palatalized or labialized).

Tones

There are three tones. The level tone is unmarked; the heavy falling tone is marked in the script by visarga and in transcription by grave accent; the 'creaky' tone is marked in the script by subscript dot, and in notation by acute accent. In addition, an abrupt (implosive or choked-off) tone occurs before the glottal stop final: this is unmarked in script. Tone marking is not consistent.

MORPHOLOGY AND SYNTAX

Noun

No grammatical gender. Where natural gender has to be specified, lexical means are employed, e.g. *má* for human females: *yá.hàŋ* 'monk' – *yá.hàŋ.má* 'nun'. *Dó* is a general plural marker: *lu* 'man', *ludó* 'people'. *Myà* is a restricted plural marker: *lumyà* 'a certain (given) number of people'. Syntactic relationships are expressed by particles following the noun. Thus, *ká* is a subject marker (literary *ði*). *Ko* is an object or directional marker, *hma* is a locative, *né* an instrumental marker: e.g. *eiŋ.hma* 'in the house'; *dou'.né* 'with a stick' (literary *hníŋ*).

POSSESSION
Literary *í* = colloquial *yέ*; Y of X is expressed as X *í/yέ* Y. This particle can be omitted; if it is, X changes tone: e.g. *θu.yέ.eiŋ* = *θú.eiŋ* 'his house'. If omitted, the objective marker *ko* induces similar tonal change.

There are several numerical coefficients, e.g. *yau'*, *ù*, for people; *kauŋ* for animals; *lòuŋ*, *chàuŋ* for objects according to shape, size, and so on. *Khú* is an all-purpose classifier which can replace any other (cf. Chinese 个/ge/).

Pronoun

The independent personal pronouns are:

> *Singular*
> 1 cuŋ.dɔ (masc.), cuŋ.má (fem.)
> 2 khìŋ.bya (formal), mìŋ (general)
> 3 θu

Plural markers are added to make the plural series. Possessives are made by adding *í/yέ*. Again, if this is omitted, the tone of the pronoun changes: *cuŋ.dɔ.yέ* = *cuŋ.dɔ́* 'mine'.

DEMONSTRATIVE PRONOUNS
di 'this'; *ho* 'that'.

INTERROGATIVE PRONOUNS
These are based on the particle *bε* + modulators: *bε.ðu* 'who?'; *ba.go* 'what?'.

Numerals

1–10: *ti'*, *hni'*, *θòuŋ*, *lè*, *ŋà*, *chau'*, *khú.ni'*, *ši'*, *kò*, *təsʰə/təse*. 20: *hni'shε*; 100: *təya*.

Verb

Verbs in Burmese may be simple, e.g. *θwà* 'to go', *sà* 'to eat'; or compound, i.e. root + root, e.g. *twé.myiŋ* 'to meet' ('meet'· + 'see'). There is no inflection for person. The general predicative marker is *ði* (coll.)/*i* (lit.). This marker is further

243

amplified by several specific markers for tense and mood: e.g. *mɛ* (future), *gɛ* (perfective), *ne* (progressive), *pyi* (inceptive). E.g.:

> təne.θə.hnai mauŋ.lu.e youŋ.hma sɔ.zɔ shin.la.*gɛ.i* 'One day, Maung Lu E came home from work early' (*təne.θə.hnai* 'one day, once'; *youŋ* 'place of work'; *hma* 'from' (postposition); *sɔ.zɔ* 'early'; *shin.la* 'to return'; *gɛ* perfective particle; *i* predicative marker).

ké/kouŋ/pi: these are used to express perfective aspect.

NEGATION

The negative marker is *mə ...phù*: e.g. *mə hmaŋ phù* 'not true'.

IMPERATIVE

Command is made more polite by addition of *pa*: e.g. *θwà.ba* 'please go'. An interrogative marker is *la*.

MODAL VERBS

Desiderative *chiŋ*; potential *ta'/hnain*; necessitative *yá*; conditional *yiŋ*: e.g. *twé.yiŋ* 'if ... meet(s)'; *θwa.yá.mɛ* '... must go'. A verbal noun is made with the *ə*-prefix (written အ = *a*, reduced to /ə/). e.g. *lou'* 'to work' – *ə.lou'* 'work' (noun); *hlá* 'to be pretty – *ə.hlá* 'beauty'.

Many verbs occur in functive–stative pairs (active–passive in Indo-European terms); the functive member has an aspirate initial which is dropped in the stative:

Functive	Stative
hcìŋ 'to make narrow'	ciŋ 'to be narrow'
hcwá 'to raise'	cwá 'to be lifted'
hnòu 'to waken'	nòu 'to be awake'
hlu' 'to set free'	lu' 'to be free'

As in Chinese, there are many four-syllable set phrases, which may be extended to six members. These often consist of formant + rhyming word, reduplicated: e.g. *kə.pya.kə.ya* 'hurriedly'.

RELATIVE CLAUSES

May be made with the particle *tɔ*:

> *θwà.dɔ̀.lu* 'the man who is going';
> *θwà.gé.dɔ̀.lu* 'the man who went' (with perfective marker *kɛ → gɛ*);
> *θwa.mɛ.dɔ̀.lu* 'the man who will go' (with future marker *mɛ*).

Subjectless sentences proliferate, as as Chinese: e.g. *Pyɔ.pyɔ.ne ðe.gè.ði* 'Live well, die miserably.'

Compounding

Burmese has a very large stock of polysyllables built up by compounding from various parts of speech. An example shows two nouns and a verb forming a third polysyllabic noun: *nyá* 'night' + *ne* 'sun' + *sàuŋ* 'to lean' → *nyá.ne.zàuŋ* 'afternoon'.

Word order

SOV is normal.

245

BURUSHASKI

INTRODUCTION

Related, so far as is known, to no other language, Burushaski is spoken by about 40,000 people in isolated and inaccessible mountain valleys in the part Indian, part Pakistani state of Jammu and Kashmir. The Burushaski (ethnonym *burušo*) appear to be the sole residue of a pre-Indo-European population inhabiting Northern India, classified by anthropologists as 'Europeanoid'. Burushaski is unwritten. Claims that a literary Burushaski may have been in use in the very early Middle Ages rest on a reference in a Tibetan source to translation from *bruža'*. Many attempts have been made to connect Burushaski with other language families – Caucasian, Dravidian, Munda, Basque, etc. – but none are convincing, and Burushaski must, for the present, rate as a language with no known congeners.

Burushaski was formerly spoken in much of what is now Dardic territory (*see* **Dardic Languages**), and shares with the Dardic group (along with certain Tibeto-Burman languages, the Pamir languages, some North-West Indian languages and one Dravidian) the areal features of the grouping known as 'Himalayan'. H. Berger (1959) has identified Burushaski words in Romany.

There are two main dialects, *burušaski* and *weršikwar*, which are mutually intelligible. The purest Burushaski is that of Hunza.

PHONOLOGY

Consonants

The series, surd stop – aspirated surd – voiced stop, is typical: e.g. /p, ph, b; t, th, d; ṭ, ṭh, ḍ; tʃ, tʃh, dʒ; k, kh, g/, etc. The dental stops and fricatives have retroflex counterparts (notated here with dots), apart from dental /n/, which has no parallel in the retroflex series.

Vowels

Long and short: i, e, a, o, u

Allophones are [ɪ, ɛ, ʌ, ə, ɔ]. Length is phonemic: cf: *γēniš* 'empress' *γeniš* 'gold'. The presence of overlong vowels has been noted by some authorities.

Tones are present in Burushaski, but so far scarcely investigated. According to Siddheshwar Varma (1931) they are comparable to the tonal system in Panjabi.

Stress

On long vowel, if present, in disyllables, but stress is weak and seems to be largely 'irrelevant' (Morgenstierne 1945, Lorimer 1935).

MORPHOLOGY AND SYNTAX

Noun

There are four classes of noun: (1) male beings; (2) female beings; (3) other animates (animals, etc.) and some objects; (4) everything not included in (1–3). e.g.

    Class 1: *hīr* 'man', *hiles* 'boy' *phūt* 'demon';
    Class 2: *gus* 'woman', *dasin* 'daughter';
    Class 3: *huk* 'dog', *hayur* 'horse';
    Class 4: *cil* 'water', *mamu* 'milk', *γeniš* 'gold'.

There are no typical class endings, though *–š*, *–č*, and *–ŋ* are often found in class 4 nouns.

    The indefinite marker *-an* is suffixed to nouns, usually in combination with the prepositive marker *hin* for classes 1 and 2, *han* for classes 3 and 4: e.g. (**hin**) *gusan* 'a woman, some woman'. The indefinite marker takes case endings (see below): e.g. *hin džat gusan.mo ha* 'an old woman's house'. *-ik* is a plural indefinite marker: e.g. *hirik* 'some men'.

NUMBER

There are two numbers. Plural markers are extremely heterogeneous – several dozen suffixes, with assimilation at junctures. Two common suffixes are *-o* and *-anc*: e.g. *balas* 'bird', pl. *balašo*; *huyēlterc* 'shepherd', pl. *huyēlterčo*; *baš* 'bridge', pl. *bašanc*; *hayur* 'horse', pl. *hayurišo*

CASE SYSTEM

Simple opposition between nominative and oblique/ergative, e.g. for *hiles* 'boy': sing. nom. *hiles*, erg./obl. *hilese*. pl. nom. *hilešo*, erg./obl. *hilešue*. In class 2 nouns, a distinction is made between ergative and general oblique case; e.g. for *gus* 'woman': erg. *guse*; general obl. *gusmo*.

    Most syntactic relationships are expressed with the help of postpositions: e.g. *gus.mu.cum* 'from the woman'; *den.iŋ.ulo* 'in the years'.

POSSESSION

The proclitic personal markers are mainly used where inalienable or organic possession is concerned. They are:

	1st person	2nd person	3rd person			
			Class 1	2	3	4
Singular	a-	gu-	i-	mu-	i-	i-
Plural	mi-	ma-		u-		u-

Examples: *ariŋ* 'my hand', *guriŋ* 'your hand'; *muriŋ* 'her hand'.

Adjective

Hardly distinguished from noun. As attribute, adjective usually precedes noun. Plural affixes attached to adjectives may be marked for class. Thus, *cūmišo* 'heavy (pl.)' with reference to classes 1–3; *cūmiŋ* 'heavy (pl.)' to class 4.

COMPARISON

A comparative is made with the postposition *cum* 'from', + positive degree: e.g. *Dža hayur īne hayurcum šua bi* 'My horse is better than his horse.'

Pronoun

The independent personal forms are:

	Singular	Oblique/ergative	Plural	Oblique/ergative
1	ǰe	ǰa	mi	mi(m)
2	ūn/ūŋ	ūŋ(e)	ma	ma(m)

The third person forms are supplied from the demonstrative series, which vary for class of referent. There are two series, proximate and distal:

	Class 1, 2	Class 3	Class 4
Proximate	kīne	guse	gute
Distal	īne	īse	īte

All with plural forms. A specific series is used only for classes 3 and 4: proximate *kōs/kōt*; distal: *ēs/ēt*.

The possessive proclitic series (see above) is used to denote direct/indirect object of verb; also, + postposition *ər*, to express a benefactive sense: e.g. *ar* 'to, for me'; *gor* 'to, for you'.

The pronominal series based on *men-*, *bes-*, etc., provide interrogative, negative, and relative forms, depending on context: e.g. *Ūŋ menan ba?* 'Who are you?'; *Besan ečam?* 'What shall I do?'

Numerals

The first three units vary for class:

	Classes 1 and 2	Class 3	Class 4
1	hin	han	han
2	āltan	ālta	ālto
3	īsken	usko	usko

4–10, all classes: *wālto, cundo, mišindo, talo, āltambo, hunčo, tōrumo*. 11–13: *turma* + class-related forms of 1, 2, 3; thereafter, *turma* + 4–9, as above. 20 *āltəran*; 30 *āltərtōrumo*; 40 *āltuwāltər*; 50 *āltuwāltər tōrumo*; 100 *tha*.

Verb

Finite forms are (a) primary (future, past tenses, imperative mood), or (b) secondary (all other tenses and moods): these secondary forms were originally compound – verb stem + *b*- auxiliary.

As in Iranian, all verbs, except the *b*- auxiliary, have two bases: past and present. The present base is made from the past by the addition of –(V)*č*/*dž*/*š*, depending on past base final: e.g. *sūyas* 'to bring', past base *su*-; present base *suč*-. The personal and class markers are prefixed or suffixed to, or infixed in, the verbal base. The verbal complex is negated by a negating prefix *a*- (with variants).

Prefixed markers are essentially the possessive markers (see above). They are in concord with the object of transitive verbs (the ergative construction), and with the subject of intransitive verbs (where they are, in fact, redundant).

Suffixed markers show person, number, and, in the third person, class. They are vocalic in the singular, V + *n* in plural: e.g. the first person singular marker is -*a*, the plural -*an*; class 2 third person singular -*u*/*o*, plural -*an*: *guyecam* 'I saw you' (-*m* is past-tense marker); *muyecum.an* 'they saw her'.

TENSE

The indicative mood has six tenses, three formed from each of the two bases. For example, from *ni(y)as* 'to go': present root *nič*-; past root *ni*.

		Singular		Plural
1		niča ba	1	niča bān
2		niča	2	ničān
3	Class 1:	ničaii	3	ničān
	Class 2:	niču bo		ničān
	Class 3:	niči bi	3	–
	Class 4:	niči bīla		—

The future tense of the same verb is: 1st p. sing. *ničam*, 2nd *ničuma*; the class-marked forms for the 3rd p. are *ničim.i*/*o*/*i*.

The past tense: *niam*, *nīma*; *nīmi*, *nīmo*, *nīmi*. The perfect has *ni(a)* + *b*-auxiliary: e.g.

present: *ǰe čamine ēirča ba* 'I'm dying of hunger'
future: *γenišan gučičam* 'I shall give you gold'
past: *badša haγurcum sōkimi* 'the emperor dismounted from the horse'

IMPERATIVE

The endings are, sing. -*ni*, pl. *nīn(a)*.

Certain verbs have class infixes, i.e. specific vocalic patterns.

NEGATION

Prefix *a*- (rarely *o*-, *ō*-): e.g. *dīca ba* 'I brought him'; *atīca ba* 'I didn't bring him'.

NON-FINITE FORMS

infinitive: past base + -*as*/*ās*;
first gerund: past base + -V*m*;
second gerund: past base + -V*š*.

Example: *Šapik **dicum** gŭsiŋanc osaljzaii* 'He sees women bringing bread' (*šapik* 'bread').

Word order

Normally SOV.

BURYAT

INTRODUCTION

This Mongolian language, closely related to Khalkha Mongolian, is spoken by about 300,000 people in the Buryat Autonomous Soviet Socialist Republic, and by, possibly, 100,000 in the People's Republic of China. It is difficult to estimate how many people speak Buryat in China, as they are not listed separately from the Khalkha and Oirat Mongolians (total for all three c. 3½ million).

In addition to a long and rich oral tradition, the Buryats now have a considerable output in several literary fields. Four main dialects are distinguished. The literary norm is based on the eastern Khori dialect.

SCRIPT

Originally the Buryats had an amended version of the vertical Mongolian character. Initial experiments with Cyrillic were made in the nineteenth century. A period of romanization in the 1930s was followed by the present Cyrillic alphabet, which contains the additional letters θ, γ, h. The Cyrillic letter н does duty for both the dental and the velar sound: /n/ and /ŋ/.

PHONOLOGY

Consonants

 stops: b (→ [w]), d, t, g (→ [γ])
 fricatives: s, z, ʃ, ʒ, x, h
 nasals: m, n, ŋ
 lateral and flap: l, r
 semi-vowel: j

/p, f, k, ts, tʃ/ occur in loan-words.

Vowels

 front: ɪ, iː
 central: y, yː, œː, e, eː, ɛ, ɛː
 back: u, uː, o, oː, a, aː

Vocalic reduction takes place in all non-initial syllables. /œ/ is notated here as *ö*.

251

The basic opposition is between central and back vowels; the high vowels /ɪ, iː/ are neutral: cf. *doloon* 'seven'; *negen* 'one'; *xorin* 'twenty'; *ygi* 'not'. Some erosion of this system is due in part to the monophthongization of old diphthongs. Thus, /aj, oj, uj/ have all become /ɛː/: cf. *axa* 'elder brother' + *tai* 'with' → *axataj* = /axatɛː/.

MORPHOLOGY AND SYNTAX

Noun

No gender, no articles. Nouns and adjectives are not formally differentiated; a noun in base form may serve as a qualifier: e.g. *modon ger* 'wood(en) house'; *aman zoxjol* 'oral literature' (lit. 'mouth creation').

PLURAL MARKERS

$(C)uud^2$: the index indicates that two allomorphs are possible, depending on vowel harmony: e.g. *seseg* 'flower', pl. *sesegyyd* (front vowel in stem); *gazar* 'place,' pl. *gazarnuud* (back vowel in stem). Similarly, $-nar^3$ indicates three possible allomorphs; this marker is used as a collective affix for humans: e.g. *dyyner* 'young people'; *axanar* 'elder brothers'.

-d is used as a plural marker after unstable *-n*, and in certain words; e.g. *mori(n)* 'horse', pl. *morid*; *nöxör* 'friend', pl. *nöxöd*.

CASE SYSTEM

Specimen paradigms of singular forms for *gal* 'fire', *dalai* 'sea'

nominative	gal	dalai
genitive	galai	dalain
dative/locative	galda	dalaida
accusative	galiije	dalaije
instrumental	galaar	dalaigaar
comitative	galtai	dalaitai
ablative	galhaa	dalaihaa

The same endings are added to plural forms. Affixes are subject to assimilation at junctures, and, of course, to vowel harmony.

The case marker precedes the possessive affix: e.g. *axa.da.m* 'to my elder brother'.

Cases may be compounded: e.g. *temeen.tei.hee* 'from the one who has the camel'; *terge.tei.tei* 'with the one who has a cart'.

Adjective

As attribute, adjective precedes noun and may take plural marker instead of noun: e.g. *jexe Ø gernyyd* = *jexenyyd ger* 'big houses'. Personal markers may be added to adjectives: e.g. *ulaanš* 'you, (who are) red'.

Pronoun

PERSONAL INDEPENDENT

Sing. 1 *bi*, ši, 3 *tere*; pl. 1 *bide(ner)*, 2 *ta(anar)*, 3 *tede(ner)*. These are declined in all cases. As in Khalkha, the oblique cases of *bi* 'I' are formed from a suppletive base, *nam-*, with a genitive in *minii*.

DEMONSTRATIVE PRONOUN

ene 'this', pl. *ede*; *tere* 'that', pl. *tede*.

INTERROGATIVE PRONOUN

xen 'who?', pl. *xed*; *juu(n)* 'what?', pl. *juud*.

Numerals

1–10: *negen, xojor, gurban, dyrben, taban, zurgaan, doloon, naiman, jyhen, arban.* 11–19: *arban + negen*, etc.; 20 *xorin*; 30 *gušan*; 40 *dyšen*; 100 *zuun*.

Verb

The Buryat verb has finite and non-finite forms. Finite forms take personal endings and function only as predicates. Non-finite forms are (a) verbal nouns which function mainly as attributives, but can take case endings and function as nouns, and (b) gerunds or converbs which are always in accessory relationship with a main verb.

There are five voices and four moods, each with specific marker (Ø in active voice and indicative and imperative moods).

VOICE

passive: *-gda²-*, e.g. *neexe* 'to open': *negdexe* 'to be opened';
causative: *-uul²-*, e.g. *jabaxa* 'to go': *jabuulaxa* 'to cause to go';
reciprocal: *-lda³-/-lša³-*, e.g. *zolgoxo* 'to meet': *zogoldoxo* 'to meet each other'.

MOODS

The indicative mood has three main tenses – present, past, future. The tense markers are: present *-na³-*; past *-ba³-/-(g)aa⁴*; future *-xa³-*. The personal markers are: sing. 1 *-b/m*, 2 *-š*, 3 *-Ø*; pl. 1 *-bdi*, 2 *-t*, 3 *-d/-Ø*. Examples from *jabaxa* 'to go':

present: *jaba.na.b/m* 'I go', *jaba.na.š* 'you go', *jaba-na* 'he goes'
past: *jab.aa.b/m* 'I went'
future: *jaba.xa.b/m* 'I shall go'

IMPERATIVE

2nd sing. = bare stem: + *-iit* for plural, with polite form in *-gtii*: *jabagtii* 'Please go.'

OPTATIVE

The marker is *-hai³-*: *jab.a.hai.bdi?* 'How about (us) going?'

DUBITATIVE
-(g)uuža²-: *unuuža.b?* 'What if I were to fall?'

GERUNDIVE AFFIXES
(Converbs): examples:

> *-ža³-* for concomitant action: e.g. *Gazaaguur garaža laptaa naadana* 'Going out, they play a ball-game.'
> *-(g)aad³-* marks action preceding that of the main verb: e.g. *Ger xaraad jabaa* 'Having seen the house, he went.'
> *-bal³-* conditional: e.g. *xarabal* 'if ... see(s)'.
> *-tar³-* terminative: e.g. *zun bolotor* 'until (it becomes) summer'.
> *-xalaar⁴-* marks action immediately preceding that of main verb – 'as soon as'; e.g. *Ger xaraxalaar jabaabdi* 'As soon as we had seen the house we went.'

NEGATION
Of indicative predicative form: *ygii* + personal marker. Cf. *jabanab* 'I go'; negative *jabana ygeib*. Other moods are negated by the particle *by*.

RELATIVE CLAUSES
Usually constructed via participial use of verbal noun forms to the left of the head-word: e.g. with *-han³*; *untaxa* 'to fall asleep, be asleep', *jerexe* 'to come'. *untahan xyn* 'someone who has fallen asleep'; *jerehen xyn* 'the person who came'. With *-xa³*: *jabaxa xargii* 'the road which ... is/are to take'. *-dag³* denotes constant or reiterated action: e.g. *jabadag xargii* 'a road which one habitually takes'.

There are four auxiliaries, the main ones being *bol-* and *bain-*, which are fully conjugated.

Postpositions

Govern the nominative, genitive, dative, or ablative cases: e.g. *gerei xažuuda* 'near the house' (with genitive); *manai gerei urda* 'in front of our house' (with genitive).

Word order

SOV is normal, but inversions are frequent.

CAMBODIAN (Khmer)

INTRODUCTION

Cambodian belongs to the Mon-Khmer sub-division of the Austro-Asiatic family. There are about 6 or 7 million speakers in Cambodia and Vietnam. The oldest inscriptions in Khmer date from the seventh century AD. From the end of the Angkor period (twelfth century) onwards, three main divisions of Cambodian literature may be distinguished: (a) Hindu influence is exemplified in the *Ream Ker*, the Cambodian version of the *Rāmāyaṇa*; in part, this is very old. (b) Buddhist influence (Cambodia became converted to Buddhism in the twelfth century). The translation of the *Tripitaka* has proved enormously influential, as, in addition to providing much of the Buddhist canon, it gave Cambodian literature a rich supply of motifs for the specifically Cambodian genre of the verse-novel. (c) the verse-novel: Cambodians seem to be particularly addicted to romantic stories of a sentimental type in which, latterly, French influence may be discerned.

SCRIPT

The Khmer script derives from a variant of Devanagari. The original Devanagari order is preserved (the retroflex and dental series have coalesced) as is the siting of the vowels; and, as in Devanagari, the consonants in their base state have a syllabic value, i.e. a back vowel inheres in each. Khmer use of this Indian material, however, introduces an essential innovation: the consonants are divided into two series or registers, in each of which one and the same vowel sign is realized differently. Thus, the system doubles the vocalic inventory (Cambodian is very rich in vowels) by giving one specific value to a vowel sign following a series 1 consonant, and quite another value to the *same* vowel sign following a series 2 consonant. Series 1 consonants are the original Devanagari voiceless stops with their aspirates (including the affricate series); series 2 consonants consist of the Devanagari voiced stops with their aspirates. For example, *kh* in series 1 represents Devanagari *kh*; *kh* in series 2 represents Devanagari *gh*. As illustration: *kh* in series 1 is 𑀘 ; *kh* in series is 𑀕𑀕 ; both can be followed by the vowel sign for long *ā*: ꠁ : but 𑀖𑀖 𑀖 is pronounced [khat] ('to polish'); 𑀕𑀕𑀕 𑀖 is pronounced [khoət] ('to prevent'). For certain consonants in series 1 there is no counterpart in series 2. In such cases, the series 1 consonant can be converted to series 2 register by means of a diacritic.

PHONOLOGY

Consonants

stops: p, ph, b, t, th, d, k, kh, ʔ
affricates: ts, tʃ
fricatives: s, h
nasals: m, n, ɲ, ŋ
lateral and flap: r, l
semi-vowels: j, w

Aspiration is phonemic: cf. *thaa* 'to say'; *taa* 'old man'.

Vowels

The vocalic system is of great complexity, requiring over 30 phonemic contrasts to be notated in close transcription. There are ten basic short vowels:

front: i, e, ɛ
central: ɪ, ə, a
back: u, o, ɔ, ɑ

Ten long vowels: the above vowels doubled: /ii, ee/, etc. Ten long diphthongs:

iə, ɪə, uə, ei , əɪ, ou, ae, aə, ao, ɔə

and three short

uə, eə, oe

Cambodian is non-tonal. Stress tends to fall on the final syllable.

MORPHOLOGY AND SYNTAX

Noun

Cambodian words have no inflection of any kind, and are not readily classifiable in terms of 'parts of speech'. There are no articles: e.g. *pteəh* means 'house, a house, the house'. Number may be inferred from the context, or expressed by such modifiers as *klah* 'some', *teəng* 'all'. For example, *pii* 'two' may be added to *teəng*: *salaa.riən teəng.pii nuh* 'those two schools' (*salaa.riən* 'house of learning').

GENDER

If necessary, gender can be expressed by such lexical additions as *proh* 'male (human)', *srəy* 'female': e.g. *koun.proh* 'son'; *koun.srəy* 'daughter'.

CASE RELATIONS

Expressed syntactically with the help of various particles, or by apposition as in the genitive: e.g. *laan əwpuk* 'father's car' (*laan* 'car'; *əwpuk* 'father'), *əwpuk neək* 'your father'; or in compound form: e.g. *tuənlee.meekong* 'the river (of the) Mekong'.

Adjective

As attribute, adjective follows noun: e.g. *salaa.riən touc* 'a small school'; *koun.srəy l'ɔɔ* 'a pretty girl'.

Pronoun

Cambodian had, and up to a point still has, a very large inventory of status-graded personal pronouns, each with correlative particles of address and response. As in the case of Lao, social change fosters the emergence of certain pronouns as neutral/polite forms of address or reference, suitable for use in most situations: e.g. for first person *khɲom*; for second person *look* (to a man), *look.srəy* (to a woman); third person *koət*. Plural forms may be made for these by adding *teəng.'ah*.

In the case of the second person, use of a title or a kinship term is preferred wherever possible. A full list of all status-graded forms is given in Jacob (1968: 158–63).

DEMONSTRATIVE PRONOUN/ADJECTIVE
nih 'this/these'; *nuh* 'that/those': e.g. *laan nih* 'this car'; *siəwphɪw tlay pram nih* 'these five (*pram*) expensive (*tlay*) books'.

INTERROGATIVE PRONOUN
neə'-naa 'who?'; *'wəy* 'what?': e.g. *Neə'naa cang tɪw məəl kon?* 'Who wants to go to the cinema?' (*məəl* 'to see, watch').

RELATIVE PRONOUN
dael, following head-word: e.g. *Khɲom miən koun.proh mənеə' dael nɪw riən nɪw laəy* 'I have a son who is still (*nɪw laəy*) at school' (*mənеə'* is the classifier for person).

Numerals

1–10: *muəy, pii, bəy, buən, pram, prammuəy, prampii, prambəy, prambuən, dɔp*; 11: *dɔp.muəy*, 12: *dɔp.pii*; 20: *məphɪy*; 30: *saamsəp*; 40: *saesəp*; 100: *rɔɔy*.

Verb

There is no inflection of any kind. Aspect, modal categories, and tense are expressed by means of auxiliary particles which may be pre- or post-verbal. Thus, *haəy* is a post-verbal particle indicating the perfective aspect; *cɔng* is a modal auxiliary expressing wish or design.

Cambodian has no genuine passive voice; many verbals can be both active and passive, the exact meaning depending on the syntactic context.

Both prefixation and infixation are used as formative processes in Cambodian. The prefix *p-/ph-*, for example, produces causatives: e.g. *dəng* 'to know' – *p.dəng* 'to let know, inform'; *deik* 'to sleep' – *ph.deik* 'to put to sleep'. Similarly, with prefix *bVn-*: *riən* 'to learn' – *bəngriən* 'to teach'.

The infix *-Vm-* makes transitives: e.g. *slap* 'die' – *səmlap* 'to kill'; *krup* 'all' – *kumrup* 'to complete'; *s'aat* 'clean' – *sam'aat* 'to clean'.

The nasal infix makes nouns from verbs: e.g. *som* 'to ask' – *smom* 'a beggar'; *klaac* 'to be afraid of' – *komlaac* 'a timid person'.

The prefix *prɔ-* suggests reciprocity: e.g. *cam* 'to wait' – *prɔcam* 'to wait for each other'.

Partial reduplication is used to express intensification or reiteration of action: e.g. *kaay* 'to dig' – *kɔkaay* 'to dig away at'.

TENSE

Action is broadly classified as perfective, imperfective, or pending:

> Perfective: expressed by *baan* or *haəy*, e.g. *Maong prambuən haəy* 'It's gone 9 o'clock'; *khɲom sdap baan* 'I understood'. This form is negated by *mɪn ... tee*: e.g. *khɲom sdap mɪn baan tee* 'I didn't understand'.
>
> Imperfective: e.g. with *kɔmpung.tae*, corresponding to Lao *kamlang*: *Khɲom kɔmpung.tae riən phiəsaa.kmae* 'I am now learning Cambodian' (*phiəsaa* 'language', < Skt. *bhāṣā*).
>
> Pending action: e.g. with *nɪng*: *khɲom nɪng tɪw pteəh* 'I shall go home'.

MODAL AUXILIARIES

E.g. *trəw* 'must'; *cɔng* 'want to': *khɲom trəw tɪw twəə.kaa* 'I have to go to work'. *craən-tae* denotes habitual action: e.g. *khɲom craən-tae tɪw psaa tɲay-can* 'I always go to market on Mondays': *dam yɔɔk krɔəp* 'to plant (*dam*) for grain'.

Prepositions

(a) simple, e.g. *nɪng* 'with', *pii* 'from', *ləə* 'on';
(b) verbs as prepositions: e.g. *tɪw* 'to go' = 'to(wards)'; *yɔɔk* 'to take' = 'by means of, with (in instrumental sense)'.

Word order

SVO.

១ ១កាលដើមដំបូងនោះមានព្រះបន្ទូល ហើយព្រះបន្ទូលគង់ជាមួយនឹងព្រះជាម្ចាស់ ហើយព្រះបន្ទូលជាព្រះជាអម្ចាស់សួរគ៌ ២កាលដើមដំបូង ទ្រង់គង់ជាមួយនឹងព្រះជាអម្ចាស់សួរគ៌ ។ ៣របស់ទាំងអស់បានបង្កើតមកដោយពីទ្រង់ ហើយគ្មានរបស់អ្វីសោះកើតមកដែលថាមិនបានបង្កើតមកដោយពីទ្រង់នោះឡើយ ។ ៤ក្នុងព្រះបន្ទូលនោះមានជីវិត្រ ហើយជីវិត្រជាពន្លឺហ៌របស់មនុស្សលោកៗ ៥ពន្លឺហ៌ បំភ្លឺហ៌ក្នុងសេចក្តីងងឺត តែសេចក្តីងងឺតមិនបានទទួលពន្លឺហ៌ទេ ។

៦មានមនុស្សម្នាក់ឈ្មោះ យ៉ូន ដែលព្រះជាអម្ចាស់សួរគ៌ចាត់ឲ្យមក ៧គាត់ បានមកសំរាប់ធ្វើជាទីបន្ទាល់ និងធ្វើជាបន្ទាល់ពីពន្លឺហ៌ ដើម្បីនឹងឲ្យមនុស្សទាំងអស់ ជឿហ៌ដោយពីគាត់ ៨គាត់មិនមែនជាពន្លឺហ៌ តែគាត់លេចមកនឹងធ្វើជាទីបន្ទាល់ពី ពន្លឺហ៌ទេ

CARIB

INTRODUCTION

In terms of geographical extent, the Ge-Pano-Carib group of languages is one of the largest in South America. In some classifications it is split into two groups, Cariban and Macro-Ge: the former, with nearly 100 languages, being centred on the Guianas and Northern Brazil, the latter stretching across Brazil into Paraguay and Patagonia. Cariban languages are spoken by about 40,000 people. The form of Cariban described here (after B.J. Hoff 1968) is spoken by 'several thousands' in Surinam. The language must be distinguished from Island Carib which belongs to the Arawakan family. Carib is unwritten.

PHONOLOGY

Consonants

The voiced and unvoiced pairs /b, p; d, t; g, k/ are present with associated nasals m, n; /ɲ/ does not seem to be present, but the palatal nasal /ŋ/ is. Also included in the inventory are the glottals /ʔ/ and /h/; /r, s, w/ and a sound which Hoff transcribes as *β̃*. All can be palatalized except the glottals.
Initial clusters consisting of nasal + stop are found, e.g. /mbo/.

Vowels

> short and long: i, ɪ, e, a, o, u

Long vowels are indicated by:. There are six diphthongs, all glides to /i/, except /au/.

MORPHOLOGY AND SYNTAX

Both nouns and verbs are related to person by a series of five personal prefixes: first person Ø, second *a-*, third *i-*; third person reflexive *tɪ-*; first person pl. incl. *kɪ-*. Examples: *Øtunda* 'my arriving'; *atunda* 'your arriving'.

Noun

Nouns occur in isolate or in *-rɪ/-ru* form, which is used, for example, when one noun is defined in terms of another: e.g. *kuri:yara* 'boat', *kasi:ri* 'cassava': *kasi:ri ku:riya:rarɪ* 'cassava boat' (with redistribution of syllabic structure).

260

Affixes added to nouns include:

-xpa and variants: 'un-/non-'; often with *i-* prefix on noun, e.g. *ka:rai* 'blackness'; *i.ka:rai.pa* 'not black'.

-koβ/-goβ is a plural marker, e.g. *wo:to* 'fish'; *wo.tokoβ* (pl.).

-mbo as a noun affix suggests a falling short of norm.

Nouns are turned into verbs by affixes with *-a* for intransitives, *-o* for transitives: e.g. *ɪxko:nɪ* 'dirt': *ɪxkonda* 'to get dirty'; *ɪxkondo* 'to make dirty'.

Adjective

Can be formed from nouns by circumfix *tɪ ... Ce*: e.g. *me:nu* 'blood' – *tɪme:un.re* 'bloody'.

Pronoun

PERSONAL PRONOUN

Free forms seem to be lacking. *See* **Verb**, below for coded personal prefixes; also above for possessive markers.

DEMONSTRATIVE PRONOUN

Here there is a basic two-way opposition between definite/indefinite and animate/inanimate. In addition, Carib has an intricate system of sub-divisions: e.g. an indefinite inanimate demonstrative pronoun can be further modulated to express relation to place (*o:we*), to direction (*o:ya*), or to neither (*o:tɪ*). In the definite series all forms are either high-vowel-initial for proximity, or low-vowel-initial for relative distance: *i:ye* 'this (def.)', with reference to direction; *mo:e* 'that (def.) yonder', with reference to place.

INTERROGATIVE PRONOUN

no:kɪ 'who?'

Numerals

1–10: *o:wiβ̄, o:ko, o:ruwa, o:kopaime, aiyato:ne, o:winduwo:pɪima, o:kotuwo:pɪima, o:ruwatuwo:pɪima, o:winapo:sikɪ:rɪ, aiyapato:ro*.

Verb

Stems are modulated by prefix or suffix for aspectual/modal senses, and can be extended by *-se/-ye* or *rɪ/-ru* where syntax requires. For example, the prefix *wos-* introduces the notion of reciprocal action: *e:ne* 'to see' – *wos.e:ne* 'to see each other'. *We-* and variants suggest that action expressed by stem does not involve second or third persons: e.g. *exke:i* 'to bake (specifically for others)'; *woxke:i* 'to be baking (for oneself?)'. The suffix *-potɪ* expresses iterative action: e.g. *e:nepotɪ* 'to go on seeing'. *-kepɪ* signals the cessation of the action expressed in verb: e.g. *ene:kepɪ* 'to see no longer'.

A typical transitive verbal complex comprises a subject personal pronominal prefix coded for pronominal object, a stem, and a temporal or modal affix. Neither the prefix nor the affix can be used without the other.

CODED PERSONAL PREFIXES

1 acting on 3:	*s(i)-*
2 acting on 3:	*m(i)-*
1 + 2 acting on 3:	*kɪs(i)-*
3 acting on 1:	Ø or *y-*
3 acting on 2:	*a, o,* or *y*
3 acting on 3:	*kɪni:/ni*

TEMPORAL/MODAL AFFIXES

-ya, -sa, -e are used with first and second person subjects acting on first, second, or third persons; *-yaβ̃, -saβ̃, -:no* are used where third person acts on first, second, or third persons.

TEMPORAL MARKERS ARE AFFIXED

-take for future; *-yakoβ̃* for past; *-yaine* for iterative action; *-se* for purpose. Examples:

with root *e:ne* 'to see':

sene:ya 'I see him'; *sene:ya:to* 'I see them'
sene:yakoβ̃ 'I saw him'
sene:yaine 'I see him repeatedly'
sene:se 'so that I may see it'
kɪne:neyaβ̃ 'he sees him'

with root *a:ro* 'to take':

saro:ya 'I take him'
maro:ya 'you take him'
kɪsa:roya 'we two take him'
ya:roya 'he takes me'

A non-personal form is made with prefix *tɪ/tu-/t-*, depending on initial: e.g. *a:ro* 'to take' – *ta:ro* 'taken'.

Copula:

		Singular	Plural
present:	1	wa	—
	2	ma:na	mandoβ̄
	1 + 2		kɪta:toβ̄
	3	maβ̄	mandoβ̄
preterite:	1	wa:koβ̄	
	2	ma:koβ̄	ma:tokoβ̄
	1 + 2		kɪta:tokoβ̄
	3	kɪna:koβ̄	kɪna:tokoβ̄

Postpostions

Examples: *pa:to* 'on the side of'; *ta* 'in'; *uwa:po* 'before', e.g. *yu:wa:po* 'before me', *ayu:wa:po* 'before you'; *wa:ra* 'like', e.g. *awa:raine* 'like you (pl.)', where *-ne* is the plural marker.

1. Lidan lagumeserun Lelerun, Lelerun lumaguiñe Bondiu, Lelerun Bondiu.

2. Ligiyameme lidan lagumeserun luma Bondiu.

3. Laduga sun katey; uati adugati lui le aduguwali.

4. Lidanguiñe ibagari; ibagari igemeri woguriña.

5. Ladururagoa igemeri lidan luburiga; ibidiati lun luburiga.

6. Ñeñen aban woguri hounahowti lumaguiñe Bondiu, John liña liri.

7. Ligiya liyabui lun ladimurehan, luagu larugougan lun hafiñerun sun woguriña.

8. Mama ligiya larugougan, lounahouña lun ladimurehan luagu larugougan.

CATALAN

INTRODUCTION

Catalan belongs to the Italik family of Indo-European. As the southern member of the rich and vigorous Ibero-Gallic culture which included Provençal, Catalan shares both French and Spanish traits. At present, it is spoken by c. 6 million people (mostly bilingual) in the north-eastern coastal strip of Spain, stretching from Roussillon and Andorra (where it has official status, along with French) through Catalonia to Valencia and the Balearics. The standard literary language is based on the Barcelona dialect. In terms of literary output, Catalan is the most important minority language in Western Europe.

Writing in Catalan dates from the twelfth century. From the troubadour period – shared with Provençal – to the fifteenth century, Catalan literature held a leading place in Europe, and two writers of genius emerged: Ramón Llull, Neoplatonic visionary and philosopher, linguist, and apostle, whose *Ars Magna* offers a kind of universal conceptive calculus, in which Christian, Islamic, and Greek paradigms are convertible and expressible in terms of each other, and whose Catalan novel *Blanquerna* (c. 1284) contains the celebrated *Llibre d'amic e amat*; and Ausias March (1397–1459), the greatest poet in the Europe of his day.

From the sixteenth to the nineteenth centuries writing in Catalan virtually ceased to exist. The Catalan *renaixença* may be dated from the re-establishment of the Barcelona *Jocs Florals* in 1859, and the romantic poetry of Verdageur. A steady output of verse and prose continued until the outbreak of the Civil War, when Catalan culture was proscribed. Since the 1970s, recovery has been sustained with the help of the rich legacy of Catalan culture in exile.

The lexicon is remarkable for the large number of monosyllables of VC, CV, CVC type: e.g. *vi* 'wine', *ma* 'hand', *be* 'sheep'; *ull* 'eye; *dit* 'finger', *blat* 'wheat'.

SCRIPT

The Roman alphabet, plus certain diacritics: grave, acute, cedilla.

PHONOLOGY

Consonants

    stops: p, b, t, d, k, g
    affricates: tʃ, dʒ

fricatives: f, v, s, z
nasals: m, n, ɲ, ŋ
laterals and flap: l, ʎ, r
semi-vowels: w, j

[ß] is a positional variant of both /b/ and /v/. *c* has three values: /s/ before *e*, *i*; /k/ before *a*, *o*, *u*; /ɣ/ before a voiced consonant.

/tʃ/ is represented in the script by *tx* or *ig*: e.g. *puig* /putʃ/; *cotxe* /kɔtʃə/.

Vowels

i, e, ɛ, a, ə, ɔ, o, u

Reductionism is an important feature of the vowel system: unstressed /e, a/ → [ə], unstressed /o/ → [u]: e.g. *patata* [pətatə], 'potato'; *forçar* [fursa], 'force' (final -*r* drops). The acute accent is used to mark the closed /e, o/; the open values /ɛ, ɔ/ are marked by the grave. The diaeresis marks a labialized vowel after /k/ or /ɣ/: *qüestio* /k°əstio/; it also marks syllabic /i/ or /u/.

Diphthongs whose second component is /i/ or /u/ are treated as monosyllables: i.e. first component + semi-vowel /w/ or /j/.

Stress

Stress is normally on penultimate of vocalic final, or on final diphthong.

MORPHOLOGY AND SYNTAX

Noun

Nouns in Catalan are masculine or feminine. The associated articles are:

	Definite		Indefinite	
	Singular	Plural	Singular	Plural
masc.	el/l'	els	un	uns
fem.	la/l'	les	una	unes

Certain prepositions fuse with the masculine definite forms: e.g. *per* + *els* → *pels*.

The plural marker is -*s*: e.g. *un gat*, pl. *uns gats* 'cats'; *el dia*, pl. *els dies* 'days'. -*os* is used for words ending in a sibilant: e.g. *el peix* 'fish', pl. *els peixos*. Addition of the plural marker may involve some change in spelling: e.g. *taronja* 'orange', pl. *taronges*; *boca* 'mouth', pl. *boques*.

Adjective

As attribute, adjective follows noun as a rule, though many of the commonest adjectives precede, e.g. *bo/bona* 'good', *gran* 'big', and agrees with it in gender and number. A typical row is: *blanc – blanca – blancs – blanques* 'white'. A few adjectives vary in meaning according to whether they precede or follow the noun.

COMPARATIVE

The comparative is made with *més* preceding adjective followed by *que* 'than'.

Pronoun

PERSONAL

The independent personal forms are: sing. *jo*, *tu*, *el/ella*; pl. *nosaltres*, *vosaltres*, *els/elles*. A polite form of address, corresponding to the Spanish *Usted/-es*, is *Vostè/-s*.

The forms given above are also the strong object forms, with one exception: in the first person singular *mi* replaces *jo*. The strong object forms are always governed by prepositions.

The weak object forms for direct and indirect object can precede or follow the verb; e.g. in the first person singular *em* → *m'* precedes the verb; *-me* → *'m* follows, if the verb form is an infinitive, an imperative, or a gerund: e.g. *li va parlar* 'he spoke to him'; *li'l donarem* 'we shall give it (masc.) to him/her/you'; *quan em va dir* 'when he told me'; *ajuda'm* 'help me'.

Frequently, a strong form (or a noun) is copied by a weak form attached to the verb: e.g. *a vostè no l'havia vist* 'I hadn't seen you'.

Combined weak forms: the grid for all persons, and numbers yields over 200 combinations, with complex rules governing the use of full and reduced forms. The indirect precedes the direct object form: e.g. *me'l dona* 'he gives it to me'; *ha de portar-nos-els* 'he has to bring them to us'; *porta-li'ls* 'take them to him'.

POSSESSIVE ADJECTIVES

E.g., in first person, *el meu – la meva – els meus – les meves*, with weak forms: *mon – ma – mos – mes*.

DEMONSTRATIVE PRONOUN/ADJECTIVE

aquest/-a/-s/-es 'this, these'; *aquell/-a/-s/-es* 'that, those'.

INTERROGATIVE PRONOUN

qui 'who?'; *què* 'what?'; *quin/-a/-s/-es* 'what, which?'

RELATIVE PRONOUN

que (invariable) is used for both subject and object; in prepositional phrases *qui* refers to persons, *què* to things. The compound forms: *el/la qual*, pl. *els/les quals* can also be used: *sobre qui = sobre el/la qual* 'about whom'; *els nois*, *que* ... 'the boys who'.

Numerals

1–10: *un/una*, *dos/dues*; *tres*, *quatre*, *cinc*, *sis*, *set*, *vuit*, *nou*, *deu*; 11 *onze*; 12 *dotze*; 13 *tretze*; 20 *vint*; 30 *trenta*; 100 *cent*.

Verb

As in Spanish, three conjugations are distinguished: *-ar*, *-re*, *-ir*.

(a) *-ar*; this, the largest class of verbs, is fairly regular. As in Spanish, some adjustment in spelling has to be made where consonants with hard and soft values are concerned: e.g. *-c-* alternates with *-qu-*: *tanco* 'I close', *tanques*.

(b) *-re*: sub-divided into classes: *-(C)Cre*, *-aure*, *-eure*, *-iure*, *-oure*; e.g. *prendre* 'take', *caure* 'fall', *creure* 'believe', *escriure* 'write', *moure* 'move'.

(c) *-ir*: certain verbs in this group add the increment *-eix-* between the stem and the endings: e.g. *llegir* 'read': *llegeixo*.

Catalan has indicative, imperative, and subjunctive moods. The indicative mood has present, imperfect, preterite, and conditional simple tenses, plus compound tenses – perfect, pluperfect, etc. – and periphrastic tenses made with the verb *anar* 'to go'. The subjunctive mood has present, imperfect, preterite, perfect, and pluperfect forms, used, as in French and Spanish, wherever doubt, negation, possibility, apprehension, or emotion colour the utterance.

PERSONAL ENDINGS
E.g. regular verb in *-ar*, *parlar* 'to speak'.

> present: sing.: *parl-o/-es/-a*; pl. *parl-em/-eu/-en*
> imperfect: sing.: *parl-ava/-aves/-ava*; pl. *parl-àvem/-àveu/-aven*
> preterite: sing.: *parl-í/-ares/-à*; pl. *parl-àrem/-àreu/-aren*
> present subjunctive sing.: *parl-i/-is/-i*; pl. *parl-em/-eu/-in*.

> The periphrastic tenses: the present-tense of the verb *anar* 'to go': *vaig, vas, va; anem, aneu, van. Vaig*, etc. + infinitive expresses a preterite sense: e.g. *Vaig arribar la setmana passada* 'I arrived last week.' *Vaig*, etc. + *a* + infinitive, forms the future: e.g. *Vaig a buscar les maletes* 'I'm going to look for the cases.'

The verbs *ésser* and *estar* (corresponding in sense and usage to Spanish *ser* and *estar*) share the same past participle – *estat. Ésser* is used with the past participle of a sense verb to make a passive: e.g. *ha estat trobat* 'has been found'; pl. *han estat trobats*.

In compound tenses, the past participle (conjugated with *haver* 'to have') is invariable, unless a third person direct pronominal object is present. Yates gives the example:

> Son boníssimes aquestes prunes; jo n'he menja**da** una i aquest se n'ha menja**des** dues o tres
> 'These plums are very good; I have eaten one, and he has eaten two or three.'

Prepositions

Several are composed of locative adverb + *de*: e.g. *dins/dintre de* 'in(side)'; *damunt de* 'above'; *sota de* 'below'.

Word order

SVO is normal.

1 En lo principi era lo Verb, y lo Verb era ab Deu, y lo Verb era Deu.

2 Ell era en lo principi ab Deu.

3 Per ell foren fetas totas las cosas, y sens ell ninguna cosa fou feta de lo que ha estat fet.

4 En ell era la vida, y la vida era la llum dels homes.

5 Y la llum resplandeix en las tenebras, y las tenebras no la comprengueren.

6 Hi hagué un home enviat de Deu ques anomenava Joan.

7 Est vingué *á servir* de testimoni pera testificar de la llum, á fi de que tots creguessen per medi d'ell.

8 No era ell la llum, sinó *enviat* pera donar testimoni de la llum.

CAUCASIAN LANGUAGES

The great majority of the languages spoken in the area between the Black Sea and the Caspian, especially in the Caucasus Mountains, appear to be indigenous to the region. The only Indo-European intruders are Ossetian and Armenian, and three Turkic languages are also present – Karachay-Balkar, Kumyk, and in the extreme south-east, Azerbaydzhani.

There are about three dozen indigenous languages, which are classified as follows:

1. Kartvelian (e.g. Georgian, Mingrelian, Svan);
2. North-West Caucasian (the Abkhaz-Adyge languages);
3. North Central Caucasian (Chechen-Ingush – the Nakh languages);
4. Dagestanian, sub-divided as:

    (a) Avar – Andi – Dido;
    (b) Lak-Dargva;
    (c) Lezgian.

One Kartvelian language – Laz – is spoken in the Trabzon area of Turkey; apart from this one outlier, all the indigenous languages of the Caucasus are spoken in USSR territory. Exile, whether voluntary (e.g. of the now extinct Ubykh people to Turkey in the 1860s, of many Kabard-Cherkes to the Near East at about the same time) or enforced (e.g. the temporary removal of the Chechen-Ingush people to Central Asia at the end of the Second World War), has done little to alter the generally static geo-linguistic picture.

See **Georgian, Laz, Mingrelian, Svan, Abaza, Abkhaz, Abkhaz-Adyge Languages, Adyge, Agul, Andi Languages, Avar, Chechen, Dagestanian Languages, Dargva, Kabard-Cherkes, Lak, Lezgi, Nakh Languages, Ubykh.**

CEBUANO

INTRODUCTION

In terms of numbers of native speakers, Cebuano, with around 10 million, rivals Tagalog as the major language of the Philippines, though it cannot compete with the 20 or 30 million who learn the latter as a second language. Cebuano and its two close congeners, Hiligaynon and Samaran, are often linked under the term 'Visayan'. The language is used to some extent in periodical literature, and in film and radio. Cebuano has a considerable number of Spanish loan-words.

SCRIPT

Roman.

PHONOLOGY

Identical to that of **Tagalog**. The stops /p, t, k/ are non-aspirated. The glottal stop is written as *q*. There are three basic vowels, /i, a, u/, with five diphthongs, /ɪ, a, u + w, y/. Short i → /ɪ/, short u → /ɔ/.

MORPHOLOGY AND SYNTAX

Noun

Nouns are proper – marked by *si* – or common, marked when subject, by *ang*, *y*, pl. *manga*. The ligature *nga/ng* is used in the construction of genitive and attributive phrases, and coalesces with a preceding vowel: e.g. *ni + nga + akuq + nga + amigu → ning akung amigu* '(this) my friend'.

Pronoun

The base series of personal pronouns is: sing. 1 *aku*, 2 *ikaw*, 3 *siya*; pl. 1 incl. *kita*, excl. *kami*, 2 *kamu*, 3 *sila*. These have genitive and dative forms, and all three sets – nominative, genitive, and dative – have short forms. In addition, there is a form for preposed genitive. Thus the complete row for the first person singular is:

Nominative		Genitive		Dative		Preposed genitive
full	*short*	*full*	*short*	*full*	*short*	
aku	ku	nakuq	ku	kanakuq	nakuq	akuq

where q = /ʔ/.

DEMONSTRATIVE PRONOUNS

Four degrees of distancing are distinguished, with reference to speaker and addressee: the nominative forms are *kiri*, *kini*, *kanaq*, *kadtu*, where *kanaq*, for example, means 'that' near addressee but not near speaker. These pronouns have correlatives marked for tense (present, past, future); for example, *kiri* 'this' (near speaker) has a present form *diqa*, a past form *diri*, and future *ari*. In addition, there are associated interrogative forms, also coded for tense: *haqin*, *diqin*, *asa*.

Numerals

The Spanish numerals are used.

Verb

As in Tagalog and Ilokano, the Cebuano verb consists of a stem or base + affixes – mainly prefixes, with a few suffixes and circumfixes. Verbal constructions are active or passive; there is a preference for passive constructions. Both active and passive conjugations have two basic versions: positive and hypothetical (sometimes called real and unreal). Each version has a specific set of prefixes. Thus for the active verb:

Mode	Positive	Hypothetical
volitional	ni-/mi-	mu-
durative	ga-/ nag-/ naga-	mag-/maga-
potential	ka-/naka-	ka-/maka-

The positive forms are used in affirmative reference to completed action or action in progress at the time of speaking. The hypothetical forms are used with reference to future or customary action, and in negative statements. For example, positive volitional statement:

mi.q.abang ni siya.g kwartu.s imung balay
'She rented a room in your house'

where *abang* means 'to rent'; *-q-* is euphonic link; *siya* is 3rd p. pron.; *-g* is the enclitic form of indefinite obj. marker *ug*; *kwartu* = Sp. *cuarto* 'room'; *imu* is 2nd p. preposed gen. *-ng-* ligature; *balay* 'house'.

Hypothetical volitional statement: e.g. ***mu**.q.abang ni siya.g* ... (as above) 'She wants to rent a room in your house'.

Hypothetical potential statement: e.g. *diq pa siya **maka**lakaw* 'He can't walk yet' (*diq* 'not'; *pa* 'yet'; *siya* is 3rd p. pron.; *lakaw* 'to walk')

PASSIVE VERB FORMS
(a) direct:

	Positive	Hypothetical
	gi-	-un
potential	na-	ma-

Cf.

> **mi**palit si P. ang Y
> 'P. bought the Y' (*mi-* form is active positive volitional; *palit* 'to buy')
> **gi**palit **ni** P. ang Y
> 'The Y was bought by P.' (passive marker *gi-* with logical sbj. in gen.)

Cf.

> **gi**tawag man (a)ku **nimu** 'you are calling me'
> **gi**tawag man ka/ikaw **nakuq** 'I am calling you'

(b) In the local passive, the locus of the action is focused. The positive markers are: *gi ... an*; the hypothetical *-an*, with potential forms. This form is also used as a benefactive, i.e. action on behalf of someone: e.g. **gipalitan** *ku si P. sa dulsi* 'I bought the candy for P.' The means or instrument of the action may also be focused. The markers of the instrumental passive are: positive *gi-*, hypothetical *i-*; also with potential forms: e.g. hypothetical: *ipalit ku kining kwarta.g X* 'I shall buy X. with this money'; *maqu kiniy akung ipalit ug X* 'This is what I'll buy X with' (*maqu* 'is').

The prefix *paN-* (where N symbolizes a nasal taking the class of the following consonant, e.g. $N + p/b = $ m), forms verbs from nouns, or indicates plurality of agent or recipient. Derivative verbs with *paN-* take all the active and passive prefixes outlined above: e.g. *bana* 'husband' – **pamana** 'to get married' (of a woman).

NEGATIVES

walaq > waq, diliq > diq, ayaw > ay. *Ayaw* negates the imperative. *Diliq* negates nouns, pronouns, adjectives: e.g. *diliq P. ang iyang ngalan* 'His name is not P.' *Walaq* negates the past tense: e.g. *waq siya **mu**qadtu sa sini* 'He didn't go to the pictures.'

Word order

Predicate precedes subject if neither is a pronoun. In positive sentences, agent may precede or follow patient.

1 Sa sinugdan mao na ang Pulong, ug ang Pulong uban sa Dios, ug Dios ang Pulong. 2 Kini siya sa sinugdan uban sa Dios. 3 Ang tanang mga butang nangahimo pinaagi kaniya; ug niadtong mga nangahimo na, walay bisan usa nga nahimo nga dili pinaagi kaniya. 4 Diha kaniya ang kinabuhi, ug ang maong kinabuhi mao ang kahayag alang sa mga tawo. 5 Ug ang kahayag nagadanag sa taliwaia sa kangitngitan, ug ang kangitngitan wala makabuntog kaniya.

6 Dihay usa ka tawo nga ginganlan si Juan,ⁿ nga pinadala gikan sa Dios. 7 Siya mianhi sa pagsaksi, sa pagpanghimatuod mahitungod sa kahayag, aron ang tanan motoo pinaagi kaniya. 8 Kini siya dili mao ang kahayag, hinonoa siya mianhi aron sa pagpanghimatuod mahitungod sa kahayag.

CELTIC LANGUAGES

INTRODUCTION

If not perhaps an Urheimat, the earliest identified point of origin for Celtic expansion seems to be the area now occupied by Austria and Bohemia, where they were the bearers of the La Tène (late Iron Age) culture, richly documented with artefacts of many kinds. From this base, the Celts spread out during the first millennium BC, westwards to Gaul, Britain, and Spain, eastwards to the Carpathians and Romania, southwards to Italy, Greece and Anatolia. In the fourth century BC they could be justifiably described by a Greek writer as one of 'the four great barbarian peoples'. Nevertheless, they lead a somewhat shadowy existence until their enforced historical debut – their defeat and subjugation at the hands of the Romans, first in cisalpine Gaul, and secondly in Gaul proper, in the first century BC.

Their somewhat unruly presence in Anatolia, where they were known as 'Galatai', is documented in the third century BC. Seven hundred years later, in the fifth century AD, the Galatians were still using their Celtic language (though St Paul had written to them in Greek). Evidence for this comes from St Jerome, the translator of the Vulgate, who recognized 'Galatian' as similar to the Gaulish language he had heard spoken in Trier in his student days.

A Celtic presence in the Iberian Peninsula is recorded by Herodotus, and attested in a corpus of inscriptions written partly in Latin character and partly in an imperfectly understood Iberian script. Two Celtic words for 'hill-fort', *briga* and *dūnum*, occur in many Iberian place-names. The distribution of these words bears witness to two strata of Celtic invaders: *briga* seems to be associated with an early wave of settlers who penetrated deep into the country, *dūnum* with a later and more restricted influx into Catalonia.

At the apogee of their expansion, about 100 BC, the Celts were in control of territory stretching from the Adriatic and the Danube to Scotland, and from the Rhine to south-western Spain. A couple of hundred years later they were everywhere on the retreat, largely subjugated, and undergoing a rapid process of assimilation. By AD 400 the erstwhile presence of continental Celtic was discernible in place-names only. It was in Britain alone that the Celts retained something of their national and ethnic identity.

Today, three of the four living Celtic languages – Irish, Welsh, and Breton – enjoy either some degree of political status, or, at least, overt support in the political arena. Irish, for example, has had joint official-language status (with English) since the foundation of the Free State in 1921 (the Irish name Eire was taken in 1937), though the language is used essentially on an internal, rather than on the international plane.

Both Welsh and Breton have been espoused by political parties or organizations, whose programmes envisage an administrative role for these languages in the future. No such political support has been forthcoming for Scottish Gaelic. All four languages are widely taught both at school and university level (Irish is an obligatory subject of the school curriculum in Eire), and their use as media for instruction in language and other subjects is apparently on the increase. All four, again, have locally run press, radio, and TV services.

Cornish and Manx are extinct: Cornish since the late eighteenth century, Manx since 1974, when the last native speaker died. The study of both languages is being actively promoted, however, and each can claim some hundreds of speakers.

The last hundred years have seen a steep decline in the numbers of speakers of Celtic languages. The statistics one finds in this connection are sometimes misleading. The number of people who 'know' Irish, for example, is usually given as about half a million. On closer examination, this figure is found to reflect those bilinguals who can *read* Irish, and who speak it as an acquired tongue. Only some 50,000 in western coastal areas actually speak the language as mother tongue, and virtually all of these are bilingual. In any case, the figures represent a substantial drop from the 1½ million who spoke Irish in the middle of the ninetenth century, of whom 320,000 were monoglot.

At the beginning of the twentieth century there was a total Gaelic-speaking population of about 230,000 in Scotland, mostly in Ross-shire and Inverness-shire, with 28,000 monoglot. Today's figure is c. 90,000, including a very small number of monoglots. There are about 3,000 Gaelic speakers in Nova Scotia. Welsh and Breton each claim about ½ million speakers; possibly none are monoglot. A few thousand people, all bilingual, speak Welsh in Patagonia.

The figures for proportional decline in the use of the Celtic languages reflect not so much a drop in populations (though emigration to North and South America has played a small part) as erosion of minority and economically weak linguistic territory by the contiguous world languages, English and French, acquisition of which is seen to be far more profitable and advantageous.

THE LANGUAGES
It was long held that Celtic stood in a special relationship with Italic, much as Baltic does with Slavonic. This thesis found some support in such linguistic phenomena as the presence of a *p/q* opposition in both Celtic and Italic (cf. Osc. *petora* for Lat. *quattuor*) and the parallel superlative formants: Lat. *-issimus* (IE *-isŭmo*), Proto-Celtic *-(i)samos*, OI-(*i*)*ssam*. For the *p/q* opposition, *see* **Proto-Celtic**, 5, below.

Proto-Celtic

In general, much of the Indo-European common fund is retained. Some points:

1. IE /*eː/ = Proto-Celtic /iː/: e.g. IE *rēgs*, Lat. *rēx/rēgis*: Goidelic, *rīks*, Old Irish, *rí* 'king'.

2. IE /*oː/ = Proto-Celtic (aː): e.g. IE *mōros = Goidelic māros, Old Irish már 'big'.
3. IE aspirated and unaspirated voiced stops are collapsed; thus OI /d/ represents both IE /*d/ and /*dh/.
4. Loss of IE /*p/, a high-frequency consonant in IE: e.g.

IE	Goidelic	Old Irish	
*pətēr	*Øaþēr	ath(a)ir	'father'
*pro-stom		Ø ross	'foothill'
*kapta		cacht	'female slave'

In initial position, /*p/ seems to have gone through an intermediate fricative stage before disappearing. This stage – /h/ – is preserved in the name of the German forest Hercynia, from *perkus 'oak' (Lat. quercus).

5. The loss of IE /*p/ was offset by the development of a secondary /p/ from IE /*kʷ/ in P-Celtic, where Q-Celtic retains /kʷ/. Cf. the equivalents for the numeral 'four': IE *kʷetvor.es, Lat. quattuor:

	Q-Celtic		P-Celtic
Old Irish	ceth(a)ir	/keːir/	Welsh pedwar < Old Welsh petguar
Gaelic	ceithir	/keːir/	Cornish peswar/peder
Manx	kiare		Breton pevar

Insular Celtic

Insular Celtic is divided into Brythonic (Welsh, Cornish, Breton) and Goidelic (Irish, Scottish Gaelic, and Manx).

The first Celtic colonizers of Britain, who arrived in the second half of the first millennium BC, were speakers of P-Celtic or Brythonic; and this remained the language of Britain up to and including the Roman period. From the seventh century onwards, Brythonic was squeezed more and more into western coastal areas by Anglo-Saxon pressure, while, at the same time, it came under attack from invaders belonging to Q-Celtic or Goidelic stock. It is not known when the Goidelic Celts reached Ireland, but it was from their base in Ireland that they attacked and successfully occupied western Scotland, north-western England, and the Isle of Man. The Celtic linguistic pattern thus established has remained virtually unchanged into modern times. Breton is a Brythonic enclave launched from Cornwall in the fifth to seventh centuries.

MUTATION

This is at once the most characteristic and the most striking feature of Insular Celtic. Phonological accommodation at syllable or word juncture is found in many languages, e.g. in the phenomenon of sandhi in Sanskrit, in Dravidian, in the juncture of article plus sun-letter in Arabic, in French, and in Portuguese. Typically, in these cases, accommodation at the juncture of two words A and B affects the final phoneme of A. For example, in French, les femmes /leː fam/ but les enfants /leːzãfã/. In Sanskrit, both final and initial my be affected.

The origin of mutation in the Celtic languages is precisely such accommodation at word juncture, but here it is specifically the initial of B that is affected. Under certain conditions, this initial shows a shift from voiceless to voiced stop, from stop to homorganic fricative or nasal, or to zero grade. These shifts were originally induced by such conditions as vocalic final of A. As the languages developed, the conditions inducing the shift were eroded and finally lost, but the mutation remained. And, since the mutations affected many of the most frequently occurring junctures, the whole system became grammaticalized, and, by analogy, extended.

Examples of the mutation system in practice will be found in the articles on the individual languages.

See **Breton**, **Cornish**, **Irish** (old and modern), **Manx**, **Scottish Gaelic**, **Welsh**.

CHAM

INTRODUCTION

Cham – spoken today by around 150,000 people in Vietnam and Cambodia – is the most important of the Chamic languages, which form part of the Western Austronesian family. The Indo-Chinese kingdom of Champa was established in the second century AD and lasted for some 1,500 years, reaching its political and cultural apogee from the sixth century onwards. Retaliation for Khmer invasions in the twelfth century resulted in the destruction of Angkor. Though of Austronesian stock, the Cham were completely dominated by Indian culture, an influence visible in their Gupta art forms and in the Cham script, which is based on Devanagari.

SCRIPT

The Devanagari-based script is mainly characteristic of Cambodian Cham.

PHONOLOGY

Consonants

The retroflex series is missing apart from signs for /ḍa, ḅa, ṣa/ in addition to the velar, palatal, dental, and labial series, the script has /ya, ra, la, va/, two sibilants, /sa/ and /ṣa/, and /ha/.

In Vietnamese Cham the Devanagari order has been lost, and the spelling is very defective: Aymonier gives the example of *sang* 'house', which is written as *pang* and pronounced as /tʰang/.

Vowels

short and long: i, a, u

/eː/, /ai/, /œ/, and /o/ also occur. The vowel system has been infected by Vietnamese, and there are several diphthongs.

MORPHOLOGY

Cham marks neither gender nor number. Natural gender is indicated either by lexical item, e.g. *amoeu* 'father', *inoeû* 'mother', or by addition of classifier, *dam* (masc.), *daraa* (fem.) for persons, *tanov* (masc.), *binai* (fem.) for animals.

There is no form of declension. Syntactic relationships are either positional, e.g. in genitive, *dii noethak tikuh* 'in the year of the rat' (*noethak* 'year'), or marked by particle, e.g. *kaa* for indirect object: *pvâch jhak kaa nhu* 'speak ill to him' (*pvâch* 'speak'; *nhu* 'he'). *Pak* indicates location: *pak thang* 'at home'; *pak nii* 'here'. *Dii* is an all-purpose marker for locative, ablative, instrumental cases: e.g. *dok dii thang* 'to stay at home'; *klaa dii laan* 'to avoid the cold'.

NOUN FORMATION
From verbs by -*n*- infix, as in Mon-Khmer:

> *pvâch* 'speak' – *panvâch* 'word'
> *dok* 'stay' – *danok* 'dwelling'
> *jiœng* 'be born' – *janiœng* 'birth'

pa- is causative: e.g. *mœtai* 'to die' – *pa.mœtai* 'to kill'. The prefix *mœ*- is heterogeneous but often indicates possession or application of something: e.g. *jruu* 'poison': *mœjruu* 'to administer poison'.

NOMINAL CLASSIFIERS
E.g. *boh* for fruits, *blah* for leaves, *ôrang* for people; *drēi*, the classifier for bodies is also used as a general pronoun.

Adjective

The attributive adjective follows the noun.

Pronoun

PERSONAL

	Singular	Plural
1	kau	gita
2	hēû	hēû
3	nhu	nhu

DEMONSTRATIVE PRONOUN
ni(i) 'this'; *nan* 'that': e.g. *ôrang ni* 'this man', *thang nan* 'that house'.

INTERROGATIVE PRONOUN
thēi 'who?'.

RELATIVE PRONOUN
k(r)ung.

Verb

Tense is indicated by particle accompanying the stem, e.g. *shi/thi* for future, *jœû* for past (Viet. *rôi*, Khmer *hœy*). The imperative marker is *bêk*.

MODAL VERBS

E.g. *truh* 'to be able', *kiœng* 'to want to'; *kau kiœng nau* 'I want to go'.

NEGATION

ôh/ô precedes or follows verb, or is reduplicated: *ôh huu = huu ôh = ôh huu ô* 'there isn't'.

Word order

SVO.

1 [1,2]Dahlau di bih, Anɨk Pô Lingik, nặn Pô Êtha, hu dok thõng Pô pajơ. Brŭk Anɨk Pô ngăk, panôch Anɨk Pô sanɨng jang yau Pô Lingik, kayua Anɨk Pô drơh yau Pô Lingik. [3]Pô Lingik bray ka Anɨk Pô pajɨng abih pakar ngŏk lingik thõng păk la tanɨh-riya. Yau năn, biăk Anɨk Pô pajɨng abih. [4,5]Anɨk Pô dok hadiup miêt miêt jang yau Pô Amɨ dok miêt miêt. Brŭk Anɨk Pô trun lôc ni pagăp yau tanrak-hadah mɨng ngŏk lingik pasang trun tamɨ dalăm libĭk sup, ngăk ka libĭk năn hadah-dai wŏk. Yau năn, Anɨk Pô pahadah hatai tian anɨk dun-ya piơh bray ka khol nhu thau djaup ka Pô Lingik.

CHAMORRO

INTRODUCTION

This Austronesian (Malay-Polynesian) language is related to the languages of the Philippines, and is spoken by about 50,000 in Guam and in some islands of the Marianas. There is a large stock of Spanish loan-words.

PHONOLOGY

Consonants

The labial, dental, and velar series are represented by non-aspirate voiceless + voiced stop + associated nasal: e.g. /p, b, m/. The palatal nasal /ɲ/ written ñ, is present, also /tʃ/, written as *ch*, and /s, l, r, h, f/ and the glottal stop. The voiced stops cannot be syllable-final, nor can /ch, l, r/; thus Spanish *verde* > *vetde*, *barco* > *batco*.

Vowels

i, e, æ, a, o, u; ao, ai

Stress

Stress on penultimate, with some exceptions.

MORPHOLOGY AND SYNTAX

The definite articles are *i* for common nouns, *si* for proper. The pronominal–verbal plural marker *man-* is transferred in stative sentences to the noun component if any: e.g. *man.mediku siha* 'they are doctors' (*siha* 'they') (*see* also **Adjective**). Juncture sandhi takes place when *man-* precedes /tʃ, s, t, k, f/.

Adjective

An adjectival attribute is linked to its noun by the ligature *na → n*, e.g. *i betde na kareta* 'the green car'; a modifying noun follows, e.g. *batkon aire* 'aeroplane'.

Dual and plural markers in stative sentences are transferred to the adjective, if any. The pronominal form is the same for both dual and plural; they are distinguished by the presence of *man-* in the plural form: e.g. *dankolo ham* 'we two are big'; *mandankolo ham* 'we (plural) are big'.

281

Pronoun

PERSONAL
Chamorro has two sets of personal pronouns:

(a) the *yo'* pronouns:

	Singular	Plural
1	yo'	excl. ham, incl. hit
2	hao	hamyo
3	gue'	siha

These are used as subject forms for intransitive/stative verbs, and as objective forms after transitive verbs.

(b) the *hu* pronouns:

	Singular	Plural
1	hu	excl. in, incl. ta
2	un	en
3	ha	ma

These are used as subject forms with transitive verbs + definite verbs + definite object: if the latter is pronominal, a *yo'* form is used: e.g. *hu li'e' **gue'*** 'I saw him'; *ha li'e' **yo'*** 'he saw me'. The *hu* pronoun is recapitulated with a nominal subject: e.g. *i famalao'an **ma** li'e i patgon* or ***ma** li'e' i famalao'an i patgon* 'the women saw the child'.

THE POSSESSIVE MARKERS
Sing. 1 -*hu*/-*ku* 2 -*mu* 3 -*na*; pl. 1 excl. -*mami*, incl. -*ta*, 2 -*miyu*, 3 -*niha*. These are used e.g. with the existential verb *guaha* to express 'to have': e.g. *guaha lepblo-mami* 'we have a book'.

A further set of personal pronouns – the *guahu*, or emphatic pronouns – may be used with agent-focused verbal construction (*see* **Verb**).

DEMONSTRATIVE PRONOUN/ADJECTIVE
Three-degrees of distancing: *este* – *enao* – *ayu*.

INTERROGATIVE PRONOUN
hayi 'who?'; *hafa* 'what?'.

RELATIVE PRONOUN
One way of making relative clauses is with the infix -*um*-. Thus, from verb *pacha* 'to touch': *i **pum**acha i lepblo* 'this one who touched the book'.

Numerals

The Spanish numerals are used as pronounced in Guam; e.g. for 12, 13, 14 *dosse, tresse, katotse*.

Verb

As in the Philippine languages, verbal constructions in Chamorro vary according to the component – agent, target, means, etc. – emphasized or focused. Thus, *-um-* is an agent-focusing marker, *-in-* is a goal-focusing marker; cf. *guahu lumi'e' i lahi* 'I (not someone else) saw the man'; *lini'e' i lahi nu guahu* 'I saw *the man*' (*nu* is a sbj. noun marker in this construction). Similarly, *na'* focuses the causative aspect of the action: e.g. *hu na'li'e' i patgon ni ga'lagu* 'I let the child see the dog'.

DEFINITE AND INDEFINITE OBJECT

This is a crucially important distinction in Chamorro. A sentence with a definite object takes a *hu* pronoun as subject; a sentence with an indefinite object takes a *yo'* pronoun as subject + *man-* prefix on verb: e.g. *hu li'e' i patgon* 'I see the child'; *manli'e' yo' patgon* 'I see a child'.

TENSE

Generally, a reduplicated form indicates imperfective action: e.g. *faisen* 'to ask' – *ma fafaisen* 'they are asking'. A non-reduplicated form is used for the perfective aspect, i.e. usually the past tense.

Future: the general marker is *para* (Sp.); in addition, 1st person singular and 1st person plural exclusive take *bai*. A *hu* pronoun is used. Example: *para bai hu li'e' i palao'an* 'I shall see the woman.' Example of passive marker *ma-* between plural marker *man-* and reduplicated stem: *manmalalalatde i famagu'on* 'the children are being scolded' (*lalatde* 'to scold').

NEGATION

The marker is *ti*: e.g. *Ti chumocho i patgon nigap* 'The child didn't eat yesterday' (*nigap*).

Word order

VSO is normal; SVO and OSV are possible, depending on focus selected.

1 Y TUTUJONÑA gaegue y Finijo, ya y Finijo güiya yan si Yuus; ya y Finijo güiya si Yuus.

2 Güiya gaegue gui tutujonña yan si Yuus.

3 Todo y güinaja sija manmafatinas pot güiya; yaguin ti pot güiya, taya ni esta mafatinas, nu y gaegue gui finatinas sija.

4 Y linâlâ gaegue guiya güiya, ya y linâlâ, güiya y candet y toatao sija.

5 Ya y candet gui jalom jomjom maniina, ya y jemjom ti matungo.

6 Y un taotao ni manafato guine as Yuus, y naanña si Juan.

7 Güiya mamaela para testimonio, para ufannae testimonio nu y candet, para ufanmanjonggue todo y taotao pot güiya.

8 Güiya ti y candet, lao mamaela para ufannae testimonio nu y candet.

CHECHEN

INTRODUCTION

Chechen is a member of the Nakh group of North-East Caucasian (the group includes Ingush and Bats). Chechen and Ingush are very closely related; until the 1930s the same literary standard was used for both. Charged with collaboration with the Nazi invaders in the Second World War, the Chechen and the Ingush were deported to Central Asia, where they remained till 1957 when the Chechen-Ingush Autonomous Soviet Socialist Republic was reinstated. At present, Chechen is spoken by about 700,000 people, Ingush by c. 190,000. Both languages are written, with periodical press and occasional books.

SCRIPT

Originally Arabic; thereafter a period of romanization, since 1938 Cyrillic + *I* as glottalization marker with consonants; by itself, it is like Arabic 'ain. The Cyrillic hard sign ъ is used to indicate hamza.

PHONOLOGY

Consonants

In general, simpler than that of the neighbouring Caucasian languages. There is no labialization; only one lateral; and the ejectives are reduced to six. There are four uvulars and two pharyngeals. Altogether 34 consonants are notated in Chechen, some of these representing positional allophones, and some sounds found only in loan-words. Intensive consonants are held (geminates). The geminate/non-geminate opposition is phonemic.

Vowels

 i, e, a, o, u

This basic series is greatly extended by palatalization, labialization, nasalization, and rounding. Desheriev (1967) lists 15 vowel signs, each representing two or more values. Magometov, quoted in Hewitt and Comrie (1981), lists 36 vowel sounds for Lowland Chechen. Typical rows are:

 a, aː, ɛ, ɛː, ã, ãː
 je, jeː, jẽ, jẽː

Stress

Normally on first root syllable.

MORPHOLOGY AND SYNTAX

Noun

There is no gender. Nouns have class, number, and case. There are six grammatical classes of noun: the noun itself is not marked for class, which is, however, reflected in verbal concord and in certain modifiers, such as adjectives and numerals.

CLASS
Markers are:

Class	Singular	Plural	Class members
1	vu	du	masculine humans
2	yu	du	feminine humans
3	du	du	
4	yu	yu	heterogeneous
5	bu	bu	
6	bu	du	

PLURAL
Markers are -*š* and -*y*: e.g. *kor* 'window' – pl. *kor.a.š*; *belxalo* 'worker' – pl. *belxaloy*; *nana* 'mother', pl. *nanoy*. The base may be extended, often with umlaut: e.g. *ča* 'bear' – pl. *čerčiy*; *lam* 'mountain' – pl. *lämnaš*.

CASE SYSTEM
Four declensions are distinguished, one criterion being the ending of the instrumental case. Specimen declension for *bedar* 'clothes', pl. *bedarš*:

	Singular	Plural
genitive	bedaran	bedariyn
ergative	bedaro	bedarša
dative	bedarna	bedaršna
instrumental	bedarca	bedaršca
inessive	bedarax	bedaršex
contrastive	bedaral	bedarel
locative	bedare	bedarška

Internal flection also occurs: e.g. *ça* 'house', gen. *çiynan*, pl. *çenoš*. There are several derivative locative cases, plus postpositional complexes in which the postpositions take specific case endings.

Adjective

As attribute, adjective precedes noun: e.g. *dika stag* 'good man' (*stag* 'man'). A few primary adjectives are marked for class. In attributive function, adjectives have two forms: nominative and a general form in -*č* + V, which covers all other cases: e.g. *ḳayn bepig* 'white bread'; *ḳayču bäpkan* 'from white bread'.

COMPARISON
A comparative is made in -*x*: e.g. *dika* 'good', *dikax* 'better'.

Pronoun

INDEPENDENT PERSONAL

	Singular		Plural
1	so	incl.	way
		excl.	txo
2	ḥo		šu
3	i/iza, hara		üš/üzaš
	(demonstrative forms)		

These are declined in all cases; specimen row, first person singular: *so, san, as, suna, söca, sox, sol, söga.*

DEMONSTRATIVE PRONOUN
As third person singular pronoun above.

INTERROGATIVE PRONOUN
mila, pl. *mülš* 'who?'; *hun* 'what?'. These are declined in all cases on suppletive bases.

Numerals

1–10: *cḥa', ši', qo', di', pxi', yalx, worh, barh, iss, itt*; 11–19: units combined with *itt*: e.g. 11 *cḥaytta*; 12 *šiytta*. 20 *tqa*; 30 *tqeitt*; 40 *šöztqa*; 100 *ḅ'e*.

Numeral + noun: noun is in the singular: e.g. *pxi stag* 'five men' (hamza drops). Certain numerals are marked for two cases preceding declined noun, e.g. *ši' – šina, šina gorwan* 'of two horses'; *di' – dea, dea berana* 'to four boys'.

Verb

Conjugation is by grammatical class, without reference to person. Mood, aspect, tense, and number are distinguished.

INDICATIVE MOOD
Specimen tenses of verb *ala* 'to say':

> present: *olu*
> future: *olur(du)*
> past: *eli* (with reference to recent past); *älla* (perfective); *olura* (imperfective); *elira* (inferential).

Intransitive verbs show concord with subject; transitive verbs show concord with object. The class markers are prefixed to primary, i.e. non-derivatory, verbal forms; infixed in composite forms. Examples:

Intransitive:

Class	Singular	Plural
1	**v**axana 'he went'	**b**axana 'they (masc.) went'
2	**y**axana 'she went'	**b**axana 'they (fem.) went'
1	**v**ux**v**irzina 'he returned'	**b**ux**b**irzina 'they (masc.) returned'
2	**y**ux**y**irzina 'she returned'	**b**ux**b**irzina 'they (fem.) returned'

Transitive:

3	co govr yügu 'he leads the horse'	
	co govraš yügu 'he leads the horses'	
4	co ṭulg baḥa 'he brings/carries the stone'	
	co ṭulgaš **d**aḥa 'he brings/carries the stones'	

In these examples (from JaNSSR, IV, 200) *co* is the ergative case of the third person singular *i/iza* 'he'.

The negating particle is *ca*: e.g. *ca vaxana* 'he didn't go'.

The other moods are: imperative, hortative, optative, and subjunctive: the optative marker is -*l*, the subjunctive -*ḥara*.

Present in -*n*, e.g. *vogun* 'going'; past: recent past form minus final vowel, e.g. *vaxan* 'having gone'; future: present participle + *dolu(n)*. These forms are used in relative clauses: e.g. *vaxan stag* 'the man who went'; *latt äxan stag* 'the man who ploughed the soil'.

Word order

Rather free; in general, S initiates sentence, V is final.

---

1. **ДУЬХХЬАР** хилла Дош, и Дош Делехь хилла, Дела Дош хилла.

2. Иза хилла дуьххьара Делехь.

3. Дерриг Цуьнгахула схьадоладелла, Цуьнан лаам боцуш долчу хӀуманийх хӀумма хилла дац.

4. Цуьнгахь хилла дахар, дахар адамийн серло хилла;

5. Серло боданехь а къега, бодано иза дӀацахьулйо.

6. Цхьа стаг хилла Дала ваийтана, цуьнан цӀе хилла Яхья.

CHEREMIS

See **Mari**.

CHEROKEE

INTRODUCTION

Cherokee is a member of the Iroquoian group of the Macro-Siouan family. The language is spoken today – entirely as a second language – by about 20,000 to 30,000 Cherokees in Oklahoma, with a residue in North Carolina. Ousted in tribal warfare from their original habitat in the Great Lakes area, the Cherokee moved south to Georgia and the Carolinas, where they proceeded to model their way of life and institutions on those of the European settlers. By the early 1800s they had achieved a remarkable degree of administrative, economic, and cultural stability. In 1828 a Cherokee weekly newspaper, the *Cherokee Phoenix*, was launched, a unique event in the annals of the American Indian. For this publication, Sequoyah's script was used (*see* **Script**, below). In the circumstances, however, it was a political and economic experiment which could not last, and the wars and rigged treaties which followed led in 1838–9 to the forcible removal of the Cherokee people to Oklahoma. Descendants of the few who escaped the 'Trail of Tears' still live in North Carolina.

SCRIPT

It was in 1819–20 that Sequoyah, a Cherokee half-breed, invented a syllabary of 86 characters, some of which are borrowed from the Roman alphabet (though with different values). The spread of literacy in this script among the Cherokees was rapid, and, in addition to the *Cherokee Phoenix*, parts of the Bible, tracts, and hymn-books soon appeared.

The script notates the vowels *a, e, i, o, u, v* = /x̃/, and 79 combinations of consonant + vowel. It does not notate vowel length, the intrusive /h/, nor the glottal stop. It is partially inconsistent; e.g. in the velar series, /ka/ and /ga/ are distinguished, the other five values are not.

W. Walker (in Crawford 1975) notes that ability to use the Cherokee syllabary is regarded as qualifying an individual to participate in Cherokee affairs. The transcription used in this article is that of Holmes and Smith in their 1976 grammar.

PHONOLOGY

Consonants

    stops: t, d, k, g, ʔ
    affricates: ts, dz/dʒ
    nasals: m, n
    fricatives: s, h
    laterals: l, ł, tl/dl
    semi-vowels: j, w

The velars /k/ and /g/ occur labalized: /k°, g°/; otherwise the labial series is absent, as are /z/ and /r/. In addition to the fricative /h/, there is an intrusive, pre-consonantal nasal /h̄/.

Vowels

    short: ɪ, ɛ, a, u, ʌ̃
    long: i, e, a, ɔ, u, ʌ̃:

The long vowels are notated here as *i:*, *a:*, etc. Following Holmes and Smith, the nasal vowel /ʌ̃/ is notated as *v*. All final vowels are nasalized.

Tone

Opposition between even tone and rising/falling; tone may be phonemic.

Stress

Long vowels may show a crescendo.

MORPHOLOGY AND SYNTAX

Noun

Nouns are divided into two classes: animate and inanimate. The distinction becomes overt only in the plural, marked for animates by *ani-/dini-*: e.g. *a.tsu.tsa* 'boy', pl. *a.ni.tsu.tsa*, where *a.* by itself is a singular prefix.

    A typical inanimate plural is made by dropping the *a-* prefix, and substituting *di/te*: e.g. *a.ye.l'.s.di* 'knife', pl. *di.ye.l'.s.di*.

    Many nouns are verbal in form: e.g. *a.tsi.lv.s.gi* 'it opens out' = 'flower'; pl. *a.ni.tsi.lv.s.gi*. An interesting point is that an adjective qualifying an inanimate noun, even if the noun itself takes the inanimate marker *di/te*, may have the animate marker: e.g. *u.ta.na tlu.kv* 'a big tree', pl. *tsu.n'.ta.na te.tlu.kv*.

POSSESSION

Alienable ownership and inalienable relatedness are distinguished. Movable goods and chattels are alienable; kinship terms and names for parts of the body are marked for inalienable relatedness. Clothing is optionally in either camp. Alienable ownership, being heterogeneous, has several markers, in contrast to relatedness, which is homogeneous.

The alienable marker is *-tse.li-* following pronominal bound forms of group 2 (see below): e.g. *a.qua.tse.li gi:tli* 'my dog'; *u.tse.li ga.lo.ge:sv* 'his farm'. Inalienable relatedness: the bound pronoun is prefixed directly to the noun: e.g. *a.gi.do.da* 'my father'; *u.do.da* 'his/her father'.

Pronoun

Only two free forms exist: *a.hyv* 'I'; *ni.hi* 'you'. Their use is optional. Bound forms: two sets, each with ten forms (three singular, three dual, three plural, one collective): e.g. set 1 with active stem *-wo:ni-* 'to speak'; set 2 with stem *-du.li-* 'to want':

Singular	1	tsi.won:ni.a	a'.wa.du.li.a
	2	hi.won:ni.a	tsa.du.li.a
	3	ga.won:ni.a	u.du.li.a
Dual	1	i.ni.won:ni.a	gi.na.du.li.a
	2	s.di.won:ni.a	s.da.du.li.a
	3	o.s.di.won:ni.a	o.gi.no.du.li.a
Plural	1	o.tsi.won:ni.a	o.ga.du.li.a
	2	i.tsi.won:ni.a	i.tsa.du.li.a
	3	a.ni.won:ni.a	u.na.du.li.a
collective		i.di.won:ni.a	i.ga.du.li.a

-a in the above paradigms is the present-tense marker.

Object pronouns coalesce with subject pronouns in pre-stem position. There is a very wide range of forms, though not all theoretically possible forms are used. Examples: *gv.yo.li:ga* 'I know you'; *tsi.yo.li.ga* 'I know him/her'; *s.quo.hl'.ga* 'you know me'; *a.gwo.l'.ga* 'he/she knows me'.

DEMONSTRATIVE PRONOUN/ADJECTIVE
hi'.a 'this' (object); *go.hi* 'this', with reference to time: e.g. *go.hi i:ga* 'this day(light)' = 'today'. *Na/na.s.gi* 'that'; *na'.ni* 'those'.

INTERROGATIVE PRONOUN
ka:ga 'who?'; *ga.do* 'what?'. Certain interrogative particles may be added to a focused word: e.g. *-ke, -tsu, -tsv*: *Ga.yo:tli.ke hi.wo:ni.a tsa.la.gi?* 'Do you speak some Cherokee?' (*ga.yo:tli* 'a little'; *tsa.la.gi* 'Cherokee').

Numerals

Sequoyah experimented with a decimal system. The numerals in use today are: 1–10: *sa.wu, ta'.li, tso:(i), nv:g(i), hi:s.g(i), su.da.l(i), ga.l(i).quo:g(i), tsu.ne:l(a), so.ne:l(a), s.go(hi)*. 11–19: analogous forms + *du.(i)*; 20 *ta.l.s.go.(hi)*; 100 *s.go.hi'.s.qua*.

Verb

Cherokee verbs may be divided into those which do not require classifiers and those which do. The latter form a small minority (a couple of dozen) and are all concerned with handling objects – picking things up, putting them down, pushing, pulling, and so on. The classifiers relate to the physical properties of objects. The basic categories are: (a) flexible objects, (b) long objects, (c) nondescript objects, (d) liquids, (e) animate objects. Thus, the English verb 'to hand something to someone' will be rendered in several different ways in Cherokee, depending on the nature of the object being handled. Cf.

gv.ne'.a 'I hand you something nondescript (probably solid)'
gv.de'.a 'I hand you something long and inflexible'
gv.nv.ne'.a 'I hand you something floppy, flexible (e.g. a cloth)'
gv.ne'.v'.si(se) 'I hand you something liquid'.

The complete grid for the verb *de.s.kv.si* 'to pass something classified (in 5 categories) to other(s)', involving singular, dual, and plural agent(s) and recipient(s), as set out in Holmes and Smith (1976: 294–6), has 175 forms.

STRUCTURE OF THE VERB COMPLEX

Prefixes – verb stem – suffixes. The main components of the prefix slot, in order, are: negative – directionals – direct object – subject, subject/object pronoun – classifiers (with certain verbs) – stem. The suffix slot includes: tense/aspect markers for durative, potential, reiterative, inferential naunces; particle indicating addressee or beneficiary of action; such particles as *doh*, which suggest various modalities of the verbal action.

NEGATIVE

One marker is *tla*, which can be resumed after the verb stem by *yi.gi*: e.g. *tla ga.ne.li yi.gi* 'he/she is not married' (*g-* is 3rd p. sing.; *a.ne.l-* is the stem, 'to live with'; *-i* is marker for recent past tense).

DIRECTIONAL PARTICLES

(In prefix slot) *da.* for approach, *wi.* for withdrawal: e.g. *da.ya'.i* 'he/she is approaching'; *wi.ga:'i* 'I am going away.'

EXAMPLES OF TENSE FORMATION

Present, future, past; first and third person singular:

tsi.wo:ni.a 'I am speaking'
ga.wo:ni.a 'he/she is speaking'
da.tsi.wo.ni.si 'I shall speak'
da.ga.wo.ni.si 'he/she will speak' (*da … si* is future marker)
a.gi.wo.ni:sv'.i 'I spoke'
u.wo.ni:sv'.i 'he/she spoke'

Word order

SOV, SVO.

1 ᏗᏓᎴᏂᏍᎬ ᎧᏃᎮᏛ ᎡᎮᎢ, ᎠᎴ
ᎾᏍᎩ ᎧᏃᎮᏛ ᎤᏁᎳᏅᎯ ᎢᏧᎳᎭ Ꭰ-
ᏁᎮᎢ, ᎠᎴ ᎾᏍᎩ ᎧᏃᎮᏛ ᎤᏁᎳᏅᎯ
ᎨᏎᎢ.
2 ᏗᏓᎴᏂᏍᎬᎢ ᎾᏍᎩ ᎤᏁᎳᏅᎯ
ᎢᏧᎳᎭ ᎠᏁᎮᎢ.
3 ᏂᎦᎥ ᎠᎱᏍᏗ ᎾᏍᎩ ᎤᏬᏢᏁᎢ, ᎠᎴ
ᏂᎦᎥ ᎠᏢᏅᎯ ᏥᎩ ᎥᏝ ᎠᎱᏍᏗ ᎾᏍᎩ
ᏄᏬᏢᏅᎾ ᏱᎩ.
4 ᎾᏍᎩ [ᎧᏃᎮᏛ] ᎬᏂᏛ ᎤᏪᎮᎢ;
ᎠᎴ ᎾᏍᎩ ᎬᏂᏛ ᏴᏫ ᎢᎦ ᎤᎾᏘᏍᏓᏁᎯ
ᎨᏎᎢ.
5 ᎠᎴ ᎾᏍᎩ ᎢᎦ-ᎦᏘᏍᏗᏍᎩ ᎤᎵᏏᎬ
ᏚᏄᏌᏕᎢ, ᎤᎵᏏᎩᏃ ᎥᏝ ᏱᏚᏓᏂᎸᏤᎢ.
6 ᎩᎶ ᎢᏳᏍᏗ ᎠᏍᎦᏯ ᎡᎲᎩ ᏣᏂ
ᏧᏙᎢᏛ ᎤᏁᎳᏅᎯ ᏅᏓᏳᏅᏏᏛ ᎨᏒᎩ.
7 ᎾᏍᎩ ᎤᎷᏨᎩ ᎧᏃᎮᏍᎩ ᎨᏒᎩ,
ᎾᏍᎩ ᎢᎦ-ᎦᏘ ᎤᏃᎮᏗᏱ, ᎾᏍᎩ ᎢᏳ-
ᏩᏂᏐᏗᏱ ᎾᏂᎥ ᎤᏃᎯᏳᏗᏱ.
8 ᎥᏝ ᎾᏍᎩ Ꮎ ᎢᎦ-ᎦᏘ ᏱᎨᏎᎢ, Ꭷ-
ᏃᎮᏍᎩᏉᏍᎩᏂ ᎨᏒᎩ ᎾᏍᎩ ᎢᎦ-ᎦᏘ.

CHEYENNE

INTRODUCTION

This Macro-Algonquian language is spoken by 3,000 or 4,000 people in Montana and Oklahoma. The language was described by R. Petter (1952).

PHONOLOGY

Consonants

Petter gives the following inventory:

stops: b/p, d/t, g/k
affricates: ts
fricatives: v/w, ç/x, h, s, ʃ, j
nasals: m, n

/q/ alternates with labialized [k°]; palatalized /t'/ alternates with the affricate [tʃ].

Vowels

ɪ, ɛ, a, o
/oː/ = [u], /a/ = [ou], /o/ = [oi], /ɛ/ = [ai]

Petter uses an acute accent to mark hiatus or glottalization, and a grave accent to denote closure on a soft /ç/: *nà* = /naç/. There are also whispered vowels which Petter denotes as °.

MORPHOLOGY AND SYNTAX

Noun

The sense of an indefinite article is provided by the *ma-* prefix: e.g. *ma.ex* 'an eye, the eye (in general)'

GENDER
The Cheyenne distinction between animate and inanimate categories surfaces in the plural marker *-eo*, specific for animates: e.g. *hetan* 'man', *hetaneo* 'men'. Natural gender can be marked by lexical items: e.g. *hetan* 'male', *hee* 'female': *hetan.eham* 'bull buffalo'; *hee.ham* 'cow buffalo'.

There are no cases.

POSSESSION

Alienable or inalienable. The alienable inanimate paradigm is:

	Singular	Plural
1	na...am	na/ni...aman
2	ni...am	ni...amevo
3	hi...am	he...amevo

Examples: *na.māme.n.am* 'my corn', pl. *na.māme.n.amoz* 'my grains'.
Inalienable possession; cf. *na.mocan* 'my shoe'; *ni.mocan* 'thy shoe'; *na.mocan.an* 'our shoe'; *na.mocan.an.oz* 'our shoes'.

KINSHIP

Many of these forms are very irregular: *nihoe* 'my father', *eijồ* 'thy father', *hèhjo* 'one's father'; *nàkohe* 'my mother', *nišq* 'thy mother'; *nanis* 'my child', *ninis* 'thy child', *naniseneo* 'my children'; *nistxeo* 'my warriors (who are with me)', *estxeo* 'thy warriors'.

Pronoun

	Singular		Plural
1	na.nēhov 'I myself'	excl.	na.nēhov.hemẻ
2	ni.nēhov	incl.	ni.nēhov.hemå
3	e.nēhov		ni.nēhov.hemā
			e.nēhov.eo

DEMONSTRATIVE PRONOUN

(a) Animate:

	Singular	Plural
1	ze.nēhov.etto 'I, who ...'	ze.nēhov.ez
2	ze.nēhov.étto	ze.nēhov.ess
3	ze.nēhov.sz	ze.nēhov.evoss

(b) Inanimate: *heto* 'this one'; *hato* 'that one'.

INTERROGATIVE PRONOUN

Animate: *nivā* 'who?', pl. *nivāseo*; inanimate: *henova* 'what?'.

Verb

Petter emphasizes the great complexity of the Cheyenne verbal system, with its limitless capacity for producing *ad hoc* forms. Some basic structures are outlined here:

TENSE
Present:

Singular		Plural
1 na.vōsan 'I see'	excl.	na.vōsan.hemě
	incl.	ni.vōsan.hemå
2 ni.vōsan		ni.vōsan.hemě
3 e.vōsan		e.vōsan.eo

Petter lists 35 temporal infixes: e.g. preterite: *-eše-*, e.g. *na.eše.vōsan*, *ni.eše.vōsan*; future: *-ze-*, e.g. *na.ze.vōsan*, *ni.ze.vōsan*. A simple past tense is made by modulation of the personal prefix: e.g. *nà.vōsan*, *nì.vōsan*, *è.vōsan*.

INTRANSITIVE VERBS
Four categories: (a) *-san* (with varients): these are duratives; (b) *-a*; (c) *-o*; (d) *-e*; these three categories differ from each other ontologically. To these forms are added several dozen endings denoting natural phenomena and human affection; e.g. *-éna* 'snow', *-tovao* 'smoke', *-oss* 'cold', *-eoxta* 'legged', *-ésta* 'eared', *-moxta* 'of feeling': *na.pev.o.moxta* 'I'm feeling good.'

Several endings such as *-etto*, *-tove*, *-nove*, form impersonal verbs; e.g. *-tove* converts nouns ending in *-toz* into verbs: *mesestoz* 'food' – *e.meses.tove* 'it is food'; *meàtoz* 'gift' – *e.meàtove.nsz* 'these are gifts'.

TRANSITIVE VERBS
Personal pronominal deixis expressed by personal prefix plus coded ending:

ni.vōm.az 'I see thee'
ni.vōm.e 'thou seest me'
ni.vōm.azemenò 'we see thee'
ni.vōm.eme 'you (pl.) see me'
na.vōm.o 'I see one'
na.vōm.on 'we (incl.) see one'
ni.vōm.on 'we (excl.) see one'

Action by third person on first or second person involves inversion of model:

na.vōm.a 'I am seen by one' = 'one sees me'
ni.vōm.ā 'thou art seen by them' = 'they see thee'
na.vōm.aen 'we are seen by one'
e.vōm.a 'he is seen by one'

Final stem consonants are subject to sandhi.

PASSIVE PARADIGM

Singular	Plural
1 na.vōm.an 'I am seen'	na.vōm.an.heme
2 ni.vōm.an	ni.vōm.an.heme
3 e.vōm.an	e.vōm.eo

INSTRUMENTAL INFIXES

E.g. *-òno* 'with a weapon'; *-éso* 'by amputation'; *-âno* 'by fire'. Examples: *na.nov.âno* 'I burn him'; *na.vov.èno* 'I wound him in the face.' These can be passive: e.g. *na.onexâhen* 'I am burned'; *na.vovehen* 'I am wounded in the face.'

MODAL FORMS OF VERB

Petter lists 35:

1. Indicative: simple assertion, e.g. *na.vōs.an* 'I see'; *na.vōm.o* 'I see one'; *na.vōm.az* 'I see myself'; *na.vōm.an* 'I am seen'.
2. Imperative: the personal prefix is dropped, e.g. *vehōmsz!* 'see me!'; *vehōmemeno!* 'see thou us!'
3. Hortative: also drops personal prefix. The suffixes are similar to those of the imperative, e.g. *vōsanehå* 'let him see'.
4. Negative: *-saa* is the characteristic, plus *-e/he* affix, e.g. *na.saa.vōsan.e* 'I do not see'; *na.saa.vōm.ohe* 'I do not see one'; *ni.saa.vōm.az.e* 'I do not see thee.'
5. Hypothetical: *-mo* + *-é/he*, e.g. *mo.na.vōs.an.é* 'it's likely I'll see'; *mo.na.vōm.an.é* 'it's likely I'm being seen'.
6. Interrogative: expressed by the negative or the hypothetical minus particles, e.g. *na.vōs.ané?* 'do I see?'

Among the remaining moods are an estimative, *na.pevatamo* 'I deem someone good'; a comitative, *na.veoxzemo* 'I go with someone'; a desiderative, *na.vōmatanotovo* 'I desire to see someone'. Further, a persuasive, a mediative, an affective, a causative, and over a dozen denoting various qualities, modes of behaviour, and appearance.

CHIBCHA

INTRODUCTION

The Chibcha described here (after Middendorf, 1890–2) has been extinct since the eighteenth century. Up to the time of the Spanish Conquest, Chibcha (or Muysca as it was also called) was the language of a centralized and organized Indian civilisation in what is now Colombia, and may have been spoken by as many as 500,000 people. Some Chibchan languages are still spoken (*see* **Macro-Chibchan**). Middendorf's description is based on grammars of the language by Lugo and Uricochea.

PHONOLOGY

Consonants

/d/ and /l/ are absent, /r/ is rare, /ts/ is present.

Vowels

The vowels are as in Spanish. /y/ is described as being between /e/ and /i/.

MORPHOLOGY AND SYNTAX

Noun

Nearly all nouns end in a vowel, usually -*a*. The following typical declension is based on Lugo:

nom.	muysca 'man'
gen.	muyscaepcua/ipcua
dat.	muyscaguaca
acc.	muyscaca
ill.	muyscan/s
abl.	muyscanynši
loc.	muyscana
instr./com.	muyscabotsa

There is no special plural ending; *mabie* 'many', may be used: e.g. *gue mabie* 'many houses'; *gue mabie ipcua* 'of many houses'.

Adjective

When independent, the adjective is declined as nominal; when attributive, invariable. Normally follows noun, but may precede. Middendorf makes the point that adjectives are usually longer than the nouns they qualify: e.g. *ie afihistatsa* 'narrow way'; *fagua chinanuca* 'shining star'.

COMPARISON
Made with *ingy* 'more': e.g. *cho* 'good', *ingy cho* 'better'.

Pronoun

PERSONAL

	Singular		Plural	
	Independent	*Enclitic*	*Independent*	*Enclitic*
1	hycha	tsy, tse, i	chie	chi
2	mue	um	mie	mi
3	—	a, as	—	a

These are declined, e.g. for *hycha*:

nom.	hycha
gen.	hycha **tse** ipcua
dat.	hycha **tse** guaca
instr.	hycha **tse** botsa
acc.	**cha**

The enclitic forms are used as possessives: e.g. *tse gue* 'my house'.

DEMONSTRATIVE PRONOUN
as – šis – ys by relative distance: 'this' – 'that' – 'that (yonder)'. These have plural forms: *anabitsa – šinabitsa – ynabitsa*.

Numerals

1–10: *ata, botsa, mica, muyca, hycsca, ta, cuhubcua, sutsa, aca, hubchihica*; 11–19: e.g. *quicha ata, quicha botsa*; 20 *quicha hubchihica*. From 21 on, *gueta* is used for 20: 21 *gueta.s asaquy.ata*; 40 *gue botsa*; 100 *gue hysca*.

The numeral follows the noun enumerated: e.g. *muysca mica* 'three men'.

Verb

Agglutinative forms with prepositive personal pronominal enclitics. There are two voices and four moods.

INDICATIVE MOOD

Present: enclitic pronoun + stem + present marker, e.g. *tse + bquy + scua* 'I do, make'; *um.bquy.scua* 'you make.'

Past: enclitic pronoun + stem + Ø, e.g. *tse.bquyØ* 'I made, did'.
Future: enclitic pronoun + stem + future marker, e.g. *tse.bquy.nga* 'I shall do, make'.

SUBJUNCTIVE
Present form + subjunctive marker, e.g. *tse.bquy.scua.nan* 'that I may do'.

IMPERATIVE
Stem only, modified, e.g. *quyu!* 'do, make!'; pl. *quyiuva!*

PARTICIPIAL FORMS
quysca 'making, doing', e.g. '(he ...) who makes, does'; past form, *quyia*; future form, *quinga*. These are used, e.g. in relative senses, with copula, *gue*: e.g. *hycha gue cha quysca* 'I am he who makes'; *mue gue ma quyia* 'you are the one who made'.

NEGATIVE
tsa/ts is affixed or infixed: e.g. *tse bquyscua.tsa* 'I do not do, make'; *tse bquy.ts.inga* 'I shall not do, make'; *cha quysca.tsa* 'I who do not ...'.

PASSIVE
To form the passive of, e.g. *tse.bquy.scua* 'I do, make', the pronominal enclitic is put in the accusative, and the verb form is slightly changed: *chan, quysca* 'he does something to me'; similarly, *man.quysca* 'he does something to you'.

The accusative forms of the enclitics can only be used if the agent is third person. If the agent is first or second person, the full form is used: e.g. *a*.quity.*cha* 'he struck me'; *mi.quity.hycha* 'you struck me'; *tse.quity.suca.mue* 'I strike you' (*-suca-* is an alternant of *-scua-*).

Chibcha used postpositions; e.g.

> *taca/chien* 'under': e.g. *guica chien* 'under the sky', *sié taca* 'under water';
> *uca/uco/uquy* 'under': e.g. *ts.uca* 'under me';
> *ubac/ubana* 'before': e.g. *ts.ubana* 'before me';
> *suca /gahan* 'behind': e.g. *ts.e.gahan* 'behind me', *i.suca* 'behind me' (*i* may replace *tse* as 1st person marker before *ch, n, s, š, t, ts*);
> *šicas* 'away from': e.g. *i./tse.šicas* '(away) from me.'

Word order
SVO is usual: cf. *to a.bca cha* 'the dog bit me'.

CHIMÚ

INTRODUCTION

Chimú, the language of the ruling stratum in Peru until the coming to power of the Incas in the fifteenth century, is of doubtful genetic affiliation, and may be an isolate. It survived into the nineteenth century, and was described by Ernst Middendorf in his great work, *Die Einheimischen Sprachen Perus* (1890). The language was unwritten, and is now extinct.

PHONOLOGY

Middendorf (1890) gives the following inventory:

Consonants

> stops: p, t, d, k; the sound marked by Middendorf as *'t* may be a glottalized /t'/ as in Aymara.
> Three velar fricatives are distinguished: *j* = Spanish /j/; *ǰ* = hard Aymara /ʝ/; *j̃* = /ç/; the affricates *ch* = /ts/, *'ch* = /tʃ/, *ts* = /ts/.

Also present are: f, w; m, n, ɲ; l, ʎ, r, rr; s, ss ('sharp s'), ʃ; h

Vowels

> long and short: i, e, a, o, u
> diphthongs: ai, ei, ui, oi

In the diphthongs, each component vowel is given its full value. Two specifically Chimú sounds are notated by Middendorf as *ä* and *ů*: both are realized as /ɛ.u/, with /ɛ/ emphasized in the former, /u/ in the latter.

MORPHOLOGY AND SYNTAX

Noun

There is no grammatical gender; natural gender is distinguished by adjunct nouns: e.g. *chisi* 'child': *ñofän chisi* 'boy child'; *mecherräk chisi* 'girl child'; *mecherräk rak* 'female jaguar'. A genitive ending is made with *-är.ō/ei.ō/ngō*, depending on noun final.

The plural marker is *-än*, which precedes the genitive marker, except when

302

this is *ngō*; *-än* is then inserted between *ng-* and *-ō*: cf. *chonkik* 'star', gen. *chonkik.är.ō*; pl. *chonkik.än*; gen. pl. *chonkik.än.är.ō*; *chelu* 'falcon', gen. *chelu.ngō*; pl. *chelu.än*; gen. pl. *chelu.ng.än.ō*. The *ō* of the genitive ending is always strongly stressed, with a hiatus between it and the preceding *-än/-är*, as though it were a postposition.

The genitive *ō* is dropped in the following circumstances:

(a) In a construct: e.g. *choj* 'boy', gen. *choj.ei.ō*; but *choj.e fanuss* 'the boy's dog', where *-ss* is the marker for a dependent nominal.

(b) Where a postposition governing the genitive is used: e.g. *uij* 'the earth', gen. *uij.är.ō*, *uij.är kapäk* 'on the earth'; *ōj* 'fire', *ōj.är nik* 'in the fire'.

(c) If the verb is passive, the agent is in the genitive case minus *-ō*: e.g. *čhuvet* 'snake', *čhuvet.är.∅ rranädo* 'bitten by the snake'; *ssonte* 'vulture', *ssonte.ng lletnädo* 'swallowed by the vulture'. Cf. *Mo an ang aio ñofär ef.ei.ō* 'This house is of-the-father of that man' (*mo* 'this'; *an* 'house'; *ang* 'is'; *ñofär* = *ñofän.är* 'of the man'; *ef* 'father'; *ei.ō*, genitive of dependent nominal).

THE DEPENDENT NOMINAL

The marker is always *-ss*, except for nouns ending in *-k*, which changes to *-r*: e.g. *manik* 'drinking vessel', dep. nom. *manir*. The dependent form is not used if the possessed object is separated from the possessor: cf. *mäiñ fanuss ang mo* 'my dog is this' = 'This is my dog'; but *mo fanu ang mäiñ* 'This dog is mine'. All dependent nominals have a genitive in *-ai.ō/ei.ō*.

Adjective

Not formally distinguished from the noun. Root adjectives are often monosyllabic, and precede the noun: e.g. *ñass* 'beautiful', *ñass tot.är.ō* 'of the beautiful face'; *ūts* 'big', *ūts nepät.är.ō* 'of the big tree'. The plural marker is added to the adjective: e.g. *ñass.än tot* 'beautiful faces'; *ūts.än nepät* 'big trees'. But in the plural genitive the plural marker reverts to the noun: e.g. *ūts nepät.än.är.ō* 'of the big trees', realized as /uc.o.nepät.än.är.ō/, where *-o-* is a euphonic infix: cf. *peñ.o.mecharräk* 'a good woman'.

COMPARATIVE

jechna 'more' + genitive case + *lekich* (postposition): e.g. *Jechna ñass.o fe ñing ja nech.är ja.ng lekich* 'The sea's water is better than the river's water' (*fe = ang* 'is'; *ñi* 'sea'; *ja* 'water'; *nech* 'river').

Pronoun

PERSONAL

	Singular	Plural
1	moiñ, gen. mäiñ.o	mäich
2	tsang	tsäich

The third person forms are supplied from the demonstrative series. These are *mo/ssio* 'this', pl. *mo.ngän/ssiong.än* 'this, these'; *aio* 'that', pl. *aiungän*.

INTERROGATIVE
eiñ 'who?'; *ech* 'what?'.

RELATIVE PRONOUN
kan.

Numerals

1–10: *onäk*, *aput*, *sopät*, *nopät*, *ejmäts*, *tsaitsa*, *ñite*, *langäss*, *tap*, *na-pong*; 11 *na-pong allo onäk*; 20 *pak pong*; 30 *sok pong*; 40 *nok pong*; 100 *na paläk*; 200 *pak paläk*.

The numeral precedes the noun, which is in the singular: e.g. *ñite.io chonkik* 'seven stars'.

Verb

THE COPULA

	Singular	Plural
1	moiñ eiñ	mäich eiš
2	tsang as	tsäich as.chi
3	aio ang	aiongän ang

There are many variant forms. *Ang/fe* can replace any of the above. In composite tenses, preferred forms are: 1 *e*, 2 *as*, 3 *fe*.

Past: the above forms plus *piñ*: e.g. *moiñ e piñ*, *tsang as piñ*. Future: the above forms plus *ka*: e.g. *moiñ e ka*.

A second substantive verb or copula is *chi*: e.g. *chi.eiñ* → *chiñ*, *chi.as* → *chis*.

CONJUGATION
Two models are possible:

(a) root + endings, coded for person and number;
(b) personal pronoun + personal marker + root.

For example, with root *tem-* 'to love, examine', present tense:

(a) *tem.eiñ*, *tem.as*, *tem.ang*; *tem.eiš*, *tem.aschi*, *tem.änang*;
(b) *moiñ e tem*, *tsang as tem*, *aiof'tem*; *mäich eiš tem*, *tsäich aschi tem*, *aiongän ang tem*.

There is only one form for the perfect: *tem.eda.iñ*, *tem.eda.s*, *tem.eda.ng*; *tem.eda.iš*, *tem.eda.schi*, *tem.eda.edän.ang*.

Future: *tiñ tem*, *täs tem*, *täng tem*, *tiš tem*, *täschi tem*, *täng tem än*.

Subjunctive: e.g. *tem.ema.iñ*, *tem.ema.s*, *tem.ema.ng*, or: *moiñ mang tem*, etc.

NON-FINITE FORMS

tem.äd 'to love', *tem.näm* 'in order to love', *tem.e.skäf* 'to have loved', *tem.e.läk/ssäk* 'loving'.

PASSIVE

är is added to the verbal stem: present-tense, *tem.är.eiñ = moiñ eiñ tem.är* 'I am loved'; passive participle, *temedo = tem.är.edo* 'loved'.

DERIVED VERBS

Causative: the infixed marker is *-ko-*, jep 'burn' (intrans.) – *jep.ko.iñ* 'I ignite'; *funo* 'eat' – *funo.ko.iñ* 'I feed'; *chi* 'to be' – *chi.ko.iñ* 'I create'.

Durative: the active participle is taken as verbal theme and conjugated, e.g. *eng* 'say' – *eng.a.päk.o.iñ* 'I always say'; *kall* 'laugh' – *kallapäkoiñ* 'I laugh all the time.'

Benefactive: the infix is *-äk/ek-*, e.g. *met* 'bring' – *met.äk.eiñ* 'I bring for/to someone'.

Privative: *-un.o/unta*, *met.uno* 'without bringing'.

Postpositions

Postpositions in Chimú govern either the base form or the genitive case. With genitive:

kapäk 'on': *llemki.ng.kapäk* 'on the mountain';
-nik/nek 'in(to)': *ñi.ng.e.nik* 'in(to) the sea' (← *ni.ng.o.nik*);
titäk 'before': *moiñ tutäk* 'before me'; *an.e tutäk* 'in front of the house';
turkich 'behind': *llemki.ng turkich* 'behind the mountain';
pän 'for': *ssiung fan.ngo pän* 'for his dog'.

With base form:

len 'with': *tsang.len* 'with you';
na 'through': *pampa.na* 'through the plains'.

NEGATION

As in Quechua, by means of circumfix, *änta...(e)sta*: e.g. *änta fe esta* 'it is not'; *Änta ang Dios esta mo jang mo ši* 'God is not the sun, the moon.'

Word order

Free. Verb + object: e.g. *moiñ e tem.edo tsang* 'I have loved you'; *tsang e tem.edo mäiñ* 'you were loved by me'.

CHINESE

By far the largest and most important member of the Sino-Tibetan family, Chinese is spoken today by about 1,200 million people in the Republic of China, in Taiwan, in Malaysia and other parts of South-East Asia, and in numerous Chinese communities all over the world. The umbrella term 'Chinese' covers several dialect groups which are broadly divided into (a) northern dialect (Mandarin), which accounts for about two-thirds of all Chinese speakers, and (b) the southern dialects including Wu, Gan, Xiang, Hakka, Yue, and Min. It is somewhat misleading to talk of 'dialects', as Chinese dialects are not mutually intelligible and should really be classified as languages.

Chinese has been a written language for about 3,500 years. Over this long time-span, pronunciation has changed very considerably, script and morphology comparatively little. Diachronically, the language may conveniently be considered under three main headings:

1. Archaic Chinese, fourteenth to eleventh centuries BC; the language of the Anyang inscriptions on animal bones and tortoise shells.
2. Classical Chinese (Wenli): broadly, the language and its literature – one of the world's most interesting and important – between the eleventh century BC and the eighth AD, with an increasingly artificial prolongation well into modern times.
3. Modern Standard Chinese: *guóyǔ* ('national language') or *pǔtōnghuà* ('common language'); essentially, the vocabulary and morphology of late Classical Chinese, pruned, enlarged, and adapted for use in a modern society. Many of the Classical characters in use have been abbreviated. An official romanization is known as *pīnyīn*.

These headings are treated in the following three articles. Pīnyīn romanization is used.

CHINESE, ARCHAIC

INTRODUCTION

The oldest recorded form of Chinese dates from the Shang Dynasty (c. 1400–1100 BC) and is known to us from oracle inscriptions on flat bones and tortoise shells used in divination. Great numbers of these have been excavated at the site of the ancient capital, Anyang, and elsewhere. Their content is largely stereotyped along the lines that one would expect to find in an economy based on agriculture: Is it going to rain? Will the harvest be plentiful? and so on. The question was written on one half of a shell, for example, which was then heated; the cracks which appeared in the other half were interpreted as the answer, and often written in. Combined as it is with a very high repetition factor, this question and answer format is of great value in the reconstruction of Shang vocabulary and syntax. About 2,000 characters have been identified, a figure which represents a much larger corpus of 'words'. This is because the Shang characters (apart from the pronouns) might be described as semantically multivalued nuclei whose valencies depend on locus and function in the utterance as a whole. Thus, 孚 (= modern 子) can mean any of the following: 'son', 'filial', 'to be filial', 'to regard oneself as filial', 'befitting a son', etc. Up to a point, the modern Chinese graph shares the polyvalence characteristic of both Shang and Classical Chinese.

SCRIPT

The three basic elements – pictographs, ideographs, and phonograms – of Chinese script are all present in the Shang script, which points to a lengthy period of anterior development.

Examples of pictographs are:

馬 (= modern 馬 *mǎ*) 'horse';

雨 (= modern 雨 *yǔ*) 'rain'.

Ideographs: e.g.

⌒ (= 下 *xià*) 'under, below';

⌣ (= 上 *shàng*) 'above, up'.

Phonograms: e.g.

来 (= 來 *lái*) 'to come'.

There is no consistency in character formation, and there are many variants.

PHONOLOGY

It is not possible to say with any degree of certainty how Shang Chinese was pronounced. In this entry, characters are given their modern Chinese values.

MORPHOLOGY AND SYNTAX

There is no inflection of any kind; Shang Chinese is a pure isolating language. Meaning depends on the due ordering of components, which are classified as auto-semantic or auxiliary. Three markers are used to indicate past (*xí*), present (*jīn*), or future time (*lái*). These also occur in an attributive capacity: e.g. *Jīn lái suì wǒ shòu nián* 'This year (*suì*) and next, we shall have harvest (*nián*).'

Pronoun

余 *yu*, 朕 *zhen*, 女 *zhu*, 乃 *nai*

are all used for first person, the first being specifically associated with the Yin ruler.

我 *wo*

is used for plural first person.

Spatial markers (*shang*, *xia*, *zhong*, etc.) are used as in later Chinese, and there are numerical classifiers.

于 *yu*

is an all-purpose preposition.

CHINESE, CLASSICAL (Wenli)

INTRODUCTION

In a narrow sense, the term 'Classical Chinese' refers to the Chinese language and its literature from the sixth century BC to the third century AD; a period which includes the lives and works of Confucius, Mencius, Lao Tzu, Han Fei, Mo Tzu, and Chuang Tzu, to mention only the six philosopher–sages who were to have such a far-reaching effect on subsequent Chinese thought. In a broader sense, Classical Chinese begins with the *Shih Ching* ('Book of Odes'), which was compiled between the eleventh and sixth centuries BC, and which was in fact co-opted, during the central period, to form one of the 'Five Classics' (*wu jing*). The other four are:

> *I Jing* ('Book of Changes');
> *Shu Jing* ('Book of History');
> *Li Ji* ('Book of Propriety');
> *Chun-Chiu* ('Spring and Autumn Annals').

After the Burning of the Books by the Qin Emperor Shi Huang Di (213 BC), when most of this material was destroyed, the text of the Classics had to be arduously reconstructed. This took place in the early years of the Han Dynasty, whose espousal of Confucianism determined the lineaments of Chinese literature for many centuries to come. In the Confucian hegemony three factors were crucial: (1) the sacrosanctity of the classical texts; (2) the examination system based on these texts and their commentaries; (3) the supremacy of the literati who expounded the classics and set the examinations.

Outside the examination halls, a succession of poets – especially in the Tang and Sung Dynasties – some of them disreputable by Confucian standards, went on producing a lot of the world's most attractive poetry.

SCRIPT

The main source for the character inventory used in the central Classical period is the *Shuo Wen* ('explain character') dictionary of the Later Han Dynasty (published c. AD 100). Here, the characters are arranged under 540 radicals (reduced to 214 in the late Ming Dynasty). The main categories of the *Shuo Wen* classification are:

1. simple characters, a few hundred in number, sub-divided into

    (a) pictographs: e.g.

    木   *mù* 'tree';

    山   *shān* 'mountain';

    門   *mén* 'gateway, door';

    (b) demonstratives: e.g.

    二   *èr* 'two',

    上   *shàng* 'above',

    下   *xià* 'below'.

2. Compound characters, sub-divided into (a) ideograms, (b) phonograms;

    (a) ideograms are made from two or more simple characters; e.g.

    坐   *zuò* 'to sit' is formed from

    人   *rén* 'man', reduplicated, placed over

    土   *tŭ* 'earth'.

    男   *nán* 'man', is made from

    田   *tián* 'field' + 力 *lì* 'power'.

    (b) phonograms – the most numerous class – are made from two elements: the radical fixing the character as belonging to this or that semantic group, and the phonetic which suggests the pronunciation. Example:

    聞   *wén* 'to hear':

    composed of radical

    耳   *ěr* 'ear' + 門 *mén*.

    That is, the following information is given: the word has to do with hearing, and should rhyme with /men/.

PHONOLOGY

Reconstruction is, of course, hypothetical. The first guide to the actual pronunciation of Classical Chinese, the *Qieyun* Rhyming Dictionary, was not published until AD 601.

Consonants

Yaxontov (1965) gives the following inventory of permissible initials:

stops: p, ph, bh, t, d, th, dh, k, g, kh, gh, ʔ
affricates: ts, tʃ, dʒ
fricatives: s, ʃ, h, x
nasals: m, n, ŋ
lateral: l

The following initials were labialized: /k°, kh°, g°, gh°, n°, x°, ʔ°/. An initial consonant could be followed by -*l* and preceded by *s*- (sonants only): e.g. *bhlak* 'white' (Mod. Ch. *bai*); *smək* 'black'; *slän* 'mountain' (Mod. Ch. *shan*).

FINALS
The nasals; /p, t, k; r/.

Vowels

front: e, ε (+ a doubtful sound, represented here by /ɪ/)
back: ə, a, o, u

Tones

An even and a rising tone; words with /p, t, k/ ending had a specific tone, the nature of which is not clear.

MORPHOLOGY AND SYNTAX

A basic distinction is between 'full' words and 'empty' words. Pronouns count as empty words, as their exact meaning can be established only by context. The empty words – particles and pronouns – account for 25–30 per cent of all the words in a text of the central Classical period.

Given the total absence of any kind of inflection, and the polyvalent nature of Chinese words (a 'word' can be almost any part of speech in a proposition), word order is clearly of paramount importance: cf. *niǎo fēi* 'the bird flies'; *fēi niǎo* 'the flying bird'; *míng kě míng* ('name' – 'can' – 'name'; i.e. noun – modal verb – verb) in the first paragraph of the *Dao De Jing*, can be glossed as: *kě míng zhī míng* (modal verb – verb – relational particle – noun): 'the name that can be named'.

Pronoun

1st person: *yu* and *zhen* are inclusive; *wu* and *wo* are exclusive;
2nd person: *ru, ro, er, nai*;
3rd person: *qi, zhi, yan*; absence of a personal pronoun indicates 3rd person.

Choice of one or another pronoun seems to have depended on criteria which are no longer always clear. *Yu* and *zhen* are typically early Classical; *wu* and *wo* are associated with the later and post-Classical period.

Verb

The presence of paired verbs has been pointed out (e.g. Yaxontov 1965:36) which are homonyms in Modern Chinese but which varied in pronunciation in the early Classical language due to the presence, in one member of the pair, of a causative or resultative formant. For example:

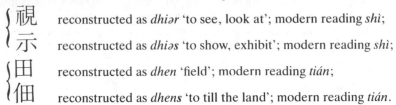

視 reconstructed as *dhiər* 'to see, look at'; modern reading *shì*;

示 reconstructed as *dhiəs* 'to show, exhibit'; modern reading *shì*;

田 reconstructed as *dhen* 'field'; modern reading *tián*;

佃 reconstructed as *dhens* 'to till the land'; modern reading *tián*.

This phenomenon has been taken as evidence for an early Chinese inflectional system which was in desuetude by the Han period.

TENSE MARKERS
Past, past anterior, future; there is also a perfective marker.

PASSIVE VOICE
May be marked by *jiàn* (modern meaning: 'to see'): e.g. *Pen-Cheng-Guo jiàn shá* 'Pen-Cheng-Guo being slain'; *Sùi sì shí ér jiàn è yān qi zhōng yě yǐ* 'If a man of forty is disliked, that is how he is going to end' (literally: 'year – four – ten – and – suffer – dislike – then – he – end – indeed – complete').

The passive may be marked by the modal auxiliary *yú*: e.g. *shā rén* 'killed men/a man'; *shā yú rén* 'was killed by men/a man'.

Other modal auxiliaries are: *neng* 'to be able', *gǎn* 'to dare': e.g. *Wú shuí gǎn yuàn?* 'Against whom dare I grumble?'

PARTICLES
These form the major sector of the

虛 詞 *xū.ci*,

the 'empty words', and they are of crucial importance in the Classical style. On an average, about a third of the characters in a *wenli* text are particles. They are sited throughout the discourse like signposts invested with three main functions.

1. Formally, they mark the onset, the suspension, and the conclusion of a proposition. In this role, they are not normally translatable.
2. They mark the preposition as negative, interrogative, or exclamatory; they intensify or limit its sense.
3. They have a large number of modal and prepositional (spatial and temporal) uses: concessive, causal, resultative, conditional, intentional, etc.

Some examples:

1. *fù* as initial particle:

> **fù** rén **zhě** jǐ yù lì **ér** lì rén
> 'The man of virtue (*rén zhě*) wishing (*yu*) himself to be established (*li*), establishes others (*ren* 'other people')'

2. *ér* as limiting agent + *yǐ fū* as final exclamatory particle:

> zǐ yūe; jūn zǐ **ér** bù rén **zhě** you **yǐ fū**
> 'The Master said: superior men (*jūn.zǐ*) who were not (*bù*) virtuous (*rén zhě*) there have been – and how!'

3. *ér* as concessive marker:

> zǐ yūe: pín **ér wú** yuàn nán
> 'The Master said: to be poor (*pín*) and yet not (*wú*) grumble (*yuàn*) is hard (*nán*)'

Example of *zhī* as objective marker for referent known to audience:

> zhī **zhī** zhě bù rú haò **zhī** zhě
> 'Those who know (*zhī*) it (= the Path) are not equal (*bù rú*) to those who love it'

CHINESE,
MODERN STANDARD

INTRODUCTION

Essentially, Modern Standard Chinese is the Northern (Beijing) form of Chinese, written in the Classical Chinese script with certain modifications (*see* **Script**, below).

During the Sung–Yuan Dynasties (twelfth to fourteenth centuries AD) *báihuà*, 'plain speech', a form of Chinese much closer to the spoken language than the *wenli* literary style, began to be used for literary purposes, e.g. in the prose passages in the Yuan drama (see, for example, the well-known *Dou E Yuan* by Guan Han-Ching). *Baihua* was also the vehicle for the prose narrative in the great Ming novels, e.g. Hong Lou Meng, the 'Dream of the Red Chamber', and Shui-hu Chuan, the 'Water Margin'.

After the fall of the Manchu Dynasty and the establishment of the Republic (1911), the movement for a national standardized language gathered momentum, accompanied by a parallel drive for the replacement of the Chinese script by some sort of phonetic alphabet. Both of these requirements were seen as indispensable first steps if universal education was ever to become a reality in China. A key part was played by the cultural revolution known as the 4 May Movement of 1919 and the implementation of the proposals for a national language first formulated by Hu Shih in the pages of the periodical *Xin Chingnian* ('New Youth'). Finally, in 1949, *báihuà* now known as *pǔtōnghuà*, 'common language' was officially adopted as the national language of the Chinese People's Republic.

SCRIPT

For a note on the origins and nature of the Chinese written character *see* **Chinese, Classical**. Modern Standard Chinese uses the same character with the following modifications:

1. Many of the ten to twelve thousand characters in use have been 'abbreviated'; i.e. the number of strokes has been reduced, often considerably, e.g. from 16 to 5, from 19 to 9: e.g.

    爲 > 为 = (co-verb): *wèi* 'on behalf of';

    難 > 难 = *nán* 'difficult';

    禮 > 礼 = *lǐ* 'propriety, ceremony'.

2. The number of radicals has been reduced from 214 to 186. Many characters used in Classical Chinese have been discarded.

The officially adopted system of romanization is known as *pīnyīn*. The tones are indicated by diacritics: macron for level, acute for abrupt rising, inverted circumflex for low rising, grave for falling.

PHONOLOGY

Consonants

INITIALS

stops: p, b, t, d, k, g
affricates: tɕ, ts, tʂ
fricatives: f, ɕ, s, ʂ, ʐ, χ
nasals: m, n, ŋ
lateral: l
semi-vowels: j, w

Phonetically /b, d, g/ are *unvoiced* and non-aspirate; /p, t, k/ are strongly aspirated. All stops occur with labialization.
/tɕ, ts, tʂ/ are notated as *j, z, zh*, with aspirated correlatives notated as *q, c, ch*. /ɕ/ is notated as *x*, /ʂ/ as *sh*, /ʐ/ as *r*, and /χ/ as *h*.

FINALS

The vowels (see below), the nasals /n, ŋ/ following various combinations of vowels, and -/r/.

Vowels

i, ɪ, ɛ, ə, a, o, u, y; pinyin /i/ is [ɪ] after the retroflex sounds. /ə/ is notated as *e* or *u*: e.g. *men* /mən/, *dun* /d°ən/.

Tones

There are four tones in Modern Standard Chinese (1) high even; (2) rising, crescendo; (3) low dipping then rising; (4) falling from high level, diminuendo.

TONAL SANDHI

A tone 3 before another tone 3 changes to 2: e.g. *suó.yĭ* 'therefore', in citation form, both *suŏ* and *yĭ* are tone 3. Second components in disyllabic words are neutralized: e.g. *xièxiĕ* 'thank you'; *wănshång* 'evening'.

MORPHOLOGY AND SYNTAX

There is no inflection of any kind. Formally, there is nothing to distinguish any one part of speech from another. Meaning in a Chinese sentence depends on due logical order assisted by certain syntactic markers such as *ba* (indicating object), *de* (many functions; see below), *le* (past marker). Grammars of modern Chinese distinguish the following parts of speech: nouns, pronouns, numerals and measure words, transitive verbs, intransitive verbs, stative verbs, resultative verbs, auxiliary verbs and co-verbs, localizers, particles.

Nouns

May be monosyllabic: these include the oldest strata of the language: e.g. *mā* 'mother'; *mǎ* 'horse'; *chá* 'tea'; *rén* 'person'; *rì* 'sun'; *mù* 'tree'. Disyllabic: *xiān.shěng* 'first-born' = 'you' (in polite address); *dì.fāng* 'place'; *Zhong.wen* 'Chinese language'; *péng.yǒu* 'friend'. Trisyllabic: *jiě.fàng.jūn* 'Army of Liberation'; *bàn.gōng.shì* 'office'. Polysyllabic: *bǎi.huò.shāng.diàn* 'department store' ('hundred-goods-business-place').

A pluralizing suffix *men* is available, but it is used only for pronouns and for groups; e.g. a speech may begin with the words *Tóng.zhì.men péng.you.men* 'Comrades and friends!' The suffix is not attached to singular nouns; i.e. *shū* 'book' or 'books'.

There are a couple of dozen classifiers for specific use with objects of various types and dimensions; they are bound forms, e.g. *běn, kuài, bēi,* etc.: *nèi liǎng běn shū* 'these two books'; *zhèi zhāng zhuōzi* 'this table'; *yí.kuài táng* 'a piece of candy'. *Ge* is an all-purpose classifier which can replace most of the others, unless the classifier is being used specifically without a referent: cf. *sì běn* 'four books' (the classifier identifies the referent as books).

Adjective

Adjectives in Chinese are stative verbs. If used attributively they precede the noun, often followed by *de*: e.g. *lì.shǐ duǎn de guó.jiā* 'a country with a short (*duǎn*) history (*lìshǐ*)'. The marker *de* is a ubiquitous and very important element in Modern Standard Chinese which has the following main functions:

1. marking attributive material, as in the above example: cf. *jīn.tián dě bào* 'today's paper';
2. to mark alienable possession: e.g. *wǒ.de shū* 'my book' (but *wǒ.Ø fù* 'my father');
3. hence, to form relative clauses preceding head-word: e.g. *wǒ.men yǐ.jīng xué.guo.de cái.liào* 'the material we have already studied' (*xué* 'to study'; *guo* = perfective marker; *cái.liào* 'material');
4. after stative verbs: e.g. *hěn dà.de zhuōzi* 'a very big table'; *hěn hǎo.de jià.qiǎn* 'a very good price';
5. as loose referent: e.g. *wǒ mǎi.de* 'the things that I bought';
6. categorizing particle in final position: e.g. *wǒ shi zuò fēi.jī lái.de* 'it was by plane that I came' = 'I came by plane'.

Pronoun

PERSONAL

Sing. 1 *wǒ*, 2 *ní/nín*, 3 *tā*; plural: add *men* to sing.: *wǒ.men*, etc. These forms function both as subject and as object: e.g. *tā gěi wǒ yi.běn shū* 'he gives me a book'.

DEMONSTRATIVE PRONOUN/ADJECTIVE, OR 'SPECIFIER'

zhèi 'this', *nà/nèi* 'that'. When these are used with nouns, classifiers are inserted between the specifier and the noun: e.g. *zhèi ge rén* 'this person'; *nèi wǔ běn shū* 'those five books'.

INTERROGATIVE PRONOUN
shúi 'who?'; *shen.me* /shəmmə/, 'what?'.

Numerals

1–10: *yi* (with movable tone), *èr, sān, sì, wǔ, liù, qī, bā, jiǔ, shí*; 12–19: *shí* + unit; 20 *èr.shí*; 100 *bǎi*; 1,000 *qiān*; 10,000 *wàn*.

Verb

Formally invariable; there are no tenses. Continuing or progressive action can be marked by *zhě*: e.g. *wǒ yuàn.yì zhàn.zhě* 'I prefer to remain standing.' Impending action may be indicated by *jiù* (*yào*); the past by *gǔo*: e.g. *Ní qǔ.**guo** Zhōng.guo.ma*? 'Have you ever been in China?' (*Zhong.guo* 'China'); *Wǒ méi qǔ.**guo*** 'I have never been there.'

PERFECTIVE ASPECT
le marks a change in a situation: e.g.

>Dōng.xǐ guì.**le** 'Things (lit. 'east–west') have become expensive'

>Wǒ.men huì shuō Zhong.guo.huà **le** 'We can speak Chinese now' (*scil.* until now, we couldn't)

>Tā hē.**le** sān píng jiǔ 'He drank up three bottles of wine'

>Qì.chē pèng.zǎi shù.shǎng **le** 'The car ran into a tree (*shù*)' (*qì.chē* 'car').

CO-VERBS
E.g. *zài* (locational), *yòng* (instrumental), *gěi* (dative), *bǎ* ('to handle something, hold in the hands'), etc. These often have to be translated by prepositions in English: e.g. *zài fàn.guǎn.r chī.fàn* 'to eat in a restaurant'; *yòng kùai.zǐ chī.fàn* 'to eat with chopsticks'; *wǒ gěi tā dǎ diàn.huà* 'I rang him'.

VERB + BOUND (LATENT) OBJECT
E.g. *kàn.shū* 'look at – book' → 'read'; *shuō.huà* 'say – word' → 'speak'; *chī.fàn* 'eat – rice' → 'eat'. These are separable: e.g. *tā kàn wan shū le* 'after he had finished reading …'

STATIVE VERBS
E.g. *dà* 'to be big', *lěng* 'to be cold': *Jīn.tiān zhēn lěng* 'It's really cold today.'

COPULA
shì: often optional in positive, obligatory in negative: e.g. *wǒ* (*shì*) *Běijīng.rén* 'I am from Beijing'; neg. *wǒ **búshì** Běijīng.rén*.

DIRECTIONAL COMPLEMENTARY VERBS
lái 'to come', *qù* 'to go': e.g. *Tā yǐ.jīng dǎ.diàn.huà.**lai**.le* 'He has already rung up (incoming call)'; *nèi.běn.shū ràng.tā mǎi.**qu**.le* lit. 'that-book – by-him – bought-went' = 'he bought the book and went off'.

317

POTENTIAL INFIX

de/bu: e.g. *kàn.de.jiàn* 'able to see'; *găn.bu.shàng* 'unable to overtake'.

NEGATION

The general marker is *bu*; the verb *yŏu* 'to have' is always negated by *méi*, never by *bu*: e.g. *Gào.sǔ tā méi.yŏu yòng.chǔ* 'It's no use telling him.'

PASSIVE

There are various markers, *bèi*, *ràng*, *jiào*, *gěi*: e.g. *tā bèi chéng.fá.le yǐ.hòu* 'after he had been punished' (*chéng.fá* 'punish'; *yǐ.hòu* 'after').

MODAL VERBS

E.g. *yīng.gāi = bì.děi* 'have to', *huì* 'can', *xiăng* 'want to', etc.: e.g. *wŏ.men yīng.gāi/bì.děi yóng.yŭan jì.dě* ... 'we must always remember ...'

Four-character expressions

The Chinese have always been very fond of using set phrases consisting of four characters. These lapidary sayings were, and are, particularly popular as birthday and festive greetings, congratulations, etc.: e.g.

蟠桃集慶

pán.táo jí.qìng, which may be translated as 'long life and happiness galore'; *pán.táo* is a reference to the peach-tree which grew by the *yáo.chí*, the Lake of Gems, in the Kunlun palace of the Queen Mother of the West. The fruit of the tree conferred immortality.

The socio-linguistic domain of a later and more mundane age is also punctuated by this persistent rhythm. Thus, in the 1960s, the vigilant proletarian had to eschew *sān xiáng yī miè* 'three capitulations and one stamping-out', observe *sì hăo lián.duì* the 'four goods', and the *sān.bā tzuò.fēng* the 'three-eight working style', and keep his eye open for *yáo.mó gŭi.guài* 'monsters and freaks' and *niú.gŭi shé.chén* 'ox-demons and supernatural snakes', i.e. people of anti-Mao persuasion.

Word order

ba: although Chinese is essentially a SVO language, SOV is not at all uncommon. The co-verb *bă* provides a way of making the object in inverted order: e.g. *wŏ bă qì.chē măi.le* 'I bought the car'.

生命之道

1 宇宙被造以前，道已經存在；道與上帝同在，與上帝相同。2 在太初，道就與上帝同在。3 上帝藉着他創造萬有；在整個創造中，沒有一樣不是藉着他造的。4 道就是生命的根源，這生命把光賜給人類。

5 光照射黑暗，黑暗從來沒有勝過光。

6 有一個人，名叫<u>約翰</u>，是上帝所差遣的使者。7 他來告訴人關於那光的事，目的要使大家聽見他的信息而相信。8 他本身不是那光，而是要為光作證。

Guóyǔ

約翰福音傳

第一章 元始有道道與上帝共在道即上帝是道元始與上帝共在也、萬物以道而造、凡受造者無不以之而造、生在道中生也者人之光、光照於暗、暗者弗識之、〇有上帝所遣者名約翰、其至為光作證使眾以之而信、約翰非光、特為光證耳、真光者臨世照萬人者也、

Wenli

CHIPEWYAN

INTRODUCTION

Chipewyan belongs to Northern branch of the Athabaskan family (*see* **Athabaskan**). It is the main Athabaskan language in Canada, but is now spoken by fewer than 5,000.

PHONOLOGY

Consonants

Central to the Chipewyan inventory of sounds is the series, voiced stop – unvoiced stop – ejective unvoiced stop + associated affricates, e.g.

    d   t   t'
    dγ   tθ   t'θ'
    dz   ts   t's'

There are five laterals, /dl, tł, t'ł, ł, l/, and five velars + labialized counterparts, /g, k, k', x, γ; gº, kº, k'º, xº, γº. Syllabic finals are /n/ and the fricative series; /r/ cannot be initial.

Vowels

    short: a, ε, e, ɪ, o, u
    long: aː, εː, iː, uː

All, except /e/, can be nasalized (shown by cedilla).
There are two tones: high, marked by acute, and low (unmarked).

MORPHOLOGY AND SYNTAX

For a general note on Athabaskan structure, *see* **Athabaskan**. Nouns in Chipewyan can be simple: e.g. *bes* 'knife', *tθε* 'stone, pipe'; + suffix: *bą́n.ε* 'war party'; or marked for inalienable possession: *sε.γú* 'my tooth'.

Verbal forms may be nominalized by the relative particle *-i*: e.g. *ya.ł.tei* 'he speaks': *ya.ł.tei.i* 'he who speaks' = 'preacher'.

Pronoun

	Singular	Possessive	Plural	Possessive
1	si	sɛ-	nuhni	nuhɛ
2	nen	nɛ-	nuhni	nuhɛ
3	—	bɛ-	—	hubɛ
obviative	—	yɛ-	—	—
indefinite	—	'ɛ	—	—

The possessive suffix ɛ́ may be added: e.g. sɛ.t̢θen.ɛ́ 'my bone'; dɛne.bą́n.ɛ́ 'Indian war party'.

Various locative and directional relationships are expressed by means of postpositions: e.g. -a 'for', -ɛ́ł 'with', t̢ṣén 'towards'. Examples: sɛ.t̢ṣén 'towards me'; sas.t̢ṣén 'towards the bear'; xíł.t̢ṣén 'towards darkness' = 'evening'.

DEMONSTRATIVE PRONOUNS
diri 'this, these'; 'ɛyi 'that, those'.

INTERROGATIVE PRONOUNS
The stem is -dla-, -dláɣ-, -dlį́- + indefinite pronoun ': e.g. 'ɛdláɣį 'who?'; 'ɛdláɣe 'what?'.

RELATIVE PRONOUN
t̢ahi 'that which'; t̢ǫhį 'the one who ...'

Numerals

There are two sets of numerals, the first for counting things, the second for persons. Thus, 'į̣láɣɛ 'one thing', 'į̣láɣį 'one person'. Velar/nasal alternation is present: taɣɛ 'three things', tane 'three people'; sasųláɣɛ 'four things', sasųláne 'four people'.

Verb

For general aperçu, see **Athabaskan Languages**. For a specific Chipewyan example, Li (in Hoijer 1946) gives the verb tǫ 'to handle a long object, such as a stick'. This neutral stem has three aspects: imperfective (tǫ), perfective (tą́) and future (tą́); the instantaneous stem also has three aspects: t̢į – tǫ – tą́; as has the durative: tén – tǫ – tą́. The customary and progressive stems have only one form each: customary t̢į́/tį́; progressive t̢į́ł/tį́ł.

CLASSIFIERS
∅, ł, l, d as in other Athabaskan languages; ł is as usual associated with transitive causative senses: e.g. kun θɛ.ł.tsi 'he has made fire' (θɛ is the perfective marker); sɛ.nɛ.ł.cɛ 'he is raising me up' (nɛ- is instantaneous action marker).

The verbal complex comprises the aspect marker, the pronominal subject and object markers, and the classifier, generally in that order. The main aspect markers are: nɛ for transitional action (Li's 'momentaneous' aspect), θɛ (or ɣɛ) for perfective, ɣwa for future aspect. The imperfective aspect has a null marker.

Theoretically, there are two sets of pronominal subject markers, which are coded for tense/aspect: one set for the Ø/ł classifiers, the other for the d/l classifiers. The two sets coincide in most persons; thus, -s- is the first person singular imperfective marker, -n(ɛ)- the second person, and Ø the third person marker in both sets.

For example, there follow the first, second and third singular persons of the Chipewyan theme cɛ...ti 'to eat':

	Imperfective	Perfect	Future
1	cɛ.s.tį̄	cɛ.γɛ.s.tį̄	cɛ.γwa.s.tį̄
2	cɛ.nɛ.tį̄	cɛ.γį.tį̄	cɛ.γwu.tį̄
3	cɛ.Ø.tį̄	cɛ.γɛ.Ø.tį̄	cɛ.γwa.Ø.tį̄

where the second person forms show assimilation of aspect and pronominal markers.

The pronominal object markers and the third person subject marker are formally identical to the pronominal possessive markers set out above (*see* **Pronoun**). The yɛ- (obviative) form is used for a third person subject. Cf. with stem t'sɛ...θ/ðir 'to wake up': t'sɛ.sɛ.nį̄.ł.θer 'he woke me up', where nį̄ is the transitional aspect marker; t'sɛ.yį̄.nį̄.ł.θer 'he woke him up'.

Noun stems – e.g. tθí 'head', na 'eye', bą́ 'war party', etc. – may be incorporated in verbal complex: e.g. Ńabą́hu.déł 'We shall go on a war party.'

1 ᒉᐅ ᐅᴎ ᐳᔑ ᐁᒐ ᓂ, ᐳᔑ ᒐᐅᴎ ᐺ, ᐁᒐ ᓂ, ᐳᔑ ᒐᐅᴎ ᐁᒐ ᓀ,
2 ᐁᒐᒐ ᒉᐅ ᐅᴎ ᒐᐅᴎ ᐺ, ᐁᒐ ᓂ,
3 ᐻᴎᑌ ᒐᐅᴎ ᒉᔑ ᐅᐅᔑ ᐃᴎ ᓂ, ᐁᒐᒐ ᐺᕤ ᒉᔑ ᐸᒐ ᓂ,
4 ᐁᒐᒐ ᐻᴎᑌ ᐅᐅᔑ ᒐᐊᒐ ᓂ, ᐁᒐᒐ ᐅᒐ ᒉᐳᒐ ᑲ ᴎᒐ ᐃᐅ ᓂ ᓀ,
5 ᴎᐱ ᐅᐅᐁ ᐃᐅ ᐸ ᒐᒐᓂ ᓂ, ᒡᕤ ᐅᐅᐁ ᐃᐅ ᐁᐅᓂᕤ ᐃᐅ ᓂ,
6 ᒐᐅᴎ ᐁᐅᴎ ᐅᒐᒐ ᐁᒐ ᒐᐸ ᐱᕤ ᓂ,
7 ᐁᒐᒐ ᒐᐅᕤ ᓂ ᐳᔑ ᴎ ᕤᒐᕤ ᐸᑲ, ᐻᴎᑌ ᐅᒐ ᐅᐅᔑ ᐅᒉᐅᴎᕤ ᐸᑲ,
8 ᐁᒐᒐ ᐳᔑ ᐁᒐ ᐃᐅ ᓂ ᒐᐅᴎ ᐊᐁᒐ ᐳᔑ ᴎ ᕤᒐᕤ ᐸᑲ,

CHOCTAW

INTRODUCTION

Choctaw is a member of the Muskogean branch of the Macro-Algonquian family. Originally, the Choctaw lands were in south-eastern Mississippi and Louisiana. Here they were in contact with the French, with whom they sided in the sixteenth- to seventeenth-century wars against the British and against other Indian tribes. In the period of white expansion westwards, the Choctaw were evicted from their homelands and exiled to Oklahoma, along with the Cherokee, the Seminole, and some other tribes. Today they number about 10,000. Choctaw is very close to Chickasaw; a trade language known as *mobilian*, based on Chickasaw/Choctaw was in use in Mississippi and Lousiana in the nineteenth century.

Translation of the Bible into Choctaw began in the early nineteenth century. A major role was played by Cyrus Byington, whose *Choctaw Grammar* – completed in 1865, after 30 years' work – was published in Philadelphia in 1870.

SCRIPT
Roman.

PHONOLOGY

Consonants

    stops: p, b, t, k
    affricate: tʃ
    fricatives: f, s, ʃ, h
    nasals: m, n
    laterals: l, ɬ
    semi-vowels: w, j

Byington (1870) distinguishes /k'/ and /x/ as allophones of /k/.

Vowels

Byington's series:

    long and short: aː, ă (= [ʌ]), eː, ɛː, iː, ɪ, oː, uː, ŭ
    nasalized: ã, ĩ, õ, ũ
    diphthongs: ai, au

The main function of nasalization seems to be to emphasize or define more closely.

Stress

Stress in polysyllables tends to penultimate.

MORPHOLOGY AND SYNTAX

Article

Suffixed -*a*/-*o* combine with a variety of particles to express different degrees and shades of specificity, distinction, sequence, and mood (optative, presumptive, etc.). Basically, -*a* seems to define, -*o* to distinguish: e.g. *wak.a* 'the cow'; *wak.o* 'a/the cow' (e.g. not a horse). -*a* + *t* forms a frequent postpositive article: *at*, *ăt*, *et*, often following -*o* + -*k*, which is a limiting and precisioning particle: e.g. *hatak okăt* 'the man/men'; *hatak okăto* 'as for the man/men'.

The articles are applied to a vocalic stem, e.g. *peni* 'boat': *peni.ăt* 'the/a boat'; *peni.o* 'a boat' (not something else); *peni.măt* 'the boat also'; *peni.oš* 'the boat already referred to'.

Noun

The noun does not change for plural; numeral can be supplied or *lawa* 'many': e.g. *wak* 'a cow'; *wak tuklo* 'two cows'; *wak lawa* '(some) cows'.

POSSESSION
Appositional, e.g. *hatak kăllo* 'a man's strength'; *iti hishi* 'leaf of a tree'; *Chahta okla* 'the Choctaw nation'. The possessive marker may be inserted for alienable possession: e.g. *Chan in chuka* 'John his house'.

Adjective

As attribute, adjective follows noun, and is marked for number. The article is then transferred from noun to adjective: e.g. *hatak ăt mintih* 'a man is coming'; *hatak ačukma yăt mintih* 'a good man is coming'. Plural forms, e.g. of *čito* 'large': *hočito*; *yuštololi* 'short': *yuštolušli*; *falaia* 'long': *hofaloha*.

The negating particle -*ik*- may be prefixed to adjectives: e.g. *hatak kăllo* 'a strong man': *hatak ikhăllo* 'a weak man'.

COMPARISON
Choctaw has an elaborate series of gradations, specifying by how much and in what way something exceeds something else.

Pronoun

EMPHATIC PERSONAL PRONOUNS

	Singular	Plural
1	ăno	excl. pišno, incl. hăppišno
2	čišno	hăčišno

The third person forms are supplied from the demonstrative series: *ilăppa*, *yămma*.

POSSESSIVE AFFIXES
Series 1: for inalienable possession; for alienable, add -*m*:

	Singular	Plural
1	sa- (si/a/o)	excl. pi-, incl. hăpi-
2	či-	hăči-
3	i-	i-

Examples: *sa*(*h*) *foni* 'my bone'; *a.ski* 'my grandmother'; *im issuba* 'his horse'.

Series 2: provides the bound forms which act as the subjects of active verbs: with variants

	Singular	Plural
1	-li (suffix)	excl. i(l)-, incl. iloh-
2	iš-	haiš-
3	Ø	Ø

Examples: *pisa.li* 'I see'; *iš.pisa*, *Øpisa*; pl. *i.pisa*, etc.

DEMONSTRATIVE PRONOUN
ilăppa 'this'; *yămma* 'that'. Adjective: *pa* 'this'; *ma* 'that'.

RELATIVE PRONOUN
The article–pronoun is used: nominative *ăt*, *ak.oš*: oblique *ā*, *akō*: e.g. *či pisa lik ăt* 'I who see thee' ('thee-see-I-who ...').

Numerals

1–10: *ačăfa*, *tuklo*, *tukčina*, *ušta*, *tahlapi*, *hannali*, *untuklo*, *untučina*, *čakali*, *pokoli*. 11–19: *auah* + unit; 20 *pokoli tuklo*; 100 *tahlepa ačăfa*.

Verb

The stem is marked for person (subject and object) and tense, and is modulated by infix to express intensive, reiterative, semelfactive, diminutive aspects and moods. For example, with stem *takči* 'tie': *tākči* 'to be busy tying'; *taiyakči* 'to tie firmly'; *tahākči* 'to keep on tying'; *tahkči* 'to tie quickly'.

The negating particle is *ik-* prefix + change, if necessary, of final vowel to *o*: e.g. *haklo* 'to hear': *ik.haklo* 'not to hear'.

STATIVE VERBS

(a) adjectival, with possessive pronominal-series subject: e.g. *ačukma* 'good': *im.ačukma* 'he has (= is) good'; *sa.kăllo.h* 'I am strong'.
(b) affective, with possessive pronoun subject: *sa.lakša.h* 'I perspire'.

ACTIVE VERBS

Take series 2 pronominal subject (*see* **Pronoun**, above) and have the following moods: indicative, imperative, subjunctive, optative, potential.

TENSE MARKERS

-tuk, recent past; *-ttok*, remote past; *-(a)či(n)*, future; *-ahinla*, potential. Examples of tense forms + pronominal subject and object:

> *takči.h* 'he, she, it ties; they tie him, her, it'
> *takči.li.h* 'I tie'
> *či.takči.li.h* 'I tie thee'
> *či.pisa.Ø.h* 'he sees thee'
> *či.takči.li.tuk* 'I have just tied thee'
> *či.takči.Ø.čī* 'he will tie thee'

Note that the pronominal object forms are provided by the possessive series, with one difference – the third person singular and plural is Ø, not *-i*.

-h is used as substantive verb or copula, affixed to any part of speech, e.g. *ŭlla* 'child': *ŭllah* 'it is a child'; *ăno* 'I': *ănoh* 'it is I'.

NEGATIVE

Formed by *k-* prefix + *-o* final: e.g. *a.ki.pisa.o(h)* 'I don't see'; *či.k.pisa.o(h)* 'you (sing.) don't see'; cf. *či.pisa.li(h)* 'I see you (sing.)'; *a.k.či.piso(h)* 'I don't see you'; *iš.pi.pisa(h)* 'you (sing.) see us'; neg. *či.k.pi.piso(h)*.

SUBJUNCTIVE

-(o)km- infix + *-a(t)*: e.g. *takčikmăt* 'if he were to tie ...'

OPTATIVE

-(o)kb- infix + *a(t)*: e.g. *takčikbăt* 'oh, that he would tie ...'

PASSIVE

Can be found in several ways from active, e.g. *hukmi* 'to burn': *holʊkmi* 'to be burned'; *bohli* 'to beat': *boa* 'to be beaten'.

Prepositions

There are directional markers and locative forms, e.g. *et-* 'hither', *pit-* 'thither'.

1. ỤMMONA ka Anumpa hʋt ahanta mʋt, Anumpa hʋt Chihowa yạ ai iba chʋfa tok: mihmʋt Anumpa hash ot Chihowa ya tok.

2. Yʋmmak inli hosh ʋmmona ka Chihowa yạ ai iba chʋfa tok.

3. Yʋmmak atuk mak ọ nan oklụha kʋt toba tok; yohmi ka nana kʋt toba tok ʋt yʋmmak ọ keyu hokʋno ik tobo ki tok.

4. Yʋmmak oka isht ai okchạya yʋt asha tok: yohmi ka isht ai okchạya yʋmmak ash ot hatak puta ka in tohwikeli ya tok.

5. Mihmʋt tohwikeli hash ot ai okhlilika yạ a tohọmmi; yohmi ka okhlilika yʋt yʋmmak ash ọ ik akostinincho ki tok.

6. Hatak Chan hohchifo hosh, Chihowa nana aiahni họ ạya tok.

7. Yʋmma pulla tuk mak ọ hatak ʋt momʋt yimma hi ọ, yʋmmak ash osh nan atokoli osh Nan-tohwikeli ash atokowa anola chị hosh ạya tok.

CHUKCHI

INTRODUCTION

Chukchi belongs, with Koryak and Itelmen, to the Chukotko-Kamchatka group of Palaeo-Siberian languages. It is spoken in the Chukchi National Region and elsewhere over a vast area, extending from the Bering Strait to the Yakut Autonomous Soviet Socialist Republic, by about 11,000 people, who fall into two groups: the Tundra Chukchi and the Maritime Chukchi. The language is in everyday use for education, administration, and journalism. Both the Chukchi and the Koryak called themselves *luoravetlat* (/ləɣʔorawətlʔat/) which means 'proper people', but the term seems to have fallen from use, as has the former specific 'women's pronunciation' of Chukchi.

SCRIPT

Cyrillic + ӈ and қ.

PHONOLOGY

Consonants

> stops: p, t, k, q, ʔ
> affricate: tʃ
> fricatives: v/ß, j, ɣ
> nasals: m, n, ŋ
> lateral: l
> roll: r

The lateral l is voiceless.

Vowels

> weak: i, e, u
> strong: e, a, o
> + ə

That is /e/ = [ɛ] is ambivalent; /ə/ is neutral. This division underlies the Chukchi

328

system of vowel harmony: the vowels in a word are drawn either from the weak or from the strong series, not from both. What is particularly interesting about Chukchi vowel harmony is that root vowels in a weak-series word are regraded to strong series when a strong-series affix is added to the word. This is in striking contrast with Altaic, for example, where it is the affix that takes its vocalic cue from the stem. This also happens in Chukchi: see verbal prefixes, below.

Examples of regrading of weak vowels before a strong-series affix are given by Skorik (1968): *keŋikupren* 'sweep-net', *γa.kaŋekopra.ma* 'with the sweep-net', where weak-series *e*, *i*, *u* have been regraded as *a*, *e*, *o*, in concord with comitative case-marker *γa...ma*. The reverse case – the regrading of strong vowels as weak – is not found.

MORPHOLOGY AND SYNTAX

Noun

Chukchi has no grammatical gender and no articles. The basic dichotomy is between human and non-human. Skorik (1968) distinguishes three declensions: (a) non-human, (b) and (c) covering human field. All distinguish number in the nominative case, but differ in their treatment of the oblique cases, of which there are eight. In the non-human declension, there is one oblique form for both singular and plural: e.g. *milger* 'gun': nom. pl. *milger.ti*; ergative (sing./pl.): *milger.e*. The comitative form *γa.melgar.ma* shows the regrading of weak-series vowels referred to above.

In the human categories, the oblique cases have distinct singular and plural forms.

Nominals can be conjugated with personal endings to denote socio-economic identity and status as regards possessions:

mik.iγəm 'who am I'
ən.pənačγ.eγət 'you are an old man'
γe.ŋinqej.iγəm 'I have son(s)'
γe.ŋinqej.iγət 'you (sing.) have son(s)'
γe.req.əturi 'what do you (pl.) own?'
γe.kupre.muri 'we own a net'

Agglutinative affixation yields further declensions expressing privative, delimiting, selective, evaluative, and other nuances.

Adjective

As predicate, adjective is treated as a stative verb: e.g. *n.itč.iγəm* 'I am heavy'; *n.itč.iγət* 'you (sing.) are heavy', etc. The attributive adjective is incorporated in nominal stems.

Pronoun

PERSONAL

	Singular	Plural
1	γəm	muri
2	γət	turi
3	ətl'on	ətri

These are declined in nine cases, and show vocalic regrading: e.g. the ergative case of *muri* 'we', is *mor.yənan*.

The possessive forms are *yəm.nin* 'my', *yən.in* 'your', *ən.in* 'his/her. The pronouns can be marked to notate a relationship to other persons – e.g. *tur.əkekine.jyəm* expresses a relationship of first person singular to second person plural, and they can even be marked for sequence or periodicity: e.g. *yəm.r'am* 'now I ...'; *yən.r'am* 'now you ...'

DEMONSTRATIVE PRONOUN

notqen 'this'; *əŋqen* 'that'. These are treated as nominals and declined according to whether they have human or non-human referents.

INTERROGATIVE PRONOUN

r'enut 'what?'; *meŋin* 'who?'.

Numerals

Numerals have base forms uncoded for person, but usually take personal affixes. The base forms for 1–5 are: *ənnen, ŋireq, ŋəroq, ŋəraq, mətləŋen*. 6–9 are compounds: e.g. 6 *ənnenmətləŋen*. 10 *mənyətken*. 20 *qlikkin*. 40 *ŋireq qlikkin*.

Verb

Transitive (ergative construction) and intransitive (nominative construction). Verbs are marked for aspect, voice, mood, tense, person, and number. Intransitive verbs show concord with subject; transitive verbs are marked for concord with both subject and object.

Two conjugational models are applied aspectually to present, past, and future tense forms:

(a) delimited/perfective: the model is personal prefix – root – suffix (in part marked for person): e.g.

tə.čejv.ərkən 'I go' (now, single occasion)
Ø.čejv.ərkət 'they go' (now, single occasion)
tre.čejv. rkən 'I shall go'
mətre. čejv. rkən 'we shall go'
mət. čejv. mək 'we went'

(b) imperfective: the model is invariable prefix – root – suffix inflected for person: e.g.

nə.čejv. iyəm 'I go' (generally, habitually)
nə.čejv. iyət 'you go' (generally, habitually)
γə.čejv. iyəm 'I was going' (generally, habitually)
γə.čejv. iyət 'you were going' (generally, habitually)

Transitive/polypersonal verb: here, the prefix is subject-related, the suffix is object-related. The complete grid for any one tense gives 28 forms: e.g. from stem *l'uk* 'to see', present-tense:

tə.l'u rkəniyət 'I see you (sing.)'
tə.l'u. rkənitək 'I see you (pl.)'
ine.l'u. rkən 'you (sing.) see me'
ne.l'u. rkəniyəm 'they see me'
ne.l'u. rkəniyət 'they see you (sing.)'

The verbal prefixes in conjugation (a) are subject to regrading in harmony with following stem vowel: e.g. *tre → tra: tra.jalyət.y'a* 'I shall go off as nomad'.

NEGATIVE

The circumfix: *(e) ...ke/ka/k* negates the root meaning of the verb. Tense and personal deixis are expressed in a following composite pronominal form: e.g. *e.piri.ke mətre.ntə.yənet* 'we shan't take them' (*piri* 'to take'; *e ...ke* = negative circumfix; *mətre-* 1st p. pl. future prefix; *yənet* = 3rd p. pl. obj. suffix).

ERGATIVE

An ergative construction is used with all transitive verbs. The logical subject is in the ergative/locative/instrumental case; the logical object in the nominative. Skorik (1968: 267) gives the following example: *tumy.e na.ntəvat.ən kupre.n* 'The comrades put the net', literally: 'by the comrades – they-put-it – the net', where *-e* is the ergative/instrumental marker, *-n* is the nominative ending.

Like some American Indian languages, Chukchi can detransitivize a transitive verb by means of the prefix *ine* (→ *ena* in the following example, because of vowel regrading): *Tumy.ət kupre.te ena.ntəvat.y'at* 'The comrades put the net', where *tumy.ət* is the nominative plural, and *-y'at* is an intransitive ending.

The rich agglutinative structure of Chukchi permits the formation of composite words comprising a series of roots; equipped with the requisite formants, a whole phrase or sentence can be nominalized.

Postpostions

These normally follow nouns in locative case. Skorik (1968, p.267) gives the following examples: *ətləy re.en.ək* 'with father'; *yəty.ək rəmaytə* 'on the other side of the lake' (where *-ək* is the locative marker).

Word order

SOV, SVO.

CHUVASH

INTRODUCTION

This, the most divergent of the Turkic languages, is spoken by a total of 1½ to 2 million people, almost equally divided between those who live in the Chuvash and those who live in the Tatar and Bashkir Autonomous Soviet Socialist Republics. Baskakov's (1966) classification assigns Chuvash to the Bulgar group of West Turkic, both of whose other constituent members – Volga Bulgar and Khazar – have been long extinct. It is interesting to note that in certain common Altaic roots where Turkic in general has /z/, Chuvash joins the Mongolian branch of Altaic in having an /r/ sound. Uralic influence can be seen in the vocabulary of Chuvash and in some aspects of the morphology (see, for example, the formation of the negative imperative).

Chuvash has been a written language since the eighteenth century. It is now used in the republic for education, local media, and literature.

SCRIPT

Several versions of the Cyrillic script have been tried over the last 200 years. The present one uses the additional letters ă, ĕ, ÿ, ç.

PHONOLOGY

Consonants

> stops: p, t, k (palatalized /t′/ occurs)
> affricate: t∫
> fricatives: f, v, s, ∫, ʒ′, x
> nasals: m, n, ɲ
> laterals and flap: l, l′, r
> semi-vowel: j

/ʒ′/, notated as ç, is described as a palatalized fricative deriving from an original affricate /dʒ/.

Chuvash has no voiced/unvoiced opposition in the stop series; /b, d, g/ are found only in loan-words.

Vowels

front: i, ε, e, y
back: ɪ, a, u, o

Short /ă/ → short /ĕ/.

VOWEL HARMONY
The general rule, front with front, back with back, obtains in Chuvash but is not consistently applied: e.g. *yultaš. amar* 'our comrade'; *xẹr.ẹmẹr* 'our daughter'. Reduced vowels (/ă, ĕ/) are unstable. In this article, reduced vowels are dotted.

Stress

On final, unless this is a reduced vowel, when stress moves to penultimate. On initial if all vowels in a word are reduced.

MORPHOLOGY AND SYNTAX

Noun

The plural marker is *-sem/-sen*: e.g. *xula* 'town', *xulasem* (no vowel harmony).

DECLENSION
Nominative = base form + eight cases; dative and accusative have fused.

genitive: -ɣ*n*
dative/accusative: -(*n*)*a*/-(*n*)*e*
locative: *-ra/-re, ta/te*
ablative:*-ran/-ren, tan/ten*
instrumental: *-pa/-pe, pala/pele*
privative: *-sạr/-sẹr*
benefactive: *-šạn/-šen*

Examples: *pürte* 'in the house'; *xulana kaj-* 'to go to town'; *šančạksar* 'hopeless'; *Ạval traktor.pa ẹžleme pultarat'* 'He can work with the tractor.'

POSSESSIVE AFFIXES

	Singular	*Plural*
1	-ạm/-ẹm/-m	-ạmạr/-ẹmẹr
2	-u/-ü	-ạr/-ẹr
3	-ẹ/-i	-ẹ/-i

Examples: *tusa.m* 'my friend'; *tusa.m.sem* 'my friends'; *tusẹ* 'his, her, their friend'. Possession can also be indicated by use of genitive case of personal pronoun (see below) either with or without possessive affix: e.g. *pirẹn yal Ø = pirẹn yal.ạmạr = yal.amạr* 'our village'.

Adjective

As attribute, adjective precedes noun and is invariable. A comparative is made with -(*ta*)*rax*/-(*te*)*rex*: e.g. *ilemlę.rex* 'more beautiful'; *pısạk. rax* 'bigger'.

Pronoun

Personal base forms with oblique bases:

	Singular	Oblique base	Plural	Oblique base
1.	epę	man-	epir/epęr	pir-
2.	esę	san-	esir/esęr	sir
3.	val	un-	vęsem	vęs-

These are fully declined: e.g. *manran* 'from me'; *manšạn* 'for me'; *siręnpe* 'by you (pl.)' *manạn vạxạt ž'uk* 'I have no time'.

DEMONSTRATIVE PRONOUN
ku 'this'; *ž'ak* 'that'; fully declined, with plural forms.

INTERROGATIVE PRONOUN
kam 'who?'; *męn* 'what?'.

Numerals

1–10: these have full and shortened forms; the latter are used to enumerate objects: they are *pęr*, *ik*(*ę*), *viž'ę*, *tạvat*, *pilęk*, *ult*, *ž'ic*, *sakạr*, *tạxạr*, *vun*; 20 *ž'iręm*. 30 *vạtạr*; 40 *xęręx*; 100 *ž'ęr*.

Verb

The Chuvash verb has four voices: active, reflexive–passive, causative, and reciprocal. There are five moods: indicative, imperative, optative, subjunctive, and concessive. The tense structure distinguishes present/future, future, and past. Aspect is not a feature of the Chuvash verb.

VOICE
Here, standard Turkic markers appear: refl./pass. in -V*l*/-V*n*, causative in -*tar*/-*ter*, reciprocal in -V*s*/-V*š*.

INDICATIVE MOOD
The present/future tense endings are: sing. 1 -*t.ạp*, 2 -*t.ạn*, 3 -*t'*; pl. 1 -*t.p.ạr*, 2 -*t.ạr*, 3 -*ž'.ž'e*. This tense is negated by -*mas*/-*mes*: thus *tavrạna.t.ạp* 'I (shall) return'; *tavrạn.mas.t.ạp* 'I do/shall return'.

The past tense has the marker -*t*/*r* plus a slightly different set of endings: e.g. *tavrạn.t.ạm* 'I returned'; *tavrạn.ma.t.ạm* 'I did not return'.

IMPERATIVE
Here there are forms for all three persons and numbers, with the verbal stem providing the second person singular form: *ęž'le*! 'work!'; *ęž'le.tęr* (3rd p.). The

first person negative form has the particle *mar*: e.g. *ęž'le.m mar* 'let me not work'. The second person uses the particle *an* e.g. *an ęž'le* 'don't work'.

The use of a prohibitive particle is alien to Turkic, though it is found in both Mongolian and Uralic.

PARTICIPIAL FORMS
Broadly divided into those with temporal significance and those with modal significance. Examples of the former are: *ęž'le.ken* '(who is) working' *ęž'le.nę* '(who) having worked'; *ęž''le.s* who will work'.

MODAL FORMS
E.g. with *malla*, giving necessitative sense; negated by *mar*: e.g. *kay.malla ž'ın* 'the man who must go'; *kay.malla mar ž'ın* 'the man who must not go'.

AUXILIARY VERBS
Used to express such modalities of action as suddenness, motion towards or away from speaker, upwards or downwards, etc.

Postpositions

Postpositions and auxiliary nouns are used, the latter declined.

Word order

SOV.

I. 1. Сӑмах ҭан малтанах пур, Вӑл Сӑмах Турӑра, Çав
2. 3 Сӑмах Хӑй Тура. Турӑра Вӑл ҭан малтанах пур. Мен
пулни пур те Ун урлӑ пулнӑ. Унсӑр пуçне нимӗн те
4 пулман. Унӑн ашӗнҭе ҭӗрелӗх пулна, çав ҭӗрӗлӗх çын-
5 сем валли çутӑ пулнӑ. Вӑл çутӑ тӗттӗмре çутатат; тӗт
тӗм ӑна хупласа илеймен.
6, 7 Тура йанӑ Іоанн йатлӑ çын пулнӑ. Хӑй урла Çут-
та пур те ӗненҭҭӗр тесе, вӑл Çутӑ çинҭен каласа
8 пӗлтерме килнӗ. Вӑл Хӑй Çутӑ пулман, Çутӑ çинҭен каласа пӗлтерме йанӑ çын анҭах пулнӑ.

CIRCASSIAN

See **Kabard-Cherkes**.

COPTIC

INTRODUCTION

Coptic – the latest form of Egyptian, which belongs to the Semito-Hamitic family – was widely spoken in Egypt from the third to the sixth centuries AD. It was never the language of administration, a role which the Greek introduced by the Ptolemies continued to discharge, even under the Roman Empire. From about 100 BC onwards the old demotic script was discarded in favour of the Greek alphabetic script, and, with the spread of Christianity, Coptic began to acquire literary status. The translation of the Bible into Sahidic Coptic (mid-third century) was of enormous importance in this respect. The large number of Greek words in Coptic is part of the legacy of the Ptolemies. By the fifth century, Coptic was the literary language of Upper Egypt; one of the best-known works in Coptic literature – the biography of Shenute, the austere abbot of the White Monastery of Atrib – which appeared about 450, is in Bohairic, the dialect of Lower Egypt.

To the Arabs who conquered Egypt in the seventh century, the terms 'Egyptian' and 'Christian' were synonymous, and the name 'Copt' derives from قبطى (qubṭi), the Arabic version of αἰγύπτιος. When Arabic replaced spoken Eygptian (from the twelfth century onwards), Coptic was retained as the liturgical language of the Coptic Monophysite Church (which had finally broken with the Byzantine Church in the fifth century). Today, there are about 5/6 million Copts. The liturgical language is not generally understood, and its replacement by Arabic has been urged. On the other hand, attempts have been made to revive Coptic as both a written and a spoken language.

There are six dialects, the most important being Sahidic and Bohairic, associated respectively with Upper and Lower Egypt. The present-day liturgical language is based on Bohairic. Here, in general, Sahidic forms are described.

SCRIPT

Thanks to the use of the Greek phonetic script, Coptic is the only form of Egyptian whose pronunciation is actually attested, and hence the great importance of the language for Egyptian philology.

Seven additional letters were borrowed from Demotic (*see* **Egyptian**) to denote sounds alien to Greek: ⲱ / ⱳ = /ʃ/, ϥ = /f/, ⳗ = /ẖ/, ϩ = ẖ, ⲭ = /dʒ/ǰ/ d′/, ϭ = /k′/, ϯ = /ti/.

z was probably pronounced as /z/, not /zd/ as in Classical Greek, ϩ = /ḫ/ is

337

for Greek ʿ (rough aspirate). The vowel marker ⁻ indicates the reduced front vowel /ə/ pronounced before the bearer consonant: thus $\overline{M}$ = /əm/. Abbreviations are frequent, especially in the case of nomina sacra: e.g. $\overline{IH\lambda}$ = ICPⲀHⲀ 'Israel'; $\overline{CⲰP}$ = CⲰTHP 'saviour'.

Doubled vowels are read as vowel + hamza: BⲰⲰN = /boːʔon/ 'bad, evil'.

PHONOLOGY

Consonants

stops: p, ḅ, t, ḍ, k, g̊
affricates: the pre-dental palatals: voiced Ⲝ = ḍ', and surd Ⳝ = tʰ are cited
  as affricates; the latter in Bohairic.
fricatives: ß, s, ʃ, h, χ
nasals: m, n
semi-vowels: j, w
lateral and flap: l, r

/p, t, k/ are aspirates; /ḅ, ḍ, g̊/ are half-voiced.

Vowels

long: eː, oː, uː
short: i, e, a, o, u, ə
long vowels are indicated here by macrons.

Stress is on the penultimate or the final syllable, long or short.

MORPHOLOGY AND SYNTAX

Coptic represents the extreme analytical stage of Egyptian. Flectional change has virtually vanished, and syntactic relationships depend on a highly developed system of articles, prefixes, prepositions, and particles.

Noun

There are two genders, masculine, and feminine. In general, the old Egyptian genders are retained. The old feminine ending -t has disappeared in the absolute state, but reappears in the pronominal state found in certain nouns (mainly denoting parts of the body), e.g. *ro* 'mouth', pronominal state *rō*: *rō.k* 'thy mouth'; *rō.f* 'his mouth'; *hē* 'body', pronominal state *hēt*.

In theory, all nouns have two states – absolute and construct (where two nouns are directly connected, with a single stress on the second member of the collocation: see genitive, below).

ARTICLE

Definite, weak form: masc. *p-*, fem. *-t*, pl. *-n*; strong: masc. *pi/pe*, fem. *ti/te*, pl. *ni/ne*. Examples: *p.rōme* 'the man', *n.rōme* 'the men'; *p.saǰe* 'the word'; *ti.polis* 'the town'; *n.halate* 'the birds'; *te.physis* 'nature'.

The indefinite article for both genders is *ou* = /w/; the plural is *hen/hən*: e.g. *w.ei* 'a house'; *hen.ei* 'houses'.

In the genitive construct, the article is attached to both components: e.g. *p.ei əm.p.ajōt* 'the house of the father'; *p.ran əm.p.ĵojs* 'the name of the Lord'; *p.kah ən.kēme* 'the land of Egypt'. In these sentences, *ən* is the genitive marker; it is *əm* before labials.

PLURAL
Marked almost exclusively by inflection in the article (see above), i.e. one and the same form of the noun serves as both singular and plural, though a few vestiges of plural inflection remain: e.g. *hōb* 'thing', pl. *hbēje*; *son* 'brother', pl. *snēj*; *ĵoj* 'ship', pl. *eĵēj*.

The category of nouns includes infinitives. Two- and three-radical nouns are most common: e.g. *sim* 'grass'; *klom* 'crown'. Four- and five-radical nouns are often reduplications of two-/three-radicals.

New formations are made by prefixation or suffixation, in the latter case showing gender: *-f* (masc.), *-s* (fem.), e.g. *sormes* 'error, delusion' (*sōrəm* 'to be mistaken').

Prefixation: e.g. *šw-* 'worthy of' – *šwmw* 'he who is worthy of death'; *šer-* 'son of' – *šerenwot* 'only son'; *bō-* 'tree of' – *bōənĵojt* 'olive tree'.

Adjective

As a separate category, the adjective does not exist in Coptic. Various verbal and nominal constructions are used: e.g. *nesōs* 'she is pretty' (< *nese-*, *nesō* 'to be pretty'). The construct formula with *ən* is frequent: e.g. *u.rōme ən.sabe* 'a man of wisdom' = 'a wise man'; *pe.f.šēre ən.wot* 'his only son'.

Pronoun

Three series: independent, suffixed, and proclitic; gender is marked in the second and third person singular:

		Singular			Plural		
		Independent	Suffixed	Proclitic	Independent	Suffixed	Proclitic
1		anok	-i/-t	ti	anon	-n	tən
2	masc.	əntok	-k/-t	k	—	—	—
	fem.	ənto	Ø/-e/-te	te	əntotən	-tən	tetən
						-tēutən	
3	masc.	əntof	-f	f	əntow	-w/-sw	se
	fem.	əntos	-s	s			

The suffixed pronouns are used with certain nouns, usually denoting parts of the human body (see **Noun**, above): e.g. *rat* 'foot, leg', *toot* 'hand', *hra* 'face': *hrak* 'your face'; *hrētən* 'your (pl.) face'.

The proclitic forms figure as the subject of adverbial clauses: e.g. *ti.həm pajōt*

'I am in my father' (John, 14.11); *nai de se.həm p.kosmos* 'but these are in the world' (John, 17.11).

DEMONSTRATIVE PRONOUN

There are three series of demonstrative pronouns, and four series of demonstrative articles. Typical of the former is the series masc. *pai*; fem. *tai*; pl. common *nai*: e.g. *Pai hən te.hweite nefšoop* 'This was in the beginning'.

The possessive prefix: masc. *pa*; fem. *ta*; pl. *na*. These precede the noun, and may be used without overt referent, as in Greek; cf. *na perro* = *ta tou pharaō* 'the things that are the Pharaoh's.

POSSESSIVE ARTICLES

Basically, the *p-*, *t-*, *n-* series plus personal markers; thus, *tes-* is the possessive article for a feminine object possessed by a feminine third person; *netən* for a plural object possessed by second person plural: e.g. *pe.k.ēi* 'your (sing.) house'; *netən.hbēje* 'your (pl.) affairs'.

INTERROGATIVE PRONOUN

nim 'who?'; *ou* 'what?'. *Nim* may be connected to a noun by *ñ* /ən/: e.g. *Nim ən.rōme?* 'What man?'; *əntək nim?* 'Who art thou? (John, 1.19); *Ou te tme?* 'What is truth?' (John, 18.38);
   aš 'who, what?': e.g. *Aš pe.k.ran* 'What is your name?'

RELATIVE PRONOUN

et/ *(e)nt*; < Egyptian *ntj*: e.g. *p.rōme et.həm p.ēi* 'the man who is in the house'; *p.rōme ete pa.jōt pe* 'the man who is my father'.

Numerals

The cardinals 1 to 10 and the lower teens have masculine and feminine forms: 1 *wa/wi*; 2 *snaw/sənte*; 3 *šomənt/šomte*; 4 *ftow/ftoe*; 5 *tiw/ti(e)*; 6 *sow/so(e)*; 7 *sašef/sašfe*; 8 *šmoun/šmoune*; 9 *psis/psit*; 10 *mēt/mēte*; 20 *juōt/juōte*; 30 *maab/maabe*; 100 *še*.

The numerals have enclitic forms used with nouns, and specific truncated forms for use after decades: e.g. *tē* 'five' following *juōt*, *maab*, etc.

Verb

The great majority of Coptic verbs are two-, three-, or four-radical. The infinitive is neutral as to voice, the transitive/intransitive opposition being alien to Egyptian. It is always masculine in gender, irrespective of whether it derives from a masculine or feminine infinitive in older Egyptian. Certain vocalic finals (*e/i*) appear where the original feminine *-t* ending has been lost.

Like the noun, the infinitive has three states: absolute, construct, and pronominal: e.g. absolute *jō* 'speak', construct *je-*, pronominal *joo*. The construct form is used with a nominal direct object, the pronominal with a pronoun.

CONJUGATION

Prefixal or suffixal. The small class of suffixal conjugations derives from the Egyptian *sjm.f* model (*see* **Egyptian**). Examples from *peje* 'say': *afei ebol pejaf naw* 'he went forth and said unto them' (John, 18.4); *pejaw naf* 'they said unto him' (John, 9.12).

PREFIXAL CONJUGATION

This is the usual conjugation pattern; the model is tense marker – personal marker – stem, e.g. *a-f-sōtəm* 'he has heard'. The inventory of tenses includes three present and three future tenses, two imperfects, a future imperfect, two perfects, and a preterite, plus a series of secondary forms. Each tense has specific affirmation and negative prefixed markers, showing gender in second and third person singular: e.g. first present:

	Singular	Plural
1	ti	tən
2	k/te	tetən
3	f/s	se

Each tense has, in addition, a neutral marker prefixed to a nominal subject. In the first present, this marker is Ø. The 1st present is negated by the circumfix *ən ...an*: e.g. *ti.sōtəm* 'I hear', *ən.ti.sōtəm an* 'I do not hear'; *k.eire* 'thou doest'; *əf.bōk* 'he goes'; *təm.bōk* 'we go'.

PERFECT

affirmative: sing. *ai, ak/are, af/as*; pl. *an, atetən, aw*;
negative: sing. *əmpi, əmpek/əmpe, əmpef/əmpes*; pl. *əmpen, əmpetən, əmpow*.

The tense characteristic is *a-*; the neutral marker is affirm. *a-*, neg. *mpe-*: e.g. *a.tetən shime sōtəm* 'your wife has heard'; *mpe.p.noute sōtəm erof* 'God has not heard him'.

PRESENT HABITUAL

affirmative: sing: *šai, šak/šare, šaf/šas*; pl. *šan, šatetən, šaw*;
negative: sing. *mei, mek/mere, mef/mes*; pl. *men, metetən, mew*.

The tense characteristic is affirm. *šare-*, neg. *mere*: e.g. *Mere.p.noute sōtəm erok* 'God is not given to hearing you'. Similarly for other primary and secondary tenses: e.g. the conditional, with affirmative markers:

sing. *ei.šan, ek.šan/er.šan, ef.šan/es.šan*; pl. *en.šan, etetənšan, ej.šan*.

The neutral marker is *eršan*: e.g. *Eršan.p.rōme šlēl p.noute na.sōtəm erof* 'If man prays, God will hear him', where *na-* is a future marker.

Conjunctive (dependent) forms have an *e-* prefix: e.g. *ef.sōtəm* 'while/as he hears'; *ef.na.sōtəm* 'while he will hear'; *ene.af.sōtəm* 'while he had heard'; *e.šaf.sōtəm* 'while he habitually hears'; *əmpat.ef.sōtəm* 'while he has not yet heard'.

COMPOUND VERBS

Infinitive in construct form + noun: e.g. *eire* 'to make', construct *ər-*: *ər.wojn* 'to illuminate' (*wojn* 'light'). Cf. John, 1.5

> auō p.wojn efərwojn həm p.kake
> 'and the light is making-to-illuminate in the darkness'.

Prepositions

Prepositions have construct and pronominal forms only, no absolute. They are simple or compound: e.g. *e-*, *ero* 'to, towards, into': *e.p.kosmos* 'into the world'; *eroi* 'to me'; *erof* 'to him'.

ən/əm marks direct object and acts as a genitive, locative, or instrumental link: e.g. *əm pei ma* 'in this place'; *p.ei əm.pa.son* 'the house of my brother'; *hən/ ənhēt* 'in, at': *həm pei wojš* 'at this time'.

COMPOUND PREPOSITIONS

These are mostly nouns denoting parts of the body, plus simple prepositions: e.g. *ro-/ro* 'mouth' + *e-/a-*; *rat/ret* 'foot' + *e*; e.g. *Afei eratəf əmpərro* 'He came to (the feet of) the emperor'.

Word order

SVO; more precisely, in a verbal sentence, temporal prefix or neutral prenominal marker + nominal subject – infinitive – direct object – indirect object.

ϧⲉⲛ ⲧⲁⲣⲭⲏ ⲛⲉ ⲡⲓⲥⲁϫⲓ ⲡⲉ. ⲟⲩⲟϩ ⲡⲓⲥⲁϫⲓ ⲛⲁϥⲭⲏ ϩⲁⲧⲉⲛ ⲫϯ. ⲟⲩⲟϩ ⲛⲉ ⲟⲩⲛⲟⲩϯ ⲡⲉ ⲡⲓⲥⲁϫⲓ. ²ⲫⲁⲓ ⲉⲛⲁϥⲭⲏ ⲓⲥϫⲉⲛϩⲏ ϩⲁⲧⲉⲛ ⲫϯ. ³ϩⲱⲃ ⲛⲓⲃⲉⲛ ⲁⲩ|ϣⲱⲡⲓ ⲉⲃⲟⲗ ϩⲓⲧⲟⲧϥ. ⲟⲩⲟϩ ⲁⲧϭ̄ⲛⲟⲩϥ ⲙ̄ⲡⲉ ϩⲗⲓ ϣⲱⲡⲓ ϧⲉⲛ ⲫⲏ ⲉⲧⲁϥ-ϣⲱⲡⲓ. ⁴ⲛⲉ ⲡⲱⲛϧ ⲡⲉⲧⲉⲛϧⲏⲧϥ. ⲟⲩⲟϩ ⲡⲱⲛϧ ⲡⲉ ⲫⲟⲩⲱⲓⲛⲓ ⲛ̄ⲛⲓⲣⲱⲙⲓ ⲡⲉ. ⁵ⲟⲩⲟϩ ⲡⲓⲟⲩⲱⲓⲛⲓ ⲁϥⲉⲣⲟⲩⲱⲓⲛⲓ ϧⲉⲛ ⲡⲓⲭⲁⲕⲓ. ⲟⲩⲟϩ ⲙ̄ⲡⲉ ⲡⲓⲭⲁⲕⲓ ⲧⲁϩⲟϥ. ⁶Ⲁϥϣⲱⲡⲓ ⲛ̄ϫⲉⲟⲩⲣⲱⲙⲓ ⲉⲁⲩⲟⲩⲟⲣⲡϥ ⲉⲃⲟⲗ ϩⲓⲧⲉⲛ ⲫϯ Ⲉⲡⲉϥⲣⲁⲛ ⲡⲉ ⲓⲱⲁⲛⲛⲏⲥ. ⁷ⲫⲁⲓ ⲁϥⲓ ⲉⲩⲙⲉⲧ-ⲙⲉⲑⲣⲉ ϩⲓⲛⲁ ⲛ̄ⲧⲉϥⲉⲣⲙⲉⲑⲣⲉ ϧⲁ ⲡⲓⲟⲩⲱⲓⲛⲓ. ϩⲓⲛⲁ ⲛ̄ⲧⲉ ⲟⲩⲟⲛ ⲛⲓⲃⲉⲛ ⲛⲁϩϯ ⲉⲃⲟⲗ ϩⲓⲧⲟⲧϥ. ⁸Ⲛⲉ ⲛ̄ⲑⲟϥ ⲁⲛ ⲡⲉ ⲡⲓⲟⲩⲱⲓⲛⲓ. ⲁⲗⲗⲁ ϩⲓⲛⲁ ⲛ̄ⲧⲉϥⲉⲣ-ⲙⲉⲑⲣⲉ ϧⲁ ⲡⲓⲟⲩⲱⲓⲛⲓ.

CORNISH

INTRODUCTION

Cornish belongs to the British (Brythonic) division of the Celtic branch of Indo-European. Old Cornish is attested in various tenth-century glosses, found in Latin MSS. Middle Cornish (fourteenth to sixteenth centuries) is well known from some 20,000 lines of source material – religious drama, ecclesiastical history, etc. The last native speaker of Cornish died in 1777. In the nineteenth century, when the first serious attempts were made to revive the written and spoken language, the model chosen was not late Cornish, heavily infected as it was with English, but the comparatively pure Middle Cornish of earlier centuries. This recrudescent language, known as Unified Modern Cornish, is the product initially of the work of Henry Jenner (1848–1934) and subsequently of R. Morton Nance. The lexical repertory provided by the Middle Cornish texts has been amplified and extended by analogy with other Celtic languages. The pronunciation adopted represents a reasoned treatment of the Middle Cornish phonological material in the light of general Celtic philology. Twentieth-century and sixteenth-century Cornish are therefore in a sense synchronic.

SCRIPT

Latin alphabet minus *i*; *x* appears in borrowings from English. The following digraphs are used: *ch* = /tʃ/, *dh* = /ð/, *th* = /θ/, *gh* = /ɣ/, *sh* = /ʃ/.

PHONOLOGY

Consonants

> stops: p, b, t, d, k, g
> affricates: tʃ, dʒ
> fricatives: f, v, ð, θ, s, z, ʃ, ʒ, χ, ɣ, h
> nasals: m, n
> lateral and flap: l, r
> semi-vowels: j, w

Labialized /k/ and /g/ occur: [k°, g°]; also a hamza-like interruption where elision of a velar fricative has taken place: *mo'a* ('very').
For mutations see below.

Vowels

i, e, a, o, u
/i/ and /ɪ/ are represented by *y*.

The letter *e* covers /eː, ɛ, ə/; *o* covers /oː, ɔ, ɔː/; *u* covers /uː, y, ʌ/.
There are several diphthongs.

Mutation

There are four types of juncture mutation in Cornish, with traces of a fifth:

(a) Soft mutation (lenition): /b/ → /v/, /d/ → /ð/, /m/ → /v/, /k/ → /g/, /gV/ → /V/, etc. As in other Celtic languages, this mutation takes place after the definite article *an* in feminine singular nouns, in masculine plural nouns denoting persons, and elsewhere: e.g.

> *mam* 'mother': *an vam* 'the mother'; *dha vam* 'thy mother'
> *dyw* 'two', *bre* 'hill': *an dhyw vre* 'the two hills'
> *bugeleth* 'shepherds': *an vugeleth* 'the shepherds'

(b) Aspiration: /k/ → /h/, /p/ → /f/, /t/ → /θ/, etc.: e.g. *pen* 'head': *ow fen* 'my head'; *tyr* 'country': *ow thyr* 'my country'.

(c) Nasalization: e.g. /d/ → /n/: *dor* 'earth': *an nor* 'the earth'.

A hard mutation: /b/ → /p/, /d/ → /t/, /g/ → /k/ (i.e. the converse of lenition) also occurs, and certain particles and adverbs generate a mixed mutation, e.g. /b/ → /f/, /d/ → /t/.

MORPHOLOGY AND SYNTAX

Noun

There are two genders: masculine and feminine. Certain endings are associated with gender: thus, abstracts in *-yeth*, nouns of place in *-va/-ek*, and nouns formed by adding *-en* to a collective plural, are feminine; abstract nouns in *-ans*, *-der/-ter*, nouns of place in *-jy/ty* and all verbal nouns are masculine.

The definite article is *an/'n*. As indefinite article, *un*, a form of the numeral *onen* 'one', is used.

NUMBER

There are about a dozen plural markers: e.g. *lu* 'army': *luyow*; *bron* 'hill': *bronyon*; *pren* 'tree': *prenyer*. Some plurals are made by internal flection: *dans* 'tooth': *dyns*.

Singular nouns can be made from collectives by addition of *-en*: e.g. *derow* 'oak-trees': *derowen* 'an oak-tree'.

There is no inflectional system. Syntactic relationships are expressed by prepositions and by apposition. The genitive is in the construct formula or appositional: e.g. *to an chy* 'the roof of the house', with elision of the definite article belonging to the possessed component.

Adjective

Not marked for gender. As attribute, adjective may precede or follow the noun; postposition is preferred, with soft mutation in concord: e.g. after feminine singular: *an vugh vorm* 'the dun cow'. Some common adjectives always precede the noun, e.g. *keth* 'same', *ken* 'other'.

COMPARISON

s or *ages* precedes the noun compared: e.g. *whecca es mel* 'sweeter than honey'.

Pronoun

The personal pronouns have independent, infixed, and suffixed forms; the latter may be reduplicated or extended.

			Independent	Infixed	Suffixed	Possessive
sing.	1		my	'm	-vy, -ma, -a	ow, am
	2		ty	'th	-sy, -jy, -ta	dha,'th
	3	masc.	ef	'n	-ef, -e, -va	y
		fem.	hy	's	-hy	hy
pl.	1		ny	'gan, 'n	-ny	agan, an
	2		why	'gas, 's	-why	agas, as
	3		y	's	-y	aga

Example of infixed pronoun: *my a'n gwel* 'I see him/it'. The infixed pronoun often recapitulates a direct object already mentioned: e.g. *an vlejen pan y's torras-hy* 'the flower (*an vlejen*) when she (*-hy*) picked it (*'s*)'.

DEMONSTRATIVE PRONOUN

Sing. *hemma/homma* 'this'; pl. *an rema*; sing. *henna/honna* 'that'; pl. *an rena*.

INTERROGATIVE PRONOUN

pyu 'who?'; 'what?' is expressed by various forms of the base *py*: e.g. *py lever* 'what book?'; *py* + *tra* ('thing') → *pandra* 'what?'

RELATIVE CLAUSE
See **Verb**, below.

Numerals

1–10: *onen/un, deu, try, peswar, pymp, whegh, seyth, eth, naw, dek*; 11 *unnek*; 12 *deudhek*; 20 *ugans*; 30 *dek warn ugans*; 30 *dek warn ugans*; 40 *deugans*; 60 *try ugans*; 100 *cans*.

The numerals *due, try, peswar* have feminine forms *dyw, tyr, peder*.

Verb

There are three moods: indicative, imperative, and subjunctive. The indicative mood has present/future, preterite, imperfect, and pluperfect tenses; the subjunctive has present/future and imperfect. The indicative and subjunctive have 3 + 3 personal forms, plus an impersonal.

Specimen conjugation of *prena* 'to buy': indicative mood:

	Singular			*Plural*			*Impersonal*
Pres./future	prena**af**	preny**th**	pren**ø**	preny**n**	preno**ugh**	preno**ns**	preny**r**
Preterite	preny**s**	prens**ys**	pren**as**	pren**en**	prens**ough**	prens**ons**	pren**as**
Imperfect	pren**en**	pren**es**	pren**a**	pren**en**	pren**eugh**	pren**ens**	pren**ys**

The pluperfect has the same endings as the imperfect, preceded by -*s*-: e.g. *prensen*. A perfect tense is made by adding the particle *re* before the preterite: e.g. *re prenys* 'I have bought'. The subjunctive has a specific set of endings.

THE SUBSTANTIVE VERB

bos/bones 'to be', has suppletive forms and a specific future:

> Present: sing. *of, os, yu*; pl. *on, ough, yns*; the impersonal form is *or*
> Preterite: sing. *buf, bus, bu*; pl. *ben, beugh, bons*; impersonal, *bes*
> Future: sing. *bydhaf, bydhyth, byth*; pl. *bydhyn, bydhough, bydhons*; impersonal, *bydher*
> Imperfect: *en/esen, es/eses, o/esa ...*
> Subjunctive: present/future: *byf, by, bo ...* Imperfect: *ben, bes, be ...*

IRREGULAR VERBS

There are several highly irregular verbs, exemplified here by the principal parts of:

(a) *mos/mones* 'to go':

> Present/future: sing. *af, eth, a*; pl. *en, eugh, ons*; impersonal: *er*
> Preterite: *yth, ythys, eth; ethen, etheugh, ethons; es*
> Perfect: *galsof, galsos, gallas; galson, galsough, galsons*; no impersonal form
> Subjunctive present/future: *yllyf, ylly, ello; yllyn, yllough, ellons; eller*

(b) *dos/dones* 'to come':

> Present/future: sing. *dof, duth, de/du*; pl. *dun, deugh, dons*; impersonal: *deer*
> Preterite: *duth, duthys, deth; duthen, dutheugh, duthons; des*
> Perfect: *devef, deves, deva; devon, deveugh, devons; deves*
> Subjunctive present/future: *dyffyf, dyffy, deffo; dyffyn, dyffough, dyffons; deffoer*

(c) *gul/gwruthyl* 'to do, make': also used as auxiliary verb 'shall, did'

> Present/future: 1st sing. *gwraf*
> Preterite: 1st sing. *gwruk*
> Subjunctive present/future: 1st sing. *gwryllyf*

(d) *ry* 'to give':

> Present/future: 1st sing. *rof*
> Preterite: 1st sing. *res*
> Subjunctive present/future: *ryllyf*

PARTICIPLES

> Present: *orth/ow* + verbal noun: e.g. *ow leverel* 'saying';
> Past: stem + *-ys*: e.g. *kemerys* 'taken'; *gwres, gwrys* 'done'.

Negative

Ny + soft mutation. The prohibitory negative is *na*.

Relative particles

A + soft mutation provides subject or object in relative sentence; e.g. *My a re dhys an lyver a dhewysyth* 'I will give you the book which you choose'; *an vugh a welys.vy* 'the cow I saw'.

Impersonal form

The characteristic is *-r*; the agent can be denoted by the particle *gans*: e.g. *redyer an lyver* 'there is a reading of the book'; *y redyer ganso* 'there is a reading by him'.

Prepositions

Simple and compound; e.g. *a* 'of, from', *rak* 'for'; *arak* 'before'; *aberveth yn* 'inside of'. Pronouns can be infixed between the components of a compound preposition. Some prepositions are followed by soft mutation; they take personal endings: e.g.

> *a*: *ahanaf* 'of me'
> *a govys*: *a'm govys* 'for my sake'; *a'y wovys* 'for his sake'
> *a ugh*: *a ughon* 'above us'
> *dhe*: *dhym* 'to me'
> *dres*: *dresough* 'over you'
> *war*: *warnough* 'on you'

Word order

SVO in nominal clauses; VSO in verbal clauses, and obligatory in subordinate clauses; OSV is possible for reasons of emphasis.

```
1   Y'n dallethvos yth esa an Ger, ha'n Ger
    esa gans Dew, ha'n Ger o Dew.
2   An keth esa y'n dallethvos gans Dew.
3   Puptra-oll a vu gwres ganso: ha hebtho ny
    vu gwres travyth a vu gwres.
4   Ynno-ef yth esa bewnans; ha'n bewnans o
    Golow tus.
5   Ha'n golow a splan y'n tewlder, ha'n tewl-
    dre ny ylly y dhyfudha.
6   Yth esa den danvenys dyworth Dew, Jowan y
    hanow.
7   An keth a dheth yn. tyyas rag dustunya a'n
    Golow may crysso pup mabden-oll dredho.
8   Nyns ova an Golow-na, mes danvenys vu rag
    dustunya a'n Golow.
```

CREE

INTRODUCTION

This is the major language of the Algonquian family in North America. It is spoken by about 60,000 Indians over a vast territory extending from Hudson's Bay in the East, across Ontario and Manitoba to Saskatchewan and Alberta, and from the grain belt northwards to Mackenzie and Kewatin. The ethnonym is *nahiyawāwak* 'the Cree people'. There are four main dialects: Plains Cree (L-dialect), Swampy Cree (N-dialect), Wood Cree in the Churchill River area, and Moose Cree, an L-dialect spoken in the Hudson's Bay country. The dialects are very largely mutually intelligible. Pre-aspiration becomes more noticeable in the western forms.

SCRIPT

The Cree syllabary was developed by the Rev. James Evans in the 1830s, and was used to print religious texts in Cree by 1840. As further modified and improved by the Rev. John Horden (author of a *Cree Grammar*), the syllabary has been subsequently used for the considerable body of Biblical translation and original devotional literature published in Cree from the late nineteenth century onwards.

PHONOLOGY

Consonants

  initial stops: p, t, k → medial b, d, g
  affricates: tʃ after short vowel/dʒ after long
  fricatives: s, ʃ, h
  nasals: m, n
  lateral: l
  semi-vowels: j, w

Pre-aspiration of /p, t, k, tʃ/ is phonemic; it is here notated as *ḥ* (' in Hives 1948). Initial nasal syllables, e.g. *ni-*, tend to /m̃/. The lateral /l/ is characteristic of the Plains dialect.

Vowels

The letters *a, e, i, o, u* are used to cover the following scale of values:

a = /ʌ/; *ā* = /aː...o/; *e* (always long) = /ɛ...e/; *i* = ı...ɛ/; *ī* = /iː/; *o* = /ɔ ...u/;
ō = /oː... uː/.

/ew/ and /aw/ occur very frequently in inflection; the /w/ is unstable.

MORPHOLOGY AND SYNTAX

Noun

Two key features in Cree are: (1) the all-pervasive dichotomy between animate and inanimate categories, which determines the morphological treatment of nouns, verbs, pronouns, numerals; (2) the use of the so-called 'fourth person' or obviative: once a third person noun or pronoun has been established as the subject or chief protagonist of a proposition, any other third person, subsequently introduced, is 'obviated' from true third person position, and is treated as a fourth person with its own complete set of verbal and nominal inflections. Thus, the ambiguity inherent in such English sentences as *He saw him going down the street* is impossible in Cree, as the verbal inflections will establish which of the two third persons was going down the street. In the Hives grammar, a story is quoted which was told to Leonard Bloomsbury by Chief Coming Day: this concerns Cree Indians who were suddenly accosted by a Blackfoot raiding party. In the English translation, the frequent references to 'they' have to be glossed: does 'they' refer to the Crees or to the Blackfoot? In Cree there is no problem: the Crees being first on the scene (and the home side) are always in the true third person; the Blackfoot are in the fourth.

ANIMATES
The category of animate nouns includes several objects which would figure rather as inanimates in many other cultural taxonomies, e.g. *apwe* 'paddle', *asam* 'snowshoe', *askihk* 'kettle'. The plural marker for animates is -(*w*)*ak*: e.g. *ahkik* 'seal', pl. *ahkikwak*; *names* 'fish', pl. *namesak*; *maskwa* 'bear', pl. *maskwak*. The affix -*skaw* is used as an indicator for large numbers of something: e.g. *sakimeskaw* 'there are large numbers of mosquitoes', a nominal form which can be treated as a verb.

INANIMATES
The plural marker is -*a*: e.g. *čiman* 'canoe', pl. *čimana*. The Indo-European accusative of a specific third person referent is given an obviative ending in Cree: e.g. *Sakihew awasisa* 'He loves-him the child' (*awasis* 'child')

LOCATIVE
In -*ihk*/*ohk*: e.g. *činamihk* 'in the canoe'; *mistikohk* 'in the tree'. The locative marker may be recapitulated in the verb by -*iši*-: e.g. *Čiman.ihk.na kit.iši.apatasin?* 'Is it in the canoe that he is working?' (-*na* is an interrogative particle).

POSSESSION

The circumfix used with animate nouns:

	Singular	Plural
1	ni(t)...m/im/om	ni(t)...(im)inan/inaw
2	ki(t)...m/im/om	ki(t)...(im)iwaw
3	o(t)...a/im	o(t)...(im)iwaw

The inanimate markers are largely similar. The *-m/-im/-om* ending replaces *-w/-y* in citation form: e.g. *okimaw* 'boss' – *nitokimam* 'my boss'; *sipiy* 'river' – *nisipim* 'my river'; *ničimaninan* 'our canoe'. The locative marker follows the possessive: e.g. *nicimaninanihk* 'in our canoe'.

Bound forms: some nouns in Cree, denoting inalienable relationship, are never used without the possessive marker: e.g. *miskisik* 'the eye' (i.e. someone's eye); *niskisik* 'my eye'; *mitanis* 'daughter'.

Double possessive: e.g. *nitanis okosisa o.čikahikan.iyiw* 'my daughter's son's axe', where *okosisa* is in the third person; *čikahikan* 'axe' is in the fourth person marked by the ending *-iyiw*.

Adjective

There are a few root adjectives, e.g. *kihči-* 'great, big', *mači* 'bad', *miywe-* 'good, fine', *oški-* 'new', but these are used mainly as prefixes in nominal compounds and as pre-verbs: e.g. *kihčimaneto* 'great spirit'; *kihči.okimaw* 'great chief'; *kihči.kami* 'sea'; *mači.kišikaw* 'it is a bad day'; *mači.pihkiskwew* 'he speaks evil'.

Most adjectival meaning are conveyed by verbal roots, e.g. *kisinaw* 'it is cold'; *čiposiw* 'it is pointed'; *napakisiw* 'it is flat'.

Pronoun

PERSONAL

The Plain Cree forms are:

	Singular	Plural
1	niya	excl. niyanan, incl. kiyanaw
2	kiya	kiyayaw
3	wiya	wiyayaw

The Plain Cree forms originally had *-l-* (*nila*, *kila*, etc.), which is preserved in Moose Cree; the Swampy Cree forms have *-n-*: *nina*, *kina*, etc.

DEMONSTRATIVE PRONOUN

awa 'this' (animate), *oma* (inanimate) with obviative forms; *ana* 'that' (animate), *anima* (inanimate) with obviative forms. These have direct and obviative plural forms.

INTERROGATIVE PRONOUN

awena 'who?'; *kekwan* 'what?'.

Numerals

1–10: *peyak*, *nišo*, *nisto*, *newaw*, *niyalan*, *nikotwas*, *niswas*, *niyananew*, *šank*, *mita*. 11–19 are formed with the linker *-asap*: e.g. 11 *mitataḫt peyakasap*. 20 *nisitonaw*; 30 *nistomitanaw*; 100 *mitaḫtomitanaw*.

Verb

Underlying the multitude of Cree verbal forms (Horden (1881) gives about 150 pages of paradigms, setting out some 2,000 forms) are certain basic oppositions:

transitive	intransitive
animate	inanimate
independent or proximate assertion	dependent (conjunct) assertion
direct personal deixis	inverse personal deixis

In general, Cree tends to use semantically densely ordered verbal units or complexes to express concepts which in languages of a different type require analytical strings of nouns, articles, verbs, adjectives, adverbs, etc. For example, the Watkins–Faries dictionary (1938) abounds in such entries as *puskwaskichāsin* 'It is a small open patch of burnt woods'; *tipiskiskum* 'Night overtakes him before he reaches his destination'; *nupokuskititimunawao* 'He breaks both its shoulder blades' (these three examples are in the older spelling used in the Watkins–Faries dictionary).

INTRANSITIVE VERBS

(a) Impersonal: there are a great many of these, e.g. *taḫkwakin* 'it is autumn'; *mispon* 'it is snowing'; *kisiwayaw* 'it's warm weather'; *kimiwan* 'it's raining'.

(b) Animate intransitive verbs are sub-divided by stem vowel into several classes. A specimen paradigm follows: indicative present of *apiw* 'he is/sits at home':

		Singular	*Plural*
1		**nitapin**	excl. **nitapinan**, incl. **kitapinanaw**
2		**kitapin**	**kitapinawaw**
3	animate	Øapiw	Øapiwak
	inanimate	Øapimakan	Øapimakanwa
4	animate	Øapiyiwa	Øapiyiwa
	inanimate	Øapimakaniyiw	Øapimakaniyiwa

The conjunct (subjunctive) form drops the personal markers, which are replaced by the invariable particle *e*, and adds a new set of endings: e.g. in the singular: 1 **e** api**yān**; 2 **e** api**yan**; 3 anim. **e** apit, inanim. **e** api**makak**; 4 anim. **e** api**yit**, inanim. **e** api**makaniyik**.

NEGATION

mola precedes the negated word(s).

TENSE MARKERS

Future: *kitta/k(a)*: e.g. *itoḥtew* 'he goes there'; *mola ni.k.itoḥtan* 'I'm not going there'.

Perfective: *-ki-* (positive), *-oḥči-* (negative): e.g. *ɵoḥčitoḥtew* 'He didn't go there.'

Potential: *-ki-* following tense marker: e.g. *ni.ki.ki.peči.toḥtan* 'I'll be able to come' (*peči-* is a directional prefix).

INTERROGATIVE MARKER

-na is added to focused word: e.g. *Kekwan weyapaḥtaman? Čiman.na?* 'What do you see? A canoe?'

INCEPTIVE PREFIX

ati-: e.g. *Ati.kimiwan* 'It is beginning to rain.'

DESIDERATIVE PREFIX

wi-: e.g. *Winipaw* 'He wants to sleep.'

DIRECT AND INVERSE VERSIONS

First and second person pronouns take precedence over third person. Thus, e.g. 'you see him' can be stated directly, *ki wapamaw*; but 'he sees you' is an inverse form in Cree, *ki wapamik*; an English approximation is 'you are seen by him', but the passive voice is misleading. To put it another way: first and second person are covered by the direct transitive conjugation *vis-à-vis* third person: e.g. *ki.wāpam.ānawak* 'we (incl.) see them'; but the inverse conjugation has to be used when a third person is subject *vis-à-vis* first or second: e.g. *ki.wāpam.ikonawak* 'we (incl.) are seen by them' = 'they see us'.

TRANSITIVE VERB

The transitive verbal form encodes subject and target, even when a noun object is overtly expressed; i.e. in Cree, a sentence of the type 'I see X', where X is a noun, appears as 'I see-it X.' The Indo-European distinction between subject and object is not relevant in Cree, which interprets the indirect object of Indo-European languages as the *direct* object, and the direct object, if expressed, as a noun in the obviative.

CONJUNCT FORM

This is the form used in dependent clauses to express state or action concomitant with, antecedent to, or following the state or action expressed in the principal clauses; i.e. a conjunct form can only be used with reference to a direct (proximate) assertion. The form has inflected endings but no personal prefixes (see paradigm, above): e.g. *pipon* 'it is winter': *e pipoḥk* 'it being winter, when it was winter', etc.; *Kit.apiñānaw e kimiwaḥk* 'As it is raining, we are (staying) at home.'

RELATIVE

ka: cf. *ililiw ka kiḥtoḥtet* 'the person who is going away'; *ililiw ka kikiḥtoḥtet* 'the person who went away'.

Roots are modulated by prefix to express motion to or away from focus, various nuances in mode of action, inception, cessation, ingress, exit, etc. For example, from root -*asiw*- 'to sail' (*pimasiw* 'he sails'), *sipweyasiw* 'he sails off', where *sipwe*- is an inceptive prefix. Cf. *sipwečaẖkwew* 'he starts the spirit on its way' = 'he dies'.

Prepositions

Cree prepositions precede nouns in the locative case. Hives (1948) gives such examples as: *peẖce* 'in'; *peẖce waskahikaniẖk* 'in the house'.

There are also a few postpositions, e.g. *isse* 'to, towards', again with locative: *waskahikaniẖk isse* 'towards the house'.

Word order

SVO is possible in nominal sentences. A verb form, incorporating all three elements, may itself be a sentence.

MAWUTCHE nistum kė ėtaw Ayumewin, mena Ayumewin kė wechāwāo Munetoowa, mena Ayumewin kė Munetoowew.

2 Āwuko owa mawutche nistum kė wechāwāo Munetoowa.

3 Kåkeyow kākwi weya kė osėtaw ; mena āka weya ȯche numoweya kākwi kitta kė osėchekatāpun ka kė osėtåk.

4 Weya kė kekeskum pimatissewin ; mena pimatissewin kė wastānumakwuk eyinewuk.

5 Mena wastāo wasetāo wunetipiskåk ; mena wunetipiskaw numoweya kė nissetowāyȯtumomukun.

6 ¶ Kė ėtaw napāo ā issitissåwat Muneto, John ā issenikasoot.

7 Āwuko owa kė pā wėtum, kitta wėtumakāt oma Wastāo, kåkeyow eyinewa kitta tapwåtumeyit weya ȯche.

8 Numoweya weya kåchewak āwuko Wastāo, maka kė issitissåwaw kitta wėtumakāt āwuko Wastāo.

(Eastern dialect)

CROW

INTRODUCTION

Crow and Hidatsa form a sub-division of the Macro-Siouan family of North American Indian languages. At present, about 5,000 speakers live in the Crow Reservation in south-eastern Montana.

PHONOLOGY

Consonants

Basic inventory with positionally determined allophones:

stops: p/b, t/d, k/g/k'/g'
affricates: tʃ/dʒ
fricatives: β, s/ʃ, z/ʒ, x, h
liquid: r/l/n

The nasals [m] and [n] are thus construed as allophones of /w/b/ and /r/l/d/. Bilabial /β/ is realized as [w, m, b].

In general, the lenis sounds are intervocalic; cf. *wiša* 'buffalo' /biža/, transcribed as *bice* by Lowie (1941).

Kaschube (1967) describes /l/ as in free variation with /r/, and probably associated with female speakers.

Vowels

Allophones are indicated:

i/ɪ, e, a/ɛ/æ/ə, o/ɔ, u

Long values are marked here, following Kaschube (1967), with : (Lowie (1941) uses ·).

Tones

Kaschube recognizes three: falling (grave accent), high (acute), low (unmarked). Syllables with high or falling tone may be stressed.

MORPHOLOGY AND SYNTAX

There is a basic division into stems and affixes. Crow stems are not marked for morphological function; that is, there is no formal difference between nouns, verbs, adjectives, particles. Stems can, however, be classified in terms of their valencies. For example, stems which are compatible with (a) personal pronominal prefixes, and (b) the imperative modal suffixes, are classified as verbs; stems which can accept (a) but not (b) are nouns.

Verbal stems are further sub-divided, by specific restraints on choice of personal pronominal prefix, into three main classes: stative, active, mixed (the mixed class combining stative and active features). Constraints of a similar nature determine nouns as denoting alienable or inalienable possession. A concatenation of stems is classed as nominal or verbal, depending on the class of the initial component.

Some examples of Crow stems: *wára* 'tree'; *-wará:* 'money'; *-warú:* 'to fight'; *wà:ra* 'winter'; *wá:ro* 'beads'; *wirá* 'water'. Stems have allomorphs (e.g. *-wará:-*/ *-waré:-*) which are functionally distributed.

Typically, a Crow word is composed of a succession of coded slots in three main sections: prefixes – stems – suffixes.

1. Prefixes include personal pronominal markers (see below), the past-tense marker *kara-*, reciprocal and demonstrative markers, and the spatio-temporal localizer *ar-*.

The personal pronominal markers, subjective and objective, are 1 *wih-*, 2 *rih-*, 3 *ih-*; all with series of functionally distributed allomorphs. The spelling is that of Kaschube (1967); Lowie (1941) uses initial allophones: 1 *bi·*, 2 *di·*, 3 *i·*. The following examples are from Kaschube:

> *wí-hà:rik* 'I finish' (*wi-* is first person marker; *-hà:ri* 'to finish'; *-k* is predicative terminator);
> *wí:a.ra.ká.k* 'you see me' (*wí* is first person object; *a...ka* 'to see' (discontinuous stem); *ra* is medial allomorph of second person pronoun);
> *wá:w.wá:ríči.k* 'I hit something' (*wá:w* indicates indefiniteness; *-ríči* 'to hit');
> *kawwá:wá:ríšši.ss.u.k* 'we didn't dance' (*kar → kaw* = past-tense marker; *wá:* indefinite marker; *wá:* 1st person pronoun; *ríšši* 'to dance'; *-ss-* = negative marker; *-u-* plural marker; *-k* predicative terminator);
> *wa.sà:škia* 'my horse' (*-sà:* is the alienable possession marker; *-škia* 'horse, dog');
> *ar.a.xap.a* 'his bed' (*ar-* = spatio-temporal localizer; *a-* = third person pronoun marker; *xap* = 'to lie down'; *-a* = singular nominalizer).

The class of inalienable nouns includes those denoting parts of the body and degrees of kinship. The pronominal marker is prefixed directly to the nominal: e.g. *wí.ía* 'my mouth'; * Øra:sa* 'his (null marker) heart'.

2. Suffixes: these include tense and modal markers, e.g. *-h*, *wáči* future markers; *-če* causative; *-i* durative; *-ku* benefactive; *-a*/*-à:ra* imperative markers. Negation markers: *-ssa-*, *ré:tá*; nominalizers: *-a* (singular), *-úa* (plural);

terminators: *-k* (finalizing), *-w/-š* (holding); agentive markers: *št* (of habitual action). Examples:

> *wá:wá:warú:w.o.h.wáči.k* 'we shall fight' (*wá:* = indefinite marker; *wá:* = first person pronoun marker; *warú* = 'to fight'; *w* + *o* = first person plural marker; *-h* + *wáči* = future markers; *-k* = predicative terminator); *wú:šišt* 'I'm in the habit of eating' (*w* = first person marker; *ú:ši* = 'to eat'; *-št* = habitual action).

Lowie (1941) gives the following paradigm of an aorist–present-tense (spelling adapted):

	Singular	*Plural*
1	ba-ka:k 'I laugh'	ba-**ku:**k
2	da-ka:k	da-**ku:**k
3	Ø-ka:k	Ø-**ku:**k

And of a discontinuous stem: *a...o:ri* 'to wait':

	Singular	*Plural*
1	a.wo:ri.k	a.wo:ru.k
2	a.ro:ri.k	a.ro:ru.k
3	o:ri.k	o:ruk

Numerals

Kaschube gives the following forms for 1–5 inclusive: *hawát, ruhp-, -rà:wí-, -šó:pá, čaxxo.* 10 is *-piraká.*

CUANG (*Cuəŋ*)

See **Juang**.

CZECH

INTRODUCTION

This Western Slavonic language is the official language (with Slovak) of the Republic of Czechoslovakia, spoken by around 10 million people. Czech and Slovak are mutually intelligible. Writing in Czech dates from the thirteenth to fourteenth centuries. Historically, Czech culture and literature are orientated towards Western Europe, rather than towards Moscow and the Orthodox Church. The first flowering of Czech literature was in the reign of Charles IV (fourteenth century), with Jan Hus playing a notable role in the formation of a standardized literary language. The suppression of Czech culture, associated with the Counter-Reformation, lasted until the late eighteenth century, when contact with Western sources was re-established, and a romantic renaissance ensued. This period culminated in the abortive revolution of 1848. From the late nineteenth century to the outbreak of the Second World War, Czech was the vehicle for a very rich and extensive literature in all genres, especially poetry (e.g. Vrchlický, Bezruč, Březina) and the novel (Holeček, Hašek, Čapek).

SCRIPT

Romanization plus diacritics. The orthography was rationalized, first by Jan Hus in the fourteenth century subsequently by the Czech Brethren in their sixteenth-century translation of the Bible.

The palatalized consonants /t', d'/ are marked by apostrophe: e.g. *ted' 'now'*, *zed'* 'wall'. /t/ and /d/ are palatalized before /i/ and /je/; the latter is then written as *ě*. The palatal n /ɲ/ is notated as *ň*.

PHONOLOGY

Consonants

    stops: p, b, t, d, k, g, + palatalized t', d'
    affricates: ts, tʃ
    fricatives: f, v, s, z, ʃ, ʒ, j, h, x
    nasals: m, n, ɲ
    lateral: l
    trill: r, ɼ (notated as *ř*).

/g/ occurs in foreign words only; in native words, Slavonic /g/ is represented by /h/; e.g. Russian *golub(ka)* = Czech *holub*. The liquids /r, l/, are syllabic: e.g. *prst* 'finger', *vlk* 'wolf'. A softened glottal stop or hamza separates vowels in final–initial contact, and in words like *naučit* 'to teach', where -*au*- is not a diphthong: *na.učit*.

Voiced consonants in final position are unvoiced: e.g. *chleb* 'bread', [xlɛ̄p]. Assimilation of unvoiced to voiced: e.g. *kdo* 'who?' [gdɔ]; *svatba* 'wedding' [svadba]. *Mě* is pronounced /mɲɛ/: e.g. *město* 'city' [mɲɛstɔ].

Vowels

> short: a, ɛ, ɪ, ɔ, u
> long: aː, ɛː, iː, uː

Long /oː/ occurs in foreign words only. /uː/ is notated as *ů*. Diphthongs: /ou/ is native, e.g. *klobouk* 'hat'; /au, eu/ occur in loan-words.

In the thirteenth/fourteenth centuries vowel mutation after soft consonants (broadly, back/low vowels were raised to front/high) gave Czech its characteristic and very distinctive sound. Thus, *žena* 'woman', *duše* 'soul', with instrumental singular *ženou*, *duší*. Similarly, *nesu* 'I carry', but *píši* 'I write' (literary form).

Stress

Stress is invariably on the first syllable.

MORPHOLOGY AND SYNTAX

Noun

Three genders, two numbers. The original six declensions (*see* **Slavonic Languages**) are preserved in Czech:

> -*i*/-*ja* feminine stems: e.g. *kost* 'bone';
> -*a*/-*ja* stems: e.g. *žena* 'woman', *duše* 'soul';
> -*o*/-*jo* masculine stems: e.g. *muž* 'man';
> -*o*/-*jo* neuter stems: e.g. *místo* 'place', *moře* 'sea';
> -*ū* stems: e.g. *církev* 'church' (feminine);
> consonantal stems (masculine and neuter): e.g. *kámen* 'stone'.

There are seven cases including a vocative. Differentiation due to phonetic constraints is very considerable; some grammars give over 250 paradigms. There follow specimen declensions of a masculine noun – *muž* 'man' – and a feminine – *žena* 'woman':

	Singular	*Plural*	*Singular*	*Plural*
nom.	muž	muži	žena	ženy
gen.	muže	mužů	ženy	žen
dat.	muži/ovi	mužům	ženě	ženám
acc.	muže	muže	ženu	ženy

instr.	mužem	muži	ženou	ženami
loc.	muži	mužích	ženě	ženách
voc.	muži	—	ženo	—

Nominative, accusative forms for animate masculine nouns differ in singular and plural from those for inanimates.

POSSESSION

Possessor follows possessed: e.g. *mapa Československa* 'a map of Czechoslavakia'. There are no articles.

Adjective

As attribute adjective precedes noun, and is in full concord with it for all cases, preserving animate/inanimate distinction. Hard adjectives show gender in the nominative ending: *-ý, -á, -é*. Soft adjectives have *-í* in all three. Examples: *nový dům* (masc.) 'new house'; *stará žena* (fem.) 'old woman'; *nové divadlo* (nt.) 'new theatre'; *moderní hotel, divadlo, budova* 'modern hotel, theatre, building'.

As predicate, adjective shows concord: cf. *nový dům – dům je nový; nové divadlo – divadlo je nové*.

POSSESSIVE ADJECTIVES

Those based on nouns denoting males and male names: *-ův, -ova, -ovo*; females: *-in, -ina, -ino*: e.g. from *bratr: bratrův pokoj* 'the brother's room'; from *sestra: sestřin pokoj* 'the sister's room'. Compare *Karlův most* 'the Charles Bridge'; *Karlova Universita* 'the Charles University'.

COMPARATIVE

In *-(ej)ší*: e.g. *bohatý* 'rich' – *bohatší; důležitý* e.g. 'important' – *důležitější*. There are the usual suppletives: e.g. *dobrý* 'good' – *lepší; špatný* 'bad' – *horší*.

Pronoun

The nominative (= subject) forms are:

sing. 1 *ja*, 2 *ty*, 3 *on/ona/ono*; pl. 1 *my*, 2 *vy*, 3 *oni*

These forms are used for emphasis and contrast only. They are declined in all cases, and have weak and strong forms; e.g. for first person singular, acc./gen. *mě*, dat. *mi/mně*, instr. *mnou*.

The possessive adjectives are marked for gender in the singular, partially in plural:

sing. 1 *můj/má/mé*, 2 *tvůj/tvá/tvé*, 3 *jeho/její*; pl. 1 *náš/naše*, 2 *vaš/vase*

The third person plural form *jejich* is not marked.

DEMONSTRATIVE PRONOUN/ADJECTIVE

ten – ta – to 'this'; pl. *ti; tamten – tamta – tamto* 'that'. *-hle* may be added: e.g. *Líbí se mi tenhle klobouk* 'I like this hat.'

INTERROGATIVE PRONOUN

kdo 'who?'; *co* 'what?' These are declined.

RELATIVE PRONOUN

který/která/které 'which, that': e.g. *kniha, která leží na stole* 'the book which is lying on the table'. Replaced in colloquial by *co*. The literary form is *jenž* (masc.), *jež* (fem. and nt.): e.g. *cíl, jenž stojí před námi* 'the aim which lies before us'.

Numerals

1 *jeden/jedna/jedno*; 2 *dva/dvě*; 3 *tři*; 4 *čtyři*. These are declined in all cases. From 5 onwards, all oblique cases are in *-i*: 5–10 *pět, šest, sedm, osm, devět, deset*. 11 *jedenáct*; 12 *dvanáct*; 13 *třináct*; 20 *dvacet*; 30 *třicet*; 40 *čtyřicet*; 100 *sto*.

Verb

Taking the third person singular as criterion, we may classify Czech verbs into three groups:

(a) *-e*: e.g. *píše* 'he writes' (infinitive: *psát*);
(b) *-á*: e.g. *dělá* 'he does' (infinitive: *dělat*);
(c) *-í*: e.g. *mluví* 'he speaks' (infinitive: *mluvit*).

The *-e* groups can be further sub-divided to include *-n-* and *-uj-* stems: e.g. *tiskne* 'he presses' (infinitive: *tisknout*); *kupuje* 'he buys' (infinitive: *kupovat*).

The past or *-l* form:

> *-e* verbs take *-l, -nul*, or *-oval*;
> *-á* verbs take *-al*;
> *-í* verbs take *-il* or *-el*.

ASPECT

As in other Slavonic languages, paired verbs. Perfective formed:

(a) by prefix: e.g. *platit* 'to pay': perf. *zaplatit*; *prosit* 'to ask': perf. *poprosit*; *končit* 'to finish': perf. *skončit*; *ptát se* 'to ask' perf. *zeptat se*.
(b) prefix + stem change: *odnést* 'take away': *odnášet*; *přinést* 'bring': *přinášet*.
(c) suppletive: *brát* 'to take': *vzít*.

Imperfectives may be formed from verbs which are inherently perfective: e.g. *padat* 'to fall': *padnout*; *dát* 'to give': *dávat*.

Example of tense/aspect structure: *psát* 'to write':

	Past	*Present*	*Future*
imperfective:	psal jsem	píši (coll. píšu)	budu psát
perfective:	**na**psal jsem	Ø	**na**píši/u

362

TENSE

Specimen present tense of a -a verb: *dělat* 'to do': imperfective:

	Singular	Plural
1	dělám	děláme
2	děláš	děláte
3	dělá	dělají

Past-tense or -*l* form: the auxiliary verb is not used in the third person. The -*l* form is marked for gender and number:

	Singular	Plural
1	čekal/-a jsem 'I waited'	čekali/-y jsme
2	čekal/-a jsi	čekali/-y jste
3	čekal/-a Ø	čekali/-y Ø

FUTURE

Future tense of auxiliary *být* = *budu* + infinitive: e.g. *budu psát* 'I shall write'. This is always imperfective. The present *form* of the perfective aspect has a future meaning: e.g. *napíšu* 'I shall write' (= have written).

IMPERATIVE

Both aspects have imperative mood: e.g. *Čtěte!* 'Read!' (imperfective); *Přečtěte cely text!* 'Read the whole text!' (perfective).

PASSIVE

(a) with *se*; this is associated with the change of transitive to intransitive: *Lidská práce mění krajinu* 'Human labour changes the countryside'; *Celá krajina se mění* 'The whole countryside is changing.'

(b) with auxiliary *být* + truncated verbal adjective: e.g. *Bly jsem vyšetřován lékařem* 'I was examined by the doctor.'

CONDITIONAL

Provided by aux. sing. *bych*, *bys*, *by*: pl. *bychom*, *byste*, *by* + -*l* form: e.g. with *rád* 'gladly': *rád bych věděl* 'I should like to know'; *rádi bychom věděli* 'we should like to know'.

PARTICIPLES

(a) present in -*cí* added to third person plural of imperfective present: e.g. *dělají*: *dělající*. The form is declined as an adjective.

(b) past active participle: -(*v*)*ší* replaces -*l* of perfective past; declined as adjective: e.g. *udělavší* 'having done, who has done'.

(c) past passive participle = verbal noun: -*ní/tí*: e.g. *děláni* 'doing'; *byti* 'being'.

Negation

The general negating particle is *ne*, prefixed to verb: e.g. *nic neslyším* 'I hear nothing' (i.e. double negative).

Prepositions

Prepositions govern nouns in the accusative, genitive, dative, locative or instrumental cases. Some, e.g. *na* 'on/in/at', *pod* 'under', *před* 'in front of', take locative or instrumental for rest in a place and the accusative for motion towards, along, etc. e.g. *jsem na poště* 'I am in the post-office'; but *jdu na poštu* 'I go to the post-office'.

Word order

SVO is basic. Subject usually omitted if pronoun. Almost all permutations of word order are possible.

Na počátku bylo Slovo, a to Slovo bylo u Boha, a to Slovo byl Bůh.

2 To bylo na počátku u Boha.

3 Všecky věci skrze ně učiněny jsou, a bez něho nic není učiněno, což učiněno jest.

4 V něm život byl, a život byl světlo lidí.

5 A to světlo v temnostech svítí, ale temnosti ho neobsáhly.

6 Byl člověk poslaný od Boha, jemuž jméno *bylo* Jan.

7 Ten přišel na svědectví, aby svědčil o tom světle, aby všickni uvěřili skrze něho.

8 Nebyl on to světlo, ale *přišel*, aby svědčil o tom světle.

DAGESTANIAN
LANGUAGES

INTRODUCTION

These languages of the North-East and North-Central Caucasus are spoken mainly in the Dagestan Autonomous Soviet Socialist Republic, with some spread into Azerbaydzhan, Georgia, and the Chechen-Ingush Autonomous Soviet Socialist Republic. They can be divided on genetic grounds into the following three large groups:

1. Avar-Andi-Dido, comprising the following languages: Avar (*see* **Avar**); the Andi sub-group, consisting of Andi, Botlikh, Godoberi, Karata, Akhvakh, Bagval, Tindi, and Chamalal; total number of speakers is around 425,000, of which Avar accounts for over 385,000; the Dido or Tsez languages: Dido, Khvarsh, Ginukh, Bezhti, Gunzib. About 10,000 speakers (Dido over 7,000).
2. Lezgian: comprising Lezgi, Archi, Tabasaran, Agul, Rutul, Tsakhur, Budukh, Udi, Khinalugh, Kryz. These are located in the south-eastern zone of the Dagestan ASSR. The total number of speakers is c. 360,000, Lezgi itself having 304,000 of this total.
3. Lak (82,000 speakers) and Dargva (227,000 speakers) are spoken in the central region of the Dagestan ASSR.

SCRIPT

The Dagestanian languages are unwritten apart from Avar, Lak, Dargva, Lezgi, and Tabasaran, which have have been used as literary languages since the 1920s, though one or two of them have literary traditions going much further back. These five languages started their post-1917 literary activity in scripts based on Arabic, switched to a Roman-based script in the 1930s, and have, since 1938/9 been using Cyrillic + the letter *I*. This letter is generally used to mark the ejective consonants characteristic of Caucasian languages. Both the Andi and the Dido sub-groups use Avar as literary language and as a lingua franca.

PHONOLOGY

Consonants

All the Dagestanian languages are characterized by extensive consonantal inventories allied to relatively simply vocalic systems. Many of them are particularly rich in dental, alveolar, velar, and lateral fricatives and affricatives, which usually occur in four- or five-term series of the type voiced member – simple aspirate surd – geminated aspirate surd – ejective simple surd – geminated ejective surd: e.g. /ʒ – tʃ – tʃtʃ – t'ʃ – t'ʃt'ʃ/. The geminated sounds are said to be 'tense' *vis-à-vis* their 'non-intensive' simple forms.

Vowels

The basic series, /a, e, i, o, u/, is extended by lengthening, nasalization, labialization, pharyngealization (in association with pharyngeal consonants). /ɛ/, /œ/ and /y/ also occur, e.g. in Bezhti.

MORPHOLOGY AND SYNTAX

The main common features of the Dagestanian languages are:

1. *Noun classes*: there are usually four of these. Class I normally comprises male human beings, class II female human beings; in certain languages this class also includes some inanimate objects. In the Andi sub-group, noun classes vary in number from five for both singular and plural in Andi and Chamalal to three in the others. Class III in Andi comprises animals. It is noteworthy that parity, as between singular and plural classes, is not conserved: thus four singular classes are usually reduced to two plural classes based on the simple opposition human/non-human. Otherwise, the taxonomies underlying the division into classes are not always clear. Dido is logical, from an Indo-European point of view:

Class	
I	male human beings
II	female human beings
III	animals, birds, plants
IV	inanimate objects

Tabasaran has only two classes: human/non-human. Gunzib, on the other hand, has six: I males, II females, III mixed bag, IV animals, V another mixed bag, VI contains only one word: *kəra* 'child'.

The class markers may appear as fossilized markers in nouns, but are regularly confined to marking concord in predicates, adjectives, etc. The class markers themselves are very regular: cf.

	Class	Avar	Andi	Dido	
Singular {	I	v	v	—	} Plural: r/l
	II	y	y	y	
	III	b	b	b	

2. *Very elaborate case systems*: about 40 'cases' can be distinguished in Tabasaran, for example. Most of these 'cases' are spatial, defining locus and relative motion in great detail. Thus, in Gunzib for example, the locatives are ordered in seven series, each with two terms specifying (a) locus and (b) motion:

1. on the surface of something
2. under something
3. in something
4. vertically with relation to something else
5, 6, 7. in varying degrees of modalities of contiguity.

3. Except in Lezgi, Agul, and Udi, verbs in Dagestanian languages are conjugated by class without inflection for person. The three exceptions ignore class. Additional differentiation by person appears in Lak, Dargva, and Tabasaran. The verbal base may also contain locative and directional markers.

For more detailed descriptions of features of Dagestanian languages, *see* **Agul**, **Andi**, **Avar**, **Lak**, **Lezgi**, **Tabasaran**.

DAKOTA

INTRODUCTION

Dakota is one of the major languages of the Siouan family. The word 'Dakota' is a Sioux ethnonym meaning 'friends/allies' and applies particularly to the Santee group, one of three groups known collectively as 'Dakota'; the other two are Nakota (Yankton) and Lakota (Teton).

Missionaries were active among the Dakota from 1819 onwards. A script for the language was worked out, and by the late 1880s the complete Bible and the *Pilgrim's Progress* had been translated into Dakota, and several school primers and readers had been provided.

Today the Dakota live in North and South Dakota, Montana, and Nebraska. There are 10,000–20,000 speakers.

SCRIPT

As used by Riggs (1893), the script has ć, ź, and ś for /tʃ, ȝ, ʃ/, ġ = /ɣ/, ħ = /χ/ and ' = hamza. The ejective consonants are marked by subscript dot.

PHONOLOGY

Consonants
In broad transcription:

> stops: p, b, p', t, d, t', k, g, k', ʔ
> affricates: tʃ, t'ʃ
> fricatives: s, ʃ, z, ȝ, x, ɣ, χ
> nasals: m, n, ŋ
> semi-vowels: j, w

Vowels

Riggs (1893) gives five vowels: /i, e, a, o, u/. Contraction and assimilation are frequent.

Stress

Stress is phonemic, usually on the second syllable; in many words on first.

MORPHOLOGY AND SYNTAX

Noun

Dakota has primary and derived nouns: examples of primary nouns are *maka* 'earth', *peta* 'fire', *ate* 'father', *ina* 'mother'. For examples of derived nouns *see* **Word formation**, below. Natural gender is marked lexically, e.g. for humans: *wića* (male), *wiŋaŋ* (female); for animals: *mdoka* (male), *wiye* (female).

For the plural, a distinction is made between animate and inanimate nouns. The former take *-pi*: e.g. *śuŋka* 'horse', *śuŋkapi* 'horses'. Inanimates do not change: e.g. *ćaŋ* 'tree(s)'. The word *tipi* 'house' is a plural form used as a singular.

The article *kiŋ* rounds off a definite phrase: e.g. *wićaśta waśte kiŋ* 'the good man'; *timdo.ku kiŋ* 'her brothers'. The plural marker, *-pi*, tends towards the end of the sentence, i.e. to the verb.

POSSESSION
Possessor precedes possessed, which may have possessive affix: e.g. *tataŋka tawote* 'buffalo his-food'. A kinship possessive is made with the suffix -(*t*)*ku*: e.g. *wićaśta ćinkśitku* 'man his-daughter'.

Adjective

As attribute, adjective follow noun. The adjective has a dual in *-uŋ-* as well as a plural in *-pi*: e.g. *waoŋśida* 'merciful': *waoŋśiuŋda* 'the two merciful ones'. The plural form may also be made by partial reduplication.

There is no formal comparative.

Pronoun

The emphatic personal pronouns are:

	Singular	*Plural*	
1	miye	uŋkiye	
2	niye	niye	} + *-pi* on pronoun or on correlative word
3	iye	iye	

The possessive forms: *mitawa, nitawa, tawa*; pl. *uŋkitawapi, nitawapi, tawapi*.

VERBAL SUBJECT MARKERS
Sing. 1 *wa-*, 2 *ya-*; pl. 1 *un...pi*, 2 *ya...pi*: e.g. **wakaġa** 'I make', **yakaġa** 'you make', **uŋkaġapi** 'we make'. These subject markers are also used with adjectives: e.g. *yaksapa* 'you are wise'.

Assimilation occurs with verbs in *yu-*: e.g. *yuwaśte* 'to make good'; *mduwaśte* 'I make good'.

OBJECT PRONOUNS
Sing. 1 *ma*, 2 *ni*; pl. 1 *un...pi*, 2 *ni...pi*: e.g. **makaġa** 'he made me'. This set is

used with certain verbs of state, feeling: e.g. *yazaŋ* 'to be sick', **mayazaŋ** 'I am sick'. Also as markers for inalienable possession: e.g. **mawe** 'my blood'; **uŋtaŋćaŋpi** 'our bodies'.

ALIENABLE POSSESSION
Marked by *-ta-* following the *ma/mi*, *ni*, etc. markers: e.g. *mitakoda* 'my friend'.

DEMONSTRATIVE PRONOUN/ADJECTIVE
de 'this', pl. *dena*; *he* 'that', pl. *hena*.

INTERROGATIVE PRONOUN
tuwe 'who?', pl. *tuwepi*; *taku* 'what?'.

Numerals

1–10: *waŋźi* (*dan*), *noŋpa*, *yamni*, *topa*, *zaptaŋ*, *śakpe*, *śakowiŋ*, *śahdoǵaŋ*, *napćiŋwaŋka*, *wikćemna*. 11 *wikćemna ake waŋźidaŋ*; 20 *wikćemna noŋpa*; 30 *wikćemna yamni*; 100 *opawiŋǵe*.

Verb

Roots are modulated by prefixes to become transitive verbs denoting specific modes of handling, manipulating, and using things: thus

ba- suggests cutting with a knife;
bo- denotes a directed impact from shot, a stick, etc.;
na- signals action performed with the foot;
pa- signals action with the hand;
ya- signals action with the mouth.

Examples from root *-ksa-* 'to break off': **baksa** 'to cut with a knife'; **yaksa** 'to bite off'.

Frequentative stem: *baksaksa* 'to slash with a knife'; i.e. reduplication.

Possessive, reflexive, dative, and benefactive stems are made by means of affixes/infixes: e.g. dative *-ki-*: *wowapi* **kićaǵa** 'writing to-him-he-made' = 'he wrote to him'.

TENSE SYSTEM
Exemplified here by transitive verb with third person singular object. first and second person subjects are marked by infix (*-wa-*, *-ya-*) or by prefix (*md- d-*). The third person subject marker is Ø. In addition to three persons, singular and plural, there is a dual form meaning 'I and you'.

There are only two tenses: an indefinite tense, not specifically marked, and a future with *-nto* affixes. Context fixes the indefinite as referring to present or past. Other tenses and moods are generated with the help of adverbs.

Examples of singular and plural of root *-ksa* 'to break off' + *ba-* prefix:

singular: 1 *bawaksa* 'I cut him with a knife', 2 *bayaksa*, 3 *baksa*;
plural: 1 *bauŋksapi*, 2 *bayaksapi*, 3 *baksapi*.

Examples with other pronominal infixes: *bamaksa* 'he cuts me with a knife'; *bawićuŋksa* 'we cut them ...; *bauŋyaksapi* 'thou cuttest us...'; *bawićuŋksa* 'we two cut them ...'

Stative verbs and adjectives take the *ma-*, *ni-* pronouns (the oblique series): e.g. with root *asni* 'to be/get well':

singular: 1 *amasni* 'I am well', 2 *anisni*, 3 *asni*;
plural: 1 *uŋkasnipi* 'we are well', 2 *anisnipi*, 3 *asnipi*.

NEGATION

The adverb *sni* is placed after verb, noun, pronoun, adjective: e.g. *waćiŋ śni* 'I don't want'; *He ćaŋ śni* 'That is not wood'.

Postpositions

For example, *ahna* 'with', *akan* 'on', *en* 'in', *ekta* 'to', *oŋ* 'because of': e.g. *oŋśika oŋ* 'because of poverty'; *tin en* 'in the house'.

Word formation

Nouns are made from other nouns, verbs, adjectives. Prefixes:

i-, instrument: e.g. *yumdu* 'to plough' – *iyumdu* 'a plough';
wa-, agent;
wo-/wića-, abstract nouns: e.g. *waśte* 'good' – *wićawaśte* 'goodness';
ta- marks genus of ruminants: e.g. *tapa* 'deer's head';
wa- refers to bears: e.g. *wapa* 'bear's head'.

The suffix *dan* forms diminutives: e.g. *hokśidaŋ* 'little boy'; *-ya* forms adverbs: e.g. *waśte.ya* 'well'.

Word order

SOV.

1 Otokahe ekta Wicoie kin hee; Wicoie kin he Wakantanka kici un, qa Wicoie kin he Wakantanka kin ee.

2 He otokahe ekta Wakantanka kici un.

3 Iye eciyatanhan taku owasin kagapi; qa taku kin tokan tanhan takudan kagapi śni.

4 Iye kin en wiconi; qa wiconi kin he wicaśta iyoyamwicaye cin hee.

5 Iyoyanpa kin hee otpaze cin en omdesya un, tuka otpaze cin he iyowinkiye śni.

6 Wicaśta wan Wakantanka eciyatanhan u śipi, he Johannes eciyapi.

7 He wayaotanin hi, Iyoyanpa kin oyake kta; hecen iye eciyatanhan owasin wicadapi kta.

8 Iyoyanpa kin he iye śni, tuka iyoyanpa kin he yaotanin kta e u śipi.

DANISH

INTRODUCTION

Danish belongs to the Scandinavian branch of Germanic family. It is the official language of the Kingdom of Denmark, where it is spoken by over 5 million people, and joint official language of the Faeroe Islands and of Greenland. For Dano-Norwegian *see* **Norwegian**.

Writing in Danish dates from about the thirteenth century. The medieval literature is notable for its rich stock of ballads. The Bible was translated into Danish in the Reformation period. An outstanding figure of the Enlightenment was Holberg, whose influence on subsequent Danish writing was fundamental. The early nineteenth century produced one writer of world stature – Søren Kierkegaard. The modern period was inaugurated by the celebrated lectures given by Georg Brandes in the period 1870–90, the impact of which was as much socio-political as cultural (*det moderne Gennembrud* – 'the modern Renaissance'). Outstanding twentieth-century writers include Kjeld Abell, Kaj Munk and Martin Nexø.

SCRIPT

Roman alphabet, 26 letters as in English, + *æ, å, ø*.

PHONOLOGY

Consonants

    stops: p, b, t, d, k, g, ʔ
    fricatives: f, v, s, ʃ, h, ð, γ, j
    nasals: m, n, ŋ
    lateral: l
    uvular trill: ʀ

All consonants are short.

The correspondence between sound and symbol in Danish is weak. *p, t, k* are aspirate /p, t, k/ only as initials. Elsewhere, *p, t, k* and *b, d, g,* tend to fuse as unaspirated /b, d, g/. Thus *lække* 'leak' and *lægge* 'lay' are both pronounced as /lεgə/; cf. in the dental series, *sist* 'last', /sisd/. /g/ is regularly elided in certain environments: cf. *nogen* 'some', /nōn/, *spørge* 'ask', /sbœrə/, *spøg* 'joke', /sbɔiʔ/, *meget* 'much', /maiəð/.

Vowels

front: i, e, ɛ, y, ø, œ
central: a
back: ɔ, o, u
neutral: ə

DIPHTHONGS
Eight glides to /u/, two to /i/.

Tone

The *stød* (glottal stop) corresponds in Danish to the acute tone in Swedish and Norwegian. The *stød* has phonemic force, as minimal pairs are thus distinguished: cf. *hund* 'dog', /hunˀ/ and *hun* 'she', /hun/.

Stress

Normally on first syllable of root word.

MORPHOLOGY AND SYNTAX

Noun

GENDER
Danish has two genders: common and neuter. The definite article is *-en* for common nouns, *-et* for neuter; *-ene* forms the plural of both genders. If, however, an attributive adjective is present, the suffixed article is dropped, and the demonstratives *den*, *det*, *de* are used instead: e.g. *hus* 'house'; *huset* 'the house'; *det store hus* 'the big house'.

NUMBER
Three possible endings: *-e*, *-(e)r*, Ø. These may be accompanied by umlaut and gemination of the final consonant: e.g. *broder* 'brother' – *brødre*; *tand* 'tooth' – *tænder*; *fod* 'foot' – *fødder*.

CASE
Only the genitive has a specific marker: *-s*. Other cases are made as in English with the help of prepositions.

Adjective

Adjective precedes noun as attribute, and takes *-t* before a neuter singular: e.g. *et godt hus* 'a good house'. For adjective with definite noun, see above.

COMPARATIVE
In *-(e)re*, with suppletive formations as in other Germanic languages: e.g. *gammal* 'old' – *ældre*; *ond* 'bad' – *værre*, etc.

Pronoun

PERSONAL

The first and second nominative forms are: *jeg*, *du*; pl. *vi*, *I*. These have objective forms: *mig*, *dig*, *os*, *der*. The third person distinguishes gender in the singular: *han*, *hun*, *den* 'he, she, it', with corresponding objective forms *ham*, *hende*, *den*. The plural is *De*, *Dem*. *De/Dem* is also the polite second person form, singular and plural.

POSSESSIVE PRONOUNS

First person *min*, *mit*, *mine*, second person *din*, *dit*, *dine*, and first person plural *vor*, *vort*, *vore*; these show concord with the object possessed. The third person forms: *hans*, *hendes*, *dens/dets* are invariable (concord, that is, with subject, not object). Similarly, the second and third person plural forms, *jeres*, *deres*, are invariable. On the analogy of *deres*, the form *vores* is replacing *vor*, *vort*, *vore*.

INTERROGATIVE PRONOUN

hvem 'who?', *hvad* 'what?'

RELATIVE PRONOUN

The interrogatives *hvem*, *hvad*, and related forms, e.g. *hvis* 'whose', are used in literary Danish, and partly in colloquial, e.g. for genitive: *Hr. Hansen, hvis broder rejser omkring i Danmark* 'Mr Hansen whose brother is travelling in Denmark'. *Som* and *der* are much used in the spoken language: *mennesker, der kan tale dansk* 'people who can speak Danish'.

Numerals

1–10: *en*, *to*, *tre*, *fire*, *fem*, *seks*, *syv*, *otte* (/-d-/), *ni*, *ti*; 11 *elleve*; 12 *tolv*; 13 *tretten*; 20 *tyve*; 30 *tredive*; 40 *fyrre*; 50 *halvtreds*; 60 *tres*; 70 *halvfjerds*; 80 *firs*; 90 *halvfems*; 100 *hundrede*.

Verb

Transitive/intransitive, weak and strong. There are active and passive voices, indicative and imperative moods, with some vestiges of a subjunctive.

NON-FINITE FORMS

Infinitive, present and past participles. The present tense for all verbs is made by adding *-r* to the infinitive in *-e*: e.g. *jeg kommer* 'I come'. There is no inflection for person or number.

The weak/strong dichotomy affects the preterite: the weak ending is *-te/-ede*, and there may be accompanying umlaut in the root: e.g. *følge* 'to follow': pres., *jeg følger*, pret. *jeg fulgte*, /fuld/.

Strong verbs have zero ending with 2- or 3-stage umlaut (including past participle): e.g. *jeg drikker* 'I drink', *jeg drak* 'I drank', *jeg har drukket* 'I have drunk'; *jeg giver* 'I give'; *jeg gav* 'I gave', *jeg har givet* 'I have given'. The umlaut sequence is often close to that in English.

PASSIVE

Two forms: *at blive* 'to become' + past participle, or *-s* added to infinitive: e.g. *han blev født 1805* 'he was born in 1805'; *huset ejes af Hr. H.* 'the house is owned by Mr H'.

IMPERATIVE

= stem; polite forms can be made by means of auxiliaries.

PARTICIPLES

Present in *-ende* /ənə/; past in *-(e)t*. The past participle can take *-en* to agree with a common gender correlative, but the modern tendency is to avoid inflection here, and to use the *-(e)t* form for both genders and both numbers.

MODAL AUXILIARIES

E.g. *få*, *ville*, *måtte*, *gøre*, *skal*, etc. are used in many ways, including formation of a periphrastic future: e.g. *jeg skal komme i morgen* 'I shall come tomorrow'.

Negation

The general negating adverb is *ikke*.

Prepositions

As in English, these may be detached from the object, and take final position in the sentence: e.g. *hvad ser du på* 'what are you looking at?'

Word formation

As in German, by prefixation, suffixation, and compounding.

Word order

SVO is normal, OVS is possible, e.g. for emphasis.

I Begyndelsen var Ordet, og Ordet var hos Gud, og Ordet var Gud.

2 Dette var i Begyndelsen hos Gud.

3 Alt er blevet til ved det, og uden det blev intet til af det, som er.

4 I det var Liv, og Livet var Menneskenes Lys.

5 Og Lyset skinner i Mørket, og Mørket fik ikke Bugt med det[1].

6 Der fremstod et Menneske, udsendt fra Gud; hans Navn var Johannes.

7 Han kom til et Vidnesbyrd for at vidne om Lyset, for at alle skulde komme til Tro ved ham.

8 Selv var han ikke Lyset, men han skulde vidne om Lyset.

DARDIC LANGUAGES

INTRODUCTION

The Dardic languages form an Indo-European language/dialect complex located in north-eastern Afghanistan (Kafiristan/Nuristan), northern Pakistan and the extreme north-western corner of India. The exact genetic status of Dardic has been the subject of some controversy. The question is whether these languages are to be seen as a sub-division of New Indo-Aryan (as the Pamir languages are of Iranian) or as a transitional stage between New Indo-Aryan and Iranian, belonging to neither but partaking of both. Sir George Grierson inclined to the latter view; Sten Konow took Dardic to be basically Iranian; while Morgenstierne regarded all Dardic languages as New Indo-Aryan except the Kafiristan group, which he treated as transitional. The route by which these languages reached their present site, and the dating of this migration, are equally uncertain. Grierson posited a passage via the Hindukush long after the main NIA–Iranian split; Morgenstierne argued for NIA immigration from the south. In general it can be said that New Indo-Aryan traits clearly outweigh Iranian features in most Dardic languages; and by far the most important member of the group – Kashmiri – shows several points of resemblance with Pahari and Lahnda, though here the influence of Urdu must be taken into account.

The three basic divisions with their components are:

> West Dardic (Kafir): Katī, Vaigalī, Aṣkun, Prasun, Demeli
> Central Dardic: Khōwār, Kalāṣa, Paṣai, Votapuri, Sumasti, Gawar(bati), Tirakhi, Citrali
> East Dardic: Kāśmīrī, Baśkārik, Garwi, Tōrwālī, Maiyã̄, Ṣiṇā, Phalūṛa

The total number of Dardic speakers is probably in the region of 3 million, with Kashmiri accounting for about 2½ million of this total. After Kashmiri come Khowar (c. 120,000), Pashai (c. 100,000), and Sina (c. 70,000).

SCRIPTS

Dardic languages are unwritten, apart from Kashmiri, which is written by the Moslem population in an expanded Arabic script, and by Hindus in either Devanagari or Sarada; this latter is a derivative of Brahmi. The Kastavari dialect of Kashmiri is written in the Kastavari script.

PHONOLOGY

Main points:

(a) Presence of nasalized vowels; nasalization may be phonemic (e.g. in Baskarik).
(b) Stops and affricates generally present in three-degree series: voiced – unvoiced – unvoiced aspirate, e.g. /b, p, p'/. This is an Indo-Aryan feature, the aspirate/non-aspirate opposition being very rare in Iranian.
(c) The presence of a retroflex series again links Dardic to Indo-Aryan; but Dardic has retroflex affricates, which are not an Indo-Aryan feature.

MORPHOLOGY AND SYNTAX

Main features:

1. Gender: the feminine -*i* marker appears generally in nominal and adjectival system.
2. Number: associated with case, i.e. unmarked in base form, marked in oblique. Presence of pluralizing suffixes in some languages.
3. Case: via postpositions, which tend to become fossilized as case endings.
4. A definite/indefinite opposition is found in nearly all Dardic languages. This is more characteristic of Iranian than of New Indo-Aryan.
5. Adjectival system: wide variation, from three markers for gender, number, and case in Kashmiri to null marker in some Central Dardic languages.
6. Pronoun: forms for first and second person are everywhere present. Third person forms are supplied by the demonstrative series which usually distinguishes three degrees of relative distance from speaker or referent. There is also a pronominal enclitic series, again an Iranian trait in the main, (but cf. **Vedic, Sindhi, Lahnda**).
7. Numerals: vigesimal system is widespread (not in Kashmiri).
8. Verb: varies from flectional system in West and Central Dardic to an analytic system, based on the use of participles plus auxiliaries, in Eastern. An anomaly here is provided by the Eastern Dardic language Sina, which has a future form marked by personal endings.

    An ergative construction is in general use for transitive verbs which make past tenses from old participial forms. Some languages have a specific ergative case in their declension system, and this marks the subject in the ergative construction. Where there is no specific ergative case, an oblique case is used. Normally, in such constructions, the verb agrees with the object; in some, however, with the subject, e.g. in Sina.
9. Both prepositions and postpositions are found, the latter being more usual.
10. Word order: SOV is normal.

DARGVA

INTRODUCTION

Dargva belongs to the Lak-Dargva sub-group of Dagestanian languages. It is also known as Dargin; the ethnonym is *dargan*. There are about 280,000 speakers in the central part of the Dagestan Autonomous Soviet Socialist Republic, bordering the Caspian Sea.

Dargva is officially classified as one of the literary languages of Dagestan.

SCRIPT

1917–28 adaptation of Arabic; thereafter experimental period of romanization till 1938, when Cyrillic + *I* and ř was adopted.

PHONOLOGY

Consonants

stops: b, p, p', d, t, t', g, k, k', ɢ, q, q', ʔ
affricates: dz, ts, t's, dʒ, tʃ, t'ʃ
fricatives: f, v, s, z, ʃ, ʒ, j, x, γ, ʕ, h, ç
nasals: m, n
lateral and flap: l, r

Vowels

i, e(ɛ), ə, a, u

/ə/ is notated as *a* or я.

MORPHOLOGY AND SYNTAX

Noun

Nouns are divided into three classes:

Class 1: male human beings; the concord marker is *v-*, *y-*, or Ø- in the singular; *b-* in the plural.
Class 2: female human beings; the concord marker is *r-* (sing.), *b-* (pl.).
Class 3: everything else; concord marker is *b-* (sing.), *d-* (pl.) or *-r-* infix (pl.).

Plural markers are *-bi*, *-ti*, *-ni*, etc.: e.g. *adam* 'man', pl. *adamti*; *dabri* 'shoe', pl. *dabrumi*. Examples of concord: *dudeš vaķib* 'father came'; *neš raķib* 'mother came'; *unc baķib* 'the bull came'.

DECLENSION

The cases in Dargva can be divided into two groups. Group 1 comprises nominative, ergative, dative, genitive, associative or comitative, instrumental, and a prepositional case used with verbs of discourse. Group 2 consists of 20 spatial frames, sub-divided into four series each with five cases:

Series 1	has five aditive cases: the endings are *-či*, *-zi*, *-hi*, etc.
Series 2	has five cases denoting locus without motion: the endings are those of series 1 + class markers.
Series 3	has five ablative cases: series 2 endings + *-ad*.
Series 4	has five elative cases: series 1 endings + class markers + *-əſ*.

In the group 1 cases, the nominative has Ø ending, the ergative adds *-li*, *-ni*, *-y*; cf. *džuz* 'book', *nuni džuz bučulra* 'I read (present-tense) the book', where *nuni* is ergative of *nu* 'I', and *b-* is the class 3 marker for *džuz*.

Either an aditive case or the ergative provides the base for the other oblique cases.

Adjective

Adjectives may appear in base form (this is normal in poetry) or take such endings as *-si* , *-a*. The modulated form takes class markers, but does not take case endings in concord with the noun qualified.

Pronoun

PERSONAL

	Singular	Plural
1	nu	nuša
2	ſu	ſuša

These are declined as nominals, but with specific endings, sometimes suppletive. Thus *nu*: erg. *nuni*, gen. *dila*, dat. *nab*, com. *nabčil*, prep. *nabčila*, instr. *nabčibli*

The third person forms are supplied by the demonstrative series, which has three degrees:

	Singular	Plural
neutral	iš	išdi
proximate	il	ildi
remote	it	itdi

INTERROGATIVE PRONOUN
či 'who?'; *se* 'what?'

RELATIVE PRONOUN
See **Verb** below.

Numerals

2–10: *ķel, ʕəbal, aval, šel, uregal, verʕal, geʕal, určemal, veçal*. 20 *γal*; 30 *ʕəbçali*, 40 *avçali*; 100 *daršal*.

The numerals can be declined as nouns.

Verb

Aspect, mood, tense, number, class, person are all expressed in a multitude of forms, all of which are based on the optative form; this has no suffixes and can be declined as a nominal, e.g. *belķ* 'that he may/might write'.

IMPERATIVE

A vocalic marker is added to the optative base. Selection of marker vowel is correlated with the third person inflections in the past tense; e.g. when this ends in *-ib/-ub*, the marker is *-a* or *-i*: *kasib* 'he took' – *kasa!* 'take!'

There are many ways of forming the imperfective aspect from the perfective, most of them involving vocalic and consonantal change: e.g. *arses* 'to fly off' – *urses* 'to be flying'. The combination of two bases (perfective and imperfective) with past, present, and future time frames generates a very wide range of verbal forms: e.g. for the past frame, a simple past, a past perfective, a past imperfective, and a past suppositive.

Examples from *vaķes* 'to come':

> simple past: *vaķibra* 'I came' (conjugated by person: 1 *-ra*, 2 *-ri*, 3 *-Ø*)
> past perfective: *vaķil(i)ri* 'I had come (before ...)'
> past imperfective: *ləvqul(i)ri* 'I was coming'
> past suppositive: *vaķi ši* 'I came (it is said)'

The latter three forms are invariable.

Specimen forms for other tenses:

> present: has both aspects: perfective *vaķil(i)ra*, *-ri*, *-say*; imperfective *ləvqul(i)ra*, *-ri*, *-say* 'I etc. am/are/is coming'
> future: *ləvqəs*, *-d*, *-n*: e.g. *ləvqən* 'he will come'
> future suppositive: *vaķiša*, *-ši*, *-s*

PARTICIPLES

The formant is *-si*, *-n*, *-ri* for the singular, *-ti* for the plural. Thus a perfective present participle is *vaķibsi-*, which is conjugated for person: *-ra*, *-ri*, *-say*. Similarly, *vaķessi* '(he) who will come'.

There are many gerundial forms: e.g. *vaķibla* 'since (he) came'; *vaķibʕella* 'when (he) came'; *vaķiblarhi* 'after (he) came'.

The formant *-n* makes participial forms denoting occupation, etc.: e.g. *luķan* 'he who is writing' → 'writer'

Particles are added to these participial/gerundial forms to express a large variety of nuances: e.g. *vaḳiliɡi* 'even though coming/having come'.

Postpositions

Postpositions in Dargva are petrified nouns; they follow various cases, including the nominative.

Word order

Basic SOV.

DINKA

INTRODUCTION

Dinka belongs to the Western Nilotic branch of Nilo-Saharan (Chari-Nile group) and is spoken by an estimated 2 million in southern Sudan and southwestern Ethiopia. The language is unwritten.

PHONOLOGY

Consonants

/p, b; t, d; tʃ, dʒ; k, g/ are present, plus associated nasals, /m, n, ɲ, ŋ/, /f, v, w, ɣ, j, r, l/ are also present. Final voiced stops tend towards voiceless /b/ → [p]. Final /tʃ/ approaches [ɟ]. In the combination /wt, wd, wn/, the /w/ is silent, but affects the pronunciation of /t, d, n/.

CONSONANT MUTATION
Final stops mutate as follows: /b,p/ → /m/, /tʃ/ → /ɲ/, /d,t/ → /n/. This takes place (a) when definite marker is added; (b) when genitive marker is added: (c) before proniminal affix; (d) before following adjective: e.g. *lyeb* 'tongue' – *lyeme* 'the tongue'; *dit* 'bird' – *dine* 'the bird' – *dindia* 'my bird' – *din did* 'a big bird'.

Vowels

iː, ɪ, eː, ɛ, ə, a, aː, ɔ, o, ou, u, uː

Tones

High, low, with rising and falling glide tones. Marked here where necessary by acute, grave, circumflex.

MORPHOLOGY AND SYNTAX

Noun

No grammatical gender. Natural gender in humans is distinguished lexically: e.g. *ran* 'man', *tik* 'wife'. *Tik* (*tek*) may also be used to denote the female of animals: e.g. *džonkor* 'horse', *tin e džonkor* 'mare'.

DEFINITE ARTICLE
-e, pl. *-ke*.

PLURAL

Most nouns do not distinguish between singular and plural: e.g. *abuok* 'gazelle(s)'. The plural form of the definite article identifies a noun as plural: e.g. *džonkorke* 'horses'. Plural may also be indicated by vowel lengthening: e.g. *tim* 'tree', pl. *tīm*; or by umlaut: e.g. *nom* 'hand', pl. *nim*; or suppletively: e.g. *tik* 'woman', pl. *dyar*.

CASE RELATIONS

Indicated by particle: e.g. *ran* 'man' (nom., acc.) *e*/*ke ran* 'of the man', *etong ran* 'to the man', *tede ran* 'from the man'.

Genitive: possessor precedes possessed: *mán nya* 'mother of the girl' (*mâ* → *mán* 'mother'). Genitive particle *e*/*ke*/*de* may be interpolated: e.g. *tin e*/*de beyn.did* 'the wife of the chief' (*beŋ-did* 'chief').

Dative: e.g. *an ači kan yek ran* 'I have given that to the man' (*yek* 'to give; *kan* 'that').

Adjective

As attribute, adjective follows noun: *ran did* 'big man'; *tin puat* 'good woman'. The predicative adjective is introduced by *a*/*e*: e.g. *bâr* 'long', *Ryen abâr* 'The ship is long'.

Pronoun

PERSONAL

Has full and abbreviated forms:

	Singular			*Plural*		
	Full	*Abbreviated*	*Possessive*	*Full*	*Abbreviated*	*Possessive*
1	ghên/an	gha/a	-dia	ghôg	gho/o/a	-da
2	yin	yi/î	-du	uêk	ue	-dun
3	yen	ye/e	-de	kêk	ke	-den

For plural possessed objects the possessive affixes are sing. *čia*, *ku*, *ke*; pl. *kua*, *kun*, *ken*.

A noun may be marked for possession either by the suffixed possessive enclitic or by the prefixed abbreviated form: e.g. *lyemdia* = **gha**.*lyeb* 'my tongue'.

The full forms set out above act both as pronominal subject and as pronominal object.

DEMONSTRATIVE PRONOUN
kan, pl. *kak* 'this, these'; *ken*, pl. *kak(a)* 'that, those'.

INTERROGATIVE PRONOUN
(*ye*)*nga* 'who?'; (*ye*)*ngu* 'what?'.

RELATIVE PRONOUN
e/*ye*/*ke*: e.g. *ran a yèk ghut* 'a man who built a house' (*yèk* 'build', *ghut* 'house').

Numerals

1–10: *tok, róu, dyak, 'nguan, wdyeč, wdetem, wderóu, bêt, wde-nguan, wtyer*;
11 *wtyer ko tok*; 20 *wtyer-rou*; 30 *wtyer-dyak*; 100 *buôt*.

Verb

Most verbs are consonant-final: e.g. *tem* 'cut', *gal* 'begin', *gam* 'believe'. Root
= infinitive = imperative.

TENSE
There are three basic tenses:

> present: the formant is *a*, e.g. *ghên a gam* 'I believe'
> perfect: *ači → či* + stem, e.g. *ghên/an ači nin* 'I have slept'
> future: *abi → bi* + stem, e.g. *an abi nin* 'I shall sleep'

PASSIVE VOICE
The stem is unchanged, the formants lengthen final vowel: e.g. *abi → abī*;
ači → ačī. The combination of pronoun + formant is subject to metathesis and
contraction, e.g. *ghên ači → ačigha → ača*. The resultant series is *ača, ači, ačé*;
pl. *ačûg, ačak, ačik*. Similarly with *ghên*, etc. + *abi*.

NEGATION
The marker is *ačí* 'distinguished by tone/stress from *ači*, the tense marker). e.g.
an ačí bi lo 'I shall not go'; *kan ačí bi loy* 'that won't be done'.
   The prohibitive particle is *dû(n)(e)*, pl. *dunke*: e.g. *dunke lo!* 'don't go! (pl.).

PARTICIPLES
Present: *a* + stem, e.g. *a čam* 'eating'; *a nin* 'sleeping'. Perfect: *či* + stem, e.g.
Či lek '(he) who has spoken?'

Word order

SOV, SVO.

---

1 NE goi goc e kaŋ ke Wet eto, ku Wet eto ke Nhialic, ku Wet eye Nhialic. 2 Yeneka to kene Nhialic ne goi goc e kaŋ. 3 Yeneke cak kaŋ kedhia; ku te cene yen kacin ke ci ca ne ka ci ke ca. 4 Pir eto ne eyic; ku pir yeneka ye yer de ran. 5 Ku yer eya ruer tecol, ku kaci cuol ye piŋ. 6 Ran e tuoc ne Nhialic, ran col Jon. 7 Yenake dule, bi koc ya le yer, bi koc kedhia biya gam ne yen. 8 Ku kacie yen eye yere, e buo bi koc biya le yere.

DRAVIDIAN LANGUAGES

INTRODUCTION

The Dravidian stock seems to have arrived in north-west India in the fifth or fourth millennium BC. Its exact provenance is not clear. A hither/central Asian origin for the language type, if not for its present bearers, finds some support in the thesis, first advanced by Caldwell in the middle of the nineteenth century, of a lexical and morphological relationship between the Dravidian and the Uralic language families. Comparison (e.g. by Burrow 1944) of certain semantic fields seems to place a lexical relationship of some kind beyond reasonable doubt; and there are structural parallels in the tense markers, the formation of the plural, the pronominal system, and the negative conjugation. Material so far deciphered at the Mohenjo-Daro and Harappa sites also suggests a connection with Dravidian.

As regards contact between Dravidian and Indo-Aryan, it seems clear that the present polarization, with Indo-Aryan in the north and Dravidian in the south of India, is of comparatively recent date. Throughout the third and second millennia BC the two families probably coexisted in the north of India, with Dravidian gradually losing ground to Indo-Aryan. There are Dravidian words in the *Rig-Veda*, and Dravidian influence is seen in such Indo-Aryan features as the development of the retroflex series, and, later, the gradual replacement of prepositions in New Indo-Aryan by postpositions.

The process was not all one-way; the major Dravidian languages are full of Sanskrit words, and, on another front, certain features of the Dravidian outlier Brahui have been attributed to contact with its Indo-Aryan neighbour Baluchi. Andronov and Emeneau have treated parallel typological features of New Indo-Aryan and Dravidian, and their mutual interaction, as evidence of the emergence of an areal 'Indian' language type, covering New Indo-Aryan, Dravidian, and Munda.

Andronov (1965) groups the Dravidian languages as follows:

	Group	Number of speakers (est.)	Location
I	Southern		
	Tamil	55 million	Tamilnad, Sri Lanka, E and S Africa, SE Asia
	Kannada	26 million	Karnataka
	Malayalam	25 million	Kerala
	Kota	a few hundred	Kotagiri Mountains
	Toda	100,000	Nilgiri area

387

	Kodagu	80,000	Mercara area
II	South-eastern		
	Telugu	60 million	Andhra Pradesh, Tamilnad
III	South-western		
	Tulu	1 million	Mangalore
IV	Central		
	Kolami		
	Naiki	150,000	border regions of Andhra Pradesh,
	Parji	(Parji, 85,000)	Madhya Pradesh, and Maharastra
	Godaba		
V	Gondwana group		
	Gondi	1½ million	border regions of Andhra Pradesh, Madhya Pradesh, and Maharastra
	Kui	680,000	Orissa
	Kuvi		
VI	North-eastern		
	Kurukh	1 million	Chhota Nagpur
	Malto	100,000	Rajmahal Hills
VII	North-western		
	Brahui	400,000	Baluchistan

Andronov (1965) gives the following time-scale for separation stages:

4000 BC: separation of Proto-Brahui
3500 BC: separation of Kurukh, Malto
2500 BC: formation of Gondwana group
1500–1100 BC: separation of Central group
1100–900 BC: separation of Telugu
mid first millenniun: separation of Tulu
turn of millennium: separation of Kannada from Tamil
AD 1000–1300: separation of Malayalam from Tamil

PHONOLOGY

In initial and medial position, Dravidian phonemes are remarkably stable over the entire domain, both diachronically and synchronically. Thus, Proto-Dravidian /t-/ is everywhere reflected as /t-/, and /p-/ very largely as /p-/. The same goes for alveolar /l/ and /r/: these are characteristically Dravidian phonemes.

Typologically, the Dravidian languages are agglutinative; there is a basic dichotomy into (a) human/rational and (b) non-human/non-rational. Gender distinction appears in the southern and south-eastern languages.

Typically, there are two basic cases, direct and oblique. Further case affixes are attached to the oblique form. The first person plural distinguishes inclusive and exclusive forms. A particularly interesting feature is the Uralic type of negative conjugation.

See **Tamil, Telugu, Kannada, Malayalam, Gondi, Brahui**.

DUTCH

INTRODUCTION

The official name of this West Germanic language is *Nederlands*. It is the official language of the Kingdom of the Netherlands, and joint official language (with French) of Belgium. There are over 14 million speakers in the Netherlands, and about 5 million in Belgium. Dutch is also the language of administration in Surinam and in the Dutch Antilles.

In the period of Germanic tribal expansion (third century AD onwards) the southern regions of what is now the Netherlands were colonized by Frankish tribes, and it was here that Old Dutch first crystallized. The transition from Middle Dutch to Modern Dutch coincided with the transfer of economic and political power to northern Holland, and the accompanying cultural polarization. It is northern (Amsterdam) usage that underlies the modern literary standard, though Brabant influence is not absent. There is a marked difference between the literary standard and the colloquials.

Writing in Old Dutch begins in the tenth century. In the subsequent history of Dutch literature three main periods may be distinguished: (a) the radiant and lyrical mysticism of fourteenth-century visionaries like Heinric van Ruysbroeck; (b) the seventeenth-century 'Golden Age'; and (c) the modern period from the mid-nineteenth century onwards: particularly rich in the social novel and in experimental verse. The novelists Multatuli, Couperus, and Schendel are outstanding. The literary monthly *De nieuwe gids* (1885 onwards) should be mentioned, as it played a seminal role in the development of Dutch culture.

SCRIPT

Roman alphabet. The standardized orthography of 1863 was revised and simplified in 1947.

PHONOLOGY

Consonants

    stops: p, b, t, d, k
    fricatives: f, v, s, z, x, γ, j, h
    nasals: m, n, ŋ
    lateral: l
    uvular flap: ʀ
    semi-vowel: ʋ

/tj/ tends towards retroflex [ʈ].

Vowels

front: i, e, ɛ, ɪ, œ, y
middle: ɵ, a, ə
back: ɑ, ɔ, o, u

There are eight diphthongs, which are glides to /i/ or /u/.

There is assimilation, both regressive and progressive, at junctures: e.g. *afbellen* [avbɛllə(n)] 'ring of'; *opvouwen* [opfɔ•və(n)] 'fold up'.

Voiced finals are unvoiced: (*ik*) *heb* → [hɛp]; *hond* → [hɔnt].

/f, s/ → /v, z/ in formation of plural, and so written: *brief* 'letter' – *brieven*; *huis* 'house' – *huizen*.

Final -*n* tends to be elided: *ziekenhuis* 'hospital' → [zikəhəys].

Intrusive /ə/: e.g. *arm* /arəm/.

Stress

Normally on first syllable, disregarding weak prefixes. In compounds, stress is not always predictable.

MORPHOLOGY AND SYNTAX

Noun

Nouns are divided into those of common gender, with singular definite article in *de*, and neuters with singular definite article *het*. For both genders the plural definite article is *de*, the singular indefinite article is *een*: e.g. *de kamer* 'the room'; *het paard* 'the horse'.

The plural marker is -*en* or -*s*: e.g. *de vrouw* 'the woman', pl. *de vrouwen*; *de prijs* 'the price', pl. *de prijzen*; *de zoon* 'the son', pl. *de zoons*.

Since final -*n* is not pronounced, the opposition between singular and plural in the case of the -*en* ending is Ø/ə.

Adjective

The attributive adjective precedes the noun and takes -*e* for common-gender nouns: e.g. *een goede man* 'a good man'; but, *een goed boek*. The predicative adjective is not inflected.

COMPARATIVE
In -*er*, superlative in -*st*. Suppletive sets parallel to those in German and English occur: e.g. *goed – beter – best*; *veel – meer – meest*.

Pronouns

PERSONAL

For each of the six personal rows (3 singular, 3 plural) there are full and reduced subject forms, full and reduced object forms. Thus:

1st sing.	ik	'k	mij	me
3rd sing.	hij	-ie	hem	'm
	zij	ze	haar	'r

In the second person there is a choice between familiar forms: *jij*, pl. *jullie* and more formal address: *u*.

POSSESSIVE

The possessive forms are:

	Singular	*Plural*
1	mijn	ons/onze
2	jouw, je	**van**jullie (dat van jullie)
	uw	
3	zijn	hun
	haar	

Note: colloquial usage: *mijn broer z'n auto = de auto van mijn broer*.

DEMONSTRATIVE

deze, dit 'this', pl. *deze*; *die, dat* 'that', pl. *die*.

INTERROGATIVE

wie 'who?', *wat* 'what?'

RELATIVE

die with reference to common gender; *dat* with reference to neuter: e.g.

... in het decadente Haagse milieu **dat** deze schrijver kende als geen ander
'... in the decadent Hague milieu which this writer knew as no other did'

... van een levendigheid, **die** voor zijn tijd volstrekt uniek was
'... a liveliness that was quite unique for his period'

After prepositions the form is *wie* for persons, *waar* + prep. for things:

de mensen **bij wie** hij wont
'the people he lives with'

de technologische prestaties **waarop** Amerika altijd trots is geweest
'the technological achievements of which A. has always been proud'

Further to relative clauses (see above): in literary Dutch, embedding of attributive (phrase) to left of head-word is permissible: e.g. *de op de agenda staande interpellaties* 'the questions on the agenda'.

Numerals

1–10: *een, twee, drie, vier, vijf, zes, zeven, acht, negan, tien*; 20 *twintig*; 21 *een en twintig*, 30 *dertig*, 40 *veertig*; 100 *honderd*.

Verb

The citation form = infinitive, ending in *-(e)n*; the stem is the infinitive form minus *-(e)n*. A long vowel in the infinitive is written doubled in the stem: e.g. *leven – leef*; *geloven – geloof*.

Dutch has active and passive voices, indicative and imperative moods. There are two simple tenses in the indicative: present and past.

Simple present: first person singular = stem; first plural and third plural = infinitive; second person singular and plural and third singular add *-t*: e.g. *ik kom – wij komen – hij komt*.

Formation of the simple past depends on whether the verb is weak or strong. Weak verbs add *-te/-ten, -de/-den* to the stem: e.g. *ik kookte – wij kookten*. Strong verbs make their past tense and past participle by means of single or two-stage umlaut: e.g.

> bidden 'pray' – bad – gebeden
> slapen 'sleep' – sliep – geslapen
> liggen 'lie' – lag – gelegen

Past participle: *ge-* + stem + *-t/d* for weak; specific form for strong has to be learnt with the verb. If the verb has a stressed prefix, *-ge-* is inserted between this prefix and the stem: e.g. *aannemen* 'accept' – *aangenomen*.

COMPOUND TENSES

These are made with specific auxiliaries: the future with *zullen*; the perfect with *zijn* or *hebben*. *Hebben* is used with transitives; intransitives involving a change of state use *zijn* (cf. *sein* with verbs of motion in German). E.g. *hij is opgestaan* 'he (has) got up'; *wij zijn naar de stad gereden* 'we drove to town'. *Zullen* and other modal auxiliaries – e.g. *laten, kunnen, moeten* – precede the infinitive they govern: e.g.

> hij is niet **kunnen** komen 'he was not able to come';
>
> hij heeft ... **laten** vallen 'he let ... drop';
>
> en ze hebben me allemaal beloofd te **zullen** komen
> 'and they all promised me they would come' (Couperus)

The modal auxiliary may even be inserted between an infinitive and its separable prefix. There are then three possibilities:

> omdat ik in Amsterdam   moet overstappen 'because I have to change in A.'
>   **over** moet stappen
>   overstappen moet

PASSIVE

Both *worden* and *zijn* are used as auxiliaries in the formation of the passive voice, the latter in the perfect tense only: e.g.

> ... zal donderdag **worden** begraven '... will be buried on Thursday'
>
> het raam is gebroken 'the window is broken' (= 'the window has been broken')
>
> uit de mededeling van thans kan **worden** afgeleid, dat ...
> 'from the present announcement it can be inferred that ...'

As dummy subject, *er* may introduce a passive sentence: e.g. *er werd veel gepraat* 'a lot of talking went on' (cf. German *es wurde viel geplaudert*).

Er also = German *da* in such constructions as: *een stuk ervan* = *ein Stück davon*, but, contrary to German usage, *er* can be separated from the preposition: *ik heb er een stuk van*.

Negation

Niet follows verb negated or its object: *ik schrijf (de brief) niet* 'I don't write the letter'; but precedes modal + infinitive groupings at end of clause: *dat boek heb ik niet kunnen koopen* 'I wasn't able to buy that book'.

Prepositions

Note that *het* cannnot be used after a preposition. Instead, *er* + prep. is used (cf. *er*, above); thus, **tegen het – ertegen*; **in het – erin*.

Word derivation

Compounds are frequent, usually two or more nouns, but other parts of speech may enter into them. Example of word-building:

> antwoord 'answer'
> **ver**antwoord**elijk** 'responsible'
> verantwoordelikj**heid** 'responsibility'

Stress may shift in compound: *tóeval* 'chance', *toevállig* 'by chance'.

Word order

SVO is normal; SOV in subordinate clauses; VSO in interrogation.

1 In den beginne was het Woord en het Woord was bij God en het Woord was God. 2 Dit was in den beginne bij God. 3 Alle dingen zijn door het Woord geworden en zonder dit is geen ding geworden, dat geworden is. 4 In het Woord was leven en het leven was het licht der mensen; 5 en het licht schijnt in de duisternis en de duisternis heeft het niet gegrepen. 6 Er trad een mens op, van God gezonden, wiens naam was Johannes; 7 deze kwam als getuige om van het licht te getuigen, opdat allen door hem geloven zouden. 8 Hij was het licht niet, maar was om te getuigen van het licht.

EASTER ISLAND

See **Rapanui**.

EFIK

INTRODUCTION

This language belongs to the Benue-Congo family. Efik and its close congener Ibibio are spoken by about 750,000 people in the Calabar area of south-east Nigeria, where the language has served as a common medium of communication between various ethnic/linguistic groups. Writing in Efik dates from 1846, when the Scottish Presbyterian Church commenced its missionary work in Calabar, and promptly set about translating parts of the Bible. A translation of the *Pilgrim's Progress* appeared in 1868. Creative writing in Efik commenced in the 1930s, and there have been several writers of note (E.N. Amuku, E.E. Okon, E.A. Edyan, and the poet Elisabeth Asibong). Efik is used for local radio services.

SCRIPT

Apart from the Roman-based alphabet provided by the missionary press, several indigenous scripts have appeared, e.g. the Nsibidhi script.

PHONOLOGY

Consonants

The labio-velar /kp/ is the syllable-initial allophone of /p/; /b/ cannot be final; /t, d, k, g, h/ are present, with /f, r, s/, and the nasals /m, n, ɲ, ŋ/. /m, n, ŋ/ appear as syllabic initials; the continuants /w/ and /j/ occur as nasal resonants.

Vowels

i/ɪ, e, ɛ, a, ɔ, o, u

There are four/five diphthongs with /i/ as second member.

VOWEL HARMONY

In prefix + stem complex, the vowel of the prefix is front or back depending on the stem vowel: e.g. *ŋ́.ke.dèp* 'I bought'; *ŋ́.kó.kùt* 'I saw'; *ŋ́.ka.nàm* 'I did', where *k*V is past marker, *ŋ́* is 1st person singular subject prefix.

Tone

Tone in Efik is 'terraced'; i.e. successive high tones decrease progressively in height. The relative pitch of low tones is not thereby affected.

There are two main tones, high and low, plus a rising and a falling tone. Tone plays a cardinal role in Efik grammar and syntax. For example, the 2nd and 3rd person subject prefixes are distinguished only by tone (*see* **Pronoun** below). All Efik stems have inherent (isolate, or dictionary) tone, which is subject to specific alteration in specific grammatical constructions.

MORPHOLOGY AND SYNTAX

There is no grammatical gender and no class system for nominals; nominals include pronouns. The noun in itself subsumes both singularity and plurality. Certain adjectives can be pluralized by prefixing a syllabic nasal: e.g. *ébot* 'goat': *èkpírì èbot* 'small goat'; *ŋ̀kpírì èbot* 'small goats' (note change of tone in noun). A few suppletive plurals are found: *éyen* 'child', pl. *ǹditɔ*; *àkámba* 'big', pl. *ìkpɔ́*.

Pronoun

The independent (long) forms are used as focused pronouns, both subject and object. The short forms are prefixed to verbs as subject:

	Singular			*Plural*	
	Focused form	*Verbal prefix*		*Focused form*	*Verbal prefix*
1	àmi	ŋ́, ń, m̀		ǹỹin	i
2	àfo	à (or harmonic allophone)		m̀bufo	è
3	èỹé	á (or harmonic allophone)		m̀mɔ́	é

That is, tone alone distinguishes second person prefix from third: *à.nam útom* 'you are working'; *á.nàm útom* 'he is working'.

POSSESSION

A variant of the focused form follows the noun, for singular possessor: e.g. *úfɔk mì* 'my house'; *úfɔk fò* 'your (sing.) house'.
In case of plural possessor, full focused form follows: *úfɔk m̀bufo* 'your (pl.) house'. Nominal possessor also follows: e.g. *úfɔk ɔ́bɔŋ* 'chief's house'.

DEMONSTRATIVE PRONOUN/ADJECTIVE
émì 'this', *órò* 'that', *ókò* 'that yonder': e.g. *úfɔk émì édì ókìm* 'this house is mine'; *émì édì ùbóm* 'this is a canoe'.

INTERROGATIVE PRONOUN
ànye 'who?'; *ǹso* 'what?'.

RELATIVE PRONOUN
None; relative-clause construction depends on whether the proposition is affirmative or negative. The affirmative relative clause is marked by *-dé*: e.g.

ḿfìri émì ì.ké.dép.dé 'the fruit which we bought'; the negative suffix is *-ké*: e.g. *ŋ́kpɔ́ émì m̀mé.ŋ.ko.fyɔ̀k.ké* 'things I didn't know'.

The negative relative is constructed on different lines, involving the reduction of the pronominal subject prefixes to three idiosyncratic forms: one for first person singular, one for second person singular and one for all other personal forms: *m̀mé – m̀mú – m̀mí*.

The *de-* form is also used after *ke* 'when', *edieke* 'if', *koro* 'because', *adaŋa nte* 'as long as', etc. : e.g. (Ward 1933: 100)

> **Ke** ndabade ntre, ŋkut owo emi esinede … 'As I dreamt thus, I saw a man who was wearing …'

> **Nte** nsaŋade ke ikɔt ererimbot … 'As I was walking in the wilderness of the world …'

Numerals

1-10: *kyèt, ìba, ìtá, ìnaŋ ìtyôn, ìtyôkyet, ìtyâba, ìtyâitá, ùsúk-kyèt, dwòp*; 11 *dwòp-e-kyet*; 12 *dwòp-e-ba*; 20 *édip*.
Numerals follow noun: e.g. *ébwa ìnaŋ* 'four dogs'.

Verb

The great majority of Efik roots are mono- or disyllabic. The root = imperative = stem for finite *prefix + stem* forms.

Perfective/imperfective action, with reference to present, past, or future, is expressed in verbal forms which combine personal prefixes, specific markers, tones, and, exceptionally, suffixes, in specific patterns. For example, for ongoing action in the present the pattern is subject prefix + stem with *low* tone: e.g. *ń.nàm útom* 'I am working' (*nám – high* tone – 'to do'); *án.nàm útom* 'he is working'.

PAST

Subject prefix + *ma* + subject prefix + stem: in this pattern the first subject prefix and the *ma* marker have the same tone; the second subject is high tone, and the stem has isolate = dictionary tone: e.g. *m̀má ń.nám útom* 'I worked'; *èmà é.nám útom* 'you (pl.) worked'.

FUTURE

Subject prefix + *ye* + stem (isolate tone): e.g. *ń.ye.bɔ́p úfɔ̀k* 'I'm going to build a house'; or, subject prefix + *dî* + stem (falling tone in monosyllable, high–low in disyllable): e.g. *Édî.kâ úfɔ̀k íbɔ̀k?* 'Is he going to go to the hospital?'

The *-di-* future is an example of what Welmers (1968) calls the 'contrastive' construction. This is found in sentences introduced by an interrogative pronoun, and also in sentences where one or another component may be optionally focused. With reference to present and past, two such constructions are possible with or without *ké* = 'is it/it is, that …'. For example, with reference to the past:

È.ké.dép ńsò
Nsò **ké** è.ké.dép   'What did you buy?'

ń.ké.dèp ḿfìri
ḿfìri **ké** ń.ké.dép   'I bought fruit'

With reference to the present:

Ànám ńsò = Nso **ké** ànam? 'What are you doing?'

ńnàm útom = útom **ké** ńnam 'I'm working'

NEGATIVE

The marker is a suffix: kV → /χ,γ/V (in Efik orthography ḥ). The basic formula is given by the negative present: subject prefix + stem + negative marker with harmonic vowel: e.g. *Ń.dí.**ge** mí* 'I'm not coming here'. Similarly for past and future, with relevant tense markers preceding stem: e.g. past, *ń.ke.dí.**ge** mí* 'I didn't come here'; future, *ń.dî.dî.**ge** mi* 'I shan't come here' (note change of stem tone).

Efik has, further, specific marker/tonal patterns for sequential, hortative, conditional, hypothetical, and customary forms.

Prepositions

Ké is an all-purpose location marker. Where closer definition is required, various nominals are used, e.g. *ésìt* 'in(side)'; *íso* 'face' → 'in front of': *k'íso*.

Word order

The constrastive pattern allows for SVO or OcSV, where c stands for the connective *ké*.

---

1 IKƆ okodu ke eritəŋɔ, IKƆ okonyuŋ odu ye Abasi,
2 IKƆ onyuŋ edi Abasi. Kpa Enye okodu ye Abasi ke
3 eritəŋɔ. Edi Enye akanam kpukpru ŋkpɔ ewɔŋɔ edi;
   ndien ke esiode Enye efep, ŋkpɔ baba kiet, eke ama
4 ɔwɔrɔ, iwɔrɔke idi. Uwem odu Enye ke idem; uwem oro
5 onyuŋ edi uŋwana owo. Ndien uŋwana oro ayama ke
   ekim; ekim inyuŋ ikanke enye.
6   Owo kiet okoto edi; Abasi osio enye ɔdɔŋ; enyiŋ esie
7 ekere John. Enye ekedi nte ntiense, ete idi ntiense inɔ
   uŋwana oro, kpaŋ kpukpru owo enim ke akpanikɔ oto ke
8 enye. Enye ikedige uŋwana oro, edi ekedi man edi ntiense
   ɔnɔ uŋwana oro.

399

EGYPTIAN

INTRODUCTION

One of the oldest attested languages in the world, Egyptian belonged to the Afro-Asiatic family, and showed several features shared in common with Semitic. The following stages in the development of Egyptian are distinguished:

1. Old Egyptian of the third millennium BC. Known from the Pyramid Texts, the most archaic form of Egyptian, and from funerary inscriptions of the fifth and sixth Dynasties.
2. Classical or Middle Egyptian, covering the period 2240–1780 BC (Dynasties 9 to 12).
3. Late Classical: 1780–1350 BC (Dynasties 13 to 18). The *Book of the Dead* was compiled in this period.
4. Late Egyptian: fourteenth to eighth centuries BC (Dynasties 18 to 24).
5. Demotic: eighth century BC to fifth century AD.
6. Coptic.

SCRIPT

The 'sacred writing' deciphered by Champollion in the 1820s is known as hieroglyphic. Several thousand hieroglyphs are known, many of them being very rare or *hapax legomena*. The hieroglyphic script is sub-divided into:

(a) Ideograms: these represent objects in purely graphic fashion with no phonetic element: e.g.

𓇳 /r'/, 'day, sun';

𓉐 /pr/, 'house'.

(b) Phonograms: these are particularized signs indicating pronunciation; e.g.

𓂋 /r/, 'mouth'

comes to function in the course of the centuries as the conventional sign for /r/, and a series of such single-valued signs ultimately produces an alphabet. At no stage of Egyptian before Coptic are vowels notated. To facilitate pronunciation, modern practice is to vocalize the Egyptian consonants with /e/. Thus, *pr* is read as /per/; *sn* 'brother', as /sen/, *nfr* 'beautiful' as /nefer/.

(c) Syllabic signs representing two or three consonants, often accompanied by phonograms: Thus,

    ⌣   /nb/, 'basket';

    ★   /sb'/, 'star'.

(d) Determinatives: these are class or function markers posted at words to suggest their semantic field. Thus, verbs of motion are often accompanied by the determinative

and words denoting liquids by the determinative

    〰〰〰

(cf. Chinese radicals, which have a similar function, though they are, of course, shorthand for characters with phonetic values). An Egyptian determinative when acting as such, has no phonetic role; it may, however, be particularized to define the object represented: it is then accompanied by a vertical stroke. Thus in

    𓄿𓆓 ⊙   /wbn/, 'rise, shine',

the sign

    ⊙

is a determinative with no phonetic value; in

    ⊙̓   /r'/

it is particularized to denote 'the sun'. Thus, a sign may function in three different ways – as ideogram, as phonogram, and as determinative.

The Egyptian script is read either vertically downwards, or horizonally left to right or right to left. Ideograms representing gods, humans, or animals act as pointers to the direction in which the script is to be read: if they face to the right of the viewer, the script is read from right to left, and vice versa. Symmetry of a purely formal nature plays an important part in the arrangement of signs. There is no punctuation.

A cursive form of hieroglyphic, known as hieratic, is attested from about 3000 BC. An abbreviated cursive, known as demotic, appears from about 800 BC onwards. While there is a one-to-one correspondence between a hieroglyph and its hieratic version, there is no such correspondence in demotic script, which is full of ligatures.

PHONOLOGY

Consonants

The consonantal inventory seems to have been as follows:
    stops: p, b, t, d, k, g, q; + glottal stop ʔ (or Arabic 'ain)
    affricates: tʃ, dʒ
    fricatives: s/z, ʃ, h, ħ, x
    nasals: m, n
    lateral and flap: l, r
    semi-vowels: j, w

Hamza is usually notated in transcription as ꜣ , here as '. The semi-vowel /j/ in initial position is notated as ỉ (also as medial). Here, /ħ/ = Ar. ح , /h/ = ه , /x/ = خ , notated as ḫ or ẖ. /tʃ/ is notated as ṯ and /dʒ/ as ḏ.

MORPHOLOGY AND SYNTAX

Noun

There are two genders, masculine and feminine. Many feminine nouns end in -t: e.g. sn 'brother', snt 'sister'. Typical Egyptian nouns are: pr 'house'; pt 'sky'; nìwt 'city'; nṯr /nečer/ 'god'.

SINGULAR, DUAL, AND PLURAL NUMBERS

The dual and plural endings are marked for gender: dual masc. -wy, fem. -ty; pl. masc. -w, fem. -wt: e.g. ' 'arm', 'wy 'two arms'; nbty 'two goddesses'; ìrty 'two eyes'.

Originally, plurality was indicated in the script by triplication, duality by duplication. This practice came to be abbreviated to three strokes for plural, two strokes for dual. Finally, the dual marker // or \\ came to be regarded as an alphabetic sign for -y. The three strokes reappear in many nouns denoting non-countable substances – provisions, tribute, salt, wine, etc.

CASE RELATIONS

Annexation: there is a direct construct case in which the qualifier immediately precedes the qualified, and an indirect construct using the inflected connective n(y), n(t), n(y)w, n(yw)t. In the direct construct the first member is definite, as in Semitic; the indirect construct permits indefinite status of either component: e.g.

(a) Direct construct: nb t'w 'the Lord of the Lands'; nbt pt 'the Lady of Heaven'; nbt sb'w 'the Lady of the stars'.
(b) Indirect construct: pr n ìnr 'an administrator's house'; 'n nṯr 'a god's hand'; sḥ n srw 'council of the nobles'.

Honorific transposition in direct construct: in the script, where gods and kings are concerned, the normal order is reversed: thus, for 'the son of the king' (normal order: s' nsw) nsw s' was written, but read as s' nsw.

Adjective

As attribute, adjective usually follows the noun, and shows concord for gender and number: e.g. *sn nfr* 'good brother'; *snt nfrt* 'good sister'. If it precedes the noun, it is invariable.
The plural marker *-w* tends to be dropped. Dual: cf. *rwty wrty* 'the two great doors' (*rwt* 'gate', *wrr* 'great') (Bullock 1979: 4).

Nisba adjectives are formed from nouns and prepositions by adding *-y*: e.g. *nìwt* 'town', *nìwty* 'urban'; *ḥr* 'on'; *ḥry* 'superior'; *m* 'in', *ìmy* 'interior'.

COMPARISON
A comparative is made with positive + *r*: e.g. *nfr r nbw* 'finer than gold'.

Pronoun

First, the independent forms with the pronominal affixes:

		Singular		Plural	
		Independent	Affix	Independent	Affix
1		ìnk	ì	ìnn	n
2	masc.	ntk	k	nttn	
	fem.	ntṯ	ṯ		ṯn
3	masc.	ntf	f	ntsn	sn
	fem.	nts	s		

There are three dual forms: 1 *ny*, 2 *ṯny*, 3 *sny*, used as suffixes. The suffixes provide the subject in conjugation: e.g. *dd.ì* 'I say'; *sḏm.f* 'he hears'. Following nouns they are possessive suffixes: *pr.f* 'his house'; *sn.s* 'her brother'. Affixed to prepositions they provide oblique cases: e.g. *n.f* 'for him'; *n.n* 'for us'; *ìrmì.st r.f* 'I did it (= *st*, see **Dependent pronouns**) to him' (Bullock 1979: 60).

DEPENDENT PRONOUNS

singular: *wì*, 2 masc. *ṯw*, fem. *ṯn*, 3 masc. *sw*, fem. *st*
dual: *ny*, *ṯny*, *sny*
plural *n*, *ṯn*, *sn*

These pronouns are used *inter alia* to provide direct objects after transitive finite forms: e.g. *dd.tw ḥ'st n ḥ'st* 'land gave you to land' (Bullock 1979:73); *rdì.n.f wì* ... 'he placed me ...' (for the *.n.* in this sentence, see **Perfective verb**, below).

DEMONSTRATIVE PRONOUN
Marked for gender and number: *pw/tw* 'this' (masc./fem.); common pl. *nw* 'this, these'; similar form with *pf/tf* 'that'.

INTERROGATIVE PRONOUN
m 'who?'; *ptr* 'what?'.

RELATIVE PRONOUN
Masc. *nty*, fem. *ntt*, pl. *ntyw*: these can be used only if the antecedent is definite:

e.g. ... **nty rdì.n.ì** *n.tn sw* 'the ... which I gave (*sw* 'it' recapitulates the relative pronoun) to you (*n.tn*)'. Where the antecedent is indefinite, no link is required: the resumptive pronoun appears in the relative clause (cf. **Arabic**).

Numerals

Numerals are treated as nominals and usually follow nouns. Theoretically, both noun and numeral are mascline singular: 1–10: *w'* (with feminine form *w't*), *snw*, *ḥmt, fdw, dìw, sìsw, sfḫ, ḥmn, psd, mḏ*; 20 *ḏwty*; 30 *m'b'*; 40 *ḥm*; 100 *štt*.

Verb

Formally, an Egyptian verb consists of two, three, four, or five root consonants: e.g. *ḏd* 'speak', *mri* 'love', *sḏm* 'hear', *wstn* 'step'. Roots are classified as weak (ending in *i, j, w*), geminate, or strong. It follows that all biliterals are strong.

The citation form is the root + the enclitic masculine pronominal marker *f*: e.g. *sḏm.f* 'he hears, heard, will hear'; pronounced /sedžemef/. Essentially, this form is a verbal noun, annexed by the third pronominal marker. It is sense-bearing, but neutral as to voice, mood, or tense. In practice, it usually serves as the active indicative present form, and is then conjugated by enclitic marker for all persons and two numbers (the dual is absorbed by the plural). The personal markers have been set out under **Pronoun** above.

The *sḏm.f* form is by far the commonest verbal form in Egyptian. The notion of tense is alien to the language, and *sḏm.f* is best regarded as an imperfective aspect indicating uncompleted or pending action. It is negated by *n* or *nn*: *nn* negates the whole proposition, *n* negates a verbal item therein.

The *sḏm.n.f* form is perfective, and usually refers to an action completed in the past. The *sḏm.f* and *sḏm.n.f* forms are illustrated in this sentence from the *Story of Sinuhe*: *ḏd.n.f'ḥ'.f ḥn'.i* 'He said that he would fight with me' (Bullock 1979: 48), where *ḏd.n.f* denotes completed action, *'ḥ'.f* imperfective/pending action. Similarly: *ḥmt.n.ì ḫpr ḫ' 'yt* 'I expected that strife would arise.'

The *sḏm.n.f* form is negated by *n*, and then acquires an imperfective meaning. Among other forms taken by the Egyptian verb are the narrative form *sḏm.in.f*, and the sequential (with future reference) form *sḏm.hrf*.

As was said above, the base form *sḏm* is neutral as to voice. It may have been specifically vocalized to express active or passive, but the script affords no clue here (cf. **Arabic**). A specifically passive form could be made in Egyptian, e.g. by the addition of the -*tw*/-*t* marker: e.g. *sḏm.tw.f* 'he was listened to'; *sḏm.tw m pr.nsw* 'it was heard in the palace'.

THE OLD PERFECTIVE

Gardiner (1969: 234) calls this the 'sole surviving relic in Egyptian of the Semitic finite verb'. Professor Bakir's (1978: 97) term 'circumstantial form' (*al-ḥāl*) is apt, as the form is neutral as to tense, used nearly always in auxiliary clauses, and, hence, essentially contingent in sense. The endings are sing. 1 -*kwì*, 2 -*tì*, 3 masc. -*w*, fem. -*tì*; pl. 1 -*wyn*, 2 -*tiwny*, 3 masc. -*w*, fem. -*tì*. Korostovtsev (1961: 60) gives the example: *gm.n.ì sw rḫ.w st* 'I found him knowing this' = '... that he knew this'.

INFINITIVE

Can be masculine or feminine (then in *-t*), and is often used with *r* to denote purpose: e.g. *r sḏm* 'in order to hear'.

PARTICIPLE

Four are distinguished, denoting active/passive single or repeated action. These are marked for gender. A common formula is: *ìn* + subject (noun or independent pronoun) + participle + complement.

Prepositions

Examples of these, e.g. *m*, *ḥn'*, *ḥr*, have appeared in sentences given above; *n* denotes the dative case: e.g. *n sn* 'to/for the brother'.

Word order

In verbal construction, VSO where S is a noun and O is direct (+ indirect) object; VOS where S is pronominalized: the formula here is V – indirect object – direct object – S pronominalized – (adverbial extension). Nominal construction: SV is normal, but may be inverted: e.g. *nfr ḥrrt* 'beautiful (is) this flower'.

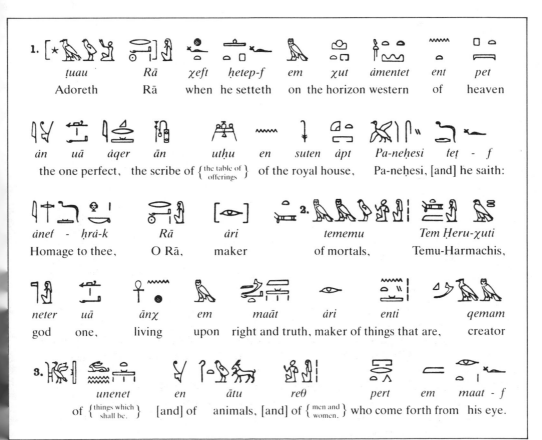

1. *ṭuau* — *Rā* — *χeft* — *ḥetep-f* — *em* — *χut* — *àmentet* — *ent* — *pet*
Adoreth — Rā — when — he setteth — on — the horizon — western — of — heaven

àn — *uā* — *àqer* — *ān* — *uthu* — *en* — *suten* — *àpt* — *Pa-neḥesi* — *teṭ - f*
the one perfect, — the scribe of { the table of offerings } — of the royal house, — Pa-neḥesi, [and] he saith:

ànef - ḥrā-k — *Rā* — *àri* — *tememu* — *Tem Ḥeru-χuti*
Homage to thee, — O Rā, — maker — of mortals, — Temu-Harmachis,

neter — *uā* — *ānχ* — *em* — *maāt* — *àri* — *enti* — *qemam*
god — one, — living — upon — right and truth, — maker of things that are, — creator

3. *unenet* — *en* — *àtu* — *reθ* — *pert* — *em* — *maat - f*
of { things which shall be. } — [and] of — animals, [and] of { men and women. } — who come forth from — his eye.

ELAMITE

See **Anatolian Languages**.

ENGLISH

INTRODUCTION

The West Germanic branch of Indo-European, to which English belongs, also includes Low German, Dutch, and Frisian. English itself derives from three Low German dialects spoken by the Angles, Saxons, and Jutes, who came from Denmark, and North Germany to settle in England from the middle of the fifth century onwards. These dialects are marked by retention of the unvoiced stops /p, t, k/, which were mutated to the corresponding fricatives /f, θ, x/, in High German, and of the voiced stops /b, d, g/, which were likewise mutated to /p, t, k/. *See* **German**: Second Sound Shift. These mutations may be illustrated by such equations as:

Low German	English	High German
dör	**d**oor	**T**ür
pad	**p**ath	**Pf**ad
ski**p**	shi**p**	Schi**ff**
hei**t**	hot	hei**ss**

Four main dialects took shape in *Englaland*, the 'land of the Angles':

1. West Saxon: spoken in the kingdom of Wessex and other parts of the south;
2. Kentish: the language of the Jutes in what is now Kent;
3. Mercian: spoken by the Angles in East Anglia and Humberside;
4. Northumbrian: the dialects of the Angles in north-east England and south-east Scotland.

Of these, West Saxon – King Alfred's *Englisc* – is by far the most important as the language in which most of Old English literature is written. (*See* **Literature**, below). In the eighth and ninth centuries a fresh Germanic influx came in the shape of Scandinavian settlers, whose Norse language provided English with many genetically homogeneous loan-words. From 1016 to 1042, England was, in fact, a Danish kingdom. On the linguistic plane, however, West Saxon preserved its ascendancy until the Norman invasion in 1066. The polarization of society which followed this upheaval was reflected in an equivalent polarization of language: as the language of the conquerors, Norman French assumed the dominant role, while West Saxon lost its privileged status, and joined other forms of Old English as a dialect of the English peasantry. Through the twelfth century there was little or no writing in Old English. The specific nature of Middle English, as it emerged and was consolidated between 1100 and 1500, is largely due to three factors:

1. The widely disparate rates at which the Old English inflectional system was lost in the various dialects. This dialectal divergence reached a point at which mutual intelligibility was severely impaired or even lost. The need for an accepted common norm became more and more urgent.
2. It has been calculated that about 10,000 French words were imported in the Middle English period, 75 per cent of which are still in use today. On the one hand, this represented a considerable enhancement of a language which found itself in a new political situation; on the other hand, it implied a corresponding loss of those Old English lexical resources which were no longer immediately useful.
3. The morphological core of the emergent language remained, however, that inherited from Old English.

By the late thirteenth century, the term 'English' refers to that compromise between the East Midland (< Mercian) and South-Eastern (< Kentish) dialects, which came to be known as the London dialect. In 1258, the accession of Henry III was proclaimed in 'English'. By the middle of the fourteenth century, English had replaced French as the language of the law (Statute of Pleading, 1362) and of education; and by the end of the century, Chaucer was using the London dialect to write one of the greatest poems in English. A hundred years later, the lineaments of Early Modern English are clearly discernible.

Periodization of Modern English is meaningful mainly on the phonological plane, and, within this field, primarily with regard to change affecting the vocalic system. The consonantal inventory remained largely the same from the early Middle English period onwards, and the principal morphological reductionist processes were virtually complete by the close of that period. Thus, Old English is marked by the possession of a rich and extensive system of Germanic inflection and a purely Germanic vocabulary; Middle English by extensive erosion of the morphological apparatus, and the intake of a large number of French words; Modern English by the near-total disappearance of inflection. Four periods in the development of Modern English are distinguished: (a) 1500–1620s; (b) to 1700; (c) to the end of the nineteenth century; (d) the twentieth century. In (c) and (d), due to political and economic factors, anglophone territory expands to global proportions, accompanied by a vast increase in the numbers of people using English as a second language. The extreme reductionism of Modern English accidence may be a contributory factor here.

Today, as the mother tongue of some 350 million people, English is demographically surpassed only by Modern Standard Chinese, which cannot, however, claim anything approaching the international status of English. The main components in this total are: USA 232 million speakers; United Kingdom 56 million; Canada 24 million; Australia and New Zealand 17 million.

In addition, English is the official language of several countries in Africa – Zimbabwe, Nigeria, Ghana, Uganda, Liberia – and the West Indies; and it has joint official status in India (with Hindi), South Africa (with Afrikaans) and Singapore (with Chinese, Malay, and Tamil). It is the accepted global medium in the travel industry and in international communications. Increasingly, a press conference of any importance, given anywhere in the world, will be in English, or accompanied by an immediate translation into English.

One and a half thousand years after Hengist and Horsa, the local dialect they brought with them from Denmark to Kent, shows every sign of becoming the planetary lingua franca in the twenty-first century.

Periodization of English literature

1. Old English: four manuscripts, dating from c. 1000, contain Anglo-Saxon poetry of the eighth and ninth centuries, including the heroic poem *Beowulf* and some lyrics. In prose, the outstanding items are the works of King Alfred, and the Anglo-Saxon Chronicle, which covers (with gaps) the period from Alfred's reign to the middle of the twelfth century.
2. Middle English: in the early period, the main body of work is in Anglo-Latin: e.g. Geoffrey of Monmouth's *Historia*. The transitional period includes the mediaeval romance *Sir Gawayne and the Grene Knight*, and John Langland's *Piers Plowman*. The period ends with Chaucer.
3. Renaissance: Shakespeare and the other dramatists (Marlowe, Webster); Spenser; lyric poetry.
4. The seventeenth century: Milton; Donne and the Metaphysical poets; Dryden; Bunyan.
5. The eighteenth century: Pope; Swift; the novelists, Richardson, Smollet, Sterne; Dr Johnson; *The Tatler* and *The Spectator*: Addison and Steele; William Blake; in Scotland, Robert Burns.
6. The nineteenth century: Byron and the Romantic movement; Wordsworth, Coleridge; Keats and Shelley; Tennyson, Browning, Matthew Arnold; the novelists, the Bronte Sisters, Jane Austen, George Eliot, Dickens, Hardy.
7. The twentieth century.

OLD ENGLISH

INTRODUCTION

Script

The earliest inscriptions are runic. Old English literature is written in an Irish version of the Latin alphabet, with specific forms for f, g, r, s. Later, two runic letters þ = /θ/, and ƿ = /w/ were added. Initially þ was used to indicate both /θ/ and the voiced counterpart /ð/, for which ð was then introduced.

PHONOLOGY

Consonants

stops: p, b, t, d, k, g
affricates: tʃ, dʒ (notated as *cg*)
fricatives: f, v, θ, ð, s, z, ʃ, x, γ, ç, h
nasal: m, n, ŋ
lateral and flap: l, r
semi-vowels: j, w

Vowels

short, ɑ, æ, ɛ, ə, œ, ɪ, ɔ, u, y
long: ɑː, æː, eː, œː, iː, oː, uː, yː
diphthongs: short: ea, eo; long: ēa, ēo

The long vowels never appear in the inflectional endings. They are indicated in the following text by macrons.

MORPHOLOGY AND SYNTAX

Noun

Old English had three grammatical genders: masculine, feminine, and neuter. A few nominal endings are coded for gender: e.g. *-a*, *-oþ*, *-dōm*, *-els*, *-scipe* are masculine; *-nes*, *-estre*, *þu*, *-ung* are feminine.

DEFINITE ARTICLE

se 'the, that'; *þes* 'this'. *Se* has fem. form *sēo*, neuter *þæt*. All three are declined in five cases on a *þ*-initial base: e.g. masculine nom. *se*; acc. *þone*; gen. *þæs*; dat. *þæm*; instr. *þȳ*. The common plural is: nom./acc. *þā*; gen. *þāra*; dat./instr. *þæm*.

Þes has fem. *þēos*, neuter *þis*. The masculine declension is: nom. *þes*; acc. *þisne*; gen. *þisses*; dat. *þissum*, *þȳs*. The common plural is: *þās*, *þissa*, *þissum*.

DECLENSION

Five cases, the instrumental sharing a form with the dative. There are three declensions: a strong declension, the weak or *-n* declension, and a group of minor and irregular declensions.

For example, masculine *a*-stem: *cēol* 'ship':

Singular		*Plural*	
nom.	se cēol	nom./acc.	þā cēolas
acc.	þone cēol		
gen.	þæs cēoles	gen.	þāra cēola
dat./instr.	þæm/þȳ cēole	dat./instr.	þæm cēolum

Feminine *o*-stem: *rōd* 'cross':

Singular		Plural	
nom.	sēo rōd	nom./acc.	þā rōda
acc.	þā rōde		
gen,.	þǣre rōde	gen.	þāra rōda
dat./instr.	þǣre rōde	dat./instr.	þǣm rōdum

-*n* declension: e.g. *guma* 'man': this declension has -(*a*)*n* in all four singular oblique cases, and in plural nom. and acc. The plural genitive is *gumena*, the dat./instr. *gumum*: e.g. *þǣm guman* 'to the man'; *þāra gumena* 'of the men'.

Minor declensions: e.g. *fōt* 'foot', pl. *fēt*; the mutated vowel appears in the sing. dat./instr. as well: *þǣm/þȳ fēt* 'to/by the foot'. Cf. *bōc* 'book', pl. *bēc*; *tōþ* 'tooth', pl. *tēþ*; *mūs* 'mouse', pl. *mȳs*.

Adjective

All adjectives have a strong (indefinite) and a weak (definite) declension. The instrumental is formally distinguished from the dative in the indefinite singular: e.g. *cwic* 'living'; fem. *cwicu*, nt. *cwic*.

The masculine oblique cases are: acc. *cwicne*, gen. *cwices*, dat. *cwicum*, instr. *cwice*. The neuter is identical, apart from the accusative, which remains *cwic*. For all three genders, the gen. is *cwicra*, the dat. *cwicum* (no instrumental).

The weak declension is used after the definite article, the demonstratives, and the possessive pronouns: e.g. *se gōda guma* 'the good man', acc. *þone gōdan guman*, dat. *þǣm gōdan guman*; pl. gen. *þāra gōdra gumena*.

Cf. Luke 15.22:

bringað raðe þone sēlestan gegierelan
'bring forth the best robe' (*raðe* 'quickly'; *sēlest* suppletive superlative of *wel* 'well (good)'; *gegierele* 'robe')

Cf. John 10.11:

Ic eom gōd hierde
'I am the good shepherd'

gōd hierde selþ his līf for his scēapum
'the good shepherd giveth his life for his sheep'

COMPARATIVE
-*ra*: *earm* 'poor' – *earmra*; *bliðe* 'glad' – *bliðra*.

SUPPLETIVE FORMS
gōd 'good' – *betra/sēlra*; *micel* 'large' – *māra*; *yfel* 'bad' – *wiersa*; *lȳtel* 'small' – *lǣssa*.

Pronoun

The first and second persons have dual forms; the third person is marked for gender in the singular, with a common plural. Cases: nom., acc., gen. dat./instr.

Singular	*Dual*	*Plural*
1 ic – mē – mīn – mē	wit – unc – uncer – unc	wē – ūs – ūre – ūs
2 þu – þē – þīn – þe	git – inc – incer – inc	gē – ēow – ēower – ēow
3 masc. hē – hine – his – him		
fem. hēo – hī – hire – hire		hī – hī – hira – him
nt. hit – hit – his – him		

Cf.

> sōþ ic secge ēow 'verily I say to you'
>
> bringað mē hider þā 'bring them hither to me' (Matthew, 14.18).
>
> and hira gōdna dæl ofslōgon 'and slew a good number of them' (*hira*)

DEMONSTRATIVE PRONOUN

See **Definite article:** *se – seo – þæt*; *þes – þēos – þis*.

INTERROGATIVE PRONOUN

Masc. *hwā*, nt. *hwæt*; declined in five cases; *hwæðer* 'what? (which of two)'; *hwelc* 'which? (of many)'.

RELATIVE PRONOUN

þe (invariable) usually preceded by appropriate form of definite article/demonstrative *se*. (Used pronominally, *se → sē-*.)

> þæt folc, þe þær binnan wæs 'the people who were inside'
>
> se hȳra, sē þe nis hierde and sē þe nāg þā scēap
> 'the hireling, that is not the shepherd, and who does not own the sheep' (*nis* 'is not'; *nag* 'does not own'; *see* **Verb**, below) (John, 15.12)

Numerals

1–10: *ān, twēgen, þrȳ, fēower, fīf, syx, seofon, eahta, nigon, tȳn*; 11 *endleofan*; 12 *twelf*; 13 *þrēotȳne*; 20 *twentig*; 21 *ān and twentig*, etc. 30 *þrītig*; 70 *hundseofontig*; 80 *hundeahtatig*; 90 *hundnigontig*; 100 *hundtēontig*.

Verb

As in other Germanic languages, Old English verbs are either strong (vocalic, i.e. displaying stem ablaut) or weak (consonantal). Most Old English verbs belong to the weak conjugation. There are three moods – indicative, imperative, subjunctive – and two basic tenses, present and past. The auxiliary verbs *wesan*, *bēon*, and *habban* are used to form a perfect, a pluperfect, and a future tense. The general negating particle *ne* precedes the verbal form, and may fuse with it: *ne habban → nabban* 'not to have'. A passive can be formed periphrastically.

STRONG VERBS

The strong verbs, which form a closed set, are divided by ablaut pattern into seven classes; examples of these (infinitive – past, third singular and plural – past particle) are:

1. rīsan – rās, rison – -risen 'rise'
2. bēodan – bēad, budon – -boden 'offer'
3. drincan – dranc, druncon – -druncen 'drink'
4. beran – bær, bǣron – -boren 'bear'
5. sprecan – spræc, sprǣcon – -sprecen 'speak'
6. faran – fōr, fōron – -faren 'go'
7. wēpan – wēop, wēopon – -wōpen 'weep'
   hātan – hēt, hēton – -hāten 'call'

All seven classes have various irregularities and sub-classes; classes 3 and 7 are particularly heterogeneous. Formation of second and third person singular present indicative from the stem often involves *i*-mutation: e.g.

cuman 'to come': cymst – cymþ
helpan 'to help': hilpst – hilpþ
grōwan 'to grow': grēwst – grēwþ

Specimen strong verb paradigm: *bīdan* 'to wait', class 1.

Indicative

present:	sing.	1 bīde, 2 bīdest, 3 bītt (<bīdþ)
	pl.	1–3: bīdaþ
past:	sing.	1 bād, 2 bide, 3 bād
	pl.	1–3: bidon

Subjunctive

| present: | sing. | 1–3: bīde; pl. 1–3: bīden |
| past: | sing. | 1–3: bide; pl. biden |

Imperative sing. *bīd*; pl. *bīdaþ*.
Participles: present: *bīdende*; past (*ge*)*biden*

WEAK VERBS

These were often formed from nouns and other parts of speech by means of the affix *-ja*, which induced *i*- mutation in the stem vowel of the resultant verb. According to the presence or absence of this mutation, Old English weak verbs are divided into two classes. Here, a specimen paradigm: *fremman* 'to perform' where the stem vowel represents a mutation from *-a-*:

Indicative

present:	sing.	1 fremme, 2 fremest, 3 freme
	pl.	1–3: fremma
past:	sing.	1 fremede, 2 fremedest, 3 fremede
	pl.	1–3: fremedon

Subjunctive

present:	sing.	1–3: fremme; pl. 1–3: fremmen
past:	sing.	1–3: fremede; pl. 1–3: fremeden

Imperative: sing. *freme*; pl. *fremma*
Participles: present *fremmende*; past *gefremed*

MIDDLE ENGLISH

INTRODUCTION

The twelfth century was the century of transition between late Old English and early Middle English. Almost nothing was written in English, and very little was borrowed from French. The English dialects ceased to reflect the original tribal divisions, and tended to polarize on an areal or typological basis into two groups: Northern (including Northumbrian and Mercian, from which latter the important Midland dialect was to emerge) and Southern (comprising West Saxon and Kentish). Each of these several components developed internally in terms of its own material, and at its own specific rate.

PHONOLOGY

The process of phonological change, by which Old English became Middle English, may, however, be broadly generalized. Some salient features are:

1. Weak vowels, especially in final position, were levelled to *e*; towards the end of the Middle English period strong diphthongs were also levelled:

Old English	*Middle English*	*Modern English*
nama	name	name /nejmɵ/
beran	beren	bear
sunu	sune	son /sʌn/
steorra	sterre	star

2. /ea/ > /æ/ > /a/: e.g. *heard* > *hærd* > *hard*: Mod. Eng. *hard*.
3. Old English long vowels were largely maintained in Middle English. /yː/ became /iː/ in Northern dialects, and subsequently standard: e.g. Old English *fȳr* > Middle English *fīr* (Mod. Eng. *fire*/faiɘ/).

   Long vowels tended to be shortened before consonantal cluster: e.g. Old English *wīsdōm* > Middle English *wisdōm*.
4. The consonantal inventory remained stable, with some changes in quantity.
5. Consonantal finals of Old English nominals were replaced by vowel finals in Middle English, originating in the oblique case: e.g. Old English *cwēn*: acc. *cwēne* > Middle English *quēne* (Mod. Eng. *queen*).

MORPHOLOGY AND SYNTAX

1. Definite article gradually reduced from the Old English inflected paradigm to the single form *þe* /θe/ > /ðə/.
2. Erosion of the article is a factor in the general loss of grammatical gender.
3. Extensive erosion of the case system; by the end of the period, only the genitive *-s* remains. Even where, for a time, a modicum of inflection persisted – e.g. in the declension of Old English feminine nouns with a plural marker in *-en* – this too was finally levelled by analogy; and a generalized plural in *-(e)s* emerges. Mutating plurals are retained: *gōs – gēs* 'goose, geese'; *mūs – mȳs* 'mouse, mice', etc., though old mutating forms in the singular are levelled.
4. The adjective becomes indeclinable.
5. Prounoun: the standard Middle English system is as follows:

		Singular		Plural	
			Oblique		Oblique
1	nom.	ī, ich	mē	wē	us
2		þow	þē	yē	yow
3	masc.	hē	him		
	fem.	shē	hir(e)	} þei	þeim
	nt.	(h)it	(h)it		hem

POSSESSIVE PRONOUNS
Sing.: mīn/mī – þīn, þī – his, hir(e)
pl.: our(e) – your(e) – þeir(e), her(e).

DEMONSTRATIVE PRONOUN
Early Middle English had a full declension for all three genders, with four cases in the singular, three in the plural. This was reduced in standard Middle English to a simple opposition between 'this, these'/'that, those'.

RELATIVE PRONOUN
The relative pronoun was standardized as *that*.

Verb

The standard Middle English strong-verb paradigm shows little change from that of Old English, apart from the levelling of *-a-* and *-o-* in inflections to *-e-*, the loss of *-þ* in the present indicative plural, and the shift from *-d-* to *-g-* in the present participle. Thus, the present tense of Middle English *bīnde(n)* 'to bind' is: sing. *bīnde, bīndest, bīnde*; pl. common, *bīnde(n)*. The past tense is: sing. *bǫnd, bounde, bǫnd*; pl. *bounde(n)*. Imperative: *bīnd, bīnd(e)*; subjunctive: pres. sing. *bīnde*; pl. *bīnde(n)*; past, sing. *bounde*; pl. *bounde(n)*; present participle: *bīndinge*; past participle: *(i)bounde(n)*.

This represents a reduction of discriminant forms from the twelve present in the Old English conjugation of *bindan*, to seven; Modern English reduces this to four.

A considerable number of Old English strong verb stems were reassessed as weak in Middle English and conjugated accordingly.

MODERN ENGLISH

INTRODUCTION

The transition from Middle to Modern English:

SCRIPT

The very weak correspondence between sound and symbol, characteristic of Modern English, is due primarily to the conservation from the late Middle English period onwards of a gallicized orthography reflecting Middle English pronunciation. The orthography was consolidated by the introduction of printing (1476), and retained through a succession of phonological changes. Variant spellings were permissible into the nineteenth century.

PHONOLOGY

Vowels

The key feature in the phonological transition from late Middle to Modern English is the so-called Great Vowel Shift, which took place in the fifteenth/sixteenth centuries. Briefly, five of the long vowels were raised by one degree; the remaining two were diphthongized:

aː > æː; ɛː > eː; eː > iː; ɔː >oː; oː > uː; iː > əi > ay; uː > aw

The new long values were subsequently (through the eighteenth and nineteenth centuries) diphthongized by the introduction of a glide to reach their present values: cf.

Middle English	Early Modern English	Seventeenth Century	Present-day
nāme /naːmə/	/næm/	/neːm/	/neːjm/ *name*
/stoːn/	/stoːn/	/stoːn/	/stōun/ *stone*
/ɔpən/	/oːpən/	/oːpən/	/ōupn/ *open*
/wiːn/	/wəin/	/wəin/	/wājn/ *wine*
/greːn/	/griːn/	/griːn/	/grījn/ *green*

Short vowels:

a > æ; ɪ, ɛ, u, ɔ unchanged through the sixteenth century
    > ɪ, ɛ, ʌ, ɔ in the seventeenth century
    > ɪ, ɛ, ɐ, ɔ in Modern English

e.g. [sune] > [sʌn] > [sɐn].

Consonants

The consonantal inventory of Modern English is:

stops, p, b, t, d, k, g
affricates: tʃ, dʒ
fricatives: f, v, θ, ð, s, z, ʃ, ʒ, h
nasals: m, n, ŋ, ɲ
lateral and flap: l, r
semi-vowels: j, w

All the stops have a measure of aspiration; /t/ and /d/ are retroflex rather than dental. All can be initial except /ŋ/; all can be medial; /h/ and /w/ cannot be final. Initial /ʒ/ occurs only in loan-words: genre /ʒãːr/.

Consonantal changes in transition from late Middle English/Early Modern English to present-day Standard:

1. /θ, s, f/ are voiced in weak syllables in the modern language: e.g. in gen. case: *mannes* /manəs/ > *man's* /mænz/; *with* /wiθ/ > /wið/
2. /c/ voiced to /dʒ/: cf. Middle English *knọwlẹ̆che* > /nɪldʒ/
3. /s/ > /z/ between weak and strong vowel: *disease* /dɪzīz/
4. Middle English /h/ represented /ç/ or /xʷ/; both lost in Modern English:

   Middle English /nɪçt/ > /nɪht/ > /nɪːt/ > /nəit/ > /najt/ *night*
   /θouxʷt/ > /θɔːt/ *thought*

5. In Modern English /r/ tends to Ø except before a vowel; this proviso includes the so-called 'intrusive r': 'law and order' pronounced as /laːwr.ənd.ɔːdə/ Cf. here = /hiə/; her = /həː/; star = /staː/
6. /l/ was elided, from the sixteenth century onwards, between a labial vowel and a consonant: e.g. *half* > /haːf/. Cf. elision of /w/ in *towards* → /tɔːdz/.
7. /k/ dropped before /n/: *know* (sixteenth century /knou/) > /nōu/.

Stress

In Old and Middle English, the main stress was on the root syllable of inflected words. In Modern English, stress may be on almost any syllable of a word in citation form; often, variants are permissible, e.g. *cóntroversy/contróversy*. In ordinary speech, stress tends to be evenly distributed over the phrasal contour, with particles, prepositions, articles in the dips. Stress is phonemic in doublets: cf. *éxtract* (noun) – *extráct* (verb); *ábsent* (adjective) – *absént* (verb).

MORPHOLOGY AND SYNTAX

The definite article is realized as /ðə/ before consonants, as /ði/ before vowels. The now prevalent use of *a/an* as an indefinite article became generalized in the Middle English period.

Noun

Only two inflections survive – the genitive -*s* = /z/ or /s/ and the plural marker -*s*, /z/ or /s/. The apostrophe is used to separate the genitive -*s* from the singular or collective noun; the genitive of a noun with -*s* plural is marked by ': thus, singular: *boy's* pl.: boys'; collective: *men's*. A few mutated plurals survive: e.g. *mouse – mice*, *goose – geese*, etc.

Adjective

All adjectives are indeclinable.

Pronoun

Up to a point, the Middle English system survives. In the first person, both singular and plural have direct and oblique forms: *I – me*; *we – us*.

In the singular, the second person is obsolete, and the plural has been levelled to a single form: *you*.

Third person: here, the gender distinction has been preserved plus oblique forms: masc. *he – him*; fem. *she – her*; nt: *it – it*. The plural is levelled to the common form: *they – them*.

Verb

Overall, there is a general reduction from the Middle English inventory to four forms: e.g. for the verb OE *bindan*, ME *bīnde(n)*, Modern English *bind*: *bind*, *binds* (3rd person present indicative), *bound* (past tense), *binding* (present participle). Archaic forms may appear in set phrases, e.g. *his bounden duty*, where *bounden* is the old past participle (*i*)*bounden*.

Extreme reductionism has led to confusion between certain verbs, e.g. between the intransitive *lie*, whose past tense is *lay*, and the transitive verb *lay*, the former being levelled to the latter: Standard *he lay there* being accompanied in sub-standard usage by **he laid there/he was laying there*. Such a confusion is impossible in German, for example, where the verbs *liegen* and *legen* have remained distinct.

Prepositions

In Old English, prepositions governed the dative, the accusative, or the genitive. The static (dative case) versus dynamic (accusative case) opposition was found, as in Modern German.

In Modern English it is natural to close a sentence with a preposition, or even two (*the man I spoke to*; *what I have to put up with*) depending on the specific requirements of the sense-verb. The practice, which is also to be found in the Scandinavian languages, has been questioned on purist and stylistic grounds. Extreme simpicity of accidence, however, merits an equivalent degree of syntactical flexibility. Together, they help to make English, with its internationally enriched vocabulary of half a million words, readily accessible to, and usable by its global community.

1. On frymðe wæs Word, and þæt Word wæs mid Gode, and God wæs þæt Word.
2. Þæt wæs on fruman mid Gode.
3. Ealle þing wæron geworhte ðurh hyne; and nān þing næs geworht būtan him.
4. Þæt wæs līf þe on him geworht wæs; and þæt līf wæs manna lēoht.
5. And þæt lēoht lȳht on ðȳstrum; and þȳstro þæt ne genāmon.
6. Mann wæs fram Gode āsend, þæs nama wæs Iohannes.
7. Ðēs cōm tō gewitnesse, þæt hē gewitnesse cȳðde be ðām lēohte, þæt ealle menn þurh hyne gelȳfdon.
8. Næs hē lēoht, ac þæt hē gewitnesse forð bære be þām lēohte.

Old English (West Saxon)

1 In the bigynnynge was the word, *that is, Goddis sone,* and the word was at 2 God, and God was the word. This was 3 in the bigynnynge at God. Alle thingis ben maad by hym, and with outen him is maad noȝt, that thing that is maad. 4 Was lyf in him, and the lyf was the liȝt 5 of men; and the liȝt schyneth in derk- 6 nessis, and derknessis tooken not it. A man was sent fro God, to whom the name 7 was Joon. This man cam in to witness- inge, that he schulde bere witnessinge of the liȝt, that alle men schulden bileue bi 8 him. He was not the liȝt, but that he 9 schulde bere witnessing of the liȝt.

Middle English (Wyclif's translation)

N the beginning was that Word , and that word was with God , and that Word was God.

2 This fame was in the beginning with God.

3 All things were made by it , and without it was made nothing that was made.

4 In it was life , and that life was the light of men.

5 And that light ſhineth in the darkneſſe and the darkneſſe comprehended it not.

6 ¶ There was a man ſent from God, whoſe name *was* Iohn.

7 *This ſame* came for a witneſſe, to beare witneſſe of that light , that all men through him might beleeue.

8 Hee was not that light , but *was ſent* to beare witneſſe of that light.

Early Modern English (the King James Version)

1 In the beginning the Word already was. The Word was in God's presence, and what God was, the Word was. [2] He was with God at the beginning, [3] and through him all things came to be; without him no created thing came into being. [4] In him was life, and that life was the light of mankind. [5] The light shines in the darkness, and the darkness has never mastered it. [6] There appeared a man named John. He was sent from God, [7] and came as a witness to testify to the light, so that through him all might become believers. [8] He was not himself the light; he came to bear witness to the light.

Contemporary English

ESKIMO-ALEUT LANGUAGES

Eskimo is spoken, in several dialect forms, over a vast area stretching from Greenland through the Arctic regions of Canada into Alaska and Siberia. Two main dialects are distinguished: Inuit in Greenland, northern Canada, and part of Alaska, Yupik in Alaska and Siberia. The total number of Eskimo speakers is estimated at c. 85,000, the overwhelming majority of whom speak Inuit. Aleut, genetically related to Eskimo, is still spoken by a few hundred people in the Aleutian Islands.

In the most recent classification of the world's languages (Greenberg 1985) Eskimo-Aleut is treated as part of a Euro-Asiatic phylum, which also includes the Indo-European family and the Altaic languages (in the wider sense, i.e. including Japanese and Korean).

See **Aleut**, **Inuit**.

ESTONIAN

INTRODUCTION

A member of the Balto-Finnic group of Finno-Ugric, Estonian is the official language of the Estonian Soviet Socialist Republic, where it is spoken by about 1 million people. There are several thousand speakers in other parts of the USSR, and some large emigré groups – for example around 70,000 in North America. The language is divided into two markedly divergent dialect groups: Northern (Tallinna keel) and Southern (Tartu keel). In their extreme forms these come close to being mutually unintelligible. The modern literary standard is based on the Northern (Tallinn) form. Centuries of German influence are reflected in the vocabulary of Estonian.

Writing in Estonian dates from the sixteenth century when religious tracts were produced in both dialects. Translation of the New Testament soon followed, and a complete Bible in 1739. A hundred years later, the appearance of Lönnroth's *Kalevala* in Finland (*see* **Finnish**) was quickly followed by the publication of a similar collection in Estonia – the *Kalevipoeg* (1857–61) edited by F.R. Kreutzwald, and by a similar upsurge of interest in the national folklore. The next important event in the history of Estonian literature was the emergence of the *Noor Eesti* group in the early twentieth century – 'Young Estonia', whose members were mainly interested in experimental verse. The period of independence in the 1920s and 1930s is the richest in Estonian literature; the main figures are the poetess Marie Under, and the novelist Anton Tammsaare, whose great novel *Tõde ja Õigus* (1926–36) offers a panoramic and detailed study of a crucial period in Estonian life, the transition from the nineteenth to the twentieth century.

SCRIPT

Roman alphabet + *ä, ö, ü, õ*; *c, f, q, w, x, y, z* occur only in recent loan-words. *õ* is a central vowel close to /ə/ but unrounded.

PHONOLOGY

Consonants

stops: p, t, k
fricatives: v, s, h

nasals: m, n
lateral and flap: l, r
semi-vowels: j

/p, t, k/ are unaspirated and voiceless, represented in the script by *b*, *d*, *g*; they are always short. When written as *p*, *t*, *k* they are long; when written with gemination: *pp*, *tt*, *kk* they are overlong.

PALATALIZATION
The palatalized consonants are /t′, n′, s′, l′/, not notated in script. The gradation from short to long and overlong, which affects other consonants as well as the stops, is accompanied by an increase in tenseness and a forward shift in articulation.

CONSONANT GRADATION
(*See* **Finnish**) exists in Estonian, although the phonological conditions which generate the phenomenon are no longer always present. For example, the typical Balto-Finnic genitive ending *-n* has been lost in Estonian; but *jalg* 'foot', still makes a genitive *jala*, representing former **jalan*.

Vowels

front: i, e, ɛ, œ, y
middle: ə (unrounded)
back: a, o, u

Like the consonants, the vowels, too, have three degrees of phonemic length; cf. *sada* /sada/, 'hundred'; *saada* /saːda/, 'they came'; *saada* /saːːda/, 'to receive'.

VOWEL HARMONY
Has been lost in Estonian, though there are residual traces in some southern dialects.

Stress

Stress is always on the first syllable. Any vowel of any length may appear in the first syllable; in subsequent syllables, only *a*, *e*, *i*, *u* appear.

MORPHOLOGY AND SYNTAX

Noun

No gender; no articles. There are two numbers and 14 cases. The plural nominative marker is always *-d*. The key case endings are:

Singular: nom. Ø; gen. a vowel; part. Ø, *-d/t*, or a vowel
Pural: nom. *-d*; gen. *-de/te/e*; part. *-d*

The other cases are all constructed on the genitive base: e.g. inessive *-s*, elative *-st*, adessive *-l*, translative *-ks*.

Some examples of case usage:

genitive: *Eesti keele õpetaja* 'a teacher of the Estonian language';
partitive: *Leiba on laual* 'There is some bread on the table';
inessive: *Mina elan linnas* 'I live in the town';
elative: *Mina tulen linnast* 'I come out of the town';
essive: *Ta töötab arstina* 'He works as a doctor';
translative: *Sõja ajal sai ta ohveritseriks* 'During the war he became an officer.'

Adjective

As attribute, adjective precedes the noun and is declined in concord with it, in most, but not all, cases: e.g. *punane raamat* 'a red book'; *punased raamatud* 'red books'; *punases raamatus* 'in a red book'; *punastes raamatutes* 'in red books'.

COMPARATIVE
-m is added to the genitive: e.g. *Tema on minust tugevam* 'He is stronger than I am.'

Pronoun

Personal independent forms: long and short:

Singular: 1 *mina/ma*, 2 *sina/sa*, 3 *tema/ta*;
Plural: 1 *meie/me*, *teie/te*, 3 *nemad/nad*.

These are fully declined in 14 cases.

DEMONSTRATIVE PRONOUN
see 'this', pl. *need*; *too* 'that', pl. *tood*.

INTERROGATIVE PRONOUN
kes 'who?'; *mis* 'what?'.

RELATIVE PRONOUN
As interrogative: e.g. *raamat, mis lamab laual* 'the book which is lying on the table'.

Numerals

1–10: *üks, kaks, kolm, neli, viis, kuus, seitse, kaheksa, üheksa, kümme*; 11 *üksteist*; 12 *kaksteist*; 20 *kakskümmend*; 30 *kolmkümmend*; 100 *sada*. The numerals 2–10 are fully declined in all cases; from 11 onwards, the decade component in the oblique forms is invariable in genitive form; the unit component is declined: e.g. 20 *kakskümmend*; inessive **kahekümnes**; illative **kahekümnesse**.

Verb

Conjugational models depend on whether the stem is mutating or not. All forms of the Estonian verb can be constructed from four basic forms:

1. 1st infinitive in *-ma*;
2. 2nd infinitive in *-da/-ta/-a*;
3. 1st person present indicative;
4. passive past participle in *-tud/-dud*.

The indicative mood has four tenses: two simple and two compound. There is no future tense. As in Finnish, the auxiliary for the compound tenses is *olema* = Fin. *olla*, with present and past forms close to those in Finnish. Again as in Finnish, all positive verb forms have parallel negative forms; but whereas the negative particle is conjugated in Finnish (*en*, *et*, *ei*, etc.), Estonian has only the single form *ei*, used with all persons and both numbers. This means that the personal pronoun must be used:

SPECIMEN CONJUGATION
kirjutama 'to write':

> Indicative present: sing. *kirjutan*, *kirjutad*, *kirjutab*; pl. *kirjutame*, *kirjutate*, *kirjutavad*;
> Indicative present negative version: *ei kirjuta* (preceded by personal pronoun);
> Indicative past: *kirjutasin*, *kirjutasid*, etc.;
> Negative: *ei kirjutanud*;
> Compound past tense: *mina olen kirjutanud*, *sina oled* ..., *mina oleme* ...;
> Negative: e.g. *mina ei ole kirjutanud*.

Note reduction in Estonian to an omnibus form of the past participle, where Finnish marks number: *olen sanonut*, *olemme sanoneet*.

MOODS

> Conditional: the marker is *-ksi-* + usual endings: e.g. *mina kirjutaksin*;
> Imperative: 2nd p. sing. *kirjuta*, 2nd p. pl. *kirjutage*; negative: *ära kirjuta*, pl. *ärge kirjutage*;
> Inferential: present, *-vat*; past, *olevat* + past participle: e.g. (*Ma kuulsin, et*) *tema õppivat ülikoolis arstiteadust* '(I hear that) he's studying medicine at the university'; *Ta sõitvat homme Moskvasse* 'So he's going to Moscow tomorrow.'

IMPERSONAL FORMS
Present in *-takse/-dakse/-akse*; past in *-ti/-di*: e.g. *linnas ehitakse maja* 'a house is being built/they're building a house in the town' (*maja* is in nominative case); *pargis jalutatakse* lit. 'it-is-gone-walking' = 'one goes walking in the park'; *räägitakse, et* ... 'it is said that ...'

PARTICIPLES

Present in -*v* (active and passive): e.g. *lugev* 'reading'; *loetav* 'being read'; *lugevad inimesed* 'people who are reading'; *loetavad raamatud* 'books that are being read'. Past in -*nud*: e.g. *Kirjutanud kirja, läks ta jalutama* 'After writing the letter he went for a walk.'

The last example also illustrates the use of the infinitive in -*ma* after verbs of motion. The infinitive in -*da* is used with such modal verbs as *oskama* 'to be able to', *tahtma* 'to want to': e.g. *Tema oskab hästi laulda* 'He can sing well.'

It is interesting to note that the partitive/accusative opposition may be used to express tense: cf.

> *ostan raamatut* 'I'm buying a/the book' (partitive case – present tense);
> *ostan raamatu* 'I shall buy the book' (accusative case – future tense).

VERBAL PARTICLES

Estonian has a rich inventory of verbal particles, whose function is (a) modification of root sense, (b) aspectual, (c) directional. They are separable: e.g. *valmis tegema* 'to complete': *ta **tegi** selle töö kiiresti **valmis*** 'He did that work quickly (and finished it)'.

Some further examples:

> *alla* 'down': *alla tulistama* 'to shoot down';
> *edasi* 'onwards': *edasi töötama* 'to go on working';
> *järele* 'after': *järele jääma* 'to be left over';
> *kinni* 'shut': *kinni võtma* 'to lay hold on'.

Postpositions

Most take the genitive case. Some occur in more than one form, inflected in line with case endings. For example, from *äär* 'margin':

> *äärde* 'towards': *Läheme mere äärde* 'We go towards the sea';
> *ääres* 'at': *Istume mere ääres* 'We sit by the sea';
> *äärest* 'from': *Tuleme mere äärest* 'We come from the sea.'

Word order

SVO is normal.

1 Alguses oli Sõna, ja Sõna oli Jumala juures, ja Sõna oli Jumal.

2 Seesama oli alguses Jumala juures.

3 Kõik on tekkinud tema läbi, ja ilma temata ei ole tekkinud midagi, mis on tekkinud.

4 Temas oli elu, ja elu oli inimeste valgus,

5 ja valgus paistab pimeduses, ja pimedus ei ole seda võtnud omaks.

6 Oli mees, Jumala läkitatud; selle nimi oli Johannes.

7 See tuli tunnistuseks, tunnistama valgusest, et kõik usuksid tema kaudu.

8 Tema ei olnud mitte valgus, vaid ta tuli tunnistama valgusest.

(Tallinna keel)

ETHIOPIC

INTRODUCTION

Ethiopic (or *Ge'ez*; *lesana ge'ez* 'the Ge'ez language') is in origin a South Arabian dialect carried to Ethiopia by the Semitic settlers who laid the foundations of the Aksumite Kingdom at some time in the last millennium BC. By the fourth/fifth century AD, Aksum had grown to be the most powerful economic and political centre in north-east Africa. It was converted to Christianity in the fourth century and Ethiopic literature is entirely and exclusively associated with the Christian Church. In these centuries, the language lost some of its South Arabian features, and gradually split into two branches – a Northern, from which Tigrinya and Tigre were to develop, and a Southern, which is the ancestor of Amharic and of several smaller Ethiopian languages (Argobba, Gafat, Sidamo, etc.).

The history of Ethiopic literature falls into three clearly defined periods:

1. The Aksum period: many pillar inscriptions of considerable historical interest, and the first Bible translation (from Greek sources). This period covers the fourth to the seventh centuries, during which Ethiopic was a living language.
2. Seventh to thirteenth centuries. After the Islamic invasions in the seventh century nothing at all seems to have been written in Ethiopic; at all events nothing remains.
3. Thirteenth to twentieth centuries. In this period a literary revival took place in Ethiopic which was no longer a living language. Bible translation recommenced, but now from Arabic sources. Original writing includes the outstanding *Kebra Nagast*, the 'Glory of the Kings', which contains *inter alia* the story of the Queen of Sheba's visit to King Solomon. There is an extensive hagiography and miracle literature, e.g. the sixteenth-century *Th'āmra Māryām*, the 'Miracles of Mary'.

SCRIPT

The Ethiopic syllabary, also used for Amharic, Tigrinya, and Tigre. This was originally a purely consonantal script. In the fourth century the system was introduced whereby the consonantal matrix is modulated to mark the vocalism. The seven orders are: *ä, u, i, ā, ē, ĕ, o*.

428

PHONOLOGY

Consonants

stops: p, p', b, t, t', d, d', k, q, g, ʔ
fricatives: f, s, s', ʃ, h, ħ, ḫ, ʕ
nasals: m, n
lateral and flap: l, r
semi-vowels: j, w

The ejectives /t', p', s', d'/ are notated as dotted letters: ṭ, p̣, ṣ, ḍ.

Vowels

ɛ, u, i, aː, eː, e, o

MORPHOLOGY AND SYNTAX

Noun

Nouns are masculine or feminine, the latter being usually marked by -(*a*)*t*. Masculine nouns are not overtly marked. The gender of a nominal is often clear from verbal and/or pronominal concord. Some nouns, e.g. *'ayn* 'eye', *sayf* 'sword', *arwē* 'wild animal', are unstable in gender.

NUMBER
Singular and plural. Certain triradical patterns are used almost exclusively as plural forms: e.g. *a*.12.*ā*.3, *a*.12.*e*.3.*t*; where 1, 2, 3 are radicals; *sayf* 'sword', pl. *asyāf*; *lebs* 'clothes', pl. *albās*; *bet* 'house', pl. *abyāt*. There are, of course, many other broken plural patterns. The sound, or unbroken plural is in -*ān*, -*āt*.

CASE
Ethiopic has retained an oblique (objective) case marked by -*a*/-*e*, but has lost both the nominative -*u* (retained in Classical Arabic) and, surprisingly, the genitive marker in -*i*.

The nominative -*u* reappears in some examples of pronominal affixation: e.g. *abu.hu* 'his father'.

Construct formula: X-*a* Y: e.g. *bet.a negus* 'the king's house'; *mangest.a samāyāt* 'the kingdom of heaven'. The genitive relationship may also be expressed by means of the relative pronoun *za*, or the preposition *la*: e.g. *gabr za.negus* 'the king's servant'; *ba.mawā'eli.hom.u la nagast za.'aksum* 'in the days of the kings of Aksum'.

Adjective

There are very few primary adjectives. Some derived adjectives are formed on such nominal formulae as 1.*a*/*e*.2.*ā*.3.*i*, e.g. *bezāwi* 'redeeming', *nabābi* 'eloquent'; or with the suffix -*awi*, e.g. *nafusāwi* 'windy', *'amānāwi* 'truthful'.

Pronoun

The independent forms with their bound objective enclitics are:

		Singular		Plural	
1		ana	-ya, -ni	neḥna	-na
2	masc.	anta	-ka	antemu	-kemu
	fem.	anti	-ki	anten	-ken
3	masc.	we'etu	-hu, -u, -o	emuntu/we'etomu	-homu, -omu
	fem.	ye'eti	-hā, -ā	emantu/we'eton	-hon, -on

The bound forms are used (a) as possessive markers, e.g. *faras.ka* 'your horse', *nesḥāhomu* 'their penitence'; (b) as objective marker, e.g. *qatal.o* 'he killed him', *qatal.ā* 'he killed her', *qatal.omu* 'he killed them'.

DEMONSTRATIVE PRONOUN/ADJECTIVE
Masc. *we'etu*, fem. *ye'eti*, pl. *we'etomu* 'this/these'; masc. *zentu*, fem. *zāti*, pl. *ellontu*, *ellāntu* 'that, those'.

INTERROGATIVE PRONOUN
mannu 'who?'; *ment* 'what?'.

RELATIVE PRONOUN
The interrogatives can be used, or the relative pronoun *za* (masc.) with feminine form *enta*, and common plural *ella/ellā*: e.g. *be'esi za.mase'a* 'the man who came'; *be'esit enta mase'at* 'the woman who came'.

Numerals

1–10: *aḥadu*, *kele'ētu*, *šalastu*, etc.: i.e. standard South Semitic forms, with feminine counterparts. As in Arabic, the law of inverse polarity holds (*see* **Arabic**). In Ethiopic, the pronominal suffix may be added to the numeral, when the referent is known to the speakers: e.g. *šalasti.**homu** 'eḍ(aw)* = *šalasti.**hu** 'eḍ (aw)* 'three trees'.

Verb

The Ethiopic verbal system has perfective and imperfective aspects; indicative, subjunctive, and imperative moods; and non-finite forms, e.g. gerund, present participle active, past participle passive, and infinitive. Gender is marked in the second and third persons singular and plural.

CONJUGATION
The perfective aspect and the gerund are suffixal; the imperfective and the subjunctive are circumfixal.

The perfective endings are largely standard South Semitic: e.g. *qatala* 'he killed': sing. 1 *qatal.ku*, 2 *-ka/-ki*, 3 *-a/-at*; pl. 1 *-na*, 2 *-kemu/-ken*, 3 *-u/-ā*.
Examples with bound pronominal object suffix: *nagar.ku.ka* 'I said to you'; *kalā'.ku.ki* 'I forbade you (fem.)'; *qatalu.w.omu* 'they killed them'.

IMPERFECTIVE
Marked by circumfixed personal affixes; stress on 1st root syllable.

		Singular	*Plural*
1		'e.qatel	ne.qatel
2	masc.	te.qatel	te.qatl.u
	fem.	te.qatel.i	te.qatl.ā
3	masc.	ye.qatel	ye.qatl.u
	fem.	te.qatel	ye.qatl.ā

The subjunctive shows accent shift and crasis; stress on prefixed marker: sing. 1 *e.qtel*, 2 *te.qtel/te.qtel.i*, 3 *ye.qtel*.

Imperative: masc. *qetel*; fem. *qetel.i*; pl. masc. *qetel.u*, fem. *qetel.ā*.

GERUND
E.g. from *nagara* 'to speak, say': *nagir.eya* 'when I said', *nagir.aka/-ki* 'when you said', *nagar.o/-a*.

DERIVED FORMS
In Ethiopic these are represented by

(a) a causative with *a-* prefix: e.g. *a.qtala* 'to cause to kill';
(b) reflexive–passive in *ta-*: *ta.qatla* 'to kill oneself';
(c) causative–reflexive in *asta-*: e.g. from *gabra* 'to do', *asta.gbara* 'to set to work'.

Intensive and durative aspects are formed, the first by gemination of the second radical, the second by lengthening the first vowel.

NEGATIVE
The marker is *'i*: e.g. *'i.qatala* 'did not kill'; *'i.yeqatel* 'does not kill'.
As in Arabic, weak and hollow verbs, and verbs with a laryngeal radical have specific paradigms.

Prepositions

Three are written prefixed to the noun: *la*, *ba*, and *'em*: e.g. *labet* 'to the house'; *la'ālama 'ālam* 'for all eternity'; *babet* 'in the house'; *bakenefa nafus* 'on the wing of the wind'; *'embeḥēr sābā* 'from the land of Saba'.
The remaining prepositions are written separately: e.g. *'enta* 'in, towards', *'eska* 'as far as, up to', *diba* 'upon', *dehar* 'after'.

Word order

VSO is normal.

ም0ራፍ፡ δ፤

፩፤   ቀዳሚሁ፡ ቃል፡ ውእቱ፡ ወውእቱ፡ ቃል፡ ኀበ፡ እግዚአብሔር፡

፪፤ ውእቱ፡ ወእግዚአብሔር፡ ውእቱ፡ ቃል፡ ወዝንቱ፡ እምቀዲሙ፡ ኀበ፡

፫፤ እግዚአብሔር፡ ውእቱ ። ኵሉ፡ ቦቱ፡ ኮነ፡ ወዘእንበሌሁሰ፡ አልቦ፡ ዘከ

፬፤ ነ፡ ወኢምንትኒ፡ እምዘኮነ፡ ቦቱ፡ ሕይወት፡ ውእቱ፡ ወሕይወትሰ፡ ብር

፭፤ ሃኑ፡ ለእጓለ፡ እመሕያው፡ ውእቱ ። ወብርሃንሰ፡ ዘውስተ፡ ጽልመት፡ ያ

፮፤ በርህ፡ ወያርኢ፡ ወጽልመትኒ፡ ኢይረክቦ ። ወሀሎ፡ አሐዱ፡ ብእሲ፡ ዘ

፯፤ ተፈነወ፡ እምኀበ፡ እግዚአብሔር፡ ዘስሙ፡ ዮሐንስ ። ወውእቱ፡ መጽአ፡
    ለስምዕ፡ ሰማዕተ ᾽ ይኩን፡ በእንተ፡ ብርሃን፡ ከመ፡ ኵሉ፡ ይእመን፡ ቦ

፰፤ ቱ ። ወለሊሁሰ፡ ኢኮነ፡ ብርሃነ፡ ዳእሙ፡ ሰማዕተ፡ ይኩን፡ በእንተ፡ ብር

፱፤ ሃን ። ዘውእቱ፡ ብርሃነ፡ ጽድቅ፡ ዘያበርህ፡ ለኵሉ፡ ሰብእ፡ ዘይመጽእ፡ ው

Ι፤ ስተ፡ ዓለም ። ወውስተ፡ ዓለም፡ ሀሎ፡ ወዓለምኒ፡ ቦቱ፡ ኮነ፡ ወዓለምሰ፡
    ኢያእመሮ ።

ETRUSCAN

INTRODUCTION

The Etruscan League of City States, bounded by the Apennines, the Tiber, the Arno, and the sea, was Rome's northern neighbour throughout the latter half of the first millennium BC. The Etruscans appear in history about 900 BC. Their period of greatest political, economic, and ideological power lay in the eighth to sixth centuries BC. The following centuries saw a gradual decline in their influence, though the city states were not finally absorbed into the Roman Empire until the first century BC. The language ceased to be used for sacral purposes at about the same time. There is no way of knowing how long it survived as a spoken language.

In spite of repeated efforts to link Etruscan with Indo-European, with agglutinative languages of the Uralic type, and with Caucasian languages, no definite relationship with any other language family has ever been established. Etruscan was written in a Greek-type script which can be read without any great difficulty. The extant material consists of:

1. the Agram mummy-wrapping in the National Museum at Zagreb; the 281 lines contains about 1,300 words;
2. several medium-length texts, e.g. the Capua tablet (250 words), the Perugia tablet (125 words), and the Lemnos tablet (35 words);
3. several thousand short stereotyped inscriptions of a votive or funerary nature.

Thanks to the repetitive nature of these short inscriptions, it has been possible to allot meanings – a few with certainty, many tentative — to some hundreds of words, and to identify, again often tentatively, a number of inflectional endings and syntactic linking agents. Certain kinship terms such as *ati* 'mother', *clan* 'son', *sex* 'daughter', *puia* 'wife', and a few other words like *zilc* 'official', *spura* 'town', *rasna* 'Etruria', may be taken as authenticated beyond reasonable doubt. Failing the discovery of a substantial digloss, an Etruscan Rosetta Stone, the most promising line of attack on the undeciphered remainder would seem to lie in the so-called 'combinatorial method'. This involves the close collation of inscriptions containing both known nuclei and undeciphered material with the artefacts bearing them, in the hope that a recurrent feature in the artefact may prove to be accompanied by a similarly recurrent item in the text. In this way, new lexical items and syntactic formants – affixes, particles, etc. – may be isolated and tentatively interpreted.

SCRIPT

West Greek in origin, written from right to left. Individual forms vary over the 700 years of usage. From the sixth century onwards, words were divided from each other by markers consisting of three or four points. There is some evidence to suggest that Etruscan was originally written in a syllabic script.

PHONOLOGY

Pfiffig (1969) gives the following inventory:

Consonants

labials: p, ph, f, v, m
dentals: t, th, n, l, r
velars: k/q, kh, h
silbilants: z, s, ś = /ç/

There are four signs for /s/ in the Etruscan script.

Vowels

i, e, a, u figure in the script; it is assumed that /o/ was also present and notated as *u*.

MORPHOLOGY AND SYNTAX

Noun

There was, apparently, no grammatical gender. The fundamental opposition seems to have been between human and non-human categories. In late Etruscan, female proper names show a gender-related inflection: *-i/-ia*. The singular nominative is not specifically marked. The plural marker is -(V)*r*, with possible change of stem vowel, which also appears in the genitive:

clan 'son' – gen. *clens* – pl. *clenar*
spura town'   pl. *spurer*

For *spura* Pfiffig gives the following declension:

	Singular	Plural
nom./indefinite acc.	spura	spurer
definite acc.	spureni	spureri
genitive	spureś-	—
	spural	—
locative	spurethi	—

There seems to have been no dative case in the Indo-European sense. Genitive endings may be compounded.

Adjective

Few adjectives are known. The qualitative adjective was formed from the noun by affixation of

-*u*/-*iu*: cf. *ais* 'god', *aisiu* 'divine';

-*n*V: cf. *suthi* 'grave', *suthina* 'funerary';

-*cva*/*khva*, etc. (allophones depending on stem-final): cf. *math* 'intoxicating drink', *mathcva* 'intoxicating'.

Pronoun

The following forms are known: first person singular *mi*, with definite accusative *mini*; third person singular *an* 'he/she', gen. *enas*.

POSSESSIVE

Forms in -*sa*/*śa* (3rd p. sing.): e.g. *arnth veluś velusa* = *Arnth Veluś* 'he of Vel'.

DEMONSTRATIVE PRONOUN

Nominative and indefinite accusative forms *ca*/*ta*, plural *cei*/*tei*, may refer to different degrees of distance. The genitive forms are *cla*/*tla*, pl. *clal*, with definite accusative *cn*/*tn*; pl. *cnl*. The locative ending is -*thi*. Examples: *cn turce murila hercnas* 'Murila Hercnas gave this' (*tur-* 'to give'); *clthi śuthiti* 'in this grave'.

INTERROGATIVE PRONOUN

ipa 'who?'; with gen. *ipas*.

RELATIVE PRONOUN

ipa.

Numerals

1–6 inclusive are known with some certainty: *thu, zal, ci, sa, makh, huth*. 8 is probably *cezp*; *semph* and *nutph* may be 7 and 9. 10 *śar*; 20 *zathrum*; 19 *thunem zathrum*; 18 *eslem zathrum*; 30 *cialkh*; 40 *sealkh*; 50 *muvalkh*; 70 *semphalkh*. The word for 100 is not known. The ordinal for 1 is *thunśna*.

The basic opposition seems to be between aspects: imperfective and perfective. From the repetitive and stereotyped nature of the Etruscan votive and funerary inscriptions, it follows naturally that few finite verbal forms occur. The only regularly recurrent forms are the first and third persons singular perfective, and the second person singular imperative.

The verbal base is often a closed monosyllable. The Agram text yields such bases as *ar* 'to make', *rakh* 'to take', *puth* 'to place, put'. This base is also the base for adjectives and nominals: e.g. from *zikh* 'to write', *zikhina* 'appertaining to writing', *zikhu* 'scribe'.

The third person singular perfective (or preterite) is one of the most securely established identities in Etruscan: *-ce*: e.g. *tur.ce* 'he/she gave'; *aval.ce* 'he/she lived'; *zilakh.ce* 'he was praetor'. The first person form is *-cun*: e.g. *thapicun* 'I cursed'. A frequent form in *-a* may be a present/imperfective third person singular: e.g. *hecia* 'he puts'; *ara* 'he makes'; *mena* 'he brings'.

An optative form in *-e* has been identified: e.g. *satene* 'let him weep'; *ame* 'let him be'.

THE COPULA

The following forms are known: *am-* 'to be': 3rd p. sing. *ama*; preterite *amce*; optative *ame* 'let him be'. *-in* has been interpreted as a medio-passive formant: e.g. *thezin* 'is sacrificed'; *zikh.un.ce* 'was written'; *utince* 'was carried out'.

SUFFIXES

Examples:

-*thur* indicates local origin: e.g. *velthur* 'from Vulci' (*vel* 'Vulci');
-*cla* makes collectives: e.g. *sacni* 'holy'; *sacnicla* 'holy place' (where holy things are);
-*tra* identifies the group; e.g. *Vipinal.tra* 'Vipinal's people/followers';
-*za* forms diminutives: e.g. *murś* 'urn', *murza* 'a small urn'.

EVEN

INTRODUCTION

Known also as Lamut, this dialect complex belongs to the Northern Tungusic branch of the Altaic group of languages. Even is spoken in the Okhotsk region of the Khabarovsk Kray, in the Magadan Oblast, and Kamchatka, by some 6,000 Evens, i.e. about half of the total Even population.

A few religious texts in Even appeared in the middle of the nineteenth century. The present literary standard is based on the Ola dialect.

SCRIPT

Since the 1930s the Cyrillic script has been used, with the addition in 1958 of ӈ, and ө/ӫ.

PHONOLOGY

Consonants

stops: p, b, t, d, k, g (q)
affricates: ts, tʃ, dʒ
fricatives: ß/w, s, j, χ, γ, h
nasals: m, n, ɲ, ŋ
laterals: l, ł, ʎ
roll: r ($\rightarrow$ d/ᵈr/rᵈ)

Vowels

The vowel system shows a symmetrical division between five soft ('bright') vowels and five hard ('dark').

hard: ɪ, e, a, o, u
soft: i, ė, ə, ȯ, u̇

All ten are short, long, or diphthongized, giving 20 + values, inadequately notated in the script: e.g. /i, iː, ɪ, ɪː/ are all notated as и in Cyrillic. The Even vowel-harmony system depends on the contrast between the hard and soft series, the hard vowels being lower in pitch and more tense than their soft counterparts. According to Novikova (1968), the hard vowels tend to be pharyngealized in some Eastern Even dialects.

437

In non-initial position, short vowels tend to be reduced or shed, a reductionism which also distinguishes many Even words from their Evenki congeners: cf. Evenki *sāre* 'they know', Even *hār*.

Stress

On long syllables; if none, on word-final syllable.

MORPHOLOGY AND SYNTAX

The orthography used here is that of Rishes and Cincius (1952) in their Russko-Evenskij Slovar'.

Noun

As in Evenki, the plural marker is *-l/-r* (stem-final *-n* drops): e.g. *dyū* 'house', pl. *dyūl*; *oron* 'reindeer', pl. *oror*. The following affixes are also used to mark plurality: *-til*, *-nil*, *-sil* (vowel harmony variable): e.g. aman 'father', pl. *amtıl*; *even* 'Even', pl. *evesel*.

SPECIMEN DECLENSION
dyū 'house' (notated as *ʒū* by Novikova (1968), and Benzing (1955)).

accusative	dyūv	ablative I	dyūduk
dative	dyūdū	ablative II	dyūgīč
adessive	dyūtkī	instrumental	dyūč
locativee	dyūlā	comitative	dyūnyun

There are also specific endings to express motion along something: *-lī/-klī*. Plural is *dyūl* + case affixes as singular.

POSSESSIVE SUFFIXES
Three-fold series depending on stem-final; e.g. the series following a final vowel is: sing. 1 *-v*, 2 *-s*, 3 *-n*; pl. 1 excl. *-(w)un*, incl. *-t*, 2 *-san*, 3 *-tan*. Examples: *dyū.v* 'my house', *dyū.s* 'your house'. These affixes are added to case affixes: e.g. *dyūdūv* 'to my house'.

To express contingent/alienable possession, the relative infix *-ng-* is used. Rishes and Cincius (1952) give the following example: *min dəlu* 'my (own) head'; *min dəlangu* 'my head (of animal killed by me)'. For *min*, see **Pronoun** below.

Adjective

As attribute, adjective precedes noun and is in concord with it for case: e.g. *ōmat dyū* 'new house'; *nyamdū dyūdū* 'in the warm house'; *bi kučukən bisəm* 'I am small'; *bu kučukər bisu* = we are small (i.e. concord for number).

COMPARATIVE

E.g. *muran oronduk əgdedmər* 'the horse is bigger than the reindeer', where *-duk* is the ablative case, and *-dmər* is an intensifying affix following *əgde(n)* 'big'.

Pronoun

PERSONAL INDEPENDENT

Sing.: 1 *bī*, 2 *hī*, 3 *nongan*; pl. 1 inc. *mut*, excl. *bū*, 2 *hū*, 3 *nongartan*. These are declined in all cases, with suppletive bases in oblique first singular and exclusive plural: e.g. for first person singular, *bī*: acc. *minu*, gen. *min* dat. *mindu*, abl. *minduk*, loc. *mindulə̄*, comitative *miññun* with three directional cases, an instrumental and an elative; e.g. *Nongan mindulə̄ dagamrīn* 'he came up to me.'

DEMONSTRATIVE PRONOUN

ərək 'this', pl. *ərəl*; *tarāk* 'that', pl. *taral*. Declined in all cases.

INTERROGATIVE PRONOUN

ngī 'who?'; *yak* 'what?'. Declined in all cases.

Numerals

1–10: *umən*, *dyūr*, *yelan*, *dɪgən*, *tunngan*, *nyungən*, *nadan*, *dyapkan*, *uyūn*, *mēn*; 11 *mēn-umən*; 12 *mēn-dyūr*; 20 *dyūrmēr*; 30 *yelanmēr*; 100 (*umən*) *nyama*.

Verb

The Even verb is marked for aspect, voice, mood, tense, person, number. Non-finite forms behave partly as verbs, partly as nominals.

ASPECT

Over a dozen markers generate various aspectual meanings in stems. For example, *-l-* is inceptive: cf. *hōng.dāy* 'to weep', *hōng.a.l.dāy* 'to burst into tears'; *-dyan-/-dyen-* is reiterative: cf. *ngəndə̄y* 'to go', *ngən.e.dyen.də̄y* 'to keep on going'.

VOICE

The active voice has no special marker. The passive voice has *-v-*, *-u-*, *-m-*: e.g. *baktāy* 'to find', *Oron mindu bak.a.v.ran* 'The reindeer was found by me' (*mindu* is dative of *bi* 'I').

CAUSATIVE

-vkan-/-vken-: e.g. *ōdāy* 'to do', *ōvkan* 'cause to be done'; *hādāy* 'to know', *hāvkan* 'let something be known'.

RECIPROCAL

-mač-/-meč-, with variants: e.g. *ukčə̄ndə̄y* 'to speak': *ukčə̄n.məč.tə̄y* → *ukčə̄n.məttə̄y* 'to converse'.

MOOD

There are indicative, imperative, subjunctive, potential, and presumptive moods. Tense is distinguished only in the indicative (present, past, future) and in the imperative (present, future).

TENSE

Unless the present tense is specifically marked for an imperfective aspect (e.g. inceptive, reiterative) it can be translated as present or past: e.g. *bi bakram* 'I find/I found'; the reasoning being that the action, if not inceptive etc., is complete.

Novikova (1968) distinguishes three classes of verb based on present indicative: (a) active verbs with affix based on *-r(a)* or variant; (b) stative verbs, with affix based on *-s(a)* or variant; (c) verbs denoting change of state, transfer, etc. with affix based on *-d(a)*, etc. Examples: (a) *ma.**ra**.m* 'I kill(ed)'; (b) *en.**sa**.m* 'I am sick'; (c) *nē.**da**.m* 'I put'.

SPECIMEN CONJUGATION

Indicative present, past, and future of *ngəndəy* 'to go':

			Present	*Past*	*Future*
sing.	1		ngən.**rəm**	ngən.rī.**v**	ngən.dī.**m**
	2		ngən.**ənri**	ngən.rī.**s**	ngən.dī.**nri**
	3		ngən.**rən**	ngən.rī.**n**	ngən.dī.**n**
plural	1	incl.	ngən.**rəp**	ngən.rī.**t**	ngən.dī.**p**
		excl.	ngən.**ru**	ngən.rī.**vun**	ngən.dī.**ru**
	2		ngən.**əs**	ngən.rī.**sən**	ngən.dī.**s**
	3		ngən.**rə**	ngən.rī.**tən**	ngən.dī.**r**

NEGATIVE FORMS

The negative verb *ədəy*, conjugated for person, tense, and mood, is used with a stable participial form of the sense-verb (based on *-r/s/d-*, *see* above): e.g. *bi hāram* 'I know', *bi əsəm hār* 'I don't know'; similarly, *hi əsənri hār*, *nongan əsni hār*; *bi əsəm dukra* 'I don't write'; *bi əču dukra* 'I didn't write'; *bi ətəm dukra* 'I shan't write'.

As in Evenki, *ač-* is an existential negator: e.g. *nongan ač hutlə̄* 'she has no children'.

PARTICIPIAL FORMS

These are tense-related, e.g. forms in *-ri*, *di/ti*, *si* with the present, in *-ča/čə* with the past, in *dnga/dnge* with the future. In the absence of a relative pronoun, these forms provide the framework for qualifying/modifying information sited on left hand of verb: e.g. *bi knigav tang.ri.v nyārīkām ittɪn* 'I saw the boy (who was) reading the book' (*tang.ri* is participial form + *-v* acc. marker).

Concomitant action is expressed by *-niqan/-niken*: e.g. *nongan, tetniken, gunin* ... 'while dressing, he said ...' *-mi* 'when ...'/'if ...': e.g. *Ngən.mi hinu ittan* 'When he came he saw you.'

Postpositions

Most of these are nouns in the locative case + possessive marker -*n*: e.g. *do* 'interior' + loc. *-lā*: *dyū dolān* 'in the house'; *oy* 'upper side': *stol oylān* 'on the table'.

There is also an extensive inventory of emotive and evaluative affixes.

Word order

SOV.

EVENKI

INTRODUCTION

Also known as Tungus, Evenki belongs to the Northern Tungusic branch of Altaic. There are are about 25,000 Evenki, and roughly half of them speak the Evenki language. The Evenki National Region is in area not far short of 1 million square kilometres, and in addition the Evenki live in the Buryat Autonomous Soviet Socialist Republic, in northern China, and elsewhere, spread over a vast wilderness extending from the Nenets area on the Yenisei to the Sea of Okhotsk and Sakhalin Island in the east. The many dialects are grouped in Northern, Southern, and Eastern main divisions. A key distinction between them lies in their respective treatment of sibilants: e.g. the verb 'to know' is *xami* in Northern, *sami* in Eastern, and *sami* or *šami* in Southern Evenki. Similarly, 'woman' is *axi* in Eastern and Northern dialects, *asi* or *aši* in Southern.

Written Evenki dates from 1931. Several Russian classics have been translated into a literary standard based on s-type dialects.

SCRIPT

After a period of romanization in the 1930s, Cyrillic was adopted; н is used to represent the velar nasal (here notated as *ng*).

PHONOLOGY

Consonants

> stops: p, b, t, d, k, g
> affricate: tʃ, dʒ
> affricatives: (f) ß, s, x, j, γ
> nasals: m, n ɲ, ŋ
> lateral: l
> roll: r

Assimilation takes place at junctures; e.g. affix initial after a nasal: *oron.vo* → *oronmo*.

Vowels

> short: i, a, ə, o, u
> long: i, e, a, ə, o, u

For purposes of vowel harmony, the vowels are classified as (a) hard: /a, aː, eː, o, oː/; soft: /ə, əː/; neutral: /i, iː, u, uː/. Vasiljevich (1958) describes Evenki vowel harmony as 'stepped'; i.e., short vowels are sensitive to an immediate preceding long vowel, and as a result vowel harmony may switch register more than once in the course of a long word.

Stress

Free; varies according to presence or absence of long vowels.

MORPHOLOGY AND SYNTAX

Noun

No grammatical gender, no articles. There are two numbers, with plural in -*l*/-*r*: e.g. *oron* 'reindeer', pl. *oror*; *bira* 'river', pl. *biral*.

DECLENSION

The endings given here for illustrative purposes have hard vowels, i.e. are in concord with roots having back vowels: case marker follows number marker:

> definite accusative: -*va*/-*pa*/-*ma*
> indefinite accusative: -*ya*/-*a*
> dative, locative: -*dū*/*tū*, eg. *biradū bidem* 'I live on the river'
> directional: -*tki*
> allative: -*lā*/-*dulā*, e.g. *xargilā* 'into the forest'
> ablative: -*duk*; -*git*/-*kit*/-*ngit*
> instrumental: -*t*/-*di*, e.g. *adilit* 'with a net'

There are further locative and directional cases.

POSSESSIVE AFFIXES

	Singular	Plural
1	-v/m	excl. -wun; incl. -t
2	-s	-sun
3	-n	-tin

A specific set of possessive suffixes with the -*ng*(*i*) marker is used to denote contingent and alienable possessions: e.g. *guləngiv* 'my hut' (= the hut I happen to be using).

In the possessive relationship, the posssessed noun, with proper affix, follows possessor: e.g. *oron dilin* 'reindeer its-head' = 'the reindeer's head'; *čalban awdannalin* 'the leaves of the birch-tree'.

Adjective

As attribute, adjective precedes noun and is inflected for number and case: e.g. *ayaldū ōmaktaldū guləldū* 'in nice new houses' (*aya* 'good'; *ōmakta* 'new'; *gulu* 'house').

COMPARATIVE
Made with *-tmar/-mar/-dimar* (with harmonic variants): e.g. *aya* 'good', *ayatmar* 'better'.

Pronoun

PERSONAL INDEPENDENT FORMS

	Singular	Plural
1	bi (oblique base, *min-*)	excl. bū, incl. mit
2	si (oblique base, *sin-*)	su
3	nungan	nungartin

These are declined in all cases.

DEMONSTRATIVE PRONOUNS
ər 'this', *tar* 'that'; plural forms: *əril, taril*. In subordinate clauses, *tar* may replace a personal pronoun: e.g. *tar əmərəkiv* 'when I came' (*əmə* 'to come'; *-rək-* is relative marker; *-v* = 1st p. sing. marker).

INTERROGATIVE PRONOUN
ngī 'who?'; *ēkun* 'what?' (plural forms: *ngīl; ēkur*).

RELATIVE PRONOUN
None in Evenki. For relative constructions, *see* **Verb**, below.

Numerals

1–10: *umūn, dyūr, ilan, digin, tunnga, nyungun, nadan, dyapkun, ēgin, dyān*; 11 *dyān.umūn*; 12 *dyān.dyūr*; 20 *dyūr.dyār*; 30 *ilan.dyār*; 100 *nyama*. Numerals take a plural noun.

Verb

Roots are transitive or intransitive, and have finite and non-finite forms. Aspect, voice, mood, tense have specific markers; in tenses, person and number are shown by affixes.

ASPECT
Perfective is unmarked, imperfective by, e.g. *-dya/ča*: *um* 'to drink', *umdya* 'to be drinking'.

VOICE
> passive marker is *-v-/-p-*, e.g. *surūv* 'to take', *surūvuv* 'to be taken';
> causative: *-vkān/-pkān/-mukān*, e.g. *gūn* 'to say', *gūnmukān* 'to cause to say';
> inceptive: *-l*, e.g. *dukū*, 'to write', *dukūlim* 'I've just started to write';
> reciprocal: *-mat*, e.g. *duku* 'to write', *dukūmat* 'to correspond'.

TENSE

The indicative mood has an aspectual present (perfective/imperfective) two past tenses, and three futures. For example, perfective present of root *ngənə* 'to go':

	Singular	Plural
1	ngənəm	incl. ngənərəp; excl. ngənəv
2	ngənənni	ngənərəs
3	ngənərən	ngənərə

Perfective past: the marker is *-čā*, e.g. *bi nungandūn dukūčāv* 'I wrote to him'; *əməčəv* 'I came'.

Imperfective past: *-ngkī*, e.g. *bi teatrildū bingkīv* 'I used to go to the theatres.'

Future (potential): *-dVngV̄*, e.g. *deng*; *əmədengōv* 'I'll come'.

NEGATIVE

The negative copula is *ə-*, inflected, + sense-verb in participial form: e.g. in present: *əsim, əsinni, əsin* (etc.) *gunə* 'I (etc.) don't speak.' The negative of the existential verb is *āčin*: e.g. *minngi oron.mi āčin* 'I have no reindeer.'

PARTICIPLES

E.g. perfective in *-čā*: *əməčə̄ bəye* 'the man who came'; imperfective in *-rī*: *bəye əməderīwən ičəm* 'I saw that the man was coming.'

There are also imperative, subjunctive, desiderative, and necessitative moods, plus an inferential or presumptive mood with an aorist and a past tense. The presumptive marker is *-rka*: e.g. *əmərkə bičən* 'He has probably come already.'

The examples given here illustrate only a small selection from the very rich inventory of affixes available in Evenki. Vasiljevich (1958) lists about 500, with examples of their usage.

Postpositions

Most of these are nouns in the locative case. In construct, following a noun, they take personal possessive markers, e.g. the third person singular *-n*: e.g.

> *oyo* 'the highest point of anything', e.g. *mō oyon* 'the top of the tree';
> *oyo.li* 'on', e.g. *dyū oyolin* 'above the house'; *dyū oyon* 'on the roof';
> *daga* 'near(ness)', *dagadu* 'near', e.g. *dyū dagadun* 'near the house';
> *dagaduvun* 'near us'.

Word order

SOV is normal.

EWE

INTRODUCTION

Ewe belongs to the Ewe-Akan sub-group of the Kwa branch of West Sudanic and is spoken by around 3 million people in Ghana and Togo, also in Benin. A literary form of Ewe (based on the Anlo dialect) has been in use since 1853, when the Norddeutsche Missionsgesellschaft started its missionary activity (Togoland was a German colony from 1884 onwards). Ewe was used as the medium of instruction in schools. Under British administration in western Togoland after the First World War, Ewe was one of five African languages selected to take part in the International African Institute competition in 1932. There is now, since independence (1954) a thriving literature in Ewe (Ferdinand Kwasi Fiawoo, Sam Obianim, S.K. Anika, etc.). The Ewe Club publishes a journal, *Togo Gedzedze* ('Light on Togo').

SCRIPT

Roman; the orthography used here is that of Diedrich Westermann (1930). The script does not reflect the many cases of sandhi assimilation at junctures.

PHONOLOGY

Consonants

Labio-dental /f, v/ are paralleled by bilabial /ɸ, ß/. m is syllabic. There is a retroflex /ḍ/, notated with subscript dot. The dental series includes /ts, dz/. There are two labio-velars /kp/ and /gb/ with simultaneous closure.
Other sounds: /p, b, w; t, d, s, z, l, r, n; ɲ, j; k, g, χ, h, ŋ/.

Vowels

a, ɛ, e, i, ɔ, o, u; ə, ɪ

These are usually short. Long vowels are indicated by doubling. All vowels can be nasalized. There are many diphthongs.

Tones

There are three level pitches and two glides: high, mid, low, rising, and falling. Tone change is a concomitant of vowel assimilation. e.g. $á + à \rightarrow â$ (falling): e.g.

ká así → *kâsí* 'touch with the hand'.

MORPHOLOGY AND SYNTAX

Noun

There is no grammatical gender. The third person plural pronominal form *wó* is used as a plural marker: e.g. *ame* 'person', pl. *amewó*; *xɔ* 'house', pl. *xɔwó*. This marker may be added to such postpositional items as adjectives and pronouns: e.g. *amewó yi = ame wóyì* 'the people went'; *lã vɔ́* 'wild animal', pl. *lã vɔ́wo* (note change of tone).

CASE
Positional. The possessive connective is *ɸé*: e.g. *fia ɸé xɔ* 'the chief's house'. Direct object follows verb and is followed by indirect object: e.g. *Éfia atí adelá* 'He showed the tree (*atí*) to the hunter (*adelá*).'

Adjective

As attribute, adjective follows noun: e.g. *xɔ nyuí* 'good house'; *tó kɔ́kɔ siawó* 'these high mountains' (mountain – high – demonstrative + plural sign). Many adjectival meanings are rendered by verbs: e.g. *kɔ́* 'to be high'; *atí kɔ́kɔ* 'high tree'; *atí lá kɔ́* 'the tree is high'.

COMPARISON
One way of expressing comparison is by using *wú* 'to surpass': e.g. *Sɔ́ lolo wú tédzi* 'The horse is larger than the donkey.'

Pronoun

Absolute (subject or object):

	Singular	Plural
1	nye	míawo
2	wò	miawó
3	éyà, yé	wóawo

These are separated from the verb either by the pronoun *é* 'he, she, it', or by the article *lá* + verb + conjoint resumptive pronoun: e.g. *nyeé kpɔ̀è* 'I (am the one who has) seen it' = 'I have seen it'; *nye lá mekpɔ̀è* 'I have seen it'.

The conjoint pronoun forms are (basic forms): sing. 1 *me*, 2 *è*, 3 *é*; pl. 1 *míe*, 2 *mìe*, 3 *wó*.

DEMONSTRATIVE PRONOUNS
si(a) 'this'; pl. *siawó*; *á*, *lá* 'the, this': e.g. *atí lá = atiá* 'the tree'.

INTERROGATIVE PRONOUNS
kâ/ka 'who, which?'; pl. *kawó*.

sì, pl. *siwó*: e.g. *lákle sì míekpɔ etsɔ lá* 'the leopard which we saw yesterday';
lákle siwó míekpɔ etsɔ lá 'the leopards which we saw yesterday'.

Numerals

1–10: *ḍeká, eve, etɔ̃, ene, atɔ̃, adé, adré, enyí, enyíḍe, ewó*; 11 *wúìḍekɛ́*; 12
wúìeve; 20 *bláavè*; 21 *bláavè vɔ́ ḍekɛ́*; 30 *bláàtɔ̃*; 40 *bláanè*; 100 *aláfá ḍeká*.

Verb

Stems are invariable and are used transitively and intransitively. Tense and
mood are generated externally. There is no passive. Examples from *yi* 'to go'.

> aorist: sing. *meyi, èyì, éyì*; pl. *míeyì, mieyi, wóyì*;
> future: formed by prefixation of *á-*: e.g. *m.á.yì* 'I shall go',
> *m.á.wɔ̃.dɔ́* 'I shall (do) work'; *á.ɸò.m* 'he will strike me'.
> habitual: *-na* suffix, e.g. *meyina* 'I generally go';
> progressive: *le* 'to be' + sense-verb + *-ḿ* suffix, e.g. *mele yiyiḿ* 'I am going';
> pret. *nɔ* (aorist of *le*) + sense-verb + *ḿ*, e.g. *menɔ yiyiḿ* 'I was in the
> habit of going';
> intentional: progressive + *gé* replacing *ḿ*, e.g. *mele yiyi gé* 'I'm about
> to go';
> imperative: *yi!* 'go!'
> jussive: *náyì* 'you are to go';
> prohibitive: *ga* infix between pronoun and verb, e.g. *mégàyi!* 'do not go!';
> verbal noun: *yiyi* 'act of going'.

E.g. with verb *ɸo* 'to strike':

éɸòm 'he strikes/struck me'	éɸò mí 'he strikes/struck us'
éɸò wo 'he strikes/struck you'	éɸò mi 'he strikes/struck you'
éɸòe 'he strikes/struck him'	éɸò wó 'he strikes/struck them'

-me- is inserted between pronoun and verb + *o*: e.g. *nyeméyì o* 'I don't go/didn't
go'.

Word formation

Noun + article: e.g. *agble* 'farm', *agbleá* 'farmer'; *ade* 'hunt', *adeá* 'hunter'.
Other formants may be inserted, e.g. *de* 'to go to': *tɔ́ɸò* 'water', *tɔ́ɸòdeá*
'boatman'.

APPOSITION

E.g. with *tɔ́* 'owner', *agbletɔ́* 'farmer' (owner of farm); with *nɔ* 'female, subject to'; *dɔnɔ* 'invalid' (subject to sickness); with *nyenye* = verbal noun of *nye* 'to be', *agbledelányenye* 'the state of being a farmer'; noun + verb + noun, e.g. *atítsògbe* 'day for felling trees'; *dɔwuame* 'starvation' ('hunger-kill-man').

MULTIPLE COMPOUND

E.g. *ɖuamewòádzekpoe* 'bite-man-he-will-go-mad' = 'scorpion'.

Word order

SVO is normal.

FAEROESE

INTRODUCTION

Originally inhabited by Celts, the Faeroe Islands were invaded in the early Middle Ages by Scandinavian settlers speaking a form of Old Norse. The development of Faeroese as a specifically divergent form of Scandinavian dates from the mid-sixteenth century, when Danish was imposed as the official language of the colony. It might be said that Faeroese is Old or Middle Norwegian as modulated by Danish. In 1947 Faeroese was given official status as the 'chief language' of the islands, which have autonomous status under the Danish crown.

A standardized orthography was first provided by the Faeroese linguist and writer V.U. Hammershaimb in the middle of the nineteenth century. Up to that point, a fairly rich folk literature had been transmitted orally. The first newspaper appeared in 1890, the first novel in 1909. The twentieth century produced some outstanding names, such as Jens Djurhuus and Heðin Brú. On the other hand, two writers of international stature, who are in fact Faeroese, Jørgen-Frantz Jacobsen and William Heinesen, have chosen to write in Danish, which still enjoys widespread usage and considerable prestige in the Faeroes.

SCRIPT

Roman with additional symbols: æ, ø, ð.

PHONOLOGY

Consonants

    stops: p, b, t, d, k, g
    affricates: tʃ, dʃ
    fricatives: f, v, ð, s, ʃ, j, h
    nasals: m, n
    lateral and flap: l, r

Written x = /ks/.

Vowels

The written inventory, with phonetic values in brackets.

short vowels: *a* (a); *á* (ɔ); *e* (ä); *i/y* (ı); *o* (ɔ); *ó* (œ); *u* (u); *ú* (ö > ü) (i); *æ* (a); *ø* (œ)

long vowels (most of these tend to be diphthongized): *a* (äa); *á* (oa); *e* (eə); *i/y* (i); *í/ý* (ui); *o* (oə); *ó* (ou); *u* (ū); *ú* (iw); *æ* (äa); *ø* (œə)

In Faeroese, there is a considerable discrepancy between the etymologically purist orthography and the actual pronunciation. Some examples are given:

ð = /j/, /w/, or /ø/: e.g. *leiða* 'lead', /laija/; *maður* 'man', /mɛawər/; *suður* 'southerly', /suər/.

g + soft vowel = /dj/ = /dʃ/: e.g. *borgin* 'town', /bordʃin/; *genta* 'girl', /dʃɛnta/; *djór* 'animal', /dʃour/.

k = /tʃ/: e.g. *kirkja* 'church', /tʃirtʃa/; or /k/: e.g. *koma* 'come', /koəma/.

hv = /k°/: e.g. *hvaar* 'where', /k°ɛar/.

a before /n, nk/ → [ɛ]: e.g. *tangi* 'spit of land', /tɛndʃi/.

long *a* → [ɛa]: e.g. *dagur* 'day', /dɛawər/.

a = /oa/: e.g. *bátur* 'boat', /boatər/.

æ in long syllable → /ɛa/: e.g. *klæða* 'clothe', /klɛa/.

MORPHOLOGY AND SYNTAX

Noun

There are strong and weak declensions; 3 genders, 2 numbers, 4 cases. For example, the strong declension of *úlvur* 'wolf':

	Singular	Plural
nom.	úlvur	úlvar
gen.	úlvs	úlva
dat.	úlvi	úlvum
acc.	úlv	úlvar

There are many variants, depending on stem and phonetic composition. The umlaut classes: *bók – bøkur, sonur – synir, gata – gøtur* are found.

Article

The independent definite article is masc. *hin*, fem. *hin*, nt. *hitt*, with plural forms *hinir, hinar, hini*. These are fully declined. As in Icelandic, these are rarely used; mainly if an attributive adjective is present: e.g. *hin gamli maður* 'the old man'.

The definite article is usually added in truncated form to the noun: e.g. *úlvurin* 'the wolf'; *drottning.ar.innar* 'of the queens'.

Adjective

As attribute, adjective precedes noun and shows full concord with it: e.g. *góðs manns barn* 'a good man's child'; *góða manna børn* 'the children of good people'.

COMPARATIVE

-(*a*)*ri*, often with umlaut: e.g. *stórur* 'big' – *størri*. Some bases are suppletive: e.g. *góður* 'good' – *betri*; *illur* 'bad' – *verri*. As attribute, the comparative is not declined.

Pronoun

The third person personal pronoun distinguishes gender: sing. 1 *eg*, 2 *tú*, 3 *hann*, *hon*, *tað*; pl. 1 *vit* 2 *tit* 3 *teir*, *tær*, *tey*. These are declined in four cases; the oblique base of first person plural is *okk-*: *okkara*, *okkum*. A polite second person is *tygum*.

DEMONSTRATIVE PRONOUN
Masc./fem. *tann*; nt. *tað*. Plural as personal plural, third person.

INTERROGATIVE PRONOUN
hvør, /k°œər/ 'who?'. The neuter form is *hvørt*.

RELATIVE PRONOUN
sum (indeclinable): e.g. *tey gomlu kvæðini, sum eru dansivísur* 'the old *kvæði*, which are dance songs'.

Numerals

1–3 inclusive: *ein*, *tveir*, *tríggir*, are declined. 4–10: *fýra*, *fimm*, *seks*, *sjey*, *átta*, *níggju*, *tíggju*; 11 *ellivu*; 12 *tólv*; 20 *tjúgu*, 30 *tríati*; 40 *fýrati*; 100 *hundrað*.

Verb

The infinitive is marked by *at*: e.g. *at sova* 'to sleep', *at skriva* 'to write'. There are active, passive, and middle voices, the latter in -*st*; indicative, subjunctive, and imperative moods; eight tenses, including perfect, pluperfect, future perfect, and past conditional. The present and imperfect tenses are simple, all the others are composite.

There are strong and weak conjugations.

STRONG CONJUGATION
Examples of ablaut classes: infinitive – third person singular present – first person singular and plural imperfect – past participle:

> renna 'to run' – rennur – rann/runnu – runnin
> sita 'to sit' – situr – sat/sótu – sitin
> standa 'to stand' – stendur – stóð/stóðu – staðin
> njóta 'to enjoy' – nýtur – neyt/nutu – notin

Personal endings: present, e.g. from *renna*: sing. 1 *renni*, 2/3 *rennur*; pl. 1, 2, 3, *renna*.

Past imperfect: sing. 1 *rann*, 2 *ranst*, 3 *rann*; pl. 1, 2, 3 *runnu*.

453

E.g. *brenna* 'to burn', *telja* 'to count':

> brenna – brennir – brendi/brendu – brendur
> telja – telur – taldi/taldu – taldur

AUXILIARIES
hava, *vilja*, *skula*, *munna*, etc.: e.g. *eg havi runnið* 'I have run'; i.e. auxiliary + neuter past participle.

PASSIVE
E.g. *eg verði heilsaður* = *eg eri heilsaður* 'I am greeted'; *vit verði heilsaðir* = *vit eru heilsaðir* 'we are greeted'.

The middle voice is generally reciprocal: *vit heilsast* 'we greet each other'.

Prepositions

These take accusative, dative, or both; some take accusative + genitive. Note the presence of a periphrastic genitive, made with the preposition *á* + dative: e.g. *hondin á honum* 'his hand'.

There are a few postpositions, e.g. *millum* 'among': *teirra millum* 'among them'.

Word order

SVO; VSO if adverbial material initiates sentence.

Í fyrstuni var orðið, og orðið var hjá Guði, og orðið var Guð.

2 Hetta var í fyrstuni hjá Guði.

3 Allir lutir eru vorðnir til við tí, og uttan tað varð einki til av tí, sum til er vorðið.

4 Í tí var lív, og lívið var ljós menniskjunnar.

5 Og ljósið skínur í myrkrinum, og myrkrið tók ikki við tí.

6 Maður kom, sendur frá Guði, hann æt Jóhannes.

7 Hesin kom til vitnisburðar, til tess at hann skuldi vitna um ljósið, fyri at allir skuldu trúgva við honum.

8 Hann var ikki ljósið, men hann skuldi vitna um ljósið.

FIJIAN

INTRODUCTION

Fijian belongs to the Melanesian sub-group of Malayo-Polynesian. The separation of Fijian and related languages from the main stream of Malayo-Polynesian seems to have taken place in the second millennium BC. There is an East/West dialect split, the standard literary language being based on the Bauan (Eastern) dialect. The official language of Fiji is English, but about 300,000 people speak Fijian, many as their second language. Local broadcasting is in Fijian, and there is a high degree of literacy in the language. Printing in Fijian (Biblical texts) dates from the 1830s.

SCRIPT

Roman, minus h, x, z. The pre-nasalized consonants are denoted as follows: /mb/ by b, /nd/ by d, /ng/ by q. /ð/ is notated as c, /ŋ/ as g, /nr/ as dr. F, j, p occur only in borrowed words.

PHONOLOGY

Consonants

    stops: p, t, k; pre-nasalized voiced: ᵐb, ⁿd, ⁿg; palatalized t', d' occur
    fricatives: ß, ð, s
    nasals: m, n, ŋ
    roll: r, ⁿr
    lateral: l
    semi-vowels: w, j

Vowels

    short and long: i, ε, a, ɔ, u

Final vowels → Ø (all Fijian words end in vowels). Vowel sequences tend to become diphthongs.

Stress

Long syllables attract stress, which in their absence tends towards penultimate. Stress is phonemic.

MORPHOLOGY

Typical Malayo-Polynesian division into bases and particles. Particles adhere in pre- or postposition to base, which is nominal or verbal depending on the valencies in the complex whose nucleus it forms.

Noun

No gender, but *see* **Class markers**. There are two articles: *o/ko* precedes proper nouns: e.g. *o Viti* 'Fiji'; the definite/indefinite article for all other nouns is *na*: e.g. *na waqa* 'a/the canoe'.

NUMBER

Common bases have a plural marker *vei* which also forms collectives: e.g. *na tiri* 'mangrove' – *na veitiri* 'mangrove swamp'; *na siga* 'day' – *na veisiga* 'days'.

Adjective

As qualifier, adjective follows noun: e.g. *vinaka* 'good': *draki vinaka* 'good weather'; *na waqa vinaka* 'the good canoe'.

Pronoun

The subject pronouns used with verbs are:

	Singular		Dual	Trial	Plural
1	(k)au.u	excl.	keirau	keitou	keimami
	—	incl.	(e)daru	(e)datou	(e)da
2	(k)o		(k)o drau	(k)o dou	(k)o nī
3	—		(e) rau	(e) ratou	(e) ra

The objective forms are very similar. Subjective forms precede the base; objective forms follow it.

POSSESSIVE

The possessive pronouns precede bases, and have singular, dual, trial, and plural forms. The first person excl. row is *noqu – neirau – neitou – neimami*. The second person base (sing.) is *nomu*, the third *nona*: e.g. *na nona vale* 'his house': *na nodratou vale* 'their (three people) house'.

These forms are used in equivalent of verb 'to have': e.g. *E dua na nona waqa* 'his canoe is one' = 'He has a canoe.'

CLASS MARKERS

The classes are: 1 neutral, 2 edible, 3 potable, 4 integral. The markers are: class 1 sing. *no*, dual, etc. *nei*; class 2 sing. *ke/qau*, dual, etc. *kei*; class 3 sing. *me*, dual, etc. *mei*.

In class 4 the class marker is suffixed to the base, which denotes a natural integration – the family, the body, a plant, etc. There are detailed rules for the proper use of terms referring to parts of these natural wholes: e.g. in kinship terms, relative status, age, degree of kinship must all be taken into account: *tama* 'father'; *tamaqu* 'my father'.

The markers are prefixed to the possessive pronominal base. Thus, *nona* in the third person refers to a neutral object – 'house': *na nona vale*; similarly *na kena uvi* 'his yam(s)', in edible class; *na mena wai* 'his water', in potable class; *na dalo kei Pita* 'Peter's taro' (edible class).

DEMONSTRATIVE PRONOUN

Three-term gradation related to person: *oqō* 'this' (near first person); *oqori* 'that' (near second person); *(k)oya* 'that' (near third person): e.g. *e na vale oqō* 'in this house (where I am)'; *e na vale oqori* 'in that house (where you are)'.

INTERROGATIVE PRONOUN

cei 'who?'; *cava* 'what?'.

RELATIVE PRONOUN

ka (referring to subject); *kina/kaya* (referring to oblique case): e.g. *na waqa ka* ... 'the canoe which ...'; *na waqa eratou ā lako kina* 'the canoe in which they sailed ...'.

Numerals

These are verbal bases: 1 *e dua na*; 2 *e rua na*; similarly, between *e* and *na*, the following are inserted for 3–10: *tolu, vā, lima, ono, vitu, walu, ciwa, tini*: e.g. *e dua na waqa* 'one canoe' (lit. 'the canoe is one'); *e na vale e rua oqō* 'in these two houses'. 20 *ruasagavulu*; 21 *ruasagavulu ka dua*; 30 *tolusagavulu*; 100 *dua na drau*.

Verb

Transitive and intransitive. Transitive verbs may be formed by adding -C*a* to base or by lengthening final vowel: e.g. *gunu* 'to drink', *gunuva* 'to drink it'; *kila* 'know', *kilā* 'to know it'. The intransitive form plus an object amounts to a stative verb: e.g. *eratou gunu yaqona* 'they are-kava-drinking' but *eratou gunuva na yaqona* 'they are drinking the kava'. -*a* → -*i* before a proper object: e.g. *eratou ā raici Viti* 'they saw Fiji'.

Tense markers precede base: *ā* for past, *na* for future: e.g. *era ā lako* 'they (pl.) went'; *era na lako* 'they (pl.) will go'.

NEGATIVE

sega is a general negative marker: e.g. *e ā sega ni lako* 'he didn't go'; *au sega ni raica* 'I haven't seen it'; *e sega ni vinaka* 'it's not good'.

MODAL PARTICLES

E.g. durative *tiko*; potential *rawa*; reiterative *tale*; *E cakacaka tiko mai Suva* 'He's working in Suva.'

PASSIVE

-a → *-i*: e.g. *e vaka-yagataka* 'he uses it', *e vaka-yagataki* 'it is used'. Cf. *au nanuma na vanua* 'I remember the land', *sā nanumi na vanua* 'the land is remembered'.

A number of particles, e.g. *dui* 'all', *dē* 'possible', *vei* (reciprocal marker), precede the verbal base; others, e.g. *vata* 'together' (comitative marker), follow.

CAUSATIVE

The formant is *vaka*: e.g. *mate* 'die' – *vaka.mate.a* 'kill'. The circumfix *vaka...taka* forms transitives: e.g. *mārau* 'happiness' – *vaka.mārau.taka* 'amusing'. *Vaka-* also indicates possession of something: e.g. *vaka.vale* 'having a house'; *na vosa vakaviti* 'the Fijian language'.

Word order

VSO; SVO.

O KOYA na Vosa sa bula e nai vakatekivu, a rau sa tiko kei na Kalou ko koya na Vosa, a Kalou ko koya na Vosa.

2 Sai koya oqo e rau sa tiko vata kei na Kalou mai nai vakatekivu.

3 Sa cakava na ka kecega ko koya: a sa sega e dua na ka sa cakavi, me sega ni cakava ko koya.

4 Sa tu vua na bula; ia na rarama ni tamata na bula.

5 Sa cila mai na rarama e na butobuto; a sa sega ni kunea na butobuto.

6 ¶ E dua na tamata sa tala mai vua na Kalou, a yacana ko Joni.

7 O koya oqo sa lako mai me dautukutuku, me tukuni koya na Rarama, me ra vakabauta na tamata kecega e na vukuna.

8 Ia ka sa sega na Rarama dina ko koya, a sa tàlai mai me tukuna na Rarama ko ya.

FINNISH

INTRODUCTION

A member of the Balto-Finnic group of Finno-Ugric, Finnish is the official language of Finland (jointly with Swedish), and joint official language of the Karelian Autonomous Soviet Socialist Republic. Finnish is spoken in Finland by around 5 million, with considerable emigré bilingual communities abroad, e.g. over half a million in North America.

The main dialectal split is into Western (South-Western, centred on Turku, and the Häme dialect, spoken by the *hämäläiset*) and Eastern (e.g. Savo dialect, spoken by the *savolaiset*). Differences between dialects are largely phonological: e.g. the /k, t, p/ stops can precede /r, l/ in Eastern forms: cf. Western *kaula* 'neck' – Eastern *kakla*; Western *eilen* 'yesterday' – Eastern *eklen*; Western *peura* 'wild reindeer' – Eastern *petra*. Also the labial final in third person singular present: Western *juo* 'he drinks' – Eastern *juop(i)*. The modern literary standard represents a successful compromise between the main dialect forms.

Finnish literature begins in 1544 with the *Rukouskirja Bibliasta* of Michael Agricola, followed in 1548 by his translation of the New Testament. Little of note followed until 1835 when Elias Lönnroth published the first version of his *Kalevala* material. The mythopoeic, ethnological, and linguistic riches revealed in *Kalevala* and its companion volume *Kanteletar* added more than one new dimension to Finnish self-awareness.

From the 1880s onwards, Finnish has been the vehicle for a rich literature in prose and verse, often fervently nationalistic but showing acute awareness of cultural crises on a European scale. Some notable names are Mika Waltari, Toivo Pekkanen, Pentti Haanpää, Paavo Haavikko, Väinö Linna, and Veijo Meri.

SCRIPT

Latin alphabet, minus *b*, *c*, *f*, *q*, *w*, *x*, *z*; plus *ä* (= /ɛ/), *ö* (= /œ/).

PHONOLOGY

Consonants

    stops: p, t, d, k
    fricatives: v, j, ṣ, h
    nasals: m, n, ŋ
    lateral and flap: l, r

CONSONANT GRADATION

This is a crucially important element in Finnish phonology and morphology, affecting all declension and conjugation patterns. A 'strong' consonant, or consonant cluster initiating an open syllable, is mutated into its 'weak' correlative, when the syllable is closed by the addition of a consonant. The phenomenon (which has many complexities) can be illustrated by comparing nouns in the nominative singular (open syllable) with their genitive forms (closed by addition of the genitive marker -n); or by comparing infinitives (strong grade) with the first person singular (weak):

Strong	Weak	Example
pp	p	loppu – lopun 'end'
tt	t	ottaa – otan 'to take'
kk	k	kukka – kukan 'flower'
mp	mm	enempi – enemmän 'more'
t	d	katu – kadun 'street'
p	v	apu – avun 'help'
k	Ø	lukea – luen 'read'

There are some important exceptions to this general rule: e.g. mutation does not take place before a long vowel (e.g. *katu* – illative *katuun*) or before the personal possessive affix (e.g. *puku* 'clothes' – *pukunsa* 'his clothes').

The process works in reverse also, i.e. strong grade is restored, for example, in the plural form of the adjective with weak grade in the singular: *rakas* 'dear' – pl. *rakkaat*.

Vowels

long and short: i, e, ε, a, o, œ, u, y

Length is phonemic. Long consonants and vowels are notated by gemination. There are 16 diphthongs: three rising – /ie, uo, yœ/, the rest falling, ending in /i, u/ or /y/.

Not more than one consonant can figure as syllable-initial (this goes even for foreign words: e.g. Stockholm becomes Tukholm) and words can end only in a vowel or one of the letters /l, n, r, s, t/. Final vowels tend to be aspirated.

VOWEL HARMONY

Back vowels /a, o, u/ are followed by back; front /ε, œ, y/ by front; /i/ and /e/ are neutral. Thus, *kymmenen* 'ten'; *omena* 'apple'; *talossa* 'in the house'; *meressä* 'in the sea'.

Formative affixes vary in orthography and pronunciation according to vowel harmony: e.g. *tuntematon* 'unknown'; *kärsimätön* 'impatient'.

MORPHOLOGY AND SYNTAX

Noun

No articles, no gender. The plural marker is -*t*, with an /-i-/ infix in the oblique cases (other than the accusative).

CASE

There are 15 cases; as illustration, the paradigm for a back-vowel noun, *talo* 'house':

	Singular	*Plural*
nominative	talo	talot
accusative	talo	talot
genitive	talon	talojen
essive	talona	taloina
translative	taloksi	taloiksi
partitive	taloa	taloja
inessive	talossa	taloissa
elative	talosta	taloista
illative	taloon	taloihin
adessive	talolla	taloilla
ablative	talolta	taloilta
allative	talolle	taloille
abessive	talotta	taloitta
comitative	—	(taloinensa)
instrumental	(talon)	taloin

Most of the cases are self-explanatory. Among the uses of the partitive are:

(a) to express indefinite quantity: e.g. *pieniä ja isoja puita* 'small and large trees';
(b) after a negative: e.g. *täällä ei ole ihmisiä* 'there's nobody here'; *en lue kirjaa* 'I don't read a/the book';
(c) after numerals: e.g. *kaksi kirjaa* 'two books';
(d) 'some': e.g. *lasi vettä* 'a glass of water'.

The adessive in -*lla*/-*lle* is used to express the verb 'to have', which is missing in Finnish: e.g. *minulla/meillä on/ei ole ystäviä* 'I/we have (no) friends'.

Adjective

As attribute, adjective precedes noun, and agrees with it in number and case: e.g. *pieni poika* 'small boy'; *pienet pojat* 'small boys'; *suuren kaupungin/suurten kaupunkien* (*ulkopuolella*) '(outside) the large town/s'.

COMPARATIVE

-*mpi* added to genitive minus -*n*: e.g. *Minä olen vanhempi kuin sinä* 'I am older than you' (*kuin* 'than').

Pronoun

Personal subject (nominative) forms: sing. 1 *minä*, 2 *sinä*, 3 *hän*; pl. 1 *me*, 2 *te*, 3 *he*. These are declined in eleven cases; e.g. the accusative forms are: *minut*, *sinut*, *hänet*; *meidät*, *teidät*, *heidät*.

POSSESSIVE AFFIXES

Sing. 1 *-ni*, 2 *-si*, 3 *-nsa/nsä*; pl. 1 *-emme*, 2 *-nne*, 3 as singular. These are added after case endings: e.g. *talossani* 'in my house'.

DEMONSTRATIVE PRONOUN/ADJECTIVES

Two-degree distinction: *tämä* 'this'; *tuo* 'that', with plural forms *nämä*, *nuo*. *Se*, pl. *ne* is neutral. All forms are declined in 12 cases.

INTERROGATIVE PRONOUN

kuka 'who?'; *mikä* 'what?'. Declined in 12 cases, the plural forms being *kutka*, *mitkä*. For all cases, the base for *kuka* is *ken-*.

RELATIVE PRONOUN

joka, pl. *jotka*, declined in 12 cases. Examples: *Tunnen kaikki, jotka asuvat tässä talossa* 'I know all those who live in this house'; *Han on mies, jonka sanaan voi luottaa* 'He is a man whose word can be relied on.'

Numerals

1–10: *yksi, kaksi, kolme, neljä, viisi, kuusi, seitsemän, kahdeksan, yhdeksän, kymmenen*; 11 *yksitoista*; 12 *kaksitoista*; 20 *kaksikymmentä*; 21 *kaksikymmentäyksi*; 30 *kolmekymmentä*; 100 *sata*.

Verb

The Finnish verb has active and passive voices and four moods: indicative, imperative, conditional, and potential. Tenses are simple (present, imperfect) or compound (e.g. perfect). There is no future tense. The language has an extensive apparatus of inflected participial and gerundial forms, including four infinitives. Compound tenses are made with the auxiliary *olla*, whose present tense is sing. *olen, olet, on*; pl. *olemme, olette, ovat*; the past tense is sing. *olin, olit, oli*; pl. *olimme, olitte, olivat*.

There is only one conjugation for all Finnish verbs; anomalies are phonological. The positive version is parallelled by a negative one. The negative marker is conjugated for person and number: sing. *en, et, ei*; pl. *emme, ette, eivät*: thus, *sanon* 'I say'; *en sano* 'I do not say'; *sanoo* 'he says'; *ei sano* 'he does not say', i.e. the sense-verb remains uninflected in the present. For past tense, see below.

Specimen conjugation of *sanoa* 'to say':

> present tense: sing. *sanon, sanot, sanoo*; pl. *sanomme, sanotte, sanovat*; negative, *en sano*, etc.;

past imperfect: e.g. sing. *sanoin, sanoit, sanoi*; here, the negative version is made with the past participle which is marked for number: e.g. *en sanonut, et sanonut, emme sanoneet, ette sanoneet*;
perfect: e.g. *olen sanonut*, negative *en ole sanonut, emme ole sanoneet*;

Conditional and potential tenses are constructed on the same principles: the former with an *-is-* infix, e.g. *sanoisin, sanoisit*; the latter with an *-e* ending, e.g. *sanonen, sanonet*, and the auxiliary *lienee* in the past, e.g. *lienen sanonut*.

Imperative: 2nd sing. *sano*; 2nd pl. *sanokaa*; in the negative, the auxiliary is *älä/älkää*: *älä sano, älkää sanoko*.

All parts of the Finnish verb can be constructed from three base forms – the infinitive, the first person singular present, and the third person singular past: e.g. *sanoa – sanon – sanoi*. In this example, the *-n* is stable: a mutating example is *tehdä – teen – teki* 'to do'.

PASSIVE VOICE

The passive stem is made from the active by the addition of *-ta/-tä, -tta/-ttä*: e.g. *sanoa* 'to say', *sanotta* 'to be said'. The passive voice is impersonal: *sanotaan* 'it is being said' → 'people say ...'; cf. *Yöllä nukutaan* lit. 'at-night it-is-being-slept' = 'People sleep at night'; *ei lauleta* 'there is no singing'; *Täällä eletään hauskasti* lit. 'here it-is-being-lived well' = 'Here one lives well'; *Antakaat, niin teille annetaan* 'Give and it shall be given unto you' (Luke, 6.38).

PARTICIPLES

(a) Present active in *-va/vä*; provides one way of making relative clauses: e.g. *Näen hänen tulevan* 'I see him coming'; *Luulen hänen tulevan* 'I think he is coming'; *suomea puhuva ulkomaalainen* 'a foreigner who speaks Finnish'.
(b) Present passive: passive stem + *-va/-vä*: e.g. *Kuulen näin sanottavan ...* 'I hear it's being said ...'; *luettava kirja* 'a book that has to be read'; *minun on tehtävä ...* 'I have to do' (where *minun* is the genitive case of *minä*).
(c) Past active: *-nut/-nyt/-neet*; used e.g. in formation of compound tenses, see above.
(d) Past passive: formed from passive stem by changing *-a-* to *-u-*, *-ä-* to *-y-*. The partitive singular of this participle indicates anterior action in the past: e.g. *Syötyä lähdettiin* lit. 'there-having-been-something-of-an-eating it-was-gone' = 'After eating, I/you/he (etc.) went away.'

The following examples show how inflected impersonal forms are used to express modality, purpose, etc.: *mitä he ovat tekemässä?* 'What are they doing?'; *Menin Amerikkaan opiskelemaan* 'I went to America to study'; *Minulla ei ole mitään tekemistä* 'I've nothing to do'; *tekemällä* 'by working'; *tekemättä* 'without working'. Motivation for the endings will be found by reference to the declension table above.

Prepositions and postpositions

Finnish has a few prepositions: e.g.

> *ilman* 'without' with partitive, e.g. *ilman aihetta* 'without cause', *ilman rahaa* 'without money';
> *paitsi* 'besides, except' with partitive, e.g. *Paitsi häntä en nähnyt ketään* 'Apart from him, I saw no one.'

Postpositions usually follow the genitive case:

> *jälkeen* 'after', e.g. *juosta jonkun jälkeen* 'to run behind someone';
> *kanssa* 'with', e.g. *lapsen kanssa* 'with the child';
> *aikana* 'during', e.g. *kahden viikon aikana* 'during two weeks';
> *edessä* 'in front of', e.g. *ikkunan edessä* 'in front of the window'.

Word formation

By formant affix: e.g. nouns from verbs:

> *-mo/-mö* 'place where': *leipomo* 'bakery', *panimo* 'brewery';
> *-ja/-jä* indicates agent: *lukea* 'to read', *lukija* 'reader';
> *-ri* indicates agent: *juoda* 'to drink', *juomari* 'drinker'.

Nouns from nouns: e.g.

> *-sto/-stö*: collective affix: *kirja* 'book', *kirjasto* 'library';
> *-nen* is a diminutive: *kukkanen* 'little flower';
> *-tar/-tär* mythopoeic female formant: *luonnotar* 'goddess of nature'; *onnetar* 'goddess of fortune'.

In a privative sense either the postposition *-(ma)ton* or the preposition *epä-*: *ajattelematon* 'thoughtless'; *epäluonnollinen* 'unnatural'.

-(t)taa/(t)tää makes verbs from any part of speech: *paimentaa* 'to tend, herd' (*paimen* 'flock, herd'); *ylittää* 'to exceed' (*yli* 'over, above').

Word order

SVO is normal but other sequences are possible; e.g. VS may follow adverbial material beginning sentence.

1 Alussa oli Sana, ja Sana oli Jumalan luona. Sana oli Jumala, ²ja hän oli alussa Jumalan luona. ³Kaikki on luotu hänen kauttaan, eikä mitään ole luotu ilman häntä. ⁴Hänessä oli elämä, ja elämä oli ihmisten valo. ⁵Valo loistaa pimeydessä, mutta pimeys ei ole sitä koskaan käsittänyt.

⁶Jumala lähetti Johannes-nimisen miehen ⁷todistamaan valosta, että kaikki kuulisivat häntä ja uskoisivat. ⁸Hän ei ollut itse valo, hän vain todisti valosta.

FRAFRA

See **Gurenne**.

FRENCH

INTRODUCTION

French belongs to the Italic branch of Indo-European. The official language of France is spoken by over 50 million in the Republic itself, by a further 4 million Walloons in Southern Belgium, and by about 6 million in Switzerland, where it is one of the four official languages. Further afield, about 6 million French speakers live in Quebec, where they form something like 80 per cent of the population, while the francophone element in New England numbers about 1 million. For most of the 5 million inhabitants of Haiti the everyday language is Creole (*see* **Pidgins and Creoles**), but theoretically French is the official language of the island. Finally, there are the sixteen francophone states running across Central Africa, in all of which French provides an official administrative and commercial medium *vis-à-vis* numerous indigenous colloquials. The total number of French speakers, including those who use it regularly as a second language, is in excess of 200 million.

Dialects

In France itself there is a broad north/south division between *langue d'oïl* (langue d'œil) and *langue d'oc*, or *occitane*; in some ways, the latter is closer to Catalan than it is to the northern dialects. Gascon in the south-west of the country is a markedly divergent occitan outlier. The sub-dialect of the Isle-de-France, known as *francien*, is the basis for the modern literary standard.

It is not too much to say that since the eleventh century French literature has provided models and set standards for the western world: an all-pervasive influence which spread in the nineteenth and twentieth centuries beyond the confines of Europe to Africa and the Far East. The history of French literature falls readily into the following six periods:

1. Eleventh to thirteenth centuries: the *chansons de geste*, including the *Chanson de Roland*; the *romans* (Arthurian cycle, *Roman de la Rose*).
2. Sixteenth century: Rabelais and Montaigne.
3. Seventeenth century: Malherbe, Descartes, Pascal, Boileau; Corneille, Molière, Racine.
4. Eighteenth century: Montesquieu; the Enlightenment and L'Encyclopédie; Voltaire, Rousseau.
5. Nineteenth century: Chateaubriand; de Vigny, Lamartine; Baudelaire, Mallarmé, George Sand, Victor Hugo, Alexandre Dumas, Gustave

Flaubert, Emile Zola.
6. Twentieth century.

SCRIPT
Latin alphabet, with three accents, circumflex, acute, and grave, and cedilla.

In the Old French period, many lexemes were, at least in writing, closer to their Latin originals than they are in Modern French, and the orthography was correspondingly more rational, with a closer correlation between sound and symbol: cf. OF *vedeir* 'see' > MF *voir*.

The period from the fourteenth to the sixteenth century brought accelerated phonetic change in which monosyllabism was a key feature, along with a consciously archaizing and sometimes misguided attempt to restore Latin orthography: e.g.

OF doit >   MF doigt   (Latin di**g**itum)
OF pie   >   MF pie**d**   (Latin pe**d**em)

The result is that the overall correspondence between pronunciation and notation in Modern French is weak; for example, /ɛ/ is notated in half a dozen different ways, and the proportion of mute letters is high. In this respect, French joins Portuguese in sharp contrast to Italian and Spanish.

In the nineteenth and twentieth centuries several attempts were made at achieving a limited rationalization of the orthography: e.g. the Beslais commissions in 1952 and 1965 which proposed *inter alia* a standardized plural marker in *-s* (i.e. the abolition of the *-x* marker) and the reduction of superfluous geminates. No action has been taken on these points.

PHONOLOGY

Consonants
stops: p, b, t, d, k, g
fricatives: f, v, s, z, ʃ, ʒ, ʁ
nasals: m, n, ɲ
lateral: l/ ļ
semi-vowels: j, w

Vowels
(a) oral: i, y, e, ø, œ, ɛ, a, ə, ɔ, o, u; + many diphthongs/triphthongs involving /j/, /w/ and /ɥ/;
(b) nasal: ɛ̃, ɔ̃, ã, œ̃

Some important features in the development of French phonology since the Old French period:

1. loss of affricates and of /h/;
2. strong tendency towards monosyllabism, involving 3 (below);

3. in Latin forms of $C_1V_1C_2(C_3)V_2C_4$ type, early loss of C_4 followed by loss in spoken French of V_2, thus generating a new final C_2/C_3.

By the rules of French prosody, final syllables which are mute in spoken French are given their full value in verse, e.g. if followed by a consonantal initial.

In word sequences whose components are closely linked by sense, e.g. article + noun, adjective + noun, verb + personal pronoun, etc., there is a follow-through between a final consonant (normally mute) and an initial vowel; in these circumstances, a voiceless fricative is voiced:

> nous allons à Paris = /nuzalɔ̃zapari/ 'we are going to Paris'
> ils ont appris = /i(l)zɔ̃tapri/ 'they have learned'

Stress

Stress tends to fall on the final syllable in citation form; in connected speech, on the focused item.

MORPHOLOGY AND SYNTAX

French has two genders – masculine and feminine – and two numbers.

Noun

Certain nominal endings are coded for gender, e.g. the following are always feminine: *-sion/-tion/-xion*; *-aison*, *-ance*; and most nouns in *-ment* are masculine. Essentially, however, gender in French is unpredictable.

A distinction between nominative (direct) and oblique case persisted throughout the Old French period, and most nouns in Modern French are derived from the oblique forms:

Latin		Old French		Modern French
noctem	>	noit	>	nuit
hominen	>	hom	>	homme
gentem	>	gent	>	gens

The plural marker is *-s*; a few nouns ending in *-eu/eau/ou* take *-x*: e.g. *le feu* 'fire' – *les feux*.

Modern French has lost all trace of declension; all syntactic relationships are expressed by means of prepositions, e.g. *de*, *à*, *pour*, etc.

Coalescence of the definite article with the preposition *de* was illustrated above. In the same way, *a + le → au, a + les → aux*. Unlike Italian, French does not permit coalescence of *de/a* with the feminine article (cf. It. della, alla).

Article

French has two articles. Both the definite and the indefinite article are marked for gender in the singular, and for number:

	Masculine	Feminine	Plural
definite	le	la	les (before vowel, *le/la → l'*)
indefinite	un	une	des 'some'

The preposition *de* coalesces with the definite article to produce the partitive articles: *de + le → du*; *de + les → des*; (*de + la* gives *de la*): thus, *du pain* '(some) bread'; *des livres* '(some) books'. But these forms are reduced to *de* if an adjective precedes the noun: e.g. *des miroirs* 'mirrors': *de grands miroirs* 'big mirrors'; *vers de nouveaux rivages* (Lamartine) 'towards new shores'.

The indefinite and partitive articles have a single negative form, *de*: e.g. *Il y a du pain* 'There is bread'; *Il n'y a pas de pain* 'There is no bread'.

Adjective

As attribute, the adjective usually follows its noun, but a few very common adjectives always precede: e.g. *bon* 'good', *mauvais* 'bad', *grand* 'big', *petit* 'small', etc. In either position, the adjective agrees with the noun in gender and number. Often, the siting of an adjective is a matter of style: cf.

> un emploi déréglé et passionnel du stupéfiant image (Aragon)
> 'a wild and passionate use of the stupefying image'

Feminine forms normally add -*e*: e.g. *lourd* – *lourde* 'heavy'. On the phonological plane, this addition very often involves activation of a mute consonant:

Masculine	Feminine
grand /grã/ 'big'	grande /grãd/
blanc /blã/ 'white'	blanche /blãš/
bon /bõ/ 'good'	bonne /bɔn/

COMPARATIVE
Made with *plus* 'more': e.g. *belle* 'beautiful (fem.)' – *plus belle*. Irregular suppletive forms are: *bon* 'good' – *meilleur*; *mauvais* 'bad' – *pire*.

Pronoun

(a) Conjunctive: first and second person have nominative and oblique forms; third person has nominative + two oblique forms, direct and indirect, with gender distinguished.

		Singular	Plural
1		je – me	nous – nous
2		tu – te	vous – vous
3	masc.	il – le – lui	ils – les – leur
	fem.	elle – la – lui	elles – les – leur

The second person plural, *vous* is used as a polite form of address for singular.

The sequential order of the conjunctive pronouns is fixed: *me, te, nous, vous* (also the reflexive *se*) precede *le, la, les*, which, in turn, precede *lui, leur*. Following all of these come the third person oblique forms: *y* (dat.) and *en* (gen.), which are used primarily with non-human referents: e.g. *J'y vais* 'I'm going there'; *Je n'en ai jamais entendu* 'I've never heard of it.'

Pronominal order changes in the imperative mood: cf. *je le/les lui/leur ai donné* 'I gave it/them to him/her/them'; but *donne-le-moi* 'give it to me'. *Moi* in the last example is the first person singular disjunctive.

(b) The forms for the remaining persons are: *toi, lui/elle*; pl. *nous, vous, eux/elles*. These are used mainly with prepositions and for emphasis: e.g. *pour moi* 'for me'; *à toi* 'to you'; *avec eux* 'with them (masc.)'.

POSSESSIVE ADJECTIVES
The singular forms show the gender of the possessed object in all three persons: *mon – ma – mes*, etc.: *mon frère* 'my brother' – *ma sœur* 'my sister'; pl. common: *mes frères*. The plural forms, *notre, votre, leur*, are not marked for gender: e.g. *leur frère/sœur*; but show number of the possessed object: *nos, vos, leurs*.

DEMONSTRATIVE ADJECTIVE
ce/cet (masc.) – *cette* (fem.) – *ces* (pl.) 'this/that'.

DEMONSTRATIVE PRONOUN
celui-ci/celle-ci 'this one', *celui-là/celle-là* 'that one'; pl. *ceux-ci/là*; *celles-ci/là*. That is, the distal member is expressed by replacing *ci* of the proximate by *là*.

INTERROGATIVE PRONOUN
qui 'who?'; *quoi* 'what?'; *qu'est-ce qui/que*.

RELATIVE PRONOUN
qui/que; *ce qui/ce que*; with oblique forms, e.g. *dont* (gen.): *un homme qui sait le français* 'a man who knows French'; *Montrez-moi les livres que vous avez achetés* 'Show me the books you have bought'; *C'est un homme que je ne connais guère* 'He's a man I scarcely know'; *une classe dont l'utilité social a disparu* 'a class whose social usefulness has vanished'.

Numerals

1–10: *un/une, deux, trois, quatre, cinq, six, sept, huit, neuf, dix*; 11 *onze*; 12 *douze*; 13 *treize*; 14 *quatorze*; 15 *quinze*; 16 *seize*; 17–19, *dix* + unit; 20 *vingt*; 21 *vingt et un*; 22 *vingt-deux*; 30 *trente*; 40 *quarante*; 100 *cent*.

Verb

There are three main conjugations, with infinitive forms ending in *-er*, *-ir*, and *-re*. *-ir* verbs are further sub-divided into (a) verbs like *finir* 'to finish', which take the infix *-iss-* in the plural forms of the indicative and subjunctive present and imperfect, and in the imperative; and (b) those like *ouvrir* 'to open', which do not.

There are indicative, imperative, and subjunctive moods. A passive voice is formed analytically by means of the auxiliary verb *être* 'to be' plus the past participle of the sense-verb: e.g. *(ses comédies) n'ont pas été écrites pour la scène* '(his comedies) were not written for the stage'.

Compound tenses are made with the auxiliary *avoir* 'to have', except for verbs of motion and reflexive verbs, which use *être* 'to be': e.g. *j'ai donné* 'I have given'; *je suis allé* 'I have gone/I went'; *Il s'est couché de bonne heure* 'He went to bed early.' Both *avoir* and *être* are highly irregular.

Specimen paradigms: *donner* 'to give' and *finir* 'to finish'; forms in regular use in modern literary and spoken French:

Present indicative:

singular	1	je donne	je finis
	2	tu donnes	tu finis
	3	il/elle donne	il finit
plural	1	nous donnons	nous finissons
	2	vous donnez	vous finissez
	3	ils/elles donnent	ils finissent

Imperfect: *je donn-ais, -ais, -ait; -ions, -iez, -aient; je finiss-ais*, etc.

Future: infinitive + the following endings: sing. *-ai, -as, -a*; pl. *-ons, -ez, -ont*: e.g. *je donnerai, il finira*.

Conditional: infinitive + imperfect endings: e.g. *je donner.ais, nous finir.ions*, etc.

Present subjunctive: sing. and 3rd p. pl. as present indicative (+ *-iss-* if present in indicative plural), 1st and 2nd pl. as imperfect: e.g. *que je donne; qu'il finisse; que nous donnions; qu'ils finissent*.

Imperative: *donne – donnons – donnez; finis – finissons – finissez*.

PARTICIPLES
Present: *donnant, finissant*; past: *donné, fini*. The past participle of verbs in *-re* is made with *-u*: e.g. *vendu* 'sold', *rompu* 'broken'.

These are regular verbs; there are, of course, many irregular verbs, some of which can be grouped, e.g. verbs in *-eler*, in *-yer*, in *-cer/-ger*.

A striking feature of these paradigms (and of French conjugation in general) is the homophonic nature of first, second, and third singular, usually shared by third plural as well. Thus, *donnais, donnais, donnait, donnaient*, are all pronounced as /dɔnɛ/; *donne, donnes, donne, donnent* as /dɔn/. It follows from this that the personal conjunctive pronouns have to be used to identify subject, a role in which they are often supported by use of the disjunctive series as well: e.g. *Moi, je veux vivre à la campagne* '(Me,) I want to live in the country.'

The subject pronoun cannot be omitted, even where, as in first person plural, the verb form itself provides sufficient identification: e.g. **nous** *avons mangé* 'we have eaten' (contrast It. *abbiamo mangiato*, and Sp. *hemos comido*).

The past historic tense (or, simple past) is found in formal literary style, though no longer in spoken or informal written style; e.g. of *donner*: sing. *je donnai, tu donnas, il donna*; pl. *nous donâmes, vous donâtes, ils donnèrent.*

The present subjunctive is used in subordinate clauses, following main verbs expressing emotion, doubt, opinion, prohibition, fear, etc.; also after certain subordinating conjunctions: *afin que* 'in order that', *quoique* 'although', *avant que* 'before', etc.: e.g. *Je crains qu'il (ne) soit mort* 'I'm afraid he may be dead'; *quoiqu'il soit pauvre* ... 'although he is poor ...'; *J'approuve qu'il le fasse immédiatement* 'I agree he should do it at once.' The imperfect subjunctive is virtually obsolete.

Negation

The standard negator is *ne ... pas*: e.g. *je ne sais pas* 'I do not know'. There is an increasing tendency, especially in spoken French, to drop the pre-verbal *ne*: e.g. *Je suis pas malade* (Sartre) 'I'm not ill'; *C'est pas ça qui manque* (Sartre) 'That's not what's missing.' In older literary style, *pas* was often omitted: e.g. *je ne sais comment cela se fait* (Maurois) 'I don't know how one does that.'

Prepositions

Apart from their function as spatial and temporal indicators – *dans le jardin* 'in the garden', *sur la table* 'on the table' *après moi* 'after me', *à la campagne* 'in the country', etc. – certain prepositions, notably *à* and *de*, are syntactically bound to specific verbal constructions:

> *commander à/défendre à quelqu'un de faire quelque chose* 'order/forbid someone to do something';
>
> *enseigner quelqu'un à faire quelque chose* 'teach someone to do something'.

Word order

SVO is basic. Simple or complex inversion occurs in certain syntactic situations.

[1] Avant que Dieu crée le monde, la Parole existait déjà; la Parole était avec Dieu, et la Parole était Dieu. [2] La Parole était donc avec Dieu au commencement. [3] Dieu a fait toutes choses par elle; rien de ce qui existe n'a été fait sans elle. [4] En elle était la vie, et cette vie donnait la lumière aux hommes. [5] La lumière brille dans l'obscurité, et l'obscurité ne l'a pas reçue.

[6] Dieu envoya son messager, un homme appelé Jean. [7] Il vint comme témoin, pour parler de la lumière. Il vint pour que tous croient grâce à ce qu'il disait. [8] Il n'était pas lui-même la lumière, il était le témoin qui vient pour parler de la lumière.

FULANI (Fulbe)

INTRODUCTION

This language (also known as Fulfulde) belongs to the West Atlantic branch of the Benue-Congo family. The total number of Fulani speakers is estimated at c. 10 million, the great majority of whom live in northern and eastern Nigeria. Others are scattered over a dozen West African states, from Chad to the seaboard.

Under the Fulani emirate of Adamawa (1806–1901) literature was mainly in Arabic. From the mid-eighteenth century onwards, a main centre of *ajami* Fulani poetry was in what is now Guinea.

PHONOLOGY

Consonants

> stops: p, b, ḅ, t, d, ḍ, k, g, q, ʔ
> affricates: tʃ, dʒ, dz
> nasals: m, n
> fricatives: f, s, h
> lateral and flap: l, r
> semi-vowels: j, w

Initial and medial /b, d, g, dʒ, j/ are frequently nasalized; notated by prefixed *m/n*. Note tendency to transfer nasalization to preceding long vowel: $C\bar{V}$ + nasalization → $C\tilde{\bar{V}}$.

PAIRED CONSONANTS

This a very striking feature of Fulani structure. The paired sets are:

b	w		dʒ	j
p	f		tʃ	s
d	r		g	w
			k	h

That is, stops are paired with their relative fricatives. *See* **Noun** below.

Vowels

> short: a, ə, ε, ɪ, ɔ, u
> long: a, e, i, o, u

476

There are seven glide diphthongs onto /j, w/.

Stress

Stress tends to long vowels.

MORPHOLOGY AND SYNTAX

Noun

No article or gender, no case system: case by position. The fundamental dichotomy in the language is human/non-human.

PLURAL

Two classes of noun are distinguished, personal and non-personal. The plural of personal nouns is formed by changing the initials as follows:

b	→ w/g	j /dʒ	→ y
ch /tʃ/	→ s	k	→ h
d	→ r	p	→ f
g	→ w/y		

These changes are reversed in the plural formation of non-personal nouns:

w	→ b/g	f	→ p
h	→ k	y	→ j/g
s	→ ch /tʃ/	r	→ d

Unvoiced ɓ, ɗ, ɣ, the nasalized consonants, and the initials of loan-words do not change in either class.

Nouns in the personal class with singular in *-o*, make a plural in *-ɓe* or *'en*: e.g. *konōwo* 'warrior': pl. *honōɓe*.

Modulation of initial consonant is accompanied by a change in final vowel. Examples:

Singular	Plural
*g*orko 'male person'	*w*orbe
*w*ordu 'dog'	*g*ordi
*d*ebbo 'female'	*r*eube
*r*euru 'bitch'	*d*ebbi

Genitive relationship is indicated by construct: *puchu lāmiɗo* 'the king's horse'; *puchu bāba māko* 'his father's horse'.

Dative precedes accusative noun, follows accusative pronoun.

Adjective

Verbal forms supply predicative adjectival sense: an attributive form is then supplied by the neutral participle, normally in *-ɗum*, often in *-dʒum* (spelled

-jum): e.g. *wōḍi* 'it is good', *bōḍḍum* 'good'; *woji* 'it is red' *bodējum/bodēdʒum/* 'red'.

The *-jum* class of noun has a personal singular form in *-jo*, with plural in *-'en* or *-ḅe*: e.g. *danējo* 'white man'; plural *ranēḅe*.

The *-jum* affix can be added to any word to form an adjectival derivative: e.g. *hande* 'today'; *handējum* 'today's', 'actual'.

A nasal initial in the noun is resumed in the adjective: cf. *mbōdi mboḍēri* 'a red snake', pl. *boḍḍe boḍēje*; *yēso woḍēwo* 'a red face', pl. *gese boḍēje*.

COMPARATIVE
Made with *ḅura* 'to excel': e.g. *Puchu ḅuri nagge* 'A horse is better than a cow'; *Leggal ḅuri towugo dou sūdu* 'The tree is taller than the house' (*dou* 'over').

Pronoun

PERSONAL INDEPENDENT PRONOUNS
Sing. 1 *min*, 2 *an*, 3 *kanko*; pl. incl. *enen*, excl. *minin*, 2 *onon*, 3 *kamḅe*. These are not used with verbs. Instead, the conjunctive forms are used:

	Singular			Plural	
	Nominative	Accusative		Nominative	Accusative
1	mi	yam	inc.	en	en
			excl.	min	min
2	a	ma		on	on
3	o	mo		ḅe	ḅe

POSSESSIVE FORMS
E.g. sing. 1 *am*, 2 *ma/māḍa*, 3 *māko*. These follow the noun: e.g. *puchu māko* 'his horse'; cf. *o yi'i mo* 'he saw him'; *o dilli bē māko* 'he went with him'.

DEMONSTRATIVE PRONOUNS
o/ḍo 'this', pl. *ḅe*; *on/ḍon* 'that', pl. *ḅen*; *to/oya* 'that (further away)', pl. *ḅeya*.

INTERROGATIVE PRONOUN
moi 'who?', pl. *ḅeye*.

RELATIVE PRONOUN
mo, pl. *ḅe*: e.g. *tigōwo mo a yi'i kengya* 'the merchant whom you saw yesterday'.

Numerals

1–5: *gōtel/go'o*, *ḍiḍi*, *tati*, *nai*, *jow*; 6–9 are based on 5: *jowēgo*, *jowēḍiḍi*, *jowētati*, *jowēnai*. 10 *sappo*; 20 *nōgas*; 30 *chappanḍe tati*; 40 *chappanḍe nai*; 100 *temerre*.

Verb

The verb has three voices: active with infinitive in *-ugo*; passive with infinitive in *-ēgo*; middle with infinitive in *-āgo*.

Perfect and imperfective aspectual system rather than tense. Thus the perfect endings in the active voice are *-i*, negative *-ai*; imperfective: *-a*, *-ata*, *-an*. *No* may be added to fix action in past.

Initial of stem changes for number: e.g. *o windi* 'he wrote', *ɓe mbindi* 'they wrote'.

SPECIMEN PARADIGM

> Present: *mi ɗon winda* 'I am writing', negative *mi windata*; *min ɗon mbinda* 'we are writing', negative *min mbindata*.
> Imperfect: *mi ɗonno winda* 'I was writing', negative *mi windatāno*; *min ɗonno mbinda* 'we were writing', negative *min mbindatāno*.
> Future: *mi wíndata* 'I shall write', negative *mi windáta*; *min mbindata*.
> Preterite I: *mi windi*, negative *mi windai*.
> Preterite II: *mi windino*, negative *mi windaino*.
> Imperative: *windu – mbinde*, negative *tā windu – tā mbinde*.

PARTICIPLES

(a) Imperfective or present: personal *bindaiɗo*, pl. *windaiɓe* 'about to write'; neutral *bindaiɗun*.
(b) Perfective: personal *binduɗo*, pl. *winduɓe*; neutral *binduɗum*.

VOICE

> Passive: not much used, active forms being preferred. Pronominal forms and initial concord as for active voice.
> Middle: pronominal forms and initial concord largely as for active voice.

DERIVATIVE STEMS

There are five of these;

> *-ina* is always transitive: e.g. *o andi* 'he knew', *o andini mo* 'he informed him';
> *-ra*, *-rV* is instrumental; *see* **Word formation**, below.
> *-tV* is intensive, or expresses the contrary of stem meaning: e.g. *maɓɓugo* 'to shut', *maɓɓitugo* 'to open';
> *-dV* has various meanings: e.g. *o jangi* 'he read', *o jangidi* 'he read through and finished'.

There are several other formants of this kind, e.g. *-tira/-indira* expressing reciprocity: e.g. *hōfna* 'to greet, *ɓe kōfnindiri* 'they greeted each other'.

Prepositions

There are a couple of dozen of these: e.g. *diga* 'from', *tana* 'without', *bāwo* 'behind': e.g. *batākewol fāgo hā alkāli* 'a letter for the judge'.

Word formation

Formation of nouns from verbs: e.g. *-ōwo* 'agent': *winda* 'to write', *bindōwo* 'writer', pl. *windōɓe*.

Noun of instrument formed from *-ra*-derived stem, with neutral endings *-ɗum*, pl. *-ɗe*; *-gal*, pl. *ɗe*; *-gol*, pl. *ɗi*: thus from *winda* 'to write': *bindirgol* 'pen', pl. *bindirɗi*; *windirde* 'office', pl. *bindirɗe*; *binduki* 'writing'.

Word order

Normally SVO.

---

1 Har fuɗɗam Wolde wonno, Wolde ɗonno wondi be Allah, Wolde nde Allah. 2 Har fuɗɗam o ɗonno wondi be Allah; 3 kala hunde fuh e mako lati; kala ɗum ko lati fuh ɗum lataki bila mako. 4 Nder mako ngēndam wonno; ngēndam ɗām ɗam annora 'yimɓe. 5 Annora kā e yaino nder nyiɓre; nyiɓre jālaki ka.

6 Wodino gorko nulaɗo ibgo e Allah, inde muɗum Yuhanna. 7 Kaŋko o wari ngam sedamku, ha o sedna annora kā, ngam ha moɓgal fuh nuɗɗina ngam mako. 8 Kaŋko o lataki annora kā, amma o wari ngam o sedna annora kā.

GAELIC

See **Scottish Gaelic**.

GAGAUZ

INTRODUCTION

Gagauz is a member of the Oguz-Bulgar sub-group of Western Turkic (Baskakov's (1966) classification). At present, there are about 150,000 speakers of Gagauz in the Moldavian Soviet Socialist Republic, and in the Odessa area of the Ukraine, with a few in Bulgaria and Romania. It was from north-eastern Bulgaria that the Gagauz moved *en masse* in the early nineteenth century, and it is to the Turkish dialects spoken there that the language is most closely related – so much so, indeed, that several authorities have considered Gagauz to be a dialect of Turkish. Structurally, this is the case, but Gagauz has been influenced by Slavonic and Romanian.

Gagauz has adopted a great many Slavonic and Moldavian/Romanian loan-words.

SCRIPT

In 1957 a script was introduced on a Cyrillic base + *ö* (= /œ/), *ÿ* (= /y/), *ä* (= /ɛ/). Very little use has been made of this script.

PHONOLOGY

Consonants

The consonantal inventory is standard Turkish but includes, in addition, the velar fricative /x/ and the dental affricate /ts/.

A notable feature of Gagauz pronunciation is the marked palatalization of consonants before front vowels: e.g. *köpek* 'dog' is [k'œp'ek'].

Vowels

front: i, e, ɛ, œ, y
back: ɪ, ɛ, a, o, u

All occur both long and short. A long vowel may be primary or secondary, i.e. due to the elision of intervocalic consonant, either historically present or still written but dropped in pronunciation: e.g. *sābi* < *sahibi* (Arabic ṣāḥib).

VOWEL HARMONY
Standard; /o, œ/ do not appear in affixation.

482

MORPHOLOGY AND SYNTAX

In general, standard Turkish, with small variations in spelling and pronunciation. Consonant elision leads to some unfamiliar forms, e.g. in the declension of *inek* 'cow': gen. *inän*, dat. *inä,* but loc. *inektä.*

The comparative degree of adjectives is made with *tā*: *tā uzun* 'longer'.

Personal pronoun: the base forms for first and second singular have the broad vowel *ä*: e.g. *bän*, *sän*, reverting to the narrower form in the oblique cases: *benim*, *beni*, etc.

A unique form is provided by the potential modal marker *nižä*: e.g. *var nižä* 'possible, can do'; *yok nižä* 'not possible, can't do'; *var nižä gideyim* 'I can go'; *yok nižä gidäsin* 'you (sing.) can't go'; *yoktu nižä gitsinnär* 'they can't go'.

Word order

Under Slavonic influence; SVO.

> 1 Келямъ ибтидаде мевджудъ иди, ве келамъ Аллахжнъ нездинде иди, ве келамъ Аллахъ иди;
>
> 2 бу келамъ ибтидаде Аллахжнъ нездинде иди.
>
> 3 Херъ шей анжнъ васитасийле вуджуде гелди, ве вуджуде гелмишъ оланларданъ ансжзъ биръ шей вуджуде гелмеди.
>
> 4 Хаятъ анде иди, хаятъ дахи адемлеринъ нуржъ иди.
>
> 5 Ве нуръ зулметде зия вериръ, зулметъ дахи анж идракъ етмезъ иди.
>
> 6 Аллахъ тарафжндапъ ирсалъ олунмушъ Иоанисъ исминде биръ адемъ варъ иди.
>
> 7 Ишбу адемъ шехадетъ ичунъ гелди, таки нуржнъ хакжнда шехадетъ етмесийле, джумле адемлеръ анжнъ васитасжйле имана гелсилнеръ.

GAN

Belonging to the Sinitic family, the Gan complex of dialects lies in Jiangxi, with some spread into adjacent regions of Hunan. About 25 million people speak one or another form of the Gan language.

The group lacks the voiced stops /b, d, g/, which are characteristic of the neighbouring Wu dialects (*see* **Wu**). Treatment of final /p, t, k/ varies from one dialect to another; retention is typical of the south of the speech area.

GARO

INTRODUCTION

This language belongs to the Baric group of Tibeto-Burman. The ethnonym is Achik. Garo is spoken in the Garo Hills area of Assam, and in adjacent parts of Bangladesh, by about 400,000 people.

SCRIPT

The Bengali script was originally used for the language (Bible translation, etc.); the Roman alphabet is now in use for some literary activity, including a long-running weekly newspaper.

PHONOLOGY

Consonants

The labial, dental, and velar series are represented by unvoiced and voiced stops + associated nasals: e.g. /p, b, m/. /ts, tʃ/ and /dz/dʒ/ are present, also /s, r/l/ and the glottal stop. The nasals /m, n, ŋ/ and /r/ have glottalized allophones.

Vowels

The vowels are /i, e, a, o, u/, with intermediate values.

Stress

Stress is phrasal.

MORPHOLOGY AND SYNTAX

Garo has no form of inflection; the accidence is entirely suffixal apart from one prefix. Formally, nominal and verbal bases differ only in their respective valencies: i.e. nominal bases are compatible with nominal affixes, verbal bases with verbal affixes. Some nominal affixes may, however, be attached to verbs expanded by certain verbal affixes.

Noun

Suffixes, e.g. *-raŋ*, are available, but their use is optional: e.g. *man.de.raŋ* 'men'. Reduplication may also be used to indicate plurality.

CASE MARKERS

E.g. *ko* for objective, *na* dative, *ni* genitive: X *ni* Y 'X's Y'. *Ni* is attached to personal pronoun to make possessive: e.g. *aŋ.ni* 'my'. The *ni* form acts as base for secondary suffixes, e.g. *gim.in* 'about': *naŋ.ni.gim.in* 'about you'.

A locative is made with *o* which also renders the verb 'to have': e.g. *aŋ.o kitap doŋ.a* 'I have a book'. Like *ni*, *o* also serves as base for further suffixation: e.g. with dative *na*: *an.ti.o.na re'aŋ.gen* 'will go to market' (*an.ti* 'market', *re'aŋ* 'to go', *gen* is future marker).

Other case makers are e.g. *ci* 'to/from', *miŋ* 'with'.

NUMERICAL CLASSIFIERS

In Garo these are sited between noun and numeral: e.g. *sak* for human beings: *man.de sak.git.tam* 'three men' (*-git.tam* 'three'). *Ge* is an all-purpose numerical classifier, equivalent to Chinese *ge*; *te* is used for buildings; *poŋ* for long, cylindrical objects, etc.

Adjective

Treated as verbal base; as attribute, adjective follows noun.

Pronoun

PERSONAL

	Singular	Plural
1	aŋ.a	excl. ciŋ.a, incl. a'n.ciŋ
2	na'.a	na'sim.aŋ
3	bi.a	u.a.maŋ/u.a.raŋ

Aŋ.a and *na'.a* have oblique forms *aŋ/na'ŋ* to which suffixes are attached: e.g. *na'ŋ.ko* 'you (acc.)'.

DEMONSTRATIVE PRONOUN/ADJECTIVE
i.a 'this'; *a.o.a.* 'that'.

INTERROGATIVE PRONOUN
sa.wa 'who?'; *ma.i.ma* 'what?'.

RELATIVE PRONOUN
A relative construction with *je* has been borrowed from Bengali: e.g. *Je.ko dok.a.ha u.an man.de o'ŋ.a* 'That is the man who was hit' (*dok* 'to hit'; *a.ha* = past-tense marker; *u.a* + *-n* = 3rd p.; *oŋ.a* 'to be').

Numerals

1–10: these are bound forms following classifiers: *-sa*, *-gin.i*, *-git.tam*, *-bri*, *-boŋ.a*, *-dok*, *-sin.i*, *-cet*, *-sku*, *-ci.kiŋ*. 20 *kor.grik*; 30 *kor.a.ci*; 40 *sot.bri*; 100 *rit.ca.sa*.

Verb

Tense and aspect markers are affixed to base: e.g.

> *eŋ* marks continuous action: e.g. *ca'.eŋ.a* 'am/is/are eating';
> *man* marks perfective aspect: e.g. *ca'.man.jok* 'has finished eating';
> *jok* past tense;
> *(a).ha* past tense;
> *gen* future marker;

NEGATION
The marker is *(gi.)ja*: e.g. *ca'.ja.ha* 'did not eat'.

IMPERATIVE
bo; negative imperative: *da* + V + *bo*.

Subordinate verbs and adverbs can be further added to base + tense markers; e.g. *on* makes temporal subordinate clauses: *u.a sok.ba.on* 'when he comes' (*sok* 'to arrive'; *ba* is a directional marker, 'hither'). There is a large inventory of adverbial affixes like *ba*: for example, *an* is the 'thither' counterpart of *ba*, indicating motion away from first person; *-pir-* suggests recapitulation, reiteration of an action; *-rim-* is comitative; *-grik-* suggests reciprocity.

Causative verbs are constructed with the affix *-at-*: e.g. *aŋ.a u.ko ca'.at.jok* 'I made him eat'; *-cim-*, desiderative marker: e.g. *ca'.gin.ok.cim* 'feel(s) like eating' (where *gin.ok* is an intentional future marker).

FORMANTS
E.g. *-gip.a-*, agent: e.g. *ca'.gip.a man.de* 'the person who eats'; *-ram-* marks locus of action: e.g. *ca'.ram* 'eating place'.

Word order

SOV is normal.

1 Chengon Kata gnangchim, aro ua Kata Isol baksachim, aro ua Kata Isolchim. 2 Uan chengon Isol baksachim. 3 Uachin pilakan ongaha; aro uni griode onggiminoni onggipa mingsaba dongja. 4 Unon janggi gnangchim, aro ua janggi manderangna seng'a ongachim. 5 Seng'a andalao tengsua; aro andala uko rim'jachim. 6 Isolni watata mande saksa rebaaha, uni bimung Johan. 7 Antangchi maikai darangan beberana mangen, seng'ani gimin saki on'na ine ua saki ongna rebaaha. 8 Uan seng'a ongjachim, indiba seng'ani gimin saki on'na (rebara).

GE'EZ

See **Ethiopic**.

GEORGIAN

INTRODUCTION

Georgian belongs to the South Caucasian (Kartvelian) group of languages, and is spoken by about 3½ million in the Georgian Soviet Socialist Republic. It has been a literary language since the sixth century AD. The Old Georgian period extends from the beginnings to the twelfth/thirteenth centuries; this period is rich in translation, mainly of religious works, and culminates in the work of the greatest Georgian poet, Shota Rustaveli, the author of the heroic epic *Vepkhis Tqaosani*, 'The Man in the Tiger Skin'.

It was not until the early eighteenth century that Georgia began to recover from the ravages of the Mongol conquest: King Vakhtang VI edited and completed the corpus of chronicles covering the dark period, known as *Kartlis Tskhovreba*, 'The Life of Georgia'. In the 1860s the drive for a unified literary language was led by three distinguished writers – Prince Ilia Chavchavadze, Akaki Tsereteli, and Vazha-Pshavela. Among modern writers, Niko Lortkipanidze and K. Gamsakhurdia are worthy of special mention.

SCRIPT

Old Georgian was written in the *xucuri* character, traditionally invented by Mesrop Mashtots, to whom the Armenians owe their script. In the eleventh century the ecclesiastical *xucuri* was replaced by the character known as the *mxedruli* 'civil', which is in use today. Georgian is the only Caucasian language to have developed its own script.

PHONOLOGY

Consonants

Central to the Georgian phonological system is the contrast between voiced, voiceless aspirate, and voiceless ejective phonemes (the latter notated with subscript dots in the text), found in the stops (three series) and the affricates (two series):

stops: b, p, p'; d, t, t'; g, k, k'; q
affricates: dz, ts, t's'; dʒ, tʃ, t'ʃ'
fricatives: v, s, z, ʃ, ʒ, x, γ, h
nasals: m, n
lateral and flap: l, r
semi-vowel: j

In the above inventory, /p, t, k/ are aspirates; /p', t', k'/ are ejectives (glottalized). Similarly for the affricates. Multiple clusters are frequent in Georgian; an example of a six-term cluster, given by Comrie and Hewitt (1981), is *mçvrtneli* 'trainer'. Such clusters have single or dual/triple release (involving shwa) depending on whether the components are homogeneous or not.

Vowels

i, ε, a, ɔ, u

Stress

On first syllable of disyllabics; in longer words, stress tends to fall on first and antepenultimate syllables.

MORPHOLOGY AND SYNTAX

Noun

There is no grammatical gender; if it is necessary to distinguish between sexes, defining terms may be added, e.g. for *švili* 'child': *važi.švili* 'boy–child' = 'son'; *kali.švili* 'girl–child' = 'daughter'.
There is no definite article. The numeral *ert* 'one', may be used as indefinite article.

NUMBER
The plural marker is *-eb-* following stem, preceding case markers: e.g. *çigni* 'book', pl. *çignebi*; *mta* 'mountain': *mtebši* 'in the mountains'. There is also an older literary plural in *-ni*: e.g. *dzma* 'brother', pl. *dzmani*.

DECLENSION
The following endings are added to consonant stems:

nominative	-i	instrumental	-it
ergative	-ma	adverbial	-ad
accusative/dative	-s	ablative	-dan
genitive	-is	locative	-ši

Vocalic stems drop *-i*, and take *-m* in the ergative.

Examples: *kalaki* 'town': *kalakši* 'in the town'; *samšoblo.dan* 'from the homeland'; *maṭareblit* 'with the train'; *Petres çigni* 'Peter's book'. The ergative in *-m(a)* is the case of the logical subject with a transitive verb in the aorist (*see* **Verb**, below).

Adjective

The attributive adjective precedes the noun, and is, in the main, invariable. Consonant stems, however, drop *-i* in the dative (e.g. *didi* 'big', becomes *did*)

491

and take the ergative -*ma*: cf. *patara*$\emptyset$ *bavšma* 'by a small child'; *didma bavšma* 'by a big child'; *ahal çigni* 'new book'; *ahal muzeumši* 'in the new museum'.

Pronoun

PERSONAL
Independent, with subject, direct and indirect pronoun markers, and possessives:

		Independent	Subject marker	Direct object	Indirect object	Possessive
sing.	1	me	v-	m	mi	čemi
	2	šen	(h) $\emptyset$-	g	gi	šeni
	3	is	-s	$\emptyset$	u	misi
plur.	1	čven	v...t	gv	gvi	čveni
	2	tkven	$\emptyset$...t	g...t	gi...t	tkveni
	3	isini	-en/-n	$\emptyset$	u	mati

Examples: *me v.çer* 'I write'; *is çer.s* 'he writes'; *čven v.çer.t* 'we write'; direct object with *xatav* 'to paint'; *šen m.xatav me* 'you paint me'; *isini gv.xatav.en čven* 'they are painting us'.

The subject marker of the first person *v-* is always dropped before the second person object marker -*g*-: i.e. **v.g.xatav šen* → *g.xatav šen* 'I paint you'. That is, the absence of a subject marker, plus the presence of a second person object marker, identifies the verb form as first person: *g.xedav* 'I see you'.

The independent forms, *me, šen, is*, etc., are declined, with little change in form; e.g. *me* is both nominative and ergative.

DEMONSTRATIVE PRONOUN/ADJECTIVE
As in Armenian, there are three degrees of distance, associated with the three persons: *es* (first person) 'this', *eg* (second person) 'that', *igi* (third person) 'that yonder'. These are declined and used for both numbers. The oblique base of *is* is *ama-*.

INTERROGATIVE PRONOUN
vin 'who?'; *ra* 'what?'; *romeli* 'which?': e.g. *Vin aris es ḳaci?* 'Who is this man?'; *Vis xatav.s axla es mxatvari?* 'Whom is this painter painting now?'

RELATIVE PRONOUN
-*c* is added to the interrogative forms: *romelic, vinc, rac*: e.g.

> is çerili, romelic me gamo.v.gzavne Tbilisidan
> 'this letter which I sent from Tbilisi'

> Ik iqo dɣes **imdeni** studentebi, **ramdenic** ik iqo gušin
> 'There were as many students here today as there were yesterday'

Numerals

1–10: *erti, ori, sami, otxi, xuti, ekvsi, švidi, rva, cxra, ati*; 11 *tert.meṭi* (*ati* → *t + ert + meṭi* 'more'); 12 *tormeṭi*. 20–99 are constructed modulo 20: thus, 20 *oci*, 30 *oc.da.ati*, 40 *or.m.oci*; 60 *sa.m.oci*. 100 *asi*.

Verb

1. In sharp contrast to the relatively simple nominal system, the Georgian verbal system is extremely complicated and difficult to describe in brief. There are two basic contrasts: verbs are (a) static or dynamic, and (b) transitive or intransitive: the latter category includes passive and middle verbs. All static verbs are intransitive; dynamic verbs may be either transitive or intransitive. Transitive verbs require the ergative construction to be used with their aorist forms, i.e. with a direct object in the *nominative* case.

2. Georgian verbs are mono- or polypersonal. For personal indices, *see* **Pronoun**, above.

3. *Conjugation*: four types are distinguished:

I   This is an active voice, and stems conjugated in it are usually transitive. Aspect is distinguished.
II Stems conjugated in this model are mostly intransitive; the second conjugation also offers one way of making passives. Aspect is distinguished.
III Denominatives are conjugated according to III. Aspect is not distinguished.
IV This is a specific conjugation for indirect verbs, whose grammatical subject is in the dative.

There is a certain amount of interchange between conjugations; e.g. verbs handled according to IV may borrow forms from II.

4. *Series and screeves*: the term 'screeve' (in Georgian *mçkrivi*) was coined by the Georgian linguist A. Sanidze to denote a finite verbal form which may be temporal (i.e. a tense), modal, or aspectual. The screeves are arranged in three series:

(a) the present–future series, comprising the following screeves: present – future – past imperfective – conditional – first subjunctive present – first subjunctive future;
(b) the aorist series: aorist – second subjunctive (optative);
(c) the perfect series: perfect – pluperfect – third subjunctive.

5. *Version*: marked by the pre-radical vowels: (∅), *a*, *i*, *u*: ∅ is neutral; *i* denotes 'for oneself'; *u* denotes action for third party; *a* is the so-called super-essive marker: action on something. Cf.

çer.s 'he writes' (neutral: no specific referential deixis);
i.çer.s 'he writes for himself', *mi.çer.s* 'he writes something for me';
u.çer.s 'he writes something for him (third party)';
v.a,çer 'I write something on something'.

6. *Pre-verbal markers*: e.g. *a-, ga-, gada-, da-, mi-/mo-, čamo-*. These function as (a) aspect markers, and (b) directional markers. E.g.

me v.çer 'I write': *me da.v.çer* 'I shall write' = 'have written' (cf. Russian perfective present form = future);
me mi.v.divar teatrši 'I am going to the theatre' (*mi-* 'thither');
me mo.v.divar sadguridan 'I am coming from the station' (*mo-* 'hither').

NEGATION
The general marker is *ar*: e.g. *arapers ar vaķeteb* 'I do nothing' (double negative). Some examples:

(a) series forms of a I conjugation verb: root *çer* 'to write':

		Singular	Plural
present screeve:	1	me vçer = I am writing	čven vçert
	2	šen Øçer	tkven Øçert
	3	is çers	isini çeren
past imperfective:	1	me vçerdi	čven vçerdit
	2	šen Øçerdi	tkven çerdit
	3	is çerda	isini çerdnen

For the conditional, the imperfective forms are preceded by *da-*: e.g. *da.v.çer.di*.

(b) series forms: aorist with logical subject in ergative: e.g. *me da.v.çer.e* 'I wrote' (*me* is the ergative case of *me* 'I'); *student.ma da.çer.a* 'the student wrote'. Optative: *student.ma unda da.çer.os* 'the student has to write' (*unda* 'must'; *-o-* is the optative ending).

(c) series: perfect: e.g. *Student.s da.u.çer.i.a çerili* 'The student has written the letter', where the *-u-* marker refers to the subject (the student) in the *dative/ accusative* case, while the *-a* marker refers to the logical object (*çerili* 'the letter') in the nominative.

POLYPERSONAL VERBS WITH SUBJECT AND OBJECT INDICES
The grid for the present screeve, for example, (either transitive or intransitive) shows 28 forms, made up as follows: four each for first and second person singular and plural; plus six each for third person singular and plural. As several of these forms would otherwise be identical, the independent forms are added: cf. *is mas Øehmareb.a* 'he helps him'; *is mat Øehmareba* 'he helps them'; *me mas v.Ø.ehmarabi* 'I help him'; *me tkven* (*v → Ø*) *g.ehmarabit* 'I help you (pl.)' (for *v → Ø*, see **Pronoun**); *tkven čven gv.ehmarebit* 'you (pl.) help us' (final *-t* is subject marker; *gv-* is object marker).

494

PASSIVE

The marker is *-i-*, *-d-*, or *-ebi-*: e.g. from *çer* 'to write': *i.çer.eb.a* 'is being written'. *-d-* is used with denominatives: e.g. *γame* 'night': *γam.d.eba* 'it becomes night' = 'night falls'.

Postpositions

These may be affixed to words in genitive, dative, or ablative case: e.g. *-tvis* 'for', affixed to genitive: *Qvela ertisatvis, erti qvelasatvis* 'All for one, one for all'; *-gan* 'from', affixed to genitive: *Visgan aris es çerili?* 'From whom is this letter?'

Affixed to dative: e.g. *-ši* 'in', *-ze* 'on, at', *-tan* 'with, at ("chez")': *kalakši* 'in the town'; *krebaze* 'at the meeting'; *dedastan* 'at one's mother's'.

Independent postpositions following genitive case:

šemdeg 'after', e.g. *gakvetilis šemdeg* 'after the lesson';
šesaxeb 'about', e.g. *Ris šesaxeb laparakobs es moçape?* 'What is this pupil talking about?';
dros 'during': e.g. *omis dros* 'during the war'.

Word order

Relatively free: SVO, SOV, OSV all occur.

1. პირველითგან იყო სიტყუა, და სიტყუა იგი იყო ღუთისა თანა, და ღმერთი იყო სიტყუა იგი.

2. ესე იყო პირველითგან ღუთისა თანა.

3. ყოველივე მის მიერ შეიქმნა, და თჳნიერ მისა არცა ერთი რა იქმნა, რაოდენი რა იქმნა.

4. მის თანა ცხოვრება იყო, და ცხოვრება იგი იყო ნათელ კაცთა.

5. და ნათელი იგი ბნელსა შინა ჰსჩანს, და ბნელი იგი მას ვერ ეწია.

6. იყო კაცი მოვლინებული ღუთისა მიერ, და სახელი მისი იოანე.

7. ესე მოვიდა მოწამედ, რათა ჰსწამოს ნათლისა მისთჳს, რათა ყოველთა ჰრწმენეს მისგან.

8. არათუ იგი იყო ნათელი, არამედ რათა ჰსწამოს ნათლისა მისთჳს.

GERMAN

INTRODUCTION

A member of the West Germanic branch of Indo-European and the official language of Germany (over 76 million speakers), German is also spoken in Austria (over 7 million) and is one of the national languages of Switzerland (c. 4 million). In addition, there are large numbers of German speakers in the Soviet Union (about 1 million), in Romania (½ million), and in Alsace-Lorraine (1½ million). The world total of German speakers is around the 100,000,000 mark.

Dialects

The Second (Germanic) Sound Shift is of fundamental importance here. During the first millennium AD, part – but not all – of the continuum of emergent German speech-forms underwent a series of phonetic mutations which can be summarized as follows:

> Proto-Germanic unvoiced stops became homorganic fricatives or affricates:
> i.e. /p, t, k/ > /f, s, x/ç/ or /pf, ts, kx/;
> voiced stops were mutated to unvoiced: /b, d, g/ > /p, t, k/.

Where these mutations were consistently carried through, the language form known as High or Upper German resulted; its emergence can be dated to, roughly, the fifth to seventh centuries. The same mutations made a partial penetration into the central German area, but left the northern dialect area untouched. Some illustrative examples:

High German	Low German	English
ich	ik	I (Anglo-Saxon: ic)
machen	maken	make
heisz	heit	hot
Apfel	appel	apple
Schiff	skip	ship

As the central German area gradually accepted the High German forms, the dialect situation was reduced to a basic opposition between High and Low German. The latter, also known as Plattdeutsch, has been used as a literary language, e.g. by Fritz Reuter (1810–74), and Klaus Groth (1819–99).

The historical development of High German falls into four main periods:

1. Old High German: from the conclusion of the Second Sound Shift onwards;

attested from the eighth to tenth centuries, notably in the sole surviving Old Germanic heroic ballad, the *Hildebrandslied*.

2. Middle High German: 1100–1350. The rich period of the courtly epic is dominated by Wolfram von Eschenbach, the author of *Parzival*, with its key concept of *mâze* – 'moderation, fittingness'; Gottfried von Strassburg, whose splendid version of the Tristan and Isolde story dates from c. 1210; and Hartmann von Aue, the author of *Der arme Heinrich*. The Middle High German period also produced the great Germanic epic of the *Nibelungenlied*, the source of Richard Wagner's *Ring des Nibelungen* tetralogy; and one of Europe's finest lyric poets, Walther von der Vogelweide.

3. Early New High German: 1350–1600: culminating in the Reformation and Martin Luther's translation of the Bible.

4. New High German: seventeenth century onwards.

It was Luther's translation of the Bible into the East Central German dialect (by then largely homogenized with High German) in the mid-sixteenth century that provided a firm basis for a standardized literary language. As he says in his *Sendbrief vom Dolmetschen* (1530): 'Ich hab mich des geflissen im Dolmetschen, das ich rein und klar Deutsch geben möchte', which may be freely translated: 'The task to which I have applied myself as interpreter has been to provide pure, clear German.' Luther succeeded; and his 'pure, clear German' became the language of the *Aufklärung*, and of Classical Weimar (Goethe and Schiller; Hölderlin), the language of *Bildung*, 'self-cultivation'. Through the nineteenth and early twentieth century it was the language of scholarship, of great prose (Adalbert Stifter, Theodor Fontane, Thomas Mann) and of some sublime poetry (Rainer Maria Rilke), until the days of the Third Reich, when German lost touch with both *mâze* and *Bildung*. In 1933 Karl Kraus ended his last poem with the line: *Das Wort entschlief, als jene Welt erwachte.*

SCRIPT

Until the twentieth century the Gothic script was used for German, both in print and in handwriting. Roman is now standard. Voiceless /s/ is notated as ß in word-final position, before final -*t*, and following a long vowel: e.g. *groß* 'big'; *läßt* 'lets'; *Füße* 'feet'.

PHONOLOGY

Consonants

>   stops: p, b, t, d, k, g, ʔ
>   fricatives: f, v, s, z, ʃ, ʒ, ç, x, h; [ç/x] are positional variants
>   nasals: m, n, ŋ
>   lateral and flap: l, r, ʀ
>   semi-vowel: j

The phonemes /ts, ps, ks, pf/ also occur, and are variously classified as affricates or as clusters.

[ç/x] as positional variants: cf. *ich* 'I' /iç/; *Buch* 'book' /bux/. The diminutive suffix *-chen* is invariably /çɛn/ whatever the preceding phoneme.

Voiced stops in word-final position are devoiced: e.g. *gab* 'gave' /gaːp/; *Tod* 'death' /toːt/.

Vowels

> front: i, iː, y, yː, e, eː, œ, œː, ɛ, ɛː
> central: ə, a, aː
> back: u, uː, o, oː
> diphthongs: ai, oi, au

MORPHOLOGY AND SYNTAX

German has three genders and two numbers. The noun has four cases.

Noun

Nominal endings are very largely coded for gender. Thus, all nouns in *-heit*, *-keit*, *-schaft*, *-ung*, and *-ion* are feminine (a very numerous class), and most nouns in *-e* are also feminine. Nouns in *-ling*, *-ich*, *-ig* are masculine; nearly all nouns in *-nis*, *-tum* are neuter (one or two exceptions), as are all nouns with the diminutive suffixes *-chen* and *-lein*. Further, most nouns with the prefix *Ge-* are neuter: e.g. *das Gebäck* 'pastry', *das Gebirge* 'range (of mountains)'.

PLURAL FORMATION
By affix: *-e/-en/-er/-s*; by stem mutation; by stem mutation + ending: e.g. *der Hund* 'dog' – *die Hunde*; *der Strahl* 'ray' – *die Strahlen*; *das Kind* 'child' – *die Kinder*; *das Wort* 'word' – *die Wörter*; *der Bruder* 'brother' – *die Brüder*; *die Tochter* 'daughter' – *die Töchter*.

Some nouns have two plural forms differing in sense: e.g. *das Wort* 'word': pl. *die Worte* 'words in connected utterance', *die Wörter* 'words' (as a plurality, e.g. in *Wörterbuch* 'dictionary').

Article

DEFINITE ARTICLE
der, *die*, *das* (masc., fem., neut.). These are fully declined in four cases; the accusative is distinguished only in the masculine: the following paradigm illustrates the declension of the article and the noun, as well as the weak declension of the adjective ('the good man/woman/book'):

	Masculine	Feminine	Neuter
Sing. nom.	der gute Mann	die gute Frau	das gute Buch
acc.	**den** guten Mann	die gute Frau	das gute Buch
gen.	**des** guten Mannes	**der** guten Frau	**des** guten Buches
dat.	**dem** guten Mann	**der** guten Frau	**dem** guten Buch
Pl. nom.	die guten Männer	die guten Frauen	die guten Bücher
acc.	die guten Männer	die guten Frauen	die guten Bücher
gen.	**der** guten Männer	**der** guten Frauen	**der** guten Bücher
dat.	**den** guten Männern	**den** guten Frauen	**den** guten Büchern

A few dozen nouns take -(*e*)*n* in all cases except the nominative (all masculine): e.g. *der Mensch* 'human being': *den*, *des*, *dem* Menschen; pl. *die Menschen*.

THE INDEFINITE ARTICLE

masculine: ein, einen, eines, einem
feminine: eine, eine, einer, einer
neuter: ein, ein, eines, einem

Adjective

As attribute, adjective precedes noun and shows concord in gender, number, and case. There are two declensions: weak, when the adjective is preceded by the definite article or other qualifier marking gender, number, and case (which is illustrated above) and strong, which is used in the absence of such a qualifier; the adjective itself then takes on the requisite markers: e.g.

	Masculine	Feminine	Neuter
nom.	guter Wein	gute Frau	gutes Brot
acc.	guten Wein	gute Frau	gutes Brot
gen.	guten Weines	guter Frau	guten Brotes
dat.	gutem Wein	guter Frau	gutem Brot

The plural endings for all three genders are: *-er*, *-e*, *-er*, *-en*.

There is also a mixed declension used after the indefinite article, the possessive adjectives *mein*, *dein*, etc., and the negating adjective/pronoun *kein*: cf. *einem guten Wein* 'to a good wine'; *einer guten Frau* 'of a good woman'.

COMPARATIVE

-er added to positive: several very common monosyllables also mutate the stem vowel: e.g. *langsam* 'slow' – *langsamer*; *lang* 'long' – *länger*; *groß* 'big' – *größer*. Suppletive: *gut* 'good' – *besser*.

Pronoun

	1	2	3
singular	ich	du	er (masc.) sie (fem.) es (neut.)
plural	wir	Ihr	sie (all 3 genders)

These are fully declined in three cases: e.g. for first person singular *ich*, acc. *mich*, dat. *mir*.

The genitive forms, e.g. *mein(er)*, *dein(er)*, etc. are very sparingly used in modern German, e.g. *es waren ihrer zehn* 'there were ten of them', though frequent in classical poetry:

> Ich denke dein, wenn mir der Sonne Schimmer
> vom Meere strahlt; (Goethe)
> 'I think of you when shimmering sunlight shines towards me from the sea'

Du and *ihr* are familiar second person singular and plural, restricted in use to certain specific socio-linguistic categories (family, school-friends, etc.). The polite form of address is *Sie* (sing. and pl.) with plural concordance; dat. *Ihnen*.

The neuter pronoun *es* is used as demonstrative and complement with the verb *sein* 'to be':

> Sind **es** deine Brüder? – Ja, sie sind **es**
> 'is it/are these your brothers? – Yes, it is they'

DEMONSTRATIVE PRONOUN/ADJECTIVE

dieser/diese/dieses; pl. *diese* 'this, these'; *jener/jene/jenes*; pl. *jene* 'that; those': e.g. *in dieser Welt* 'in this world'; *in jenen Tagen* 'in those days' (dative endings after preposition *in*: see **Preposition**).

The neutral form *dies* may be used as an all-purpose demonstrative pronoun: e.g. *dies sind meine Schwestern* 'these are my sisters' (cf. Russian, *eto*).

INTERROGATIVE PRONOUN

wer 'who?', *was* 'what?'.

Wer has accusative and dative forms: *wen*, *wem*; both *wer* and *was* have a genitive: *wessen*.

RELATIVE PRONOUN

Two forms are used: (a) *der*, *die*, *das*; pl. *die*; (b) *welcher*, *welche*, *welches*; pl. *welche*. The (a) form is more usual; the masculine and neuter genitive form is *dessen*; the feminine and plural genitive form fluctuates between *deren* and *derer*: e.g. *es folgten acht Monate, während derer* ... 'eight months followed, during which ...'

The extended form, *derjenige/diejenige/dasjenige*, pl. *diejenigen*, is also available.

Numerals

1–10: *eins, zwei, drei, vier, fünf, sechs, sieben, acht, neun, zehn*; 11 *elf*; 12 *zwölf*; 13 *dreizehn*; 14 *vierzehn*; 20 *zwanzig*; 21 *einundzwanzig*; 22 *zweiundzwanzig*, etc. 30 *dreißig*, 40 *vierzig*; 100 *hundert*.

The numeral *eins*, when used before a noun, takes the form *ein/eine/ein*, and is declined like the indefinite article: e.g. *das kostet nur eine Mark* 'that costs only one mark'; *einer der Beamten* 'one of the officials'; *eines Morgens* ... 'one morning'.

Verb

German verbs are transitive or intransitive; formally, weak or strong. There are three moods: indicative, subjunctive, and imperative, in two voices: active or passive. The active voice has two simple tenses, present and past, and several compound tenses, made with such auxiliaries as *haben* 'to have', *sein* 'to be', *werden* 'to become'. The passive voice is entirely analytical.

The auxiliary *sein* is used to conjugate verbs denoting a change of state or place. All verbs conjugated with *haben* are transitive: cf. *ich **habe** ihm das Buch gegeben* 'I have given/gave him the book'; *ich **bin** in die Stadt gefahren* 'I drove to town' (change of place). (For position of verbal components in these examples, *see* **Word order**, below).

WEAK VERBS

The past tense is formed by adding *-te* to the stem; the past participle by prefixing *ge-* to the stem, i.e. the infinitive minus *-en*. For example, infinitive: *machen* 'to make'; stem: *mach-*; past tense: *machte*; past participle: *gemacht*. Similarly: *holen* 'to fetch' – *holte* – *geholt*; *sagen* 'to say' – *sagte* – *gesagt*.

STRONG VERBS

The past tense is made by ablaut, i.e. mutation of stem vowel. The past participle may resume either the stem vowel or the past-tense vowel, or may exhibit a further mutation: cf.

	Past	*Past participle*
lesen 'read'	las	gelesen
fließen 'flow'	floß	geflossen
empfehlen 'recommend'	empfahl	empfohlen
gehen 'go'	ging	gegangen

Specimen paradigms of indicative present and past tenses of weak (*holen*) and strong (*gehen*) verbs.

		Singular	*Plural*	*Singular*	*Plural*
present:	1	ich hole	wir holen	ich gehe	wir gehen
	2	du holst	Ihr holtet	du gehst	Ihr gehet
	3	er holt	sie holen	er geht	sie gehen
past:	1	ich holte	wir holten	ich ging	wir gingen
	2	du holtest	Ihr holet	du gingst	Ihr ginget
	3	er holte	sie holten	er ging	sie gingen

Certain stem vowels also mutate in the second and third persons singular of the present tense of strong verbs: e.g.

/ē > ī/: *lesen* 'read': *ich lese, du liest, er liest*
/a > ä/: *fangen* 'catch': *ich fange, du fängst, er fängt*
/o > ö/: *stoßen* 'push': *ich stoße, du stößt, er stößt*

The present subjunctive is always regular; e.g. of *tragen* 'to carry': *ich trage, du tragest, er trage*; *wir tragen, ihr traget, sie tragen.*

The past subjunctive adds -e to the past indicative first and third persons singular, and mutates the stem vowel if possible: e.g. *ich trüge, du trügest, er trüge,* etc.

German verbs, transitive and intransitive alike, are simple, as *tragen,* or take a separable or inseparable prefix. The following prefixes are inseparable, *be-, emp-, ent-, er-, ge-, ver-, zer-,* and, therefore, do not take prefixed *ge-* to form the past participle:

> empfehlen 'recommend': ich empfehle – ich empfahl – ich habe **emp**fohlen
> geschehen 'happen': es geschieht – es geschah – es ist **ge**schehen

The following prefixes are variable, i.e. separable or inseparable: *über-, durch-, hinter-, unter-, um-, voll-, wider-, miß-, wieder-.* A verb which is used with one of these nine prefixes in an inseparable capacity has normally a secondary or derived sense. Compare with *legen* 'to lay', *setzen* 'put, place':

separable:

> wir setzten (mit der Fähre) **über**
> 'we crossed (by ferry)'

> sie hatte dem Kinde eine Decke über**ge**legt
> 'she had laid a blanket over the child'

inseparable:

> er **über**setzte das Buch/er hat das Buch über∅setzt
> 'he translated the book'

> ich habe es mir noch mal über∅legt
> 'I had second thoughts about it'

Preposition

The prepositions in German govern the genitive, the dative, or the accusative. Nine very common prepositions take either the accusative or the dative, depending on sense. For example:

with gen.	während **des** Krieges 'during the war'
with dat.	seit **dem** Krieg(e) 'since the war'
with acc.	er ging durch **den** Wald 'he went through the wood'

variable: e.g. *in*:

> er wohnt in **der** Stadt 'he lives in the town' (locus of action does not change)

> er ist in **die** Stadt gefahren 'he drove to town' (change of locus)

> das Buch liegt auf **dem** Tisch 'the book is lying on the table'

> er hat das Buch auf **den** Tisch hingelegt 'he laid the book on the table'

Word order

The rules governing German word order are strict, especially as regards the relative positioning of verbal components:

1. In a principal clause; basic order with a simple tense is SVO: e.g. *Ich gebe ihm das Buch* 'I give him the book.' If the tense is compound, the non-finite component goes to the end: e.g. *Ich habe ihm das Buch gegeben* 'I have given/ gave him the book.' If the sentence is introduced by anything other than the subject, e.g. by adverbial material, inversion is obligatory: e.g. *Gestern habe ich ihm das Buch gegeben* 'Yesterday I gave him the book.'

Use with modal verb; e.g. *müssen* 'to have to': e.g. *Er muß in die Stadt fahren* 'He has to go to town.'

If a compound tense is used, both sense-verb and modal auxiliary close the sentence in infinitive form: e.g. *Er hat in die Stadt fahren müssen* 'He (has) had to go to town.'

2. Relative clause: the auxiliary in a compound verb form now follows the participle: e.g. *Ich weiß, daß er in die Stadt gefahren ist* 'I know that he has gone to town'. But the auxiliary precedes the sense-verb if a modal verb is used: e.g. *Ich weiß, daß er in die Stadt hat fahren müssen* 'I know that he (has) had to go to town'; *In unserem Kreise hat er sich nicht mehr sehen lassen können* 'He was not able to let himself be seen again in our circle.'

In *oratio obliqua* the subjunctive is used: e.g.:

assertion:

Das billigt er nicht, aber er kann es verstehen
'He does not approve of this, but he can understand it.'

reported speech:

Er billige das nicht, aber er **könne** es verstehen.

---

1 Im Anfang war das Wort, und das Wort war bei Gott, und Gott war das Wort.
²Dasselbe war im Anfang bei Gott.
³Alle Dinge sind durch dasselbe gemacht, und ohne dasselbe ist nichts gemacht, was gemacht ist.
⁴In ihm war das Leben, und das Leben war das Licht der Menschen.
⁵Und das Licht scheint in der Finsternis, und die Finsternis hat's nicht ergriffen.
⁶¶Es war ein Mensch, von Gott gesandt, der hieß Johannes.
⁷Der kam zum Zeugnis, um von dem Licht zu zeugen, damit sie alle durch ihn glaubten.
⁸Er war nicht das Licht, sondern er sollte zeugen von dem Licht.

GERMANIC LANGUAGES

INTRODUCTION

Towards the close of the second millennium BC, tribes speaking the Proto-Germanic dialect of Indo-European seem to have been located in the Baltic area centring on Southern Sweden. When and whence these tribes reached this habitat remains something of a mystery (*see* **Indo-European Languages**).

It is significant, however, that, *vis-à-vis* the parent stock, Germanic is one of the most divergent of all the twelve branches of Indo-European. The divergence is evident both on the lexical and on the phonological plane. At least 30 per cent of the vocabulary of Common Germanic is non-Indo-European in origin, and, surprisingly, this sub- or adstrate third is largely made up of everyday words connected with hunting, sea-faring, farming, social organization, etc. – all of these being semantic fields amply furnished elsewhere with Indo-European roots. The case here for linguistic miscegenation is strong.

PHONOLOGY

Consonants

Evidence for this is also forthcoming on the phonological plane. The phonological watershed between the Indo-European matrix and the Proto-Germanic language is marked by

(a) the First or Germanic Sound Shift;
(b) a concomitant or closely subsequent shift to initial primary stress;
(c) a consequent erosion in, and ultimately loss of, final unstressed syllables.

The crucially important and far-reaching First Sound Shift seems to have been complete by the middle of the first millennium BC. It can be summarized as follows:

1. Unaspirated and aspirated voiceless stops merge to yield the corresponding fricatives in Proto-Germanic; the palatal/velar distinction is lost:

$$\left.\begin{array}{l} \text{/p, t, } \hat{k}\text{/q, q}^w\text{/} \\ \text{/ph, th, } \hat{k}h\text{/qh, q}^wh\text{/} \end{array}\right\} \quad > \quad \text{/f, } \theta\text{, } \chi^h\text{, } \chi^w\text{/}$$

2. Voiced unaspirated stops are unvoiced; again, the palatal/velar distinction is lost:

$$\text{/b, d, } \hat{g}\text{/g, g}^w\text{/} > \text{/p, t, k, k}^w\text{/}$$

3. The voiced aspirated stops become voiced fricatives:

/bh, th, ĝh/gh, gʷh/ > /ß, ð, γ, γʷ/

For example, using Latin and Gothic:

p > f	Latin	pēs	Gothic	fotus	English	foot
t > θ		trēs		þreis		three
ƙ > χ		canis		hunds		hound
b > p	IE	*dheub		diups		deep
d > t	Latin	decem		taihun		ten
g > k		genus		kuni		kin
g > k		iugum		juk		yoke
bh > ß > b	IE	*bhrāter		broþar		brother

The voiced and unvoiced fricatives in Proto-Germanic appear as positional allophones, depending on the position of the primary stress in the Indo-European matrix form. Thus, where /t/ is neither initial nor immediately preceded by the primary stress, it becomes /ð/ in Proto-Germanic; if preceded by stress, it becomes /θ/. For example:

IE *pətér (Sanskrit pitár, Greek patér) – Gothic fāðar

but

*bhráter (Sanskrit bhrátr, Latin fráter) – Gothic broþar

This reflex relationship is known as Verner's Law, after the Danish linguist who first identified it.

Changes in the vocalic structure of Proto-Germanic, relative to the parent stock, can be briefly summarized: the Indo-European short vowels /ă, ŏ, ɜ̆/, merged to give Proto-Germanic /ă/; /aː/ and /oː/ merged to give /ō/; syllabic /r, l, m, n/ were expanded to yield /ur, ul, um, un/.

The Second Sound Shift is a local German phenomenon, complete by the end of the Old High German period, by which High German became differentiated from the Low and (up to a point) the Central German dialects (*see* **German**).

Historically, the Germanic languages fall into three groups:

(a) North Germanic: represented today by the Scandinavian languages, Icelandic, and Faeroese. The old literary language is known as Old Norse or Old Icelandic. North Germanic is attested in runic inscriptions from the third century onwards.

(b) West Germanic: the contemporary representatives are English, German, Low German (*das Plattdeutsche*), Dutch/Flemish, Frisian, Afrikaans, Yiddish; historical stages of English and German are represented by Anglo-Saxon, Middle English, Old and Middle High German. English has many regional variations which have proliferated on a global scale, as dialectal differentiation within the confines of Britain itself has shrunk.

(c) East Germanic: the languages of the Goths, Vandals, Burgundians, etc. who installed themselves throughout Southern Europe following the collapse of the Roman Empire. Their languages are all extinct. The earliest connected text in a Germanic language is provided by the Bible translation into Gothic of Bishop Wulfilas in the fourth century AD.

The global diffusion of English gives Germanic the widest territorial distribution of any language family. About 450 million people speak Germanic languages, with English accounting for about 75 per cent of this total.

MORPHOLOGY AND SYNTAX

Noun

The Indo-European inventory of three genders, three numbers, and eight cases, was reduced to three genders, two numbers, and four cases (nominative, accusative, genitive, dative). Traces of a dual are found in Old Norse and in Old English pronominal forms. The nominal declension system was reduced, with a corresponding gain in the prepositional inventory. The pronominal system remained relatively unaffected *vis-à-vis* the Indo-European model. A Germanic innovation is the formal distinction between strong and weak adjectives, the latter being used with the definite article.

Verb

The rich verbal apparatus of the Indo-European core languages – Sanskrit, Greek, Latin – is cut down in Proto-Germanic and the daughter languages to a formal contrast between past and non-past; a future tense is formed with the help of auxiliary verbs. The medio-passive was lost, except in Old Norse; Gothic retains a passive. The subjunctive mood merged with the optative. The innovatory importance of the sound shift on the phonological plane is matched in the morphology by the highly disinctive ablaut series of strong verbs (*see* **German**, **Gothic**, **Old Norse**, etc.). Germanic weak verbs make their past tenses with the help of a dental formant, /t/d/.

In the older Germanic languages – Gothic, Old Norse, Old and Middle High German, Anglo-Saxon – finite verbal forms were coded for person and number, though not exclusively: i.e. some endings were duplicated. For example, in Old Norse, present and past tenses of *gefa* 'to give':

	Singular			Plural		
Present:	1 gef	2 gefr	3 gefr	1 gefum	2 gefið	3 gefa
Past:	1 gaf	2 gaft	3 gaf	1 gáfum	2 gafuð	3 gáfu

Coded inflection is largely retained in Icelandic and in modern standard German; cf. the corresponding forms of German *geben* 'to give':

	Singular			Plural		
Present:	1 gebe	2 gibst	3 gibt	1 geben	2 gebt	3 geben
Past:	1 gab	2 gabst	3 gab	1 gaben	2 gabt	3 gaben

In English, the three Scandinavian languages, and in Afrikaans, the inflectional system has been greatly reduced by syncretic processes, often to a single form for each tense. Thus, in English, the past tense has *gave* for all six forms; the present tense has *give*, with -*s* added for the third person singular.

GILYAK

See **Nivkh**.

GOṆḌI

INTRODUCTION

Goṇḍi belongs, in Andronov's (1978) classification, to the Gondwana group of the Dravidian family, a group which includes Kui, Kuvi, Koṇḍa, and Pēngō. Goṇḍi is much the largest of the non-literary Dravidian languages, and is spoken at present by at least 1½ million people in Madhya Pradesh, Maharashtra, Andhra Pradesh, and Orissa. There are several dialects.

PHONOLOGY

Consonants

> stops: p, b, t, d, ṭ, ḍ, k, g
> affricates: tʃ, dʒ
> fricatives: v, j, s, h
> nasals: m, n, ṇ, ŋ
> lateral and flap: l, r, ṛ

All stops and affricates have corresponding aspirates: /ph, bh/, etc. Retroflex consonants are notated with dots.

Vowels

> long and short: i, e, a, o, u

Subrahmanyam (1968) points out a kind of vowel harmony in CVCV̄C forms: e.g. *mosōr* 'nose'; *perēk* 'rice'.

MORPHOLOGY AND SYNTAX

Noun

There are traces of a feminine ending in *-āṛ/-ī*: e.g. *pōrāṛ* 'mother-in-law', but the opposition masculine/non-masculine is characteristic, and indeed general in the Gondwana group. A typical masculine ending is *-āl*: e g. *āndāl* 'blind man'.

NUMBER

A masculine plural ending is *-īr/-ūr*: e.g. *kāṇḍīr* 'boys'. Non-masculine plural endings are *-ng*, *-(ī)k*: e.g. *ḍuvvalīk* 'tigers'; *marāk* 'trees'; *kork* 'fowls'.

CASE SYSTEM

The case markers are added either to the base or to the base plus augment, this augment being *-d-/t/ṭ/n/* or Ø: e.g.

> with accusative/dative ending *-un*: e.g. *ḍuvval.d.un* 'the tiger (acc.)', 'to the tiger';
> with instrumental/locative ending *-e/-ē*: e.g. *nār.t.ē* 'in the village'; *nār.k.n.ē* 'in the villages';
> with ablative ending *-(n)āl*: e.g. *nā(r).ṭ.nāl* 'from the village'.

The genitive ending is coded for the masculine/non-masculine dichotomy.

Pronoun

PERSONAL INDEPENDENT

1 sing. *(n)annā*; pl. excl. *(m)ammāṭ/marāṭ*, incl. *aplō*; 2 sing. *imma/(n)immē*; pl. *immāṭ/mirāṭ*. That is, *-a-* is first person marker + *n* (sing.)/*m* (pl.); *-i-* is second person marker.

The third person forms are supplied from the demonstrative series, in which Subrahmanyam (1968) distinguishes proximate and distal forms:

	Masculine	*Non-masculine*
proximate:	sing. vēr, pl. vīr	sing. id, pl. iv
distal:	sing. vōr, pl. vūr	sing. ad, pl. av

INTERROGATIVE PRONOUN

Masc. sing. *bōr*, pl. *būr*; non-masc. sing. *bad*, pl. *bav*.

Numerals

1–7: *undī, raṇḍ, mūnd, nālūŋ, siyyūŋ, sārūŋ, ēṛūŋ*: these are non-masculine forms; the masculine forms add *-ī/-ōr* to modified bases. 1 and 2 are suppletive, *vorōr, ivvīr*; 4 *nālvīr*, etc.

From 8 inclusive onwards, Marathi numerals are used: e.g. 8 *āṭh*; 9 *nav*; 10 *daha*.

Verb

Inflected forms are made with base + tense marker + personal ending. The personal endings are (all with several allophones):

		Singular	*Plural*
1		-ōn/-ā	excl. -ōm; incl. (future only) -āṭ
2		-ī	-īṭ
3	masc.	-ōr	-ēr
	non-masc.	-ā	-ān

That is, third person distinguishes gender.

TENSE

Markers are:

past: *-t-/-ṭṭ-*
present/future: *-ānt-/-nt-*
future: *-(a)k/-(ā)n-/-ār-*

Examples: *aṭṭ.ṭ.ōn* 'I cooked'; *un.ṭṭ.ōn* 'I drank'; *vā.k.ā* 'I'll come'; *sī.nt.ōn* 'I'm giving, will give'.

NEGATIVE

The marker is *-v-/-ō-*, the latter for use with non-second person: e.g. *veh.v.ī* 'you (sing.) will not tell', pl. *veh.v.īṭ*; *sūṛ.ō.n* 'I don't/will not see'; *sūṛ.ōr* 'he does/will not see'.

IMPERATIVE

2nd sing./pl. *-ā/-m/-Ø*: e.g. *sūṛ.ā*, *sūṛ.āṭ* 'see!'

PARTICIPLES

There are several participles; some of the endings are illustrated here: past, *tin.džī* 'having eaten'; present, *tin.džēr* 'eating'; conditional, *vā.t.ēkē* 'if/when you came'.

A verbal noun form in *-māṛ/-vāḷ* (active or passive) is used to make relative clauses: e.g. *veh.vāl māynāl* 'the man who tells'; *veh.vāl vēsūṛī* 'the story that is told'.

Postpositions

Usually follow the augumented base: e.g.

aggā 'in, near': e.g. *kay.d.aggā* 'in the hand';
karūm 'near': e.g. *marā.t.karūm* 'near the tree';
tarsō 'with, by': e.g. *vōr.n.tarsō* 'with/by him';
phorō 'on': e.g. *marā.t.phorō* 'on the tree';
roppō 'inside': e.g. *kuhī.t.roppō* 'in the forest'.

Word order

SOV.

(१) मुन्ने ते बचन मत्ता अनि बचन परमेश्वर-
त्-संगने मत्ता अनि वचन परमेश्वर मत्ता । (२) इद्दे मुन्ने
ते परमेश्वर-त्-संगने मत्ता । (३) सब कुछ श्रोना कैदाल पैदा
आता, अनि जो कुछ पैदा आता आपिनाल श्रोन मीचुक
बड़ांगे भी हुल्ले पैदा आयो जो पैदा आता । (४) श्रोन
रोपा जीवन मत्ता अनि अद जीवन आदमीड़ा वेर्चीं मत्ता ।
(५) अनि वेर्चीं सीकाटीते चमके माइता अनि सीकाटी तान
नाश¹ हुल्ले केवो ॥

(६) परमेश्वर-त्-इगाताल राँहुतल वोड़ुल आदमी
वातुल अनि श्रोना पड़ेाल येाहुन्ना मत्ता । (७) एल आदमी
गवाही सीयाले वातुल — अद वेर्चीं ता गवाही सीश्राले,
कि सब आदमींड़ श्रोना द्वारा बिश्वास केवीड़ । (८) श्रोल
तना अद वेर्चीं हुल्ले आयोल, पर परमेश्वर श्रोन अद वेर्चींता
गवाही सीयाले राँहुतुल ।

GORONTALO

INTRODUCTION

This Austronesian language is spoken in the north-eastern peninsula of Sulawesi (Celebes) by about 1 million Moslems. The ethnonym is Holontalo (the sound /r/ is not in the language).

SCRIPT

If written, the Roman alphabet is used.

PHONOLOGY

Consonants

    stops: p, b, t, d, k, g, q, ʔ
    affricates: tʃ, dʒ
    fricative: h
    nasals: m, n, ŋ
    lateral: l
    semi-vowels: w, j

Pre-nasalized stops: e.g. /mb, nt, ng/. /s, n, r/ occur in loan-words.

Vowels

    short: i, ɛ, a, ɔ, u
    long: i, ɛ, a, ɔ

All finals are vocalic with diphthong glides, e.g. ọö, iö /wə, jə/.

MORPHOLOGY AND SYNTAX

Noun

No gender; stems are potentially nominal or verbal. The singular can be stressed by addition of the numerical *tuwawu/tu.a.u* 'one'. There is no plural formant: *dadata* 'many' may be used, and reduplication occurs.

    U is often used as an article, together with demonstrative: e.g. *U alo bo.tie mo.piohu tutu* 'This food (*alo*) is very (*tutu*) good (*mo.piohu*)', where *bo.tie* is the demonstrative pronoun/adjective.

POSSESSION

Positional, e.g. *bihu auhu* 'the shore of the ocean' (*auhu* = Indonesian laut). The connecting particle *li* may also be used: e.g. *o/u bele li pani* 'the house (*bele*) of the smith'; *loia li amo.lio* 'the speech of his father' (*-lio* is third person suffix).

Adjective

As attribute, adjective follows noun: e.g. *bele mo.piohu* 'fine house'; *huidu mo.langgato* 'high mountain'; *hualimo talaa* 'silver ring'.

Pronoun

Personal independent with enclitic suffixes:

	Singular		*Plural*	
1	wau/wātija	-(q)u	incl. ito, excl. ami/-lami/-to/-nto	
2	(j)iö	-mu	timongoli	-limongoli
3	tiö	-(l)io	timongolio	-limongolia

DEMONSTRATIVE PRONOUN/ADJECTIVE

Based on stems *ti/ta*: *bo.tia/-tie* 'this, these'; *bo.ito* 'that, those'. These follow the noun: e.g. (*u*) *tau bo.tia* 'this man'.

INTERROGATIVE PRONOUN

ti.ta 'who?'; *wo.lo* 'what?'.

RELATIVE PRONOUN

tā: e.g. *wadala tā pangola* 'a horse which is old'; *Wau/wātija tā mo.hama, jiö tā mo.delo* 'I am the one who takes, you are the one who brings'; *Wātija tā mo.mintaqā bulua boito* 'I am the one who will pick up the box.'

Numerals

1–10: *o-ēnta*, *o-luo*, *o-tolu*, *o-pato*, *o-limo*, *o-lomo*, *o-pitu*, *o-walu*, *o-tio*, *o-pulu*. 11 *mo.pulu wa u tuau*; 20 *dulo pulu*; 30 *to(w)ulo pulu*; 100 *mo-hetuto*.

Verb

Prefixes, often compounded, play a crucial role in Gorontalo verb structure.

TENSE MARKERS

Present *he*; past *lo(ti)*; future *mo(ti)* = imperfective marker. Examples: *Tiö he mo.kaladža to ilēngi* 'He works in the garden'; *Tei Ako he mo.luladu* 'Ako is writing now'; *Ti mama he mo.tubu* 'Mother is cooking'; *Wātija lo.tuluhē to bele.lio ohui* 'I slept at his house last night'; *Wātija mo.tuluhē toqutōnu?* 'Where shall I sleep?' Cf. *Ti mama dīla **mo**tubu ila* 'Mother isn't going to cook rice' (*dīla* 'not'); *Ti mama dīla **lo**tubu ila* 'Mother didn't cook rice.'

Perfective marker is *ma-*: e.g. *teli* 'buy', *mateli* 'have bought'; *Tete ma.ti.lumeteo* 'The cat has run away.' The imperfective marker *mo-* is also used with adjectival verbs: e.g. *Wadala.mu mo.hata* 'Your horse is thin.'

Imperative/necessitative marker is *po*: e.g. *po(ti).huloqolo!* 'sit down!': *Po.laö jiö ode hulondtalo* 'You have to go to Gorontalo.' This marker is reduplicated for emphasis: e.g. *Dīla popo.langgata batanga tota ngopohidža* 'Do not place yourself above others.'

Future necessitative: *mapopo-*, e.g. *mapopo.teli.ja.mu* 'to be bought by you'.

Potential: *loö*, e.g. *loö.teli* 'be able to buy'.

Passive infix: *-il-* e.g. *mo.delo* 'to bring', *mo.d.il.elo.lio* 'it was brought by him'.

Causative prefixes: *mopo-*, *ləpo-*, *popo-* for present, past, future: e.g. *Tiö mopo.teteqo* 'He will make it run' (= drive a car); *Tiö lopo.teteqo* 'He made it run.'

Prepositions

Li 'of, by', e.g. *ilā li Ali* 'eaten by Ali'; *to* 'at', e.g. *to Hulondtalo* 'at/in Gorontalo', *towātija* 'at my house' (= 'chez moi'); *londto* 'from', e.g. *londto wātija* 'from me'.

Word order

SVO.

GOTHIC

INTRODUCTION

Gothic belongs to the Germanic family. In the fourth century AD the Visigoths were settled along the lower course of the Danube and in neighbouring areas, having moved there from a homeland in southern Sweden; and it was here that Bishop Wulfila worked as a missionary and translator, first north of the Danube, and after 348 south of the river in Roman territory. Wulfila seems to have translated most of the Bible into Gothic, and our knowledge of the language rests on the extensive fragments which have survived. The manuscripts date from about the sixth century and were found in northern Italy, brought there presumably by the Ostrogoths. There are two main collections – the *Codex Argenteus* in Uppsala University, and the *Codices Ambrosiani* in Milan. A form of spoken Gothic survived in the Crimea until the eighteenth century.

SCRIPT

Basically, a Greek uncial plus graphs from Latin and Runic. Þ = /θ/.

PHONOLOGY

Consonants

    stops: p, b, t, d, k, g
    fricatives: f, v, s, θ, ð, z, h, γ
    nasals: m, n, ŋ
    lateral and flap: l, r
    semi-vowels: w, j

/b, d, g/: pronunciation depends on position in word; cf. *barn* /barn/, 'child'; *sibun* /sivun/, 'seven', where /-v-/ is a bilabial [ß]; *augō* /auγoː/, 'eye'; *dag* /dax/, 'day'; *drigkan* /driŋkan/, 'to drink'. The dental and velar stops, /m, n, s, l, r, θ/ occur geminated. [k°] and [h°] occur. /h/ may represent [ç] or [x].

Vowels

i, eː, a, aː, oː, u, uː

/ɛ/ and /ɔ/ were probably present, notated as digraphs *ai* and *au*. /m, n, l, r/ function as vowels in certain words, i.e. as /m̩, n̩, l̩, r̩/.

MORPHOLOGY AND SYNTAX

Noun

Nouns are masculine, feminine, or neuter, singular or plural, with four cases.

a-, *ō-*, *i-*, and *u*-stems follow the standard Indo-European strong-declension model. There is also a weak declension comprising *n*-stems.

Example of *a*-stem declension: *dags* 'day' (masculine):

	Singular	*Plural*
nominative	dags	dagos
accusative	dag	dagans
genitive	dagis	dagē
dative	daga	dagam

Examples of case usage:

Accusative: bigētun þana siukan skalk hailana
'they found the sick servant whole' (*hailana* is acc. of adj. *hails* 'whole'; *þana* is acc. of demonstrative *sa* 'that')

Genitive: ahmins weihis fulls 'full of the Holy Ghost'.
Partitive genitive: jah ni was im barnē 'and they had no children'.
Dative: jah qaþ du þamma mann þamma gaþaursana habandin handu
(Mark, 3.3) 'and he said to the man which had the withered hand' (*du* is prep. 'to'; *habandin* is participle + dat. ending).

Adjective

The adjective has strong and weak declensions (as nouns). Both are exemplified in the sentence above: *bigētun þana siukan skalk hailana* (*siukan* is weak after *þana*, and *hailana* is the strong declension accusative).

The singular masculine strong declension is illustrated here by *blinds* 'blind': nom. *blinds*; acc. *blindana*; gen. *blindis*; dat. *blindamma*. The singular weak forms are: nom. *blinda*; acc. *blindan*; gen. *blindins*; dat. *blindin*.

COMPARATIVE

The comparative is made with *-iz-/-oz-*: e.g. *swinþs* 'strong', comp. *swinþoza*.

The usual suppletive bases are found: e.g. *gōþs* 'good' – *batiza*; *mikils* 'big' – *maiza*; *ubils* 'bad' – *wairsiza*.

Pronoun

PERSONAL

		1st person	2nd person	3rd person		
				Masc.	*Fem.*	*Nt.*
Singular	nom.	ik	u	is	ita	si
	acc.	mik	uk	ina	ita	ija
	gen.	meina	eina	is	is	izōs
	dat.	mis	us	imma	imma	izai
Dual	nom.	wit	—			
	acc.	ugkis	igqis			
	gen.	—	igqara			
	dat.	ugkis	igqis			
Plural	nom.	weis	jus	eis	ija	—
	acc.	uns(is)	izwis	ins	—	ijōs
	gen.	unsara	izwara	izē	—	izōs
	dat.	uns(is)	izwis	im	im	im

DEMONSTRATIVE PRONOUN/ADJECTIVE
sa 'this' (masc.) with nt. *þata*, fem. *sō*. These are declined normally: e.g. *sa*: *þana*, *þis*, *þamma*.

INTERROGATIVE PRONOUN
Masc. *hºas*; neuter *hºa*; fem. *hºo*: fully declined.

RELATIVE PRONOUN
Masc. *sæi*; nt. *þatei*; fem. *sæi*; fully declined: e.g.

> þu is sunus meins sa liuba, in þuzei waila galeikāida (Mark, 1.11)
> 'thou art my beloved Son, in whom I am well pleased'

Numerals

1–10: *ains, twai, þrija, fidwōr, fimf, saiha, sibun, ahtau, niun, taihun*; 12 *twilif*; 14 *fidwōrtaihun*; 20 *twai tigjus*; 40 *fidwōr tigjus*; 100 *taihuntēhund*.

Verb

The Gothic verb has two voices, active and passive; two moods, indicative and subjunctive; two tenses, present and preterite; three numbers.

For the indicative and subjunctive present there is a synthetic passive: e.g. *nasja* 'I save': pass. *nasjada* 'I am saved'; subj. pass. *nasjaidau*. Elsewhere, the passive voice is made analytically with past participle (passive) plus auxiliaries *wairþan* or *wisan*.

CONJUGATION

Strong or weak according to the form taken by the preterite:

strong (a) ablaut: six classes; (b) reduplication; (c) ablaut + reduplication; weak: -*da*/-*ta* (this is a Germanic innovation).

Strong

(a) The ablaut classes can be illustrated by giving the infinitive, the first person singular and plural preterite, and the past participle: e.g.
niman – nam, nēmum – numans 'take'
hilpan – halp, hulpum – hulpans 'help'
giban – gaf, gēbum – gibans 'give'

(b) Reduplicating class: e.g. *haitan – haihait, haihaitum – haitans* 'call'.
(c) Ablaut + reduplication: *grētan – gaigrot – grētans* 'weep'.

Present indicative and subjunctive: e.g. of *niman* 'take':

Indicative:

sing.	1 nima	2 nimis	3 nimi
dual	1 nimos	2 nimats	
pl.	1 nimam	2 nimiþ	3 nimand

Subjunctive:

sing.	1 nimau	2 nimais	3 nimai
dual:	1 nimaiwa	2 nimaits	
pl.	1 nimaima	2 nimaiþ	3 nimaina

The first person indicative preterite forms are: sing. *nam*; dual: *nēmu*; pl. *nēmum*; and in the subjunctive: sing. *nēmjau*; dual: *nēmeiwa*; pl. *nēmeima*.

Passive:

	Singular			Plural
indicative:	1 nimada	2 nimaza	3 nimada	1, 2, 3 nimanda
subjunctive:	nimaidau	nimaizau	nimaidau	nimaindau

The passive dual is not attested.
Imperative: 2nd sing. *nim*; pl. *nēmuþ*; dual: *nimats*; + 3rd p. forms, singular and plural.

Weak

The first person forms of a weak verb, *nasjan* 'to save', are given as illustration:

indicative present: *nasja*; dual: *nasjōs*; pl.: *nasjam*
subjunctive present: *nasjau*; dual: *nasjaiwa*; pl.: *nasjaima*
indicative preterite: *nasida*; dual: *nasidēdu*; pl. *nasidēdum*
subjunctive preterite: *nasidēdjau*; dual: *nasidēdeiwa*; pl.: *nasidēdeima*
passive: *nasjada*; subjunctive passive: *nasjaidau*

Prepositions

Prepositions govern accusative or dative or both; some govern both + genitive.

---

20 Aþþan ni bi þans bidja áinans, ak bi þans galáubjandans
   þaírh waúrda izē du mis,

21 ei allái áin sijáina, swaswē þu, atta, in mis jah ik in þus, ei
   jah þái in uggkis áin sijáina, ei sō manasēþs galáubjái þatei
   þu mik insandidēs.

22 Jah ik wulþu þanei gaſt mis, gaſ im, ei sijáina áin swaswē
   wit áin siju.

23 Ik in im jah þu in mis, ei sijáina ustaúhanái du áinamma,
   jah kunnei sō manasēþs þatei þu mik insandidēs, jah ſrijōdēs
   ins, swaswē mik ſrijōdēs.

24 Atta, þatei atgaſt mis, wiljáu ei þarei im ik, jah þái sijáina
   miþ mis, ei saſƕáina wulþu meinana þanei gaſt mis, untē
   ſrijōdēs mik ſaúr gaskaſt ſaírƕáus.

25 Atta garaſhta, jah sō manasēþs þuk ni uſkunþa; iþ ik þuk
   kunþa.   Jah þái uſkunþēdun þatei þu mik insandidēs.

26 Jah gakannida im namō þeinata jah kannja, ei ſriaþwa þōei
   ſrijōdēs mik, in im sijái jah ik in im.

(John 17: 20-6)

GREEK, CLASSICAL

INTRODUCTION

Greek belongs to the Hellenic branch of Indo-European. With a written record extending over 3,400 years, it has the longest attested history of any Indo-European language, and is rivalled globally only by Chinese.

It was early in the second millennium BC that the first wave of Indo-European-speaking invaders reached the Greek Peninsula, the Peloponnese, and some of the islands, and settled. Homer calls them the *Achaioi*. Their speech seems to have formed the basis for the dialect subsequently known as Ionic. Little is known about the autochthonous 'Pelasgian' people whom they displaced or absorbed, but it is to the presumably non-Indo-European Pelasgian language that Greek owes such consonantal clusters as -*nth*- and -*ss*-, which proliferate in place-names and names of plants: e.g. *Korinthos*, *Zakinthos*; *akantha* (thorny bush).

This Bronze Age civilization, known as Mycenaean, lasted approximately from 1500 to 1100 BC. During this period, the language was notated in the so-called Linear B script, which was based on a non-Indo-European Cretan model (Linear A). The Linear B character was deciphered by Michael Ventris and John Chadwick in 1952.

In the eleventh century BC the Mycenaean civilization was disrupted by the Dorian invasions into western Greece. There followed a considerable redistribution of population involving dispersal of dialects. Linear B ceased to be used. For three centuries there is no written record.

In the ninth/eighth centuries BC the Homeric poems were written in the Ionic dialect and in a new script based on the North Semitic alphabet, with specific signs for the five vowels. Thus the creation of a literary standard in the shape of two of the world's greatest poems coincided with the introduction of what is arguably the world's most efficient and adaptable writing system.

Ionic blended into the Attic dialect of Athens, and the scene was set for the unparalleled period of creativity which followed – the seminal years of the whole of Western culture: a period which includes Aeschylus, Sophocles, Euripides, Aristophanes, Sappho, Anakreon, Pindar, Menander, Plato, Aristotle, Demosthenes, Herodotus, Thucydides, and Xenophon.

Towards the end of the first millennium BC a modified Attic Greek emerged as *hē koinē dialektos*, or 'common speech', a form which was to survive for a thousand years as the language of the Hellenistic period, based first on Alexandria and then on Byzantium. It is this form which provides the basis for the *katharevousa* (*see* **Greek, Modern Standard**).

Dialects

Many dialects flourished in the Classical and Hellenistic periods, and are attested in thousands of inscriptions found all over the Greek world, which includes apart from Greece itself, Asia Minor, the Adriatic seaboard, Southern Italy, Sicily, Egypt, and parts of the Middle East. Four dialects are important:

1. Ionic, the dialect used in the Homeric poems and in Hesiod.
2. Attic, the language of the Classical period.
3. Doric/Dorian, the language of Sparta. Doric is marked by certain archaic features, e.g. the retention of long *ā* in words like *mātēr* 'mother' where Ionic and Attic have *mētēr*. In Attic literature, Doric was used for choral lyric poetry, and to superb comic effect in the Lysistrata of Aristophanes.
4. The dialect known as Aeolic, spoken in Thessaly and in some of the islands, e.g. Lesbos, was used by Sappho. A curious trait in this dialect is the presence of /p/ for Attic /t/ in such words as *pisyres* 'four' for Attic *tessares*. Aeolic also retained the digamma ϝ = /w/: cf. Mycenaean *woiko* = Aeolic ϝ*oikos* = Attic *oikos* 'house'.

SCRIPT

Athens adopted the Ionic form of the North Semitic script in the early fifth century. The digamma had ceased to function in Ionic/Attic in pre-historic times, and is therefore absent from the standard script. Its historical presence is of importance in scansion.

PHONOLOGY

Consonants

stops: p, ph, b, t, th, d, k, kh, g
fricatives: s (in later Greek + f (< ph), θ (< th), χ (< kh))
nasals: m, n, ŋ
lateral and flap: l, r

There are three composite fricatives: /zd/, /ks/, /ps/; notated as ζ, ξ, ψ. Note that voiced aspirates are missing.

Vowels

iː, ɪ, ɛː, ɛ, aː, a, ɔː, o, uː, yː, y

Vocalic onset is accompanied by rough (ʻ) or soft (ʼ) breathing. Rough onset is indicated here by h-.

DIPHTHONGS

ai, au, eu, ɛi, ɛu, oi, yi, ɔi

PITCH MARKS

From 200 BC on, under the influence of the Alexandrine grammarians pitch accents are used: high (acute), low (grave), and high to low (circumflex). The tonic stress falls on one of the last three syllables. In the nominal system, accentuation is usually consistent with citation form; in the verbal system, stress is governed by rules and is therefore theoretically predictable.

MORPHOLOGY AND SYNTAX

Greek has three genders and three numbers: the dual is preserved in the Attic nominal system throughout the classical period; in the verbal system it is practically limited to the second and third person.

Definite article

Masc. *ho*, fem. *hē*, nt. *to*; declined in three numbers and four cases: nominative, accusative, genitive, dative: e.g. masc. *ho – ton – tou – tō*; fem. *hē – tēn – tēs – tē*. Dual: nom./acc. *tō*, gen., dat. *toin* are regularly used for all three genders, though specific feminine forms, *tā*, *tain*, existed. Plural: masc. *hoi – tous – tōn – tois*; fem. *hai – tās – tōn – tais*; nt. *ta – ta – tōn – tois*.

The article – especially the neuter plural *ta* – can be used without an overtly expressed referent: e.g. *ta tōn polemiōn* 'the (things, i.e. assets) of the enemy'; *ta en Spartē* 'the (events) in Sparta'; *pros tous eukolōs ekpherontas ta autōn* 'to those who talk lightly about their own affairs' (Epictetus: IV, XIII).

Declension

There are three declensions of nominals including adjectives and participles:

1st decl. *ā* stems: masc. *-as/ēs*, fem. *ā/ē*: e.g. masc. *ho politēs* 'the citizen';
    fem. *hē xōrā* 'the land', *hē timē* 'the honour'.
2nd decl. *-o/ō* stem: masc. *-os* (with some feminines); neuter *-on*: e.g. masc.
    ho logos 'the word'; fem. *hē nēsos* 'the island'; nt. *to dōron* 'the gift'.
3rd decl. the consonantal declension comprising all nouns not in 1st or 2nd:
    e.g. masc. *ho phylaks* 'the watchman', *ho salpingks* 'the trumpet', *ho*
    poimēn 'the shepherd', *ho sōtēr* 'the saviour'; fem. *hē lampas* 'the lamp',
    hē elpis 'the hope'; nt. *to peras* 'the end', *to sōma* 'the body'.

Specimen declension: *ho politēs* 'the citizen':

	Singular	*Dual*	*Plural*
nom.	ho politēs	tō polītā	hoi politai
acc.	ton polītēn	tō polītā	tous polītās
gen.	tou polītou	toin polītain	tōn polītōn
dat.	tō polītē	toin polītain	tois polītais

Declension is, on the whole, remarkably regular and symmetrical; there are, of course, many irregularities.

Some examples of case usage (apart from primary functions):

Accusative:

cognate accusative, e.g. *hamartīma hamartanein* 'to sin a sin', *grafēn graphesthai* 'to bring an indictment';

accusative of specification: e.g. *Hellēnes eisi to genos* 'they are Greeks by race'.

Genitive:

partitive genitive with many verbs: e.g. *hoiagathei tōn anthrōpōn* 'the good (ones) among the men';

with verbs of perception: e.g. *eleutheriēs geusamenoi* 'having tasted of freedom' (Herodotus), *toutōn tōn mathēmatōn epithymō* 'I long for this learning' (Xenophon);

with ablative nuance: e.g. *Hē nēsos ou poly diekhei tēs ēpeirou* 'The island is not far distant from the mainland'; *epistēmē khōrizdomenē dikaiosynēs* 'knowledge separated from justice' (Plato);

genitive of cause, source: e.g. *Zdēlō se tou nou, tēs de deilias stygō* 'I envy you for your mind but detest you for your cowardice' (Sophocles: *Electra*).

Dative:

of benefit or disadvantage (*dativus commodi et incommodi*): e.g. *Pas anēr autō ponei* 'Every man labours for himself' (Sophocles: *Ajax*), *Solon Athēnaiois nomous ethēke* 'Solon made laws for the Athenians';

causal and instrumental use: e.g. *logō* 'in word', *ergō* 'in deed', *horōmen tois ophthalmois* 'we see with our eyes';

agent: e.g. *eksetasai ti pepraktai tois allois* 'to ask what has been done by the others' (Demosthenes);

time: e.g. *tē autē hēmera apathanen* 'he died on the same day'.

Adjective

The adjective agrees in gender, number, and case with noun, and as attribute, precedes it: e.g. *ho sophos anēr* 'the wise man', gen. *tou sophou andros*, dat. *tō sophō andri*, pl. gen. *tōn sophōn andrōn*. Similarly, all participles in *-os*.

Some adjectives are irregular, e.g. *megas* 'big': acc. *megan*, gen. *megalou*, dat. *megalō*.

COMPARATIVE

In *-teros/-tatos*: e.g. *pikros* 'bitter' – *pikroteros/pikrotatos*.

Pronoun

PERSONAL

The personal pronouns are:

	Singular	Dual	Plural
1	egō	nō	hēmeis
2	sy	sphō	hymeis
3	aitos/autē/auto	autō/autā/autō	spheis; autoi/autai/auta

These are declined in all cases; e.g. first person singular: *egō – eme – emou – emoi*. The dual accusative = nominative; the genitive/dative forms are first person *nōn*, second *sphōn*.

DEMONSTRATIVE PRONOUN

outos/autē/touto; pl. *outoi/autai/tauta* 'this, these'; *hode/hēde/tode*; pl. *hoide/haide/tade* 'that, those'. *Ekeinos/-ē/-o* can also be used for 'that, those'. The demonstratives have dual forms and are declined in all cases.

INTERROGATIVE PRONOUN

tis, ti 'who? what?', declined in three numbers and all cases.

RELATIVE PRONOUN

hos, hē, ho; dual *hō* (all three genders); pl. *hoi, hai, ha*: e.g. *egō hos touto epoiēsa* 'I who did this'; *Edēlōse touto **hois** epratte* 'He showed this by what he did' (pl. dat.); *Touto ouk epoiēsen, en ō ton dēmon etimēsen an* 'He did not do this in which he might have honoured the people' (Demosthenes).

Numerals

1–4 inclusive: *eis, dyo, treis, tessares/tettares*; these are declined; the feminine of *eis* is *mia*, the neuter *hen*.

5 upwards are indeclinable: 5–10 *pente, heks, hepta, oktō, ennea, deka*; 11 *endeka*; 12 *dōdeka*; 13 *treis kai deka*; 20 *eikosi(n)*; 21 *eis kai eikosi*; 30 *triakonta*, 40 *tessarakonta*; 100 *hekaton*.

Verb

The Greek verb had three voices: active, middle, and passive; medio-passive forms with active meaning are known as deponent verbs.

There are four moods: indicative, imperative, subjunctive, optative; the indicative mood has seven tenses: present, imperfect, perfect, pluperfect, aorist, future, and future perfect.

TENSE SYSTEM

The basic nine stems, with their associated tenses:

1. present: present, imperfect (active, middle, and passive);
2. future: future (active and middle)
3. first aorist: first aorist (active and middle);
4. second aorist: second aorist (active and middle);
5. first perfect: first perfect, pluperfect (active);
6. second perfect: second perfect, pluperfect (active);
7. perfect middle: perfect and pluperfect (middle), future perfect (passive);

8. first passive: first aorist, future (passive);
9. second passive: second aorist, future (passive).

Few verbs have both the first and second forms of any tense; hence, most verbs have only six stems, while many have fewer.

Verbs are further sub-divided into two categories: in (a) the root stem is stable throughout the tense system; in (b) the root stem is specifically modulated to accommodate the various tense stems.

A further division is into (a) vowel stems, e.g. *phile-* 'to love', and (b) consonant stems, e.g. *trib-* 'to rub', *graph-* 'to write', *peith-* 'to prevail upon'.

PRINCIPAL PARTS
Theoretically, all forms of a Greek verb can be constructed from the following items: first person singular of the present, the future, the first aorist, and the perfect in the indicative active; the first person singular of the perfect middle and the aorist (passive); first person singular of second aorist (active or middle) if present. Examples, from *leipō* 'to leave' and *phainō* 'to show':

> leipō, leipsō, leloipa, leleimmai, eleiphthēn, elipon
> phainō, phanō, ephēna, pephangka/pephēna, pephasmai, epanthēn

DEPONENT VERBS
The principal parts are the first person singular of the present, the future, the perfect, and the aorist (all indicative); e.g. of *ergazdomai* 'to work':

> ergazdomai, ergasomai, eirgasamēn, eirgasmai, eirgasthēn

CONJUGATION
Involves selection of the correct stem, the relevant personal endings in three numbers, the use of the augment in the imperfect and aorist indicative, and the use of the reduplicating prefix in the perfect system. In this way, over 500 forms are generated in a typical conjugation.

Specimen conjugation: *leipō* 'to leave'

1. present system:

    active: present: *leípō*; imperfect: *éleipon*; subjunctive *leípō*; optative *leípoimi*; imperative: *leîpe*; infinitive: *leípein*; participle: *leípōn*.
    middle: present: *leípomai*; imperfect: *eleipómēn*; subjunctive *leípōmai*; optative *leipoímēn*; imperative: *leípou*; infinitive: *leípesthai*; participle: *leipómenos*.
    passive: as middle.

2. future system:

    active: future: *leípsō*; optative *leípsoimi*; infinitive: *leípsein*: participle *leípsōn*.
    middle: future: *leípsomai*; optative *leipsoímēn*; infinitive: *leípsesthai*; participle: *leipsómenos*.

3. none.

4. second aorist system:

active: *élipon*; subjunctive *lípō*; optative *lípoimi*; imperative: *lípe*; infinitive: *lipeîn*; participle: *lipṓn*.

middle: *elipómēn*; subjunctive *lípōmai*; optative *lipoímēn*; imperative: *lipoû*; infinitive: *lipésthai*; participle: *lipómenos*.

5. none.

6. second perfect and pluperfect:

active: *léloipa*; subjunctive *leloípō*; optative *leloípoimi*; infinitive: *leloipénai*; participle: *leloipṓs*.

7. perfect and pluperfect:

middle: *léleimmai*; subjuctive *leleimménos ō*; optative *leleimménos eíēn*; imperative: *léleipso*; infinitive: *leleîphthai*; participle: *leleimménos*.

future perfect: *leleípsomai*; optative *leleipsoímēn*; infinitive: *leleípsesthai*; participle: *leleipsómenos*.

8. first future passive: *leiphthḗsomai*; optative *leiphthēsoímēn*; infinitive: *leiphthḗsesthai*; participle: *leiphthēsómenos*.

first aorist passive: *eleíphthēn*; subjunctive *leiphthô*; optative *leiphtheíēn*; imperative: *leíphthēti*; infinitive: *leiphthênai*; participle: *leiphtheís*.

The *-th-* characteristic of the passive system is a Greek innovation in the structure of Indo-European.

Certain irregularities are due to internal sandhi in consonant-stem verbs; e.g. from *trībō* 'rub', perfect **tetribmai → tetrimmai*, etc.

The vocalic collocations *aō*, *eō*, *oō* are contracted in the present and imperfect: e.g. *timaō → timō* 'honour'; *dēloō → dēlō* 'manifest'.

Verbs in *-mi* form a special class, with irregularities in the present and second aorist systems.

PERSONAL ENDINGS
Basic inventory:

(a) Active

		Primary tenses	*Secondary tenses*
sing.	1	mi (ō)	n
	2	s	s
	3	si (ti)	—
dual	2	ton	ton
	3	ton	tēn
pl.	1	men (mes)	men (mes)
	2	te	te
	3	nsi (nti) asi	n, san

(b) Middle and passive

sing.	1	mai	mēn
	2	sai	so
	3	tai	to
dual	2	(s)thon	(s)thon
	3	(s)thon	(s)thēn
pl.	1	metha	metha
	2	(s)the	(s)the
	3	ntai	nto

Imperative

		Active	*Middle and passive*
sing.	2	thi	so
	3	tō	(s)thō
dual	2	ton	(s)thon
	3	tōn	(s)thōn
pl.	2	te	(s)the
	3	ntōn/tōsan	(s)thōn/(s)thōsan

The primary tenses referred to in the above table are the present, perfect, future, and future perfect; the secondary tenses are the imperfect, the pluperfect, and the aorist.

Oratio obliqua: accusative and infinitive (marked for tense/aspect): e.g. *phēsi tous andras apelthein* 'he says that the men went away'; *nomizdō se mōron einai* 'I think you're stupid'; *Apangelleis moi pollous toi epibouleuein* 'You tell me that many are plotting against you' (Diogenes Laertius, I.64).

Or tense sequence after *hoti* 'that': following primary tenses, an indicative form retains mood and tense: e.g. *legei hoti graphei/egraphen/egrapsen* 'he says that he is writing/was writing/wrote'. After secondary tenses the optative may replace the indicative forms: e.g. *Eleksan hoti pempseie sfas ho Indōn basileus* 'They said that the king of the Indians had sent them' (Xenophon).

NEGATION

ou is general negator in both independent and indirect sentences. *Mē* negates the imperative and the subjunctive.

Prepositions

Four – *anti* 'against', *apo* 'from, for', *ek(s)* 'out of', *pro* 'before' – take the genitive: e.g. *apo toutou tou khronou* 'from that time' (Xenophon); *onar ek Dios estin* 'the dream comes from Zeus' (*Iliad*).

Two – *en* 'in', *syn* 'with' – take the dative: e.g. *ton Periklea en orgē eikhon* 'they held Pericles in anger' = 'were angry with Pericles' (Thucydides).

Four take the genitive or accusative: *dia* 'through', *kata* 'below', *hyper* 'over', *meta* 'among': e.g. with gen.: *meta zdōntōn* 'among the living' (Sophocles); with accusative: *meta straton ēlas' Akhaiōn* 'he drove into the army of the Achaeans' (*Iliad*).

Six take genitive, dative, or accusative: *amphi* 'about', *epi* 'on, upon', *para* 'by, near', *peri* 'around', *pros* 'at, my', *hypo* 'under': e.g. *hypo*

> with genitive: *ta hypo gēs* 'the things that are under the earth' (Plato: *Apology*);
> with dative: *hypo tē Akropoli* 'under the Akropolis' (Herodotus);
> with accusative: *ēltheth' hypo Troiēn* 'you came to Troy' (*Odyssey*).

Word order

Generally SVO, but almost any order is possible.

---

¹_{iii} **1** Ἐν ἀρχῇ ἦν ὁ λόγος, καὶ ὁ λόγος ἦν πρὸς τὸν θεόν, καὶ θεὸς ἦν ὁ λόγος. **2** οὗτος ἦν ἐν ἀρχῇ πρὸς τὸν θεόν. **3** πάντα δι᾽ αὐτοῦ ἐγένετο, καὶ χωρὶς αὐτοῦ ἐγένετο ⌜οὐδὲ ἕν⌝⸳. ὃ γέγονεν⸳¹ **4** ἐν αὐτῷ ζωὴ ⌜ἦν, καὶ ἡ ζωὴ ἦν τὸ φῶς □τῶν ἀνθρώπων⌟⸳ **5** καὶ τὸ φῶς ἐν τῇ σκοτίᾳ φαίνει, καὶ ἡ σκοτία αὐτὸ οὐ κατέλαβεν.

²_{iii} **6** Ἐγένετο ἄνθρωπος, ἀπεσταλμένος παρὰ ⌜θεοῦ, ⌝ ὄνομα αὐτῷ Ἰωάννης⸳ **7** οὗτος ἦλθεν εἰς μαρτυρίαν ἵνα μαρτυρήσῃ περὶ τοῦ φωτός, ἵνα πάντες πιστεύσωσιν δι᾽ αὐτοῦ. **8** οὐκ ἦν ἐκεῖνος τὸ φῶς, ἀλλ᾽ ἵνα μαρτυρήσῃ περὶ τοῦ φωτός.

GREEK,
MODERN STANDARD

INTRODUCTION

Modern Greek belongs to the Hellenic branch of Indo-European. It is the official language of Greece, where it is spoken by over 10 million people, and joint official language of Cyprus; in addition, there are large Greek-speaking communities in many countries. A dialect of Greek is still spoken in few villages in Calabria.

For many centuries Greece presented the classic example of a *diglossia*. Two Greek languages were in use: (a) Demotic, the spoken language deriving from the Hellenistic koine, as modulated and developed in the Byzantine period and during the following centuries of Turkish domination; and (b) Katharevousa, the consciously archaizing language of administration, religion, education, and literature. Katharevousa itself was written on more than one stylistic level, ranging from a semi-puristic register (advocated, for example, by Adamantios Koraïs in the early nineteenth century; a demotic base plus classical enhancement) to a high-flown literary style which was almost indistinguishable from Classical Greek. Curiously enough, the creation of an independent Greek state in 1830 proved a setback for the pro-demotic camp, as the linguistic issue became confused with political interests. Thus, from the mid-nineteenth century to the 1970s Greek continued to exist on two or even three linguistic planes, the selective use of which depended on socio-linguistic factors. Key stages in the gradual ascendancy of Demotic are:

1. The 'militant demoticism' of Psycharis (1854–1929): identification of Demotic as the expression of the modern Greek ethos: γλώσσα και πατρίδα είναι το ίδιο, 'language and fatherland are one and the same thing'.
2. 1910: Educational Society founded to promote the use of Demotic in education; countered by recognition in the 1911 Constitution of Katharevousa as the official language of the Greek State.
3. 1917: Venizelos government introduces use of Demotic in elementary schools.
4. After several setbacks – e.g. the 1952 Constitution and the Emergency Law of 1967, both of which endorsed the 1911 ruling – Demotic has now been finally and formally recognized as the spoken and written language of Greece.

SCRIPT

The 24 letters of Classical Greek, plus digraphs for certain sounds, e.g.

mp = /b/: *mpaino* = /bɛnɔ/, 'I go in';
nt = /d/: *ntunomai* = /dinɔmɛ/, 'I dress';
gx = /ŋx/: *sugxronos* = /siŋxrɔnɔs/, 'contemporary';
ts = /ts/

PHONOLOGY

Consonants

stops: p, b, t, d, k, (g) + palatalized k'
affricates: ts, dz, ks/gz, ps
fricatives: f, v, θ, ð, s, z, x, γ
laterals and flap: l, ʎ, r
nasals: m/m', n/ŋ
semi-vowel: j

/g/ is rare.

Vowels

i, ɛ, a, ɔ, u

The former distinction between long and short vowels has been lost. All unstressed syllables are short; stressed syllables may be slightly longer or half-long. A reduction to /ə/ before or after stressed syllable is frequent. Vocalic reduction has led to considerable divergence between sound and symbol; the sound /i/, for example, is notated in no less than six different ways: η, ι,υ,ει,οι,υι.

If the digraphs *ai, oi* are to be pronounced as diphthongs, the *i* is marked by a diaeresis: e.g. *roloï 'watch'; kaïmaki* 'cream'.

Stress

Until recently, stress in both Demotic and Katharevousa was marked by acute, grave, and circumflex accents, a legacy from the musical pitch of Ancient Greek. In 1982, a monotonic system of accentuation was introduced by the Greek Ministry of Education; this uses the acute alone to mark stress. Use of the circumflex seems to be optional. The grave has been discarded along with the aspiration markers (*spiritus asper* and *spiritus lenis*) traditionally provided for vocalic initials.

Sandhi

Sandhi at word juncture is a fundamental feature of Greek pronunciation: e.g.

/n/ + /k/ → [ŋg]: e.g. *ston kipo* [stɔŋg ipɔ], 'in the garden'
/n/ + /b/ → [mb]: e.g. *ðen mporei* [ðɛmbɔri], 'he cannot'
/n/ + /ks/ → [ŋgz]: e.g. *ðen ksero* [ðɛŋg zɛrɔ], 'I don't know'

Crasis takes place at vocalic junctures.

MORPHOLOGY AND SYNTAX

Noun

Greek has three genders, masculine, feminine, and neuter. Some guidance as to gender may be given by the ending of a word. Thus, words ending in *-os*, *-as*, *-is* are usually masculine; words in *-i*, *-a* are typically feminine; words in *-o*, *-i*, *-ma* typically neuter.

ARTICLES
There are two articles: the indefinite article is: masc. *enas*, fem. *mia*, neut. *ena*. The definite article is: masc. *o*, pl. *oi* /i/; fem. *i*, pl. *oi* /i/; neut. *to*, pl. *ta*. This article is declined: see declension of noun, below.

DECLENSION
There are three declensions according to ending; the consonantal stems, so plentiful in Katharevousa, have been largely reduced to their accusative forms: *i elpis* 'hope' > *elpida*; *filaks* 'guard' > *filaka*.

Three typical paradigms follow: masc., *o pateras* 'father', fem., *i kardia* 'heart', neut., *to vuno* 'mountain':

Singular	nom.	o pateras	i kardia	to vuno
	gen.	tou patera	tis kardias	tou vunou
	acc.	ton patera	tin kardia	to vuno
Plural	nom.	oi pateres	oi kardies	ta vuna
	gen.	ton pateron	ton kardion	ton vunon
	acc.	tous pateres	tis kardies	ta vuna

Katharevousa formants may reappear in plural endings: e.g. *psaras* 'fisherman' – *psarades*. Notice also such forms as *to kreas* 'meat', gen. *tou kreatos*; *to γramma* 'letter', gen. *tou γrammatos*.

Adjective

As attributive, adjective precedes noun, with concord for gender, number, case: e.g.

nom.	o kalos pateras	i kali mitera	to kalo paidi
gen.	tou kalou patera	tis kalis miteras	tou kalou paidiou
	'the good father('s)'	'the good mother('s)'	'the good child('s)'

Most Greek adjectives end in *-os*, *-i/-a*, *-o*. Other endings are found, e.g. *ziliaris* 'jealous' – fem. *ziliara* – neut. *ziliariko*; pl. masc. *ziliarides*.

COMPARATIVE
In *-teros* (inflected) or with *pio* + positive: thus from *psilos* 'high': *psiloteros* = *pio psilos*.

Pronoun

PERSONAL
The personal pronouns have full, oblique, and two short forms, one of which is used as possessive marker, the other as objective pronoun. These forms are:

	Singular			*Plural*		
	Full	*Oblique*	*Short*	*Full*	*Oblique*	*Short*
1	ego	emena	mou, me	emeis	emas	mas
2	esu	esena	sou, se	eseis	esas	sas

The third person is marked for gender: masc. *autos* /aftɔs/, fem. *auti* /afti/, neut. *auto*. These are declined like the definite article, except that the feminine plural has *autes* – *auton* – *autes* /aftɛs/, etc.

POSSESSIVES
Example: *o pateras mou* /ɔ patɛraz.mu/, 'my father'.

DIRECT OBJECT
*ðen **m**. endiaferei* 'It doesn't interest me'; *mas katalave* = 'he understood us'. Also as indirect object: *Sas aresoun ta taksiðia?* 'Do you like travelling?'; *telefonese mas* 'call us'.

DEMONSTRATIVE PRONOUN
autos, *auti*, *auto* 'this' (*see* **Personal pronoun**, above). The non-proximate series is *ekeinos*, *ekeini*, *ekeino*.

INTERROGATIVE PRONOUN
pyos – pya – pyo 'who?', with plural forms, e.g. *Pyos eina autos o anθropos?* 'Who is that man?'; *ti* 'what?'.

RELATIVE PRONOUN
Is marked for gender, e.g. *o opyos – o opya – to opyo*; and is declined like *autos*. The alternative forms *pou* and *o, ti* are indeclinable: e.g. *o neos pou irθe* 'the young man who came'; *o neos pou eiða* 'the young man whom I saw'; *o, ti θeleis* 'whatever you want'; *to spiti to opyo koitazeis* = *to spiti pou koitazeis* 'the house you are looking at'.

Numerals

1–10: *enas* '1', is fully declined (fem. *mia*) and provides the indefinite article; *duo* '2' /ðiɔ/ is indeclinable; *treis* '3' and *tessereis* '4' are declined. Thereafter indeclinable. 5–10: *pente, eksi, epta, okto, ennea, deka*; 11 *endeka*; 12 *dodeka*; 20 *eikosi*; 30 *trianta*; 40 *saranta*; 50 *peninta*; 100 *ekato*.

Verb

The basic division is into perfective and imperfective aspects. The perfective base is made from the imperfective base by addition of *-s*, with accompanying assimilation depending on stem final: vowel $+ s \rightarrow s$; $z + s \rightarrow s$; $f + s \rightarrow ps$; $g/\gamma + s \rightarrow ks$. Thus:

Imperfective base	*Perfective base*
γrafo 'I write'	γra**ps**o
ðiavazo 'I read'	ðiava**s**o
ðialeγo 'I choose'	ðiale**ks**o

There are two conjugations: in (a) the stress falls on the root syllable preceding the ending; in (b) stress falls on the ending. For conjugation (a) the formation of the perfective aspect, as set out above, is regular; in conjugation (b) the formative element is *-is*: e.g. *milo* 'I speak' – *miliso*.

From the imperfective base the following tenses are made (verb *khano* 'I lose').

present: sing. *khano, khaneis, khanei*; pl. *khanoume, khanete, khanoun*
future: auxiliary + present forms: *tha khano*, etc. (*tha* is invariable)
past imperfect: augment in sing. 1, 2, 3, and in pl. 3: e.g. *ekhana, ekhanes, ekhane*; pl. *khaname, khanate, ekhanan*
imperfect subjunctive: particle *na* + present: *na khano* 'that I lose'
conditional: auxiliary *tha* + past imperfect forms
optative: *na* + past imperfect forms
participle: *khanontas*
imperative: sing. *khane*, pl. *khanete*; negative: *mi(n)* + subjunctive.

Tenses made from perfective base:

past definite: again the augment is in the singular and the third person plural: e.g. sing. *ekhasa, ekhases, ekhase*; pl. *khasame, khasate, ekhasan*
future definite: *tha* + perfective base + *imperfective* endings: e.g. *tha khasoume* 'we shall lose'
perfect: auxiliary *ekho* 'I have' + past participle: e.g. *ekho khasei* 'I have lost'

MIDDLE VOICE

The *-Vmai* ending has three distinct functions:

(a) deponent: *kaθomai* 'I sit'
(b) reflexive: *ntunomai* /dinɔmɛ/, 'I dress (myself), get dressed'
(c) passive: *vlepetai* 'it is seen'

The present-tense endings, e.g. for *khanomai*, are: sing. *khan-omai, -esai, -etai*; pl. *-omaste, -este, -ontai*

The perfective stem ends in -θ with assimilation: *khaθika, khaθikes*, etc.: e.g. *sinantiθikame ksana meta ti sinaulia* 'we met again after the concert'.

PARTICIPLES
Active present *khanontas*, past *khasei*; passive present *khamenos*, past *khaθei*.

MODAL VERBS
Examples:

prepei na ton vlepo taktika 'I must see him regularly' (*prepei* 'must, should')

prepei na ton ðo simera 'I must see him today' (*ðo* is the suppletive perfective base of *vlepo* 'I see')

θelo na sou ðoso mia simvouli (*θelo* 'I want')
'I want to give you some advice' (*ðoso* is the perfective base of *ðino* 'I give')

m'aresei na maθaino γlosses 'I like learning languages' (*m'aresi* 'it pleases me')

prepei na maθo ellenika 'I must learn Greek'

Prepositions

Prepositions are simple or compound: e.g.

simple: *se* 'in(to)', which coalesces with the article: e.g. *ston, stin, sto*; *me* 'with'; *meta* 'after'; *prin* 'before'.
compound: e.g. *istera apo* 'after'; *ðipla se* 'alongside'; *pamo se* 'upon'.

Most govern the accusative, five the genitive; one *-kata-* takes either the accusative or the genitive, with change in meaning: e.g. *sto spiti* 'in the house, at home'; *stin Aθina* 'to/in Athens'; *kata ton polemo* 'during the war'; *meta ton polemo* 'after the war'; *apo tin Anglia* 'from England'; *me ta poðia* 'with the feet', i.e. 'on foot'.

Word order

SVO is basic; OV with S understood is frequent: e.g. *tin eiða* 'I saw her'.

1 Απ' όλα πριν υπήρχε ο Λόγος
κι ήταν ο Λόγος με το Θεό,
κι ήταν Θεός ο Λόγος.
²Απ' την αρχή ήταν αυτός με το Θεό.
³Μέσον αυτού δημιουργήθηκαν τα πάντα,
κι απ' όσα έγιναν
δεν έγινε τίποτε χωρίς αυτόν.
⁴Αυτός ήταν για τα δημιουργήματα η ζωή, ⁽ᵃ⁾
κι ήταν η ζωή αυτή το φως για τους ανθρώπους.
⁵Το φως αυτό έλαμψε μέσα στη σκοτεινιά του κόσμου,
μα η σκοτεινιά δεν το δέχτηκε. ⁽ᴮ⁾
⁶Ο Θεός έστειλε έναν άνθρωπο που τον έλεγαν Ιωάννη· ⁷αυτός
ήρθε ως μάρτυρας για να κηρύξει ποιος είναι το φως, ώστε με τα λόγια
του να πιστέψουν όλοι. ⁸Δεν ήταν ο ίδιος το φως, ήρθε όμως για να
πει ποιος είναι το φως.

GUARANÍ

INTRODUCTION

Guaraní belongs to the Tupí-Guaraní group of the Andean-Equatorial family. It is spoken by about 2 million people in Paraguay, where it has semi-official status along with the official language, Spanish. The Paraguayan Guaranís are the descendants of Tupí tribes who migrated to the Paraguay River area in the fifteenth century. Guaraní has been a written language since its use in the Jesuit communities in Paraguay in the sixteenth and seventeenth centuries.

SCRIPT

The Roman alphabet with diacritics. A standardized orthography was agreed at the Montevideo Congress in 1950.

PHONOLOGY

Consonants

stops: ^{m}b, p, ^{n}d, t, k, g, ʔ
affricate: dʒ
fricatives: v, ʃ, h
lateral and flap: l, r
nasals: m, n ɲ
semi-vowels: j, w

Neither /b/ nor /d/ occurs apart from as the pre-nasalized phonemes. /ʃ/ is notated as *x*, /dʒ/ as *j*.

Vowels

i, e, a, o, u, y

All occur nasalized, usually marked in Guaraní script by diaeresis: *ï*, *ë*, etc. Length is not phonemic.

/y/ is a pharyngeal unrounded vowel resembling /ɯ/ or /ɪ/. Guasch (1956) compares it to the Russian ы. Its nasalized allophone is the characteristic Tupí-Guaraní sound.

537

Stress

Stress is, in general, unmarked on final vowel or diphthong.

MORPHOLOGY AND SYNTAX

Guaraní has no grammatical gender, nor is there a definite article. Increasing use is being made, however, of the two Spanish articles, *la* for the singular, and *lo* for the plural: e.g. *lo mitä* 'the children'. The numeral *peteï* may serve as an indefinite article for a singular noun, *umi* (a plural demonstrative) for the plural: e.g. *peteï mitäkuna paraguai* 'a Paraguayan girl'. Similarly, a demonstrative may be used as a definite article: e.g. *pe kokue jara jagua* 'the farmer's dog' (*kokue* = *chacra* 'small farm'; *jara* 'master'; *jagua* 'dog').

Noun

Initial *t-* and *h-* are movable or 'oscillating' consonants, changing to *r-* after first or second personal pronouns used as possessives, and in the inverse construct which is the Guaraní (and Tupí) genitive: cf. *toba* 'face' – *xe.roba* 'my face' (*xe* = first person pronoun); *tera* 'name' – *xe.rera* 'my name'; *oga* 'house' – *Tuparoga* 'house of God'. Many nouns which originally had a *t-* initial, are now fixed in the *r-* form.

NUMBER
The plural marker is *-kuera* (→ *nguera* by assimilation, e.g. after nasal vowel): e.g. *jagua* 'dog', pl. *jaguakuera*; *mitä* 'child', pl. *mitänguera*.

GENITIVE
By juxtaposition, the inverse of the Spanish order, with *t-/h-* shift: e.g. *tuva sombrero* 'father's hat'; *Ko tapo mba'e yvyra rapo.pa*? 'This root is the root of which tree?' (*yvyra* 'tree').

Pe is used to mark a direct or indirect object, and also as a locative marker: e.g. *Jagua omuna mbarakajape* 'The dog chases the cat'; *Pe karai ome'ë avati kavajupe* 'The man (*karai*) gives maize (*avati*) to the horse'; *i.koty.pe* 'in his (*i.-*) room'; *ipopekuera* 'in his hands' (*po* 'hand').

Adjective

Adjective follows noun: *peteï kure ka'aguy hü* 'a wild black pig'; *Paraguai ñane retä porä* 'Paraguay, our lovely country' (*tetä* 'country').

Pronoun

Subject, possessive, direct and indirect object sets are distinguished (*see also* **Verb** prefixes, below):

			Subject	Possessive	Direct object	Indirect object
sing.	1		xe	xe	xe	xeve
	2		nde	nde	nde/ro	ndeve
	3		ha'e	i/in/ij/h(i)	ixupe	ixupe
pl.	1	incl.	ñande	ñande	ñande	ñandeve
		excl.	ore	ore	ore	oreve
	2		peë (pende)	pende	pende/po	peëme
	3		ha'e kuera	*as sing.*	ixupekuera	ixupekuera

Examples: *xe*/*nde kavaju* 'my/your horse ...'; *ñande ra'ykuera rera* 'the number of our sons' (*ta'y* 'son', *tera* 'number'). The base forms take postpositions: e.g. *xe.hegui* 'of me'; *xe.rehe* 'for me'; *xe.ndive* 'with me'.

DEMONSTRATIVE PRONOUN
Ranges through several degrees from *ko*/*ko'ä* 'this' (here and now), to *aipo(v)a* 'that' (unseen and unknown). Plural forms: *äva*; *umi*.

INTERROGATIVE PRONOUN
avapa 'who?'; *mba'epa* 'what?'.

Numerals

Guaraní forms are used for the first four numerals: *peteï, moköi, mbohapy, irundy*. Thereafter, Spanish numbers are used, though Guaraní forms exist (set out, for example, in Guasch (1956)).

Verb

There is a broad division into two classes of verb, which the Spanish writers on Guaraní call (a) *verbos areales*, and (b) *verbos xendales*.

(a) *verbos areales*: these are active/transitive, with invariable stem and personal prefixes as subject markers: these are sing. 1 *a-*, 2 *re-*, 3 *o-*; pl. 1 (incl.) *ja-/na-*, (excl.) *ro-*, 2 *pe-*, 3 *o-*. A sub-group has 1 *ai-*, 2 *rei-*, etc.: e.g. (*xe*) *a.guata* 'I walk', (*nde*) *reguata* 'you walk'.

Tense markers are added: *va'ekue* (past), *va'erä* (future): e.g. *re.japo.va'ekue* 'you did'; *re.japo.va'erä* 'you will do'. There is also a continuative form: *a.japo aina* 'I am doing'; *Mba'epa re.japo reina?* 'What are you doing?'

Objective pronouns: first and second person forms precede the verb, third person forms follow: e.g. *nde xejuhu* 'you meet me'; *ha'e nde.juhu* 'he meets you'; *xe ajuhu ixupekuera* 'I meet them'.

(b) *verbos xendales*: these are stative forms, in which the independent pronoun precedes an adjectival or nominal stem. If the stem initial is *t-/h-*, the shift to *r-* takes place for first and second persons: e.g. with *tasy* 'sick': *xe rasy* 'I am sick'; *nde rasy* 'you are sick'; but, *hasy* 'he is sick'.

Both types of verb are negated by means of *nda-* ... *i*, as in Tupí: *nd.ai.pota.i*

'I don't want'; *nde.rei.pota.i* 'you don't want'; *nda.ore.rasy.i* 'we are not ill'.

There are, of course, numerous secondary tenses, e.g. a perfect with *kuri*: *ajapo/rejapo kuri* 'I/you have done'; and a second future in *-ne*: *ajapone* 'I shall do'.

Guaraní has two verbs meaning 'to be': (a) *aime* 'I am in/at a place'; (b) *aiko* 'I am (+ adverb)'. There is no copula; 'I am' + adjective or noun = juxtaposition: e.g. *xe tujama* 'I am old'. Nouns may be marked for tense (cf. Tupi): *-kue* (past), *-ra* (future): *mburuvixakue* '(he) who was boss/chief'; *mburuvixara* '(he) who will be boss/chief'; *mburuvixarangue* 'someone who was expected to become chief but did not'.

RELATIVE CLAUSE

va/gua: the referent is the subject or direct object of relative clause: e.g. *amo karai oho.va amongotio* 'that man who is going over there' (*oho* is third person singular of irregular verb *aha* 'go'); *amo karai a hexa.va amo* 'the man I see there'. *Ha* is used with reference to an indirect object: e.g. *amo karai a me'ë.ha* ... 'the man to whom I give ...'; *amo tava aju.ha.gui* 'that village from which I come'. Cf. *Kova.pa re.jogua va'erä?* 'Is this what you intend to buy?'; *Kova pa re.jogua va'ekue?* 'Is this what you bought?'

Imperative, conditional, potential, causal, affective moods and several modalities of motion, etc., are expressed with the help of an extensive inventory of particles.

Word order

SVO, VOS.

---

1 Cuando todo comenzó, ya existía la Palabra; y aquel que es la Palabra estaba con Dios y era Dios. En el principio, pues, él estaba con Dios. Por medio de él, Dios hizo todas las cosas; nada de lo que existe fue hecho sin él. En él estaba la vida, y esta vida era la luz para los hombres. Esta luz brilla en la oscuridad, y la oscuridad no ha podido apagarla.

Hubo un hombre a quien Dios envió, llamado Juan, que vino como testigo para hablar de la luz, para que todos creyeran por medio de lo que él decía. Juan no era la luz; era solamente un testigo enviado para hablar en favor de la luz.

GUJARATI

INTRODUCTION

Gujarati is a Western New Indo-Ayran language and is the official language of the state of Gujarat, where it is spoken by about 25 million people. It also spreads into Maharashtra, and is spoken by Gujarati communities in every major city in India. The total number of speakers is estimated at around 30 million.

Gujarati took shape from the Gurjara Apabhraṁsa between the tenth and thirteenth centuries AD. The literature dates from the fourteenth century with mediaeval verse centring on the Rādhā–Kṛṣṇa theme.

Modern writing in Gujarati started in the late nineteenth century along with a new literary standard language, based on the Baroda dialect, as its medium. The influence of Mahatma Gandhi's writings in Gujarati can hardly be over-estimated. An outstanding modern poet is Umāśankar Jośī.

Bhili and Khandesi, spoken together by around 4 million people, are usually regarded as variant forms of Gujarati, but by some authorities as languages in their own right. Apart from this questionable point, Gujarati is remarkably homogeneous over its spoken area.

SCRIPT

The specific variant of the Devanagari script used by Gujarati discards the horizontal line above the letter sequence, which is standard in Sanskrit and Hindi.

PHONOLOGY

Consonants

stops: p, b, t, d, ṭ, ḍ, k, g; all with aspirated values: ph, bh, etc.
affricates: tʃ, tʃh, dʒ, dʒh
fricatives: v/w, (f), s, ṣ, ʃ, h
laterals and flaps: l, lh, ḷ, r, rh
nasals: m, mh, n, nh, ṇ, ṇh, (ɲ), ŋ)
semi-vowels: j, w

/dʒ/ and /dʒh/ are represented as *j* and *jh*; retroflex sounds with a subscript dot.

Vowels

i, e, ɛ, ə, a, ɔ, o, u

Most occur nasalized. Each vowel is realized in four allophones, depending on position in word. These variants are not phonemic. Vowels may be accompanied by a kind of breathy 'murmur', which is perhaps associated with elision of intervocalic consonants.

Stress

Stress is barely perceptible.

MORPHOLOGY AND SYNTAX

Noun

Gujarati distinguishes masculine, feminine, and neuter genders. Gender may be identifiable from ending: thus, -o is typically masculine, -ī and -ā are feminine, -ū is neuter. An exception is provided by the many nouns of profession, nationality, etc. which have a masculine form in -ī: e.g. *kaṇbī* 'peasant', *maḷī* 'gardener'. There are no articles.

NUMBER
The plural marker -o is added to the oblique base; this is normally identical to the nominative base, which is also the citation form. Masculine nouns in -o, however, make their oblique base in -ā: e.g. *ghoḍo* 'horse', obl. base *ghoḍā-*.

DECLENSION
There are six cases. Specimen declension of *kūtro* 'dog':
Singular

>nom. kūtro
>gen. kūtrāno (masc.), -nī (fem.), -nū (neuter) (i.e. the genitive behaves as
>   an adjective)
>acc./dat. kūtrāne
>instr. kūtrāe
>abl. kūtrāe
>abl. kūtrāthī
>loc. kūtrāmã̄

The plural adds the same affixes to the pluralized stem: e.g. *kūtrā.o.-no, -nī*.

GENITIVE
Examples: *chokəra.no bāp* 'the boy's father'; *ghar.nī orḍī* 'the room of the house'; *mahātmā Gandhījī.no āśram* 'Mahatma Gandhi's ashram'.
   The ablative may be used in such passive constructions as *bāpthī aje kām nahi thāy* 'from father today work not done' = 'Father did no work today.'

Adjective

Adjectives in -*o* show concord for gender, number, and case. Other adjectives are indeclinable, e.g. *sundar* 'beautiful'.

Pronoun

Personal base forms:

	Singular	Plural
1	hū	ame (excl.), āpṇe (incl.)
2	tu	tāme, āp
3	te/ā (demonstratives)	teo/āo

These are declined in five cases. The oblique base of *hu* is *man-*.

POSSESSIVE PRONOUN
Sing. *māro, tāro*; pl. *amāro, tamāro*; these show concord.

DEMONSTRATIVE PRONOUN
ā 'this', *te* 'that', with plural forms.

INTERROGATIVE PRONOUN
The base form *koṇ* appears as *kyo* (masc.), *kaī* (fem.), *kyū* (neut.), with plural forms.

RELATIVE PRONOUN
Sing. *je*, pl. *jeo*, declined in all cases, e.g. gen. sing. *jenū*, pl. *jenmū*; with correlatives in *t-* form in principal clause: e.g.

je maṇəsne mē pəysa apya **te** pəṭel.no bhaī che
'The man to whom I gave the money is the village officer's brother' (*pəṭel* 'village officer')

Jyāre mumbaī jao **tyāre** māre māṭe ā be pustak lāvajo
'When you go to Bombay (*mumbaī*) (then) bring me those two books' (*māṭe* 'for' (postposition); *pustak* 'book')

Numerals

1–10: *ek, be, traṇ, cār, pãc, cha, sāt, āṭh, nav, das*; 11 *agiār*; 12 *bār*; 13 *ter*; 14–19 are unpredictable forms; 20 *vīs*; 30 *trīs*; 40 *cālīs*. The individual forms for 21 to 99 are unpredictable, though decade + 9 is always linked to the following decade: e.g. 48 is *əḍtālīs* (i.e. based on *cālīs*) but 49 is *ogaṇpacās*, based on *pacās* '50'. 100 *so*.

Verb

The infinitive ending is -*ū*: e.g. *karvū* 'to do'; this is the citation form.

MOODS
Indicative, imperative, subjunctive, conditional, presumptive.

Indicative mood: specimen tense formations:

Present: stem + personal inflections: e.g., for *karvū* 'to do': sing. 1 *hū karū*, 2 *tu kare*, 3 *te kare*; pl. 1 *ame karīe*, 2 *tame karo*, 3 *teo kare*. A progressive form is made from this by recapitulating the endings in the auxiliary verb *chū*: e.g. *hū karū chū, tu kare che*.

Perfect:
(a) Intransitive verb, *āvvū* 'to come': perfective participle, marked for gender and number, + *chū*: *hū āvyo/-ī/-ū chū* = *hū āvelo/-lī/-lū chū* (*chū* is conjugated).
(b) Transitive verb: *karvū* 'to do': subject in oblique (instrumental) case. The participial form agrees with the object in gender and number: e.g. *mē karyū che, tē karyū che* = *mē/tē karelū che* 'by-me, by-you was done'.

Past habitual: pronoun + imperfective participle, marked for gender and number: e.g. *hū karto/-tī/-tū* 'I was in the habit of doing'; pl. *ame kartā/ -tī/-tã̄*.
Past perfective: intransitive: *hū āvyo/-ī/-yū* = *hu āvelo/-lī/-lū* 'I came'; transitive: *mē, tē ...karyū/karelū*.
Future: sing. 1 *hū karīš*, 2 *tu karše*, 3 *te karše*; pl. *karīšu, karšo, karše*.

The presumptive, subjunctive, and conditional moods are made by combining the perfective/imperfective participles with auxiliaries: e.g. in subjunctive: *hū āvto/-tī/-tū hoū* 'I may (not) come'.

PASSIVE
In *-ā-*, e.g. from *karvū*, *karāvū* 'to be done'. Conjugated as in active.

CAUSATIVE
-āv/-āḍ added to stem: e.g. *karāvvū* 'cause to do'.

NEGATION
The negative form of the copula – sing. *chū, che, che*; pl. *chīe, cho, che* – is *nathī* /nəhiː/, which is invariable: e.g. *malik ahī nathī* 'the master is not here'; *teo bīmār nathī* 'he is not ill'; *avta nathī* 'he doesn't come'. The particles *na* /nə/, *nahi* /nəhi/ negate personal and impersonal forms of the verb in which the copula is not used: e.g. *Kūvamã̄ kapaḍā dhovā nahi* 'Clothes are not to be washed in the well' (*kūvo* 'well'; *kapaḍū* 'cloth'; *dho* 'to wash'). *Mā* is used to form a negative imperative.

Postpositions

These may follow either the base form of the noun, or one of the oblique cases. For example, with *par* 'on', *baso khursi par* 'sit on the chair', where *khursi* is in the base form.

Several postpositions follow the feminine genitive case in *-nī*: e.g. *ā bāḷak.nī taraph* 'in the direction of that boy'.

Word order

SOV is normal.

૧ સૃષ્ટિના આરંભ પહેલાં **શબ્દ**નું અસ્તિત્વ હતું. તે ઈશ્વરની સાથે
૨ હતો, અને જે ઈશ્વર હતા તે જ તે હતો. · **શબ્દ** ઈશ્વરની સાથે
૩ આરંભથી જ હતો. · તેના દ્વારા જ ઈશ્વરે બધાનું સર્જન કર્યું, અને
તે સર્જનમાંની કોઈપણ વસ્તુ તેના સિવાય બનાવવામાં આવી
૪ ન હતી · **શબ્દ** જીવનનું ઉદ્ભવસ્થાન હતો અને એ જીવન માનવી
૫ પાસે પ્રકાશ લાવ્યું. · આ પ્રકાશ અંધકારમાં પ્રકાશે છે, અને અંધકાર
તેને કદીએ હોલવી શકતો નથી.

૬, ૭ ઈશ્વરે પોતાના સંદેશવાહક યોહાનને મોકલ્યો. · તે લોકોને એ પ્રકાશ
વિષે સાક્ષી આપવા આવ્યો; જેથી બધા માણસો આ સંદેશા સાંભળીને
૮ વિશ્વાસ કરે. · યોહાન પોતે એ પ્રકાશ ન હતો, પરંતુ પ્રકાશ વિષે તે
૯ સાક્ષી આપવા આવ્યો હતો. ·

GURENNE

INTRODUCTION

Also known as Frafra, Gurenne belongs to the Gur (Voltaic) group of the Niger-Congo phylum. It is spoken in north-eastern Ghana, with some spread into Burkina Faso and Togo, by about a quarter of a million people.

SCRIPT

Gurenne may be written in Roman script.

PHONOLOGY

Consonants

stops: p, b, t, d, k, g; with two labio-velars: kp, gb and two palatalized:
/k′/ = [tj], /g′/ = [dj]
fricatives: f, v, s, z, γ
nasals: m, n, ɲ, ŋ, ŋm
lateral and flap: l, r
semi-vowels: j, w

/h/ occurs in loan-words.

Vowels

short or long: i, ɪ, e, ɛ, a, æ, o, ɔ, u, ʊ

There are two series of long vowels: /iː, eː, aː, oː, uː/, and /i'i, e'e, a'a/, etc., that is, vowel + glottal stop + echo. Both /m/ and /ŋ/ are syllabic and tone-bearing. All vowels are subject to weak or strong nasalization.

Tones

Gurenne has five tones: mid-even, high, low, rising, and falling. Terraced tone is a feature of Gurenne pronunciation: relative to an initial high tone, subsequent high tones tend to drop in pitch through an utterance. Low tones are not affected and remain constant in relative pitch.

MORPHOLOGY AND SYNTAX

Noun

Gurenne has five noun classes; these are semantically heterogeneous, and the class marker is affixed to the stem, in contrast to Bantu practice. The classes are:

	Singular	*Plural*	*Example*
1	-a	-ba	nera 'man', pl. nereba
2	-ka	-se	bua (< buka) 'goat', pl. buuse
3	-de	-a	yelle (< yelde), 'word, thing', pl. yela
4	-ko	-to	zuo (< zuko) 'head', pl. zuto
5	-bo	-i	naafo 'cow', pl. nii

The class markers for 3 singular and 4 singular and plural have many variants. Class 3 singulars have C + *e/i*; class 4 singulars and plurals have C + *o/u*. Class 3 plural is stable in -*a*.

Many nouns are hybrid as regards class, with singular in one class, plural in another: e.g. *mabia* 'brother' is singular class 2, the plural *mabito* is class 4. Some plurals are suppletive, e.g. *bia* 'child' (class 2), pl. *komma* (class 1).

The class marker is dropped (a) from the possessor noun in the genitive construct: e.g. *na.ba* 'chief', *bia* 'child': *na.∅ bia* 'chief's son'; *Guren.ga* 'Gurenne man', *yire* 'house': *Guren.∅ yire* 'a Gurenne man's house'; and (b) from the noun when an attributive adjective follows. The class marker is then transferred to the adjective; e.g. with *paale* 'new', *nere paale.ga* 'new man'.

Kinship terms form a special class of noun in Gurenne, and often have a very extensive range of meaning; e.g. *deema* which has over two dozen meanings, ranging from 'mother-in-law'/'father-in-law' to 'husband of mother's brother's daughter's daughter'.

The article *la* follows the noun.

Adjective

Theoretically, the adjective should take all 5×2 class endings, and some in fact do so, e.g. *paale* 'new', *som* 'good'. For most adjectives, however, one singular and one plural ending suffice in all five classes.

Pronoun

PERSONAL PRONOUNS
The third person is marked for class:

		Full form	*Short form*		*Object*
singular	1	mam	ma		m
	2	fom	fo		f
plural	1	tomam		to	
	2	yamam		ya	

	Singular		Plural	
	Full	Shortened	Full	Shortened
3rd p. class 1	enga	a – e	bamma	ba
2	ka	ka	se	se
3	de	de	a	a
4	ko	ko	to	to
5	bo	bo	i	i

The shortened forms have high tone as possessives, low tone as verbal subjects. Examples: *m puuse fo* 'I thank you (sing.)'; *a bote ka* 'he/she loves her/him', neg. *a ka bote ka* (**ka** = neg. marker); *mam ka nye yebaa la* 'I have not seen the leopard' (*nye* 'to see'; *yebaa* 'leopard'; *la* = article).

DEMONSTRATIVE PRONOUN

Proximate: class marker + vowel lengthening + *-na*: e.g. *nere eena wa* 'this man (here)' (*wa* is the demonstrative adjective); similarly *bi kaana wa* 'this child', pl. *bi seena wa* 'these children'; *zi boona wa* 'this fish', pl. *zi iina wa* 'these fish'.

The distal pronoun is formed by duplicating the class marker, with *n/m* linker: thus in cl. 2 sing. *ka.n.ka*, pl. *se.n.se*; cl. 4 sing. *ko.n.ko*, pl. *to.n.to*.

INTERROGATIVE PRONOUN

anne 'who?'; *bem* 'what?'.

RELATIVE PRONOUN

mina: e.g. *mina n tare lon yinga* 'he who has a single piece of land' (*tare* 'have'; *lon* 'land'; *yinga* 'single'; *n* is a co-ordinating particle).

Numerals

Here, the normal Gurenne order, stem – class marker, is reversed; the numeral stems are added to the class marker. Thus, *-yemena* '1' appears, depending on class, as *ayemena*, *kayemena*, *deyemena*, etc., e.g. *nera ayemena* 'one man'. Similarly with *-yi* '2': *nere.ba ba.yi* 'two men', *bon.se se.yi* 'two donkeys'. The remaining stems 3 to 9 are: *-ta, -naase, -nuu, -yoobe, -yopoe, -nii, -wæ*; 10 is *pia*, which is invariable for all classes: e.g. *nereba pia* 'ten men', *bonse pia* 'ten donkeys'. 11–19: e.g. *pia la ayemena*. Class is ignored, and *pia* is invariable, though it changes tone (both syllables low when = '10'; both syllables high through teens and upwards). 20 *piseyi*; 30 *piseta*; 40 *pisenaase*; 100 *kwabega* /kɔbega/.

Verb

The stem is uninflected; tense is indicated by markers, e.g.:

present: the affirmative marker is *la*; *la* is discarded when the negating particle *ka* is used: e.g. *m ye la* 'I go', *m ka ye* 'I don't go'; *fo ye la* 'you (sing.) go';

past imperfective: the marker is *daa*: e.g. *ka dela* 'he is', *ka daa dela* 'he was', *ka daa dagge* 'he wasn't'. Where a time-fixing adverb is present, no marker is necessary: e.g. with *zaa* 'yesterday': *m zaa kenge* 'I went yesterday';

perfect: *ya* or *pon* may be used: e.g. *mam pon di* 'I have already eaten', *ka nye ya* 'he has received'.

IMPERATIVE

The stem acts as a singular imperative; the plural is stem + -*ya*. An indirect imperative is made with *vam/vamya*: e.g. *Vamya te to kenge daa* 'Let's go to the market' (*te* 'so that'; *to* 'we'; *daa* 'market'). This imperative is negated by *da*: e.g. *da vam te to kenge daa* 'let's not go ...'.

CAUSATIVE

The marker is *se/sa*.

Postpositions

Examples: *zia/zian* 'with, at': *to so zian* 'with our father, at our father's'; *poore* 'after, behind': *taae mam poore na* 'follow me' (*taae* 'follow'; *na* 'hither').

There is a localizer in -*n*: e.g. *daa* 'market': *daan* 'at market'; *moen* 'in the jungle'; *diadeon* 'in the restaurant'.

Word order

SVO: e.g. *a karenge la gongo* 'he reads (*karenge*) a book (*gongo*)', where *la* is a pleonastic affirmative particle following the verb.

1 Teŋa wa pin'inluŋɔ na, Se'em te Ba Daa Yi'ira Yelehom la daa pon bɔna mɛ. A daa bo mɛ la Na'ayenɛ. Enŋa me n de Na'ayenɛ. 2 A daa bo mɛ la Na'ayenɛ di pin'inluŋɔ na. 3 Enŋa zuo te Na'ayenɛ daa naam sɛla woo. Dagɛ la bonɔ ayena me n daa naam, han dagɛna la enŋa zuo. 4 Te Yelehom wa zuo te nɛreba tara nyɔvose'ere n ka tare ba'ahegɔ Na'ayenɛ zen'en. Te nyɔvoore wa ana wo nɛɛhom bɔ'ɔra nɛreba. 5 Nɛɛhom wa daana wa la wa'an teŋa wa zuo me na. Halee lika la n kelom bɔna la, gee nɛɛhom la kelom nɛɛre mɛ.

6 Te Na'ayenɛ daa tom boraa kayema na. A yu'urɛ daa de la Yon. 7 A daa wa'ana te a yele la nɛreba nɛɛhom la yele. A daa wa'ana te a yele ba te nɛra woo wom gee sakɛ yetɔgom la. 8 Gee Yon mea daa dagɛ nɛɛhom la. Enŋa daa wa'an me na te a yele nɛreba nɛɛhom la yele.

HAIDA

See **North American Indian Isolates**.

HAITIAN CREOLE

See **Pidgins and Creoles**.

HAKKA

Hakka is a member of the Sinitic family. The Hakka are the descendants of northern Han stock who migrated during the twelfth century to southern China, where they are now very widely distributed. They have long since abandoned their own form of Northern Chinese for the speech forms of their southern neighbours. The total number of Hakka speakers is estimated at something under 40 million.

Hakka has no voiced stops. The surd–aspirate series is represented by /p, p', t, t', k, k'/, with the affricates /ts, ts'/. There is no /r/. /k/-final is frequent.

Hakka has six vowels and six tones. The tonal system is *sui generis*, in that syllables with initial nasal or /l/ are frequently first (level) tone, a sequence normally eschewed in Sinitic languages.

HATTIC

See **Anatolian Languages**.

HAUSA

INTRODUCTION

This, the major language of West Africa, belongs to the Chadic branch of the Afro-Asiatic phylum. It is spoken as mother tongue by over 20 million people, and used as second language and lingua franca by at least another 10 million, and is one of the official languages of the Republic of Nigeria.

Writing in Hausa dates from the religious and literary revival associated with the Sokoto Empire established by the Fulani Usman dan Fodio in 1809. Hausa was written in Arabic script, and this *ajami* tradition lasted in general until the British occupation of Nigeria introduced the Roman script in the early twentieth century. Locally, in northern Nigeria, *ajami* writing persists. Traditional Hausa literature consists largely of verse chronicles and homiletic tracts. Prose fiction began to appear in the 1930s, drama slightly later. Poetry retains its popularity and is often broadcast.

The Kano dialect is the basis of the literary language. Very many Arabic loan-words have been integrated into Hausa; borrowing from English is also extensive.

SCRIPT

Roman alphabet; neither vowel length nor tones are marked.

PHONOLOGY

Consonants

    stops: b; t, d; c, ɟ; k, g; palatalized k′, g′; labialized k°, g°
    glottalized/implosives: ɓ, ɗ, ƙ; ƙ′, ƙ°
    fricatives: f, j, s, z, ʃ, w, f′, h
    nasals: n, m, ŋ
    lateral: l
    flap/roll: r, ɽ

All initial vowels have glottal onset (hamza). Retroflex /ɽ/ is notated here with a subscript dot.

Vowels

short and long: i, e, a, o, u

Short /e/ = [ɛ], short /i/ = [ɪ], short /o/ = [ɔ], short /a/ = [ɐ]. Diphthongs: /ai, au/.

Tones

Two main tones, high and low, with a secondary falling tone. Tone is phonemic. Intonation is also of the greatest importance in Hausa: three cardinal intonational patterns are distinguished: declarative (stepped descending), interrogative, and vocative.

MORPHOLOGY AND SYNTAX

Noun

There are two genders, masculine and feminine, identifiable as such only in singular. Most nouns not ending in -*a*/-*aa* are masculine.

The plural takes many forms, usually involving extension and/or rearrangement (on broken plural lines; *see* **Arabic**) of singular ending, plus tonal change. In the following examples, tone is marked for illustrative purposes: *túnkìyáa* 'sheep', pl. *túmáakíi*; *sírdìi* 'saddle', pl. *síràadáa*; *gàrmáa* 'plough', pl. *gárèemáníi*; *gàríi* 'town', pl. *gárúurúwàa*. A frequent formation is the replacement of the final vowel of the singular by *ō.C.ī*, where C is the final consonant of the singular or its reflex: e.g. *taasaa* 'bowl', pl. *taasooshii*; *kaasuwaa* 'market', pl. *kaasuwooyii*. Many words have more than one plural form.

THE CONSTRUCT STATE
That is, linkage by *na → n* (masc.), *ta → r* (fem.), pl. -*n*. These linking elements are used in the following ways:

(a) To form the possessive relationship: e.g.

   masc. *abooki.n ubaa* 'the friend of the father' (*abookii* 'friend');
   fem. *goona.r ubaa* 'the field of the father';
   pl. *mutaane.n garii* 'the people of the town'.

(b) To link preceding attributive adjective to noun: e.g.

   masc. *babba.n gidaa* 'the big house' (*gidaa* is masculine, although ending in -*aa*);
   fem. *saabuwa.r makarantaa* 'the new school';
   pl. *saababbi.n littattaafai* 'the new books'.

(c) To link noun with enclitic demonstrative: e.g. *gari.n nan* 'this town'; *koofa.r nan* 'this door'.

(d) To link noun and possessive marker: e.g. *dooki.n.sa* 'his horse'; *goona.r.mu* 'our farm'.

(e) In relative-clause structure (see below).

Adjective

There is no distinction between adjectives and other nominals. Attributive nominals precede the noun they qualify, and are in gender and number concord with it. (See examples, above).

Pronoun

PERSONAL

			Base form	Dative	Possessive
Singular	1		ni	mini	-na
	2	masc.	kai	maka	-ka
		fem.	ke	miki	-ki
	3	masc.	shi	masa	-sa
		fem.	ita	mata	-ta
Plural	1		mu	mana	-mu
	2		ku	muku	-ku
	3		su	musu	-su

The base forms have direct-object forms which are identical except for second singular, *ka/ki*; and third feminine, *ta*. The pronominal forms, plus linking element, underlie the verbal tense markers (see below). The possessive enclitics combine with the construct markers to provide separable possessives: *nawa, naka; tawa, taka*, where *-wa* is variant of *-na*: e.g. *Gida.n na.mu nee* 'This house is ours.'

DEMONSTRATIVE PRONOUN/ADJECTIVE

wannan (masc. and fem.) 'this', pl. *waɗannan* 'these'; *wancan* (masc.), *waccan* (fem.) 'that'; pl. *waɗancan* 'those'. *Nan* 'this, these' and *can* 'that, those' follow noun + construct marker: e.g. *wannan dookii = dooki.n nan* 'this horse'.

INTERROGATIVE PRONOUN

waa 'who?'; *mee* 'what?'. These combine with particles *nee* and *cee* to form sing. *waanee, waacee*, pl. *su waanee*: e.g. *Su waanee nee suka tafi goona?* 'Who (pl.) went to the field?'

RELATIVE CONSTRUCTION

Two constructions are used:

(a) with *da* (invariable): headword + *n/r* link + *da*: e.g. *gida.n da sarkii ya gina* 'the house that the chief built' (for *ya gina, see* **Verb**, below);

(b) *da* + *wa* → sing. masc. *wanda*. fem. *wadda*, pl. *waɗanda*; here, no linker is used: e.g. *yaaroo wanda ya zoo* 'the boy who came'.

Numerals

1–10: *ɗaya, biyu, uku, huɗu, biyar, shida, bakwai, takwas, tara, gooma*. 11 (*gooma*) *sha ɗaya*, 12 (*gooma*) *sha biyu*; 20 *ashirin*; 30 *talatin*. Arabic forms are used for decades. 100 *ɗarii*.

Verb

All Hausa verbs end in a vowel, and are invariable as regards tense or aspect, person, and number. The final vowel is, however, coded for transitivity and intransitivity, causativity, and certain modal nuances (see below). Specific realizations for aspect, version, person, etc. are generated via pre-verbal markers (based on the pronominal series) plus auxiliary verbal elements. One classification of Hausa verbs uses the third person plural form of these pronominal markers as indices of the various aspects and versions.

There are perfective, imperative, subjunctive, future, continuative, and habitual aspects; direct (indicative) and relative versions, affirmative, and negative; three singular and three plural + an impersonal form; the second and third singular forms are marked for gender.

DIRECT (INDICATIVE) VERSION

Perfective aspect: the pronominal series used here is illustrated with the stem *zoo* 'to come': sing. 1 *naa zoo,* 2 *kaa/kin zoo,* 3 *ya/ta zoo;* pl. 1 *mun zoo,* 2 *kun zoo,* 3 *sun zoo.* The impersonal form is *an:* e.g. *an zoo* 'one came'.

Formally, the pattern for other aspects is largely similar. Thus, e.g. for the first future, in which the auxiliary *zaa* precedes a specific set of markers:

	Singular	Plural
1	zan zoo	zaa mu zoo
2	zaa ka/ki zoo	zaa ku zoo
3	zai/zaa ta zoo	zaa su zoo

The direct continuative uses the auxiliary *naa* following a specific set of markers, and preceding the verbal noun: eg. *inaa zuwa* 'I am coming'; *kanaa/kinaa zuwaa; yanna/tanaa zuwaa.*

RELATIVE VERSION

The perfective and the continuative aspects have relative versions which are used in the formation of relative clauses: e.g. sing. 1 *na zoo,* 2 *ka/kika zoo,* 3 *ya/ta zoo;* pl. 1 *muka zoo,* 2 *kuka zoo,* 3 *suka zoo.* Examples: *mutaanen da suka zoo jiya* 'the people who came yesterday' (*jiya* 'yesterday'); *abin da ya cee jiya* 'what he said yesterday' (*cee* 'to say'). As the first of these examples shows, even when a nominal head-word is present, the pronominal copy is necessary.

SUBJUNCTIVE

The subjunctive marker is *su:* e.g. *su zoo* 'let them come'.

NEGATIVE

All affirmative forms, some of which are illustrated above, have negative counterparts; e.g. the negative form of the direct perfective *naa zoo* etc. is *ban zoo ba, ba ka zoo ba, ba ki zoo ba,* etc. The subjunctive negative is in *kada +* pronominal marker: e.g. *kada in zoo* 'lest I come'.

Hausa has nothing comparable to the derived stem system of Arabic, but certain terminal vowels plus accompanying tonal patterns are associated with specific meanings. Thus ⸱aa verbs are always transitive, e.g. *gìrbaa* 'to harvest'; ⸱-a verbs are usually intransitive, e.g. *shìga* 'to enter'. Some in ⸱-i have centrifugal meaning, e.g. *tàfi* 'to go away'. Similarly, *-èe* verbs are transitive or intransitive, often with intensification of root meaning; *-ar* verbs are often causative, e.g. *sayar* 'to sell' (= cause to buy); many verbs in *-oo* have centripetal significance, e.g. *zoo* 'to come'; ⸱u verbs are intransitive and passive, e.g. *tàaru* 'to be gathered together'.

Prepositions

Prepositions are simple, derivative, or compound. Derivative prepositions are nouns specifying location. They take the construct markers; *cikii* 'stomach': *ciki.n* 'in(side), into': *yaa shiga cikin gidaa* 'he went into the house'; *gabaa* 'breast': *gaba.n* 'in front of'.

Word formation

By affixation or compounding. Examples of affixation: *mai-* denoting presence of object or quality; *maras-* denoting its absence, e.g. *hankalii* 'mind', *mai.hankalii* 'intelligent', *maras.hankalii* 'unintelligent'; *ba-* denoting ethnic origin, profession, e.g. *ba.haushee* 'a Hausa', *ba.tuuree* 'European, English'.

Compounding: e.g. noun + noun with construct *-n*: *jirgii* 'boat' + *samaa* 'sky': *jirgin samaa* 'aircraft'; or + *kasaa* 'land': *jirgin kasaa* 'train'.

Compound + prefixed form: e.g. *tauraro.mai.wutsiya* 'star with a tail' = 'comet'.

Word order

Normally SVO.

1 ¹ Tun fil azal akwai Kalma. Kalman nan kuwa tare da Allah yake. Kalman nan kuwa Allah ne. ² Shi ne tun fil azal yake tare da Allah. ³ Dukan abubuwa sun kasance ta gare shi ne, ba kuma abin da ya kasance na abubuwan da suka kasance, sai ta game da shi. ⁴ Shi ne tushen rai, wannan rai kuwa shi ne hasken mutane. ⁵ Haske na haskakawa cikin duhu, duhun kuwa bai rinjaye shi ba.

6 Akwai wani mutum da Allah ya aiko, mai suna Yahaya. ⁷ Shi fa ya zo shaida ne, domin ya shaidi hasken, kowa yā ba da gaskiya ta hanyarsa. ⁸ Ba shi ne hasken ba, ya zo ne domin ya shaidi hasken.

HAWAIIAN

INTRODUCTION

Hawaiian belongs to the Eastern Polynesian branch of the Malay-Polynesian family (*see* **Polynesian Languages**). English is the official language of the State of Hawaii (the fiftieth State of the USA), and probably less than 1½ per cent of the population – i.e. about 15,000 – retain a command of the Hawaiian language. Some effort is being made to halt its decline. An uncontaminated form of Hawaiian is still spoken on the island of Ni'ihau.

There is a considerable body of traditional literature; the *Kumulipo* creation myth is especially notable. Bible translation dates from 1839.

Hawaiian exhibits an extreme case of phonological reductionism, with only eight consonants surviving from the Proto-Polynesian inventory. Together with five vowels, these eight consonants can form 45 of the monosyllabic particles which play a crucial role in Polynesian syntax.

SCRIPT

Roman alphabet + ' for glottal stop.

PHONOLOGY

Consonants

w, m, p, l, n, k, h, ʔ

Vowels

a, e, i, o, u

MORPHOLOGY AND SYNTAX

Noun

For a general note on Polynesian morphology, *see* **Polynesian Languages**. In Hawaiian, the nominal complex has the following preposited items:

(a) prepositions: include possessive markers, neutral and emphatic (the *o/a* dichotomy; *see* **Possession** below); the subjective marker *'o*, the agentive *e*, the relative *i*; the relational particles *me* 'with', *ma* 'at, in', *mai* 'from', *aa* 'as far as'.

(b) determinatives: comprise the articles: *ka/ke*, the definite article singular, plural *naa*; *he*, the indefinite article; *a*, the personal article.

(c) number markers: *mau, po'e, kau* are plural markers. *Wahi* is one of several paucal markers.

Adjective

The adjective is not separately distinguished. Nominal qualifiers follow the noun: e.g. *mauna loa* 'long mountain'; *aloha nui* 'much *aloha*'. Elbert's (1979) term is 'adjectival stative'; it may correspond to English adjective or adverb: e.g. *he kanaka maika'i* 'a **good** man'; *ua hana maika'i* '... worked **well**'.

Pronoun

PERSONAL
Here a dual number is distinguished:

		Singular	*Dual*	*Plural*
1	incl.	—	kaaua	kaakou
	excl.	au/wau	maaua	maakou
2		'oe	'olua	'oukou
3		'oia	laaua	laakou

Examples: *'ike kaaua* 'we (= you and I) know'; *'ike 'ia 'oia e kaaua* 'he was seen by us (= you and me)' (*'ia 'oia* = third person subject form; *e* is agentive marker).

POSSESSION
The possessive pronouns are formed from the following elements: definite/ indefinite marker + possession marker (-*a*- for alienable, -*o*- for inalienable possession) + personal marker: e.g. *kokaakou* 'our (yours and mine)', inalienable; *kana* 'his/hers', alienable. The *k*- forms are also possessive adjectives. Ø-forms and *n*- forms are also used, *inter alia*, like the *k*-forms, to express the verb 'to have' which is missing in Hawaiian: e.g. *he keiki kau* 'I have a child'.

Alienable/inalienable possession: as Elbert (1979) puts it, -*a*- forms indicate that ownership has been brought about by the possessor; the -*o*- forms show that the possessive relationship is not primarily due to the contingent possessor: e.g. *kaana keiki* 'his child' (-*a*- form, as the child is begotten by him), *ko'u kupuna* 'my grandparent'; *ka heana **a** ke ali'i* 'the chief's victim' (lit. 'the dead body caused by the chief'), *ka heana **o** ke ali'i* 'the chief's corpse' (examples, from Elbert 1979).

In the socio-religious terminology of the traditional Hawaiian culture, -*a*- forms were characteristic of subordinate relationships; -*o*- forms of dominant relationships, e.g. of divine action.

Three-degree series by relative distance: (*kee*)*ia* 'this' – (*kee*)*naa* 'that' – (*kee*)*laa* 'that (yonder)': e.g. *i keeia kanaka* 'to this person', *ua hale laa* 'that house' (*ua* recapitulates a noun already mentioned).

INTERROGATIVE PRONOUN
wai 'who?'; *aha* 'what?': e.g. *'o wai ke kumu?* 'Who is the teacher?'; *'o wai kou inoa?* 'What's your name?'

Numerals

The basic numerals 1–10 are *kahi, lua, kolu, haa, lima, ono, hiku, walu, iwa, 'umi.* These are usually preceded by a general classifier, *'e.* The classifier *'a* is used in the names of days: e.g. *poo'akahi* 'Monday', *poo'alua* 'Tuesday', etc. 11 *'umi kuumaa-kahi*; 12 *'umi kuumaa-lua*; 20 *iwakaalua*; 30 *kana-kolu*; 40 *kana-haa*; 100 *hanele*. Examples: *'elua i'a* 'two fish'; *'elua au mau i'a* 'my two fish'.

Verb

Verbal bases are compatible with certain particles, nominal and verbal, which precede it. There is a basic division into active and stative verbs. For nominal particles, see above. The verbal particles include:

Aspect:	inceptive	ke
	perfective	ua
	progressive	e...ana
		ke...nei
		ke...na
Tense:	past	i
	non-past	e

plus markers for imperative and subjunctive moods, positive and negative. Examples: *Ua hele ke kanaka i Lalato'a* 'The man went to Rarotonga' (*hele* 'to go'; *kanaka* 'man'); *ke kali nei au* 'I'm waiting'; *E hele ana 'oe?* 'Are you going?'

The passive voice is marked by the particle *'ia + e* or *i*: e.g. *Ua inu ke kanaka i ka lama* 'The man drank the rum' (*inu* 'drink'; *lama* 'rum'); *Ua inu 'ia ka lama e ka kanaka* 'The rum was drunk by the man' (*e* is the agentive case marker).

NEGATIVE
'a'ole + verb: e.g. *'a'ole i hele ke kanaka* 'The man did not go.'

Word formation

Verbs and nouns take certain prefixes which modify the meaning in various ways: e.g. *ho'o* and its alternants are causative: cf. *hele* 'to go', *ho'ohele* 'to cause to go, set in motion'; *'ai* 'to eat', *hoo'ai* 'to feed (trans.)'. *Aka* suggests a slow or careful approach: e.g. *aka'ai* 'to eat deliberately'.

563

The particle *'ana* and the suffix *-na* act as nominalizers: the suffix may have a regressive effect on the stem vowel(s): e.g. *hau* 'to strike', *haauna* 'a blow'; *hiki* 'to arrive', *hikina* 'the east'.

Word order

VSO is normal in verbal sentences. SVO occurs for emphasis on S.

I KINOHI ka Logou, me ke Akua ka Logou, a o ke Akua no ka Logou.

2 Me ke Akua no hoi ia i kinohi.

3 Hanaia iho la na mea a pau e ia; aole kekahi mea i hanaia i hana ole ia e ia.

4 Iloko ona ke ola, a o ua ola la ka malamalama no na kanaka.

5 Puka mai la ka malamalama iloko o ka pouli, aole nae i hookipa ka pouli ia ia.

6 ¶ Hoounaia mai la e ke Akua kekahi kanaka, o Ioane kona inoa.

7 Hele mai la oia i mea hoike, i hoike ai ia no ua malamalama la, i manaoio ai na kanaka a pau ma ona la.

8 Aole no oia ka malamalama, aka, ua hele mai ia e hoike i ka malamalama.

HEBREW

INTRODUCTION

In the North-Western branch of Semitic in the first millennium BC, a distinction is made between Canaanite and Aramaic. By far the most important member of the Canaanite group is Hebrew, known from a rich literature which can be broadly periodized as follows:

1. The Bible: earliest material c. 1200 BC, latest c. 200 BC. This period includes the Babylonian exile, 587–538, and the Persian rule, 538–333.
2. The Dead Sea Scrolls and related material: these are mainly Essene writings dating from the time of the Maccabees around the turn of the millennium. Also worthy of mention is the historian Flavius Josephus (first century AD).
3. The rabbinical literature of the early centuries AD. By this time, Hebrew was no longer a spoken language, and much of the rabbinical literature, e.g. the *Talmud* and the *Targum*, is in Aramaic and based on oral tradition (cf. the hadith in Islam). Central to these writings, however, is the *Mishnah*, a first-century collection of Hebrew treatises on Jewish law.
4. The mediaeval period: the outstanding figure is Moses Maimonides (1135–1204), whose main works in Hebrew are the *Mishne Torah*, a monumental codification of Jewish law, and the *More Nevukhim*, translated by Maimonides himself from his Arabic original *Dalālat al-ḥā'irīn*, the 'Guide for the Perplexed'.

For the modern revival of Hebrew, *see* **Ivrit**.

SCRIPT

The Aramaic script in which the Old Testament was written is based on a Phoenician prototype, adopted by the Israelites around 1000 BC. Like Arabic, this script runs from right to left. Originally, vowels were not marked, though three consonants, yodh, waw, and he, came to be used to notate long vowels, especially finals: yodh representing /iː, eː/, waw /oː, uː/, and he /aː/. In the seventh century AD the Massoretes – Jewish scholars working to preserve the Hebrew text of the Old Testament with maximum fidelity – introduced the system of vocalization known as the Massoretic or Tiberian. Since the consonantal structure of the text was regarded as sacred and could not be adapted in any way, vowel points were written above or below the consonants. The vocalization as now preserved represents, therefore, the pronunciation of Hebrew in the seventh century AD, and there are some grounds for believing that the original pronunciation of Hebrew was somewhat different. In addition to the long vowels mentioned above, the Massoretic system marks short /i, e, a, o, u/, plus simple shwa and three shwa augments, /ĕ, ă, ŏ/.

A key deficiency in the system is the use of ִ for both simple shwa and zero vocalization.

PHONOLOGY

Consonants

stops: p, b, t, d, ŧ, k, g, q, ʔ
affricate: ts
fricatives: f, β, θ, ð, s, z, ꭍ, ʃ, χ, γ, ʕ, h, ɦ
lateral and flap: r, l
nasals: m, n
semi-vowels: j, w

The stops /b, g, d, k, p, t/ have spirant allophones: [β, γ, ð, x, f, θ] notated in transcription as b̲, g̲, d̲, k̲, p̲, t̲. The six stops are primarily syllable-initial, and become spirants following vowels: bayit̲ 'house': ba.bayit̲ /bə.ßajiθ/, 'in a house'.

The dotted letters ṭ, ṣ are the emphatics; ḥ represents /ɦ/.

Vowels

long and short: i, e, a, o, u + shwa /ə/ and shwa augments /əᵃ, əᵒ, əᵘ/.

Stress

Stress is generally on the final syllable, otherwise on penultimate. Stress can be marked in the script.

MORPHOLOGY AND SYNTAX

Noun

Hebrew has two genders (masculine and feminine) and three numbers; the dual is used mainly for naturally paired items, e.g. parts of the body: einayim 'two eyes'; reglayim 'two feet'.

Masculine nouns often end in a consonant and have -im plural marker: e.g. ṣuṣ 'horse', pl. ṣuṣim. Irregularly, some masculine nouns have the feminine plural marker -ot̲, e.g. 'ab̲ 'father', pl. 'ab̲ot̲; others have a modified stem: 'iš 'man', pl. 'anašim.

Typical feminine singular endings are -ah, et̲/at̲, but many nouns with consonantal endings are feminine: e.g. 'eš 'fire', 'erec 'earth', yad̲ 'hand', regel 'foot', nepeš 'soul', ḥereb̲ 'sword'. The feminine plural marker is -ot̲: e.g. nepeš 'soul', pl. nepešot̲.

The dual endings are, masc. -ayim, fem. -at̲ayim.

DEFINITE ARTICLE

h- + V, where V is a vowel depending on the nature of the following initial and its vocalization: cf. *hā.'iš* 'the man'; *ha.ḥereḇ* 'the sword'; *he.hārim* 'the mountains'; *he.ḥāg* 'the festival'.

CASE

The accusative is marked by the particle *'eṯ*: e.g. *bərešiṯ bara' 'elohim 'eṯ ha.šamayim v'eṯ ha.'arec* 'In the beginning (*resiṯ*) God created (*bara'*) heaven and earth.'

The genitive relationship is expressed by means of the construct formula: the noun denoting the possessed object, shortened or compressed as far as possible, precedes the possessor: e.g. *qol ha.'elohim* 'the voice of God'. The feminine construct form restores the *-ṯ* ending: e.g. *torah* 'law', construct, *toraṯ-*: *toraṯ YHVH* 'the law of Jehovah'; *'iššeṯ ha.'iš ha.toḇ* 'the wife of the good man'. As in Arabic, the noun in construct cannot take the article. The masculine plural and dual ending in the construct is *-ei*: e.g. *'elohei ha.šamayim və 'elohei ha.'arec* 'the God of heaven and of earth'.

Adjective

As attribute, the adjective follows the noun, with concord in number and gender. If the noun is definite, the article is resumed with the adjective: e.g. *ha.'iš ha.toḇ* 'the good man'; *ha.'iššah ha.toḇah* 'the good woman'; *ha.'anašim ha.toḇim* 'the good men'. As predicate, the adjective usually precedes the noun: *toḇ ha.'iš* 'the man is good'. Adjectival qualification may also be expressed by construct noun plus nominal: e.g. *har ha.qodeš* 'mountain of holiness' = 'the holy mountain'.

Pronoun

Independent personal forms with enclitics (possessive):

		Singular		Plural	
		Independent	*Enclitic*	*Independent*	*Enclitic*
1		'ani/'anoḵi	-i	'anaḵnu	-enu
2	masc.	'attah	-ḵa	'attem	-ḵem
	fem.	'att	-eḵ	'atten	-ḵen
3	masc.	hu'	-o	hem/hemmah	-am
	fem.	hi'	-ah	hennah	-an

The possessive enclitics are added to the construct form: e.g. *dabar* 'word', *dəḇar.i* 'my word', *dəḇar.enu* 'our word'; with feminine noun, e.g. *šanah* 'year', *šənaṯ.i* 'my year', *šənaṯ.enu* 'our year'. For plural of possessed object, yodh appears in the possessive suffix: *dəḇar.einu* 'our words'.

DEMONSTRATIVE PRONOUN/ADJECTIVE

Masc. *zeh*, fem. *zoṯ*, pl. *'elleh* (common) 'this, these'; masc. *hu'*, pl. *hem*; fem.

hi', pl. *hen(nah)* 'that, those'. These follow the noun and take the article: e.g. *ha.'iš ha.zeh* 'this man'; *ha.'iššah ha.zot* 'this woman'.

INTERROGATIVE PRONOUN

mi 'who?'; *mah* 'what?'. These are indeclinable. *Ha-* in various forms, depending on phonetic follow-up, initiates an interrogative sentence (cf. Arabic *hal*): e.g. **ha.ṭobah ha.'arec?** 'Is the land good?'

RELATIVE PRONOUN

'ašer, indeclinable: e.g. *vayasem šam 'et ha.adam 'ašer yacar* 'and he put there the man whom he had formed' (Genesis, 2.8); *ha. 'ir'ašer yaṣə'u mimennah* 'the city from which they came'. A participial construction may also be used: e.g. *ha.'iš ha.yošeb* 'the man who is sitting'.

Numerals

1–19 have masculine and feminine forms; 1–10 have both construct and absolute forms. Thus, for '2':

	Absolute	*Construct*
masculine	šənayim	šənei
feminine	šətaim	šətei

Example: *va.ya'aš elohim 'et.šənei ha.mə'orot ha.gədolim* 'and God made the two great lights' (*ma'or* 'light': masc. noun with fem. pl.).

3–10: masculine forms in singular absolute; these forms modify *feminine* nouns: *šaloš, 'arba', ḥameš, šeš, šeba', šəmoneh, teša', 'ešer*. The feminine form adds *-ah* to a slightly modified form of the masculine: e.g. from *šeš*, fem. *šiššah*. The feminine forms qualify *masculine* nouns: compare *šeš našim* 'six women', **šiššah** *'anašim* 'six men'; **šaloš** *banot* 'three daughters'; **šəlošet** *banim* 'three sons'.

Verb

Hebrew verbs are strong or weak: in the former, the (triliteral) root is stable throughout the base conjugation and the derived forms. Weak verbs belong to any one of the following categories: (1) one radical is a guttural; (2) first or third radical is aleph; (3) first radical is nun; (4) first radical is yodh or waw; (5) hollow verb (second radical is yodh or waw); (6) geminated verbs.

The Hebrew verb, like the Arabic, is marked for aspect rather than tense; i.e. perfective contrasts with imperfective. Aspect coalesces with tense in the sense that the perfective aspect is very often equivalent to a past tense, the imperfective to a present or future.

The two aspects combine and complement each other in the narrative tense known as the waw-consecutive, which is a cardinal feature of Old Testament Hebrew. The first verb in such a narrative sequence is in the perfective, while following verbs, continuing the narrative, are in the imperfective – even with switch of subject. In this way, successive actions are effectively linked to initial action: the effectiveness is, of course, lost in translation, e.g. *qam ha.'iš wa.y.yomer.* 'and the man arose and **says**' (= said) ...'. Conversely, a future-orientated proposition starts with an imperfective verb, and continues with perfective forms. The consecutive-waw, as the conjunction is called, is followed by gemination of the imperfective personal prefixes (*see* **Conjugation**, below) except in the first person singular, where the vowel of waw is lengthened before *'e-*. The sequence is broken by a negative (the negative particle is *lo*), and must then be re-initiated by a perfective or imperfective take-off point.

CONJUGATION
The basic *binyan* or 'structure' of the Hebrew verb is known as the Qal form. Here, as illustration, the perfective and imperfective aspects of the root *KTB* 'write':

			Perfective	Imperfective
singular	3	masc.	kātab 'he wrote'	yiktōb 'he writes/will write'
		fem.	kātəbah	tiktōb
	2	masc.	kātabta	tiktōb
		fem.	kātabt	tiktəbi
	1		kātabti	'ektōb
plural	3		kātəbu	masc. yiktəbu, fem. tiktobnah
	2	masc.	kətabtem	tiktəbu
		fem.	kətabten	tiktōbnah
	1		kātabnu	niktōb

The other *binyanim*, the derived 'structures', are:

1. *niphal*: this is the passive of the *qal*, and is marked by the prefix *n-*: e.g. *niktab ha.dabar* 'the word was written'.
2. *piel*: this is the factitive of the *qal*, forming transitive verbs: it is marked by gemination of the second radical, thus corresponding to Arabic II: *qadeš* 'holy', *qiddaš* 'to sanctify'. It also forms verbs from nouns: e.g. *dabar* 'word', *dibber* 'to speak'.
3. *pual*: the passive of the *piel*: e.g. *biqqeš* 'to seek', *buqqaš* 'he was sought'.
4. *hiphil*: the causative of *qal*: e.g. *šama'* 'to hear', *hišmi'a* 'he caused to hear'.
5. *hophal*: the passive of the *hiphil*: e.g. *hoktab* 'it was caused to be written'.
6. *hithpael*: reflexive of *piel*; also reciprocal: e.g. *hitra'u* 'they looked at one another'.

The imperative has forms for second person masculine and feminine, both singular and plural. The jussive coincides largely with the imperfective (slightly truncated), is not used in the first person and has a specific negative particle: *al tiqtol* 'do not kill'. (It is interesting that in Exodus 20 the negative commandments are in the imperfective with the negative particle *lo*: i.e. a general exclusion, rather than contingent prohibition: *lo tircāh* 'thou shalt not slay'; *lo tignob* 'thou shalt not steal'. But cf. Exodus 20, 16: *dabər-'atāh 'immānu wa.nišmā'āh wa.'al.yidaber 'immānu 'elohim* 'speak thou with us and we will hear; but let not God speak with us'.

PARTICIPLES

The active participle of the *qal* has the form *koteb* 'writing'; the passive is *katub* 'written'.

Prepositions

(a) Bound forms: *bə* 'in', *lə* 'to', *kə* 'like'. These replace the *h-* of the article: e.g. *b.e.harim* 'in the mountains'; *l.a.melek* 'to the king'.
(b) Hyphenated forms: e.g. *'el* 'to(wards)', *'al* 'on, over, against', *taḥat* 'under', *'aharei* 'after'. These have a specific set of personal pronominal enclitics, e.g. *'elaw* 'to him'.
(c) Free forms: e.g. *lipne* 'near'.

Word order

VSO is standard, SVO frequent.

אָ ¹ בְּרֵאשִׁית הָיָה הַדָּבָר וְהַדָּבָר הָיָה אֵצֶל הָאֱלֹהִים וֵאלֹהִים הָיָה הַדָּבָר. ² הוּא הָיָה בְּרֵאשִׁית אֵצֶל הָאֱלֹהִים. ³ הַכֹּל נִהְיָה עַל-יָדוֹ וּמִבַּלְעָדָיו לֹא נִהְיָה כָּל אֲשֶׁר נִהְיָה. ⁴ בּוֹ הָיוּ חַיִּים וְהַחַיִּים הָיוּ הָאוֹר לִבְנֵי הָאָדָם. ⁵ הָאוֹר מֵאִיר בַּחֹשֶׁךְ וְהַחֹשֶׁךְ לֹא הִשִּׂיגוּ.

⁶ אִישׁ הָיָה שָׁלוּחַ מֵאֵת אֱלֹהִים וּשְׁמוֹ יוֹחָנָן. ⁷ הוּא בָּא לְעֵדוּת, לְהָעִיד עַל הָאוֹר כְּדֵי שֶׁעַל-פִּיו יַאֲמִינוּ הַכֹּל. ⁸ הוּא לֹא הָיָה הָאוֹר; הוּא בָּא לְהָעִיד עַל הָאוֹר.

(Gen. 1: 1–8)

HINDI

INTRODUCTION

A New Indo-Aryan language, Hindi has been the official language of India (along with English) since 1947. In terms of numbers it is by far the most important of the New Indo-Aryan languages. It is estimated that as many as 225 million people speak Hindi as mother tongue in the states of Bihar, Haryana, Himachal Pradesh, Uttar Pradesh, Madhya Pradesh, and Rajasthan, and several millions more speak it as a second language. In addition, there are considerable Hindi-speaking communities in many parts of the world.

In origin, Hindi stems from the same Khaṛī Bolī group of dialects which underlies its alter ego – Urdu. For a note on the historical development of these twin forms, *see* **Urdu**.

The *Rāmcaritmānas* of Tulsi Dās (late sixteenth/seventeenth century) written in the Avadhī dialect, is generally regarded as the first outstanding work in the Hindi literary tradition. In Hindi, the transition from traditional poetry to the treatment of contemporary themes in adequate language, lagged, on the whole, behind parallel developments in Bengali and Urdu. The first genuinely modern writer of any stature in Hindi was Hariścandra Bhārtendu (1850–85). With the advent of Premcand (1880–1936) Hindi prose writing, in the shape of the socio-political novel and short story, came of age. During the twentieth century his work was followed by the *āñcalik upanyās* school of novels of social criticism. Through the mid-twentieth century the *nayī kavitā* and *nayī kahānī* – the 'new poetry' and the 'new story' – movements have flourished, both preoccupied with man's predicament in a modern society.

SCRIPT

Devanagari, retaining Sanskrit conjuncts. *See* **Sanskrit**.

PHONOLOGY

Consonants

The consonantal grid is essentially as in Sanskrit. The retroflex /ḷ/ is not in Hindi; /f, z, x, γ, q/ occur in loan-words.
The opposition between the aspirate and the non-aspirate series is carefully observed, as is the opposition between the dentals and the retroflex sounds.

Vowels

   short: ɪ, ə, ʊ
   long: i, e, ɛ, a, ɔ, o, u

All occur nasalized. The digraph *ai* = /æ/; *au* = /ɔ/.

Stress

Stress is not phonemic.

MORPHOLOGY AND SYNTAX

Noun

Hindi has no articles. There are two genders, masculine and feminine. A typical masculine ending is *-ā*: e.g. *laṛkā* 'boy', *beṭā* 'son'. Typical feminine endings are *-ī, -iyā*: e.g. *laṛkī* 'girl'. Nouns with consonantal endings may be of either gender: e.g. *din* 'day' is masculine, *mez* 'table' is feminine. Sanskrit nouns retain their original gender.

CASE SYSTEM
Basically, there are two cases, direct (nominative) and oblique, plus two numbers, singular and plural. Nouns ending in the characteristic vowels *-ā/-ī* are declined as follows:

	Masculine		*Feminine*	
	Singular	*Plural*	*Singular*	*Plural*
direct	laṛkā	laṛke	laṛkī	laṛkiyāṁ
oblique	laṛke	laṛkoṁ	laṛkī	laṛkiyoṁ

(nasalized forms like *laṛkoṁ* can also be transcribed as *laṛkõ*).
Athematic nouns like *din*, *mez* do not change for singular oblique, but take *-eṁ* and *-oṁ* in the plural.

This system is extended by a series of postpositional markers: e.g. *ko* which marks the definite direct or indirect object: e.g. *us ādmī ko* 'to that man'; *Kisān ghoṛe ko ḍhūṁṛh rahā hai* 'The farmer is looking for the horse.'

The genitive relationship is expressed by means of the link *kā, kī, ke*, depending on gender and number of nouns possessed; this link follows the oblique case: e.g. *laṛke kī pustak* 'the boy's book', *laṛkoṁ kī pustakeṁ* 'the boys' books'.

Other case relations are expressed with the help of such postpositions as *se* 'from', *meṁ* 'in', *par* 'on', *tak* 'up to, as far as', *ne* 'by' following the oblique case: e.g. *in laṛkoṁ kī bahnoṁ ko* 'to the sisters of these boys'.

Adjective

As attribute, adjective precedes the noun; adjectives ending in *-ā* in the masculine singular behave like *kā*: all other adjectives are invariable, i.e. the feminine form in -*ī*, for example, does not change to -*e* in the oblique: e.g. *us choṭe gāṁv meṁ* 'in that small village'.

Pronoun

PERSONAL

The basic forms with their oblique cases are: sing. 1 *maiṁ – mujh*; 2 *tū – tujh*; pl. 1 *ham – ham*; 2 *tum – tum*. The third person forms are supplied from the demonstrative series: *yah* 'this', *vah* 'that'. These have oblique forms in *is/us*.

A more formal and polite second person form is *āp*, e.g. *āp.ke beṭe* 'your son' (honorific plural) taking plural concord in verb. Used also with reference to third person.

INTERROGATIVE PRONOUN

kaun 'who?', *kyā* 'what?'

RELATIVE PRONOUN

jo, obl. *jis* (declined), with correlative *vah*: e.g. *Jo kitab us mez par hai, vah* ... 'The book that is on the table, (it) ...'; *ham.ne jin ādmiyoṁ.ko kal yahaṁ dekhā thā, ve* ... 'The men we saw here yesterday, (they) ...' (for use of agentive case with perfective verb, *ne*, *see* **Verb**, below; *ko* is the accusative particle; *ve* is plural of *vah* 'that').

Numerals

1–10: *ek, do, tin, cār, pāṁc, chah, sāt, āṭh, nau, das*; 11 *gyārah*; 12 *bārah*; 20 *bīs*; 30 *tīs*; 40 *cālīs*; 100 *sau*.

The intermediate forms are not predictable. As in other New Indo-Aryan languages, decade + 9 anticipates the following decade; thus, 38 is *aṛtīs*, continuing the *tīs* '30' decade, but 39 is *untālīs* anticipating *cālīs* '40'.

Verb

The division into finite and non-finite forms is basic:

Non-finite forms:

infinitive:	-nā
gerundive:	-nā
present/imperfective participle:	-tā ⎫
past/perfective participle:	-ā ⎬ declined for gender and number
conjunctive participle:	-kar(ke)

Finite forms:

1. Synthetic: the Old Indo-Aryan flectional system is represented in Hindi by the following:

(a) The imperative: 2nd sing. = base; 2nd pl. (associated with *tum*) in -*o*. A more formally polite imperative/request is made with -*ie* (associated with

573

āp): e.g. *Yah kām abhī kījīe* 'Could you please do this work now.'
(b) The subjunctive: the endings are sing. 1 *-ūṁ*, 2 *-e*, 3 *-e*; pl. 1 *-eṁ*, 2 *-o*, 3 *-eṁ*: e.g. *caleṁ* 'let's go/shall we go?'; *maiṁ kyā karūṁ*? 'What am I to do?'
(c) The future (not, strictly speaking, synthetic) is made by adding the affix *-ga/-gī/-ge* to the subjunctive endings: e.g. *maiṁ dūṁge* 'I shall give'; *ham caleṁge* 'we shall go'.

2. Compound tenses with auxiliary *hūṁ*:

(a) with imperfective participle (marked for gender and number) + *hūṁ* (inflected)

general present: *maiṁ caltā hūṁ* 'I go'; *ham calte haiṁ* 'we go';
imperfect past: *maiṁ caltā thā* 'I went'; *ham calte the* 'we (masc.) went';

(b) with perfective participle (marked for gender and number) + aux.

perfective present: *maiṁ calā hūṁ* 'I have gone';
perfective past: *maiṁ calā thā* 'I had gone'

3. Perfective participle conjugated as preterite tense: e.g. *maiṁ calā* 'I went'; *ham calīṁ* 'we (fem.) went'. The perfective participle forms of five irregular verbs are very important: *karnā* 'to do' – *kiyā*; *lenā* 'to take' – *liyā*; *denā* 'to give' – *diyā*; *jānā* 'to go' – *gayā*; *honā* 'to be' – *huā*.

4. Aspectual forms with secondary auxiliaries: stem + aux.[2] + aux.[1]: e.g. a durative aspect with *rahnā* 'to remain': *maiṁ cal rahā hūṁ* 'I was going'; *ham cal rahe haiṁ* 'we (masc.) were going' (stressed as *cál.rahā.hūṁ*).

Similarly, with modal auxiliaries: e.g. *saknā* 'to be able', *cuknā* 'to complete', *milnā* 'to receive': *maiṁ hindī bol saktā hūṁ* 'I can speak Hindi'; *maiṁ khā cukā hūṁ* 'I've finished eating'.

5. Passive voice: perfective participle of sense-verb + *jānā* 'to go': e.g. *Hindī bhārat meṁ bolī jātī hai* 'Hindi is spoken in India' (*bhārat*).

6. Causative: a formal progression often produces transitive and causative verbs from an intransitive stem; the causative marker is *-vā-*: cf.

marnā 'to die', *mārnā* 'to kill', *marvānā* 'to have someone killed';
bannā 'to be made', *banānā* 'to make', *banvānā* 'to have something made'.

AGENTIVE CASE WITH TRANSITIVE VERBS IN PERFECTIVE FORM
The subject is in the oblique case + *ne*, the verb is in concord with the object: e.g. *Is laṛke ne kitāb paṛhī thī* 'The boy read the book' (*kitāb* is fem.). In this construction, the postposition *ne* follows the oblique form of the third personal pronoun, but the nominative (direct) form of the first and second: cf. *maiṁ.ne/ tū.ne/us.ne patr likhā* 'I/you/he/she wrote the/a letter', where *likhā* agrees with *patr* (masculine). However, if a definite object marked by *ko* is present, the verbal form is that of third person singular, construed as an impersonal. An example is given in the section on the relative pronoun, above; cf. *maiṁ.ne un logon.ko pahle dekhā thā*. 'I had seen these people before'.

Postpositions

Some of the most important have been mentioned in the foregoing sections.

Word order

SOV.

१ आदि में शब्द* था;––शब्द परमेश्वर के साथ था और शब्द परमेश्वर था। २ वह आदि में परमेश्वर के साथ था।

३ उसके द्वारा सब वस्तुओं की उत्पत्ति हुई, और जो कुछ भी उत्पन्न हुआ उसमें से एक भी वस्तु उसके बिना उत्पन्न नहीं हुई।

४ उसमें जीवन था † और यह जीवन मनुष्यों की ज्योति था।

५ ज्योति अन्धकार में प्रकाश देती रही, परन्तु अन्धकार उस पर कभी विजयी नहीं हुआ।

६ परमेश्वर ने एक व्यक्ति को भेजा। उसका नाम यूहन्ना था। ७ यूहन्ना साक्षी देने के लिए आए कि वह ज्योति की साक्षी दें जिससे सब लोग उनके द्वारा ज्योति पर विश्वास करें। ८ वह स्वयं ज्योति नहीं थे, किन्तु ज्योति के सम्बन्ध में साक्षी देने आए थे।

HITTITE

INTRODUCTION

Hittite is the oldest attested Indo-European language, and the most important member of the Anatolian branch of Indo-European. The other members are Luwian, Palaic, Lydian, and Lycian.

The Hittite-Luwian peoples seem to have entered Anatolia (present-day Turkey and north Syria) late in the third millennium BC, displacing an indigenous population whose language was not Indo-European (*see* **Anatolian Languages, Hurrian**). Whether the Hittite invaders came from the east via the Caucasus, or southwards from the Balkans and Greece, is not clear. A Palaic document refers to the sun 'rising out of the sea'. Through the second millennium BC the Hittite kingdom was one of the most powerful in the Near East. The capital city was Hattusas, the modern Boğazköy, about a hundred miles east of Ankara. From 1905 onwards, excavation at this site yielded over 25,000 clay tablets, many of them inscribed in two known languages, Sumerian and Akkadian; the great majority, however, in a hitherto unknown language. The fact that the same cuneiform character was used for all three made for relatively rapid decipherment of the new language, and during 1915–19 Hrozný demonstrated that 'Hittite' was an Indo-European language.

The Indo-European identity of Hittite was initially obscured by two factors: the presence of a large non-Indo-European lexical element; and, second, the absence of that degree of synthetic inflection which might reasonably have been expected in an Indo-European language older than Homeric Greek and Vedic Sanskrit.

The exotic element in the vocabulary would be readily explicable as a substratum dating from the transit period or from prolonged sojourn in a non-Indo-European linguistic environment, or both, were it not so extensive – much larger than, for example, the Dravidian element in New Indo-Aryan. Nor is there any convincing explanation for the surprising simplicity of the morphological system.

The Boğazköy material dates mainly from the New Kingdom period of Hittite history (c. 1400–1300 BC) though it includes copies, made during this period, of much older material dating from the Old Kingdom, and going back as far as 1800 BC. The Hittite ethnonym was *nasi-*: *nasili* 'in the language of Nesa'.

SCRIPT

Cuneiform, very close to Old Akkadian. That is to say, Hittite was written in a script originally designed to notate a radically different phonological system. Sumero-Akkadian ideograms and determinants appear in it, and these are semantically useful in that they help to determine meaning. At the same time, they give no clue (unless they are accompanied by phonetic *furigana* – *see* **Japanese**) as to how they were pronounced in Hittite. For example, the Sumero-Akkadian phonogram ⫶⫶ *DUMU* is known to mean 'son, child' but its Hittite pronunciation is unknown. Ideograms are also found accompanied by cuneiform phonetic complements indicating case; e.g. *EN* 'lord, master'; *EN-an* (acc.), *EN-i* (dat.).

In transliteration, Sumero-Akkadian ideograms and phonograms are notated in capitals.

PHONOLOGY

Consonants

stops: p, t, k; with geminated series pp, tt, kk
affricate: ts
fricatives: z, ʃ, h/ɦ (notated as ḫ/ḫḫ)
nasals: m, n
lateral and flap: l, r

Geminated consonants are tense.

F. de Saussure's hypothesis (1879) that loss of certain laryngeal sounds, originally present in Proto-Indo-European, could account for regular phonetic differentiations in the daughter languages, seemed to find support in the Hittite phonological system, where ḫ/ḫḫ appears in positions predicted by the theory; cf.

Hittite paḫḫar	Greek pur	English fire
Hittite ḫaštai	Greek osteon	Sanskrit asthi, Latin os

Vowels

i, e, a, u

The absence of /o/ is striking.

MORPHOLOGY AND SYNTAX

Noun

In Late Hittite there are two numbers, two genders (common and neuter) and six cases (Old Hittite had seven). Forms naturally vary over a time-span of 1,500 years; the following table of endings may be taken as typical:

	Singular		Plural	
	Common	Neuter	Common	Neuter
nominative	-š	-n, Ø	-eš, aš, uš	-a, i, Ø
accusative	-n	—	-uš	—
genitive	-aš	—	-an, aš	—
dative	-ai, a, i, Ø	—	-aš	—
locative	-a, i, Ø	—	-aš	—
ablative	-az	—	-az	—
instrumental	-it	—	-it	—

Specimen nouns:

a/ā stems: *antuhša* 'human being', *atta-* 'father';
i-stems: *tuzzi-* 'army', *ḫalki-* 'grain';
u-stems: *heu-* 'rain', *genu-* 'knee';
n-stems: *henkan* 'death'; *tekan* 'earth';
l-stems: *waštul* 'sin'.

In contrast to other Indo-European languages, *r/n* stems are fairly common in Hittite (cf. Latin, *femur – femoris* 'thigh'):

wātar 'water', gen. *wetenaš*, pl. *widar* (cf. Greek *hudor – hudatos*);
paḫḫar 'fire', gen. *paḫḫwenaš*;
ešḫar 'blood'; gen. *ešḫanaš*.

Adjectives

In general, inflected as nominals.

Pronoun

The first person singular pronoun is variously attested as *uk*, *uga*, *ukka*, with oblique forms such as *ammuk(ka)*; a genitive *ammēl*, e.g. *ammēl UKU-as* 'my man'; and an ablative *ammēdaz* occur. Plural first person forms are *wēš*, acc. *anzēl*; second person *zik*, *zig(ga)*, gen. *tuēl*, dat./loc. *tuga/tugga*, abl. *tuēdaz*. The third person is more fully attested: *apas* (common), *apāt* (neuter), with oblique cases: gen. *apēl*, dat./loc. *apēdani*, abl. *apēz*, instr. *apit*. The third person plural forms are *apē*, *apūš*.

Enclitic forms for direct and indirect objects:

	Singular	Plural
1	-mu	-naš
2	-ta/ -du	-šmaš
3	-ši	-šmaš

The possessive enclitics are characteristic of older Hittite: sing. 1 *-mi/-mu*, 2 *-ti/-ta*, 3 */ši*; pl. 2/3 *-smi*. These take case endings: e.g. with *atta-* 'father': *attaššin* 'his father (acc.)'.

DEMONSTRATIVE PRONOUN
kāš (1st p. orientated), pl. *ke, kuš*; *apāš* (2nd and 3rd p. orientated), pl. *ape, apuš*.

INTERROGATIVE PRONOUN
kuiš 'who?'; pl. *kueš*.

Numerals

Only the following are known: 2 *dā-*, 3 *tri-*, 4 *meiu-*, 7 *šipta-*.

Verb

In comparison with Vedic Sanskrit and Homeric Greek, Hittite has a remarkably simple verbal system: there are two voices, active and middle; two moods, indicative and imperative; and two tenses, present–future and past.

INDICATIVE
There are two sets of present–future endings for the singular: *-mi, -ši, -zi*, and *-hi, -ti, -i*. The two sets coalesce in the plural to give the single set: *-weni, -teni, -anzi*. The past endings are: *-(n)un/(h)un, -s/-t, -t(a)*; pl. *-wen, -tel-in, -el-ir*.

SPECIMEN CONJUGATION
iya- 'to do':

> present–future: sing. 1 *(t)iyami*, 2 *(t)iyaši*, 3 *(t)iyazi*; pl. 1 *(t)iyaweni*,
> 2 *(t)iyateni*, 3 *(t)iyanzi*;
> past: sing. 1 *(t)iyanun*, 2 *(t)iyat*, 3 *(t)iyat*; pl. 1 *(t)iyawen*, 2 *(t)iyatten*, 3 *(t)ier*.

THE MIDDLE VOICE
The endings are: present–future: sing. 1 *-hahari*, 2 *-ta(ti)*, 3 *-tari*; pl. 1 *-waštati*, 2 *-duma*, 3 *-antari*. The past endings in the middle voice are closely similar to the present series.

IMPERATIVE
Used in both voices; the active endings are: sing. 1 *(a)llu*, 2 *-Ø*, 3 *-du*; pl. 1 *-wen*, 2 *-tel-in*, 3 *-andu*. The endings in the middle-voice imperative are close to those of the middle present.

The infinitive ends in *-anzi* or *-anna*. A verbal noun is made with *-war*, a supine with *-wan*, and a participle in *-ant-* (passive in transitive verbs, active in intransitives).

Postpositions

Some signify either locus or directed motion into/towards that locus: e.g. *piran*: *GIŠBANŠUR-i piran* 'before the table' (locus), or 'towards the front of the table'. Similarly, *anda(n)* 'in(to)': *E-ri anda(n)* 'in(to) the house'.

With other postpositions a distinction is made: e.g. *HUR-SAG-i šēr* 'on the mountain'; *HUR-SAG-i šarā* 'up to the top of the mountain'.

HOPI

INTRODUCTION

Hopi belongs to the Pueblo group of the Uto-Aztecan branch of the Aztec-Tanoan phylum. Linguistically, the Pueblo group is heterogeneous, containing, in addition to Hopi, Tewa and Keresan languages and Zuni, whose genetic status is not clear. Culturally, the Pueblo Indians are the modern representatives of the Anasazi-Pueblo civilization – a major Indian culture extending from the early years of the first millennium AD to modern times, which reached its climax in the 'cliff-dwelling' culture of the eleventh to fourteenth centuries. At present Hopi is spoken by about 2,000 Indians in northern Arizona. The language is unwritten. The form described by Whorf (1946) is the Toreva dialect.

Much has been written about the Hopi perception of time and space. Hopi is, of course, not unique in making a distinction between a Heraclitean flux of point events on the one hand, and the relative stability of durative events on the other; but few languages are so well equipped to map this distinction on to their morphological structure. Point events – momentary flashes, sparks, movements, ripples – occur *in* a spatio-temporal field which is not materially altered by them; and Hopi avoids what Whitehead called the fallacy of 'misplaced concreteness' by refusing to confer the stability of nominalization upon them. Rocks, mountains, and the desert are nominals; point events are mapped in the form of verbals, which do not even need umbral indices (contrast English '*it* poured', 'it flashed'). The same goes for cyclical events: to a Hopi, 'summer' is not a nominal, nor could it be the subject of a sentence; it can only be a temporal adverbial: 'when-it-was-summer'.

Durative events can be nominalized, however, in so far as they (a) are bounded spatio-temporal entities, and/or (b) affect their spatio-temporal locus by superimposing their own determinateness upon it.

PHONOLOGY

Consonants

The plosives /p, t, c, k, k°, q/ are accompanied by their pre-aspirated counterparts /'p, 't/, etc. and by the nasal series /m, n, ɲ, ŋ, n°/. Further, Whorf (1946) lists what he calls 'desonants': /w̥, m̥, n̥, l̥, y̱/, which are described as 'voiceless continuants'. Glottal stop ʔ.

Vowels

a, ɛ, ɪ, ou, œ, i

A following consonant causes a vowel to be abruptly cut off.

There are three tones, high, middle, and low. Elision, contraction, and assimilation are frequent.

MORPHOLOGY AND SYNTAX

Parts of speech:

(a) Nouns, verbs, pronouns, plus what Whorf calls 'ambivalents', i.e. forms with both nominal and verbal features. All of these are heavily inflected.
(b) Adjectives, numerals, and adverbs: these latter are either of space – Whorf's 'locators' – or of time and degree, Whorf's 'tensors' (not in the mathematical sense).

Noun

There are three classes: animate, inanimate, vegetative. The noun is inflected for case (nominative/accusative), state (absolute/construct), and, where this does not conflict with Hopi cosmology, for number. Animate and inanimate nouns may be marked for dual, paucal, and multiple number. The vegetative category has one general plural marker -*qölö*. The Hopi notion of plurality applies to entities that can be simultaneously grouped and counted; clearly, this rules out temporal concepts.

Specimen conjugation for root *pa·sa* 'field' (inanimate):

		Singular		Plural (multiple)	
		Nominative	Accusative	Nominative	Accusative
absolute		pa·sa	pá·sat	pá·vàsa	pá·vàsat
construct	1	'ivása 'my field'	'ivásay	'ivá·vàsa	'ivá·vàsay
	2	'é'pàsa	'é'pàsay	'é'pà·vasa	'è'pà·vasay
	3	pá·sa'àt	pá·sayàt	—	—

Further case relationships are expressed by suffixes, e.g. -*mem* (comitative), -*h* (partitive), -*vnî'qaY* (comparative).

Adjective

Adjectives in Hopi are restricted to such qualitative concepts as 'cold', 'rough', etc. They cannot map shape or configuration: point configuration is a verbal, and durative configuration is expressed by an ambivalent form, (usually a *k*-class verb, see below).

Pronoun

The personal forms have a base form, three nominal forms (nominative, objective and possessive) and about a dozen locative/directional forms. The base forms are:

	Singular	*Plural*
1	'ine-	'itame-
2	'e-	'eme-
3	'a-	'ame-

SPECIMEN DECLENSION

First person: nom. *ne'*; obj. *ney*; poss. *'i-*; loc. *'ine'pe*; all. *'inemi*; ill. *'inemiq*; abl. *'ineŋaq*.

DEMONSTRATIVE PRONOUN

Examples: base *pa-'*; nom. *pam*; pl. *pema*. The base for the oblique cases is *p*V + nasal, e.g. illative *paŋsok*. The demonstrative agrees with the noun in case: thus, *paŋsok ki·'soŋmiq* 'into (the interior of) that house' (*-soŋ-* links the root *ki·* 'house' with the suffix *-miq*).

Verb

The verb is intransitive or transitive; in the latter, if no overt direct object is present, a third person object is implied.

Different collocations of stress, extension by suffix, and contraction of stem produce four conjugations. The most important extension is that provided by the *k*-class verbs – the 'eventive' voice, described by Whorf (1946: 173) as 'a rich vocabulary of CVCV roots which denote ... characteristic visual outlines and figural arrangements'. The spectrum here extends from momentary manifestations which do not affect their field, to semi-durative configurations which do, qualifying thereby for status as 'ambivalents': verbals with certain nominal properties. An essive voice reports a measure of concretion plus prolongation of an event; the cessative voice records its cancellation. With the 'extended dynamic voice' Hopi is even equipped to notate the switch from a neutral background field to a force-field, exerting influence on the event denoted by the verb. The possessive voice defines a subject in terms of its valencies: e.g. *siwa yta* 'has a younger sister', or with a modifier, 'is younger-sistered'.

Aspects are marked by stem suffixes in ordered sequence. The simplex aspect with Ø marker refers either to a point event or to a durative, depending on the semantic content of the stem. The inceptive aspect is always with reference to a point event; all other aspects are durative.

The 'segmentative aspect', found only in the *k*-class verbs, converts a point event into a recurrent or cyclical spatio-temporal configuration. Aspects may be compounded to notate even more subtle facets of Hopi perception and Hopi cosmology. In addition, several modes classify spatio-temporal events in terms of concomitance, sequentiality, agency, etc. The transrelative mode copes specifically with subject-switching.

Word order

SOV.

---

1 1 Ayáq yayhniwhqat epeq God Lavayiat pay ep'e; pu Lavayi God ámuma; pu pay Lavayi God.

2 Pu pay pam hak piw yayhniwhqat epeq God amum yanta.

3 Sohsoy himu put ahpiy yukilti; pu qa himu yukiwtaqa put qa ahpiy yukilti.

4 Pam nãp nahpiy qatsit pasiwta; pu pay pam qatsi sinmuy amumi tãlat anta.

5 Noqw tãla qatãlat ep tãlawva; noqw qatãla put qa tõka.

6 Noqw hak tãqa God aṅqw ayatiwa; nihqe John yan mãtsiwa.

7 Pam hak hihta tuawi'taniqe õviy pitu, Tãlat tuawi'taniqee, sohsoyam put ahpiy tũtuptsiwaniqat õviy'o.

8 Pay pam qa pas pas pám himu Tãla; pam put Tãlat tuawi'taniqe ayatiwa.

HUNGARIAN

INTRODUCTION

Hungarian belongs to the Finno-Ugric branch of Uralic, and is the official language of the Republic of Hungary. There is also a large Hungarian-speaking minority in Transylvania (Erdély) and the total number of speakers is between 12 and 14 million. The ethnonym is Magyar: *a magyar nyelv* 'the Hungarian language'.

From an original homeland in the Urals, where their closest congeners still live (*see* **Khanty, Mansi**) the Magyar tribes moved westwards to reach the Carpathians and the Danube in the ninth century AD. Under the leadership of Árpád, the *honfoglalás* 'settlement' was completed by 896. The oldest monuments in Hungarian are the *Halotti Beszéd* ('Funeral Oration') of c. 1200, and the *Ó-Mária Siralom* ('Lament of Mary') dating from about a hundred years later. The fifteenth century saw a brilliant renaissance period in the reign of Matthias I Corvinus. National disaster at Mohács, where the Hungarians were defeated by the Turks, was followed by a long, slow recovery until the early nineteenth century, when the revolutionary movement produced two great poets, Petőfi Sándor and Arany János. The social and economic transformation of Hungary from the 1860s onwards brought the conditions for a tremendous upsurge in cultural creativity, both qualitative and quantitative, and Hungarian can now lay claim to one of the world's great literatures.

SCRIPT

Roman alphabet, minus *q, w, x, y,* + diacritics for vowel length and quality: peculiar to Hungarian is the notation of long /œ, y/ as *ő, ű*.

PHONOLOGY

Consonants

    stops: p, b, t, d, ɟ, k, g
    affricates: tʃ, dʒ
    fricatives: f, v, s, z, ʃ, ʒ, j, h
    nasals: m, n ɲ, ŋ
    lateral and flap: l, r

All consonants can be long or short; if long, they are written doubled. At junctures, assimilation takes place: unvoiced → voiced before voiced: e.g. *nép*

'people' + *dal* 'song': *népdal* /neːbdal/, 'folksong'. And vice versa: voiced →
unvoiced before unvoiced: e.g. *zseb* /ʒɛp/, 'pocket' + *kendő* 'kerchief':
zsebkendő /ʒɛpkendœ/, 'handkerchief'.

Vowels

For reasons of vowel harmony, the vowels are divided into:

high: i, e, œ, y
low: a, o, u

All have corresponding long values (indicated by acute accent). As regards
vowel harmony, /i, iː/ are neutral and can be used with either high or low vowels;
e.g. *virág* 'flower', *piros* 'red'. /e, eː/ may also occur with low vowels. In general,
however, the front/back opposition is observed: cf.

a ház 'the house', *a házban* 'in the house';
a víz 'the water', *a vízben* 'in the water';
adtam 'I gave', *kértem* 'I asked'.

Hungarian short /a/ is close to the value [ɒ]; long /a/ is [aː]. Theoretically, there is
a distinction between open and closed short /e/: [ɛ] and [e]. In Budapest
Hungarian the distinction is not observed. /œ/ and /y/ are notated here as *ö* and
ü.

Liaison of final consonant to initial vowel of following word is a marked
feature of Hungarian pronunciation: e.g. *nem akarok ebédelni* /ne-ma-ka-ro-
ke-bé-del-ni/, 'I don't want to have lunch'.

Stress

Stress is invariably on first syllable.

MORPHOLOGY AND SYNTAX

Noun

There is no grammatical gender; the pronoun *ő*, for example, means 'he/she'.
Where necessary, nouns signifying natural distinction of gender may be added:
e.g. *a tanár* 'the teacher', *a tanárnő* 'the female teacher' (*nő* 'woman').

The definite article is *a/az*, the latter form before vowels: e.g. *az ember* 'the
man'. The definite article is invariable for number: e.g. *a kép* 'the picture', pl. *a
képek*. The article is assimilated to postpositions, as e.g. *a házban* 'in the house':
**az.ban a házban* → *abban a házban* 'in that house'.

The plural marker is *-k* linked to consonantal stems by a harmonic vowel: e.g.
a házak 'the houses'; *a könyvek* 'the books'; *az ablakok* 'the windows'.

CASE SYSTEM
Agglutinative affixes on stem, with harmonic vowels where necessary. With
certain endings, assimilation at juncture takes place (see, e.g. comitative case in

the following paradigm). In the plural, the endings are added to the *-k* marker.

Singular	nominative	a bor 'the wine'	a víz 'the water'
	accusative	a bort	a vízet
	dative	a bornak	a víznek
	illative	a borba	a vízbe
	comitative	a borral	a vízzel

The comitative ending is *-val/-vel* → *-ral/-rel* after *-r*, → *-zal/-zel* after *-z*, etc.

Variants: some stems change for certain oblique cases, e.g. *tó* 'lake', acc. *tavat*.

Adjective

As attribute, adjective precedes noun and is invariable: e.g. *piros virág* 'red flower', *piros virágok* 'red flowers'; *egy mezőgazdasági kérdés* 'an agricultural question'; (*megoldás*) *ezekre a mezőgazdaságió kérdésekre* '(solution) to these agricultural questions'.

All adjectives can be used as nouns, and are then declined fully: e.g. *a magyar nép* 'the Hungarian people'; *a magyarok* 'the Hungarians'.

COMPARATIVE
(Harmonic vowel) + *-bb*: e.g. *nehéz* 'heavy', *nehezebb* 'heavier'. Some comparatives are suppletive, e.g. *sok* 'many', comparative *több*.

Pronoun

	Singular			*Plural*		
	Nominative	Accusative	Enclitic	Nominative	Accusative	Enclitic
1	én	engemet	-m	mi	minket	-unk/ünk
2	te	tégedet	-d	ti	titeket	-tok/tek
3	ő	őt	-i/e	ők	őket	-ik

Te and *ti* are familiar. The polite second person is *Ön* or *Maga*, with third person concord. Oblique forms are made by adding the enclitic markers to the case endings; e.g. *nekem* 'to me', *neked* 'to you'; *bennem* 'in me', *bennünk* 'in us'. The possessive markers are closely similar, but precede the case endings: e.g. *könyvem* 'my book'; *házunk* 'our house'; *egy barátom* 'a friend of mine'; *zsebemben* 'in my pocket'; *a városainknak* 'of our cities'. These endings also provide the Hungarian equivalent of the verb 'to have': *könyvem van* 'I have a book' (lit. 'my-book is'); *könyvem nincs* 'I don't have a book'. Where one possessive follows another, the second has the *-nak/-nek* ending: e.g. *a tanárom barátjá.nak a könyve* 'my teacher's friend's book' (where *-já-* marks possession by *tanárom* 'my teacher', and *-nak* signals the pending possessive ending *-e*).

DEMONSTRATIVE PRONOUN/ADJECTIVE
ez 'this', pl. *ezek*; *az* 'that', pl. *azok*: e.g. *ez a könyv* 'this book'; *azok a virágok* 'those flowers'; *ennek az iskolának a tanulói* 'the pupils of this school'.

ki 'who?'; *mi* 'what?'.

RELATIVE PRONOUN
aki/ami/amely/amelyik: e.g. *az ember, aki beszél* 'the man who is speaking'; *az ember, akiről beszéltem* 'the man I spoke about'.

Numerals

1–10: *egy, két/kettő, három, négy, öt, hat, hét, nyolc, kilenc, tíz*; 11 *tizenegy*; 12 *tizenkettő*; 20 *húsz*; 30 *harminc*; thereafter by addition of *-van/-ven*: e.g. 40 *negyven*; 50 *ötven*; 100 *száz*.

Numerals are followed by a noun in the singular: e.g. *hat könyv* 'six books'; *tíz ember* 'ten men'.

Verb

Stems are inherently transitive or intransitive, and can be converted or extended by various modal and aspectual formants: e.g.

> *-tat/-tet* makes causatives: *csinál-* 'to do, make', *Peter ruhát csináltat* 'Peter has a suit made';
> *-kozik/kezik/közik* makes reflexives: e.g. *véd* 'to defend', *védekezik* 'to defend oneself';
> *-gat/-get* is frequentative: e.g. *beszél* 'to speak', *beszélget* 'to converse'.

The passive voice is no longer used in Hungarian; many stems are paired for transitive/active and intransitive/passive meanings: e.g. *nyít-* 'to open' (trans.) – *nyílik* 'to open (intrans.)/be opened'; *rejt-* 'to hide' (trans.) – *rejlik* 'to be hidden'.

There is a very extensive system of pre-verbal particles or prefixes, which are separable, as in German. Some of the commonest are: *be-* 'into'; *ki-* 'out of'; *le-* 'down'; *át-* 'through'; *vissza* 'back'; *meg-* is the perfective marker. Thus *megy* 'he goes', **be**megy 'he goes into'; *lép* 'he steps', **ki**lép 'he comes out'; *írja* 'he writes', **le**írja 'he writes down'; *fordul* 'he turns', **vissza**fordul 'he turns back'.

SEPARABILITY
Illustrated with verb *tenni* 'to do' + *meg-* (present third singular is *tesz*):

> *hosszú utat tett **meg*** 'he's come a long way';
> *mindent **meg**tenne értem* 'he'd do anything for me';
> ***meg** kell tennem* 'I have to do it';
> *nem tesz **meg*** 'he won't do it'.

MOODS
Indicative, conditional, and a subjunctive/imperative.

Indicative: present and past tenses are made by means of personal endings added to the stem. There are two sets of these endings, one for definite, the other for indefinite complement. A subordinate clause introduced by *hogy* 'that', counts as definite. The endings are illustrated with the stem *ad-* 'give':

		Present		Past	
		Indefinite	*Definite*	*Indefinite*	*Definite*
singular	1	adok	ado**m**	adtam	adtam
	2	adsz	ado**d**	adtál	ad**tad**
	3	ad	ad**ja**	adott	ad**ta**
plural	1	adunk	ad**juk**	adtunk	ad**tuk**
	2	adtok	ad**játok**	adtatok	adtátok
	3	adnak	ad**ják**	adtak	adták

Thus *újságot olvasok* 'I read **a** newspaper'; *az újságot olvasom* 'I read **the** paper.'

First person singular subject + second singular object are encoded in the ending *-lak/-lek*: e.g. *kérlek* 'I ask you'; *szeretlek* 'I love you'.

A future tense is made with the auxiliary *fog-* ('to catch') + infinitive in *-ni*: e.g. *adni fogok/fogom* (depending on whether complement is definite or indefinite) 'I'll give'. The present with *meg-* prefix may also have future sense: e.g. *megkérdezem a tanártól* 'I'll ask the teacher' (lit. 'from the teacher').

Conditional: the marker is *-n-* + harmonic vowel: e.g. *adnám* 'I'd give' (definite object); *kérnék* 'they would ask'.

Imperative/subjunctive: the marker is *-j-*: note the sandhi of *j* with certain sibilants: *s + j → ss*; *sz + j → ssz*; *z + j → zz*: e.g. *olvas-* ('read') + *j → olvassa* 'read' (definite object). A polite request is made with *legyen szíves* 'please': e.g. *legyen szíves, olvasson* 'please read' (indefinite). *Fontos, hogy megírjam a levelet* 'It's important (*fontos*) that I write the letter.'

Imperative in *-ó/-ő*: e.g. *a dolgozó ember* 'the working man'. The form is much used as a nominal: e.g. *a dolgozók* 'the workers'. The perfective participle is identical with third person singular past indefinite: e.g. *adott* 'he gave' → 'given'; *egy ismert író* 'a well-known writer'.

The participial form in *-va/-ve* denotes a state of affairs; it is often used with the auxiliary: e.g. *Az üzletek be vannak csukva* 'The shops are closed'; *A televíziót nézve elaludtam* 'While watching television I fell asleep.'

NEGATIVE
The general marker is *nem*; *ne* is used with the imperative/subjunctive: e.g. *nem megy* 'he doesn't go'; *ne menjen* 'don't go'. Negation is reduplicated: e.g. *Nem dolgoznak sehol sem*, lit. 'They're not working nowhere neither' = 'There's nobody working anywhere.'

Postpositions

For example, *mellett* 'beside', *fölött* 'above', *alatt* 'below'. They are reduplicated with demonstratives: e.g. *ez alatt a szék alatt* 'under this chair'. The postpositions take the personal markers, and show a three-way opposition for motion relative to speaker or other referent: e.g. *mellettem* 'beside me'; *mellém* 'in my direction'; *mellőlem* 'from beside me'; *fölöttem* 'above me'; *fölém* '(moving) over me'; *fölülem* 'from above me'.

Word order

SOV is basic, but order is free.

---

1 [1] Kezdetben volt az Ige, és az Ige az Istennél volt, és Isten volt az Ige. [2] Ö kezdetben az Istennél volt. [3] Minden általa lett, és nélküle semmi sem lett, ami létrejött. [4] Benne élet volt, és az élet volt az emberek világossága. [5] A világosság a sötétségben világít, de a sötétség nem fogadta be. [6] Megjelent egy ember, akit Isten küldött, akinek a neve János. [7] Ő tanúként jött, hogy bizonyságot tegyen a világosságról, és hogy mindenki higgyen általa. [8] Nem ő volt a világosság, de a világosságról kellett bizonyságot tennie.

HURRIAN

INTRODUCTION

This ancient Anatolian language is of unknown affinity. Clearly non-Indo-European, it is very close to Urartian (*see* **Urartian**). The Hurrian people seem to have entered Anatolia and the north Mesopotamian area during the third millennium BC. It is possible that at least one wave of Hurrians came in via Armenia. The apogee of their power was reached in the second millennium BC, when they ruled the kingdom of Mitanni. They disappear from the historical scene in the sixth/fifth century BC. Their language is known from second-millennium texts excavated at a number of places in the Near East – Mari on the Euphrates, Amarna in Egypt, Boğazköy in Turkey, and Ugarit on the Syrian coast.

While attempts to establish a genetic relationship between Urartian-Hurrian and the Karthvelian languages have not met with general agreement, the case for some connection with the Nakh languages of Dagestan seems to be more promising.

SCRIPT

Mainly Akkadian cuneiform. Some Hurrian texts have been found in the Ugaritic proto-alphabet (*see* **Ugaritic**).

PHONOLOGY

Consonants

Paired stops – a surd and its geminate – are characteristic of Hurrian: e.g. /p – pp, t – tt, k – kk/. Sonant or semi-vowel pairs are also found: /w – ww, l – ll, ḫ – ḫḫ, Z – ZZ/.

The sibilant series is indeterminate; notated here by capitals S, Z.

Other phonemes: /m, n, r, d, g, γ/.

Vowels

i, e, a, o, u, ə

MORPHOLOGY AND SYNTAX

Noun

There is no grammatical gender. The noun has two numbers, with a plural form in *-a-* or *-aZ*. Eight or nine cases are distinguished. Some case endings:

	Singular	Plural
absolute	Ø	-aZ
ergative	-(u)S	-aZuS
genitive	-we	-aZ(w)e
dative	-wa	-aZ(w)a
ablative	-dan	—

ARTICLE

Sing. *-ne*, pl. *-na*. This article usually precedes the case marker, but may follow it. The following example shows an ergative construction + article: *SawuSka.we.na.aZuS Sije.na.aZuS* 'by (the agency of) the waters of (the goddess) Sawuska', where the plural ergative marker follows the article (pl. *-na-*), which, in the first word, follows the genitive marker *we-*: *ardi.ne.we.na Ḫatti.ne.we.na* '(the gods) of the town of Hatti'.

Adjective

There are certain adjectival formants: *-u/-oḫḫe*, e.g. *hijar.oḫḫe* 'golden'; *-u/ -ozzi*, e.g. *aStuzzi* 'female'; *-ye*, e.g. *ḫurwo.ye* 'Hurrian'.

Pronoun

First person: the base form is *iSte*, with ergative *iZaS*, genitive *Zowe*. The second person is known only in its ergative form, *weS*, and its genitive, *we.we*. No third person pronouns are attested.

POSSESSIVE ENCLITICS

	Singular	Plural
1	-iww	iww.aZ
2	-w	—
3	-ija	-ijaZ

DEMONSTRATIVE PRONOUN
andi 'this'; *anni* 'that'.

RELATIVE PRONOUN
(i)ja/je.

Numerals

The following are known: 2 *Sin*; 4 *tumni*; 7 *Sinda*; 10 *eman*.

Verb

A Hurrian verbal form is a complex of strictly ordered markers following a (possibly augmented) base. The slot sequence is (D'akonov 1979):

1. extension of base: *-ar/-al/-ug*, etc. (*cf.* **Urartian**);
2. aspect marker: *-u/oZ-* (perfective), *-ed-* imperfective;
3. this slot has a *-t-* marker when no direct object is present;
4. the *-st-* marker: in Urartian this is perfective; its meaning in Hurrian is doubtful;
5. plural marker;
6. transitive/intransitive markers: *-i-* (trans.), *-u/o-* (intrans.);
7. negation: *-wa-*, *-kk-*;
8. unreal conditional marker;
9. mood marker;
10. subject marker: *-a-/-if-*;
11. subject plural marker: *-Za*.

ICELANDIC

INTRODUCTION

Icelandic belongs to the Germanic branch (Scandinavian sub-division) of the Indo-European family. It is the official language of Iceland, where it is spoken by about a quarter of a million people. While its Scandinavian congeners have carried reductionism to extremes, Icelandic remains close to Old Norse. This is partly due to its geographical position as an outlier. More important, however, and the major factor in its linguistic conservatism, was the presence in Iceland of the saga literature of the thirteenth and fourteenth centuries. What was kept alive was not merely a grammatical system but one of the world's great literatures. The narrative sweep, the moral power, and the sheer human interest of the sagas clearly inform the genre in which modern Icelandic writers have excelled – the epic novel, as practised by Halldor Laxness, Þ. Þórðarson, G. Hagalín, and O.J. Sigurðsson. Modern Icelandic literature has also produced many outstanding poets.

Dialectal differences are not great. The main division is between *harðmæli* in Northern Iceland, and *linmæli* in Southern Iceland (including Reykjavik). This division centres on the pronunciation of the plosives /p, t, k/ between vowels: in *harðmæli* as aspirates [pʰ, tʰ, kʰ] and in *linmæli* as almost voiceless [b̥, d̥, g̊].

SCRIPT

Gothic until the nineteenth century. Now Roman alphabet + æ, ö, þ, ð.

PHONOLOGY

Consonants

The core of the Icelandic consonantal system is provided by the five-term series of labial, dental, and velar stops: weak non-aspirate – hard non-aspirate – weak aspirate – strong pre-aspirate – strong post-aspirate; e.g. the labial series /b̥ – p – b̥ʰ – ʰp – pʰ/. In addition, there is a palatalized velar series, in which, however, the weak aspirated member */g̊ʰ/ is missing. The remaining phonemes in the consonantal inventory are:

fricatives: f, v, þ, ð, s, ç, γ, χ, h
nasals: voiced m, n, ŋ, ŋ'; unvoiced m̥, n̥, ŋ̊, ŋ̊'
lateral and flap: l, l̥, r, r̥
semi-vowel: j

593

The Icelandic phonological system is of extreme complexity, and the sound–symbol correspondence is correspondingly weak. The graph *k* for example represents the following nine values, depending on phonetic environment: /k, k′, kʰ, ʰk, k′ʰ, g, g′, χ, Ø/; e.g. *kalla* /kʰaḍla/, *aska* /aska/, *ekla* /ɛʰkla/, *kær* /k′ʰaiːr̥/, *veski* /vɛsk′i/, *skammur* /sgamːyr/, *skyr* /sg′iːr/; *slikt* /slixtʰ/, *velkt* /vɛl̥tʰ/.

Long consonants are pronounced doubled.

Vowels

> front: i, ɪ, ɛ
> central: ɣ/y, œ, a
> back: u, ɔ, o

Vowels tend to be diphthongized (vowel + /i/) before *-gi/-gj*: e.g. *boginn* /bɔiɣɪn/, 'crooked, bent'.

Stress

Always on first syllable, even in loan-words: *prófessor*. Both ablaut and umlaut are very frequent in Icelandic words, the former in the strong-verb system, the latter in declension.

MORPHOLOGY AND SYNTAX

Noun

There are three genders: masculine, feminine, and neuter. The definite article is free or bound. The free article is used with a noun which is also defined by an adjective; the bound article is affixed, e.g. when a possessive pronoun follows the noun: e.g. *hinn góði maður* 'the good man'; *bókin þín* 'your book'. The free article is:

	Masculine	*Feminine*	*Neuter*
singular	hinn	hin	hið
plural	hinir	hinar	hin

These are declined in four cases: the genitive forms are: *hins, hinnar, hins*, with a common plural for all three – *hinna*.

The bound form is made by dropping the *h(i)-* of the free article: *hestur.inn* 'the horse', plural *hestar.nir*.

GENDER

Many endings are specific, e.g. all nouns in *-ir*, *-inn*, *-ingur* are masculine and all nouns in *-ning*, *-ung*, *-ja* are feminine. But no generally applicable rule can be given.

DECLENSION

Weak or strong; the weak declension comprises nouns ending in a vowel. Typical weak declensions: *tunga* (fem.) 'tongue', *vetur* (masc.) 'winter'; strong: *hestur* (masc.) 'horse'

	Singular	Plural	Singular	Plural	Singular	Plural
nom.	tunga	tungur	vetur	vetur	hestur	hestar
acc.	tungu	tungur	vetur	vetur	hest	hesta
dat.	tungu	tungum	vetri	vetrum	hesti	hestum
gen.	tungu	tungna	vetrar	vetra	hests	hesta

Adjectives

The adjective agrees with noun in gender, number, and case. The adjective has strong and weak declensions: weak if the article or a pronoun is present. For example, the strong declension of *glaður* 'glad' is:

singular	glaður	glaðan	glöðum	glaðs
plural	glaðir	glaða	glöðum	glaðra

COMPARATIVE

The comparative is made with -(*a*)*ri*, and is always weak: e.g. *rikari* 'richer'. The usual suppletive forms are found: e.g. *góður* 'good' – *betri*; *gamall* 'old' – *eldri*; *lítill* 'small' – *minni*.

Pronoun

The base forms are:

	Singular	Plural	Honorific plural
1	ég	við	vér
2	þú	þið	þér

The third person is marked for gender:

singular	hann	hún	það
plural	þeir	þær	þau

These are declined in four cases: e.g. *ég, mig, mér, mín*.

The genitive forms of these personal pronouns – *mín, þín*, etc. – are used mainly after prepositions, and as the objective forms after certain transitive verbs: e.g. *ég vænti þín* 'I await you', *ég vænti hennar* 'I await her', *til þín* 'to you', *meðal þeirra* 'among them'. The possessive pronouns are marked for gender: e.g. *bókin mín* (fem.) 'my book', *bækurnar minar* 'my books'.

DEMONSTRATIVE PRONOUN/ADJECTIVE

Masc./fem. *þessi*, neut., *þetta* 'this'; masc. *sá*, fem. *sú*, neut., *það* 'that'. All these forms are declined in four cases, singular and plural.

hver /χɛːr/ 'who?'; *hvad* /χaːð/ 'what?'

RELATIVE PRONOUN
sem (indeclinable): e.g. *maðurinn, sem ég sá* 'the man who I saw'; *maðurinn, sem sá mig* 'the man who saw me'.

Numerals

1–10: 1 to 4 inclusive are marked for gender: 1 *einn/ein/eitt*, 2 *tveir/tvær/tvö*, etc. 5–10: *fimm, sex, sjö, átta, níu, tíu*; 11 *ellefu*; 12 *tólf*; 20 *tuttugu*; 21 *tuttugu og einn*; 30 *þrjátíu* (*þrír tugir*); 40 *fjörutíu* (*fjórir tugir*); 100 *hundrað*.

Verb

Verbs in Icelandic are weak or strong. There are active, passive (analytical), and middle (in *-st*) voices; indicative, imperative, and subjunctive moods.

TENSE
The present and preterite are simple, other tenses are formed by means of the auxiliary verbs: *hafa* 'have', *vera* 'be', *verða* 'become', etc. The non-finite forms are: the infinitive, and present and past participles.

WEAK VERB
Four groups are distinguished by phonological criteria; the key forms are the infinitive, the first person singular preterite, and the past participle. Examples of each class are given here; the forms shown are the infinitive, the first person singular present tense, the first person singular and plural preterite, and the past participle in its masculine form:

1. telja 'to count' – tel – taldi/töldum – talinn
2. heyra 'to hear' – heyri – heyrði/heyrðum – heyrður
3. segja 'to say' – segi – sagði/sögðum – sagður
4. elska 'to love' – elska – elskaði/elskuðum – elskaður

Most weak verbs belong to class 4. The present and preterite of *elska* are:

	Singular			*Plural*		
present	1 elska	2 elskar	3 elskar	1 elskum	2 elskið	3 elska
preterite	elskaði	elskaðir	elskaði	elskuðum	elskuðuð	elskuðu

In the subjunctive present, *i* replaces *a* of the indicative present: e.g. *elski, elskir*, etc. The past subjunctive is the same as the indicative past. The present participle is *elskandi*; past participle, *elskaður*.

STRONG VERB
Here there are seven classes, according to seven types of ablaut. The classes are set out here, showing infinitive, first person singular/plural of present, first

person singular/plural of preterite, past participle: the ablaut sequence is marked by bold typeface.

1. lita 'look' – lit/litum – **leit**-/litum – litið
2. brjóta 'break' – brýt/brjótum – **braut**/brjutum – brotið
3. verða 'become' – verð/verðum – **varð**/**urð**um – orðið
4. bera 'bear' – ber/berum – **bar**/**bár**um – borið
5. gefa 'give' – gef/gefum – **gaf**/**gáf**um – gefið
6. fara – 'travel' – fer/förum – **for**/forum – farið
7. falla 'fall' – fell/föllum – **féll**/**fél**lum – fallið

Conjugation of a strong verb: *gefa* = 'to give' (ablaut class 5):

	Singular			*Plural*		
present	1 gef	2 gefur	3 gefur	1 gefum	2 gefið	3 gefa
preterite	gaf	gafst	gaf	gáfum	gáfuð	gáfu

Subjunctive: present, e.g. *gefi, gefir*; past, e.g. *gæfi, gæfir*.
Participles: present, *gefandi*; past, *gefinn*.

MIDDLE VOICE
The characteristic is *-st*: e.g. *kallast* 'to be called'. The middle voice has reflexive, reciprocal, and passive sense: cf. *klæðast* 'to get dressed': *þeir heilsast* 'they greet each other'; *finnast dæmi til, að ...* 'an example can be found for ...'; *brjótast fyrir einhverju* 'to fight for something'.

PASSIVE
Auxiliary *vera* 'to be' + past participle of sense-verb, coded for gender: e.g. *bókin var gefin mér* 'the book was given to me'.

MODAL AUXILIARIES
kunna, munu, skulu, mega, eiga/átt, vilja, etc.: e.g.

> *ég kann ekki að gera það* 'I can't do that';
> *hann sagðist mundu koma* 'he said he would probably come';
> *ég má ekki hugsa til þess* 'I can't think about this';
> *þu átt að læra íslenzku* 'you ought to learn Icelandic'.

Negation

The general negating particle is *ekki* /ɛʰk'iː/ following the verb.

Prepositions

> With accusative: *um, á, í, undir, eftir, fyrir*, etc.
> With genitive: *til, án*; directionals, *sunnan* 'southwards', *norðan* 'northwards', etc.
> With dative: *að, hjá, gegn, handa*, etc.

Examples with accusative: *á borðið* 'on the table'; *ganga á fjöll* 'to go into the mountains'; *hann fer í garðinn* 'he goes into the garden'; *það er gott fyrir sjúklinga* 'that is good for invalids'.

Examples with dative: *hann er hjá mér* 'he's with me'; *kaupa eitthvað handa einhverjum* 'to buy something for someone'.

Word order

SVO.

Í UPPHAFI var Orðið og Orðið var hjá Guði, og Orðið var Guð.

2. Það var í upphafi hjá Guði.

3. Allir hlutir eru fyrir það gjörðir, og án þess er ekkert til orðið, sem til er.

4. Í því var líf, og lífið var ljós mannanna;

5. Og ljósið skín í myrkrinu, og myrkrið meðtók það ekki.

6. ¶ Maður nokkur var sendur af Guði, hann hèt Jóhannes.

7. Þessi kom til vitnisburðar, til þess að vitna um ljósið, svo allir tryðu fyrir hans vitnisburð.

8. Ekki var hann ljósið, heldur átti hann að vitna um ljósið.

IGBO

INTRODUCTION

Igbo is usually assigned to the Kwa group of Niger-Congo languages, though certain affinities with the Bantu language Efik have been pointed out. It is spoken by around 10 million people, in a variety of dialects spread over southern Nigeria, from Onitsha and Owerri to Calabar. 'Central Igbo' is a compromise standard based on the Onitsha-Owerri dialect. Writing in Igbo, as distinct from Bible translation, dates from 1932 when Pita Nwana's story *Omenuko* won a prize in a competition run by the International African Institute. From the 1970s on there has been a steady growth in the output of Igbo novels, plays, and verse. Igbo writers have also been prolific in English.

SCRIPT

Romanization dates from the inception of missionary activities in the mid-1850s. A standardized orthography was introduced in 1961. The sound–symbol correspondence is weak; e.g. the letter *s* represents /s/, s'/, /š/ and /š'/.

PHONOLOGY

Consonants

stops: /p, ph, b, bh/; these occur palatalized: /p', ph'/, etc.
/t, th, d, dh/; the palatalized dentals: /c, ch, ɟ, ɟh/;
/k, kh, g, gh/; the velars occur labialized: /k°, kh°/, etc.
fricatives: /f, v, s, z, γ, h/; these occur (except /γ/) nasalized: /f̃, ṽ/, etc. /s, z, h/ occur both palatalized and nasalized: /š', ž', h̃'/; /h̃/ also labialized, /h̃°/.
lateral: l
roll: r
nasals: m, n, n', ŋ, ŋ°
semi-vowels: j, w
implosives: kp, gb

Vowels

i, ɪ, ɛ, a, ɔ, o, ɵ, u

Notated as: *i, i̧, e, a, o̧, o, u̧, u.*

599

VOWEL HARMONY
i, e, o, u are compatible with each other; similarly, *ị, a, ọ, ụ.*

Tones

Three level tones are distinguished: high, mid, and low. The mid level tone is constrained in that it can only follow a high, i.e. no monosyllable can be mid level. Two or more non-level tones, i.e. rising/falling, are also present. Tonal contours are not fixed, and relative pitch varies considerably in the course of an utterance. Furthermore, lexical tone or citation form changes in certain environments.

Tone in Igbo is of cardinal phonemic importance.

In this description, high tone is unmarked, low tone is marked with a grave accent, mid level with a dash (').

MORPHOLOGY AND SYNTAX

Noun

Nouns fall lexically into tonal classes: e.g. for disyllables, high–high, low–high; high–low, low–low. Similarly for tri- and quadrisyllables. In various syntactic relationships, e.g. in genitive construction and in conjugational patterns, lexical tone is subject to change in specific ways: cf.

m chị anụ 'I bring meat';
m̀ chị anụ 'Do I bring meat?';
m̀ chị anụ́ 'I don't bring meat'.

Meaning is thus a function of tonal pattern and word position.

There is no plural form.

Adjective

Adjectives may be formed by tonal modulation from verbs and other parts of speech: e.g. from *ịjọ́* 'to be bad', is formed *ojo/ojoọ́* 'bad'; cf. *ọma* 'good'. There are few words of this type in Igbo. Any nominal can, of course, act as a modifier and follow another nominal: this collocation is equivalent to the genitive relationship: e.g. *ụlọ̀ ezè* 'house-chief' = 'chief's house'; *ụlọ̀ eghú* 'goat-shed'; *àla ụ́dho* 'land of peace'; *àlà ezè* 'chief's domain'.

Pronoun

PERSONAL

		Separable	Inseparable
singular	1	mụ, m	m
	2	gi	i/ị
	3	ya	o/ọ

impersonal e/a

plural	1	anyị
	2	unù
	3	h̄a

The inseparable forms occur only as bound forms for verbal subject. There is also an emphatic form: àmị̂, àgị̂, àyâ; anyî, unû, h̄â.

The separable forms act also as possessives: tone depends on noun modified: cf. *nnà m* 'my father'; *nne ḿ* 'my mother'; *nnà gị* 'your father'; *nne gị* 'your mother'; *isi ḿ* 'my head'; *isi gị* 'your head'.

Examples of object pronoun: *nyètu ḿ yá* 'give it to me'; *jùo yá* 'ask him'; *dèe yá* 'write it'; *ži yá ùwe m* 'show him my clothes'.

DEMONSTRATIVE ADJECTIVES
à 'this', *ahụ̀* 'that'. Emphatic forms: e.g. *àmị̂, àgị̂*.

INTERROGATIVE PRONOUNS
These have specific tonal patterns: *ònye/òchu* 'who?'; *gịnị* 'what?': e.g. *ònyê bịà-rà?* 'Who came?'

Numerals

1–10: *otù, àbụọ̀, àtọ, ànọ, ìse, ìsiì, àsaà, àsatọ̀, tolú, ìri.* 11 *ìri nà otù;* 12 *ìri nà àbụọ̀;* 20 *ohu;* 30 *ohu nà ìri;* 40 *ohu àbụọ̀;* 50 *ohu àbụọ̀ nà ìri;* 100 *ohu ise.*

Verb

Formally simple, the Igbo verb structure is of great tonal complexity. The infinitive is marked by the high-tone prefix *i-* or *ị-*, harmonizing, that is, with the stem vowel, which is either middle or low tone: e.g. *i.sị* 'to cook', *ị.nụ̀* 'to hear', *i.zù* 'to meet'.

The infinitive is negated by replacing *i-/-ị* with *e-/a-* (depending on vowel harmony) and adding the suffix *-ghi/-ghì*: e.g. *i.kè* 'to distribute', negative *e.kè.ghì*.

A participial form is made with harmonic prefix *e-/a-*; this form is conjugated by one of several auxiliaries, e.g. *ị.nà* 'to do, make': *ọ nà.è.sị anụ̀* 'she is cooking meat' (tone of prefix changes from *e* to *è*). Simple forms take this participial form to express protracted or habitual action: e.g. *mụ nà.a.chị anụ* 'I (usually) brought meat'.

The exact meaning – aspectual, modal, temporal – of an Igbo verb depends on the presence or absence of certain prefixes and suffixes; the stem itself is not inflected in any way. Tonal sequence also varies depending on whether a statement is or is not initiatory.

IMPERATIVE
No prefix, certain suffixes may be used: e.g. *gwa ḿ* 'tell me!'; *gà.wa ahịa* 'set off for market!' (where *-wa* is an inceptive suffix),

ASPECT

VSO/SVO imperfective aspectual assertion: a pronominal vowel prefix is used in VSO, absent in SVO: cf. *a.chị m̀ anụ* 'I am/was carrying some meat', *m chị anụ* 'I am/was carrying some meat'.

SVO perfective: with *-rV* suffix, where V copies the stem vowel: cf. *m sì.rì anụ* 'I cooked some meat', *m hù.rù enyi* 'I saw an elephant'.

The directional suffix *te/ta* may be added: e.g. *ọ bù.tè.rè abọ* 'he brought the basket' (to a specific place), where the form *te* is demanded by vowel harmony (within the *i, e, o, u* group) and *-vR* copies it: *te.re*.

SVO perfective with *e-/a-* prefix, plus open vowel suffix and *la/le* suffix: e.g. *anyị è.sì.e.le anụ* 'we have cooked meat'. The pronominal prefix *e-/a-* is dropped if the pronominal subject preceding the verb is monosyllabic: *m sị.e.le anụ* but *e.sị.e.le m̀ anụ* 'I have cooked meat'.

All affirmative forms have correlative negative forms. The prohibitive usually has the *-le/-le* suffix. In negative assertion, *e-/a-* is prefixed to the verb, and *-ghi* is added. This *e-/a-* is a verbal prefix, not to be confused with the pronominal prefix *e-/a-* discussed above: e.g. *Ewu atá.ghi ji ányị* 'The goat (*ewu*) didn't eat our yams (*ji*).'

Narrative form: this form takes up the thread of discourse from a preceding primary form, with no recapitulation of subject: absence of overt subject induces tonal change in both verbs and nouns.

Subordinate verb forms differing from primary forms in tone, are used to make affirmative and negative conditional and relative clauses: e.g. a relative affirmative clause with change of subject:

> *unù tìsị ùwe* 'you wear clothes'
> *ùwe unu tìsị dị mmà* 'the clothes are you wearing are good'
>
> *ewû tàrà ji* 'the goat ate yams'
> *ji ewu tàrà rìrì nne* 'the yams the goat ate were many'

Preposition

na/la 'on, in' is an all-purpose preposition: e.g. *ọ nọ nà London* 'he is in London', where *na* changes to *nà* (low tone) because of following consonant (non-nasal). Preceding a vowel, *na* is assimilated to the vowel in both tone and quality, and is written as *n'*: e.g. *na ụlọ̀ → n'ụlọ̀* 'in the house'.

Word order

See **Verb**, above.

1 NA mbu ka Okwu ahu diri, Okwu ahu na, Cineke di-kwa-ra, Okwu ahu buru kwa Cineke. 2 Onye ahu na Cineke diri na mbu. 3 Ekere ihe nile site n'aka-Ya ; ekegh kwa otù ihe obula nke ekeworo ma Onogh ya. 4 Nime Ya ka ndu diri ; ndu ahu buru kwa Ihè nke madu(pl). 5 Ihè ahu we nāmu n'ociciri ; ociciri ahu ejidegh kwa ya. 6 Otù nwoke putara, onye ezitere site n'ebe Cineke no, ahà-ya bu Jon. 7 Onye ahu biara igba amà, ka owe gbara Ihè ahu amà, ka madu nile we site n'aka-ya kwere. 8 Ya onweya abugh Ihè ahu, kama obiara ka owe gbara Ihè ahu ama.

ILOKANO

INTRODUCTION

This Austronesian language (Malayo-Polynesian branch) is spoken in the Philippines (northern Luzon and elsewhere) by from 4 to 6 million people, i.e. exceeded only by Cebuano and Tagalog. Ilokano is used for press and radio.

SCRIPT

Adapted from Spanish. *c* before *e* and *i* is pronounced as /s/.

PHONOLOGY

Consonants

There is a very simple consonantal inventory of the labial, dental, and velar voiced and unvoiced stops with their associated nasals, plus the semi-vowels /w, j/, and /r, s, l/.

Vowels

i, e, a, o, u

Stress

Stress may be phonemic; *see* **Adjective**, below.

MORPHOLOGY AND SYNTAX

As typically in the languages of the Philippines, noun, pronoun, and verb are correlated in a syntactic nexus determined by the category of focus (*see* **Tagalog**). The Ilokano account of an action will focus the agent, the patient, the beneficiary, or the means or locus of such action; and for each option a specific verb form is available with correlated pronouns.

Noun

Nouns are proper or common, with singular and plural markers: *ni* and *da* for proper nouns, *ti* and *dagiti* for common. The same markers can be used as

604

possessive-relational links: *ni Pedro* 'Peter's'; *ti ubing* 'of the child'; *dagiti ubbing* 'of the children'.

Mainly by reduplication: e.g. *sabong* 'flower', pl. *sabsabong*. This extends even to loan-words: e.g. *maestra* 'teacher', pl. *mamaestra*. The plural form is not necessary if a plural demonstrative is present: e.g. *balasang* 'lady', pl. *babbalasang*; *balasang dagitoy* 'these ladies'.

Adjective

There are two forms, simplex, e.g. *dakkel* 'big', and *na*-prefix form, e.g. *nalukmeg* 'stout', *napintas* 'beautiful'. Again, the plural form is by reduplication: *dadakkel, lulukmeg*. The adjective and noun are connected by *a* (before consonants) or *nga* (before vowels): e.g. *nalukmeg nga ubing* 'a fat child'.

COMPARISON
A comparative is made, also by reduplication: cf. *napínpintás* 'more beautiful' (distinguish from *napipintás*, the plural form). Further, the comparative form has two stress points, the plural only one.

Pronoun

There are four series:

(a) sing. 1 *siak*, 2 *sika*, 3 *isu*; dual. *data*; pl. 1 incl. *datayo*, excl. *dakami*, 2 *dakayo*, 3 *isuda*. These are used e.g. with 'agent-focus' verbs as subject/ nominative pronouns.
(b) the *ak* series: identical to *siak* series minus the *si-/da-* prefix: sing. 3 is Ø.
(c) the *ko* series: sing. *ko, mo, na*; dual *ta*; pl. *mi, tayo, yo, da*. Used e.g. with *-en* verbs (target-focus).
(d) the *kaniak* series: e.g. *kaniak, kenka, kenkuana*, the oblique series.

DEMONSTRATIVE PRONOUN
Three degrees of distancing, singular and plural forms: *daytoy* 'this', *dayta* 'that', *daydiay* 'that yonder': pl. *dagitoy, dagita, dagidiay*.

INTERROGATIVE PRONOUN
sino 'who?'; *ania* 'what?'.

RELATIVE PRONOUN
Example with *ti*: *Siak ti agsurat* 'I am the one who will write.'

Numerals

The native series 1–10: *maysa, dua, tallo, uppat, lima, innem, pito, walo, siam, sangapulo*. 11 *sangapulo ket maysa*; 20 *duapulo*; 30 *tallopuo*; 100 *sangagasut*.
    The Spanish numerals are also in use.

Verb

As in Tagalog, Ilokano verbs are classified by their determinant affixes: *ag-/-um-* verbs, *-en* verbs, *i...-an* verbs, etc.

ag-/-um- verbs: verbs with these affixes are agent-focused, and use the *(si)ak* pronominal series: e.g. *ag.basa ak* 'I read'; *ag.takder Ø* 'he/she stands'. A progressive form is made by reduplication: e.g. *ag.tak.tak.der* 'he/she goes on standing'. The past form is made with *nag-*: e.g. *nag.saludsod* 'he asked'.

-um- verbs are also agent-focused, and take the *siak* series: e.g. *gatang* 'buy', *g.um.atang ka* 'you buy'; *inom* 'drink', *um.inom tayo* 'we (incl.) drink'. The progressive is again by reduplication: e.g. *tumulong* 'to help', prog. *tumultulong*.

-en verbs are target-focused; they are used with the *ko* series of pronouns: e.g. *lutuen* 'to cook (something specific)', *lutuen ta ti karne* 'we two cook the meat'; *kitaen ti ubing ni Pedro* 'the child looks at *Pedro*'.

i-/iya- verbs are also target-focused.

pag- verbs are means/instrument-focused: e.g. *pag.surat mo daytoy* 'use this to write with'. The *pag*-verbs use the *ko* series. The past tense is in *pinag-*.

The *i-...-an* verbs are used when the beneficiary of an action is in mind: e.g. *i.gatang.an na kami iti singsing* 'he/she buys us (excl.) a ring'. Here, since the beneficiary is focused, the *siak* series is used for 'us' while the agent 'he' is in the *ko* series.

maka- verbs denote ability to perform the action expressed by the stem.

VERBAL NOUN

panag- + stem, *or i-* + partial reduplication + base. These forms are used to make future and past tense formations with the help of marked adverbials, e.g. adverbial + *-nto* (future); + *idi* (past): e.g.

> kaan**onto** ti isasangpet **da** = kaan**onto** ti **panag**sangpet **da**?
> 'When will they arrive?'

> kaano **idi** ti isasangpet **da**?
> 'When did they arrive?'

1 Idi punganay addan ti Sao ket ti Sao adda iti Dios, ket ti Sao, Dios. 2 Isu idi punganay adda iti Dios. 3 Babaen kencuana napaadda dagiti amin a banag, ket amin a napaaddan saanda a napaadda no di babaen kencuana. 4 Adda idin kencuana ti biag, ket ti biag isu ti silaw cadagiti tao. 5 Ket aglawag ti silaw iti sipnget, ket saan nga inabac ti sipnget.

6 Adda idi maysa a tao a ti naganna Juan a naibaon nanipud iti Dios. 7 Ket daytoy immay maipuon iti panangsacsi, tapno mangpanecnec maipapan iti silaw, tapno babaen kencuana mamati coma dagiti isuamin. 8 Saan nga isu ti silaw no di ket isu immay tapno mangpanecnec maipapan iti silaw.

INDO-ARYAN
LANGUAGES (New)

See **New Indo-Aryan Languages**.

INDO-EUROPEAN
LANGUAGES

INTRODUCTION

The Indo-European family of languages comprises the following twelve branches:

1. Indic: including Vedic, Sanskrit, the Prakrits, and the New Indo-Aryan languages (NIA); the Dardic languages form a peripheral and controversial grouping within this branch.
2. Iranian: including Avestan, Old Persian, Middle Iranian (Pehlevi, etc.), the modern Iranian languages (Persian, Kurdish, Pashto, Ossetian, etc.), and the Pamir languages.
3. Anatolian: Hittite, Luvian, Palaic, Lydian, etc.; all extinct.
4. Armenian.
5. Hellenic: including Linear B Greek, Homeric and Classical Greek, New Testament Greek, and Modern Greek.
6. Albanian: formerly regarded as the sole survivor of an Illyrian branch.
7. Italic: including Latin-Faliscan, Oscan-Umbrian, Venetic, the modern Romance languages.
8. Celtic:
   (a) Continental Celtic (in Gaul, the Iberian Peninsula, and Central Europe; Galatian in Anatolia; all extinct);
   (b) Insular Celtic: (i) Goidelic: Irish, Gaelic, Manx; (ii) Brythonic: Welsh, Cornish, Breton.
9. Tocharaic (extinct).
10. Germanic:
    (a) East Germanic: Gothic;
    (b) North Germanic: Old Norse, Icelandic, the modern Scandinavian languages:
    (c) West Germanic: Old and Middle High German, Low German, Anglo-Saxon, English, modern German, Dutch, Frisian, Afrikaans; Yiddish.
11. Baltic: Lithuanian, Latvian; Old Prussian (extinct).
12. Slavonic:
    (a) South Slavonic: Old Church Slavonic, Macedonian, Bulgarian, Serbo-Croat;
    (b) East Slavonic: Russian, Ukrainian, Belorussian;
    (c) West Slavonic: Polish, Czech, Slovak, Lusatian, Slovene.

In terms of their primary expansion, that is, as located about 2,000 years ago, the Indo-European languages covered a territory stretching from Ireland to Assam, and from Norway and central Russia to the Mediterranean, the Persian Gulf, and Central India. Secondary expansion in the last four hundred years, by conquest and colonization, has placed Indo-European languages, especially English, Spanish, Portuguese, Russian, and French in every corner of the globe. The sole major language area still largely untouched by Indo-European is that occupied by its sole quantitative rival – Chinese.

As regards textual attestation, the Indo-European languages can be divided into four groups:

1. Primary stratum: centring round the second millennium BC: Hittite, Vedic, Linear B Greek.
2. Secondary stratum: first millennium BC: Greek, Sanskrit, Avestan, Old Persian, Latin, Oscan, Umbrian.
3. Tertiary stratum: first millennium AD: Gothic, Old Irish, Tocharaic, Old Church Slavonic, Armenian, early North and West Germanic.
4. Modern period: from 1000 to present: the mediaeval and modern New Indo-Aryan languages, Iranian, Romance, Germanic, Slavonic, Celtic, and Baltic languages; Modern Greek, Armenian; Albanian.

The position of Lithuanian in this tabulation is anomalous; though it is attested from no earlier than the fifteenth century AD, it belongs by virtue of its exceptionally archaic structures to the primary or, at least, the secondary stratum.

A genetic relationship between the classical languages, Greek, Latin, and Sanskrit, was identified in the late eighteenth century by Sir William Jones, who correctly postulated a 'common source' for these three languages, and suggested that Celtic, Iranian, and Germanic might well be connected. The genetic relationship was first scientifically codified and set out on a comparative basis by Franz Bopp, whose major work – *Vergleichende Grammatik des Sanskrit, Zend, Armenischen, Griechischen, Lateinischen, Lithauischen, Altslawischen, Gothischen und Deutschen* – was published in 1833. ('Zend' in Bopp's title refers to **Avestan**, *q.v.*) In the following half-century, comparative Indo-European linguistics made rapid strides in several fields: phonology (Pott, Saussure), reconstruction of Proto-Indo-European (Schleicher); lexicography (Fick), and comparative morphology (Brugmann, Delbrück, Rask). This period of comparative Indo-European studies culminates in the great *Grundrisz der vergleichenden Grammatik der indo-germanischen Sprachen* (5 vols, 1886–1916) by Karl Brugmann and Berthold Delbrück. The comprehensive, enormously detailed and theoretically well-ordered picture presented here of Proto-Indo-European and its reflexes, was shaken in some respects by the discovery of Hittite, in the early years of the twentieth century. In particular, a brilliant piece of theoretical insight, put forward by Saussure some fifty years earlier, seemed to find confirmation in the new language. Saussure had argued that certain ablaut sequences in the Classical Indo-European languages could be explained by assuming the presence in the parent language of what he called '*coefficients sonantiques*' – probably laryngeals – which were subsequently lost: and now here was Hittite with two laryngeals, written as *ḫ* and *ḫḫ* in the

Akkadian cuneiform script, precisely where the theory predicted they should be found: cf. Hittite *ḫarkiš* 'white' – Greek *argēs*.
Lehmann (1952) notated four laryngeals as /x, γ, h, ʔ/.

Hittite differs, of course, so markedly from its coevals in this oldest stratum of Indo-European (it might be compared to Samoyedic *vis-à-vis* Uralic), and is so evidently under non-Indo-European influence, that not all authorities accept the laryngeal theory as it stands (cf. Krahe 1966: 101). Nevertheless, one to three laryngeals figure in the more recent, authoritative reconstruction of the Indo-European phonological system by O. Szemerényi (1980) which contains:

Consonants

> stops: labial, dental, and velar four-term series with four-way distinction of voiced/unvoiced and aspirate/non-aspirate: e.g. /p – p^h – b – b^h/. The velar series has palatalized and labialized correlatives: /k', k'^{h}, g', g'^{h}; k^w, k^{wh}, g^w, g^{wh}/.
> fricatives: /s, h/ (a reduction from Brugmann's system);
> resonants: /j, w, m, n, l, r/;
> syllabic liquids: /n̥, m̥, l̥, r̥/, long and short

One to three laryngeals.

Vowels

> /i, e, a, ə, o, u/; long and short, except /ə/ which is short only;
> diphthongs: ei, ai, oi; eu, au, ou.

If we take the highly inflected and mythopoetically rich Indo-Iranian reflex as close to, and typical of, the parent language, it is clear that we then have to postulate an anterior period of development lasting some five thousand years. In its final stage before the break-up, Proto-Indo-European seems to have had three genders, three numbers, and probably eight cases (as in Sanskrit). Adjectives were treated as nouns. First and second personal pronouns were present, with the third personal forms supplied from the demonstrative series; all were declined in all cases. The verb had two voices and four moods, with both finite and non-finite forms, and very elaborate marking for person and number.

Over the two centuries since its identification, the comparative study of the Indo-European family has tended to centre round the great classical languages of India, Greece, and Rome, with Germanic, Celtic, and Slavonic as important auxiliary fields. The discovery of Hittite, a primary stratum language with a phonological and morphological apparatus about as far removed from its coeval Vedic as could well be imagined, has awakened interest in the Anatolian area as an alternative cradle of Proto-Indo-European, which, it was increasingly felt, had been reconstructed perhaps all too exclusively in the Aryan (Indo-Iranian) mould. (For example, of all the Indo-European languages, Sanskrit alone displays a phonological system of almost artificial perfection, with five positional series, each of which has five modes of articulation.)

Typological reconstructions have now been put forward which include four typically Caucasian ejectives (glottalized obstruents) as bases for voiced and unvoiced plain and aspirated stops: e.g. /ṭ – d/dʰ – t/tʰ/.

A typological equation between a theoretical reconstruction of Proto-Indo-European and languages of the **Abkhaz-Adyge** (*q.v.*) type does not, of course, imply any sort of genetic relationship. The premise that the proto-language had ejectives, however, does offer promising solutions for certain highly technical problems in the daughter languages; and the ejective model is, in fact, fundamental to the phonological apparatus of the main Indo-European language in the Caucasus area – Armenian.

Pari passu with the reconstruction of the Proto-Indo-European language went the quest for an 'Aryan' homeland, speculation on its nature, and the creation of scenarios for the primary diffusion process. One of the most influential was that advanced by Professor V. Gordon Childe (1926, *The Aryans*). Childe used the archaeological evidence provided by the so-called Corded Ware culture, together with the linguistic evidence of isoglosses – common Indo-European roots delineating the flora, fauna, and climate of the putative homeland – to fix an Aryan radiant in what is now the Ukraine, at a time close to the onset of the Bronze Age. Thus, artefacts were identified with a tribe, the tribe with a language. Today, amplified by much new evidence, the Kurgan thesis (so called after the burial mounds in the Ukraine: the Turkic word *kurgan* means 'tumulus', 'mound') has been given a fresh lease of life in the impressive work of Marija Gimbutas. From a Pontic source, so runs the scenario, mounted warrior–sages fanned out in the late Neolithic period to dispense conjugation and declension, the horse, the wheel, and Indo-European kinship systems, including the husband's in-laws, to agglutinating and isolating humanity. In some ways, this thesis ties up with the image of Aryan superiority built into the Indo-Iranian sector of historical Indo-European. In the *Rig-Veda*, Indra smites dusky aboriginals: e.g. in Hymn 12 of Book II:

yo dāsaṃ varṇam adharaṃ guhākaḥ
'(Indra) who has subjected and made to vanish the non-Aryan colour'
(where *akar*, the root aorist of *kṛ* to do, has to be understood)

If this point is worth making, it is because the subjugation of more primitive societies by a dominant elite is a feasible mode of language diffusion; and certainly, Indo-European languages spread into India from the north. The account given in the *Rig-Veda* is, naturally, partisan, however. Thus, Indra is also described as: *yo apo vavṛvāṃsaṃ Vṛtraṃ jaghāna* 'who slew Vṛtra who had enclosed the waters', ostensibly a victory for the dominant elite. The fact is, however, that this seems to refer to the destruction of the dams which supplied the great cities of Mohenjo-Daro and Harappa with water: the ruin, that is, of the technologically advanced pre-Aryan Indus civilization by invading pastoral nomads.

Alternative scenarios featuring Anatolia as an Urheimat have been put forward. Thus, T.V. Gamkrelidze and V.V. Ivanov (1986), while accepting a Pontic radiant for Balto-Slavonic, Celtic, Germanic, and Italic contingents, as postulated by Gimbutas, regard this as a *secondary* staging-post for an advance into Europe; the original homeland is placed in Anatolia and the Lake Van area, and antedates the Pontic stage by some 3,000 years. From this viewpoint, Indo-European diffusion falls into three categories: (a) the proto-Europeans move out to sojourn in the Pontic area before starting to colonize Europe c. 3000 BC; (b) the proto-Indo-Iranians move eastwards through Iran towards India; (c) the Hittites, the Greeks, and the Armenians stay put: that is, Hellas was colonized by Greeks from Anatolia, not vice versa.

In the total absence of concrete evidence for these speculations, Gamkrelidze and Ivanov rely on comparative reconstruction, pointing to the undoubted presence of Semitic roots in Indo-European, and adducing alleged parallels from various Caucasian languages. Not all linguists find either these parallels or, indeed, the thesis itself convincing.

Colin Renfrew (1988) also places the Urheimat in Anatolia, whence, c. 6500 BC, peasant farmers with agrarian and stock-breeding skills, spread slowly (a few kilometres per annum) north and westwards to the Ukraine and to central and northern Europe. In other words, Indo-European languages are *in situ* for thousands of years, instead of being swiftly spread by mounted warriors. Concurrently, farmers (in the exact sense of the word – i.e. not pastoral nomads) speaking Proto-Afro-Asiatic, and, possibly, Proto-Dravidian, make their economically elite way by comparable pathways to north Africa and the East. In both of these scenarios the time-scale changes dramatically; starting about 3000 BC the mounted warrior–sages had taken something over a thousand years to colonize the Indo-European speech area as it appears in the second and first millennia BC; by wheelbarrow it took much longer.

Not that the early Indo-European farmer travelled necessarily on his own. If the Georges Dumézil school is to be believed, both the warrior and the priest, if not actually alongside him, were not far behind. Dumézil saw early Indo-European society as informed throughout by what he called *les trois fonctions*. These are:

(a) the sacerdotal power, or spiritual authority; the indispensable basis of
(b) the temporal and military power;
(c) the sustaining power: the providers and distributors of food.

In the Indian tradition, where they are designated as 'colours' (*varṇa*: see quote from *Rig-Veda*, Book II, Hymn 12, above) the three functions are embodied as follows: (a) *brahman*; (b) *kṣattriya*; (c) *vaiśya*. And a congruent tripartite system is found in the Avesta: (a) *āθravan*; (b) *raθaēštā*; (c) *vāstryō fšuyant*. The terms in (c) form a syzygy, which Emile Benveniste (1969) translates as *celui des pâturages*, and *celui qui s'occupe du bétail*. In the Hellenic sources, Plato (*Critias*) lists the following functions: (a) *hiereis*; (b) *makhimoi*; (c) *geōrgoi* and *dēmiourgoi*. Comparable triads can be found in Umbrian (in the Iguvine Tables), in Ferdousi's Shāh Nāmeh, in Celtic, and elsewhere.

INDONESIAN

INTRODUCTION

Indonesian is a member of the Austronesian family. Two main forms of the Malayan stock are spoken and written in South-East Asia and the islands of the archipelago: (a) Bahasa Indonesia, the official language of Indonesia, spoken by around 170 million; (b) Bahasa Malaysia, the official language of Malaysia, Singapore, and the Sultanate of Brunei, spoken by around 20 million. Phonologically and morphologically, the two forms are virtually identical. Nor is there much variation in vocabulary, though local differences are frequent. The description that follows is specifically of Bahasa Indonesia.

As far back as in the ninth to twelfth centuries AD Malay was in use as the administrative language of Hindu rule in Sriwijaya (south-east Sumatra). It continued to be so used through the following centuries under the Sultans of Malacca: on the one hand, as Classical Malay, the highly organized vehicle of a rich and extensive literature, and on the other as the lingua franca for the many peoples who lived in the area. In this second form it was known as *Melayu Pasar* – 'Bazaar Malay'.

In the early years of the twentieth century it seemed likely that Dutch would emerge as the language of administration, higher education and the cultural media in the archipelago, and, in line with this, the claims of Dutch were promoted even by Indonesian intellectuals (e.g. the Budi Utomo Association). Resistance to this policy grew *pari passu* with the rise of nationalism, and in 1928, at a conference in Batavia, the ideal of a national language was first promulgated. For such a national language there could be only one base – Malay, by far the most widely used and understood of all the languages of Indonesia. Curiously, by banning the use of Dutch, the Japanese occupation fuelled this movement. On 17 August 1945, Bahasa Indonesia was officially adopted as the national language of the Republic of Indonesia.

SCRIPT

Roman alphabet. A 'perfected spelling' was recommended by the Indonesian Ministry of Education in 1972. The main change here is that *y* everywhere replaces the *j* previously used under Dutch influence: e.g. *jang* > *yang*. *j* and *c* now represent the voiced and unvoiced affricates.

Modern Bahasa Malaysia is also written in *rumi*, the *jawi* (Arabic) script being reserved for religious texts.

PHONOLOGY

Consonants

> stops: p, b, t, d, k, g, ʔ
> affricates: tʃ, dʒ
> fricatives: f, s, ʃ, x, h;
> nasals: m, n, ɲ, ŋ
> lateral and flap: l, r
> semi-vowels: j (notated as *y*), w

Vowels

> i, ɪ, e, ə, a, ɔ, o, u

The letter *i* represents /i/ and /ɪ/; the letter *e* represents /ɛ/, /ɪ/, or /ə/; *o* represents /o/ or /ɔ/.

Stress

On the penultimate syllable, unless this contains an *e*-pepet (short *e*), no longer specifically marked in Bahasa Indonesian.

MORPHOLOGY AND SYNTAX

Roots are largely disyllabic. In the absence of prefixation, which encodes nominal and verbal properties, it is not possible to tell by inspection whether a disyllable is a noun, an adjective, a verb, or a numeral: cf. *gambar* 'picture' (noun); *hitam* 'black' (adjective/stative verb); *goreng* 'to fry' (verb); *tujuh* 'seven'.

Noun

Nouns are not marked for gender or number. Lexical means may be used to specify gender where necessary; and again, if necessary, number can be shown by reduplication (never if a numeral is present): e.g. *barang-barang itu* 'these things'; *penyakit-penyakit tropis* 'tropical diseases'; *sumber-sumber militer* 'military sources'.

DEFINITE/INDEFINITENESS
There are no articles, but the demonstratives *itu* and *ini* may be used as recapitulatory topicalizers, whose referents are known to the audience: e.g. *Undangan itu akan dipenuhi tahun ini juga* 'The invitation will be taken up this year' (the *undangan* 'invitation', having already been mentioned in the discourse; *akan* is future formant; *tahun* 'year').

All case relations are expressed by means of prepositional constructions or by apposition: e.g. *rumah makan* 'house-eat' = 'restaurant'; *pusat kebudayaan* 'cultural centre'; *buku petunjuk kota* 'guide book to the town'.

NOMINAL FORMATION BY AFFIXATION
Examples:

-*an*: forms resultatives, e.g. *tulis* 'to write' – *tulisan* 'something written'; *ajar* 'to teach' – *ajaran* 'doctrine'.

ke...-an: frequently used to form abstract nouns from adjectives and root nouns, e.g. *bangsa* 'people' – *ke.bangsa.an* 'nationalism'; *berani* 'brave' – *ke.berani.an* 'courage'.

pe + nasal: indicates agent or instrument, e.g. *pahat* 'to carve' – *pemahat* 'sculptor'; *laut* 'sea' – *pelaut* 'seaman'.

per/pen...an: abstract nouns formed by these two circumfixes may differ in respect of voice: e.g. from *kembang* 'develop': *per.kembang.an* 'development' (the passive result of a process), *pen.gembang.an* 'development' (the active process of developing something).

Adjective

As attribute, adjective follows noun, though quantifying modifiers precede: e.g. *orang baik* 'good man'; *banyak orang* 'many people'.

COMPARISON
The comparative is made with *lebih...dari(pada)*: e.g. *Malam ini lebih dingin daripada kemarin* 'Tonight is colder than yesterday.'

Pronoun

1st person: sing. *saya/aku*; pl. excl. *kami*, incl. *kita*;
2nd person: sing. *kamu/engkau/saudara/anda*; these are also plural forms;
3rd person: sing. *dia/ia*; pl. *mereka*. *Beliau* is a polite third person form.

Saundara is a generally acceptable form of polite address; *anda* is increasingly used when addressing an impersonal audience, e.g. on radio or television. *Aku*, *kamu*, and *dia* have enclitic forms: *-ku*, *-mu*, *-nya*.

Either the full form of the pronoun or its enclitic can be used as possessive: e.g. *rumah saya* = *rumah.ku* 'my house'; also as object, direct or indirect: e.g. *dia sudah menyurati saya* = *dia sudah menyurat kepada saya* = *dia sudah menyurati.ku* 'he has written (to) me'; *saya akan tinggal dengan dia/dengan.nya* 'I shall live with him'.

DEMONSTRATIVE PRONOUN/ADJECTIVE
itu 'this, these'; *ini* 'that, those'.

INTERROGATIVE PRONOUN
siapa 'who?'; *apa* 'what?'. *Apa* is used as an introductory interrogative particle: e.g. *Apa mereka belum makan?* 'Haven't they eaten yet?'

RELATIVE PRONOUN
yang: e.g. *pemilihan yang akan datang* 'the forthcoming election' ('which will come').

Numerals

1–10: *satu*, *dua*, *tiga*, *empat*, *lima*, *enam*, *tujuh*, *delapan*, *sembilan*, *sepuluh*; 11 *sebelas*; 12 *dua belas*; 13 *tiga belas*; 20 *dua puluh*; 30 *tiga puluh*; 100 *seratus*.

Classifiers

The lengthy inventory of numerical classifiers formerly used in Malay has been reduced in both languages, in Indonesian to three: *seorang* for humans; *seekor* for animals; and *sebuah* for things. Even of these, use is optional: e.g. *dia (seorang) wartawan* 'he is a journalist'.

Verb

The verb in Indonesian is not marked for person, number, or tense. Aspect and tense can be indicated by adverbial markers (see below). There is no copula. Roots are modulated by affixation. Verbs are stative, intransitive, or transitive. A transitive verb takes both a *me*(N)- prefix and a *di-* prefix; i.e. a transitive verb can be both active and passive.

VERBAL FORMANTS
Examples:

1. *ber-*: this is a formant for very many intransitives and statives, e.g. *bermain* 'to play'; *berhenti* 'to pause'; *bersumber* 'to originate in'.
2. *me*(N)-, usually with *-kan* affix: dynamic/transitive formant of wide semantic range. N here stands for a nasal, homogeneous with initial of root word: i.e. the prefix can be *me-*, *men*, *mem*, *meng*, or *meny*: Cf. *jalan* 'walk' – *men.jalan.kan* 'to drive (a car), to carry out'; *hidup* 'to live' – *meng.hidup.kan* 'to enliven, to switch on (the radio)'; *luas* 'wide' – *me.luas.kan* 'to spread'; *meng.amuk* 'to run amuck'. Initial *p*, *t*, *k*, *s* are dropped when *men-* is prefixed: e.g. *tangis* → *men.angis* 'to weep, cry'.
3. *mem-* acts as a subject focus marker prefixed to *per-*: cf. *kenal* 'to become friendly with' – *memper.kenal.kan* 'to introduce'; *lihat* 'to see' – *memper.lihat.kan* = *me.lihat.kan* 'to show'.
4. *di-* can be described as an object focus marker, or, in Indo-European terms, as a passive marker: e.g. *di.tunggu ke.datang.an.nya* 'his arrival is expected'; *dutabesar di.terima oleh Menteri Luar Negeri* 'the ambassador was received by the foreign minister' (*oleh* 'by'); cf. *memper.timbang.kan* 'to take into consideration', *di.timbang.kan* 'to be taken into consideration'.

NEGATIVE
The general negating particle is *tidak* preceding the word negated. A negative imperative is made with *jangan(lah)*: e.g. *janganlah baca buku itu* 'don't read that book'.

TENSE MARKERS
Imperfective *masih*, *sedang*; perfective *sudah*. The future tense marker is *akan*.

Prepositions

Indonesian uses prepositions: e.g. *di* 'in, on, at'; *untuk* 'for'; *kepada* 'to' (a person).

Word formation

In recent years, many compounds have been formed from the initial syllables of component roots in a name, title, or designation consisting of several words: e.g. *Jatim = Jawa Timur* 'East Java'; *Dubes = duta besar* 'ambassador'; *Hankam = Pertahanan dan Keamanan* 'Defence and Security'.

Word order

SVO.

1 Maka pada awal pertama adalah Kalam, dan Kalam itoe bersama-sama dengan Allah, dan Kalam itoelah djoega Allah.

2 Adalah Ia pada moelanja beserta dengan Allah.

3 Segala sesoeatoe didjadikan Oléhnja, maka djikalau tidak ada Ia, tiadalah djoega barang sesoeatoe jang telah djadi.

4 Didalamnja itoe ada hidoep, dan hidoep itoelah terang manoesia.

5 Maka terang itoe bertjahaja didalam gelap, maka gelap itoe tiada sadar akan Dia.

6 Maka adalah seorang jang disoeroeh oléh Allah, namanja Jahja.

7 Ialah datang memberi kesaksian, hendak menjaksikan hal terang itoe, soepaja sekalian orang pertjaja oléh sebab Dia.

8 Maka ia sendiri boekan terang itoe, melainkan hendak menjaksikan hal terang itoe.

INGRIAN

See **Balto-Finnic Languages**.

INUIT

INTRODUCTION

Inuit belongs to the Eskimo-Aleut family. There are two main divisions of Eskimo: Eastern, known as Inuit or Inupiaq, and Western, known as Yupik. Each of these divisions is a dialectal continuum, with a rather sharp dividing line between them. Inuit and Yupik are mutually unintelligible. The dividing line lies roughly along the 64° parallel in Alaska. To the south and west of this line Yupik extends towards the Aleutians, and into Siberia. The main Yupik dialect – Central Alaskan – is spoken by about 15,000 people, and literary and pedagogical material in it is produced under the aegis of the University of Alaska. Obsolescent in most of its territory, Yupik seems to be just holding its own in Central Alaska. The situation as regards Inuit is very different. It is spoken by over 60,000 people, 45,000 of whom are in Greenland, where Inuit is now the official language: *kalaallit oqasii*, 'the language of the Greenlanders'. In Canada the language is spoken by c. 16,000, with another 5,000 in Alaska.

West Greenlandic Inuit is the primary language of instruction in schools in Greenland, which means that the number of Inuit speakers is on the increase. Most Greenlanders, especially urbanized adults, are, of course, bilingual in Danish and Inuit.

Literature in West Greenlandic dates back to the religious texts produced in the eighteenth century. Today there is a fairly prolific output in most genres – newspapers, magazines, novels, school books, etc.

SCRIPT

Roman. In the mid-nineteenth century Samuel Kleinschmidt standardized the spelling of Greenlandic words on an etymological rather than a phonetic basis. In 1973 a new, phonetically more accurate, orthography was introduced.

PHONOLOGY

Consonants

    stops: p, t, k, q
    fricatives: v, s, (ʃ), j, γ, h, ɹ/ʁ
    nasals: m, n, ŋ, N
    lateral: l

/N/ is a voiced uvular, notated as *rng*.

Vowels

a, i, u (with hamza onset)

These have several allophones induced by phonetic environment. Thus, /a/ →
[ɛ], /i/ → [ɪ], /u/ → [ɔ].

MORPHOLOGY AND SYNTAX

Inuit words are divided into nominals, verbals, and particles. Inflection in
nominals and verbals is always by affix; there are about 400 affixes in the
language (listed in Fortescue 1983).

Noun

The Inuit noun is marked for number, case, and possessive relationship. A noun
is in the absolute case when it is the subject of an intransitive verb, in the relative
(ergative) case when it is the subject of a transitive verb.

Specimen of inflectional paradigm:

	Singular	*Plural*
absolute	-q/-t/-k/Ø	-(i)t
relative	-(u)p	-(i)t
instrumental	-mik	-nik
allative	-mut	-nut
locative	-mi	-ni
ablative	-mit	-nit
circumstantial	-kkut	-tigut
equative	-tut	-tut

Affix initials are subject to sandhi (assimilation, accommodation) at junctures.

Examples:

allative: *umiarsuar.mut* 'by ship';
ablative: *qiia.nir.nit* 'from the cold' (*-nir* is a nominalizing particle on verbal
stem);
instrumental: *savim.mi.nik* 'with his knife';
circumstantial: *ullaa.kkut* 'in the mornings', *unnua.kkut* 'at night'.

POSSESSION
There are two sets of endings, depending on absolute or relative status of head-
noun. Thus in the phrase *niviarsia.**p** ikinnguta.**ata** qimmi.**a*** 'the girl's friend's
dog' the second noun, *ikinnguta* 'the friend', has the relative possessive marker
-ata as *ikinnguta* is in relative relationship to the first noun *niviarsia* 'girl', which
has the absolute possessive marker *-p*. Similarly, *qimmi* 'dog', has the primary
third person possessed marker *-a*. Cf. *piniartu.**p** irnir.**a** pani.**a**.lu* 'the hunter's
son and daughter' (*lu* 'and'); *piniartu.**p** irnir.**ata** pani.**a**.lu* 'the hunter's son and
his (the son's) daughter'. Further, there is a specific set of endings for oblique
object possessed.

Adjective

There is no adjective as a separate category in Inuit. The predicative function is discharged by stative verb, the attributive function by the intransitive participle form (nominal): e.g. *illu.at kusanar.puq* 'their house is pretty' (*-at* = 3rd p. poss. abs.; *kusanar* (verb) 'to be pretty'; *puq* = 3rd p. sing. indic.).

Attributive follows noun: e.g. *inuit pikkuris.su.t* 'clever people' (*pikkuris* (verb) 'to be clever'; *su* = intrans. participle affix; *t* = pl. marker).

Pronoun

The free personal forms are:

	Singular	Plural
1	uanga	uagut
2	illit	ilissi
3	una	uku

The third person forms are demonstratives. These pronouns are declined in all cases. Thus for first person singular: *uanga – uanga – uannik – uannut – uanni – uannit – uakkut – uattut*. For subject/object fused forms in transitive verb, *see* **Verb**, below).

DEMONSTRATIVE PRONOUN

The complex orientational/directional deictic system of Eskimo in general has been reduced in West Greenlandic to a simpler grid based on relative proximity: *manna* 'this' – *una* 'that' – *innga* 'that yonder'; with further series indicative of relative height, compass point, or visibility.

The demonstratives form plurals and are declined in all eight cases in both numbers. *Ta-* may be prefixed to any demonstrative form whose coreferent has already been focused: e.g. **tamanna** 'this (here) (item) we've been talking about'.

INTERROGATIVE PRONOUN

kina 'who?'; *suna* 'what?'. Declined in eight cases, singular and plural.

RELATIVE PRONOUN

None. *See* **Relative clauses**, below.

Numerals

Native Eskimo words exist for 1–20. For numbers over 12, Danish equivalents are used, pronounced as in Danish or as converted to Inuit phonology. The indigenous series is: 1 *ataasiq*; 2 *marluk*; 3 *pingasut*; 4 *sisamat*; 5 *tallimat*; 6 *arvinillit*; 7 *arvini(q)-marluk*; 8 *arvini(q)-pingasut*; 9 *qulingiluat*; 10 *qulit*; 11 *aqqanillit*; 12 *aqqani(q)-marluk*. Continued on *aqqani-* base to 15; then *arvirsani-* base + units to 20, which is *arvirsani(q)-tallimat*.

The numerals are declined: e.g. *ukiuni sisamani* 'in four years'; *qimmit qaqurtut marluk taakku* 'these two white dogs' (*qimmi* 'dog'; *qaqurtu* 'white'). The old Eskimo dual is not used in West Greenlandic.

Verb

Inuit verbs are intransitive, transitive, or semi-transitive. A definite direct object following a transitive verb is in the base case: *tuttu taku.aa* 'he saw the caribou' (*tuttu* 'caribou'; *taku-* 'see'; *-(v)aa* inflection encoding transitive action by third person subject on third person object, both singular); an indefinite or non-focused object is in the instrumental case and follows a transitive stem now furnished with intransitive endings: e.g. *tuttu.mik taku.vuq* 'he saw a caribou', where *-vuq* is the intransitive third person ending. The stem *taku-*, with a specific infix, may also behave as a semi-transitive, again with intransitive inflection, and object in the instrumental: *tuttu.mik taku. **nnip**.puq* (with juncture assimilation, *-vuq* → *-puq*). Finally, the word denoting the object can itself take a verbalizing affix, e.g. *-si-*, plus the intransitive endings: e.g. *tuttu.si.vuq* which amounts to 'he caribou-ed', 'he became caribou-seeing'. (See Fortescue 1984: 86.)

PASSIVE VOICE

The marker is *-niqar-*; the object of the active verb becomes the subject of the converted verb, while the subject of the active verb may appear in the ablative case: Fortescue gives the following examples: *Inuit manuq taku.aat* 'The people saw the polar bear'; *Nanuq (inun.nit) taku.niqar.puq* 'The polar bear was seen by the people'; cf. *taa.**niqar**.tar.puq* 'it is called' (where *-tar-* is habitual action marker); *apiri.**niqar**.tar.punga* 'I'd be asked'.

MOOD

Inuit has primary (indicative, imperative/optative, interrogative) and several subordinate moods, the latter including a causative and a conditional. With each mood are associated (a) a set of intransitive endings; (b) a set of inflections coded for transitivity, person, and number; and (c) a specific mood marker; e.g. *va/var* (indicative), *gu/ku* (conditional), *li/la* (optative). The intransitive indicative paradigm shows the following endings:

	Singular	Plural
1	-vunga	-vugut
2	-vutit	-vusi
3	-vuq	-pput

while the correlative transitive paradigm has 28 forms notating person and number deixis: e.g. *-vara* (1st p. sing. subject acting on 3rd p. sing. patient; *-varma* (2nd p. sing. subject acting on 1st p. sing. patient). Specimen forms from the optative paradigm are: *-lara* (1st p. sing. acting on 3rd p. sing.), *-lakkit* (1st p. sing. acting on 2nd p. sing.).

Conditional: the intransitive singular forms are: 1 *-guma*, 2 *-guit*, 3 *-ppat*: e.g. *ilaa.ssa.guit* 'if you come' (*ssa* is future marker).

There are specific infixed markers for various modal senses, e.g. potential, inceptive, and desiderative: e.g. potential *-sinnaa-*: e.g. *kalaallit qallunaatut uqalus.**sinnaa**.gamik* 'Greenlanders (*kalaallit*) who can speak (*uqalus*) Danish (*qallunaatut*)'.

TENSE

The unmarked indicative can be construed as present or past, depending on context. *Sima*, *nikuu* are used as past-tense markers: e.g. *Nuum.miis.sima.vunga* 'I've been to Nuuk'. The future is marked by *-ssa-* (with others): e.g. *aalla.ssa.agut* 'we shall leave'.

Several affixes, e.g. *-qqu-*, *-tit-*, *-sar-*, convert intransitive into transitive verbs.

ASPECT

Fortescue (1983) lists about 50 'affixes concerned with aspect'. Some of the markers are:

> perfective: *riir*, *tikit*
> imperfective: *riar*
> habitual: *tar/sar*
> progressive: *giartur*
> iterative: *qattaar*

NEGATIVE

nngit negates sentences (sandhi at junctures): e.g. *tuku.**nngil**.aa* 'he didn't see him' (*-aa* is trans. ending for 3rd sbj. acting upon 3rd obj., both sing.); *paasi.**nngil**.aa* 'he didn't understand it'. The infix may be doubled: e.g. *tiki.**nngi**.ssa.**nngil**.anga* 'I'll not not-come' = 'I'll definitely come'.

RELATIVE CLAUSES

Participial forms replace adjective and relative pronoun, both absent in Inuit: e.g. *niviarsiaq kalaallisut ilinnia.lir.**suq*** 'the girl who has begun learning Greenlandic' (*lir* is inceptive marker; *suq* = intrans. participle); *Nuum.miir.**suq** niviarsiaq* 'the girl from Nuuk'; *illu purtusu.nngit.**suq*** 'a house that is not tall'.

Postpositions

Various nominals are used as postpositions: e.g.

> *ilu* 'interior': *illup ilu.a.ni* 'in the house' (*-a-* is poss. marker);
> *silat* 'outside of': *uqaluvvi.**up** silata.a.ni* 'outside the church';
> *quli-* 'above': *quli.tsin.nit* 'above us'.

Word order

Fairly free.

¹ pilerkàrneráne oкauseк iрок, oкauserdlo Gùtimīрок, oкau-
-serdlo Gùtiuvoк.   ² táuna pilerkàrneráne Gùtimīрок.   ³ sùt ta-
-marmik táussumùna píngorput; táussumùna píngitsumik atautsi-
-migdlùnît píngortoкángitdlat píngortut.   ⁴ inūssut táussumanī-
-рок, inùssutdlo inuit кáumaркutigàt.   ⁵ кáumaркutdlo târtumut
кaumavoк, tàrmiutdle ilasiaríngilàt.   ⁶ inuk Gùtip autdlartitarà
Juánasimik atilik.   ⁷ táuna tikiúpoк nalunaiáisavdlune, кáumaркut
nalunaiáissutígísavdlugo,   tamaisa   táussumùna   ugpeркuvdlugit.
⁸ táuna кáumaркutauvdlune píngilaк, kisiáne кáumaркut nalunaiái-
-ssutigísagamiuk.

(Greenlandic)

IRANIAN LANGUAGES

In its origins, this satem branch of Indo-European is very closely associated with the Indic branch. Apart from the evident parallels in religion and mythology, the language of the oldest stratum of the Gathas (*see* **Avestan**) is close enough to Vedic Sanskrit to suggest a fairly recent common ancestor. It seems likely that a stage of Indo-Iranian unity, centred in or near an Indo-European homeland in what is now the Ukraine, lasted into the third millennium BC. Exactly how and when the two groups reached their present locations is not clear; a Caucasian passage is one possibility. By the time the *Rig-Veda* was composed, however, in the middle of the second millennium, the Aryan kindred were already settled in northern India, and a comparable dating for Iranian colonization of Iran seems plausible.

The ethnonym of the Iranian-speaking tribes was *ar(i)ya* (Sanskrit: *ārya* 'of one's own tribe; honourable, noble') from which are derived Modern Persian *Irān*, Tadzhik *eron*, Ossete *Iron*.

As now distributed, the core languages – Persian, Dari, Baluchi, Pashto, Kurdish – lie in a broad band stretching from Pakistan to Turkey. The outliers are few – Ossete in the Caucasus, Tat in Azerbaydzhan, and the Pamir language Sarikoli in the CPR. The group can be classified dialectally and diachronically as follows:

(a) South-West Iranian
1. ancient and middle Iranian: Old Persian; Pehlevi;
2. modern: Persian, Dari, Tadzhik, Tat, with several smaller dialects including Luri and Bakhtyari.

(b) North-West Iranian
1. ancient and middle Iranian: Median, Parthian;
2. modern: Kurdish, Baluchi, Talysh, with many dialects.

(c) Eastern Iranian
Northern:
1. ancient and middle Iranian: Avestan, Sogdian, Khwarezmian;
2. modern: Ossete, Yagnob;
Southern:
1. ancient and middle Iranian: Khotanese Saka, Bactrian;
2. modern: Pashto, Pamir languages.

Typological grouping by dialect does not always correspond to present-day geographical location. For example, Ossete is a North-East Iranian language but is, in fact, the most north-westerly member of the family. As a North-West

Iranian language, Baluchi is similarly uncharacteristically placed on the south-eastern flank.

PERIODIZATION

Ancient Iranian: end of second millennium BC to fourth/third century BC; Middle Iranian: third century BC to eighth/ninth century AD; Modern Iranian: to the present day.

The close similarity between the oldest strata of Indic and Iranian was pointed out above. With the passage of time, however, the two families diverged very considerably, and no modern Iranian language is intelligible to a New Indo-Aryan speaker, or vice versa (though a special case might be made out for Classical literary Urdu, for example, which had a considerable number of Persian loan-words). Within the Iranian family itself, while Persian, Dari, and Tadzhik form a closely homogeneous group, the mutual intelligibility factor is, in general, rather low.

Vis-à-vis the Indo-European parent language, Iranian shows the following sound shifts:

1. IE /*p, t, k/ > Iranian /f, θ, x/ (Indic /p, t, k/)
2. IE /*ph, th, kh/ > Iranian /f, θ, x/ (Indic /p, t, k/)

That is the Indo-European voiceless stops and their aspirated counterparts were collapsed in Iranian to form the series of homorganic fricatives.

3. The voiced aspirated stops */bh, dh, gh/ were unvoiced in Iranian to give /b, d, g/ (in Indic the aspiration was retained).
4. IE *s > Iranian h; s/s after */i, u, r, k/: e.g.

Avestan	frā;	Sanskrit	pra- Greek **pro**, Latin **prō**- (prefix meaning 'in front of', 'on behalf of' etc.)
Avestan	yaθa	Sanskrit	yathā, 'as'
Avestan	brātar	Sanskrit	bhrātar 'brother'
Avestan	ahmi	Sanskrit	asmi 'I am'

5. IE /*a, e, o, ṇ, ṃ/ (all short) > Iranian /a/; the corresponding long values > Iranian /aː/: e.g. IE *dekṃ > 'ten' Avestan *dasa*, Sanskrit *daśa*; Latic *decem*, OCh. Slav. *deset'*.

IE /*ə/ > Iranian /i/; e.g. *pəter* > Iranian *pitā*; Latin *pater* 'father'.

In the modern languages, the West Iranian voiced stops /b, d, g/ are represented in East Iranian by the corresponding fricatives /β, ð, γ/; and Western /p/ is represented by /f/: cf. Persian *pedär* – Ossete *fida/fəd*.

Between ninety and a hundred million people speak Iranian languages, over half of this total being provided by Persian. As might be expected, all the present-day representatives of the family share a considerable number of Arabic words.

See **Avestan; Persian, Old; Pehlevi; Baluchi; Kurdish; Ossete; Pashto; Pamir Languages; Persian; Shughn-Roshan; Tadzhik; Talysh; Tat.**

EASTERN MEDIAEVAL IRANIAN LANGUAGES

INTRODUCTION

The Iranian imprint in Central Asia dates from the satrapies established beyond the Amu Darya by the Achaeminids: Suguda (in Greek, *Sogdianē*) and Uvarazmish (in Greek, *Chorasmia*). By the time that the Silk Road came to be used for commercial and cultural communication between India, China, and the West (Rome and Byzantium) several of the main staging-posts thereon, such as Kashgar, Yarkand, Khiva, and Khotan, were inhabited by Iranian-speaking populations. Three of their languages, all fairly close to each other, are known to us from archaeological excavations carried out in the twentieth century. They are:

1. Sogdian: after forming part of the Kushan (Tocharian) realm, and sharing in its Mahāyāna Buddhist culture, Sogdiana fell, first to the Sasanids, then to the western Turks (sixth century AD) and finally to the Sāmānid dynasty. The so-called Ancient Letters, which were found on the Great Wall of China date from the fourth century AD, but most of the extant Sogdian material is of much later date (eighth to tenth centuries). The main find was in the Zerafshan valley in 1933. Here, as elsewhere, Buddhist, Christian, and Manichaean religious texts and documents in Sogdian were found. With each of these denominations is associated a specific variety of the Aramaic alphabetic script, and what appears to be a specific socio-linguistic identity. For example, in marked contrast to the Manichaean material, the Christian documents suggest an appeal to the wider masses of Sogdian society (Oranskij 1963, after Henning 1958).

2. Khwarezmian: Chorasmia was conquered by the Arabs in the sixth century, and our main source of textual material in the Khwarezmian language is provided by Arabic works of the twelfth/thirteenth century – e.g. Zamakhšari's *Muqaddimatu'l adab*, which contains Khwarezmian glosses in Arabic script. Earlier specimens of the language were found in Khiva, the site of the ancient capital, Khwarazm; these date from the third to the eighth centuries.

3. Khotanese Saka: Khotan, the ancient Hvatana, lies in Chinese Turkestan (Xīnjiāng) between the Kunlun and the Takla Makan desert. Here, and in Tumshuk, a considerable corpus of Buddhist literature, dating from the seventh to the tenth centuries was found. Khotanese was written in the Indian Brahmi character.

Mention should also be made of Bactrian, about which very little is known. The few inscriptions found in northern Afghanistan are in a variant of the Greek character, and date from the second century AD.

PHONOLOGY

The Khotanese Saka consonantal inventory has three symmetrical series consisting of surd – voiced stop – voiceless fricative – voiced fricative: /p, b, f, ß; t, d, θ, ð; k, g, x, γ/. Also present are the affricates: /ts, dz, tʃ, dʒ/; the fricatives /s, z, ʃ, ʒ/ with the pharyngeal /ħ/; the semi-vowels /j/ and /w/; and /m, n, r, l/.

The Sogdian inventory is closely similar, but here the voiced stops appear to be used only after nasals; /l/ is absent. A Sogdian characteristic is the retention of surd stops in intervocalic position.

MORPHOLOGY AND SYNTAX

Noun

Sogdian had definite and indefinite articles which vary according to gender (masculine or feminine), case, number, and denominational affiliation: e.g. nominative masculine singular: Buddhist 'γw, Manichaean/Christian xw.

SPECIMEN DECLENSION
Khotanese Saka, *dastä* 'hand' (cf. Persian *dast*).

	Singular	*Plural*
nominative	dastä	dasta
accusative	dastu	dasta
genitive	dasti	dastānu
instrumental/ablative	dastäna	dastyau
locative	dīśta	dastuvo
vocative	dasta	dastyau

Feminine nouns: e.g. *kantha* 'town' (nom., acc.), pl. *kanthe*. Oblique endings as in masculine paradigm. The Khwarezmian plural ending was *-ina*.

Adjective

Adjectives are marked for gender and case in both Sogdian and Saka, and partially for number: e.g. Saka *dirä*, fem. *dira* 'bad', declined like *dastä*. The adjectival inflections are unstable, and tend, in later stages of the language, to be omitted. The comparative marker is Saka *-tarä*, Sogdian *-t(a)r*, with many variants: e.g. Manichaean Sogdian *čn škr' n'mr.tr* 'sweeter than honey'.

Pronoun

The personal pronoun has independent forms with two cases, and enclitic forms. The Sogdian paradigm is:

	Independent (singular = plural)		Enclictic	
	Direct	Oblique	Singular	Plural
1	'zw	mn'	-my	-mn
2	tγw	tw'	-f(y)	-fn
3	xw	w(y)nyy	-šy(y)/-šw	-šn

These are Manichaean forms. The oblique form of the independent pronouns may be used as a possessive: e.g. *mn' w'xš* 'my words'.

DEMONSTRATIVE PRONOUN
Several variants. In Sogdian, the forms *x-/w-*, each with oblique base, are used as indefinite articles. In Saka, masc. *ṣä*, fem. *ṣa*, pl. *ttä*, *tte*: declined in six cases on base *tt-*.

Numerals

Khotanese Saka 1–10: *śśau* (fem. *śśa*), *duva* (fem. *dvi*), *drai*, *tcahora*, *paṁjsa*, *kṣä(tä)*, *hauda*, *haṣṭa*, *nau*, *dasau*; 20 *bistä*; 30 *därsä*; 100 *satä*. The Sogdian numerals vary according to religious affiliation; e.g. for 3, Manichaean *'δry(y)*; Buddhist *δry*; Christian *šy *θrē*.

Verb

The characteristic Iranian division into present and past bases is found, the former generating the present indicative, the subjunctive, the optative, the imperative, and the present participle. The past tense, the past participle, and the infinitive are formed from the past base.

Sogdian and Khwarezmian retain an imperfect constructed on the present base. Also noteworthy in these two languages is a transitive perfect, formed with the auxiliary verb *δār* 'to have', from transitive verbs: e.g. *θfart δāram* 'I gave', *θfart δārt* 'he gave'.

In all three languages the verb is marked for person, number, tense, and mood; Khotanese Saka adds gender (marked in the past tense) and voice.

Sogdian indicative present: root *var-* 'to carry, take':

	Singular	Plural
1	varam	varim
2	vari	varta
3	vart	varand

Sogdian imperfect:

	Singular	Plural
1	varu	varim
2	var	varθ
3	vara	varand

The negative marker is *nē*; prohibitive, *mā*.

Prepositions and postpositions

All three languages use both pre- and postpositions. Sogdian is perhaps the only known language in which a writer's religion can be identified from the prepositions he uses: cf. Buddhist *čnn*, Manichaean/Christian *čn*, Manichaean *čwn* 'from, than' (as used in example in **Adjective** above).

IRISH

INTRODUCTION

A member of the Goidelic branch of Celtic, Irish is the first official language of the Republic of Ireland, with English. The Gaéltacht – the area where Irish is spoken – is not continuous; there is a broad division into a southern belt (Waterford, Cork, Kerry) and a northern (Connemara, Galway, Mayo, Donegal). About 30,000 people speak Irish in one form or another, none of them monoglot. There is a very considerable degree of divergence between the dialects. A standard orthography was adopted in 1948.

The centuries covering the transition from Old Irish to Modern Irish – 1200 to 1600 – produced a lot of fine bardic verse. Thereafter there was a period of decline, relieved by the work of three outstanding poets: Ó Bruadair in the seventeenth century, Aogán Ó Rathaille and Brian Merriman in the eighteenth. There has been a small but significant revival in the twentieth century – e.g. the short stories of Liam O'Flaherty.

SCRIPT

The Old Irish minuscule formerly used for Irish, has been replaced by the Roman alphabet, minus the letters *j, k, q, v, w, x, y, z*. In the Irish script the spirants were marked by superscript dot; the Latin script uses the letter h: thus Irish *ċ* = Latin *ch* /χ/. Long vowels are marked by acute.

PHONOLOGY

Consonants

With 18 letters to represent some 60 phonemes, Irish has one of the least efficient writing systems in use. The basic consonantal inventory is:

> stops: b, p, d, t, g, k; palatalized: b', p', d', t', g', k'
> fricatives: f, v, s, ʃ, x, γ, h; palatalized: f', x' (ç), γ' (→ [j])
> nasals: m, n, ŋ; palatalized: m', n', ŋ'
> lateral and flap: l, r; palatalized: l', r'
> semi-vowel: w

The non-palatalized consonants are associated with the 'broad' vowels, /a, o, u/, long and short; the palatalized with the 'slender' /i, e/. In other words, the vowels determine and indicate the palatal or non-palatal nature of consonants.

Vowel

The vowel series is:

slender: ɪː, ɪ, eː, ɛ, æ
broad: aː, a, oː, ɔ, uː, u
neutral: /ə/

The notation is highly redundant and inefficient: /oː/, for example, is variously represented as *ó*, *ói*, *eo*, *eoi*, *omh*, *omha(i)*. There are several diphthongs.

Stress

Stress is usually on the first syllable.

Mutation

(a) Lenition: (*see* also **Scottish Gaelic**). In Modern Irish, the stop to spirant mutation is observed in the initial of singular feminine nouns, following the definite article, the singular genitive of masculine nouns, after the singular series of possessive adjectives (except third feminine), after certain prepositions, numerals, and particles in the construct relationship, etc.: e.g.

bean 'woman': *an bhean* /ən vʹæn/, 'the woman';
crann 'tree'; *barr* 'top': *barr an chrainn* /bar.ən xrinʹ/ 'the top of the tree';
mac 'son': *mo mhac* /mo wak/ 'my son'; *hata an fhir bhig* 'the small man's hat'.

(b) Eclipsis (nasalization): this mutation takes place in noun initials after the plural possessive adjectives, after certain numerals, in the dative singular and the genitive plural, after the preposition *i* 'in'; in verbs after certain particles, after the negative relative *nach*, etc.: e.g.

ár 'our'; *cairde* 'friends' (sing. *cara*): *ár gcairde* /ār garʹdʹə/, 'our friends';
seacht 'seven'; *capall* 'horse': *seacht gcapall* /śæxt gapəl/, 'seven horses';
i 'in': *teach* 'house': *i dteach* /i dʹæx/, 'in a house'.

As will be seen from these examples, the sound resulting from eclipsis is marked in the script by a digraph: $p \rightarrow bp$, $t \rightarrow dt$, $c \rightarrow gc$, $b \rightarrow mb$, $d \rightarrow nd$, etc.

(c) The *h*- prefix: used with vocalic initials, after the article *na*, after *a* 'her', after certain prepositions and particles, and after *de* 'day': e.g.

aos 'age': *a haois* /a hisʹ/, 'her age';
Aoine 'Friday': *De hAoine* /dʹē hinʹə/, 'Friday' (lit: 'day of Friday');
ean 'bird': *na hein* /nə hēnʹ/ 'the birds'

(d) *t*- prefix: in masculine singular nouns with vowel initial, after definite article: e.g.

aran 'bread': *an t-aran* 'the bread';

and s- → ts- /t/ in feminine singular nominative and masculine genitive singular: e.g.

> seachtan (fem.) 'week': an tseachtain /ən tʹæxtən'/, 'the week'.

MORPHOLOGY AND SYNTAX

Two genders: masculine and feminine. Apart from a few linked endings, gender is not predictable. The definite article is *an* (sing.), *na* (pl.). The phonetic changes outlined above have to be borne in mind when the article is added.

Noun

There are five declensions in the literary standard, with three cases: nominative/ accusative – genitive – vocative. A few nouns have specific forms for the dative. Plural forms are divided into (a) strong (one form for all three cases) and (b) weak (nominative/genitive). The following examples show typical plural formations for each declension:

> 1st declension: *an capall bán* 'the white horse': pl. *na capaill bhána*; pl. gen. *na gcapall bán* 'of the white horses'.
> 2nd declension: *cloch* 'stone' (fem.): pl. *na clocha troma* 'the heavy stones'.
> 3rd declension: *ríocht* 'kingdom': pl. *na ríochtaí*; *gamhain* 'calf': pl. *na gamhna*.
> 4th declension: *iascaire* /iəsgir'i/, 'fisherman': pl. *iascairi*.
> 5th declension: *cathair* /kahir'/, 'city': pl. *na cathracha*.

CASES

Example: second declension noun, *an chloch* (fem.) 'the stone' (west Munster dialect):

	Singular	Plural
nominative/accusative	an chloch	na clocha
genitive	na cloiche	na gcloch
dative	don chloich	dosna clochaibh

The vocative has to be learnt: with masculine nouns of the first declension it is the same as the genitive singular; with feminine nouns of the first declension it is the same as the nominative. The preposed vocative particle *a* causes lenition: e.g. *Cáit > a Cháit!* 'Hi, Kathy!'

POSSESSIVE CONSTRUCT

As in Semitic, the possessed noun comes first, minus its article: e.g. *fuinneog an t-seomra* 'the window of the room'. In masculine nouns, the initial of the possessor noun is mutated, and a final broad consonant is mutated into the corresponding slender. Thus, from *aggart* 'priest': *teach an tsagairt* /ən tagər't/, 'the house of the priest'.

Adjective

As attribute follows noun, with concord for gender, number, and case. Thus, *fear mór* 'big man': gen. *fir mhóir* 'of a big man'; pl. *fir mhóra* 'big men': *fearaibh móra* 'to big men'.

Adjectival qualification may also be expressed by prefix: *dea-, so-* 'good', *droch-, do* 'bad': e.g. *dea.scéal* 'good news'; *do.líonta* 'hard to fill' (cf. Sanskrit *su-, dus-*).

In the first three declensions the adjective is modified to form a comparative, e.g. *deacair* 'difficult' – *deacra*; *fada* 'long' – *faide*. *Níos* precedes the comparative in a verbal sentence with *tá* 'is': e.g. *tá* X *níos faide ná* Y 'X is longer than Y'.

Some comparatives are suppletive: *olc* 'bad' – *measa*; *beag* 'small' – *lú*; *maith* 'good' – *fearr*.

Pronoun

PERSONAL
The independent subject forms are:

		Singular	Plural
1		mé	muid
2		tú	sibh
3	masc.	sé	siad
	fem.	sí	

These are also the object forms, except in the third person where *e/i* and *iad* replace *sé/sí* and *siad*: cf. *chonaic mé thú* 'I saw you'; *chonaic tú é* 'you saw him'.

POSSESSIVE ADJECTIVES

> sing. 1 *mo/m'*, 2 *do/d'*, 3 *a* (these induce lenition)
> pl. 1 *ár*, 2 *bhur*, 3 *a* (these induce eclipsis, i.e. voicing or nazalising of initial consonant)

A series of important prepositions combine with the personal pronouns, e.g. *ag* 'at': *agam, agat, aige/aici...* to express 'to have': e.g. *ta leabhar **agam*** 'I have a book' ('a book is at me').

DEMONSTRATIVE PRONOUN/ADJECTIVE
Three degrees of relative distance: *seo* 'this', *sin* 'that', *siúd* 'that yonder': e.g. *an fear seo* 'this man'.

INTERROGATIVE PRONOUN
cé 'who?'; *céard* 'what?': e.g. *Cé/céard a chonaic sé?* 'Whom/what did he see?'

RELATIVE PRONOUN

(a) Direct: *a* + lenition: e.g. *an obair a bhí sibh a dhéanamh* 'the work you were doing' where *dhéanamh* /jeːnə/ is the verbal noun of *deinim* 'I do'.

(b) Indirect: *a* + eclipsis, or, *ar* + lenition: e.g. *am buachaill a bhfuil a athair tinn* 'the boy whose father is ill'.

Numerals

1–10: *a haon, a dó, a trí, a ceathair, a cúig, a sé, a seacht, a hocht, a naoi, a deich* /ə d'e/; 11 *a haon déag*; 12 *a dó dhéag*; 13 *a trí déag*; 20 *fiche*; 30 *tríocha*; 40 *daichead*; 50 *caoga*; 100 *céad*. There is a specific series of numbers, 1–10, for persons. These end in -(*e*)*ar* < *fear* 'man': e.g. *seis.ear* 'six persons'.

Verb

In striking contrast with Old Irish, most verbs are regular in the modern language. There are two conjugations: I comprising monosyllabic stems with a future tense in -*fidh*/-*faidh* /ə/; and II polysyllabic stems with future tense in -(*e*)*oidh* /ɔ/. As regards inflection, there is considerable divergence among the various dialects; on the whole, the southern dialects (Munster) are more conservative, and here synthetic forms tend to be retained which are replaced by analytic forms in the north and west.

The tense/mood structure consists of indicative present (progressive or habitual), past habitual, preterite, future; conditional, subjunctive, imperative. Where analytic reductionism has produced an identical form for more than one person, the personal pronouns have to be added.

A key role is played by the verbal noun, whose form is not predictable; over a dozen different formulations are possible. Among the commonest are: -(*e*)*adh*, -*áil*, -*e*, -*t*. For example, from *bris* 'break', VN *briseadh*; from *tóg* 'take', VN *tógáil*, from *ith* 'eat', VN *ithe*; from *labhair* 'speak' VN *labhairt*. Uses of the verbal noun will be illustrated in the following description of the tenses.

Present progressive: auxiliary + subject + *ag* + VN; e.g. *tá mé ag léamh* 'I am reading'; *tá thú ag obair* 'you are working'. The same formula can be used in the past (*tá* → *bhí*) or future (*ta* → *beidh*).

Present habitual: in Galway and the north, only the first person singular and plural have synthetic forms: e.g. from *dún* 'to shut', *dúnaim* and *dúnaimid*. second and third persons have VN *dúnann* followed by personal pronouns – *tú*, *sé/sí*, *sibh*, *siad*. In Munster, synthetic forms may be retained for second singular and third plural.

Preterite: here again there is dialectal variation: in Galway, the initial is lenited: *dún* – *dhún*, *mol* – *mhol*, and this single form is followed by the personal pronouns, *except* in the first person plural, which has the synthetic form *dhún.amar*, 'we closed', *mhol.amar* 'we praised'. In Munster, the form is *do dhúnas*, *do dhúnais*, etc.

Future: the future form, as given above, + personal pronouns, again with an exception for the first person plural: *molfaidh mé/tú/sé/sí*, etc. but *molfaimid* in first person plural. The conditional endings are close to those of the future; the subjunctive is in *-a/-e* (depending on whether stem vowel is broad or slender).

Dependent forms: these occur with only a few verbs, but these few have a very high frequency rating, e.g. the auxiliary *tá*, whose dependent forms are:

(a) with negative *ní*: present: *níl*; past: *ni raibh* /n'i ro/;
(b) after interrogative particle *an*: present: *an bhfuil* /ə wil'), past: *an raibh*;
(c) after negative interrogative particle *nach* (as after interrogative);
(d) after relative link *go* (as b, c)

Thus, *bhí thú ann* 'you were there'; *An raibh tú ann?* 'Were you there?'

The autonomous form: the regular endings for all persons and both numbers are: present: *-t(e)ar*; past; *-adh*; future: *-far* /hər/. The past form does not take lenition. The autonomous form takes an object: *briseadh an fhuinneog* /ən iŋ'oːg/ can be rendered in English as 'they broke the window' or 'the window got broken'. A more exact translation would be 'breaking-occurred with relation to the window': cf. *dúntar an dorus* 'closing-occurs with relation to the door'; *óltar deoch* 'drinking-occurs with relation to a dram'. (Cf. Finnish and Estonian forms like *annetaan*, *räägitakse*, etc.)

Irish has several very common and very irregular verbs, with dependent forms, e.g. *téigh* 'to go', with independent pret. *chuaigh mé*; dependent pret. *ní dheachaigh mé*: future: *rachaidh mé*: VN: *dul*. There are similar thematic complications with *feic* 'to see', pret. *chonaic*; *déan* 'to do', pret. *rinne*; *tar* 'to come', pret. *tháinig*.

Prepositions

We have already seen the preposition coalescing with the personal pronouns to produce forms like *agam* 'I have', *againn* 'we have', etc. Similarly, with *de* 'from': *díom* 'from me', *díbh* 'from you (pl.)', etc.; *i* 'in': *ionam* 'in me', *ionat*, etc. This preposition combines with the article to form *san*: *san ardeaglais* /sən ardægləʃ/, 'in the cathedral'. Other examples: *ar* 'on': *orm, ort, air*; *as* 'out of': *asam, asat, as*.

Word order

VSO is basic.

1 Bhí an Briathar(1) ann i dtús báire
agus bhí an Briathar in éineacht le Dia,
agus ba Dhia an Briathar.
²Bhí sé ann i dtús báire in éineacht le Dia.
³Rinneadh an uile ní tríd
agus gan é ní dearnadh aon ní dá ndearnadh.
⁴Bhí beatha ann
agus ba é solas na ndaoine an bheatha.
⁵Agus tá an solas ag taitneamh sa dorchadas,
ach níor ghabh an dorchadas é.
⁶Bhí fear a tháinig ina theachtaire ó Dhia, agus Eoin a ba ainm dó. ⁷Tháinig sé ag déanamh fianaise chun fianaise a thabhairt i dtaobh an tsolais chun go gcreidfeadh cách tríd. ⁸Níorbh é féin an solas ach tháinig ag tabhairt fianaise i dtaobh an tsolais.

IRISH, OLD

INTRODUCTION

Old Irish is a Q-Celtic language, and the oldest attested form of Goidelic. It is known to us from (a) about 300 inscriptions in the Ogam runic script, dating from the fourth to the eighth centuries, and (b) an extensive corpus of very fine poetry and prose (eighth to twelfth centuries), a central place being taken by the splendid heroic romance, the *Tain bo Cúailnge* (seventh century). The main sources for these early works are the twelfth-century *Leabhar na h-Uidhe* ('The Book of the Dun Cow'), the twelfth-century *Book of Leinster* and the fourteenth-century *Yellow Book of Lecan*. The ninth-century *Book of Armagh*, containing the most ancient translation of the New Testament into Irish, should also be mentioned.

SCRIPT

The Roman alphabet was introduced in the fifth century. As a notation for Old Irish it is highly inadequate: mutation is only partially marked. The acute accent is used to mark long vowels, e.g. *sin* 'that', *sín* 'weather', and to identify true diphthongs: *céo* 'mist, fog'.

The letter *c* serves to notate initial /k/; medial and final post-vocalic plosives /b, d, g/ are notated by *p, t, k*: e.g. *fotae* /fode/, 'long'. Medial and final *b, d, g* notate the homorganic voiced fricatives: /v/ß, ð, γ/: e.g. *dub* /duv/, 'black'. /χ, f, θ/ are represented by *ch, ph, th*. Geminated *ll, nn, rr* are energetically pronounced held sounds, represented in transcription by *L, N, R*. Dotted consonants: *ṡ* = /h/, the lenited form of /s/: e.g. *son* 'sound' – *a ṡon* /ə.hon/; *ḟ* = Ø the lenited resultative of /f/: e.g. *fuil* 'blood' – *a ḟuil* /ə-ul'/.

PHONOLOGY

Consonants

The neutral or basic inventory of consonants is:

    stops: p, t, k, b, d, g
    fricatives: f, s, θ, ð, χ, γ
    nasals: m, n, N
    lateral and flap: L, R, l, r

Parallel to the basic series is the palatalized series: /p', t', k'/, etc. Certain consonants may also have had a labialized value.

Vowels

long and short: i, e, a, o, u

Plus eight long and three short diphthongs.

Mutation

Lenition: marked for the occlusives *p*, *t*, *k* → *ph*, *th*, *ch*. The spirant resultatives of lenited *b*, *d*, *g*, /v, ð, γ/, are not marked in the script, nor are those of other consonants. Similarly, the nasalized (eclipsed) values of the stop series are only partially notated: *b*, *d*, *g* → *mb*, *nd*, *ng*.

MORPHOLOGY AND SYNTAX

Three genders: masculine, feminine, neuter. Traces of a dual number are preserved, always accompanied by the numeral *da* 'two', with plural concord: e.g. *a dib crannaib* 'from two trees'; *in da ḟer moir* 'the two big men'.

Definite article

Masc. *in*, fem. *ind*, nt. *a*; pl. *ind – inna – inna*. The article is declined in four cases: nominative, accusative, genitive, dative, with little variation from the nominative form: thus, masc.: *in – (s)in – ind – (s) ind*. The three plural oblique cases have the same forms for all three genders: *inna/isna – inna – (s)naib*.

Noun

The noun is declined in the same cases as the definite article, plus a vocative. About a dozen types of declension are distinguished, according to stem; in several of these, only the genitive singular is significantly inflected. Example: a feminine *ā*-stem: *aram* 'number':

	Singular	Plural	Dual
nominative/vocative	áram	áirmea	ár(a)im
accusative	áram	airmea	—
genitive	áirme	áram	áram
dative	ár(a)im	áirmib	áirmib

In general, Old Irish declension shows a gradual levelling out of the nominative/accusative opposition, and a reduction of final vowels to /ə/.

Some nouns are highly irregular, e.g. *ben* 'woman': gen. sing. *mná*; pl. nom. *mná*, gen. *ban*, dat. *mnáib*.

POSSESSIVE CONSTRUCT

Possessed (minus article) precedes possessor: e.g. *claideb ind ḟir* 'the man's sword', *claideb inna fer* 'the men's swords'; cf. *son cíuil* 'the sound of music'.

Adjective

As attribute, adjective follows noun, agreeing with it in gender and number. With regard to initial mutation, adjectives behave as nouns do after the article. Like nouns, adjectives are classified according to stem. Examples: *in mathair oac* 'the young mother'; *a crann n-ard* 'the high tree'; *isnaib cathaib móraib* 'in the great battles'.

COMPARISON

A comparative is made by adding *-(i)u* to the positive, usually with palatalization: e.g. *sen* 'old' – *siniu*. The dative case follows the comparative: e.g. *ard. u slébib* 'higher than mountains'. Several comparatives are suppletive: e.g. *maith* 'good' – *ferr*; *már* 'big' – *máo*; *olc* 'bad' – *messa*.

Pronoun

The pronominal system can be set out as (a) independent forms, and (b) three sets of infixed/suffixed forms. The independent forms are:

sing. 1 *mé*, 2 *tú*, 3 masc. *(h)é*, fem. *sí*, nt. *(h)ed*;
pl. 1 *sní*, 2 *sí*, 3 *(h)é*.

These have emphatic forms (the spelling varies):

		Singular	*Plural*
1		meisse	snisni
2		tussu	sissi
3	masc.	(h)é.som	
	fem.	si.ssi	(h)ésidi
	nt.	(h)ed.ón	

The first set of infixed forms appears as sing. 1 *m*, 2 *t*, 3 *a – s – a*; pl. 1 *n*, 2 *b*, 3 *s*. These follow most of the pre-verbal particles: e.g. *ro-cluinethar* 'he hears'; *rom-chluinethar* 'he hears me'.

The second series has a dental prefix *t/d*: sing. 1 *tom/dom/tum*, 2 *tot/tat* … It follows certain pre-verbals such as *ad, aith, com*: e.g. *ad-cí* 'he sees'; *atot-chí* 'he sees you (sing.)'.

The third series has a *d-* prefix + the same endings as the second series; it is used in relative clauses: e.g. *in fer no-**dom**-chara* 'the man who loves me'; *in fer no-**da**-cara* 'the man who loves her'.

All singular forms are followed by lenition, except third person masculine, which is followed by nasalization, as is third person feminine in the first series (*s*); the feminine forms in the other two series do not affect the following consonant.

Third-person singular simple verbs may also take suffixed pronominal forms: e.g. *beirthium* 'he carries me'; *beirthiut* 'he carries you'.

Pronominal markers are attached to certain prepositions: e.g. *lem* 'with me', *dim* 'from me', *duit* 'to you': e.g. *Scél lem dúib* 'tidings – with me – to you (pl.)' = 'I have news for you'. Compare the eleventh-century *Invocation of the Holy*

Spirit (Murphy 1970: 52):

> In Spirut nóeb immun, innunn ocus ocunn
> 'May the Holy Spirit be about us, in us and with us.'

DEMONSTRATIVE PRONOUN/ADJECTIVE

(a) Indeclinable postpositional: *sa/sa* 'this', *sin* 'that': e.g. *in fer.sin* 'that man'; *ind fir.so* 'these men'.

(b) Deictic particle *-í* added to definite article: e.g. *indí.sin* 'these' (masc.); *donaib-í* 'to those'.

INTERROGATIVE PRONOUN

cía 'who?'; *cid* 'what?' The particle *in* introduces a positive question; the negative form is *in(n)ád*; e.g. *in cruthaigedar Día domun do duiniu?* 'Does God create the world for a man?'

Numerals

1 *oén*: indeclinable, compounds with following noun which is lenited: *oénfer* 'one man'. 2 *da*; 3 *tri*; 4 *cethir*: these are declined. 5–10: *cóic, sé, secht, ocht, noí, deich*: these are indeclinable. 11–19: *déac* (genitive plural of *deich*) is added: e.g. *di huair déac* '12 hours'; *tri fir deac* '13 men'. 20 *fiche*; 30 *tricho*; 40 *cethorcho*: these are nouns followed by genitive plural, e.g. *tri ferdruíd, trí bandruíd* 'three druids and three druidesses'.

Verb

The Old Irish verb is immensely complex, and no more than a few pointers to its structure can be attempted here.

1. Verbs are weak or strong; a distinguished feature is the presence or absence of a vocalic ending in the conjunct third person: cf.

> strong: *as.beirø* 'says' (< Indo-European stock);
> weak: *marba* 'kills' (Goidelic innovation).

2. Both strong and weak verbs have absolute and conjunct forms. Absolute forms are not preceded by particles: e.g. *Móraid Conn slógu* 'Conn praises a host.' Conjunct forms are preceded by such particles as *ni* (negating): e.g. *ní móraø Conn slógø* 'Conn does not praise a host.' (Examples from Quin 1975.)

3. Compound verbs are formed by means of prepositional prefix: this acts in the same way as the particles referred to in (2), and the verb is therefore in conjunct form: root *biru* 'bear, bring': compound: ***do.biur*** 'I bring'. The form *-biur* is said to be 'bound', as it cannot stand alone.

4. Stems: there are present, subjunctive, *f*-future, *s*-future, *s*- and *t*- preterite stems. The *s*-preterite is common in weak verbs, the *t*-preterite in strong verbs, and there is a reduplicated preterite, e.g. *cingid* 'he strides', pret. ***cechaign***: ***Cechain in duine in salm*** 'The man sang the psalm'.

Principal parts of strong verbs: some examples (in third person singular):

	Present	Present subjunctive	Future	Preterite	Verbal noun (variable gender)
'sing'	canid, -cain	-cana	-cechna	cechain	cétal (nt.)
'break'	bongid, -boing	-bó	-biba	bob(a)ig	búain (fem.)
'take'	gaibid, -gaib	-gaba	-géba	ga(i)b	gabá(i)l (fem.)
'run'	rethid, -reith	-ré	-ré	rdith	riuth (masc.)

5. Personal endings: indicative present and preterite of *berid* 'carries':

> present singular: 1 *biru*, 2 *biri*, 3 *berid*; plural: 1 *bermai*, 2 *beirthe*, 3 *berait*; preterite singular: 1 *biurt*, 2 *birt*, 3 *bert*; plural: 1 *bertamar*, 2 *bertaid*, 3 *bertar*.

6. Verbal particles: e.g. *no/nu* with unbound forms: e.g. *No marbadfiru* 'He was killing men'; *No crenainn ech* 'I bought a horse'; *No scríbmais libru* 'We wrote books'. The particle *ro* has perfective force: e.g. *Ro marb in fer* 'He has killed the man'.

7. Deponent verbs in *-r* (*cf.* **Latin**): e.g. *labraithair* 'speaks'. The passive form is third person only, used as an impersonal verb, which can take an object: e.g. *no.m.marbthar* 'there is a killing with reference to me' = 'I am killed'.

8. Relative clause: leniting (after nominative or accusative referent), nasalizing (after accusative referent); the referent must be third singular/plural or first plural. Examples from Quin (1975: 54):

> in fer **ch**eles in claideb 'the man who hides the sword'
>
> in claideb **ch**eles in fer 'the sword the man hides'
>
> in fer **nád ch**eil in claideb 'the man who does not hide the sword'

The nasalizing relative is also used to indicate modality, the 'how' of an action: e.g.

> in gabál **ng**aibes in catt in lochaid
> 'the seizing, by-way-of which the cat seizes the mouse'

9. Verb 'to be':

> sing. 1 *at-to*, 2 *at-tai*, 3 *at-tá*; pl. 1 *at.-táam*, 2 *at.táaid*, 3 *at-táat*.

Negative: *fil* is used, + infixed **accusative** pronoun (original meaning of *fil* is 'sees'):

> sing. 1 *ním-fil* 2 *nít-fil*, 3 *ní-fil*; pl. 1 *nín-fil*, 2 *níb-fil*, 3 *nís.fil*.

Copula:

> sing. 1 *am*, 2 *at*, 3 *is*; pl. 1 *ammi*, 2 *adib*, 3 *it*

Bound form: *ní-ta*, etc.: e.g. *Adib céili, nítad ríg* 'You are companions, not kings.'

Prepositions

Prepositions take various cases; e.g. (*h*)*i* takes the accusative for motion into something, the dative for rest in a place. *Co* 'with' takes the dative: e.g. *co claidbib* 'with swords'. Examples: *is.ind fid* 'in the wood'; *a dib crannaib* 'out of two trees'; *a sidib* 'from the fairy mounds'; *cen brón, cen dube, cen bás* 'without sorrow, without grief, without death' (description of *Tír nan Óg* 'Land of Youth').

Word order

VSO is basic.

644

ITALIAN

INTRODUCTION

Belonging to the Italic branch of Indo-European, Italian is the official language of the Republic of Italy and is spoken today by over 50 million people, if the dialect form spoken in Sardinia is included. In addition, Italian is one of the three official languages of Switzerland, and is spoken in large communities in North and South America, in North Africa, and elsewhere, which probably add 5 or 6 million to give an overall total of about 60 million.

A dialectal division of Italy running roughly along the line of the Northern Appennines has long been recognized (see, for example, Dante, *De Vulgari Eloquentia*, X). To the north of this line are Piedmontese, Lombardian, Venetian, etc.; to the south lie Tuscan, Umbrian, Neapolitan, Calabrese, and Sicilian. In spite of the homogenizing influence of the standard language used by the media, most of the dialects are still very much alive, and many Italians use the language on two socio-linguistic levels – the local dialect in the family circle and among friends, Standard Italian on all more formal occasions. Certain dialectal features differ markedly from the standard norm, e.g. in the north, the palatal fricative reflex of Low Latin *pl-* as /tʃ/: e.g. /tʃatsa/ for standard *piazza*; and, in the south, the interdental fricatives of Tuscan, e.g. /θ/.

The earliest textual example of written Italian dates from the tenth century. In the ensuing 300 years, poetry was written in several dialects, until Tuscan was suddenly transmuted into one of the world's great literary languages by the genius of Dante Alighieri (1265–1321); the *Divina Commedia* was written between 1310 and 1314. Petrarca and Boccaccio complete the trio of great fourteenth-century writers. The prestige thus conferred upon Tuscan – specifically Florentine – usage ensured its adoption in the nineteenth century, when political union brought the question of a unified national language to a head. Alessandro Manzoni, who presided over the committee (1868) which took this decision, was himself impelled to rewrite his masterpiece *I Promessi Sposi* in Florentine Tuscan (the original version was in Manzoni's native Lombardian dialect; Tuscan version 1840).

SCRIPT

Latin alphabet; *j*, *k*, *w*, *x*, *y* appear in foreign words only.

PHONOLOGY

The Florentine standard inventory is given.

Consonants

stops: p, b, t, d, k, g; labialized /k/: [k°]
affricates: ts, dz, tʃ, dʒ
fricatives: f, v, s/z, ʃ
nasals: m, n, ɲ, (ŋ)
lateral and flap: l, ʎ, r
semi-vowel: j, w

/ɲ/ is notated as *gn*: e.g. *ogni* 'each' = /ɔɲi/; /k/ is notated as *c*/*ch*; /w/ is notated as *uo*: *uomo* 'man' = /wɔmo/, or *ua*: *acqua* 'water' = /akwa/. The letter *z* is unvoiced /c/ or voiced /dz/: e.g. *zucchero* /tsukɛrɔ/ 'sugar'; *zelo* /dzɛlo/ 'zeal'. The distinction may be phonemic.

Vowels

i, e, ɛ, a, ɔ, o, u

/e,ɛ/ and /o,ɔ/ contrast in stressed syllables. Typically, Italian words end in vowels.

Stress

Stress is frequently on the penultimate syllable, but there are many exceptions: e.g. the third person singular past definite is always stressed on the final, as are many words marked with final grave: e.g. *virtù*, *caffè*, etc. Antepenultimate stress appears in infinitives like *vèndere* 'to sell', in the third person plural present indicative form (*màndano* 'they send'), and in many words like *mèdico* 'doctor', *àngelo* 'angel', *piròscafo* 'steamer'.

MORPHOLOGY AND SYNTAX

Italian has two genders and two numbers.

Noun

Nominal endings are, up to a point, coded for gender: e.g. most nouns in -*o* are masculine with plural in -*i*: e.g. *il bambino* 'the child' – *i bambini*; and most nouns in -*a* are feminine with plural in -*e*: e.g. *la stella* 'the star' – *le stelle*. These categories are not exclusive, however: cf. *la mano* 'the hand', pl. *le mani*; *il poeta* 'the poet', pl. *i poeti*.

Most nouns in -*e* are masculine: e.g. *il fiume* 'the river' – *i fiumi*, and all in -*zione*, -*gione*, -*udine* are feminine.

There is no declensional system; syntactic relationships are expressed by prepositions which typically coalesce with the articles, e.g.

a 'to' + *il* → *al*: similarly, *ai*, *agli*, *alla*, *alle*.
in 'in' + *il* → *nel*: similarly, *nei*, *negli*, *nella*, *nelle*.
con 'with' + *il* → *col*: similarly, *coi*, *cogli*, *colla*, *colle*.

Articles

The definite article is marked for gender and number: masc. *il – i*; fem. *la – le*. Before vocalic initial, both *il* and *la* become *l'*; *lo* is the form taken by the masculine article before such frequent initials as /ɲ/ and *s* + consonant: conditions which also change the plural *i* to *gli*: e.g. *lo squillo* 'ringing', *gli scopi* 'the aims'.

The indefinite article is masc. *un(o)*, fem. *un(a)*, with pl. forms: masc. *dei/degli*, fem. *delle*.

Adjective

The adjective agrees in gender and number with the noun, which it may precede or follow; some adjectives, e.g. of nationality, colour, always follow. A few very common adjectives have shortened forms used before masculine nouns beginning with a consonant (subject to the same constraints as those affecting the use of the definite article): e.g. *un bel dì* 'a fine day'; *un bello specchio* 'a beautiful mirror'.

COMPARATIVE
più + *di*: e.g. *Questa ragazza e più bella di quella* 'This girl is prettier than that one.'

The customary suppletive forms are found with very common adjectives: *buono* 'good' – *migliore*; *cattivo* 'bad' – *peggiore*; *poco* 'little' – *meno*; *grande* 'big' – *maggiore*.

Pronoun

The Italian pronominal system has (a) independent forms, showing a formal/informal distinction in the second and third persons. Thus, second person singular *tu* is informal, contrasting with *voi* 'you' (sing. or. pl. informal). In the third person formal *egli/ella* are distinguished from informal *lui/lei*; the plural of both is *loro*. The form chosen as the most acceptable for polite address, however, is *lei* (sing.), pl. *loro*, though *voi* is acceptable, especially in the south.

Secondly (b) sets of disjunctive and conjunctive pronouns, the latter subdivided into accusative and dative forms. Thus:

	Singular			*Plural*		
independent:	1 io	2 tu	3 lui, lei	1 noi	2 voi	3 loro
disjunctive:	me	te	lui, lei	noi	voi	loro
conjunctive: acc.	mi	ti	lo, la	ci	vi	li, le
dat.	mi/me	ti/te	gli/glie/le	ci/ce	vi/ve	loro

The *-e* forms are used before *lo, la, li, le*, and *ne* 'of it' (= Fr. *en*): e.g. *gli + lo* → *glielo*: *glielo diedi* 'I gave it to him'.

Conjunctive forms follow an infinitive, whose object they form: e.g. *volevo dar.glie.lo* 'I wanted to give it to him'.

Pronominal complexes, consisting of *si* → *se* or *ci* → *ce* + *la* or *ne*, follow certain verbs: e.g. *dar.se.la a gambe* 'to take to one's heels'; *metter.ce.la* 'to do one's utmost'.

POSSESSIVE ADJECTIVES

These are accompanied by the article, precede the noun, and show number and gender, except *loro* 'your/s, their/s', which is invariable: e.g. *il mio, la mia, i miei, le mie*, etc. but *il Loro, la Loro, i Loro*, etc.

DEMONSTRATIVE PRONOUN/ADJECTIVE

questo 'this', *quel(lo)* 'that'. These are marked for gender and number: e.g. *questo/quel ragazzo* 'this/that boy'; *quella ragazza* 'that girl'.

INTERROGATIVE PRONOUN

chi 'who?'; *che* 'what?'

RELATIVE PRONOUN

il quale, la quale, i quali, le quali; che (indeclinable): e.g. *la ragazza che vedi* 'the girl (whom) you see'; *il libro che sto leggendo* 'the book which I am reading'.

Numerals

1–10: *uno/una, due, tre, quattro, cinque, sei, sette, otto, nove, dieci*; 11 *undici*; 12 *dodici*; 13 *tredici*; 20 *venti*; 30 *trenta*; 40 *quaranta*; 100 *cento*.

Verb

Italian verbs may be conveniently divided into three conjugations: (a) verbs in *-a*; (b) verbs in *-e*; and (c) verbs in *-i*. Verbs in *-e* are further sub-divided into two classes, depending on whether the stem or the ending is stressed: e.g. *chièdere* 'to close'; *sedère* 'to sit'. Verbs in *-i* may be regular or may take a stem augment, *-isc-*. An important group of *-e* verbs has irregular forms in the past definite: e.g. *prendere* 'take' – *presi*.

Verbs are transitive or intransitive, and there are indicative, imperative, and subjunctive moods. Both the indicative and the subjunctive have present and imperfect tenses; the indicative has in addition a past definite, a future, and a conditional. The non-finite forms include the infinitive, a gerund, and present and past participles. The gerund and the past participle combine with auxiliaries such as *stare* 'be', *avere* 'have', *essere* 'be' to form composite tenses: e.g. a progressive: *sto scrivendo* 'I am writing'; *stavo dicendo* 'I was saying'; and a perfect: *abbiamo mangiato* 'we have eaten'; *sono andato* 'I went'.

The basic verbs of motion – *andare* 'go', *venire* 'come', *partire* 'depart' *entrare* 'enter', etc. – are always conjugated with *essere*. Some verbs expressing motion, e.g. *correre* 'run', may be conjugated with either *avere* or *essere*, depending on sense.

SPECIMEN PARADIGM
1st conjugation verb, *mandare* 'to send':

Indicative mood

> present: mand-o, -i, -a; -iamo, -ate, -ano (stress on penultimate syllable, except in third person plural)
> imperfect: mandav-o, -i, -a; -amo, -ate, -ano
> past definite: mandai, mandaste, mando; mand-ammo, -aste, -arono
> future: mander-o, -i, -a; -emo, -ete, -anno
> conditional: mandere-i, -sti, -bbe; -mmo, -ste, -bbero

Subjunctive mood

> present: mand-i, -i, -i; -iamo, -iate, -ino
> imperfect: mandass-i, -i, -e; -imo, mandaste, mandassero
> imperative mood: -, manda, mandi; mandiamo, mandate, mandino
> gerund: mandando; past participle: mandato

PASSIVE
Can be made analytically by means of such auxiliaries as *essere*, *venire*, *andare* followed by the past participle: e.g. *Il manoscritto è andato perduto* 'The manuscript has been lost'; *Le città vengono bombardate* 'The cities are being bombed.'

Wherever possible, Italian prefers the impersonal construction with *si*: e.g. *Si parla inglese qui* 'English is spoken here.'

Negation

The general negating particle is *non* preceding the verb; negation may be duplicated or triplicated: e.g. *Non voglio niente* 'I don't want anything' (lit. 'nothing'); *Non lo vuole nessuno* 'No one wants it' (lit. 'doesn't want').

Prepositions

Simple, e.g. *di*, *a*, *con*, *per*, etc.; or compound: *davanti a* 'in the presence of, in front of'; *di lato a* 'beside'; *al di sopra di* 'above'. As in French, certain verbs take specific prepositions before a following infinitive; e.g. *dimenticare di* 'to forget', *cominciare a* 'to begin to': e.g. *mi sono dimenticato di avvertirti* 'I forgot to let you know'; *cominciare ad andare* 'to start walking'.

Word order

Depending on emphasis, SOV, VOS, VSO are all possible.

[1] Al principio,
prima che Dio creasse il mondo,
c'era colui che è « la Parola ».
Egli era con Dio;
Egli era Dio.
[2] Egli era al principio con Dio.
[3] Per mezzo di lui Dio ha creato ogni cosa.
Senza di lui non ha creato nulla.
[4] Egli era vita
e la vita era luce per gli uomini.
[5] Quella luce risplende nelle tenebre
e le tenebre non l'hanno vinta.
[6] Dio mandò un uomo:
si chiamava Giovanni.
[7] Egli venne come testimone della luce
perché tutti gli uomini,
ascoltandolo,
credessero nella luce.
[8] Non era lui, la luce:
Giovanni era un testimone della luce.

ITELMEN

INTRODUCTION

Itelmen was formerly known as Kamchadal. The Itelmen live or lived – they are now virtually extinct – in the Koryak National Okrug in Kamchatka. The language belongs to the Chukotko-Kamchatkan group, and was unwritten, apart from a brief experimental period in the 1930s.

PHONOLOGY

Consonants

The consonantal inventory is rather more elaborate than those of Chukchi and Koryak. The voiced plosives are missing but /p, t, k, q/ + their palatalized counterparts occur, as does the glottal stop. The voiceless uvular fricative is represented by χ. There are three laterals, including /ḻ/.

Vowels

The vowel system is simple:

i, e, a, ə, o, u

MORPHOLOGY AND SYNTAX

Noun

Nouns are classified as human or non-human. Seven or eight cases are formed; the plural marker is 'n: e.g. *sleč* 'eagle', pl. *sle'n*.

Specimen declension: *wač* 'stone'; singular:

nominative	wač
locative	wač.ank
instrumental	wa.l
dative	wač.anke
ablative	wačan.x'al
comitative	k'wa.čom
causative	wačan.ket

The plural nominative is *wa'n*; locative *wa'nk*, etc.

Pronoun

PERSONAL PRONOUNS

Sing. 1 *kəmma*, 2 *kəzza*, 3 *'ənna*; pl. 1 *muza'n*, 2 *tuza'n*, 3 *itχ*. These are declined in 14 cases, including an ergative.

Numerals

Only 1–4 have been retained: *kŋiŋ, kasχ, č'oq, č'aaq.*

Verb

Itelmen has monopersonal (intransitive) verbs with six personal forms, and polypersonal (transitive) verbs with 28 personal forms in each of three moods: indicative, subjunctive, and imperative/optative.

TENSES

The past tense marker is Ø; present -*s/z*-; future, -*al'*-. The aspect marker precedes the tense marker; e.g. -*kzo*- is the durative aspect marker, so present tense in durative aspect is marked by -*kzo.s*-.

Examples of polypersonal paradigm of *ančpəs* 'to teach someone':

1st person – 2nd	*t.ančp.γen* 'I teach you'
2nd person – 1st	*Ø.ančp. məŋk* 'you teach me'
3rd person – 1st	*Ø.ančp.γomnen* 'he teaches me'
1st plural – 2nd	*n.ančp.γen* 'we teach you'

NEGATION

Formed analytically, e.g. by means of the negating particle *qam* preceding the sense-verb in the invariable form in -*kaq*: *qam vetatkaq* 'I don't work/did not work'; 'you don't/did not work', etc. Person and tense are inferred from the context.

Prepositions

There are no native prepositions, but Itelmen has borrowed a few from Russian.

Word order

SVO, SOV both occur. If S is a personal pronoun, it is in the ergative case: cf. *kmənvən tančpčen p'eč* 'I taught the boy' where *kmənvən* is the ergative case of *kəmma*, the first person pronoun.

IVRIT

INTRODUCTION

Modern Hebrew, or Ivrit, belongs to the Semito-Hamitic branch of the Afro-Asiatic phylym. The rebirth of Hebrew, as a spoken language, from the literary Hebrew which was used in the Mediterranean area for a thousand years, began in eastern Europe in the mid-nineteenth century and was transplanted to Palestine with the arrival there of Jewish settlers from Russia. The pioneer role in this process was played by Eliezer Ben-Yehuda (1858–1922). In 1948 Ivrit was officially adopted as the national language of the State of Israel. The pronunciation represents a compromise between Ashkenazi (Northern and Eastern) and Sephardic (Southern, specifically of Spain) models.

Essentially, Ivrit is the Hebrew of the *Torah*, plus enormous lexical expansion and many phonological and morphological modifications. These modifications are more or less radical, depending on the register of speech or writing. Thus, formal literary style may use forms approximating to Classical Hebrew, which are quite inappropriate in colloquial parlance. For example, the rules governing the alternation of consonants are observed in literary style, ignored in the colloquial. In step with this division, two varieties of orthography are in use: *xaser*, conservative, i.e. classical, spelling without the pointing; and *male*, used in the press, with the vowels /o/ and /u/ written with *vav*, /i/ with *yod*.

The thousands of new items with which the Hebrew lexicon has been enriched are in part derived from Semitic roots, in part loan-words.

SCRIPT

Classical Hebrew basis.

PHONOLOGY

Consonants

    stops: p, b, t, d, k, g, ʔ
    affricates: ts
    fricatives: f, v, s, ʃ, z, x, h
    nasals: m, n
    lateral and flap: l, r, ʀ
    semi-vowel: j

Ivrit has a very extensive range of initial and medial clusters: e.g. /gz, cd, pc, pg, cx/. Certain clusters are realized with the help of a schwa vowel: thus, nd- /nᶜd/. /tʃ, dʒ/ occur in loan-words.

Vowels

> i, ɪ, e, a, o/ɔ, u, ə
> diphthongs: /oa/ = [oə], /ua, ea, ia/.

MORPHOLOGY AND SYNTAX

Noun

Ivrit has two genders, masculine and feminine; and three numbers, singular, dual, and plural. The dual is used mainly for naturally paired objects: the ending is *-aim*: *eynaim* 'two eyes'; and units of time: *šnataim* 'two years'. The dual takes the plural form of the verb. The masculine plural ending is *-im*, fem. *-ot*: e.g. *xaver* 'comrade', pl. *xaverim*. There are a few exceptions, e.g. *'avot* 'fathers'.

The definite article is *ha-*.

CONSTRUCT FORMS

(*See* **Semito-Hamitic Languages**): many nouns governed by a following noun, or by a personal pronominal suffix, undergo a kind of stretto modification: thus, *šalom* 'peace, welfare', *šlom ha.mišpaxa* 'the welfare of the family'; *bayit* 'house', **bet** *ha.sefer* 'house of the book' ('school'); *braxa* 'blessing', **birkat**.*i* 'my blessing'; *'erec* 'country', *'arc.i* 'my country' (in *birkati*, the *-t-* is the Semitic feminine ending which reappears in the construct).

The construct, which is the natural Semitic way of expressing the genitive relationship, is giving way (as in Maltese) to an analytical construction with the particle *šel*: e.g. *ha.bayit šelo* 'his house', *ha.bayit šel Dov* 'Dov's house'.

ACCUSATIVE

A definite object after a transitive verb is signalled by the particle *et*: e.g. *ten.li et.ha.sefer* 'give me the book'; *tisgor et.ha.delet* 'close the door' (*sefer* 'book'; *delet* 'door').

Adjective

The attributive adjective follows the noun, and agrees with it in gender and number. The article is resumed: e.g. *ha.binyan ha.gadol* 'the big building'; pl. *ha.binyanim ha.gədolim*. Adjectives have construct forms.

COMPARISON

A comparative is made with *yoter*, + *mi* 'from': e.g. *Dov yoter xazak mi.Moše* 'Dov is stronger than Mose.'

Pronoun

The basic personal forms are followed here by their objective and possessive suffix forms:

		Singular			*Plural*		
1		ani	oti	-i	anu	otanu	-enu
2	masc.	ata	otxa	-xa	atcm	ctxcm	-xcm
	fem.	at	otax	-ex	aten	etxen	-xen
3	masc.	hu	oto	-o	hem	otam	-am
	fem.	hi	ota	-a	hen	otan	-an

An alternative set of objective forms is affixed to the verb. These are almost identical to the possessive forms; the first person singular is *-ni* instead of *-i*.

The possessive forms are added to nouns in the construct: e.g. *Ma šlom.xa?* 'How is your health?' (to a man); *ma šlom.ex?* (to a woman).

Objective forms: cf. *yekabel otxa = yekablexa* 'he will receive you (masc.)'.

DEMONSTRATIVE PRONOUN/ADJECTIVE

ze (masc.), *zot* (fem.), pl. *'ele* (common), following the noun, and taking definite article: e.g. *ha.sefer ha.ze* 'this book'; *ha.anišim ha.'ele* 'these people'.

INTERROGATIVE PRONOUN

mi 'who?'; *ma* 'what?'.

RELATIVE PRONOUN

ašer: e.g. *ha.yeled ašer diber ivrit* 'the boy who spoke Hebrew'.

Numerals

The feminine forms are used in counting: 1–10: *'axat, štayim, šaloš, 'arba, xameš, šeš, ševa, šmone, teša, 'eser*. Teens are formed by construct + 10: e.g. *'axat.'ešre, šteym.'ešre, šloš.'ešre*. 20 *'ešrim*; 30 *šlošim*; 40 *'arba'im*; 100 *me'a*.

The numbers 3 to 10 inclusive have the following alternative forms: *šlošet ha-* 'three of'; *'arba'at ha.* 'four of'; *xamešet ha.* 'five of', etc. Cf. *šaloš oniot* 'three ships'; *šlošet ha.oniot* 'the three ships'.

The law of inverse polarity obtains (*see* **Arabic**).

Verb

As in other Semitic languages, the radical is usually a triliteral, though two- and four-literal radicals abound.

Formally, the aspectual system of the Classical Hebrew verb is retained, but this is construed in Ivrit as a tense system with past- and future-tense forms. There is also a present tense formed on different lines. The derived versions of the stem (the binyanim, *see* **Hebrew**) are also retained.

THE TENSE SYSTEM

Past tense: stem + affix, marked for person and number, additionally, in second and third persons singular and plural, for gender.

Future tense: prefix + stem + affix (in second and third masculine/feminine plural and second feminine singular).

Present: *me-* is prefixed to the masculine singular imperative; marked for gender and number.

As illustration, the tense system of *DBR* 'to speak':

Imperative: masc. sing. *daber*; fem. sing. *dabri*, masc. pl. *dabru*, fem. pl. *daberna*.

			Singular	*Plural*
Future:	1		**a**.daber	**ne**.daber
	2	masc.	**te**.daber	**te**.dabr.**u**
		fem.	**te**.dabr.**i**	**te**.daber.**na**
	3	masc.	**ye**.daber	**ye**.dabr.**u**
		fem.	**te**.daber	**te**.daber.**na**
Past:	1		dibar.**ti**	dibar.**nu**
	2	masc.	dibar.**ta**	dibar.**tem**
		fem.	dibar.**t**	dibar.**ten**
	3	masc.	diber	dibr.**u**
		fem.	dibr.**a**	dibr.**u**
Present:		masc. sing. **me**daber	masc. pl. **me**dabr.**im**	
		fem. sing. **me**daber**et**	fem. pl. **me**.dabr.**ot**	

THE BINYANIM

For more detail, *see* **Hebrew**. Here, some examples of Ivrit usage.

(a) *nif'al:* the prefix is *ni-*: the form expresses the passive or intransitive of the *pa'al* (active) form: *patax* 'he opened' – *niftax* '… was opened'; *moxer* 'he sells' – *nimkar* '… is sold'; *šalxu oti la.malon* 'they sent me to the hotel'; *nišlaxti la.malon* 'I was sent to the hotel'.

(b) *hif'il:* the prefix is *h-*; *hif'il* is itself the causative binyan of *pa'al*; it is used to form causatives: e.g. *šama'ti* 'I heard' – *hišma'ati* 'I proclaimed'; *gadal* 'he grew' – *higdil* 'he enlarged (something)'.

(c) *hitpa'el:* the prefix is *hit-*, with extensive assimilation at junctures. The form makes intransitive verbs from transitives, with extension to passive sense: e.g. *šina* 'he changed something' – *hištana* 'he changed' (intrans.); *šiamen* 'he bored someone' – *hištaamamti* 'I was bored'.

There are several examples in the above of consonant alternation, involving *b/v*, *p/f*, *k/x*. In this context, the alternation affects first and second radicals. The general rule is that initial *b*, *p*, *k* become *v*, *f*, *x* in non-initial position and in specific phonological environments:

ptax 'open!' (imperative) – *tiftax* 'you will open'
bikašti 'I asked' – *le.vakeš* 'to ask'
pne 'turn!' (imperative) – *tifne* 'you will turn'

NEGATION

The general marker is *lo*: e.g. *hu yaqia maxar* 'he'll arrive tomorrow'; *hu lo yaqia maxar* 'he'll not arrive tomorrow'. *'eyn* negates the existential verb *yeš* 'there is/ are', and the present: e.g. *ani medaber* 'I speak' – *'eyneni medaber* 'I do not speak'; *eyn lak adam še.eyn lo šaa* lit. 'there is not to you (*lak*) a man (*adam*) that (*še*) has not his hour (*šaa*)', i.e. 'no man but has his hour'.

Prepositions

These take the personal possessive affixes: e.g. with *avur* 'for': *avuri* 'for me', *avurenu* 'for us'. Some fuse with the article, e.g. *le* 'to': *le + ha → la*, e.g. *la.doar ha.merkazi* 'to the main post-office'.

Word order

SVO is basic; a pronominal S is, of course, not always necessary.

ילפני שנברא העולם היה המשיח עם אלוהים. הוא היה עם
אלוהים מבראשית, והוא עצמו אלוהים.· יהוא ברא את כל הקיים — אין
דבר שלא נברא על־ידו. ייש בו חיי נצח, וחיים אלה העניקו אור לבני־
האדם. יחייו הם האור הזורח והמאיר בחשכה, והחשכה אינה יכולה
להתגבר על אור זה.
יאלוהים שלח אדם בשם יוחנן להעיד שישוע המשיח הוא האור
האמיתי, כדי שכולם יאמינו בו. יייוחנן עצמו לא היה האור; הוא רק
נשלח לזהות את האור האמיתי שבא לעולם כדי להאיר לכל בני־האדם.

JAPANESE, CLASSICAL

INTRODUCTION

The Neolithic culture known as the Joomon lasted about 6,000 years in Japan, to be followed in the third century BC by the Yayoi neolithic culture, which lasted about 500 years. According to one school of thought, the Joomon people were the aboriginal inhabitants of Japan, and the ancestors of the Ainu people, who were ousted by the Yayoi, the ancestors of the modern Japanese. The archaeological evidence is not conclusive, however, and nothing is known about either the Joomon or the Yayoi language. What is clear is that Old Japanese, as it first appears in the eighth-century documents, is characterized by a sparse phonological system, a polysyllabic lexical structure, and an agglutinative morphology, features which qualify the language equally well for inclusion in either the Altaic or the Malayo-Polynesian areal type. Japanese philologists are much concerned with identifying 'Yamato' words – i.e. pristine Japanese words, as the core of their language. As attested, however, even the oldest Japanese stratum does not seem to be entirely free of Chinese loan-words.

PERIODIZATION OF CLASSICAL JAPANESE

1. c. AD 400–794: this is the Nara period, including the 180 years when the Yamato court had its seat in the then new city of Nara. To this period belong the oldest known works in Japanese – the *Man'yooshuu* (an anthology of about 4½ thousand short poems) and the *Kojiki* ('Record of Ancient Things'), a collection of myths and pseudo-history. Both of these works were compiled in the eighth century.

2. In 794 the court moved to Heian. The Heian period, which lasted until 1191, saw the great efflorescence of Classical Japanese literature. A major formal innovation was the introduction of narrative prose for fiction and the essay/diary. At its best, this literature is often of extraordinary charm and refinement: it is enough to mention the *Genji Monogatari* and the *Murasaki Shikibu Nikki*, both by the Lady Murasaki Shikibu (c. 1000) and the delightful 'Pillow Book' (*Makura no Sooshi*) by the Lady Sei Shoonagon, who was at the Heian court between 990 and 1000.

3. Classical Japanese was still being used by scholars in the nineteenth century. In point of grammatical and lexical detail, of course, usage fluctuated and changed over this long period, but it is not too much to say that *bungo(tai)*, Classical Japanese, is the vehicle of a great literature extending over some 1,200 years. Apart from the Heian classics, particular mention must be made of the

Noo dramatist Zeami (fifteenth century), the *kabuki* playwright Chikamatsu Monzaemon (seventeenth/eighteenth century), and the seventeenth-century poet and diarist Matsuo Bashoo.

SCRIPT

The Chinese morphemic script reached Japan via Korea in the third/fourth century AD. For Japanese, a polysyllabic and inflected language, a morphemic script designed for a monosyllabic and non-inflecting language, could be utilized in either or both of two ways:

(a) *kun*: the Chinese character was simply used for its Japanese semantic equivalent. Thus, the Japanese word *yama* 'mountain' could be notated as

山 , the Chinese graph for 'mountain' (*shan* in Chinese).

(b) *man'yoogana*: the *kun* method worked, up to a point, for bare stems. For the representation of Japanese inflections, verbal endings and nominal particles, certain Chinese characters were selected as *phonetic approximations*, regardless of their meaning: e.g., to notate the Japanese particle *no*, widely used to mark the genitive relationship, a Tang Chinese character, whose pronunciation was approximately similar, was chosen. There was no consistency; at least a dozen Chinese graphs are used for the Japanese particle *ka*.

Most of the Heian classics are written, however, in hiragana, a phonetic cursive based on Chinese characters. Being phonetic, this script, up to a point, reflects Heian pronunciation. The orthography was not stable.

PHONOLOGY

Consonants

Heian Japanese had the following consonantal inventory:

> stops: p, b, t, d, k, g
> fricatives: (F) → h, s, z, h
> nasals: m, n
> flap: r
> semi-vowels: j, w

Vowels

In its earliest stages, the language had an eight-vowel system consisting of /i, e, a, o, u/, plus allophones of [i, e, o], which are notated in the literature on Old Japanese as ï, ë, ö. These seem to have been lower, less tense than *i, e, o*. Many words now written with *o*, for example, had *ö* in Old Japanese: cf. *tökörö* 'place', Modern Standard Japanese *tokoro*; *kökörö* 'heart', Modern Standard Japanese *kokoro*.

By the Heian period, this eight-vowel system had been reduced to five, with the reduction of /i/ï/ to /i/, /e/ë/ to /e/, /o/ö/ to /o/.

Combining the consonantal and vocalic rows, we get a grid of open syllables which provide the phonemes of Japanese. In early Old Japanese there were 112 such syllables, reduced in Heian Japanese to about 70: e.g. for the series based on *k*, *ka* – *ki* – *ku* – *ke* – *ko*. In Modern Standard Japanese, allophones have arisen in the grid, e.g. in the *t* series, *ti* has become /tʃi/ and *tu* has become /tsu/. Similarly, in the *s* row, Modern Standard /ʃi/ was probably /si/.

MORPHOLOGY AND SYNTAX

Japanese words were traditionally divided into two categories: indeclinable words (including nouns, pronouns, particles, adverbs, conjunctions, interjections) and declinable words (comprising verbs and adjectives). There are no articles; gender is absent.

Noun

Since the noun is uninflected, syntactic relationships have to be expressed by means of particles: e.g. *no* for genitive, *ni* for dative, *o* for accusative: e.g. *tsuki no to no hito ga* 'people of the capital of the moon' (*ga* is a subject marker); *kaze no ne o kiku* 'to hear the sound of the wind'; *ashibiki no yama no anata ni* 'on the other side of the feet-tiring mountain' (more on *ashibiki* and *anata*, below).

Compounds are readily formed: e.g. *yama.bito* 'mountain people' (/hito/ → [bito]); *matsu.kaze* 'wind in the pines'.

NUMBER
The noun itself is neutral as to number: e.g. *kaze* 'wind(s)'. Certain pluralizers occur, e.g. *-tachi*, *-domo*, *-ra*: *kami.tachi* 'gods'.

Adjective

See **Verb**, below.

Pronoun

First person forms are *a/wa/ware*; *a* has a possessive form in *a.ga*, *wa* in *wa.ga*: e.g. *a.ga ko tobisitsu* 'my child flew away' (= 'died'); *wa.ga imo(ko)* 'my little sister' (i.e. 'my mistress'); *ware wa sabishi* 'I am lonely'.

A second person form is *na/nare*: e.g. *nare mo, are mo* 'both you and I'. *Kimi* is also used: e.g. *kimi.ga mi.pune no* 'of your (hon.) boat' (/fune/ → [pune], 'boat'). *Kimi* 'my Lord' may be used for third person honorific: e.g. *kimi mo kimasa.zu* 'even though my Lord does not come'.

No specific third person pronoun is attested.

The pronoun was relatively unimportant in Classical Japanese, as verbs were themselves so coded for either respect or deference that deixis was usually manifest: deferential expressions were clearly first person-orientated, while respectful or honorific language could only imply a second person addressed or a third person referred to.

In the Heian period the form *anata* 'on that (other)side' comes to be used as a second person pronoun (and still means 'you' in Modern Standard Japanese).

DEMONSTRATIVE PRONOUN/ADJECTIVE
ko(re), *so(re)*; adjective: *ko(no)*, *so(no)*.

INTERROGATIVE PRONOUN
ta(re) 'who?'; *nani* 'what?': e.g. *Kore wa tare desu ka*? 'Who is this?'

RELATIVE PRONOUN
None; for formation of relative clause, *see* **Verb**, below.

Numerals

The earliest numerals show an ablaut relationship with their doubles: 1 *pitö*: 2 *puta*; 3 *mi*: 6 *mu*; 4 *yö*: 8 *ya*. This does not apply to *itsu* 5, *nana* 7; 9 is rare; 10 *töwo*. In the Heian period, the *hito-*, *futa-*, *mi-* series came into use (*see* **Japanese, Modern Standard**).

Verb

The verb has neither person nor number. Stems are not 'conjugated' in the sense in which this word is used with regard to, e.g., Indo-European languages. They are modulated in two stages:

Stage 1: stems are differentiated into six aspectual/modal bases: e.g. from the stem *yuk-* 'to go', the six bases are (1) *yuku*, (2) *yuku*, (3) *yuki*, (4) *yuka-*, (5) *yuke*, (6) *yuke*. Not all verbs make their bases in the same way; thus, for *tabe-* 'to eat' the series is *tabu*, *taburu*, *tabe*, *tabe-*, *tabure*, *tabe*. These bases have specific functions:

1. Base 1 is predicative/affirmative: *yuku* 'go'/'goes', *kaku* 'write/s', e.g. *waga uma nadumu* 'my horse stumbles'; *kari ga kaeru* 'wild geese are returning'; *hototogisu naku* 'the cuckoo(s) is/are singing'.
2. Base 2 provides the attributive form which precedes nouns and is used in the formation of relative clauses: e.g. *ware no yuku tokoro* 'the place I go to'; *waga omou hito wa* 'the person I care for'.
3. This base provides the conjunctive or suspended form, used to hold verbs in a serial utterance until the last verb, which alone can be in conclusive, i.e. predicative, form (base 1). (Cf. the role of the participle in Altaic languages, especially **Turkic**.) Use of this base is largely responsible for the inordinately long sentences frequent in Classical Japanese. A simple example: *Hana saki tori naku* 'While flowers bloom the birds sing'.
4. Imperfective base: action has not taken place or will not. Hence it is also the base used for the negative. This is the only base that can never be used

independently; it is always followed by a temporal or modal particle: e.g. *tabe.mu* 'will eat'; *tabe.zu* 'does not eat'; *tabe.ba* 'if ... eat(s)'; *waga koromo iro ni simete.mu* 'my garment will be dyed'.

5. The perfective form: usually followed by *ba* or *do(mo)*: e.g. *kake/kakeba* 'has/have written'.
6. Imperative (rare).

Stage 2: the first four primary bases take auxiliary verbal suffixes expressing tense, voice, plus certain nuances. Some of these suffixes have already been seen in the illustrations to base 4, above: *mu, zu, ba*. There is a distinction here, however: some suffixes, e.g. *mu* and *zu*, are themselves declinable, and are therefore subject to the primary modulation; *ba* is not declinable.

There are about 30 declinable auxiliary verbal suffixes; *mu* (future tense) and *zu* (negative) have already been mentioned. Other examples are:

> -*ramu*: expresses conjecture, hearsay, surprise, e.g. *tsuki o miru.ramu* 'is/are (I suppose) looking at the moon'; *Yama.ji koyu.ramu?* 'Is/are ... really going to take the mountain path?'
> -*rashi*: 'looks like, seems to be', e.g. *Yama ni shigure furu.rashi* 'It looks as though a shower is falling on the mountain.'
> -*keri*, -*nu*, -*tsu* give a perfective meaning.

ADJECTIVAL VERBS
Predicative base in -*shi*, attributive in -*ki*: thus, from *taka*- 'to be high': *yama takashi* 'the mountain is high'; *takaki yama* 'the high mountain'. An attributive adjective often fuses with the noun to form a compound: e.g. *oo.yumi* 'great sea'; *ko.gawa* 'small river'; *shira.kumo* 'white cloud(s)'. The adjective may be the second component: e.g. *ashi.biki* 'foot-tiring' (this is a *makura.kotoba*, a 'pillow-word' or set expression, frequently applied to a mountain).

Honorific language

Classical Japanese had an extensive repertory of nominal and verbal forms graduated to cover various socio-linguistic situations. Thus, *tamau* 'to bestow on an inferior', assumes an agent to whom respect is due; its correlative is *matsuru* 'to offer to a superior', the agent being of lowly status.

Word order

SOV is normal but not obligatory.

JAPANESE,
MODERN STANDARD

INTRODUCTION

(For a note on genetic affinity, *see* **Japanese, Classical**). Today, Japanese is spoken by about 120 million, in Japan and by large Japanese communities in several parts of the world. The Ryu-Kyu language spoken in the Okinawa Prefecture is a dialect of Japanese. In Japan itself, several local dialects persist, some of which are unintelligible to outsiders, but all Japanese in Japan are taught *hyoozyun-go*, the 'standard language'.

For a note on the early literature, *see* **Japanese, Classical**.

The political, economic, and social upheaval brought about by the Meiji Restoration in 1868, could not fail to be reflected in new attitudes to literature in Japan, and the ensuing century saw a remarkable efflorescence of the novel as the relevant medium both for the naturalistic narrative and for social and psychological analysis. Themes were drawn from Sino-Japanese sources and from a great variety of western models, ranging from Zola and the Russian novelists to Kafka and Rilke, and Japanese treatment of this material is equally eclectic, covering the familiar fields of naturalism, surrealism, alienation, and existentialism, and adding a peculiarly Japanese vein of morbid lyricism. Distinguished names abound; the following cannot fail to be mentioned: Natsume Sooseki, Shimazaki Tooson, Mori Oogai, Abe Kooboo, Kawabata Yasunari, Akutagawa Ryuunosuke, Mishima Yukio.

SCRIPT

The 'standard language' is written in a combination of Chinese characters and the two Japanese syllabaries: hiragana (derived from a cursive writing of Chinese characters) and katakana (originally a kind of shorthand for mnemonic purposes).

Hiragana is used for verbal inflection and nominal particles, postpositions, etc. Katakana is used primarily for foreign words, particularly Anglo-American words which proliferate in Modern Japanese. It is also the script for telegraphese. Chinese characters figure as root words, both verbal and nominal. For example, in the complex verb form *asobanakereba.narimasen* '... have to play...' the root *aso-* 'play' is notated as the Chinese character

遊 (*yóu* 'to play')

while the remaining ten syllables (negative conditional plus negative present indicative) are in hiragana (*-n* is syllabic). Most Chinese characters used in Japanese have more than one pronunciation; a basic distinction is made between *on-yomi*, the Sino-Japanese reading (which itself may have several variants) and the *kun-yomi*, the native Japanese reading. The *on-yomi* reading of the character meaning to 'to play', given above, for example, is *yu*. Reference to this character in the dictionary (no. 4726 in Nelson's *Japanese–English Dictionary*) will show that out of about 80 compounds listed, only 25 per cent or so give

遊   its *kun-yomi* pronunciation (*aso-*); everywhere else, *yu* is used.

In 1946, an official list of 1,850 Chinese characters was adopted as the desirable inventory for everyday purposes. In 1981, this list was extended to almost 2,000. Chinese characters not included in this list are accompanied in print by their hiragana readings.

PHONOLOGY

Consonants

> stops: p, b, t, d, k, g
> fricatives: s, z, h
> nasals: m, n, ŋ
> flap: r
> semi-vowels: j, w

Vowels

> i, e, a, o, u

These provide the basic inventory in terms of the vowel X consonant grid (*see* **Classical Japanese**). However, allophones arise in the grid: in the *s* series the fricative /ʃ/, in the *t* series the affricates /ts/ and /tʃ/, and in the *z* series the affricate /dʒ/. These are notated in the usual transcription, and here, as *sh, ts, ch, j*. Thus, *hajimemashite* 'how do you do' is /hadʒimemaʃte/. For the complete grid, see the Japanese script chart.

Again, for all consonants apart from /d/ and /w/ there is a three-term palatalized series; e.g. *kya, kyu, kyo*. In the *s* row the palatalized values are realized as /ʃa – ʃu – ʃo/; in the *t* row as /tʃa – tʃu – tʃo/, and in the *z* row as /dʒa – dʒu – dʒo/.

Final *-n* is realized as nasal [ŋ], without nasalization of the preceding vowel. That is to say, final *n* is syllabic: *Nihon* 'Japan' is pronounced /ni.ho.ŋ/.

In the transcription used here, long vowels are written doubled: e.g. *oo*. They are twice the length of single vowels; the difference is phonemic.
There are several diphthongs. When final or in contact with an unvoiced consonant: /u/ is reduced to Ø: e.g. *suki* 'likes, is fond of' → /ski/; *arimasu* 'is' → /arimas/.

665

Stress

Japanese has a pitch-accentuation pattern in place of tonic stress. Syllables flow evenly: a long syllable is two moras, a short syllable is one mora. Pitch is not marked; if it were, the marker would be on the last syllable of a high-pitch sequence, preceding a drop: e.g. *wakarimasen deshita* 'didn't understand': /wa$_n$karimasen.deshita/.

MORPHOLOGY AND SYNTAX

There is no grammatical gender; no articles. A plural marker exists but this is used mainly with pronouns. Reduplication is possible. The word *takusan* 'many', is often used: e.g. *Kuruma wa takusan arimasu ne?* 'There are lots of cars, aren't there?'; *shashin o takusan torimashita* 'took lots of photographs'.

Noun

Nouns are invariable. Syntactic relationships are expressed by means of particles. The most important of these are:

wa: this is a focusing agent, which identifies or recapitulates the topic, e.g. *watashi no kaisha **wa** Oosaka ni arimasu* '(as for) my business (it) is in O'.

ga: subject marker, e.g. *soto **wa** ame **ga** futte imasu* '(as for) outside, the rain is falling'; *ano hito **wa** se **ga** takai desu* '(as for) that man, stature is tall' = 'that man is tall'.

ni: locative, aditive, dative, e.g. *kooen ni* 'in the park'; *imooto ni* 'to sister'; *sakura o mi **ni** ikimasu* 'go to see the cherry blossom'.

o: object marker, e.g. *asa-gohan **o** tabemashita* 'ate breakfast'; *e-hagaki **o** takusan kaimashita* 'bought many postcards'.

no: genitival relationship, e.g. *watashi **no** heya wa* 'my room'; *Tookyoo wa Nippon **no** shuto desu* 'Tokyo is the capital of Japan'.

de: instrumental, e.g. *hikooki **de** 'by plane'; *denwa **de** 'by phone'.

Adjective

See **Stative verb**, below. An attributive adjective precedes the noun: e.g. *yuumei-na haiku wa* 'a famous haiku'; *takai yama wa* 'a high mountain'.

Pronoun

In general, pronouns are avoided in Japanese, especially as regards the second person. Here, the addressee's name followed by *san* should be used: e.g. *Oota.san wa nani o tabemasu ka?* 'What are you having (to eat)?' (addressing Mr Oota)

Watashi, pl. *watashitachi* are acceptable first person forms; *anata* has restricted use as a second person form.

Third person: *anohito* or *anokata* 'he/she'; *kare* 'he', *kanojo* 'she'.

DEMONSTRATIVE PRONOUN

kore 'this', *sore* 'that', *are* 'that (further away)'. The demonstrative adjectives are *kono* 'this', *sono* 'that', *ano* 'that (further away)'.

INTERROGATIVE PRONOUN

dare 'who?'; *nani* 'what?'. The final particle *ka* makes a sentence interrogative: e.g. *Sono hito wa Nippon-jin desu ka* 'Is that man (is he) a Japanese?'

RELATIVE PRONOUN

See **Verb**, below.

Numerals

There are two parallel sets of numbers, native Japanese and Chinese: 1–10: Jap. *hito-, futa-, mi-, yon-, itsu-, mu-, nana-, ya-, kokono-, too*; Ch. *ichi, ni, san, shi, go, roku, shichi, hachi, ku/kyu, juu*. In enumeration, the Chinese numerals have to be combined with appropriate classifiers, e.g. *-hon* for long objects, *-satsu* for books, *-nin* for people. There are a couple of dozen of these, usually with assimilation at junctures: e.g. with *-hon*: *ippon* 'one' (e.g. pencil); *nihon* 'two' (pencils); *sanbon* /sambon/, 'three' (pencils). Numeral + classifier usually follow the referent: e.g. *Ki wa roppon arimasu* 'There are six trees (*roku + hon →* *roppon*).

11 *juu-ichi*; 12 *juu-ni*; 20 *ni-juu*; 30 *san-juu*; 100 *hyaku*.

Verb

There are three classes of verb: vowel stems, consonantal stems, and a small class of irregular verbs (six members). For inflectional purposes, the six bases of Classical Japanese are retained in slightly modified form:

Base	1	2	3	4	5	6
vowel class	mi	mi	miru	mire	miro	miyoo
consonant class	kaka	kaki	kaku	kake	kake	kakoo
irregular	shi/sa	shi	suru	sure	seyo/siro	shiyoo

Base 1: this is used in the formation of the negative, e.g. *minai* 'not to see', and the causative, e.g. *kakaseru* 'to cause to write'.

Base 2 provides the base for the present and past polite forms, and the desiderative: e.g. *mimasu* 'sees'; *mimashita* 'saw', *mitai* 'wants to see'.

Base 3: citation form, used as infinitive. Plain present tense.

Base 4: provides the conditional form in *-eba*, e.g. *mireba* 'would see'; *kakeba* 'would write'.

Base 5: imperative plain form, e.g. *kake!* 'write!'; this is permissible only in reported speech.

Base 6: prospective or hortative, e.g. *motto benkyoo shiyoo to omotte imasu* 'I'm thinking of doing some more studying' (*benkyoo*). This form is associated with first person only (but citation form + *deshoo* – base 6 of *da* 'to be' – is general: e.g. *Taroo wa kyoo kuru deshoo* 'Taroo will probably come today').

THE -TE/-DE (GERUND) FORM

In verbs ending in *-ru*, *-te* replaces *-ru*: *deru* – *dete* 'having gone out'. In *-u* verbs, root *k/g* are elided, *-de* appears after a sonant: *kaku* 'write' – *kaite*; *shinu* 'die' – *shinde*; *narabu* 'line up' – *narande*. There are some irregular forms: *suru* 'do' – *shite*; *kuru* 'come' – *kite*.

This form is much used with the auxiliary *iru/aru* to express a continuing state of affairs: e.g. *Nani o shite imasu ka* 'What is/are … doing?' It is also used as a holding suffix in a serial utterance involving several verbs; each of these then ends in *-te/-de*, the final verb alone taking the finite ending:

Hiru-gohan o tabete, oka ni nobotte, mati o mimashita
'Having eaten lunch, we climbed up the hill and looked at the town'

Tamago o too katte, niwa e dete, hiru-gohan o tabemashita
'(I, we, etc.) bought a dozen eggs, went into the garden and had lunch'

The parallel with the Turkic languages is striking.

PRESENT AND PAST POLITE FORMS, POSITIVE AND NEGATIVE

present: *-masu* /mas'/, e.g. *kakimasu* 'writes'; neg. *kakimasen* 'doesn't write';

past: *-mashita* /mash'ta/, e.g. *kakimashita* 'wrote'; neg. *kakimasen deshita* 'didn't write'.

There is a great wealth of agglutinative affixes; some of the most important are:

-eba: conditional, e.g. *ame ga fureba* 'if it rains';

-tara: temporal, e.g. *hiru-gohan o tabetara* 'when (I, we, etc.) eat, have eaten lunch';

-eba + *ikemasen/narimasen*: obligation, e.g. *Watashiwa Tookyoo e ikana-kereba narimasen* 'I have to go to Tokyo';

-tai: desire, e.g. *Watashi moo tabetai desu* 'I want to eat too.'

PASSIVE

Infixes *-are-*, *-rare-*, e.g. *taberareru* 'be eaten'; *kakareru* 'be written'. An agent, if overtly expressed, takes the postposition *ni*: e.g. *Watashi wa kinoo ame **ni** furareta* 'By the rain (*ame*) I-was-rained-on yesterday.'

CAUSATIVE

The infixes are *-ase-*, *-sase-*, e.g. *tabesasete imasu* 'is feeding (trans.)'. Passive and causative may be combined: e.g. *Watashi wa ka-choo-san **ni** Oosaka e ik.**ase**.**rare**.mashita* 'I was made to go to Osaka by my department boss.'

STATIVE VERBS

Examples: *takai* 'it is high'; *omoshiroi* 'it is interesting'. As attributes, these precede the noun. As predicates they are conjugated: past *omoshiro.katta* 'it was interesting'; negative past *omoshiroku.nakatta* 'it wasn't interesting'.

RELATIVE CLAUSES

Relative clauses are placed in attributive position to the left of the head-word: e.g., using *o-tenki* 'weather', *warui* 'bad', *tokoro* 'place', *o-tenki ga warui tokoro* 'a place where the weather is bad'. Ambiguity may arise, as the deixis is not specific in Japanese: e.g. *tegami o okutta hito wa* 'the man who sent us the letter', *or* 'the man to whom the letter was sent'.

Nominalizing agents such as *toki* 'time', *koto* 'thing', are used to form other types of relative clause (verb in plain form): e.g. *asa hito ni atta toki ni wa ...* 'when you meet someone in the morning ...' (*asa* 'morning'; *au* 'to meet'); *Kare wa sensoo ga owatta **to iu koto** o shiranakatta* 'He didn't know (the thing) that the war had ended.'

HONORIFIC PREFIXES

O-, *go-* are attached to nominals and to adjectives: e.g. *Anata no **o-too-san** no **go**-iken wa doo desu ka?* 'What is your (hon.) father's (hon.) opinion?' A verbal form is made honorific by substituting *o-/go-* + base 2 + *narimasu*: *Yamada-san wa kore o **o-kaki ni** narimashita* 'Mr Yamada wrote this'; cf. for first person (never hon.): *watashi wa kore o kakimashita* 'I wrote this'.

Postpositions

Examples: *kara* 'from', *made* 'as far as', *de* 'in, with'.

Word order

Typically SOV.

1 初めに言（ことば）があった。 言は神と共に
あった。言は神であった。

2 この言は初めに神と共にあった。

3 すべてのものは，これによってできた。 できたものの
うち，一つとしてこれによらないものはなかった。

4 この言に 命があった。 そして この命は 人の光で
あった。

5 光はやみの中に輝いている。 そして，やみはこれ
に勝たなかった。

6 ¶ここにひとりの人があって，神からつかわされて
いた。その名をヨハネと言った。

7 この人はあかしのためにきた。 光についてあかしを
し，彼によってすべての人が信じるためである。

8 彼は光ではなく， ただ， 光についてあかしをする
ためにきたのである。

JAVANESE

INTRODUCTION

Javanese belongs to the Malayo-Polynesian branch of Austronesian, and is spoken by between 50 and 60 million people in central and eastern Java. The language has been influenced, first, by Sanskrit, then, from the fifteenth century onwards by Arabic, and finally, since about 1600, by Dutch. The influence of Malay, in the shape of Bahasa Indonesia, has increased since the latter became the official language of Indonesia.

For the older language and literature, *see* **Javanese, Old**. By the thirteenth/ fourteenth century Old Javanese was no longer a spoken language, though it continued to be used for literature. Of particular interest in the Middle Javanese period is the *babad* literature dealing with the traditional history of Java. This period culminates in the impressive figure of Jasadipurva, the eighteenth-century court poet whose work was a major factor in the emergence of the Surakarta, or Solo, dialect as the basis of modern literary Javanese.

The *wayang* – the traditional Javanese puppet theatre – draws on both Hindu and Islamic sources for its themes: e.g. on Jasadipurva's reworking of the Old Javanese version of the *Mahābhārata*, Book III (*vanapurvan*).

The twentieth century has seen the growth of the social novel and other western genres; certain influential writers in this field, e.g. Senggono and Subagijo, use ngoko (*see* **Speech levels**, below). In general, however, Javanese has been more conservative than Bahasa Indonesia.

SCRIPT

The *čarakan* script was used exclusively until replaced by romanization in the twentieth century. In 1926 a standardized orthography was adopted, revised in 1972.

Speech levels

Javanese is a two-tier language. The socio-linguistic constraints which operate in many languages with regard to pronominal usage, for example, are applied in Javanese to all parts of speech, nouns, verbs, adjectives, prepositions. The two main levels are: *ngoko* or colloquial; *krama* /krɔmɔ/, 'elevated'.

Ngoko is basic Javanese in the sense that it is picked up by the child at home. From school age on, however, the Javanese child has to acquire the additional and rather extensive krama lexicon for use in certain prescribed socio-linguistic situations – by young people to their elders, on formal occasions, when addressing strangers or social superiors, and so on. A compromise solution is increasingly being developed in the shape of krama madya – more formal than ngoko, less stilted than krama.

All three forms have virtually identical grammar and syntax; the differences are purely lexical. For any given referent, krama may have the same word as ngoko, an enhanced form, or a completely different word: e.g.

Ngoko	Krama	English
wit	wit	tree
prakara	prakawis	occasion
asu	segawon	dog
omah	griya	house
wong	tiyang	man

Use of ngoko is steadily encroaching on the krama preserve. The Javanese press uses ngoko in general. Krama itself has more than one register.

PHONOLOGY

Consonants

> stops: p/b, t/d, ʈ/ɖ, k/g, ʔ
> affricates: tʃ/dʒ/, t'/d'
> fricatives: w, s, j, h
> nasals: m, n, ɲ, ŋ
> lateral and trill: l, r

Since the voiced/unvoiced values are almost indistinguishable, the stops and affricates are set out in pairs. According to Uhlenbeck (1949), the voiced member is slightly aspirated. Initial /k/ = [q]; final /k/ = /ʔ/. No final is voiced.

Vowels

> i, ɪ, e, ɛ, a, ə, ɔ, o, u

/ə/ is known as *e*-pepet; it appears in unstressed syllables, /a/ in penultimate and final syllables → [ɔ]: e.g. *nagara* /nəgɔrɔ/, 'country'.

There are no diphthongs; contingent vowels are pronounced separately.

Stress

Stress is on the penultimate syllable unless this is *e*-pepet: e.g. *berás* 'polished rice'.

MORPHOLOGY AND SYNTAX

(N = ngoko, K = krama.)

Noun

No gender; there are no articles or plural markers; to suggest plurality N *akeh*, K *kathah* 'many' may be used. A collective can be made by reduplication: e.g. *sedulur-sedulur* (sometimes written *'sedulur 2'*) 'a group of friends'.

POSSESSIVE RELATIONSHIP
See **Pronoun**, below.

Adjective

The attributive adjective follows the noun and is invariable: e.g. N *omah gedhé* = K *griya ageng* '(a/the) big house'.

COMPARATIVE
N. *luwih*, K *langkung*: e.g. N *luwih dhuwur* = K *langkung inggil* 'higher'.

Pronoun

Independent personal forms and possessive enclitics:

	Personal	Possessive
1	N aku, K kula	N -ku, K kula
2	N kowé, K sampéyan	N -mu, K sampéyan
3	N dhèwèké, K piyambakipun	N -e, K -ipun

There are no specifically plural forms: e.g. N *omah**ku*** = K *griya kula* 'my house(s)', 'our house(s)'; N *omahé* = K *griya**nipun*** 'his house(s)', 'their house(s)'; cf. N *sapiné wong iki* = K *lembu**nipun** tiyang punika* 'that man's cow'.

DEMONSTRATIVE PRONOUN
N *iki*, K *punika* (pronounced /menikɔ/): 'this', 'that'.

INTERROGATIVE PRONOUN
N *sapa*, K *sinten* 'who?'; N *apa*, N *punapa* /menɔpɔ/ 'what?'. The introductory interrogative particle is N *apa*, K *punapa*.

RELATIVE PRONOUN
N *kang/sing*, K *ingkang*: e.g. N *Iki wong kang arep adol omahe* = K *Punika tiyang ingkang badhé sade griyanipun* 'That is the man who wants to sell his house' (*arep* = *badhé* 'will'; *adol* = *sade* 'sell').

Numerals

For the cardinals 1 to 5 there are distinct N/K sets: N *siji, loro, telu, papat, lima* = K *setunggal, kalih, tiga, sekawan, gangsal*; 6 to 9 show common N/K forms: *enem, pitu, wolu, sanga*. 10 = N *sepuluh*, K *sedasa*; 11 = N/K *sewelas*; 12–15 separate N and K forms; 16–19 common forms; 20 is N *rongpuluh*, K *kalihdasa*; 30 N *telungpuluh*, K *tigangdasa*; 100 N/K *saratus*.

Verb

A few Javanese verbal stems are used in primary form, e.g. N *takon* = K *taken* 'ask'; N *ana* = K *wonten* 'be located', but the great majority of stems undergo initial nasalization before they can function as verbs. Vocalic initials take prefix *ng-*, e.g. *iris* – *ngiris* 'to cut'; consonantal initials take homorganic nasal, e.g. *buru* – *mburu* 'to hunt'; *sapu* – *nyapu* 'to sweep'; *rembat* – *ngrembat* 'to yoke'. These stems are neutral as to tense or aspect, and, since there is nothing resembling a conjugational system, adverbial markers preceding the verb may be used to indicate tense, e.g. N *tau* = K *nate* for remote past; N *wis* = K *sampun* for past; N *bakal, arep* = K *badhé, adyeng* for future. Example: K *Ratu sampun.nitih mengsah.hipun* 'The prince has overcome his enemy' (*mengsah* 'enemy').

THE -I SUFFIX

This establishes a directional relationship between a verb and its locus of action or its direct object: e.g. *linggih* 'to sit' – *nglinggihi* 'to sit on (something)'; *-tulis* 'to write' – *nulisi kertas* 'to write on paper'.

PASSIVE

In general, the passive construction is preferred in Javanese, and there are several passive forms:

(a) The personal passive; the prefixes are N 1 *tak-*, 2 *kok-*, 3 *di-*; K 1 *kula*, 2 *sampeyan*, 3 *dipun*: e.g. N *Layang iki **taktulis** 'This letter is being written by me'; N *Woh iki **dipangan** wong iki* = K *Woh punika **dipun** tedha tiyang punika* 'This fruit is being eaten by this man.'

(b) Neutral passive: this is characteristic of the literary style – *-in-* infix, e.g. *tinulis* 'to be written'.

(c) Chance or accidental passive: formed with *ke...an* circumfix, e.g. N *maling* 'thief' – *kemalingan* 'to be robbed', K *pandung* 'thief' – *kepandungan* 'to be robbed'; N *udan* 'rain' – *kodanan* 'to be caught in the rain', K *jawah* 'rain' – *kejawahan* 'to be caught in the rain'.

(d) Two passives are coded for aspect: *ka-* perfective; *-um-* imperfective.

IMPERATIVE

In N only, as imperative forms would be incompatible with K usage. The N suffixes are *-a*, *-(n)en* for passive verbs, *-ana* for *-i* verbs.

CAUSATIVE

The suffixes are N *-aké-*, K *-aken*: e.g. N *sopir itu nglakok**aké** montore* = K *sopir punika nglampah**aken** montoripun* 'the driver starts his engine'.

NEGATIVE

N *ora*/K *mboten* negate verbs: N *dudu*/K *sanès, dede* negate nouns: e.g. N *aku dudu wong Inggeris* = K *kula sanès tiyang Inggeris* 'I'm not English'; N *aku ora isa basa Jawi* = K *kula mboten saged basa Jawi* 'I don't speak Javanese'.

AFFIXES
Examples:

-an, an all-purpose affix, usually with loss of initial nasalization; often indicates result of verbal action, or the instrument used: e.g. *nimbang* 'to weigh' – *timbangan* 'scales'.

ka...an makes abstract nouns, e.g. *sugih* 'rich' – *kasugihan* 'wealth'.

pa-: indicates agent, e.g. N *nulis* 'to write' – *panulis* 'writer'; K *nyerat* 'to write' – *panyerat* 'writer'.

pa...an: locus of action, e.g. N *turu* 'to sleep' – *paturon* 'bedroom'.

sa + pa-: extent, range, e.g. *mbedhil* 'to shoot' – *sapambedhil* 'range limit for a shot' → 'as far as ...'.

suffix *-en* forms adjectives, e.g. *uwan* 'grey hair' – *uwanen* 'grey-haired'.

Prepositions

Examples: *ing* 'in', *saking* 'from'. Composite prepositions like *ing duwur* 'up', *ing isor* 'down' are also adverbials.

Word order

Varies according to whether construction is active or passive. S normally precedes V.

---

1 Ing kala purwa Sang Sabda iku ana, déné Sang Sabda iku nunggil karo Gusti Allah, sarta Sang Sabda iku Gusti Allah. 2 Wiwitané Pandjenengané iku nunggil karo Gusti Allah. 3 Samubarang kabèh dumadiné déning Sang Sabda, lan samubarang kang dumadi ora ana sawidji-widjia kang ora didadèkaké déning Sang Sabda. 4 Sang Sabda kang kedunungan urip, sarta urip iku kang dadi pepaḍanging manungsa. 5 Anadéné Sang Paḍang nelahi sadjroning pepeteng, lan ora kalinḍih déning pepeteng iku. 6 Ana prija rawuh kautus déning Allah asmané Jokanan. 7 Rawuhé dadi saksi, kapatah neksèni bab Sang Paḍang, supaja dadia lantarané wong kabèh paḍa pratjaja. 8 Pandjenengané iku dudu Sang Paḍang pijambak, mung kapatah neksèni bab Sang Paḍang.

JAVANESE, OLD
(KAWI)

INTRODUCTION

This is the only Austronesian language whose earlier forms are attested in written record in the shape of an extensive corpus of texts. Herein lies the great importance of Old Javanese. The language makes its first appearance in a legal document dated AD 804, and it reaches its apogee in the rich output of creative literature and re-creation of Sanskrit originals, which continued from the tenth to the fifteenth century. These are the centuries of Indic cultural domination in Sumatra and Java, and it is hardly surprising to find that about a third of Kawi vocabulary consists of Sanskrit roots (always in base form). This imported element does not, however, prevent the language from being, structurally, pure Malayo-Polynesian, close, in many respects, to Modern Javanese. Even the Sanskrit roots are acclimatized, so to say, in a Javanese setting; one might compare the harmonious symbiosis of Arabic words and Persian syntax.

The great period of Old Javanese writing is bound up with the Śailendra and Majapahit Dynasties in eastern Java. On the collapse of the latter, in the face of advancing Islam, the centre of gravity of Old Javanese culture moved to Bali, where it is still preserved as a living entity.

THE LITERATURE
Three main divisions may be recognized:

(a) Recensions of parts of the *Mahābhārata*. These are never exact translations – rather, one might call them restatements of the epic material in Javanese terms.
(b) Didactic fables or cautionary tales, loosely based on such sources as the *Pañcatantra* and the *Jātakas*.
(c) Narrative texts: these combine myth and history of the Javanese people; e.g. the *Pararaton*, an account of the Majapahit Dynasty, and the *Tantu Panggĕlaran*, which is a creation myth.

SCRIPT

The Old Javanese script is not the same as the Modern Javanese one. The old script has signs for the Sanskrit aspirates, which are alien to Javanese but which were necessary for the notation of Sanskrit loan-words.

PHONOLOGY

Consonants

> stops: p, b, t/th, ḍ/ḍh, t/th, d/dh, k, g
> affricates: tʃ, dʒ
> fricatives: s, ṣ, ʃ, j, w, h
> nasals: m, n, ɲ, ŋ
> lateral and flap: l, r

Retroflex consonants are notated here as ṭ, ḍ, ṣ.

Vowels

> a, aː, i, uː, ə, e, o, œ, ṛ, ḷ

/ṛ/ and /ḷ/ were probably realized as [rə], [lə]. ĕ as /ɐ/.
Little is known about the actual pronunciation of Old Javanese. Long vowels are indicated by a macron in the following text, e.g. ū.

Sandhi in compounds and elsewhere is partly Sanskrit and partly Javanese.

MORPHOLOGY AND SYNTAX

No gender, number, or case: e.g. *wwang* 'man'/'people'. If greater precision is necessary, an indefinite article can be made with the numeral 'one': e.g. *sa.tunggal wwang* 'a man'; pl. with *akweh* 'many': *akweh wwang* 'people'.

The particle *ng/ang* is used as a topicalizing device, suggesting that the noun to which it is affixed is definite, and known to listener or reader. The all-purpose preposition *i*, with variants *ning, ing, ring, ri, ni*, serves as a linking particle in possessive relationships: e.g. *wwe ning samudra* 'the waters of the ocean'; *warna ning kuda* 'the horse's colour'.

DERIVATIVE NOUNS
Examples:

> *pa-*: *naḍah* 'to eat' – *pa.naḍah* 'eating' (noun);
> *-an*: *dum* 'to divide' – *duman* 'a part';
> *ka-*: *pĕjah* 'to die' – *kapĕjah* 'death'; *doh* 'remote' – *kadohan* 'a far-off place';
> *ka...an* makes abstract nouns: *panas* 'hot' – *ka.panas.an* 'heat'; *ling* 'word' – *ka.ling.an* 'intention'.

Adjective

Invariable, follows noun: e.g. *sila item* 'black rock'.

Pronoun

Not marked for number or gender:

	Singular and plural	Enclitics
1	aku, dak, tak, kami, sun	-ku/-ngku
2	ko, kamu, sira, kita	-mu
3	ya, sira	-nya/-(n)ira

Plus an inventory of honorific and periphrastic forms. The enclitics are sometimes used to replace a verb: e.g. *nātha ling.nya* 'the king his-word' = 'the king said'.

DEMONSTRATIVE PRONOUN
iki 'this' – *iku* 'that' – *ika* 'that yonder'.

INTERROGATIVE PRONOUN
syapa 'who?'; *apa* 'what?'.

RELATIVE PRONOUN
ikang: e.g.

> Mangaliwati sireng Ksīrārṇawa ikang punuter de ning dewāsura
> 'They sailed across the (sea of) K, which the gods and the asuras had made stormy'

Numerals

1–10: *tunggal, rwa, telu/tiga, pat/papat, lima, nem, pitu, wwalu, sanga, sapuluh*; 11 *sawĕlas*; 12 *rwa wĕlas*; 20 *likur*; 21 *salikur*; 30 *telung puluh*; 100 *atus*.

Verb

The Kawi verb has no tenses, nor is it marked for person; the context is the only guide.

Active and passive voices are, however, formally distinguished by affixation or infixation. For example, *ang-/am-* are prefixes, *-um-* is an infix, forming active transitive verbs from nouns. Certain initials, especially labials, are discarded when the prefix is added: cf. *panas* 'warm' – *amθanas.i* 'to heat'; *santwa* 'respect' – *sumantwa* 'to show respect to'. The passive is made either by *-in-* infix, or by *ka-* prefix: e.g. *ton* 'to see' – *tinon* = *katon* 'to be visible'. *Paha* → *maha* makes transitives/causatives: e.g. *lĕbā* 'pleasant' – *mahalĕbā* 'to make desirable'.

-akĕn, -i: these important suffixes signal the presence of direct object(s), locus of verbal action, and accompanying dynamic movement or change: e.g. *hana* 'there is/are': *mang.han.ākĕn* 'to create'; *ya tanuwuh.akĕn krodha sang gurupatni* 'this arouses the anger (*krodha*, Sanskrit loan-word) of the teacher's wife (*gurupatni*, Sanskrit loan-word)'; *wwang mangaliwat.i Yamuna* 'people swimming across the Jumna'.

NEGATIVE

The particle is *tan* (with variants): e.g. *Sugyan tan wruha kita ri kami* 'Perhaps you do not know me' (*sugyan* 'perhaps, if'; *wruh-* 'to know').

The last sentence illustrates one usage of the linking particle *i/ri/ning*, etc., i.e. to mark the direct or indirect object: e.g. *ri kami* '(to) us'. This particle has many prepositional usages, e.g. *ing hawan* 'on the road'; *i sedeng* 'at that time'; *i sor* 'down below'; *in gruhur* 'above'. Its role as a genitival linking particle has already been mentioned.

Word order

SVO/VSO; when the latter is used, the exact meaning has usually to be elucidated from associated particles and from the context: cf. the sentence given above in illustration of the relative pronoun, where both components – the principal and the relative clause – are verb-initial.

JUANG (Cuəŋ)

INTRODUCTION

A member of the Juang-Dai branch of the Tai family, Juang enjoys official status as a major minority language of the People's Republic of China, and is spoken by about 13 million people in the Juang Autonomous Region of Guangxi (established in 1958). Other groups of Juang live in Yunnan, Guizhou, and Guangdong. All Juang are bilingual. The literary standard is based on Wuming usage (Northern dialect).

SCRIPT

Until the 1950s Juang was occasionally written in a script based on Chinese, in which Chinese characters were freely and arbitrarily adapted, truncated, and compounded. The closest parallel is perhaps with the chữnom script used formerly in Vietnam (*see* **Vietnamese**). In the 1950s a roman-based script with additional signs was adopted. Among the additional letters are five indicating tones 2 to 6. In this article, the Arabic numerals are used.

PHONOLOGY

As in Chinese, the phonemes of Juang are divided into two classes – initials and finals. A Juang syllable may be (a) a vowel or diphthong; (b) an initial consonant + vowel or diphthong; (c) as (b) + a permissible final; (d) vowel or diphthong + permissible final. Permissible finals are the nasals and the stops /p, t, k/ which are not released; that is, they become implosives.

Consonants

stops: p, b, t, d, k, ʔ; k', k°
fricatives: f, ç, s/θ, h
nasals: m, n, ɲ, ŋ, ŋ°
laterals: l, r/ɣ
semi-vowels: j, w

The Serdyučenko (1961) table of consonants includes /ʔ/ but it is not clear whether this is indeed a glottal stop or a hamza-type onset /ʕ/ e.g. preceding *j*, *w*, *b*, *d*: /ˈj, ˈw, ˈb, ˈd/

There is no dental /s/; ç is used to notate a palatalized /c/.

In some Juang dialects, initial clustering of the Thai type is tolerated: e.g. *ml*, *pl*; in the standard language, these tend to be reduced and palatalized; e.g. /pl/ > [p'].

The labialized /ŋ°/ is a characteristic Juang sound.

Vowels

The basic vowels are:

i, e, ə, a, ɯ, o, u

All may be long or short, except /e/ and /a/ which are short only. Short /o/ is notated as *θ*.

Tones

Some authorities specify six tones, others eight including two 'checked tones' used with /p, t, k/ finals. The tone markers are placed immediately after words, e.g. *wun2* 'man'; *ma4* 'horse'. Tone 2 is low falling, 3 high even, 4 falling, 5 mid-rising, 6 low rising.

MORPHOLOGY AND SYNTAX

Noun

As in Chinese, the parts of speech in Juang may be classified in terms of nominals, verbals, and particles. A further division is into free and bound forms. Apart from many lexical items, Juang has borrowed from Chinese certain structural features, e.g. the relational particle *-de* (the Juang form is *ti6*), e.g. to form a genitive case which coexists with the standard Juang appositional genitive: cf. *səɯ kou* (book – I) = *kou də səɯ* 'my book'. Other case relations are positionally determined. A plural form may be made for nouns denoting persons by means of a specific classifier.

Juang has a great many classifiers. These precede the noun, e.g. *bon3* for books, *diu2* for rivers, *lau4* for old people. The classifier *ən* has become an all-purpose classifier, equivalent to the Chinese *ge*. A specific classifier may replace its referent nominal: e.g. *bon3 kou* 'my book' (the classifier *bon3* fixes the referent as a book).

Adjective

Adjective follows noun as in Thai: e.g. *va diŋ* 'red flower'; *ko saŋ* 'high tree'. It may be intensified by reduplication: e.g. *diŋdiŋ* 'brilliant red'.

681

Pronoun

The personal pronouns are:

	Singular	Plural
1	kou/gou	tou, rəu2
2	mɯŋ2	sou
3	te	k'əŋte

As possessive forms these follow the noun: e.g. *na2 kou* 'my field'; *bi6 sou* 'your clothes'.

DEMONSTRATIVE PRONOUNS
nei4 'this'; *hən4* 'that'. Again as in Thai, these follow the noun.

INTERROGATIVE PRONOUN
bou4 ləɪ2 'who?'; *ki6 ma2* 'what?'.

Numerals

1–10: *tei, soŋ, sam, sei5, ha3, rŏk, cət, bet, kou3, cip*; 11 *cip it*; 12 *cip soŋ*; 20 *nei6 cip*; 30 *sam cip*; 40 *sei5 cip*; 100 *bak* (Chinese *băi*).

Verb

Stems may be simple or compound: e.g. *gu6* 'do', *sieŋ3* 'think'; *ro4nau* 'know' (*ro4* 'know' + *nau* 'speak'). Stems may be reduplicated – type xxyy is common: e.g. *bəibəimama* 'come'.

There are no tenses or personal endings; hence, personal pronouns are always necessary. Tense is inferred from the context (e.g. the presence of adverbial indicators) and from certain aspectual markers, e.g. *lo* denoting completed action (cf. Chinese *le*); other perfective markers are *kwa5* and *liu4/leu*; e.g. *kɪn* 'eat' – *kɪn.liu4* 'ate up'.

to4/ta3 may be prefixed to stem to denote customary action: e.g. *ta3təm* 'to plough'.

Juang has an elaborate system of modal co-verbs (resultative, directional, potential, etc.): e.g. *tei3 = kam3* 'be able to'; *ɪŋdaŋ* 'have to' (Chinese); *n'ien6* 'want to'.

COPULA
/tɪk/, notated as *duug*, is used between nominals: e.g. *soutu rəu2 duug Bəkgiŋ* 'our capital is Beijing'; *ən ran2 nei4 duug hakdaŋ* 'this building is a school'.

NEGATION
The negating particle *bou3* precedes verb: e.g. *bou3 gu6* 'not work'.

Prepositions

Examples: *da3* 'from, out of'; *vi6* 'for'; *vi6liu4* 'on account of'. *Doi5* is used to indicate indirect object: e.g. *doi5 te gaŋ3* 'to tell him'.

Vocabulary

The basic Tai stock is supplemented with many borrowings, both ancient and modern, from Chinese.

Basic Tai words are: *bo6* 'father', *me6* 'mother', *wun2* 'man', *ma* 'dog'. Ancient Chinese loan-words include *mu* 'eye', *lu* 'way', *ma4* 'horse'. Modern Chinese loan-words: e.g. *cinciu* = Ch. *zhèngzhì* 'politics'; *ban6fap* = Ch. *bànfǎ* 'method, procedure'.

An interesting group of compounds takes the form AB, where A is a general generic term particularized by B: e.g. for birds the generic term is *rŏg*: e.g. *rŏggum3* 'female quail'; *rŏgbieghag* 'white crane'; *rŏgbit* 'duck'.

Word order

SVO.

KABARD–CHERKES

INTRODUCTION

Kabard–Cherkes belongs to the Abkhaz-Adyge group of North-West Caucasian, and is spoken by between 300,000 and 350,000 people in the Kabard-Balkar Autonomous Soviet Socialist Republic and in the Karachay-Cherkes Autonomous Region. A literary norm, based on the dialect of Bol'šaya Kabarda dates from 1924.

SCRIPT

Since the late 1930s, Cyrillic + *I*, which is used to mark the ejective consonants.

PHONOLOGY

Consonants

plosives: b, p, p', d, t, t', g°, k°, k°', q, q', q°, q°', ʔ
affricates: dz, ts, t's, dʒ, tʃ, t'ʃ
fricatives: v, f, f', z, s, ź, ś, ś', ʒ, ʃ, γ, x, x°, ʁ, χ, ʁ°, χ°, h/ħ
nasals: m, n
lateral and flap: l, ł, l', r

In the following description, the ejective consonants are marked with subscript dot: i.e. /t'/ is notated as t. The alveo-palatal series of fricatives /ź, ś, ś'/ is notated here as $\bar{z}, \bar{s}, \bar{s}'$.

Vowels

Kabardian has been variously described as vowel-less (Kuipers 1960), as having a basic opposition between /ə/ and /a/aː/ (Jakovlev 1923), and as having one single vowel /a/. Šagirov (1967) gives the following list:

high: i, u
middle: e, ɪ, o
low: ɛ, a

This is also the inventory given by Kardanov in the 1955 Russian–Kabard dictionary.

The basic Kabardian vowels seem to be /a, ɪ, ɛ/; the other vowels as listed by Šagirov are secondary formations involving the semi-vowels /j, w/. In this entry, *a* is used as a generalized sign for the basic Kabardian vowel sound, whose values range over /a, ɪ, ɛ/.

MORPHOLOGY AND SYNTAX

Noun

Nouns are definite or indefinite. All nominals are declined in three cases, according to one paradigm: nom. in *-r*, erg. in *-m*, instr. in *-ča*.

CASE

The ergative figures as logical subject with a transitive verb; the logical object is in the nominative case: e.g. *šaǩ°em šɪxɪr yɪnčaš* 'by the hunter – the deer – killed'. The *-m* form may also be the direct or indirect object with both transitive and intransitive verbs, depending on the opposition between dynamic and stative versions: e.g. *šaler radiom yoda'we* 'the boy listens to the radio'; *sa txɪłɪm sodže* 'I read the book'.

Postpositional or instrumental case: in *-ča* (notated in Cyrillic script with *kI*): e.g. *qarandaš.ča* 'with a pencil' (Russian loan-word).

NUMBER

The plural marker is *-xa*: e.g. *žɪɣ* 'tree', pl. *žɪɣ.xa.r*; *wɪner* 'house', pl. *wɪnaxar/wɪnexer*.

Adjective

As attribute, adjective follows noun: e.g. *psɪ šɪ'a* 'cold water'; *zawe šɪ'ja* 'cold war'.

COMPARISON

A comparative is made with *neχ*: e.g. *neχ jən* 'bigger'; *Mo wɪnem neχra mɪ wɪner neχ jənš* 'This house is bigger than that one.'

Pronoun

	Singular	Plural
1	sa/se	da/de
2	wa/we	fa/fe

These have no specific ergative forms. The possessive adjective forms are sing. *si – wi*, pl. *di – fi*: e.g. *si q°eš* 'my brother'.

The third person possessive forms, sing. *yey*, pl. *yay*, are always accompanied by a nominal or pronominal referent in the ergative case: e.g. *abɪ i/abɪ yey* 'his': *abɪ i wɪne* 'his house' (*abɪ* is the ergative of the demonstrative *ar*).

686

DEMONSTRATIVE PRONOUN/ADJECTIVE
ar 'this'; *mɪr* 'that'; *mor* 'that (further away)'. The adjectival form is shortened:
a/*mɪ txɪłɪr* 'this/that book'.

INTERROGATIVE PRONOUN
xet 'who?'; *sɪt* 'what?'.

RELATIVE PRONOUN
The same as the interrogative; or participial construction may be used: e.g.
stolɪm teł txɪłɪr 'the book which is lying on the table' (Russian loan-word).

Numerals

1–10: *zɪ*, *ṭu*, *šɪ*, *pḷɪ*, *txu*, *xɪ*, *blɪ*, *yi*, *bɣu*, *pšɪ*. *Zɪ* precedes the noun; 2–10
inclusive follow noun in affixed form: e.g. *wɪne.š* 'three houses'; *çɪx°ɪpš* 'ten
men'. 11 *pšɪ.ḳ°.z*; 12 *pšɪ.ḳ°.ṭ*; 20 *ṭoš*; 30 *šaš*; 100 *ša*.

Verb

Transitive (with ergative construction), intransitive (with nominative); this
opposition is complicated by the parallel opposition between dynamic and static/
stative verbs.

Intransitive verbs can be transitivized by the prefix *ɣa-* (causative): e.g. *maḳ°a*
'he goes' – *ya.ɣ.aḳ°a* 'he sends (someone)'.

VOICE
Kabardian verbs have active, passive, reflexive, and reciprocal voices.

MOOD
Indicative, imperative, optative, presumptive, concessive.

NON-FINITE FORMS
Infinitive, participles (active and passive), gerund.

TENSE
All moods have present, past, and future tenses. Person is marked by prefix
which is also coded for number: e.g. *sa ar słaɣ°aš* 'I saw him'; *da ar tłaɣ°aš* 'we saw
him'. Similarly for second person singular: *w*/*b*/*p*; pl. *f*.

CONJUGATION
The basic model is personal pronoun – personal marker – tense characteristic –
stem: e.g. indicative mood, active, present tense, positive, of dynamic verb with
root *džɪn* 'learn' (the tense marker when the subject is first or second person is
-o-):

    sa txɪłɪr s.o.dž 'I learn, study the book';
    wa txɪłɪr w.o.dž 'you learn, study the book';
    da txɪłɪr d.o.dž 'we learn, study the book'.

This tense is negated with the affix *-rqɪm*: e.g. *sa txɪłɪr z.džɪ.rqɪm* 'I don't study
the book.'

Stative verb, monopersonal, e.g. *txan* 'to write': *sa s.o.txa* 'I write'; *wa w.o.txa* 'you write'; *da d.o.txa* 'we write'.

There are several past tenses, each representing a different segmentation of past time in respect of aspect, mode, and duration. Some examples with the verb *ḳ°en* 'to go', present, *s.o.ḳ°e.r*:

> past perfective: *sa sɪḳ°aš* 'I went';
> past imperfective: *sa sɪḳ°e(r)t* 'I was going';
> past anterior: *sa sɪḳ°at* 'I had gone'.

Future: the characteristic is *-nu-*: e.g. *sa sɪḳ°e.nu.š* 'I shall go'; *da dɪ.laža.nu.š* 'we shall work'.

NOMINAL CONJUGATION
Examples: *sa sɪ.ucit'el'.š* 'I am a teacher' (Russian loan-word); *wa wɪ.ucit'el'.š* 'you are a teacher'.

IMPERATIVE
Base, or personal marker + base: e.g. *sa.reḳ°a!* 'let me go!' *f.txɪ!* 'write!'

PREVERBS
These are directional markers, prefixed to verbs: e.g.

> *šā-* indicates locus under something, movement from under something;
> *da-* indicates locus within;
> *q°a-* indicates locus behind;
> *fa-* indicates locus at end of something.

An example: *q°atɪn* 'to stand behind someone/something'.

Participles: intransitive, e.g. from *txen*, *txer* 'writing'; transitive with prefix *zɪ-*, e.g. *zɪšar* 'leading (someone)'.

The passive characteristic is *-za-*: e.g. *sa sɪ.za.džar* 'read by me'; *wa wɪ.za.džar* 'read by you'. Future: *sa sɪ.za.dža.nu.r* 'what will be read by me'.

GERUND
Examples: *sa.dž.aw* 'I (while) reading ...'; *da.dž.aw* 'we (while) reading ...'.

Postpositions

In Kabardian these are not clearly differentiated from nominals and verbals; they may be declined. Examples: *dež* 'at, of', e.g. *nɪbžeɣ°m dež* 'at/of (my) friend', *Muhamad i ḳ°ašɪm dež šī'aš* 'Muhamad was at his brother's place'; *nes* 'as far as, up to', e.g. *qalam nes ḳ°e* 'go to the town'. In these examples, *nɪbžeɣ°.m* and *ḳ°ašɪ.m* are both in the *-m* case.

Word order

SOV is basic.

KACHIN

INTRODUCTION

Burmic group of Sino-Tibetan. The Kachin area forms the northernmost administrative unit in the Union of Burma (capital Myityina). There are about 160,000 speakers in Burma, and possibly 80,000 in China. The ethnonym is Tsingpho. The many dialects can be grouped in three main divisions: (a) Tsingpo, (b) Maru, (c) Nung.

SCRIPT

A Roman alphabet with diacritics was provided for Kachin by O. Hanson in 1896. The diacritics mark the reduced vowels; the tones are not marked. A revised and simplified script for Kachin as spoken in China was worked out in the 1950s. Hanson's script used here, marks the aspirates as *hp*, *ht*, *hk*.

PHONOLOGY

Consonants

> stops: non-aspirate: p, b, t, d, k, g; aspirate: p', t', k'; retroflex p, ḅ, ḳ, g,;
>   aspirate p', ḳ'
> affricates: ts, tʃ, dʒ
> fricatives: f, v, s, z, ʃ, ʒ, h
> nasals: m, n, ŋ; m', n'
> lateral: l
> semi-vowels: w, j

Both sets of stops palatalized: e.g. /p', b', p''/ (excluding the dentals).

Vowels

> i, e, ə, ă, a, ɑ, o, u

Tones

The dialect described by Puzitski (1968) has three tones (not marked): mid-level, high-level, mid-falling. Tone is phonemic.

MORPHOLOGY AND SYNTAX

Noun

Nouns are indeclinable, and there is no grammatical gender. If necessary, lexical means are used to specify male/female, e.g. *-la-* for male, *-num-* for female: e.g. *kăsha* 'child': *lakăsha* 'boy', *numkăsha* 'girl'; *myenla* 'Burmese man', *myennum* 'Burmese woman'. A similar pair for animals is *la/yi*: e.g. *gumrala* 'stallion', *gumrayi* 'mare'.

The particle *ni* acts as a pluralizer: e.g. *măsha ni* 'people'; *gumra ni* 'horses'. A plural may also be made by reduplication.

Adjective

Invariable; adjective may precede or follow noun; if following, it takes relative marker *ai*: e.g. *sănat gălu* 'long rifle'; *gălu ai sănat* '(which is) long rifle'.

COMPARATIVE

Made with *hta grau*: e.g. *Ngai a kumra gaw wora hta grau kăba ai* 'My horse is bigger than that one' (*ngai a*, see **Pronoun**, below; *gaw*, subject marker; *wora*, demonstrative pronoun; *kăba* (verb) 'to be big').

Pronoun

PERSONAL INDEPENDENT

	Singular	Dual	Plural
1	ngai	an	anhte(ng)
2	nang	nan	nanhte(ng)
3	shi, hkri	shan, hkan	shanhte(ng), hkanhte

POSSESSION

First and second person singular have specific possessive forms, *nye*, *na*: e.g. *nye nta* 'my house'; *na sha* 'your child'. All three persons also make a possessive by means of the particle *a/ai*: e.g. *nang a nta* 'your house'; *shi a gumra* 'his horse'.

DEMONSTRATIVE PRONOUN

Three-degree graduation: *ndai* 'this' – *dai* 'that' – *waw* 'that yonder'; with a plural, *ndaini* 'these'. Another series of demonstratives takes into account position in vertical plane relative to speaker: e.g. *wora* (on the same level as speaker), *htawra* (higher than speaker), *lera* (lower). Example: *ndai laika = laika ndai* 'this book'.

INTERROGATIVE PRONOUN

kădai 'who?'; *kăra* 'what?'; with plural in *-ni*, or reduplication.

RELATIVE PRONOUN

ai is used: e.g. *ngai hpe karum ai masha* 'the man (*masha*) who (*ai*) helps (*hpe karum*) me'.

Numerals

1–10: *lăngai, lăhkawng, măsum, măli, mănga, kru, sătnit, măsat, chăhku, shi*; 20 *nkum/hkum*; 30 *sum shi*; 40 *măli shi*; 100 *lă sa*.

Numerical classifiers are used: collectives (e.g. *hpun* 'a herd') and measure words (e.g. *lin* 'a vessel'). The numeral follows the classifier: e.g. *saupa lin lahkawng* 'two measures of water'.

Verb

The invariable base is followed by grammatical markers which generate distinctions of aspect, mood, tense, and – exceptionally for a Sino-Tibetan language – person. For example, in imperfective aspect, *galaw* 'to do', present tense:

	Singular	Plural
1	ngai gălaw nngai	anhte gălaw gă ai
2	nang gălaw ndai	nanhte gălaw mă ndai
3	shi gălaw ai	shihte gălaw mă ai

In perfective aspect, past tense: e.g. sing. 1 *ngai gălaw sa ngai* 'I did'; pl. 1 *anhte gălaw sa ga ngai* 'we did'.

These grammatical markers are also coded for subject/object relationship; e.g.

> *de ai* encodes action by 1st p. sing. on or for 2nd p. sing.: *ngai nang hpe jaw de ai* 'I give you this' (*hpe* (postposition) 'to, for');
> *mi ai* encodes action by 2nd or 3rd p. sing. on 1st p. sing.: *shanhte ngai hpe tsun mi ai* 'they speak to me'.

Similarly in hortative mood and interrogative version: *shi sa u ga!* 'let him go!'; *Shi hpa ra ai ta* 'What does he want?' Cf. *Nang namsi sha n ni* 'Do you eat fruit?' (imperfective aspect; *n ni* = 2nd on 3rd); *Nang namsi sha sa ni* 'Did you eat the fruit? (perfective aspect: *sa ni* encodes action by 2nd on 3rd; *sha* 'eat', cf. Tibetan /za.ba/).

TENSE MARKERS
Future *na*, e.g. *shi sa na ai* 'he will come'; past *yu*.

MODAL AFFIXES
Continuative *nga*; inchoative *wa*; terminative *tawn*; potential *lu/dang*: e.g. *ngai gălaw lu nngai* 'I can do this'; *ngai gălaw lu na* 'I shall have to do this'.

NEGATIVE
The marker *n* precedes the verb, e.g. *n gălaw* 'not to work'. The prohibitive marker is *hkum*: e.g. *hkum sa!* 'don't go!'

Word order

Fixed SOV; indirect object precedes direct.

1   Shawng npawt ĕ, Mungga nga ai, dai Mungga mung, Kărai Kăsang hte rau nga ai rai nna, dai Mungga gaw, Kărai Kăsang

2 rē ai rai.   Dai gaw shawng npawt ĕ, Kărai

3 Kăsang hte rau nga ai.   Shi kaw nna arai yawng măyawng tai wa ai rē; shi hta nna, ntai ai arai lăngai mi muk, n tai ai rai.

4 Shi hta nsoi nsa rawng ai; dai nsoi nsa

5 chyawm gaw, măsha ni a nhtoi rē.   Dai nhtoi gaw, nsin hta a htoi nga ai; nsin chyawm gaw, dai hpe n hkap la wu ai.

6 Kărai Kăsang shăngun dat ai, Yawhan

7 mying ai măsha lăngai mi, sa ra ai.   Dai wa gaw sakse tai na sa ai; mahkra shi kaw nna kam mu ga, dai nhtoi a lam shi sakse

8 hkam na rai.   Shi gaw dai nhtoi n rai, dai nhtoi a lam sakse hkam na shi sa ai.

KALMYK

INTRODUCTION

Kalmyk belongs to the Oyrat branch of Mongolian. In the seventeenth century the Kalmyk left their Central Asian homelands and moved westwards, finally to settle along the lower Volga; it is here that most of them now live, in the Kalmyk Autonomous Soviet Socialist Republic. The number of speakers is put at c. 140,000. During the Second World War, the Kalmyk were one of the minority peoples deported to central Asia on a charge of collaboration with the enemy. The Kalmyk ASSR was re-established in the late 1950s.

There is a sizeable Kalmyk population, probably around 5,000, in the Xinjiang-Uigur Autonomous Region of the CPR.

SCRIPT

Till the mid-seventeenth century a variety of the vertical Mongolian script was used. Cyrillic was adopted in 1924, and again in 1939, after the experimental romanization in the 1930s. Non-initial short vowels are not notated in the script: thus *uls* = /uləs/. Additional letters, *h, җ, ц, ə, θ, γ, ӊ*.

PHONOLOGY

Consonants

    stops: (p), b, t, d, k, g
    affricates: ts, tʃ, dʒ
    fricatives: (f), s, (z), ʃ, ʒ, j, x, h
    nasals: m, n, ŋ
    lateral and flap: l, r

Vowels

    long and short: i, ε, ə, a, y, œ, o, u

There are no diphthongs. /y/ is notated here as *ü*; /œ/ as *ö*.

VOWEL HARMONY

Front vowels followed by front, back by back, with /i/ neutral. /ε, o, œ/ long and short, are found only in first syllables; in following syllables they tend to be neutralized, /ε/ and /œ/ to /y/ or /ə/, /o/ to /a/ or /u/.

MORPHOLOGY AND SYNTAX

Noun

The noun is marked for number and case. Vocalic stems take a plural marker -*s*: e.g. *xarada* 'swallow', pl. *xaradas*. Other pluralizing affixes are -*ud*/-*üd*, -*mud*/-*müd*, -*čud*/-*čüd*: e.g. *nökəd* 'comrade', pl. *nökədmüd*; -*nr*: e.g. *bagš* 'teacher', pl. *bagšnr* /bagʃənər/.

There are nine cases, including the nominative base with null marker; the other cases may be illustrated with the noun *mal* 'cattle': gen. *malin*; dat./loc. *mald*; acc. *malig*; instr. *malar*; abl. *malas*; conj. *malla*; com. *malta*; adit. *malur*. The same endings are added to the plural: e.g. *nökədmüdin* 'of the comrades.'

As in Khalkha (*see* **Mongolian, Modern**), the reflexive possessive (-*n* added to inflected stem, e.g. *malasən* 'from one's own cattle') and the double declension (especially genitive + comitative) are frequent.

Adjective

Adjective precedes noun as attribute and is invariable.

Pronoun

Independent forms with oblique bases and possessive markers:

	Singular			Plural		
	Nominative	Oblique base	Possessive	Nominative	Oblique base	Possessive
1	bi	nan-	-m	bidn	man-	-mdn
2	či	čam-	-čn	tadn	tan-	-tn

The first person plural has an alternative nominative form, *madn*. Third person forms are supplied from the demonstrative series: *ęn* 'this', *ter* 'that'.

INTERROGATIVE PRONOUN
ken, 'who?'; *yun* 'what?'.

Numerals

1–10: *negn, xoyr, hurvn, dörvn, tavn, zurhan, dolan, nəəmn, yisn, arvn*; 20 *xörn*; 30 *hučn*; 40 *döčn*; 100 *zun*. Decimal system.

Verb

In general, close to Khalkha (*see* **Mongolian, Modern**). The Kalmyk verb is marked for aspect (durative, intensive, etc.), five voices (active, passive, hortative, reciprocal, co-operative), two moods (indicative, imperative), tense, person, and number. Overt tense marking is restricted to the indicative mood and the participial forms.

INDICATIVE MOOD

Present and past tense forms are distinguished. The markers are: general present -na/-nə; past -v; past anterior -la/-lə. To the stem and tense marker is added the personal affix for first or second person:

	Singular	Plural
1	-v	-vdn
2	-č	-t

Thus, *naad.na.v* 'I play'.

A progressive present is made with the participial form in -*č*/-*dž* + shortened auxiliary: e.g. *bič.dž.ənəv* 'I am writing'.

The participles and gerunds, or converbs, express various modes and stages of conjoint, contemporary, anterior, successive action; for detail of the closely similar Khalkha system, *see* **Mongolian, Modern**.

A general negating particle is *ǫs*.

Postpositions

Follow nominative, genitive, or comitative cases.

Word order

SOV is basic.

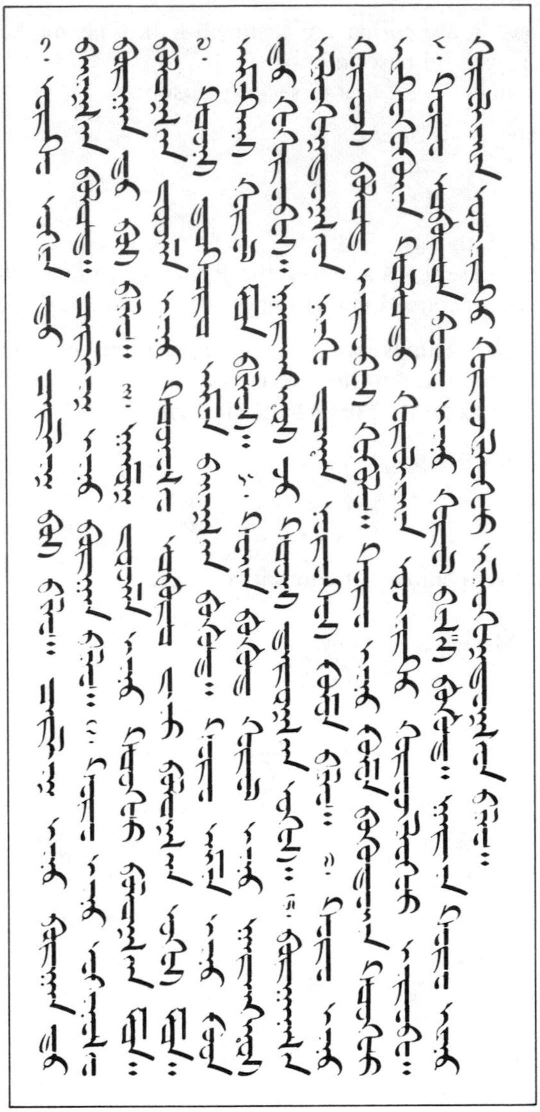

KANNADA (Kanarese)

INTRODUCTION

As regards number of speakers, Kannada comes in third place among the Dravidian languages after Telugu and Tamil; as regards age and quality of literary tradition, it runs Tamil a close second. The most important work in the early period is the *Kavirājamārga*, a rhetorical Sanskritized treatise, enlivened by glimpses of the Kannada people and their customs. Worthy of particular mention is the splendid *vacana* poetry of the Vīraśaiva saints – free verse of mystical and gnomic import in colloquial Kannada – produced in the tenth to twelfth centuries. With its extensive output of novels, drama, and verse, Modern Kannada literature is one of the most flourishing in southern India.

Kannada is the official language of the State of Karnataka. The number of speakers is estimated at about 24 million.

SCRIPT

The syllabary derives ultimately from Brahmi via the transitional script which also underlies Telugu. Order and content are as in Devanagari.

PHONOLOGY

Consonants

> stops: p, b, ṭ, ḍ, t, d, k, g
> affricates: tʃ, dʒ
> fricatives: v, s, ṣ, ḷ, ʃ, j, h
> nasals: m, n, ɲ, ŋ, ṇ
> lateral and flap: l, ḷ, r, ṛ

/ḷ/ is the retroflex fricative which tends to be pronounced as [l] in Modern Kannada. Similarly, /ṛ/ tends to [r]. The stops have aspirated values, not usually found in pure Kannada words. The affricates also have aspirated values. Retroflex phonemes are notated here with a dot: e.g. /ḍ/ = ḍ.

Vowels

> long and short: i, e, a, o, u
> diphthongs: ai, au

Stress

Light stress on first syllable. All Kannada words end in vowels.

Sandhi

/j/ and /v/ are widely used in vocalic juncture: e.g. *guru* + *-u* → *guruvu* 'guru, teacher'; *ā* + *ūṭa* → *āvūṭa* 'that food'; *huli* 'tiger' + *-inda* (instr. affix) → *huliyinda* 'by the tiger'.

MORPHOLOGY AND SYNTAX

Noun

Kannada has three genders: masculine, feminine, and neuter. A typical masculine ending is *-anu*, typical feminine *-aḷu*. Plural markers are *-aru*, *-kaḷu/ galu*. Thus, *sēvaka.nu* 'male servant', and *sēvaka.ḷu* 'female servant', share the plural form *sēvaka.ru*; cf. *maravu* 'tree', pl. *mara.gaḷu*; *ūru* 'village', pl. *ūru.gaḷu*. A reduplicated plural of respect is found: e.g.*dēv.aru.gaḷu* 'gods'.

DECLENSION
There are seven classes: given here is the specimen declension of *sēvaka* 'servant':

	Singular
nominative	sēvakanu
accusative	sēvakanannu
instrumental	sēvakaninda
dative	sēvakanige
genitive	sēvekana
locative	sēvakanalli
vocative	sēvakanē

Plural forms are as singular, with *-r-* replacing *-n-*: e.g. nom. *sēvakaru*, acc. *sēvakarannu*.

Adjective

As attribute, adjective is invariable, preceding noun: e.g. *doḍḍa ūru* 'a big town'.

Pronoun

The first person singular is *nān(u)/nā*, with pl. *nāvu*; similarly, the second person forms are sing. *nīnu/nī*, with pl. *nīvu*. The third person forms are marked for gender: masc. *avanu/ivanu*; fem. *avaḷu/ivaḷu*, in the singular; they share a common plural form: *avaru/ivaru*. The neuter third person form is sing. *adu/idu*, pl. *avu(gaḷu)/ivu(gaḷu)*.

In the declension of the first person singular form, *nān(u)* the base for the oblique cases remains *nann*-: e.g. gen. *nanna*, acc. *nannannu*.

DEMONSTRATIVE PRONOUN
ī/intha 'this'; *ā/antha* 'that'.

INTERROGATIVE PRONOUN
Masc. *yāvanu*, fem. *yāvaḷu*; they coalesce as *yāru* 'who?'; *yāvudu* 'what?'.

RELATIVE PRONOUN
None in Kannada; *see* **Verb**, below, for formation of relative clause.

Numerals

The numerals 1–5 inclusive have each two forms reflecting gender. The neuter series is *ondu*, *eraḍu*, *mūru*, *nālku*, *aidu*; the corresponding masculine/feminine forms are *obba*, *ibbaru*, *mūvaru*, *nālvaru*, *aivaru*. From 6 onwards, there is only one form for each numeral. 6–10: *āru*, *ēḷu*, *eṇṭu*, *ombhattu*, *hattu*. 11 *hannondu*; 12 *hanneraḍu*; 13 *hadimūru*; 20 *ippattu*; 21 *ippattondu*; 30 *muvattu*; 40 *nālvattu*; 100 *nūru*.

Verb

Fundamental to the structure of the Kannada verb is the verbal noun series comprising the infinitive, the gerunds, and the participles. For the stem *māḍu* 'to do, make', the forms are:

infinitive: *māḍa*;
gerunds: present *māḍuttā*; past *māḍi*; negative *māḍade*;
participles: present *māḍuva*; past *māḍida*; negative *māḍada*.

For many Kannada verbs, the form of the verbal noun is not predictable; cf. *koḍu* 'to give' – *koṭṭu*; *koḷḷu* 'to take' – *koṇḍu*; *nāgu* 'to laugh' – *nakku*.
There are three moods: indicative, imperative, suppositional.

INDICATIVE MOOD
Present tense (marker -*(u)tt*); past tense (marker -*(i)d*); future tense (marker -*(u)v*). Thus, from stem *māḍu* 'to do':

		Present			Past			Future	
		Sing.	Pl.		Sing.	Pl.		Sing.	Pl.
1	māḍutt.	-ēne	-ēve	māḍid	-ēnu	-evu	māḍuv	-enu	-evu
2		-īye	-īri		-e	-iri		-e	-iri
3 masc.		-āne }	-āre		-anu }	-aru		-anu }	-aru
fem.		-āḷe }			-aḷu }			-aḷu }	
nt.		-ade	-ave		māḍitu	-uvu		-udu	-uvu

NEGATIVE CONJUGATION
The personal affixes are added directly to the root, without infixed marker. The

negative form thus produced does duty for all three tenses: thus, the present, past, and future negative indicative of *māḍu* is:

		Singular	Plural
1		māḍenu	māḍevu
2		māḍe	māḍiri
3	masc.	māḍanu ⎫	māḍaru
	fem.	māḍalu ⎭	
	nt.	māḍadu	māḍavu

IMPERATIVE MOOD

Here the verb is marked for three persons, singular and plural, without distinction of gender in the third person: e.g. sing. 1 *māḍuve*, 2 *māḍu*, 3 *māḍali*; pl. *māḍōṇa* (with variants), *māḍiri*, *māḍali*.

SUPPOSITIONAL MOOD

Made by adding the personal affixes to the stem extended by the past-tense characteristic vowel *-i*: e.g. *māḍ.i.y.ēnu* 'I may/might do'.

NON-FINITE FORMS

Present–future participle: *māḍuva* 'doing, is doing, will be doing'. Past participle: *māḍida* 'was doing'. Pronominal endings may be attached to these forms to produce verbal nouns marked in third person for gender: e.g. *māḍuva.v.anu* 'he who does'; *māḍuva.va.aḷu* 'she who does'. Similarly in the negative conjugation: *māḍada* 'who is not doing'; *māḍada.va.aḷu* 'she who is not doing/did not do'.

The participial forms are used in the formation of relative clauses; the forms themselves are neutral as to voice: cf. *pāṭhavannu ōdida huḍuganu* 'the boy who read the lesson'; *huḍuganu ōdida pāṭhavannu* 'the lesson read by the boy'.

Postpositions

Nouns, participles, pronouns, etc. governed by postpositions are usually in the genitive case: e.g. *oḍane* 'along with', *nanna + oḍane → nannoḍane* 'along with me'; *horatu* 'apart from', *nanna horatu* 'apart from me'.

Word order

SOV.

೧   ఆదియల్లివాక్యవిర్ఱ్తు అవాక్యవుదేవరసంగడకూడా

౨   యిర్ఱ్తుమర్ఱ్తలవాక్యవీదేవరు ‖ అదులదియల్లదేవ

౩   రసంగడకూడాయిర్ఱ్తు ‖ సమస్తవులదరకృయ్యవుం

     టాయికుమర్ఱ్తుఆదద్దెల్లాఅహరిందలల్లడెబ్యేశి వందు

౪   నువుంటాదద్దిల్ల ‖ అదరల్లిఴీవవుంటుమర్ఱ్తలఆఴీవపు

౫   మనుష్యరిశేబ్యశాఇర్ఱ్తు ‖ ఆబేశఫులంధకారదల్లి ప్ర

     కాశిశికుఆదరశిలలంధకారవులదరంనక్ర హిగణల్లవు ‖

౬   యోవాననెంబితుసరుల్లవుక్కమనుష్యరుదేవర

౭   కృయ్యకఴిహిసపట్టను ‖ అసురెనకృయ్యక్సమస్తరువి

     క్వాశిసువదాగేబేశకగేసాఊ కొదసాఊయాగిింద

೮   ను ‖ అవనులబేశకల్లఆదరశిలబేశకగేసాఊ కొడువ

೯   దక్ఴిందను ‖

KARACHAY-BALKAR

INTRODUCTION

Baskakov's (1966) classification puts this language in the Kipchak-Oguz subdivision of the Kipchak group of Turkic languages. Both the Karachays and the Balkars use the ethnonym *alan*, which would link them to the Scythian tribes who inhabited the area between the Black Sea and the Danube in the Middle Ages. The language of the fourteenth-century *Codex Cumanicus* is close to Karachay-Balkar.

Today, about 160,000 people speak Karachay-Balkar in the Karachaev-Cherkess Autonomous Region and in the Kabardian-Balkar Autonomous Soviet Socialist Republic; the language is used in local media, radio, and newspapers, and some books have been published. Loan-words from Ossete, Kabardian, Arabic, and Persian are fairly numerous.

SCRIPT

Cyrillic + *ý* which denotes the bilabial sonant /ß/.

PHONOLOGY

Consonants

The consonantal inventory is standard Turkic (*see* **Turkic Languages**).

Vowels

    front   rounded: yu, yo
            unrounded: i, e
    back   rounded: u, o
            unrounded: ı, a

That is, /œ/ and /y/ are absent. This division underlies the vowel harmony system of Karachay-Balkar: front is followed by front vowel, back by back, and rounded by rounded: e.g. *kyok.yubyuz* 'our sky'.

Stress

Stress is on the final syllable, displaced by affixation; e.g. by negative marker to preceding syllable: *kelmék* 'to come', *kél.me.gen.di* 'he didn't come'.

MORPHOLOGY AND SYNTAX

Noun

In general, standard Turkic. The plural marker is *-la/-le*, i.e. with loss of final *-r*, which reappears, however, in medial position: e.g. *atla* 'horses', *atlarim* 'my horses'.

The genitive and accusative ending is *-n*V^4, i.e. *-n* + one of four possible vowels; the dative affix has nine variants by assimilation and vowel harmony.

The predicative personal endings and the possessive mrkers are all standard, the latter varying from two possible forms in the third person plural – *-larɪ/-leri* – to eight in the second and first persons plural and third person singular: cf. *ana.gɪz* 'your (pl.) mother'; *džurt.uɣuz* 'your (pl.) homeland'.

Adjective

Standard; a comparative is made in *-raq/-rek*: e.g. *Umar Xalitden uzun.raq.dɪ* 'Umar is taller than Xalit' (ablative case). As in Turkish, intensification is expressed by partial reduplication, with harmonic consonant: e.g. *sap.sarɪ* 'very yellow'; *qap-qara* 'pitch-black'.

Pronoun

Standard, but note third person plural *ala*, with loss of final *r*.

Numerals

Standard, but there is some wavering between the decimal and the vigesimal systems: thus, *on* is 10; 20 may be *eki on* = 2×10, or *bir džɪyɪrma* (cf. Turkish *yirmi*); 40 is *tyort on* = 4×10 or *eki džɪyɪrma* = 2×20.

Verb

Standard Turkic pattern, with passive in *-V*^{10}*l/n*; causative in *-d/tV*^{4}*r*; reciprocal in *-V*^{5}*s*; reflexive in *-V*^{5}*n*, with variants: e.g. *ayɪrɪl* 'be separated'; *keltir* 'to bring' ('cause to come').

TENSE STRUCTURE
The present–future tense has a link vowel between stem and ending:

Singular	Plural
bar.a.ma 'I go'	bar.a.bɪz
bar.a.sa	bar.a.sɪz
bar.a.dɪ	bar.a.dɪla

The past definite marker is *-dɪ-*: e.g. *ayt.dɪ.m* 'I said'; *ayt.dɪn...* 1st pl. *ayt.dɪ.q*. The auxiliary *tur-* is used to make the present progressive, plus the gerund in *-a/-e/-i/-y*: e.g. *išley **tur**.a.ma* 'I am working at present'.

There are two futures: the first, or presumptive, future tense has the infix -*ır/ir*: e.g. *al.ır.bız* 'we shall (probably) take'. The second, or definite, future has -*lıq/-nıq/-rıq*: e.g. *al.lıq.bız* 'we shall take'.

Postpositions

These govern all cases except the accusative. E.g. with dative: *deri* 'up to', 'as far as', e.g. *yuj.ge deri bar.dı.m* 'I reached home'; with ablative: *arı* 'beyond', e.g. *kyopyur.den arı* 'beyond the bridge'; with genitive: *amaltın* 'because of', *seni amaltın* 'because of you'.

Word order

As normal in Turkic.

---

1. Исса келиб синагогагъа киреди; анда уа къолу къу-рушхан биреу бар эди.

2. Алайдагъыла, Исса шабаткюн аны сау этгени болса, аны сылтау этиб Иссаны терслер акъыл бла, Аны ызындан къарайдыла.

3. Исса ол къолу къурушханнга: ортагъа чыкъ—дейди.

4. Алайдагъылагъа да: шабаткюн игилик этгенми игиди, огъесе джаманлыкъ этгенми? Джанны къутхаргъанмы, огъесе аны джойгъанмы? Алай болгъанлыкъгъа ала, джукъ айтмай, тынглайдыла.

5. Тёгерекдегилени джюреклерини къатылыгъына ачый, алагъа хыны къарай, Исса ол сакъатха: къолунгу узат—дейди. Ол да къолун узатады, олсагъат огъуна сакъат къолу ол башха къолу кибик, сау болады.

6. Фарисейле, тышына чыгъыб дженгил огъуна иродчула бла бирге, Иссаны джояр ючюн кенгеш этедиле.

7. Алая Исса Кесини сохталары бла бирге алайдан тенгиз таба кетеди; Аны ызындан Галилеядан, Иудеядан,

8. Иерусалимден, Идумеядан эм да Иорданны арыджанын-дан кёб халкъ джыйын болуб тебредиле. Аны кибик, Тир бла Сидонну тёгереклеринде джашагъанла да, Аны неле этгенлерин эштиб, уллу джыйын болуб Аннга келе эдиле.

(Mark 3: 1–8)

KARAKALPAK

INTRODUCTION

In Baskakov's (1966) classification, Karakalpak is placed in the Kipchak-Nogay sub-division of the Kipchak group of Western Turkic languages. It is spoken by about 280,000 people in the Karakalpak Autonomous Soviet Socialist Republic (created in the 1930s), which lies to the south and west of the Aral Sea. There are two main dialects, which are not widely divergent. The literary standard is based on the North-Eastern dialect. The language is used in the local media – radio, television, newspapers, and periodicals – and some books are published.

SCRIPT

Karakalpak was first written (from 1924 onwards) in an adapted Arabic script. The experimental romanization periód in the 1930s was followed by an expanded Cyrillic script, which, as amended in 1957, is in use today. The additional non-Cyrillic letters are: ә, ғ, қ, ң, ө, ү, ў, х.

PHONOLOGY

Consonants

> stops: p, b, t, d, k, g, q
> affricates: ts, tʃ
> fricatives: w, v, f, s, z, ʃ, ʒ, j, γ, x, h
> nasals: m, n, ŋ
> lateral and flap: l, r

Vowels

> front: i, ε, ə, œ, y; back: i, a, ɔ, u

VOWEL HARMONY

Back–back and front–front sequence is rigorously observed. Theoretically, rounded should always be followed by rounded, and unrounded by unrounded, but according to Baskakov this is only partially observed.

MORPHOLOGY AND SYNTAX

In general, Karakalpak is close to standard Turkic model (*see* **Turkic Languages**; **Turkish**).

The plural marker is *-lar/-ler*: e.g. *Qaraqalpaqlar* 'the Karakalpaks'.

Assimilation in the declension system yields several initials for most case affixes, plus harmonic change in vowel; thus, the genitive takes the following forms: *-nɪn, -nin, -dɪn, din, -tɪn, -tin*. Hereafter, the index convention is followed.

The possessive affixes are standard. The adjective makes a comparative in *-ɪraq/-irek*.

The first person singular pronoun is *men*, with oblique cases formed on this same base.

The numerals are standard, with some variant spellings, e.g. *žeti* 7 = Turkish *yedi*; *žigirma* 20 = Turkish *yirmi*.

Verb

Four voices with standard markers, e.g. *-Vn/l* for passive: *alɪn* 'to be taken', *-t/d.i/ɪ.r* for causative: *keltir-* 'bring' (*kelmek* 'to come').

Frequentative or irregular action can be marked by *-qɪla*[4]: e.g. *at-* 'to shoot', *atqɪla-* 'to fire at intervals'. An intensifying infix is *-ɪnqɪra-*[2].

There is a large inventory of participial and gerundial forms, marking tense, aspect and mood: e.g. *alɪp* 'having taken'; *ala* 'taking'.

There are two sets of personal endings, full and truncated. The full endings are used, for example, in the simple present, e.g. *al.a.man* 'I take'; and in the present progressive with the auxiliary *žatɪr*, e.g. *men alɪp.žatɪr.man* 'I am taking'; and again the future tense with the future partipicial marker *-žaq*, e.g. *men al.a.žaq.man* 'I shall take'.

The short endings appear, for example, in the past definite: e.g. *men al.dɪ.m* 'I took'. Other forms: *men al.ar edim* 'I'd have taken'; *al.sam* 'if I take'; *al.γay.man* 'let me take'.

As in Turkic generally, the participial forms are used in the construction of relative clauses: e.g. *Men seniŋ bar.ma.i.žayɪn.dɪ bilemen* 'I know that you won't go', where *senin* is the genitive of the second person singular pronoun *sen*; *-ma-* is the negative infix; *-žaq/žay-* is the future marker; *-n* is the genitive inflection; *-dɪ* marks the accusative; *bil.e.men* 'I know'.

Postpositions

Standard Turkic inventory.

KARELIAN

INTRODUCTION

Karelian belongs to the Balto-Finnic group of Finno-Ugric. There are about 100,000 speakers in the Karelian Autonomous Soviet Socialist Republic. It is not known even approximately when Finno-Ugric speaking tribes reached and settled in the Karelian Isthmus, but they were certainly there in the early Middle Ages, when *karjalaiset* are first mentioned in Russian chronicles. The following centuries saw Karelian expansion towards the White Sea, and southwards towards Lakes Ladoga and Onega and the Valdai Hills. In 1323 a new frontier line between Novgorod Russia and Sweden divided the Karelians into two groups: those to the east of it are the ancestors of the present-day Karelians, while those to the west of it merged with other groups to form the nucleus of the modern Finnish nation.

The earliest record of Karelian is a spell against lightning, scratched on a piece of birch-bark dating from the thirteenth century. Apart from some translation of religious texts, Karelian has never been used for written literature. It should be pointed out, however, that it was in Karelia, particularly in the Uhtua area, that Elias Lönnroth was able to draw on the vast riches of Karelian folklore for the material which he subsequently reworked to form the *Kalevala*. Post-Lönnroth collections often preserve more clearly the Karelian nature of the texts.

There are three main dialects: Karelian proper, Olonets (*aunuksen kieli*), and Lud, the latter being close to Veps (*see* **Balto-Finnic Minor Languages**). The three dialects vary in their treatment of consonant gradation; it is close to the Finnish standard in Karelian proper, and virtually absent in Lud (cf. Veps). The dialects also vary in lexicon: e.g. Karelian *kirpu* 'flea' (Finnish *kirppu*) is *čonžoi* in Olonets and *sonzar'* in Lud.

The official languages for administration, education, and the media in the ASSR are Finnish and Russian.

SCRIPT

If written, Karelian uses a Roman base plus diacritics.

PHONOLOGY

Consonants

stops, p, b, t, d, k, g
affricates: tʃ, dʒ
fricatives: v, s, z, ʃ, ʒ, s', z', j, h
nasals: m, n, ɲ
lateral: l, l'
flap: r, r'
semi-vowel: w

/t', d'/ occur, i.e. palatalized; and /p, t, k/ occur geminated: /pp, tt, kk/. /tʃ/ also occurs geminated.

CONSONANT GRADATION
In Karelian proper, consonant gradation is largely as in Finnish standard (for detail, *see* **Finnish**), i.e. strong grade in open syllables, weak grade in closed. As examples of divergence from Finnish standard:

	Genitive	*Finnish*	
mečča 'forest'	mečän	metsä	metsän
joki 'river'	joven	joki	joen
sada 'hundred'	šuan	sata	sadan
hammaš 'tooth'	hambahan	hammas	hampaan

Vowels

i, e, ɛ, a, œ, o, y, u

All combine to form diphthongs. /ɛ/ is notated here as *ä*, /œ/ as *ö*, /y/ as *ü*.

VOWEL HARMONY
/a, o, u/ followed by like; similarly /ɛ, œ, y/. /e/ and /i/ are neutral.

MORPHOLOGY AND SYNTAX

Noun

The plural marker is *-t* in nominative and accusative; in oblique cases *-i-* is infixed, extended to *-loi-/-l'öi-* in certain phonetic environments: e.g. from *mua* 'earth' (Finnish *maa*), ablative *mualoida*.

DECLENSION
Thirteen cases are made by agglutinative suffixation. There is one general paradigm for all nouns, anomalies occurring in the partitive only. There are, of course, phonetic variants. As an example, *hammaš* 'tooth': the consonant gradation is *-mm-/-mb-*, with *-mm-* appearing in nominative, accusative, and

partitive singular only. Thus, e.g. gen. *hambahan*, iness. *hambahašša*, abl. *hambahalda*; plural: *hambahat*, gen. *hambahin*, part. *hambahie*.

Adjective

As attribute, adjective precedes noun, and has concord in case and number. A comparative is made in *-mbi-*: e.g. *l'evie* 'wide' – *l'eviembi*.

Pronoun

PERSONAL INDEPENDENT

	Singular	Genitive	Plural	Genitive
1.	mie	miwn	müö	miän
2	šie	šiwn	t'üö	t'iän
3	hiän/že	hän'en/žen	hüö	hiän

These are declined with five oblique cases; e.g. of *mie*, *miwn*: acc. *miwn*, ill. *miwh*, adess. *miwla*, part. *milma*.

DEMONSTRATIVE PRONOUN
t'ämä 'this', *tua* 'that', *že* 'that' (already mentioned)'. Plurals in *n'ämä*, *nua*, *n'e*. Declined with three oblique cases.

INTERROGATIVE PRONOUN
ken 'who?'; *mi* 'what?'. Three oblique cases. The interrogative pronouns are also used as relative pronouns.

POSSESSIVE PRONOUNS
oma is affixed to the genitive of relevant pronoun: e.g. *miwn-oma* 'my', *šiwn-oma* 'your'. The personal markers in second and third persons, *-š* and *-h*, are used for close kin only. The first person marker, *-n'e/-n'i*, *-zen'i*, is described by Makarov (1966) as a term of endearment or a diminutive only: e.g. *tuattozen'i* '(dear) daddy'.

Numerals

1–10: *üks'i*, *kakši*, *kolme*, *n'el'l'ä*, *viiz'i*, *kuwži*, *šeiččimen*, *kahekšan*, *ühekšän*, *kümmenen*; 20 *kakšikümmen'd'ä*; 100 *šada*.

Verb

Finite and non-finite forms; active and passive voices; positive and negative versions. There are four moods; the indicative mood has four tenses, two simple and two compound. The subjunctive and the potential moods have two tenses each. The fourth mood is the imperative, present only.

SPECIMEN CONJUGATION

šanuo 'to say'; indicative mood, present tense:

	Positive		Negative	
	Singular	Plural	Singular	Plural
1	šanon	šanomma	en šano	emmä šano
2	šanot	šanotta	et šano	et'ť'ä šano
3	šanow	šanotah	ei šano	ei **šanota**

IMPERFECT

Sing. *šanoin, šanoit, šano*; pl. *šanoimma, šanoja, šanottih*. The negative is *en, et*, etc., *šanon*, with distinctive form in third plural *ei šanottu*. The perfect and pluperfect are made with the auxiliary *olen, olet*, etc. Again, the third person plural has a specific form: *ei olla šanottu* (perfect).

SUBJUNCTIVE

šanoz'in, sanoz'it; neg. *en, et šanois'*.

POTENTIAL

šanonnen, šannonet; neg. *en, et šanonne*; both with distinctive forms in third person plural: *ei sanottais', šanottanne*.

IMPERATIVE

šanokko(is), pl. *šanokkua(kkois)*; neg. *el'a šano, el'giä šanokkua*.

Participial and gerundial forms and usage correspond closely to those in Standard Finnish: e.g. the inessive of the declined infinitive, in *-eššä/-eššä*, expresses concomitant action; the illative in *-mah/-mäh* inceptive action, the elative in *-mašta/-mäštä* motion from or out of something: e.g. *Hiän tulow l'eikkuamašta* 'He comes back from the reaping.'

Prepositions and postpositions

Karelian uses both prepositions and postpositions; e.g. postposition: *miwda vaššen* 'in relation to me'; preposition: *ennen üöd'ä* 'before nightfall'. The case system is, of course, rich enough to express many meanings requiring prepositions or postpositions in other languages; e.g. *talvekši* 'in winter'.

Compounding

As in Finnish, compounding is a highly productive source of lexical enrichment: noun (in nom. or gen.) + noun, adjective/adverb + noun: cf. *keviä.vihma* 'spring rain'; *vihma-keviä* 'a rainy spring'.

Word order

As in Finnish.

KAREN

INTRODUCTION

Spoken by about 2 million people in south-east Burma and western Thailand, this language complex is certainly of Tibeto-Burman stock, but typologically diverges up to a point – e.g. in word order – from its Bodic, Baric, and Burmic congeners. The main forms are Sgaw and Pho Karen. There is a sizeable body of religious and pedagogic literature in Sgaw, which also has periodicals and some creative writing, along with a local radio service.

SCRIPT

A Latin-based notation for Sgaw Karen dates from the mid-nineteenth century. The Mon script has also been used.

PHONOLOGY

Consonants

The dental series is represented by /t, th, d, θ, n, l, r, s, sh, z/, where /th/ and /sh/ are aspirates. The labial, palatal and velar series have unvoiced unaspirate and aspirate stops + associated nasals; the labial series has in addition the voiced stop /b/. The glottal stop and h are present, also the semi-vowels j and w, and the fricative /γ/.

Vowels

i, e, ε, ʉ, ə, a, ɔ, o, u

Tones

High, mid, and low. Tone is affected by a final glottal stop. Tone is phonemic: e.g. *pγa* 'person', *pγà* 'old'.

MORPHOLOGY AND SYNTAX

There are five main classes of word. Nominal and verbal bases are not formally distinguished, and differ only in terms of their valencies. The class of attributes (adjectives) is included in the verb. The other three main classes are: pronouns, numerical classifiers, and particles.

Noun

Nouns are simple or compound: *γî* 'house', *tàsháyî* 'hospital' (*tà* 'item'; *shá* 'sick').

Attributes follow the noun in genitive or adjectival relationship: e.g. *kə'sɜ̀phó* 'hill people' (*kə'sɜ̀* 'mountain'); *lì' γɔ tə' bé' 'i* 'this red book' (*lì'* 'book'; *γɔ* 'red'; *tə'* 'one'; *bé'* = numerical classifier for books).

There is a very large inventory of classifiers, which follow the numeral.

Pronoun

First and second persons independent forms are *jɛ*, *nɛ́* in the singular, with plural forms *wɛ́* and *θúwɛ́*. There are objective and subjective possessive forms. The third person forms are made periphrastically: e.g. in singular, by using *pγa* 'person'.

DEMONSTRATIVE PRONOUN/ADJECTIVE
'i 'this'; *ne* 'that'. These follow noun + attribute phrase.

INTERROGATIVE PRONOUN
mə'ta(γa) 'who?'; *mə* 'what?' *di* 'what?'.

RELATIVE PRONOUN
The all-purpose particle *lɔ́* is used: e.g. *'ə'má lɔ́ 'ə'dó'tà γe* 'a wife who is pretty' (lit. 'whose figure is good').

Numerals

1–10: *tɔ́*, *khí*, *θɔ́*, *lwì*, *jɛ̀*, *xɣ́*, *nwí*, *xɔ'*, *khwí*, *tə'shi*. These precede the classifiers.

Verb

In a typical verbal complex the main verb occupies the nucleus, with modal verbs and auxiliaries to the left, and attributes, auxiliary verbs, and aspectual markers to the right.

The modal verbs include *θá* expressing intention; *plé* expressing permission. Auxiliary verbs: e.g. *θé/kɛ́*, both expressing potentiality: 'can, be able'. Modal and aspectual auxiliaries: *wi* perfective; *di'* imperfective; *dɔ'* continuous action; *kə'* future.

NEGATION
Expressed by *tə'* (...*bá'*): e.g. *kə' lɛ bá'* 'will definitely go' (*bá'* is the aspectual auxiliary emphasizing action); *lɛ tə' θé* 'cannot go'; *tə' lɛ bá'* 'definitely did not go'; *lɛ tə' γe!* 'don't go!' (lit. 'go not good').

Prepositions

Lá is a general preposition with several meanings (used also as relative pronoun): e.g. *láwètə'kú* 'in Rangoon'. Exceptionally for a Tibeto-Burman language, Karen has no postpositions.

Word order

Again exceptionally for a Tibeto-Burman language, SVO.

(Sgaw dialect)

KASHMIRI

INTRODUCTION

By far the most important of the Dardic languages, Kashmiri is the official language of the Indian state of Jammu and Kashmir. The number of speakers is estimated at 3 million. The ethnonym is /kʼaʃiːrʸ/. For controversy surrounding the exact genetic status of Kashmir and the other Dardic languages, *see* **Dardic Languages**.

Alone among the Dardic languages, Kashmiri has a literary tradition dating from the thirteenth/fourteenth century. The earliest Kashmiri poetry was written by the poetess Lal Ded in the fourteenth century; later, two of the best writers in a specifically Kashmiri genre, the *lol* ('love') lyric, were also women – Haba Khotun in the sixteenth century and Arnimal in the eighteenth century.

SCRIPT

Originally, Kashmiri was written in the Sharada version of Devanagari. It is now written in the Urdu version of the Arabo-Persian script, with specific adaptations for Kashmiri phonemes.

PHONOLOGY

The Kashmiri phonological system is of considerable complexity. The following grid displays the basic phonemes, disregarding secondary articulation values. For these, see the notes following the grid.

Consonants

 stops: p, ph, ṭ, ṭh, t, th, k, kh, b, ḍ, d
 affricates: c, č
 fricatives: s, ṣ, ʃ, z, ʒ, h
 nasals: m, n
 lateral and flap: l, r
 semi-vowels: j, w

Notes
1. Stops: this is the familiar NIA series, minus the voiced aspirate member. All stops (including the aspirates) occur palatalized: /pʼ, phʼ, bʼ/, etc., and all, except the labials, occur labialized: /t°, th°/, etc.

2. Affricates: Kashmiri has a dual series of affricates: (a) a dental series (single focus) based on /c/ pure and aspirated, each of these with palatalized and labialized correlatives: /c, c', c°, c', c'', c'°/ (six terms); (b) a palatal series based on /č/, pure and aspirate, with labialized correlatives (four terms). The base phoneme (dual focus) for this series is represented by Zakhar'in and Edel'man (1971) as čǰ.

The Kashmiri affricates appear to have a homorganic sibilant fricative onset. Examples given in Zakhar'in and Edel'man include (here simplified): *bučh* 'it stung, bit', transcribed as /bᵒu-ʋ-s-čh/. Similarly, for a voiced affricate: *baji* 'more, bigger', /bᵒəʒdʒi/.

3. Initial clusters are articulated with the help of epenthetic vowels, which harmonize with stem vowel: *drog* 'dear' /doroʋg°/.

4. /s, z, h, l, r, w/ occur palatalized; /s, z, ʃ, h, l, r/ occur labialized.

5. /m', n', n°/ are present.

The complete grid comprises 69 phonemes. In this entry, the retroflex phonemes are denoted by subscript dot; e.g. /ḍ/ = ḍ.

Vowels

> short: ɪ, ə, a, o, u, œ, y
> long: iː, eː, aː, oː, uː

These are basic values; all occur nasalized, and all, especially the short vowels, have many variants. Close transcription of Kashmiri is exceedingly complicated; here, a simplified approximation is used. (Long vowels are notated here as ī, ē, etc.)

The Kashmiri vocalic system has two distinctive features:

(a) Regressive assimilation, whereby the root vowel is modified by the affix (cf. *Uygur*): e.g. *pūth'* 'book'; oblique base, *poṭh'ɪ*.
(b) The so-called matra vowels – ultra-short medial and final vowels – historically present; now mute, they nevertheless induce the regressive assimilation described in (a). The matra vowels are written in index position: e.g. *host"* 'bull elephant'.

MORPHOLOGY AND SYNTAX

Noun

Kashmiri has two genders, masculine and feminine. Gender is very unstable. A typical masculine ending is -"; fem. -ⁱ/ᵘ: both of these matra vowels mark palatalization of the preceding consonant.

Virtually all nouns ending in the singular in a palatalized consonant are feminine.

PLURAL FORMATION

Some examples illustrating affixation and stem change: *māl* 'garland', plural *māl.ı*; *wat* 'way' – *wat.ı*; *mōl* 'father' – *məl'*; *rāt* 'night' – *rəc*; *bud* 'old woman' – *budžı*.

Where singular and plural do not differ, plurality is indicated by verbal concord: e.g. singular *cūr čhuh ā.mut* 'the thief came'; plural *cūr čhıh ā.mıt* 'the thieves came'.

DECLENSION

Four models: two masculine (-" and non-") and two feminine: e.g. masculine in -":

	Singular	*Plural*
nominative	gur" 'horse'	gurⁱ
oblique I	guris	guren
oblique II	guri ⎫	guryau
agentive	gurⁱ ⎭	

Oblique I provides the direct object; oblique II and the agentive are used as subject of transitive verb.

GENITIVE

The inflected postpositions *-h/sund*, *-un*, *-uk* are used. Some examples: *məl'sund gur* 'father's horse'; *məl'sınd' gur^j* 'father's horses'; *məl'sınd'ıs gur'ıs p'ath* 'on father's horse'; *māl'an.hınd'aw gur'aw p'ath* 'on the horses of the fathers'.

Adjective

As attribute, the adjective precedes the noun with which it is in concord for gender, number, and case; e.g. nom. *boḍ" mahanyuv"* 'big man'; obl. *I baḍis mahanvis*; pl. *baḍⁱ mahanivⁱ*. Cf. *baḍıs gāmas manz* 'in the big village'; *baḍ'aw gāmaw manz* 'from big villages'.

COMPARATIVE

Example: *yıh gur hum'ı gur'ı čhuh boḍ* 'this horse is bigger than that one', where *hum'ı gur'ı* is in obl. II.

Pronoun

	Singular		*Plural*	
	Nominative	*Oblique*	*Nominative*	*Oblique*
1	boh	me	asⁱ	ase
2	cə	ce	tohⁱ	tohe

The third person forms are supplied from the demonstrative series.

The personal pronouns have enclitic forms used with verbs: e.g. *di.m* 'give me' (where *.m* marks the first person indirect object); *wučh".h.as* 'they saw me'

716

(.*h* marks the third person agentive; .*as* is first person direct object).

Demonstrative: the series has five degrees of relative distance, ranging from *yɪh* 'this (close at hand)' to *suh* (remote, invisible). All are fully declined.

INTERROGATIVE PRONOUN
k'ah 'who, what?'

RELATIVE PRONOUN
Masc. *yus*, fem. *yossa*, inanimate *yɪh*; pl. *yɪm* (masc.), *yɪma* (fem.).

Numerals

1–10: *akh, zᵃh, trih, cor, panc, ṣah, sath, aiṭh, nav, dah*; 11 *kāh*; 12 *bāh*; 13 *truwāh*; 20 *wuh*; 21 *akawuh*; 22 *zᵃtōwuh*; 29 *kunatrᵃh*; 30 *trᵃh*; 100 *hath*.

Verb

Non-finite forms

> infinitive in -*un*: e.g. *wučhun* 'to see';
> present participle in -*ān*: e.g. *wuchān* 'seeing'; this form is invariable;
> past participle: four forms covering recent to remote past: e.g. *wučhᵘ*; to these forms, the perfective aspect marker -*mutᵘ*- (inflected for gender and number) can be added;
> gerund in -*ɪth*: *wučhɪth* 'having seen, seeing'.

Synthetic forms inherited from Indo-Aryan are represented in Kashmiri by the present–future tense with the following personal endings: singular 1 -*a*, 2 -*akh*, 3 -*i*; plural 1 -*aw*, 2 -*iw*, 3 -*an*, and by the imperative mood.

All other tenses are constructed by conjugating the relevant participle with an auxiliary, *čhus/ās*, marked for person, gender, and number. The present tense of *čhus* has, for example, the following first person forms: singular, masculine *čhus*, feminine *čhes*; plural, masculine *čhɪh*, feminine *čheh*: e.g. *čhus wuchān* 'I see'; *čhɪh wučhān* 'we see'. The negative form is *wučhan.ay*

Future *ās*- + participle: *āsɪ wučhān* 'I shall see'.

The past tense of the auxiliary is based on *os-/əs*-: e.g. *ōsus wuchān* 'I was seeing'. In the past tenses, the non-finite form (apart from the present participle) agrees with the subject of an intransitive verb, with the object of a transitive. The subject of the transitive verb is then in the agentive case (*see* **Pronoun**, above) and may be recapitulated by a personal enclitic marker affixed to the participle: e.g. *me wučhu.**m*** 'I saw him' (i.e. *me* 'by me'; *wučhᵘ* past participle of verb 'to see'; Ø third person implied; -*m* first person oblique enclitic).

Irregularities due to phonetic accommodation, vowel harmony, and other requirements abound in the system.

PASSIVE
The oblique case of the infinitive combines with the verb *yun* 'to come': e.g. *wučhana yunᵘ* 'to be seen'.

Postpositions

The case system is reinforced by an extensive inventory of postpositions, which follow the oblique cases; e.g. *k'ath* 'on', *guris k'ath* 'on the horse'; *sūtin* 'with', *Məlis sūtin āv* 'He came with his father.'

Word order

Rather free; SVO is frequent.

۰ در اِبتِدا اُوس کلام تَہ کلام اُوس خُدائس سنیتِ تَہ کلام اب ١

اُوس خُدا ۰ يِمَى اُوس در اِبتِدا خُدائس سنیتِ ۰ ساری چیز سپن ٢

تَهنٚدی وسیٚلہ سنیتِ پیٚدٕ تَہ تَهنٚدٕ بغیر سپن تَہ کِهہ نٚہ پیٚدٕ یہ پیٚدٕ ٣

سپن ۰ زِندگی آس تَس اَندٚر تَہ سُہ زِندگی آس اِنسائن ہُنٚد نوٚر ٤

۰ تَہ نوٚر چھُ تاریکیہ اندر پرزٚلان تَہ تاہیٚکیہ کُرنٚہ سُہ دریافت ۰ اک ٥

شخصہ اُوس خُدایہ سنٚدٕ طرفٕ سوٚز نَہ آمٚت یٚس یُوحنّا ناو ٦

اُوس یہہ آو گواہیہ ہَنٚدٕ خاطرٕ زٕ نوٚرس پٹھ دیہ گواہی ٧

یٹھ ساری تِمٚنٚدٕ وسیٚلہ اِعتِقاد آنٚ ۰ شَہ اُوسنٚہ سُہ نوٚر ٨

بلکہ نوٚرس پٹھ اُوس گواہی دِنہ آمٚت

KASHUBIAN

This member of the Lekhitic or Pomeranian branch of West Slavonic is spoken by about 200,000 people in the region of the Gulf of Danzig. The Lekhitic group, whose most important member is, of course, Polish, included Polabian (extinct since the eighteenth century) and Slovincian (still spoken by a few people in the 1900s). Of the smaller members of the group, Kashubian alone has, to some extent at least, resisted assimilation to German and Polish speaking populations. The Poles regard Kashubian as a dialect of Polish.

Three dialects of Kashubian are recognized. Phonologically the most interesting is the northern dialect which has movable stress and phonemic quantity. In the central dialect, stress is on the penultimate as in Polish; in the southern, on the initial as in Czech and Slovak.

A striking feature of the verbal system is the analytical perfect with the verb 'to have' as auxiliary, as in German: e.g. *ja mom widzel* = Gm. *ich habe gesehen* 'I have seen'.

In the late nineteenth and early twentieth centuries some attempt was made to establish a literary standard in Kashubian. Since 1956 the Organyzacia Zrzeszenia Kaszubskiego has been publishing the periodical *Kaszube*.

KAWI

See **Javanese, Old**.

KAZAKH

INTRODUCTION

In Baskakov's (1966) classification, Kazakh is placed in the Kipchak-Nogay group of Western Hunnic Turkic. There are over 6 million speakers in the Kazakh Soviet Socialist Republic, and about half a million in the Xinjiang-Uygur Autonomous Region of the CPR. The Kazakh literary language dates from the early nineteenth century (Abay Kunanbayev, 1845–1904, is regarded as its founding father), though traditional folk-poetry is older.

SCRIPT

Until the 1930s Kazakh was written in the Arabic script. A period of experimental romanization followed. Since 1940, Cyrillic with nine additional letters: ə, ғ, қ, ң, θ, ұ, ү, h, i.

PHONOLOGY

Consonants

 stops: p, b, t, d, k, g, q
 affricates: ts, tʃ/dz′
 fricatives: f, v, s, z, ʃ, ʒ, x, γ, h
 nasals: m, n, ŋ
 lateral and flap: l, r
 semi-vowels: w, j

Vowels

 front unrounded: i, e
   rounded: œ, y
 back unrounded: ɪ, a
   rounded: o, ŭ

/œ/ and /y/ are here notated as ö and ü respectively. Assimilation, both progressive and regressive, takes place, internally and at junctures.

VOWEL HARMONY

(a) Palatal vowel harmony is strictly observed: front with front, back with back: cf. front, *mektep.ler.imiz.niŋ* 'of our schools'; back, *qalam.dar.ɪnɪz.nɪŋ* 'of your pens'.

(b) Labial: the rounded/unrounded opposition is less strictly observed, and is usually disregarded beyond the third syllable of a word: e.g. *önerpazdarɪmɪz* 'our skilled workmen'.

Stress

Stress tends to be on the final syllable, but never on copula affixes.

MORPHOLOGY AND SYNTAX

In declension, formation of plural, treatment of adjective, the pronominal system, and the numerals, Kazakh conforms to the general Turkic pattern. The plural marker is *lar*[6], (i.e. six variants), with *l/d/t* initial and *a/e* according to vowel harmony.

Noun

Some examples of case usage:

genitive: e.g. *el.imiz.diŋ astana.sɪ* 'the capital of our country';

accusative: distinguishes definite object from indefinite, e.g. *Men kitap oqɪdɪm* 'I read (past) a book'; *Men kitaptɪ oqɪdɪm* 'I read the (specific) book';

dative of purpose: e.g. *Bala.lar balɪq alauya ketti* 'The boys went to catch fish';

locative: may express possession, coupled with verb 'to be', e.g. *Sašada qɪzɪq kitap var* 'Sasha has an interesting book';

ablative: e.g. *Üy kirpišten salɪndɪ* 'The house is built of brick';

instrumental/comitative in *-men*[3]: e.g. *qarɪndašpen* 'with a pencil'.

Verb

A simple present is made for only four verbs: *tur-* 'to stand'; *otɪr* 'to sit'; *žür-* 'to go'; *žatɪr-* 'to lie'. A compound present and several other tenses are made by means of the *-p/-ɪp*[2] gerund of the sense-verb plus inflected form of one of these four auxiliaries: e.g. *žazɪp otɪr* 'he is writing', *oqɪp otɪrsɪzdar* 'you (sing./pl.) are reading'; negative *oqɪp otɪr.gan žoqsɪz*.

The first person singular affixes are *-mɪn*[4]; pl. *-mɪz*[6]; second person *-sɪŋ*[2]; pl. *-sɪŋdar*[4]. The third person form has a null affix, except in the past tense, where it has *-dɪ*[4].

Past definite: synthetic form with *-dɪ-* marker: e.g. *kör.di.m* 'I saw'; analytical form: *γan*[4] + copula: e.g. *žaz. γan.sɪŋ* 'you were writing', where *γan*[4] is the past marker: cf. *ber.il.gen* 'given', *kel.gen* '(who) came'.

A presumptive future is made with the marker $-ar^3-$ + the copula: e.g. *bar.ar.sıŋ* 'you will (presumably) go'; a definite or intentional future with $-maq^6$ + copula: usually with $-sı^2-$ infix: e.g. *kel.mek.ši.siŋ* 'it is up to you to come'/ 'your intention is to come'.

As elsewhere in Turkic, the participles are used to make forms corresponding to relative clauses in other languages: e.g. the present participle in $-tın^2$: *kel.e.tin kisi* 'the man who is coming'.

The negative marker is ma^6: e.g. *al.ma.dı* 'he didn't take'; *emes* and *žoq* are used with compound tenses: *ol kel.gen žoq* 'he didn't come.

COPULA

The endings are, sing. 1 $mın^6$, 2 $sıŋ^2$, 3 $\emptyset$; pl. 1 $mız^6$, 2 $sızdar^2$, 3 $\emptyset$. These are negated by *emes*: e.g. *men qazaqpın* 'I am a Kazakh'; *ol qızmetši emes* 'he isn't a worker'.

Postpositions

Many are standard Turkic: e.g. *sabaqtan soŋ* 'after the lesson'; *qarındaš stol üstinde žatır* 'the pencil is lying on the table' (note vowel harmony neutralization in *üstinde*); *bala.m turalı ǝngime* 'a story about my son'.

Word order

SOV.

١ سوز اثك الگس يدين بولغان، سوز خداكسامن بولغان؛

٢ سوز خداك بولغان ، اول الگس يدين خداك من بولغان؛

٣ باسليق نرسه اونوثك آسرقالى جاسرتلفان، نه

٤ غنا بولسه ده اونان باستقه بولو نبانغان ، اوندا تيس كتلكى

٥ بولغان ، اول تيس كتلك آده غه جاسريق بولغان ، جاسريق
تاسل شغيدا جاسه تيسراب تورسنمان ، قسا گغى اونوتياتنا

٦ بيتس المه دك، خداى اثك جبه سگن بس كس بولغان ،

٧ اونوثك آت يميس، اول جاسريق تورسا سيندا گورا ليق
بسو گه كلگن ، اونوثك آسرتيل باسليق آدم نا نسيس ابو؛

٨ اول اوزو جاسريق بولمغان ، تلك جاسريق تلك تورسا

٩ سيندا گورا ليق بسو گه جبه سالگن، دونيانه كيلوشس باليق
آدم داسادك جاسريق تلاتن شيين جاسريق بولغان

KET

INTRODUCTION

This is the sole remaining representative of the Yeniseyan group of languages, the other members of which – Arin, Assan, and Kott – died out in the early nineteenth century. The Kets live along the middle reaches of the Yenisei in the Krasnoyarsk Kray, and number less than a thousand. In several ways – e.g. in its class system of nouns, the presence of internal flection, and the extraordinary complication of the verbal system – Ket is quite unlike any other Siberian language; indeed, it seems to be unrelated to any other known language. Attempts have been made to link it with Sino-Tibetan, with Basque, and with Caucasian. Ket is unwritten.

PHONOLOGY

Consonants

    stops: p, b, t, d, k, g, q, ɢ, ʔ
    fricatives: v, s, s′, j, x, γ, ʁ, (h)
    nasals: m, n, ɲ, ŋ
    lateral and flap: l, l′, r, r′

All stops occur palatalized as allophones, except /q, ɢ, ʔ/.

Vowels

    high: i, ɪ, u
    mid: e, ɛ, ʌ, ɔ, o
    low: a (œ)

/a/ = [æ]. Vowels can be long or short; the difference is phonemic. Recent research goes to show that Ket also has a phonemic tonal system. /ɛ/ is notated here as ẹ; ə is represented by ə.

Stress

Stress is moveable, and again may be phonemic, in that it distinguishes, for example, number and person.

MORPHOLOGY AND SYNTAX

Noun

Three noun classes are distinguished: masculine, feminine, and neuter. The class of masculine nouns includes, apart from male humans, most male animals, some birds, nearly all fishes, some insects, all trees, large wooden objects, and the moon; the feminine class includes some animals (fox, hare, squirrel, etc.), three kinds of fish, and the sun. Everything else is in the neuter class. Nouns themselves are not overtly marked for class; concord is established via verbal forms, predicative adjectives, etc.

NUMBER

The plural is formed in several ways: masculine and feminine classes coalesce in the plural.

(a) by suffixation: (vowel) + *n/n'*, e.g. *ut'* 'mouse', pl. *ut'n'*; *am* 'mother', pl. *amaŋ*;
(b) internal flection: e.g. *tip'* 'dog', pl. *tap'*;
(c) by vowel lengthening;
(d) by stress transfer;
(e) by suppletion: e.g. *k'ęt* 'person', *d'ęŋ* 'people'; *dɪl'* 'child', *kʌt* 'children'.

CASE SYSTEM

Seven cases are distinguished by suffixation: e.g.

the dative/aditive case has dental + (harmonic?) vowel + *na*: e.g. *am* 'mother' – *amdiŋa*; *on* 'father' – *obdaŋa*;
ablative: dental + vowel + -*l'*: e.g. *amdil'* 'from the mother';
benefactive: dental + vowel + -*nt'* (often + -*æn*), e.g. *amdiŋt'* = *amdiŋtæn* 'on behalf of, for the mother'. Cf. in plural: *amıŋ.naŋt'* 'for the mothers'.

Adjective

A petrified formant, -*l'*, is found in some adjectives: e.g. *s'ęl'* 'bad'; *xol'* 'short'; *qil'* 'wide'. The attributive adjective precedes the noun, and may take plural marker. The predicative adjective is marked for person, and, in the third person, for class: e.g. *at' qæ.r'i* 'I am big'; *u qæ.ɣu* 'you are big'; *bu qæ.r'u* 'he is big'; *bu qæ.r'æ* 'she is big'.

Pronoun

PERSONAL INDEPENDENT

		Singular	Plural
1		at'	ət'n'
2		u/uk	əkŋ
3	common:	bu	buŋ

These are declined in five cases: e.g. for 1st sing., aditive *aviŋa*, ablative *avil'*, locative *aviŋt'*, comitative *ar'as'*.

Personalizing prefixes marking possession, relatedness to, etc.

		Singular	Plural
1		(a)b-	na/næ, ət'næ
2		(u)k-	na/næ, əknæ
3	masc.	da-/dæ, buræ-	na/næ, buŋnæ
	fem.	d-, bur-	—

Examples: (*a*)*bam* 'my mother'; (*u*)*kam* 'your mother'.

DEMONSTRATIVE PRONOUN

Three degrees of relative distance ('this' – 'that' – 'that yonder') are distinguished, fully declined: masculine series: *kir'* – *tur'* – *qar'*; fem. *kir'æ* – *tur'æ* – *qar'æ*; pl. *kin'æ* – *tun'æ* – *qan'æ*.

INTERROGATIVE PRONOUN

anæ(t) 'who?', pl. *anætæŋ*; *akus'* 'what?'. The interrogative series is fully declined.

Numerals

The forms for 1–5 inclusive have class markers:

> neuter: *qus'am*, *ɪn'æm*, *doŋæm*, *siyæm*, *qayæm*;
> masculine: *qogd'*, *ɪn'aŋ*, *do:ŋ*, *si:ŋ*, *qa:ŋ*;
> feminine: *qogd'æ*;

6–10 have one form for all three classes: 6 *as'*; 7 *on's*; 8 is *ɪn'æm bəns'aŋ qus'* '10 minus 2'; 9 is *qus'æm bəns'aŋ qus'* '10 minus 1'; 10 *qūs'*.

Verb

The main features of the very complicated system described by Kreinovič (1968) are here set out.

Roots are integral or split: the following four models are found:

(a) integral root in final position; all deixis by prefixation;
(b) split root consisting of two root morphemes
(c) split root with derivatory element preceding root; deixis by prefix/infix;
(d) split root with derivative element following root; deixis by prefix/infix.

The complete table of personal prefixes and infixes shows 64 forms. Formally, they can be divided into two groups of first and third person forms: the D-group and the B-groups:

D-group				B-group			
Prefixes		Infixes		Prefixes		Infixes	
1	2	3	4	1	2	3	4
d-/d-	di-/du-	-r-/-a-	-a-/-Ø-	ba-/bu-	bo-/bu-	ba-/a	bo/o

The second person forms in both D and B are based on *k-*. The third person markers shown in the table are masculine exponents. There are feminine and neuter correlatives.

D-group:

1: subject exponents in verbs of all types;
2: subject exponents in base-final verbs;
3: subject and object exponents;
4: subject exponent in intransitive verb; object exponent in intransitive/ reflexive verb.

B-group:

1 and 2: subject exponent;
3 and 4: subject and object exponent.

In base-final verbs, both series precede the base; in split-root verbs (bases X and Y) first series precedes base X, second series follows; base Y is final.
Examples:

(a) D-group exponent as subject: base *-it* 'to sneeze' (base-final): *di.j.it, ku.j.it, du.j.it* 'I sneeze', 'you sneeze', 'he sneezes'.
(b) Base + derivative: *di-* 'hide oneself': *di.ri.tn, di.u.tn* 'I'll hide'.
(c) D-group exponents as subject and object; split base: *usqit* 'to warm', *d.us.qi.r.it* 'he warms me'; *d.us.qi.u.t* 'he warms you'.
(d) B-group as subject exponent; *sa:l* 'to spend the night': *ba.γ.i.s.sæl* 'I spend the night'; *ku.γ.i.s.sæl* 'you spend the night'.
(e) B-group exponent as direct object; base *-uŋ* 'to see': *ba.t.uŋ* 'sees me'; *ku.t.uŋ* 'sees you'; *dæŋ.t.uŋ* 'sees us'.

Plurality of subject can be marked at end of verbal complex by (γ) + vowel + *-n/ŋ*: e.g. from base *totæt* = to praise: *to.ba.γæ.t.iγin* 'they praise me'.
Since Ket has no accusative case, the subject/object relationship has to be elucidated by the personal exponents within the verbal complex. Kreinovič gives an example involving the word *bis'sæp* 'sibling' (male or female):

bis'æp bis'æp d.i.t.uŋ 'the brother sees the sister'
bis'æp bis'æp dæ.a.t.uŋ 'the sister sees the brother'

In the first sentence, *d.i.* indicates action by third masculine on third feminine: 'he – her'; in the second sentence, *dæ.a.* indicates action by third feminine on third masculine.

MOOD AND TENSE
In origin, *l, l', n, n'* were perfective markers. They appear as past-tense infixes and in the imperative mood. The imperative forms are marked for subject and object of action (in transitive verbs) showing person, class, and number, and for modality (single or repeated action, etc.). Other modalities of action – inceptive, terminative, semelfactive, etc. – may also be expressed. The present–future tense infixes are Ø, *-s-*, *-a-*.

NEGATIVE

bən' precedes the verb: e.g. *bu bən' daʁij* 'he doesn't laugh'; *bu bən' daʁol'ij* 'he didn't laugh'.

The elaborate participial and gerundial apparatus characteristic of so many Siberian languages is completely absent in Ket, but the infinitive has a great many forms, both primary and derivative.

Postpositions

Nominal derivatives with possessive affix are used.

Word order

SOV occurs, as in example given above: *bis'æp bis'æp d.i.t.uŋ* 'the brother sees the sister', though this could also be construed as OSV. OVS also occurs; Kreinovič gives the following example: *abam dūtæt b'ep* 'brother/son-in-law (*b'ep*) beats (*dūtæt*) my mother (*abam*)'.

KHAKAS

INTRODUCTION

Classified by Baskakov (1966) as a member of the Uygur-Oguz group of Turkic languages. There are between 50 and 60 thousand speakers in the Khakas Autonomous Region, which lies just north of the Tuva Autonomous Soviet Socialist Republic in Krasnoyarsk Kraj. The name 'Khakas' dates from the 1920s; previously, the Khakas were known as Abakan or Minusinsk Tatars. Use of a literary standard also dates from the early years of Soviet rule. The language is now used in local radio and television and the press, and there is a small literature.

SCRIPT

Cyrillic was adopted in 1939, after an experimental period of romanization. There are six additional letters: i, ö, ÿ, ғ, ц, ң, ч.

PHONOLOGY

Consonants

    stops: p, b, t, d, k, g
    affricates: ts, tʃ, dʒ
    fricatives: f, v, s, z, ʃ, ʒ, j, x, γ
    nasals: m, n, ŋ
    lateral and flap: l, r

Vowels

    front: i, e, œ, y
    back: ɪ, a, o, u

Consonants are either hard – associated with back vowels – or soft – associated with front vowels. Two /i/ sounds are distinguished by relative degree of closure, the more narrow being denoted in the script by the Cyrillic letter и, the half-narrow by the Roman i. /i/ is short only; all other vowels can be either long or short. Here, the difference between the two soft /i/ sounds is ignored. /œ/ is notated as ö, /y/ as ü.

VOWEL HARMONY
Normal Turkic pattern, /i/ is neutral. Labialization of endings is not notated in the script: cf. *tülgü* + *-ni* = /tylgyny/ 'the fox' (acc.).

MORPHOLOGY AND SYNTAX

See also **Turkic Languages**.

Noun

The plural marker is *lar*[6] (*l-/n-/t-* + *a/e*): e.g. *tura.lar* 'houses'.

DECLENSION
Standard Turkic endings, with allophones varying from eight in the dative to two in the instrumental. To the usual six cases, Khakas adds an aditive in *-sar*[4], and an instrumental in *-nan*[2].

The possessive affixes and the predicative affixes are standard: e.g. *min toɣɪsčɪbɪn* 'I am a worker'; *ol toɣɪsčɪ∅* 'he is a worker'.

Pronouns

The pronominal system is standard Turkic for the most part; a relative pronoun exists (*kem* 'who', *nime* 'what'), though relative clauses are made, as is usual in Turkic, by means of participial forms: *see* **Verb**, below.

Numerals

Standard: 1 *pir*; 2 *iki*; 3 *üs*. 20 is *čibirgi*, 40 *xɪrɪx*; 100 *čüs*.

Verb

Five moods, four voices; the present-tense system has three forms, the past-tense system has six, and there is a future.

The voice markers are standard Turkic: e.g. passive *-il/-ɪl*: e.g. *pas-* 'to write', *pazɪl* 'to be written'. Causative: *-tir*[4], e.g. *al-* 'to take', *aldɪr* 'to cause to be taken'.

PARTICIPIAL FORMS
Examples: *uzup.čatxan ōlax* 'the sleeping boy/the boy who is asleep'; *čōxtaɣ an* → *čōxtān kizi* 'the man who was speaking/had spoken'; *kiligen mašina* 'the car that is coming'.

Postpositions

Standard Turkic, as is word order.

KHALKHA

See **Mongolian, Modern**.

KHANTY

INTRODUCTION

Khanty belongs to the Ob'-Ugric branch of Finno-Ugric (along with Mansi and Hungarian). In the nineteenth century the people and the language alike were known as Ostyak. There are at present about 15,000 speakers of the language in the Khanty-Mansi National Region and the Yamal-Nenets National Region. Khanty shows marked dialectal variation. In particular, one dialect – Vakh – is highly idiosyncratic, in that it has vowel harmony based on a rigid opposition between back and front vowels, with no neutral middle ground, and, in addition, a semi-ergative construction, unique in Uralic. The agent of a Vakh transitive verb is marked by the locative ending -nə – but the direct pronominal object is in the accusative, and the verb is in concord with the agent–subject.

Here the Central Ob' dialect is described.

SCRIPT

Early missionary attempts to provide a script for Khanty covered several dialects, and were in general on a Roman basis. Since 1937 Khanty has been written in Cyrillic + a hooked n (ӈ) for /ŋ/, (notated here as *ng*). The reduced vowel /ə/ is notated as ы or и.

PHONOLOGY

Consonants

    stops: p, t, k + palatalized t'
    fricatives: s, ʃ, s', x
    nasals: m, n, ɲ, ŋ
    lateral and flap: l, r
    semi-vowels: j, w

Vowels

The vocalic system is based on two oppositions: (a) between the long vowels: /eː, aː, oː, uː/; and the short vowels: /i, a, o, u/. All of these occur with pre-palatalization: /ji, je, ja/, etc. (b) Between all the above vowels and the reduced vowel /ə, jə/ which is never initial. In this article, /ə/ is notated as ę.

733

MORPHOLOGY AND SYNTAX

Noun

Khanty has three numbers: singular, dual, and plural. The dual marker is *-ngẹn*; the plural *-t/-ẹt*.

Three cases: nominative (unmarked), dative/aditive, locative/instrumental: e.g. *xot* 'house':

	Singular	Dual	Plural
nominative	xot	xotngẹn	xotẹt
dative/aditive	xota	xotngẹna	xotẹta
locative/instrumental	xotnẹ	xotngẹnnẹ	xotẹtnẹ

POSSESSIVE ENDINGS
The grid shows singular/dual/plural possessor with singular/dual/plural possessed object, for all persons, i.e. 27 possible forms. Example for first person with singular, dual, and plural referents: *mẹsem* 'my cow'; *mẹsemẹn* 'my two cows'; *mẹsew* 'my cows'; cf. *mẹsngẹtuw* 'our (pl.) two cows'; *mẹstatẹn* 'our (dual) cows'. The possessive forms are declinable.

Adjective

As attribute, adjective is invariable. There is no comparative form.

Pronoun

There are singular, dual, and plural personal forms:

	Singular nominative	Dual nominative	Plural nominative
1	ma	min	mung
2	nang	nẹn	nang
3	tuw	tẹn	tẹw

These have accusative and dative cases; e.g. for *ma*: acc. *manẹt*, dat. *manẹm*.

DEMONSTRATIVE PRONOUN/ADJECTIVE
tamẹ 'this', *tomẹ* 'that', *sit* 'that (yonder)'. A shortened form is used attributively before nouns: e.g. *tam xot* 'this house'.

INTERROGATIVE PRONOUN
xoy 'who?'; *muy* 'what?'; fully declined.

Numerals

1–10: *yit/yiy, katn/kat, xutẹm, nyatẹ, wet, xut, tapẹt, nẹvẹt, yaryang, yang*. 11 *yixosyang*; 12 *katxosyang* (where *-xos'-* is a postposition meaning 'around'); 20 *xus*; 30 *xutẹmyang*; 100 *sot*.

Verb

Like Mansi and Hungarian, Khanty has definite and indefinite conjugations. The inflections of the definite conjugation are coded for person and number for both subject and object, and are very similar to the inflections of the possessive declensions. Cf. *tusem* 'I brought him'; *tustam* 'I brought them'; *tusemen* 'we two brought him'; *pontetten* 'you two will place them'. Both intransitive and transitive verbs may be conjugated in the indefinite conjugation.

The Central Ob' dialect has indicative and imperative moods, and the indicative mood has two tenses: present–future and past. As illustration, the present–future endings, indicative mood, of *tuta* 'to bring':

	Singular	Dual	Plural
1	tutem	tutmen	tutuw
2	tuten	tutten	tutte
3	tut	tutngen	tutet

The characteristic of the past tense is *-s-*: e.g. from *tuta*: *tusem* 'I brought' – *tusen* – *tus*; dual: e.g. *tusmen*; pl. e.g. *tusuw*.

PASSIVE VOICE

The characteristic is *-ai/ei* infix + indefinite conjugation endings: e.g. present–future *kett.ai.m* 'I am/shall be sent'; past *ket.s.ai.m* 'I was sent'; *ket.s.ai.ten* 'you two were sent'.

IMPERATIVE

Second person only, in all three numbers and both conjugations. The dual and plural forms are not differentiated for definiteness/indefiniteness.

NON-FINITE FORMS

The infinitive is in *-ta*. Participles: present in *-te*, past in *-em*: e.g. *werte* 'doing/being done'; *manem* 'having gone'. Gerund is in *-man*: e.g. *werman* 'doing'. These participial forms can be conjugated with personal affixes and case endings: e.g. *wertemne* 'when I do'; *wertewne* 'when we do'; *wertemenne* 'when we two do'; *wermemne* 'when I did'. They are used attributively: e.g. *rupette xo* 'working man, man who works'; *rupetem xo* 'a/the man who worked'.

ASPECT

The inchoative characteristic is *-me-*: e.g. *xuxetta* 'to run' – *xuxet.me.ta* 'to start running, run off'. The semelfactive characteristic is *-emt/-eme*; the reiterative has *-eyt-*.

The general negating particle is *ant-* preceding the verb; the imperative is negated by *at*: e.g. *at mana!* 'don't go!'

Postpositions

Examples:

xosę 'at, around', e.g. *xop xosę* 'at the boat';
xuwat 'along', e.g. *yoxan xuwat* 'along the river';
pata 'for', e.g. *tow pata* 'for the horse'.

Word order

SOV is normal.

---

9 Nen sidy sagat poikśat: muń azieu, turmet och-tyna ultot! nyń jemyń nemen muń choźa jemyń at ull;

10 At jogodl nyń turum nubten; nyń kažen at ull i mu ochtyna chody turum ochtyna;

11 N'ań muń mosta levypaseu mija muńeu tam chadl ochtyja;

12 I esla muńeu muń kreklau, chody i muń eslylu kuteuna kreklau;

13 Pa al esla muńeu chuzipsaja pidta, no muńeu šavyja kuľ eľta; nyń choźą ull turum nubyt i vey i symyltypsa nubyt chuvat, jena.

14 Chun channe-chojeta ly kreklal eslta pidleta, i nen turum azen esll nyńylana;

15 A chun channe-chojeta ly kreklal eslta an pid-leta, i nen turum azen an esll nen kreklan.

(Matt. 6: 9–15)

KHASI

INTRODUCTION

Khasi is usually classified as a branch of the Mon-Khmer family of Austro-Asiatic languages. It is spoken in northern Assam by anything up to half a million people. There are four dialects, the main one being the Pnar dialect.

SCRIPT

A Roman script was provided by missionaries in the nineteenth century, and this has been utilized in the twentieth century to provide a small literature. Devanagari is also used.

PHONOLOGY

Consonants

The main framework is provided by the series /p, ph, b; t, th, d; k, kh, Ø/; with their associated nasals /m, n, ŋ/, though the voiced velar is missing. /dʒ/ is present with its nasal /ɲ/. Further, the sonants /r, l/, the sibilants /s, ʃ/, the semi-vowels /w, y/, the glottal stop /ʔ/ and the fricative /h/.

Prefixed formant syllables have a sonant (nasal or liquid) as vocalic component: e.g. *hn-*, *kn-*, *pn-*, *sl-*, *khl-*, etc. The nasal is assimilated to the class of the following consonant, thus *tn- + p- → tmp-*.

Vowels

Basically:

   i, ɪ, e, ɛ, a, o, ɔ, u

These can be short, long, half-long, raised, lowered. In her grammar of Khasi, Rabel (1961) lists 32 phonemic values of the basic vowels.

Stress

Stress tends towards final syllable of both word and phrase.

737

MORPHOLOGY AND SYNTAX

Roots in Khasi are largely ambivalent and can be treated as nominals or verbals.

Noun

There are two numbers, singular and plural; and two genders, masculine and feminine/neuter. The gender markers, *'uu* for masculine and *ka* for feminine/ neuter are also the third person pronouns: the common plural is *kii*. Examples: *'uu kpaa* 'father, the/a father'; *ka kmi* 'mother, the mother, a mother'; *'uu khlaa* 'tiger'; *ka miaw* 'cat'; *'uu bseɲ* 'snake'. *'ii* can be used as a marker expressing endearment: e.g. *'ii miaw* 'pussy'.

POSSESSION
The possessive relating particle is *joŋ* /dʒon/: e.g. *'uu khuon joŋ ka knthey* 'the woman's son'. All attributes follow head-word.

Pronoun

		Singular	Plural
1		ŋa	ŋii
2	polite	phii }	phii
	familiar	pha }	
3	masc.	'uu }	kii
	fem.	ka }	

DEMONSTRATIVE PRONOUNS
These are compound forms, the personal pronouns being prefixed to six bases which give four degrees of relative distance plus two of relative locus above or below that of speaker. Thus, e.g. *'uutu* 'that man (near you)', *katu* 'that woman/thing'.

INTERROGATIVE PRONOUNS
These are compounds made from the personal pronouns plus the interrogative base *'ey*: *'uu'ey* 'who?' (male), *ka'ey* 'who?' (female)/'what?'.

RELATIVE PRONOUN
ba can be used with recapitulation of personal marker: e.g. *kii khuon kii ba ...* 'the children who ...'.

Numerals

1–10: *wey/šii, 'aar, laay, saaw, san, hnriw, hnɲew, phra, khndaaw, khat.* 11–19: *khat-* + units. 20 *'aarphew* (where *-phew* is another word for 10); 30 *laayphew*; 100 *šiispa'*.

Verb

There is no inflection. The following tense markers are used:

customary action in past:	*la*
perfective	*la'*
future	*'n/sa*
continuous	*na*

Ya is an object marker, optional where one object is concerned, obligatory in the case of two: e.g. *'uu hiikay ya ŋa ka ktien pharen* 'he teaches me English'. (Rabel, 1961: 124).

The verb is negated by *'m*, which is affixed to the pronoun if there is a pronominal subject, to the verb if not. In the past tense, *šm* replaces *la*: e.g. *ŋi.m šm yatip* 'we didn't know'.

MODAL MARKERS

ya reciprocal; *pn* causative: e.g. *tip* 'to know' – *pntip* 'to make known'. Bound forms may be pre- or post-verbs: e.g. with the verb stem *baam* 'to eat': *naŋ.baam* 'to keep on eating'; *šaj baam* 'to be accustomed to eating'. Examples of post-verbs: *kaay* 'to do (something) for pleasure'; *lem* 'to share'; *baam kaay* 'to eat for eating's sake'; *lej lem* 'to go together'.

Prepositions

Examples of directional prepositions: *na, ha, ša*. These are used with or without gender marker/article: e.g. *'uu lej ša ka skul* 'he goes to the school'.

Word formation

Compounds are freely made: noun–noun, noun–verb, verb–verb, verb–noun: e.g. *ka šnon* 'village' + *ka kndon* 'corner': *ka šnon.kndon* 'an out-of-the way village'. Imitative compounds are based on such patterns as Ab-Ac, Abc.Abd: e.g. *khuon.kur khuon.kmi* 'respectable people' (*kur* 'mother's relatives'); *kren thu'.khana kren thu'.khade'* 'to gossip' (*kren* 'to speak'; *thu'.khana* 'to tell a story').

Reduplication is much used in Khasi, e.g. in adverbial expressions, often with ablaut; Rabel (1961) gives several examples, e.g. *khliŋkhliŋ khlaŋkhlaŋ* 'to look around'.

Word order

SVO; inversion is possible in principal clause, if preceded by subordinate clause.

১ কাবানুঙ্ক কাঙ্কিন লাতন্ কাঙ্কিন বঙওরেই রক্কাট

২ লাতন্ পাতে কাঙ্কিন ওরেই হি। কাতা মিন্নুঙ্ক

৩ রক্কাট বঙওরেই লাতন। বণ্ডু কাজিঙ্বু তাকাতা
লালাখাও পাতে কাট২ লালাখাও হাপ্তে জুঙ্কা
কারেই কাজি৹বুক গ্নেয্কাতা কাবালাখাও কাম্চুম্ল।

৪ হাপ্তে জুঙ্কা কাবাইম কাতা কাবাইম কাজুঙ্কিবিঙ

৫ কাবাসায়। কাতা কাবাসায় হাক্কাবাইয়ঙওঞ
লালাসায় পাতে কাবাইয়ঙওঞ কাতা কাম্চুম্রি।

৬ ওয়োহন হাক্কাক্কেঙ ওরেই নাঙরেই ওবালাম্হা

৭ ওলাতন্ বণ্ডু ভঙতা ওট্টেই২ নাপুন্কানে ওতা কাজুঙ
কাবাসায় কাপুয়ান বান্আয় ওরেই ওসাক্ষী বান্
৮ ওলাঙওআন। ওতা কাতা কাবাসায় এম্ পাতে কাজুঙ
কাতা কাবাসায় কাপুয়ান বান্আয় ওলালাতন।

KHMER

See **Cambodian**.

KIRGIZ

INTRODUCTION

In Baskakov's (1966) classification, Kirgiz appears as the Kirgiz-Kipchak sub-group of Eastern Hunnic. The language is spoken by 1½ or 2 million people in the Kirgiz Soviet Socialist Republic, and in adjacent areas of the Uzbek, Tadzhik, and Kazakh SSRs. The Kirgiz also live in the Xinjiang-Uigur Autonomous region of the CPR, and in western regions of the Mongolian People's Republic. Smaller communities are found in Afghanistan and Pakistan.

In the eighth/ninth century AD the Kirgiz were located in the Upper Yenisei region, and it is presumably to their culture that we owe the Orkhon-Yenisei inscriptional material discovered there in the seventeenth century.

Kirgiz folk literature possesses one of the world's longest poems – the *Manas* epic – which runs in one version to half a million lines. The epic mixes heroic myth with a colourful account of actual happenings in the history of the Kirgiz people. Sections of the *Manas* are sung on festive occasions by *manasčiler*.

The modern literature dates from the 1920s. Primary and secondary education are provided in Kirgiz, which is also used in local media, radio, television, and journalism.

SCRIPT

Originally Arabic; Cyrillic since 1940.

PHONOLOGY

Consonants

    stops: p, b, t, d, k, g (q)
    affricates: ts, tʃ, dʒ
    fricatives: (f, v) s, z, ʃ, (ʒ) j, x, (ɣ)
    nasals: m, n, ŋ
    lateral and flap: l, r

Vowels

Kirgiz has one of the most symmetrical vowel systems in Turkic:

	Unrounded	*Rounded*
front	(ə, əː), ɛ, ɛː, i, iː	œ, œː, y, yː
back	a, aː, ɪ, ɪː	o, oː, u, uː

/œ/ is notated here as *ö*, /y/ as *ü*. Long vowels are indicated in the text by macrons: e.g. *ī*.

VOWEL HARMONY
Is systematically observed: front with front, back with back, rounded with rounded: cf. declensions of *konok* 'guest', and *töö* 'camel':

nominative	konok	töö
accusative	konoktu	töönü
genitive	konoktun	töönün
dative	konokko	töögö
locative	konokto	töödö
ablative	konokton	töödön

The accusative marker *-nı* appears in twelve variants: four with *n*- initial, four with *d*- and four with *t*-; the locative and ablative in eight.

MORPHOLOGY AND SYNTAX

Declension, the personal affixes, the possessive markers, the treatment of adjectives, the pronominal system and the numerals are all standard Turkic in pattern and individual forms (*see* **Turkic Languages**). The verb has simple and composite (participial) forms. Unusually, the third person plural of the first preterite takes an *-iš-* infix: e.g. *kaldı* 'he remained': *kal.ıš.tı* 'they remained'; *kal.ıš.pa.dı* 'they did not remain'.

Adjective

As attribute, adjective precedes noun and is invariable. Comparative in *-irek*[2], with compared form in ablative: e.g. *kara attan tezirek* 'faster than the black horse'.

Pronoun

Standard Turkic forms. The third person shows optional forms, *al/ol* (sing.), with oblique cases, e.g. gen. *anın/onun*, and pl. *alar/olor*, gen. *alardın/olrdun*.
   The possessive markers are standard: e.g. *atım* 'my horse'; *kitebim* 'my book'; *emgekči.ler.din el aralık künü* 'the international day of the workers (*el* 'nation'; *ara.lık* 'between').

DEMONSTRATIVE PRONOUN/ADJECTIVE
bul/bu 'this'; *usul* 'that'; declension is standard.

INTERROGATIVE PRONOUN
kim 'who?'; *(n)emne* 'what?'; declension is standard.

Numerals

Standard; 20 is *jıyırma* = Turkish *yirmi*.

Verb

Standard Turkic pattern throughout (*see* **Turkic Languages**). The negating infix is *-ba-* with allophones: e.g. *džazmak* 'to write', neg. *džazbamak*.

The personal endings can be sub-divided into (a) full forms, and (b) short forms:

	Singular		Plural	
	Full	*Short*	*Full*	*Short*
1	-min	-m	-biz	**-k**
2	-siŋ/-siz	-ŋ/ŋiz	-siz(der)	-ŋer/ŋizder
3	(-t)	—	—	—

Examples of verb formation:

present/future definite: *-e/a-*, e.g. *džaz.a.m* 'I write, I'll write';

future presumptive: *-er/ar*, e.g. *kal.ar.bɪz* 'we'll (presumably) stay'; *Kal.ba.s.sɪŋar* 'You won't stay?';

present progressive: gerund of sense-verb + auxiliary *tur-/džat-*, e.g. *okup turam* 'I'm reading now';

past definite: *-dɪ/di-*, e.g. *kaldɪm* 'I stayed'; *kal.ba.dɪ.ŋɪzdar* 'you didn't stay';

conditional: *-se/sa-*, e.g. *kelsem* 'if I come';

desiderative/optative: *-gey/gay-* + auxiliary *ele-*.

Passive, causative, and co-operative markers are standard. The co-operative marker -Vš- reappears in the third person plural forms of several tenses; cf. *džaz.ɪš.at* 'they write'; *džaz.ɪš.tɪ* 'they wrote'.

The negative particle *emes* is conjugated to negate certain tenses: e.g. *okuču emesmin* 'I was not in the habit of reading' (*okuču-* is past habitual). Note the form *-gende* etc. which makes temporal clauses of concomitant action: e.g. *karɪganda* 'when he grows old …'.

Postpositions

Standard, governing base case, ablative, dative, or accusative.

بدايتده كلمت بار ايردي و كلمت خدايده
اردي و كلمت خدا ايردي ۞ ۲ وهمان بدايتده ايردي
الله‌ده ۳ ۞ وسيله‌سي برله هر نرسه بولدي و آ نيسيز هيچ بر
نرسه بولمادي كه بولدي ۞ ۴ آ نده حيات بار ايردي و
اول حيات آ دملرننك روشنيسي ايردي۵۞و اول روشني
قرانكلقده يالدورايب دورا و قرانكلق آ ني (ايچنده)
توتمادي ۞ ٦ بر آدم خدادان مرسول بولدي كه اسمي
يحيا ايردي ۞ ۷ همان شهادت اوچون كيلدي (يعني)
نورغه شهادت بيرمك اوچون كه سببندان همه ايمان
كبدورالر ۞ ۸ شول نور داكول ايردي لكن شول نورغه
شهادت بيرمك اوچون كيلدي ۞

745

KOMI

INTRODUCTION

The Permic branch of Finno-Ugrian includes, apart from Udmurt, the two forms of Komi: Komi-Zyryan and Komi-Permyak. They are mutually intelligible. Most Komi-Zyryan live in the Komi Autonomous Soviet Socialist Republic in the northern Urals; the Komi-Permyak live further to the south, in the Komi-Permyak National Area. The total number of speakers of both forms is put at about 400,000.

Komi is one of the two Uralic languages whose past history is actually documented. In the second half of the fourteenth century St Stephen of Perm, Bishop of the Russian Orthodox Church and missionary to the Permic peoples, translated parts of the Bible and the liturgy into Komi, using a script which he himself had prepared from Greek and Cyrillic elements. Both script and literary language were known to no more than a few clerics, and both, accordingly, were soon forgotten. The extant material is, however, of great philological importance, as it represents by far the oldest written record of a Uralic language (if the markedly divergent and therefore unrepresentative Hungarian is discounted). This material falls into two divisions: (a) late seventeeth-/eighteenth-century copies in Cyrillic script containing passages from the Acts of the Apostles and from St John's gospel, along with some liturgical material; (b) texts in St Stephen's script inscribed on two ikons – the Holy Trinity Ikon in the church of Vožem, and the Pentecost Ikon (now lost).

The language of the Old Permic texts is quite close to Modern Komi.
From the middle of the nineteenth century onwards, Komi has produced a small but flourishing literature with one or two outstanding figures, e.g. the poet I.A. Kuratov, who translated several English, French, and German authors into Komi.

The forms described in this article are those of Komi-Zyryan.

SCRIPT

Cyrillic with additional letters i and ö.

PHONOLOGY

Consonants

stops: p, b, t, d, k, g; t', d'
affricates: (dz), tʃ, tʃ', dʒ, dʒ'
fricatives: v, s, z, ʃ, ʒ, s', z', j
nasals: m, n, ɲ
laterals and flap: l, l', r

Consonants marked with the palatalization sign ' differ materially in articulation from their non-palatalized counterparts.

Vowels

i, e, ɪ, œ, a, o, u

/œ/ → [ə].

A dental consonant may be followed by a palatalized or a non-palatalized /i/. In the former case, /i/ is denoted by the Cyrillic letter и; in the latter case, by the letter i. In this article, hard /i/ is denoted by a dot under the preceding consonant.

Stress

Theoretically, stress is on the first syllable, but is mobile and non-phonemic.

MORPHOLOGY AND SYNTAX

Noun

The noun has two numbers, the plural marker being *-yas*: e.g. *kerka* 'house', pl. *kerkyas*; *vöv* 'horse', pl. *vövyas*.

Sixteen cases are distinguished in the literary language; for *yort* 'comrade', e.g. gen. *yortlön*, dat. *yortlı*, acc. *yortös*, instr. *yortön*. The possessive affixes are sing. 1 *-öy*, 2 *-ıd*, 3 *-ıs*; pl. 1 *-nım*, 2 *-nıd*, 3 *-nıs*. These affixes may precede or follow the case ending; cf. *yortöylön* 'of my comrade'; *yorttögıd* 'without your comrade'.

Adjective

As attribute, adjective precedes noun and is invariable: e.g. *bur mortlön* 'of the good man'. The predicative adjective tends to be in the instrumental, and may have a specific plural form in *-ös'*: e.g. *vövyas yonös'* 'the horses are strong'.

Pronoun

Personal: sing. 1 *me*; 2 *te*; 3 *siyö*; pl. 1 *mi*; 2 *ti*; 3 *nayö*. These are declined in all cases, e.g. for *me*: gen. *menam*, dat. *menım*, acc. *menö*.

DEMONSTRATIVE PRONOUN
tayö 'this'; *şiyo* 'that'.

INTERROGATIVE/RELATIVE PRONOUN
koḍi 'who?'; *mɪy* 'what?'.

Numerals

1–10: *ötik*, *kɪk*, *kuim*, *nyol'*, *vit*, *kwayt*, *sizim*, *kökyamɪs*, *ökmɪs*, *das*; 11 *das öti*; 12 *das kɪk*; 20 *kɪz'*; 30 *komɪn*; 40 *nelyamɪn*; 100 *syo*.

Verb

The verb has aspect, mood, voice, tense, number, and person; positive and negative versions. As specimen, the present indicative, affirmative and positive, of *gižnɪ* 'to write':

	Positive		Negative	
	Singular	Plural	Singular	Plural
1	giža	gižam	og giž	og gižöy
2	gižan	gižannɪd	on giž	on gižöy
3	gižö	gižöni	oz giž	oz gižnɪ

The future tense is closely similar in the affirmative, identical in the negative. There are two past tenses, one of which is an inferential: e.g. *gižis* 'he wrote'; *gižöma* '(it seems that) he wrote'. This inferential tense has no first person form.

NEGATION
As will be seen from the above example, the verb is negated by means of a conjugated negative auxiliary, plus a stem form marked for number.

ASPECT
Semelfactive, reiterative aspects are marked, but the distinction between perfective and imperfective is not observed.

VOICE
Causative with a dental marker, e.g. *-öd*; reflexive with a sibilant. The infinitive can take personal endings: e.g. *munnɪm og vermɪ* 'I can't go'; *munnɪd on vermɪ* 'you can't go'.

Postpositions

Komi uses postpositions: e.g. *berd-* 'near', *vör berdɪn* 'near the forest'; *dɪrji* 'during', *voina* (Russian loan-word) *dɪrji* 'during the war'; *gögör* 'about', *vit lun gögör* 'about five days'; *moz* 'like', *udžalö oš moz* 'he works like a bear'.

Word order

SVO seems usual.

Въ началѣ было Слово, и Слово было у Бога, и Слово было Богъ.

2. Оно было въ началѣ у Бога.

3. Все чрезъ Него начало быть, и безъ Него ни что не начало быть, что начало быть.

4. Въ Немъ была жизнь, и жизнь была свѣтъ человѣковъ.

5. И свѣтъ во тьмѣ свѣтитъ, и тьма не объяла его.

6. Былъ человѣкъ, посланный отъ Бога; имя ему Іоаннъ.

7. Онъ пришелъ для свидѣтельства, чтобы свидѣтельствовать о свѣтѣ, дабы всѣ увѣровали чрезъ него.

8. Онъ не былъ свѣтъ, но былъ *посланъ*, чтобы свидѣтельствовать о свѣтѣ.

(Komi-Zyryan)

749

KOREAN

INTRODUCTION

Korean has been variously connected with Dravidian, Austronesian, Palaeo-Asiatic, Chinese, and, most convincingly, with the Altaic languages, with which it certainly shares many grammatical features. How many of these resemblances are areal or typological, however, is a moot point, and the exact genetic affinity of Korean remains questionable. The Chinese element is very large but essentially alien. Comparison with Japanese yields a surprising wealth of morphological and syntactical similarities, but the two languages seem to have developed in parallel, rather than to be derived from a common genetic source.

Modern Korean derives from the ancient Korean Han dialect, which ousted its rival congeners thanks to the rise to political dominance of the Silla state, where it was spoken. It is spoken today by between 50 and 60 million people in North and South Korea, and in Korean colonies in China, Japan, and elsewhere. The literary norm is based on the Seoul dialect.

Until the nineteenth century Chinese was the main language of literature in Korea, and little seems to have been written in Korean. A favourite genre was the *sijo*, – a kind of ruba'i, with seven- (three + four) or eight-syllable lines. Among the most famous exponents of the *sijo* were Yun Səndo (seventeenth century), Chəng Ch'əl (sixteenth century), and Kim Sijang (eighteenth century). In the twentieth century the novel has become the main forum for the literary handling of social issues. The best-known practitioners include Yi Kwangsu and Yi Injik.

SCRIPT

In the fifteenth century the fourth Yi king of Korea, King Sejong, commissioned his scholars to produce a phonetic alphabet of 28 letters, and soon the first work in the new script, the 'Songs of Flying Dragons' was published. Chinese script continued, however, to be used for notating Korean until well into the nineteenth/twentieth century. The so-called 'mixed script' uses the indigenous alphabet plus Chinese characters; this method of writing was abandoned in North Korea after 1945, and attempts are being made to phase it out in South Korea.

PHONOLOGY

Consonants

stops: /p, t, k/, with aspirates /ph, th, kh/, and glottalized /p', t', k'/
The glottalized values are written as *pp*, *tt*, *kk*, and are sometimes
described as 'implosives'. The same triad is found in the affricates: /tʃ,
tʃh, tʃ'/.
fricatives: s, s', h
nasals: m, n, ŋ
lateral and flap: l, r
semi-vowels: j, w

In final position, members of the dental triad, the affricates and the sibilants are
all realized as /t/; final /k, kh, k'/ → /k/; final /p, ph, p'/ → /p/. Intervocalic /p, t, k/
→ [b, d, g].
Korean has an elaborate system of consonantal assimilation; e.g. stops
preceding a nasal are assimilated to that nasal: e.g. *pakmulkwan* 'museum' →
/panmulgwan/. In this article, /tʃ/ and its allophone /dʒ/ are notated as *c*, /tʃh/ as
ch, /tʃ'/ as *ch'*.

Vowels

The basic inventory is:

i, e, ε, ɪ, ə, a, u, o

plus allophones /œ, y/. The script provides for notation of the vowels preceded
by /j/ and by /w/, i.e. palatalized and labialized series. [ɔ] and [ʌ] are allophones
of /ə/. Korean shows some traces of vowel harmony.

MORPHOLOGY AND SYNTAX

Noun

The nominative/subject particle, corresponding to the Japanese *ga*, is *-i*
(following a consonant) or *ka* (following a vowel): e.g. *saram.i* 'the man'. Six
oblique cases are formed by agglutinative affix (not inflection):

genitive	saramɪi
accusative	saramɪl
dative	sarameke
locative	(saramesə)
instrumental	saramɪro
comitative	saramkwa

In itself the noun is neutral as to number. A plurality marker is *-tɪl/-dɪl*. A
focusing agent or topicalizer, corresponding to Japanese *wa*, is *-(n)ɪn*: e.g. *Kɪ
saram.ɪn Hankuk mal.ɪl kalɪchi.lə kassɪmnita* 'As for that man, he went to
teach Korean.'

751

Compound nouns are readily formed by apposition: e.g. *chaek.pang* 'book-store'; *chaek-sdang* 'reading table'; *chaek.kaps* 'price of books'; *Hankuk.salam* 'Korean person'.

Adjective

A participial form in *-n* provides attributive adjectives which precede the noun: e.g.

khɪ.ta 'to be big': *khɪn* 'big', *khɪn kənmul* 'big building';
pissa.ta 'to be expensive': *pissan* 'dear', *pissan chaek* 'expensive book'.

Pronoun

Until comparatively recently personal pronouns were avoided in Korean in favour of various circumlocutions, e.g. with *mom* 'body': *i mom.i* 'this body' = 'I'. In the modern language, pronouns are respect-graded: first and second person singular forms in respectful/formal language are: *cə*, *tangsin*; *na* is an acceptable form for first person singular in more informal language. For the third person the demonstrative *kɪ* is used, often plus *saram*, *puin*: e.g. *kɪ saram.ɪn* 'he', *ki puin.i* 'she' (cf. *ano hito wa* in Japanese). A polite form of address is *sənsaeng* = Chinese *xiānsheng*.

The pluralizing marker *-tɪl* can be added.

DEMONSTRATIVE PRONOUN/ADJECTIVE
Three degrees: *i* 'this', *chə* 'that', *kɪ* 'that yonder'.

INTERROGATIVE PRONOUN
nugu 'who?', *myəch* /myət/, 'what?'.

RELATIVE PRONOUN
None; *see* **Relative constructions** in **Verb** (below).

Numerals

The indigenous Korean numerals 1–10 are: *han(a)*, *tu(l)*, *se*, *ne*, *tasəs*, *yəsəs*, *ilkop*, *yətəl*, *ahop*, *yəl*. For the teens, these are added to *yəl*: e.g. 11 *yəl-hana*. 20 *sɪmu(l)*; 30 *səlhɪn*; 40 *mahɪn*; 100 *paek*.

A Chinese series 1–10 is also used: *il*, *i*, *sam*, *sa*, *o*, *yuk*, *chil*, *phal*, *ku*, *sip*.

Verb

With half a dozen basic agglutinative components which can be added to the stem, plus a large number of possible affixes, a Korean verb can appear in literally hundreds of forms. The basic structure can be set out as: stem – grade marker – tense/mood/aspect marker – finite indicative or interrogative marker: e.g. *kalɪchi – si – kess.imni – ta* 'will teach' (honorific register).

Neither person nor number is marked; i.e. failing a nominal subject, the personal pronoun must be used.

STEM

This can be one-, two- or three-syllable: e.g. *mək-* 'eat'; *pissa-* 'be expensive'; *kalɪchi-* 'teach'. Compounds are made with *ha-/hae-* 'to do', *po-* 'to see', and other verbs, following either a noun or a verbal form: e.g. with noun: *kongpu ha-* 'to study' (Japanese *benkyō suru*); with verbal: *mul po-* 'to inquire' (*mu.ta* 'inquire', *pota* 'to see').

GRADE

There are several socio-linguistic levels; a broad division is into plain, informal polite, formal polite, and honorific. For example, in the present tense, the informal polite style has a form close to the stem, + *yo*; the formal polite style has the infixed characteristic *-mn-*: cf.

Stem	Informal polite	Formal polite	Respectful
ha 'to do'	hae yo	hamnita	hasɪmnita
iss 'to be'	issə yo	issɪmnita	issɪsɪmnita
o- 'to come'	wa yo	omnita	osimnita

Some verbs have suppletive stems for respectful/honorific usage: e.g. *mək* 'to eat': hon. *capsusita – capsusɪmnita* 'eat(s)'. The plain style has its own specific set of endings, used in the family and at school: senior to junior, elder to younger, and so on.

TENSE MARKERS

The informal and formal style present has been illustrated above. The past tense characteristic is *-ss-*; past anterior *-ssəss-*; future *-kess-*: e.g. in formal polite style: *ilkəssɪmnita* 'read' (past tense); *patəssəssɪmnita* 'had taken'; *kalɪchi.si.kess.ɪmnita* 'will teach' (hon.).

IMPERATIVE/HORTATIVE MOOD

Typical endings are *-iyo* and *-ita*: e.g. *cusipsiyo* 'please give'; *kapsita* 'let's go'. The verb stem + *ki* is a verbal noun: *Hankukmal(ɪl) paeuki* '(the) learning (of) Korean'.

NEGATION

There are several interesting constructions:

1. *an* preceding finite form: e.g. *hakkyo.e kamnita* 'goes to school', *hakkyo.e an kamnita* 'doesn't go to school';
2. stem + *ci-* + *anh-*: e.g. *ka.ci anh.simnita* 'doesn't/don't go';
3. stem + *ci-* + *mot hamnita*: e.g. *kaci mot hamnita* 'doesn't/don't go';
4. stem in *-l* form + *su* + *əps*: e.g. *kal su əpsɪmnita* 'can't go'.

INTERROGATIVE

The general characteristic is *-kka, kka yo*: e.g. *əti.e kasɪmnikka* 'Where is/are … going?'; *Tapang.e kal kka yo* 'How about going to a tearoom?'

MODAL CONSTRUCTIONS

There are many of these: e.g.

-(*i*)*lə* 'in order to', e.g. *Hankuk mal.ıl paeu.lə* 'in order to learn Korean';
    chinku.lıl mannalə wassımnita 'came to meet a friend' (*chinku*);

-(*i*)*ly ko* + *ha*-: 'intend to', e.g. *Hankuk.e kalyəko haessımnita* 'intended
    to go to Korea';

-*ko* + *siph*-: 'want to', e.g. *yənghwa.lıl poko siphsımnita* 'wanted to see
    a film';

-*myən*: 'if', e.g. *Hankuk.e ka.myən* 'if ... go(es)/went to Korea'; *maekcu.lıl*
    wənhasimyən 'if you'd like a beer';

stem in -*l* + *su iss*-: 'be able to', e.g. *kal su issımnita* 'can go';

-(*i*)*ni kaa*: 'because', e.g. *ton.i əpsınikka* 'because ... has/have no money'.

Participial forms in -*n* (for present and past) and -*l* (future) are used
attributively: e.g. *nae.ka paeu.nın mal* 'the language which I am learning';
nae.ka ilk.ıl chaek 'the book which I'm going to read'; *hal il.i manhsımnita* 'the
work which has to be done is much' = 'there's a lot of work to be done'. These
forms can be passive: e.g. *mannal salam* 'people who are going to be met'.

Postpositions

Examples: *hakkyo aph e* 'in front of the school'; *i nyən cən.e* 'before two years'
= 'two years ago'; *Səul esə Pusan kkaci* 'from Seoul to Pusan'.

Word order

SOV is normal.

처음에두가이스퍼도가 하ᄂ님파함긔하니두난곳하

나님이라이도가처음에 하나님파함긔하미만믈이말미

여라지므스니지은하나 토말미지안깨지오미업나니

라ᄂ에셩명이사니이싱명이사람의빗치되여빗치어두

온뎌빗치오되여드오되나아지못하다라한사람이기스니

하나님이보낸바일흠은요인니라와셔간증이되문빗츨위

하여간증하여ᄉ사람이뎌로말미여빗가하나ᄃ가빗치ᄂ

이요오직빗츨위하여간증하엿나니다

KORYAK

INTRODUCTION

In terms of numbers this is, after Chukchi, the largest member of the Chukotko-Kamchatkan group of Palaeo-Siberian languages. It is spoken by about six or seven thousand people in the Koryak National Area in north Kamchatka, and along the Bering Sea coast as far as Cape Navarin. Since 1936, a written form, based on the Chavchuven dialect, has been notated in Cyrillic script with additional letters for /q/ and /n/.

Two closely related languages, Alyutor and Kerek, both now virtually extinct, were until recently regarded as dialects of Koryak.

It is noteworthy that not all neologisms in the language are straight loans from Russian; many are calques on Russian words, using native Koryak resources.

PHONOLOGY

Consonants

> stops: p, t, k, q, ʔ
> affricate: tʃ
> fricatives: w, v, j, γ, ʕ
> nasals: m, n, ŋ
> lateral: l

/t, n, l/ also occur palatalized: /t', n', l'/.

Vowels

> i, ɪ, e/ɛ, a, o u

In this article, /ɛ/ is represented as ę.

VOWEL HARMONY
Very close to that of Chukchi (*see* **Chukchi**).

MORPHOLOGY AND SYNTAX

Noun

A dual number is distinguished throughout the grammatical system, though, in the noun, it is formally marked only in the absolute/nominative case. Elsewhere in the nominal declension it seems to be identical to the plural. Human and non-human categories are distinguished, giving two declensions: the first comprises all nouns in the non-human category, plus nouns denoting humans in so far as they are general, i.e. do not refer to specific persons. These are covered by the second declension.

The dual marker is *-t* or *-u/-ę*: e.g. *qoya.t* 'two reindeer'; *kayŋɪ.t* 'two bears'.

For nouns ending in a vowel, the plural marker is *-v'* (with variants); *-u* is added to nouns ending in a consonant. Both plural endings tend to be realized as /w/: e.g. *ŋavɪqqalyu.v'* 'girls'; *tɪnup.u* 'hills'.

DECLENSION

The first declension has eleven cases which are neutral as to number, apart, of course, from the nominative or absolute case which is marked for dual or plural. Thus, for *qoyaŋa* 'reindeer', dual *qoyat*, plural *qoya.v'* /qoyaw/, the paradigm shows, for example, an ergative *qoya.ta*; a locative *qoya.k*; an ablative *qoya.ŋqo*; a comitative *ga.qoya.ma*.

In the second declension, the plural forms are distinguished from the singular by the presence of *-yɪk(a)-*; and the ergative and locative cases, separate in the first declension, share a single form: e.g. for *appa* 'father':

	Singular	Plural
ergative/locative	appa.nak	appa.yɪk
ablative	appa.na.ŋqo	appa.yɪka.ŋqo
dative	appa.na.ŋ	appa.yɪk.ɪŋ
aditive	appa.na.ytɪŋ	appa.yɪka.ytɪŋ

The second declension has eight cases.

Adjective

Qualitative adjectives are constructed on the model *nɪ* + stem + *qin*: e.g. *nɪ.męyɪŋ.qin* 'big'; *nɪ.ŋlɪ.qęn* 'smoky'. These forms are then conjugated for person and number: e.g. *nɪ.X.y.gɪm* 'I am X', *nɪ.X.y.gi* 'you (sing.) are X', where X is a quality. Similarly with nouns: e.g. *ęn'piči.y.gɪm* 'I am a father', *ęn'piči.y.gi* 'you (sing.) are a father'. There are corresponding negative versions.

Pronoun

	Singular	Dual	Plural
1	gɪmmo	muyi	muyu
2	gɪčči	tuyi	tuyu
3	ɪnno	ɪčči	ɪčču

These are fully declined: e.g. the ergative of first person singular is *gɪmnan*, of first person plural *močgɪnan*.

DEMONSTRATIVE PRONOUN

Three degrees: *v'uččin* 'this' (proximate) – *ɪnnin* 'that' – *ŋaen* 'that yonder'.

INTERROGATIVE PRONOUN

mẹki 'who?' (declined in second declension); *yɪnnɪ* 'what?'.

Numerals

1–10: *ɪnnẹn, ŋɪččeq, ŋɪyoq, ŋɪyaq, mɪllɪŋẹn, ɪnnan.mɪllɪŋẹn, ŋiyaq.mɪllɪŋẹn, ŋiyoq.mɪllɪŋẹn, qonʕayčɪŋkẹn, mɪngɪtkẹn.*

Verb

The infinitive ending is *-k(kɪ)*; there are indicative, subjunctive, and imperative moods. The indicative has a present, two past tenses, two futures. The dual is everywhere formally distinguished. The conjugational system is essentially one of prefix – stem – personal ending, e.g. from *tɪlẹk* 'to go':

Present:

	Singular	Dual	Plural
1	tɪku.lẹ.ŋ	mɪt.ku.lẹ.ŋ	mɪt.ko.la.laŋ
2	Øku.lẹ.ŋ	Øku.lẹ.ŋtɪk	Øko.la.laŋtɪk
3	Øku.lẹ.ŋ	Øku.lẹ.ŋi	Øko.la.laŋ

Here *lẹ* is the stem of the verb and *la* is an allophone.

Similarly for other tenses and moods: e.g. the perfective past has a *t-* prefix in the singular, *mɪt-* in dual and plural; the suffixes end in *-k/-i*. The imperative has *mɪ.lẹ.k* 'that I may go, let me go'; *qɪ.lẹ.gi* 'go!'.

TRANSITIVE VERB + OBJECT

The endings encode subject/object deixis: e.g. with verb *liʕuk* 'to see':

tɪku.lʕu.gi 'I see you (sing.)'
tɪku.lʕu.ŋtɪk 'I see you two'
kinẹ.lʕu.ŋ 'you (sing.) see me'
nẹku.lʕu.gi 'he sees you'
nẹku.lʕu.gɪm 'they see me'

The complete grid has over 80 forms.

ERGATIVE CONSTRUCTION

Agent in instrumental case: e.g. *igẹ tɪmnẹn qoyaŋa* 'the wolf killed the reindeer', (*-ẹ* is instr. ending for bases ending in a consonant; *qoyaŋa* is abs./nom. case; *tɪmnẹn* 'he/it killed him/it').

NEGATION

The Koryak verb is negated by combining a negative marker (*uiŋẹ*), the *ẹ/ a....kelka* form of the sense-verb, and a conjugated auxiliary (transitive or intransitive): e.g. *ɪnno uiŋẹ ẹ.yemk.ẹ itti* 'he didn't come'; *gɪmmo uiŋẹ avẹtat.ka titɪk* 'I didn't work'; *ɪnno uiŋẹ avẹtat.ka itti* 'he didn't work'.

Word order

Free; SVO is normal.

KPELLE

INTRODUCTION

Kpelle belongs to the Mande group of Niger-Congo. It is spoken by around 700,000 people in Liberia, with some spill-over into Guinea.

PHONOLOGY

Consonants

In addition to /p, b, f, v, w, m/, there are labio-velars /kp/ and /gb/. In the dental series, /s/ and /z/ tend to palatal fricatives /ʃ, ʒ/. There are two *d* sounds, one of which alternates with *l* and *r*. The fricative /ɣ/ and the nasals /ɲ/ and /ŋ/ are present. Nasals + stops are subject to sandhi at junctures, e.g. /-n/ + /t-/ → [nd]. Clustering occurs, e.g. *kplikpli* 'cat-fish'.

Vowels

The phonemes are:

    long or short: i, ɪ, ɛ, a, ɔ, o, u

Vocalic length is phonemic, though homonyms are also usually distinguished by tone. Nasalized vowels in contact with a non-nasal consonant are marked: ã, ɛ̃, etc.

Tones

High, low, rising, falling; not usually marked in script.

MORPHOLOGY AND SYNTAX

Noun

There is no grammatical gender. A noun is made definite by mutation of initial and addition of *-i*: e.g. a voiceless initial mutates to its voiced counterpart: e.g. *folo* 'sun' – *voloi* 'the sun'. Nasal consonants do not mutate but add *-i*: e.g. *nyɛ* 'fish' – *nyɛi* 'the fish'. Further examples: *ba* 'rice' – *mbai* 'the rice'; *lɔwɔ* 'bush' – *ndɔwɔi* 'the bush'; *wulu* 'tree' – *ŋgului* 'the tree'.

PLURAL

-*ŋa* is added: e.g. *ta* 'town'; *taŋa* 'towns'; *daŋai* 'the towns'. Plural marking is largely optional. A generic plural is made with *-bela*: e.g. *kpɛlɛnu* 'a Kpelle man'; pl. *kpɛlɛbela* 'Kpelle people'.

GENITIVE

Appositional; possessor precedes possessed: e.g. *kaloŋ ta* 'chief's town'. The personal pronoun may be interpolated: *kaloŋ a ta*.

Adjective

As attribute, adjective follows noun, e.g. *wulu koya* 'high tree', and takes the same mutations: *ŋgului goyai* 'the high tree'.

Pronoun

The independent forms used with the copula/existential verb are:

	Singular	Plural
1	nyá	kwiá
2	yɛ́	ká
3	nyà	diá

Example: *kpɛlɛnu ba nyà* 'I am a Kpelle'

SUBJECT, OBJECT, AND DATIVE FORMS
The past-tense set:

	Singular			Plural		
	Subject	Object	Dative	Subject	Object	Dative
1	ŋá	ŋá	mê	kú	kú	kúà
2	í	í	ya	ká	ká	kâ
3	è	∅ (see below)	mè	dí	dí	díà

The third person singular object pronoun is indicated by mutation (as in nominals) of the initial of the verb: e.g. *kâ* 'to see' – *dí gà* 'they saw him'; *paa* 'to kill' – *dí baa* 'they killed him'.

DEMONSTRATIVE PRONOUN/ADJECTIVE
Examples: *ŋɛi* 'this'; *ti* 'that'.

INTERROGATIVE PRONOUN
gbɛ 'who?'; pl. *gbɛni* 'what?'.

There is no *relative pronoun*: a relative clause is indicated by raised tone + *-i* final: e.g. *bɛlɛi nyin a lɔmui* 'the house which he enters' (*nyin* 'that', demonstrative; *lɔ* 'enter'; *mu* 'lower part, under', cf. *bɛlɛi mu* 'in the house').

Numerals

1–5: *taaŋ, felɛ, saba, naaŋ, lɔlu*; 6 *lɔl mai da*; 7 *lɔl mai felɛ*; 10 *pu*; 11 *pu kao tɔnɔ*; 20 *pu felɛ*; 100 *pu pu*.

Verb

There is no inflection. Tenses are generated by tonal change in root + specific sets of pronominal markers + auxiliaries:

aorist: pronominal series sing. *ŋà, yà, à*; pl. *kwà, kà, dà* + root, e.g. *pa – à pá* 'he has come';

past: subject series (as above, *see* **Pronoun**) + root, e.g. *è pà* 'he came' (note change of tone in root);

progressive: aorist series + root + *-i*, e.g. *à pái* 'he's coming';

future: *pai* is placed before root; aorist pronominal series, + *-i*: e.g. *ŋà pái kái* 'I shall see'.

NEGATION

The general negative marker is *fé*: e.g. *ŋa fé pani* 'I did not come'; *vè pani* 'he did not come'.

There are various ways of emphasizing a tense form, e.g. the aorist by means of *gba*: this produces a perfective aspect. Similarly, the verb *kɛ* 'to do', can reinforce another verb: e.g. *na (fe) kɛ mɛni* 'I heard/did not hear'.

Postpositions

Examples: *su* 'in' – *zu* 'in him'; *pol* 'behind' – *bol* 'behind him'; *pɔ* 'with' – *bɛlɛi pol* 'behind the house'.

Word order

SVO: e.g. *Sulɔno e kwɛni pili* 'The boy threw a stone' (*sulɔno* 'boy'; *pili* 'stone'; *kwɛni* = 'throw'; *e* is the third person pronoun copying the nominal subject). A pronominal indirect object may be final: e.g. *e X fe me* 'he gave X to me'.

1 Gɔ́ɔ pelanii Ŋóoi e kɛ̀ naa. Ŋóoi nyaŋ e kɛ̀ Ɣâla kɔlɛ. Nyaŋ Ŋóoi e kɛ̀ a Ɣâla. ² E kɛ̀ Ɣâla kɔlɛ a gɔ́ɔ pelanii. ³ Sɛŋ kélee e kpɛ̀tɛ zârai. Sɛŋ da kelee fe kɛ ni a gbɛtɛɛ ŋ́éi pôlu ma nyii kɛ̀ a gbɛtɛɛi. ⁴ Fúlu-laa e kɛ̀ gbonôi. Nyaŋ vúlu-laai e kɛ̀ a núu-kpune ŋɔkwaa-ponɔɔ. ⁵ Gwaa-ponɔɔi a fòlo gbínii su. Nyaŋ gbínii fe tá niiŋ ni.

⁶ Núu tɔ̀nɔ e kɛ̀ naa. Ɣâla e dɛ̀ɛ. Ñáa ɓe kɛ̀ a Zɔ̂ɔ. ⁷ E pà sêre-faa kɛ mɛni ma, e gwaa-ponɔɔi maa sêre-faa kɛ, a gɛɛ núu kelee é láa la zârai. ⁸ Ve kɛ ni a gwaa-ponɔɔi. Kɛ́lɛ, e pà a gɛɛ é gwaa-ponɔɔi maa sêre-faa kɛ́.

KUMYK

INTRODUCTION

Kumyk belongs to the Kypchak-Polovets group of Turkic languages (Baskakov's (1966) classification). With over 180,000 speakers in the Dagestan Autonomous Socialist Republic, Kumyk is one of the six literary languages of Dagestan.

SCRIPT

Following initial experiments with Arabic and romanization, Cyrillic has been used since the late 1930s. The Cyrillic hard and soft signs are used to modify base letters; thus, *o* + soft sign = /œ/, *u* + soft sign = /y/, notated here as *ö* and *ü* respectively.

PHONOLOGY

/c/ figures in an otherwise standard Turkic inventory (*see* **Turkic Languages**), plus the glottal stop which is, for example, a realization of script *t*: e.g. *atlɪ* /aˀlɪ/, 'rider'.

VOWEL HARMONY
Both palatal and labial, e.g. *qɪzardaš.ɪm* 'my sister', *güčlüsüz* 'you are strong (pl.)'.

MORPHOLOGY AND SYNTAX

Standard Turkic models throughout; *see* **Turkic Languages**.

Noun

In the nominal declension, the genitive case ending is -*n*V⁴, i.e. the normally present final -*n* has been dropped, making the genitive and accusative forms identical: *atnɪ* 'of the horse/the horse (acc.)'

Verb

Some examples of tense structure:

> present: gel.e.men 'I come'
> past (a): gel.gen.men 'I have come'
> past (b): geldim 'I came'
> imperf.: gel.e.edim 'I was coming'
> future: gel.er.men 'I shall come'
> conditional: gel.sem 'if I come'

PARTICIPLES

gel.e.gen 'coming, who is coming'; *gel.gen* 'who came'; *gel.e.žek* 'who will come'.

INFINITIVE

gel.mek 'to come'; negative: *gel.me.mek* 'not to come'.

٢١ صونك, آنتك آناسى وقارداشلارى كلدبلر, و
(اوى ننك) قير ياننه نوروب, آنى چاقرمغه آدم
٢٢ ييارديلر. وآنتك آبلانه سنه اولتورغان خلق, اوغار
آيتديلار: «مونه حاله, آنانك وقارداشلارنك كلوب,
٢٣ قيرده سغه قارائيلار» ۰ اول ده اولارغه جواب
بروب: «آنام وقارداشلارم كيملردر؟» ديدى ۰
٢٤ وآيلانه سنه اوتورغانلارغه قراب, «مونه حاله,
٢٥ آنام وقارداشلارم ۰ زيرا هركيم الله ننك مُرادين غام
ابتسه; اُولدر قارداشم وقزقارداشم وآنام» ديدى ۰

(Mark 3: 31–5)

!KUNG (!Xu)

INTRODUCTION

!Kung belongs to the Northern Khoisan group of languages. It is spoken by upwards of 10,000 Bushmen in the Botswana, Angola, Namibia frontier regions, on the north-western fringes of the Kalahari Desert.

The language has been reduced to writing in various forms of notation. An official orthography was approved by the Language and Publications Board of South West Africa in 1969. The orthography adopted in this article follows that of Snyman (1970).

PHONOLOGY

Consonants

About a hundred consonantal phonemes are distinguished, evenly divided between egressive (non-click) and ingressive (click) inventories. This large number of phonemes (the world record, as far as is known) is achieved in both inventories by means of extensive secondary articulation.

The egressive inventory has bilabial, alveolar, palatal, and velar series. The aveolar series, for example, is based on the simple plosives /t/ and /d/. Velar aspiration is added to give /tx/, laryngeal aspiration to give /th/, and ejective velar aspiration to give /tx'/; the voiced correlatives are /dγ/ and /d'h/; this latter phoneme is preceded by unreleased glottalization.

Analogous surd and voiced sets, each with from four to seven members, are provided by the bilabial plosives (based on /p/, /b/), the velar plosives (based on /k/, /g/), the alveolar affricates (based on /ts/, /dz/) and the palatal affricates (based on /tʃ/, /dʒ/. Together, these sets provided 31 phonemes.

The fricatives are relatively simple: /ß, s, z, ʃ, ʒ, x, ɦ/. There are six phonemes based on /m/, including a laryngeal aspirate /mɦ/, glottalized onset /ʔm/ and two phonemes involving 'interruption': *m.m* = /m'm/, where ' represents a kind of glottal *Bebung*, and *m̰.m̰* = /m'm/ in which pharyngeal friction is added to interruption (*see* **Vowels**, below).

The ingressive or click inventory has dental, alveolar, and palatal rows. The dental row has ten fricatives and three nasals based on the dental click, which is notated as |. The alveolar row has eleven plosives and three nasals based on the alveolar click ǂ. The palatal row has eleven plosives based on the palatal plosive click !, and eleven affricatives and six nasals based on the palatal fricative and nasal click ||.

The palatal plosive series is given here in illustration:

!	!x	!h
!?	!x?	!?h
g!	g!γ	g!h
	g!γ?	g!?h

Vowels

Here the basic division is into nasal and non-nasal (oral) series.

short vowels: i, e, a, o, u

/a/ and /o/ also occur accompanied by pharyngeal friction to produce a kind of croaking sound. Snyman (1970) calls these 'pressed vowels', and notates them as a̧ and o̧. The long vowels include all the short vowels except /e/ – /iː, aː/, etc.

A third series of vowels involves interruption; notated as *a.a* or *a'a*.

The above sets are oral. The nasal sets include: (a) short vowels: as oral without /e/; (b) long vowels: /ãː, a̧ː, ɔ̃ː, õː, ũː/; (c) rising and falling diphthongs: e.g. /eĩ, oĩ, wã/; (d) interrupted homorganic or disparate pairs: e.g. /ã.ã/.

MORPHOLOGY AND SYNTAX

A detailed and very finely differentiated taxonomy of the Bushman habitat is reflected in the vocabulary of !Kung.

Noun

Singular and plural numbers are not normally distinguished, but plural markers are available if required, e.g. *-mhi, -si/-sī*: ≠*'aama* 'snake', pl. ≠*'aamhi*; *!a'o* 'leopard', pl. *!a'osi*

There is no inflection for case. Syntactic relationships are expressed by means of postpositions; e.g. *n!om !'o* 'on the rock'; *n!om dī* 'under the rock'; *tš'u n!eng* 'inside the house'; *tš'u ts'i* 'in front of the house'.

Adjective

Modifier follows modified, attached to it by a *-wa/-ya* glide, which behaves very like the Iranian *ezafe*; e.g. |*ao* 'buffalo' + |*xwa* 'alive': |*aowa* |*xwa* 'the live buffalo'; |*hwe* 'horse' + |*'lom* 'beautiful': |*hweya* |*'hom* 'the beautiful horse'. The plural connective is *-sa*; e.g. |*aosa* |*xwa* 'the live buffaloes'; |*hwesa* |*'hom* 'the beautiful horses'.

Any verb in !Kung can function thus, as what Snyman calls 'adnouns' in modifier position connected by glide link, and it is in the this way that relative clauses are made: e.g. |*hwe* + *'m* → |*hweya 'm* 'the horse which is grazing'; *žu.wa kwa̧ n!'hei* 'the person (*žu*) who fears (*kwa̧*) a lion (*n!'hei*)'.

Pronoun

PERSONAL

	Singular	Plural
1	mi	e!a, m!a (with variants)
2	a	i!a, i
3	ha	(dependent on class: see next section)

Singular and plural forms of the third person are related to specific Bushman taxonomies which are not always identifiable in Indo-European terms. The *ha-* (sing.) – *si* (plural) class comprises human beings; the *ha–hi* class covers birds, reptiles, insects; the *ha–ha* class covers articles of everyday use. There are many sub-groupings, which are presumably explicable in terms of specific features of the environment. Some examples from Snyman:

		Class
žu|'hwa	'Bushman'	ha–si
da'ama	'child'	ha–si
||a'e	'monkey'	ha–hi
!wã!wã	'arrow shaft'	ha–ha
šamanga	'maize'	ha–hi
‡'aama	'snake'	ka–ka

These class distinctions are reflected in the possessive constructions: e.g. *mi hisi* 'my ...' (plural objects belonging to the *ha–si* class); *a masi* 'your ...' (plural objects belonging to the *ha–ha* class).

DEMONSTRATIVE PRONOUN AND ADJECTIVE

he, ke 'this'; *to'a* 'that'; *uuto'a* 'that yonder'. The *-wa/-ya* glide is used as a connective: e.g. *n\|ei* 'head' – *n\|eiya ke* 'this head'.

INTERROGATIVE PRONOUN

hažwe/hažwi 'who?'; *hatše/hatšii* 'what?'. These require the general interrogative marker *re, ba, xae* (with variants): e.g. *Hatše **ba** ‡'aama n!ei?* 'What does the snake bite?'

Numerals

1 *r\|e'e* or *n\|wi*; 2 *tsã*; 3 *n!eni*. Examples: *žu n\|e'e* 'one person'; *e tsã* 'we two'; *gumi n!eni* 'the three animals'.

Verb

Verbs are transitive or intransitive. There is no inflection, nor are there any auxiliary verbs. Regular transitive verbs do not show concord with object: cf. *zo n!ei !'hwã* 'the bee stings the man'; *zo n!ei n\|\|ae* 'the bee stings the men'. But, irregularly, concord may be shown with number of object: e.g. *mi g!xa g!we* 'I take off the shoe'; *mi šwe g!wesi* 'I take off the shoes'.

A causative is made with *n≠ei*: e.g. *N!aro-kx'ao n≠ei-ge'eya de'ebi* 'The teacher (*n!aro-kx'ao*) makes the children (*de'ebi*) sing (*ge'eya*).

TENSE

In the absence of inflection of any kind, temporal adverbs are necessary. Some of these may precede or follow the subject. Some examples from Snyman: *ka |ao !haa-tsi* 'the buffalo is charging now (*ka*)'; *|ao n||aāha !haa-tsi* 'the buffalo charged long ago'.

IMPERATIVE

The imperative is usually followed by a benefactive pronoun, e.g. *na* 'to/for me', *ko* 'for other': cf. *eiya na 'msi* 'Mother gives me food'; *na 'msi* 'give me food'.

NEGATIVE

The verb is generally negated by negative adverbs, e.g. *|wa, |wi, |ao*: *mi ho !'hwā* 'I see the man'; *mi |wa ho !'hwā* 'I do not see the man'.

COPULA

o; e.g. *g!heī o mi ga* 'the tree is mine'; *g!heīsi o mi gasi* 'the trees are mine'; *mi o žu|'hwā* 'I am a Bushman'.

Post-verbal particles generate modal senses – reciprocal, comitative, instrumental, benefactive.

Word order

SVO.

---

31. Te Yesu ǁ'ā ha t<u>a</u>e kota ha tsīsī tsia ha, xabe si!a
    ǀwa g!a'ama tš'u te ǁxwaa žú te hi !'eu ha.

32. Te žúsa ≠hhi !hoo nǁhomi ha, te si!a ǀwa ha te ko:
    Ye'ao, a t<u>a</u>e kota a tsīsī gea ts'i te !'eu a.

33. Xabe ha meni si!a te ko: Hažwe re o mi t<u>a</u>e te
    hažwe sī ne o mi tsīsī ?

34. Te ha se nǁhomi ha !'e ko žú te ko: Si!asa he
    o mi t<u>a</u>esī kota mi tsīsī.

35. Khhama žwa du tšisa !Xu ku kare o mi !o kota mi
    !wui kota mi tsī kota mi t<u>a</u>e.

(Mark 3: 31–5)

KURDISH

INTRODUCTION

Kurdistan, where this North-West Iranian language is mainly spoken, covers large contiguous areas of Turkey, Syria, Iraq, and Iran. Kurds are also resident in north-eastern Iran (Khorasan), Baluchistan, and in the Armenian, Azerbaydzhani, and Turkmen Soviet Socialist Republics of the USSR. Estimates as to the total number of speakers vary widely; possible around 10 million people speak one or another form of Kurdish. The main dialects are Sorani (Iraq and Iran), and Kurmandji (Turkey, USSR, Syria).

Political and social fragmentation is reflected in the language, which has no recognized standard form, and which is or has been written in a variety of scripts – Arabic, Cyrillic, Roman, Armenian. Sorani has semi-official status in Iraqi Kurdistan, where it is the language of primary education and of the local media. Poetry has been written in Kurdish since the thirteenth century.

SCRIPT

Sorani Kurdish is written in Arabic script plus the Iranian innovations and two letters for the specifically Kurdish sounds ŗ and ļ: inverted circumflex on Arabic r, l. The inverted circumflex is also used on a y or w bearer to denote the vowel phonemes /o/, /ə/, /ɛ/. Arabic *hā* is used to denote /ĕ/; thus, for example, the word *ferheng* 'dictionary' is written as فەرهەنگ.

In Cyrillic, /ɪ/ is represented by the Cyrillic soft sign ь; /ə/ by ə. In Sorani, the orthography is that codified by Taufiq Wahby in the 1920s, as subsequently modified by Iraqi Kurdish scholars. Treatment of certain phonemes e.g. of medial and final /iː/ and /uː/ is not always consistent.

PHONOLOGY (of Sorani)

Consonants

> stops: p, b, t, d, k, g, q, ʔ
> affricates: tʃ, dʒ
> fricatives: f, v, s, ʃ, z, ʒ, x, γ, ħ, h, ʕ = Arabic 'ain.
> nasals: m, n, ŋ
> laterals and flaps: l, ļ /ɫ/, r, ŗ /r/.
> semi-vowels: j, w

/k/ and /g/ have palatalized allophones. *r* is single-flap /ɾ/; *r̲* is rolled /r/.

Kurmandji makes a distinction between the non-aspirates /p, t, k, ʃ/ and their aspirated counterparts, /ph, th/, etc.

Vowels

short: ɪ, ɛ, ʊ
long: i, e, a, o, u

Ö is a diphthong, /əɛ/. The short vowels are unstable. Long vowels are indicated here by a macron, e.g. *ō*.

MORPHOLOGY AND SYNTAX

Noun

The definite article is -(*y*)*eke*: e.g. *bazar̲.eke* 'the market'; *dē.yeke* 'the village'. The indefinite article is *ēk*/*ē*: e.g. *pē.yēk* 'a foot'.

Gender is not distinguished grammatically; if necessary, natural gender can be marked lexically: e.g. *shēr.ī.nēr* 'lion', *shēr.ī.mē* 'lioness'. In Kurmandji, gender (masculine, feminine, common) is distinguished and marked by correlative changes in the izafe. (*See* **Persian**).

NUMBER
The usual plural marker is -*an*: e.g. *wul̲at.an* 'countries'. The definite article precedes -*an*: e.g. *žin.ek.an* 'the women'.

POSSESSION
The ezafe -*ī*/-*y* links two nouns in genitive relationship: e.g. *xel̲k.i.r̲ožhel̲at* 'the peoples of the Middle East'; *mela.y.mizgewt* 'the mullah of the mosque'. The ezafe is to be distinguished from the linking vowels, *e*, *ö*, *a*, *o*, *ē*, used e.g. in composite nouns: *būm.e.lerze* 'earthquake' (here, the linker *e* coalesces with the Arabic article: *al.ard̲* 'the earth'); *kič.e.čaw.r̲eš.eke* 'the black-eyed girl' (*čaw* 'eye'; *r̲eš* 'black').

(In the Kurdish spoken in the USSR nouns form oblique cases: e.g. *gavan* 'shepherd', oblique, *geven*.)

Adjective

As attribute, adjective follows noun and is invariable. It is linked to its noun by the ezafe: e.g. *utel.i.baš* 'good hotel'; *šar.ek.i gewre.y taze* 'a big modern town'; *žin.ek.i kurd.i ǰiwan* 'a beautiful Kurdish woman'.

COMPARISON
A comparative is made with -*ter*: e.g. *sur* 'red' – *sur.ter*.

Pronoun

The personal pronouns with their enclitics are:

	Singular		Plural	
1	min	-(i)m	ēme	-man
2	to	-(i)t	ēwe	-tan
3	ew	-ī	ewan	-yan

The verb 'to be' is expressed by the following enclitic endings: sing. 1 -*m*, 2 -*y*, 3 -*ye*; pl. 1 -*yn*, 2 -*n*, 3 -*n*. The negative form is not enclitic: e.g. *nim* 'I am not', *nit*, etc.

The enclitic forms are used as possessive affixes, e.g. *čaw.an.it* 'your eyes', and as direct-object forms between prefix and root in the present tense and the subjunctive mood: e.g. *de.m.bīn.ē* 'he sees me'.

DEMONSTRATIVE PRONOUN
em.e (proximate), *ew.e* (non-proximate); pl. *ewane*.

DEMONSTRATIVE ADJECTIVE
em – ew; in Kurmandji a circumfix, e.g. *'əm.pyaw.ə* 'this man'.

INTERROGATIVE PRONOUN
či 'who?'; *čī* 'what?'.

RELATIVE PRONOUN
ke + definite -*e* + ezafe: e.g. *ew kitēb-e.y ke to de.y.bīn.ī* 'the book which you see (it)'.

Numerals

1–10: *yek, dū, sē, čuwar, pēnč, šeš, ħewt, hešt, no, de.* 11 *yazde*; 12 *duwazde*; 20 *bīst*; 30 *sī*; 40 *čil*; 100 *sed*.

Verb

As in Persian, the Kurdish verbal system is built up on the two-base pattern, the present base underlying the present–future tense, the present subjunctive, and the imperative; the past base supplies the three past tenses. The past base is obtained by dropping the -*in* ending of the infinitive; the present base is not predictable: e.g.

girtin	'to catch'	– girt	– gir
kuštin	'to kill'	– kušt	– kuž
dītin	'to see'	– dīt	– bīn

The personal endings for intransitive verbs are: sing. 1 -(*i*)*m*, 2 -*ī*/*y*(*t*), 3 *ē*(*t*); pl. 1 *īn*, 2 -*in*, 3 -*in*. Some examples of verb forms:

present tense: *de* + present stem + personal ending, e.g. *de.kew.im* 'I fall'; in negative version *na* replaces *de*: *na.kew.im*;

present subjunctive: *bi* + present stem + personal ending, e.g. *bi.kew.im* 'I may fall';

preterite: past stem + personal ending – third person marker here is *∅*, e.g. *kewt.im* 'I fell', *kewt* 'he fell'; negative: *ne.kewt(im)*;

perfect: past stem + -*uw*- + personal ending, e.g. *kewt.uw.im* 'I have fallen'; negative: *ne.m.kewt(im)*;

imperfect: *de* + past stem + personal ending, e.g. *de.kewt.im* 'I was falling'; negative: *ne.m.kewt*;

a pluperfect is made with the past stem of *hebun* 'to be', e.g. *kewt.i.bū.m* 'I had fallen';

an unreal conditional with the particle -*aye*, e.g. *bi.kewt.im.aye* 'if I had fallen'.

TRANSITIVE VERB

In the past tense the transitive verb is in concord with the object, and the agent is denoted by personal affix attached to that object; if no object is present, the agent marker is attached to the verb: cf. with object: *name.yek.im nūs.ī* 'I wrote a letter'. The agent markers are the enclitic forms of the personal pronouns (see above): cf. *nard.it.im* 'you (sing.) sent me'; *nard.im.it* 'I sent you (sing.)'; *nard.man.in* 'we sent you/them'. Examples with no object present: *xward.im* 'I ate', *xward.man* 'we ate'; neg. *ne.m.xward* 'I didn't eat', *ne.man.xward* 'we didn't eat'.

PASSIVE

The characteristic is -*r*-, with -*ē* for the present, -*a* for the past; thus, from *nūsīn* 'to write': *nūsran* 'to be written'; past stem: *nūsra*; present stem: *nūsrē*.

The causative characteristic is -*din*: e.g. *šikan* 'to break' (intrans.) – *šikandin* 'to break' (trans.).

The past participle is made by adding -*ū*/-*w* to the past base. Enclitic personal markers are added to this participle to form the perfect tense: e.g. *hat.uw.im* 'I have come'.

Prepositions

Prepositions may be simple, e.g. *be* 'to', *bo* 'for'; or complex, e.g. the circumfix *le...da* 'in': *le kurdistan.i.emro da* 'in modern Kurdistan', where the circumfix encloses the ezafe phrase, which is felt as a unit. Similarly, *legel...da* 'with': e.g. *legel dostim da* 'with my friend'.

Word order

SOV is normal.

له ابتدا كلمه بوو آو كلمه له لای خدا بوو
هر آو كلمه خدا بوو ۲   هر آو وله ابتدا له
لای خدا بوو ۳   وبجز خواهش آو وچشئ
ئه موجودات وجودنات ۴   له آو وحيات
بوو وحيات نور انسان بوو ه ونور له تاريكی
تا بان بوو ونار بكی آو وادراك نكرد ء شخصئ
له لای خدا ئنات و رسالت نا وی بجی بوو
۷   آو وازای شهادت هات تا ونور شهادت
بنت ناگشت له واسط آو وایمان بارن ۸
آو وآو نور نبو بلكه هات تا ونور شهادت
بنت

LADAKHI

INTRODUCTION

Along with Balti and Purik, Ladakhi belongs to the Western sub-group of Bodish languages (Sino-Tibetan family), and is at present spoken by about 65,000 people in the Baltistan-Ladakh area of the state of Jammu and Kashmir. There are several dialects, with an approximate standard form in the Central dialect of the Leh area. Both phonologically and morphologically Ladakhi is close to Tibetan, and Classical Tibetan is used for literary purposes. In recitation or oration, however, written Tibetan may be realized as Ladakhi.

SCRIPT

Ladakhi Buddhists use the Tibetan characters.

PHONOLOGY

Consonants

Ladakhi has three-term series of the type voiceless stop – aspirate – voiced stop: e.g. /p, ph, b; t, th, d/. The retroflex series is present, along with /r, ʈ, l, ļ/ and a murmured lateral /l/, which Sanyakta Koshal (1979) notates as £. ß, ð, γ occur as allophones of /b, d, g/. Other sounds: the affricates /ts, tsh, dz, tʃ, tʃh, dʒ/, the fricatives /s, z, ʃ, ʒ/, the nasals /m, n, ɲ, ŋ/ and the semi-vowels /j, w/.

Vowels

    i, e, a, o, u, ə

The back lax vowel /ʊ/ also occurs. It is not clear to what extent the tonal patterns of Tibetan are retained, if at all, in any of the Ladakhi dialects.

MORPHOLOGY AND SYNTAX

In general, close to Tibetan.

Noun

Feminine gender is marked by *mo*: cf. *nəs.skor.pə* 'pilgrim'; *nəs.skor.mə* 'female pilgrim'.

Plural markers: *kun, gun, sək*: e.g. *khəŋ.pə* 'house', pl. *khəŋ.pə.gun*. *Məŋ.pə* 'many', may also be used: e.g. *lə.dəks.pə.məŋ.pə* 'many Ladakhis'.

Case is expressed by suffixed particle. Both the ergative and the genitive cases are marked by *yi* after a vocalic final; after a consonantal final, assimilation takes place: e.g. *ləm* 'road' – gen./erg. *ləm.mi*; *yul* 'village' – gen./erg. *yul.li*; *rgyəb* 'back' – gen./erg. *rgyəb.bi*. The Tibetan ergative marker in *-s* is found in certain dialects, but is absent from standard Ladakhi.

In Tibetan *gcig/zhig/cig* appear as allophones of the indefinite article (i.e. the numeral 'one'); in Ladakhi, *čig* is used as the numeral, *žig* as the indefinite article.

Adjective

As attribute, adjective follows noun, preceding plural and case markers: e.g. *khəŋ.pə rde.mo.gun.nə* 'in the beautiful houses'.

Pronoun

The personal pronouns are:

	Singular	Plural
1	ŋə	incl. ŋə.təŋ (gun); excl. ŋə.žə (gun)
2	khyot/khyo.rəŋ	khyod.gun/khyot.kun; khyo.rəŋ (gun)
3	kho/khoŋ	kho.gun

There are several honorific forms, especially for 2nd person.

DEMONSTRATIVE PRONOUN
Three degrees of distance: *i* (proximate), *o.te* (distal), *te* (obviative).

INTERROGATIVE PRONOUN
su 'who?'; *kə*, *či* 'what?'.

Numerals

Close to the Tibetan series: 1–10: *čik, ñis, sum, ži, sŋə, tuk, (r)dun, rgyət, (r)gu, (r)ču*; 11 *ču.čik*; 12 *ču.ñis*. 100 *rgyə*.

Verb

Stems are simple (monosyllabic) or complex. Particles are suffixed to express tense (present, past, future), aspect (perfective, imperfective), mode (narrative, progressive, inferential, dubitative, etc.).

The copula is *dug* or *yod*; negative *med*. Allomorphs of *yod*: *-əd* added to vocalic final; C*əd*→*t* added to consonantal final C: e.g. root *sil-* 'read' + *yod* → *sil.lət*

Specimen forms of *sil-* 'to read':

(a) Basic tense frames:

	Affirmative	*Negative*
present	sil.lət	sil.lə.met
present continuous	sil.lin.yot	sil.lin.met
past	sil.lət.pin	sil.lə.met.pin
perfect	sils	mə.sils
future definite	sil.lin	mi.sil

(b) Each tense frame is further differentiated, e.g. to specify whether a statement is a general assertion or a report based on personal experience. Thus, for the present-tense frame:

	Affirmative	*Negative*
general assertion	sil.lət	sil.lə.met
reported action as observed	sil.**duk**	sil.lə.mi.**duk**
continuous observed action	sil.lin.duk	sil.lin.mi.duk
historical present	sil.lə.nok	sil.lə.mə.nok

There is no inflection for person or number. According to Sanyukta Koshal (1979), however, certain forms may vary in nuance, depending on person. Thus, used with a third person subject, the *tshuk* form, for example, is a simple narrative tense; used with a second person subject, it indicates the speaker's surprise at some impending action by this second person; used with a first person subject, it expresses the realization that an intended but unperformed action by first person would have been undesirable.

All tenses have a parallel honorific system; e.g. in the present: *sil.lə.dzəd.dət* 'Your Honour reads'; neg. *sil.lə.dzəd.də.met*.

MODAL AUXILIARIES
Potential *thub*; desiderative *gos*; permissive *nen.dig*. These follow the stem: e.g. *sil.thub.bət* 'can read'; neg. *sil.thub.bə.met*.

IMPERATIVE MOOD
-s is added to vocalic stems, Ø to consonantal; + *šik* for plural: e.g. *səl* 'give' (2nd p. sing.), *səl.šik* (2nd p. pl.).

The subject of a transitive verb is in the ergative case: e.g. *i.mi.yi šiŋ čəd.duk* 'by that man – wood – being cut' = 'that man is (I see) cutting wood'; *lə.me gon.pə žəŋ.ŋə* 'the monk will build the monastery' (*lə.mə*, erg. *lə.me*).

Postpositions

These follow noun or noun phrase in genitive case, and may themselves take case markers: e.g.

pər 'between': e.g. *Khəŋ.pə.ñis.si pər.lə sən yot* 'There is a street between the two houses';

skyil 'in the middle of': e.g. *Nǝm.khe skyil.li skǝr.mǝ čǝn.mo duk* 'There is
   a big star in the middle of the sky';
ldǝn 'beside': e.g. *sǝr.ri.yi ldǝn.lǝ* 'beside the eastern mountain'.

Word order

SOV.

(Mark 3: 31–5)

LAHNDĀ

INTRODUCTION

Lahndā is a member of the North-Western group of New Indo-Aryan; the name means 'western'. 'Lahndā' is an umbrella term covering an extensive group of dialects, spoken, in all, by upwards of 20 million people in western Pakistan; more precisely, in the 400 mile wide strip of territory extending from Rawalpindi to Behawalpur. The two most important dialects are Multāni and Siraiki, both of which belong to the southern group of dialects. Multāni is associated with the ancient city of Multān, an early Aryan centre of sun-god worship, and latterly an Islamic strong-point. Some portions of the Adi Granth and Sikh scriptures, are in Lahndā. At present, both Multani and Siraiki are used for literary purposes, including periodicals. Towards their eastern periphery, Lahndā forms blend gradually into the phonologically close Panjabi.

SCRIPT

As might be expected, since the great majority of its speakers are Moslems, Lahndā is written in the Arabic-Persian character plus certain additions and modifications: e.g. ب for /bb/, ڋ for /dd/, etc. For Multāni, the old *laṇḍa* character (related to the *šarada* script of Kashmir) may still be used.

PHONOLOGY

Consonants

The labial, dental, palatal, retroflex, and velar stops appear in five-term series with asociated nasals: /p, p', b, b', bb, m; t, t', d, d', dd, n/, etc. That is, in contrast to the normal New Indo-Aryan series, the Lahndā series include the geminate sonant. /q/ with its associated fricatives /x/ and /ɣ/ are also present exemplifiying Arabic and Persian influence. The inventory also includes retroflex /ḷ/ and /ṛ/.

Vowels

short: i, ə, a, u
long: iː, e, ɛ, uː, o, aː

All occur nasalized. Diphthong: /au/.

Tones

There are two tones, with variations in some dialects. In the script, *h* marks the non-even tone.

MORPHOLOGY AND SYNTAX

Noun

Old synthetic forms have been more extensively preserved in Lahndā than in e.g. Panjabi.

Two genders, masculine and feminine, are grammatically distinguished. Typical masculine endings are *-a*, *-u* (long or short) and -C; typical feminine endings *-i*, *-ī*, -C. Vowel endings may be nasalized. There are many ways of marking plurality; change of vocalic final, e.g. *-a* → *-e* is common. Consonantal finals often add nasalized vowel.

There are singular and plural numbers, both having direct and oblique stems.

CASE SYSTEM

Synthetic case forms, e.g. locative in *-e*, are usually supported by agglutinative formants, e.g. *kū̃*. The synthetic form itself, if consonant-final, may show umlaut induced by loss of historically present vowel. Smirnov (1970) gives the following examples: *buškā* 'bundle of clothes': acc. *buške kū̃*; *muṇḍur* 'stump': acc. *muṇḍar ā̃h*.

Use of the analytical form confers definiteness on the noun, and is therefore equivalent to use of a definite article.

The genitive relationship is expressed by the relating particle *nā/nā̆/dā*.

Adjective

As attribute, adjective may precede or follow noun. Those in *-ā* agree with noun; consonant-finals are indeclinable.

Pronoun

The Multāni forms are:

>   Singular: 1 *mā̃* 2 *tū̃* 3 *e/o*, *īh/ūh*
>   Plural: 1 *assā̃* 2 *tussā̃* 3 *e/o*, *īh/ūh*
>   Possessive: *meḍā* 'my'; *assāḍā* 'our', etc.

With Sindhi and Kashmiri, Lahndā shares a system of pronominal enclitics, not found elsewhere in New Indo-Aryan. These are used with both nominal and verbal stems. Further, they combine with an ossified negative particle to provide a specific negative conjugation. The enclitic pronouns can denote subject, indirect or direct object, and genitive relationship. They are marked for number, but not gender:

	Singular	Plural
1	-Vm, -s	-se, -hse
2	-(v)ī	-(n)/-(V)e
3	-s, -su	-n(en)

e.g. subject: *Mele gäose* 'We went to market'; object (indirect): *Hukm ḍittā hāse* 'We were given an order.'

DEMONSTRATIVE PRONOUN

The vocalic gradation series *e-, i-, u-* combines with consonants *h/n* to produce such forms as: *e* 'this', *in* 'these', *ūh* 'those', etc.

INTERROGATIVE PRONOUN

kaun 'who?'; *keā* 'what?'

RELATIVE PRONOUN

jo, jeṛā, jehṛā, etc.: e.g. *e zamīn jeṛī mäde kol he...* 'This land which I have...' These have oblique forms.

Numerals

Close to the Panjabi numerals and equally unpredictable. A specific feature is the geminated initial in, e.g. *ḍḍŭ* 2, *ḍḍāh* 10, *bbārhǎ* 12.

Verb

The verb has personal and impersonal forms. The main impersonal forms are:

infinitive: in -Vṇ, etc.: e.g. *pīvuṇ* 'to drink'
imperfective participle: in -Vndā: e.g. *karendā* 'doing'
perfective participle: in -Vā: e.g. *geā* 'having done'. This form may be active or passive
gerund in -ī, etc. often with supporting formant: e.g. *karī kä* '(having) done'

Personal forms. The present tense of the auxiliary verb *hovuṇ* 'to be' is: sing. *ã, ī, e*; pl. *ã, o, in*. All these forms may be preceded by *h-*. The present tense of other verbs is made by conjugating their present participle with these forms of *hovuṇ*. Change of auxiliary from *hovuṇ* to *karuṇ* 'to do', *rahuṇ* 'to remain', etc. produces other aspectual forms – repetitive, resultative, habitual, etc.

Past: an analytical form is made by conjugating the imperfective or perfective participle with the past tense of *hovuṇ*: e.g. *āhus, āhis*.

Future: for the future there is a standard set of sigmatic endings on the formula -VsV/Ṽ: e.g. *āusǎ* 'I shall come'.

ERGATIVE

The construction exists but is preferably replaced by a pronominal suffix construction, where the subject of the action appears as a pronominal suffix. It is noteworthy that an ergative construction with the gerundive (nom. form in -nā/-ṇā) can be used with reference to the future.

IMPERATIVE
Second person singular = root; plural = root + V; many dialectal variations.

SUBJUNCTIVE
Synthetic form or participle + auxiliary. The synthetic endings are close to the present forms of *hovuṇ* (see above): e.g. *šarbat piyālā pīve* 'let him/her drink a glass of sherbet'.

PASSIVE
A synthetic form is made in *-i/-ī*: e.g. in future: *paṛīsī* 'it will be torn up'.

NEGATIVE
nā is a general negator.

Postpositions

Postpositions express many syntactic relationships: e.g. genitive, *šaks **nī** zamīn* 'the man's land'. The *kŭ* formant counts as a postposition: e.g. *putr ŭ kŭ ākhiā* 'the son said to him'; *parbhat kŭ* 'in the morning'.

Word order

SOV is usual.

(۱) مُنڈھ وچ کلام ہا اتیں کلام خدا دے نال
ہا اتیں کلام خدا ہا (۲) ایہو مُنڈھ وچ خدا دے
نال ہا (۳) سبھے شائیں اُوندوں پیدا تھیاں اتیں کِنی
شئے پیدا نہ تھئی جو سوا اُوندے پیدا تھی تھئی (۴) حیاتی
اُوں وچ ہائی اتیں او حیاتی آدمیں دا نُور ہائی (۵)
اتیں نُور اندھارے وچ چمکدا ہے اتیں اندھارے
اُوں کوں نہ سنجاتا (۶) ہک شخص خدا دی طرف
کنّوں چھٹیا گیا جیندا ناں یوحنا ہا (۷) او اگاہی ڈیونڑ
دے کیتے آیا جو نُور تے اگاہی ڈیوے تانجو سب
لوک، اُوندے وسیلے ایمان آنڑن (۸) او اوہو نُور نہ ہا
پر نُور دے اُتّے اگاہی ڈیونڑ آیا

(Multāni dialect)

LAK

INTRODUCTION

Lak belongs to the Lak-Dargva group of Dagestanian languages, and has about 80,000 speakers in Central Dagestan. It is one of the five literary languages of Dagestan.

SCRIPT

The Arabic script was used for the earliest writings in Lak, which date from the middle of the eighteenth century (translations from Persian). In the mid-nineteenth century, P.K. Uslar designed a Cyrillic-based alphabet for Lak, but this failed to replace Arabic. The present Cyrillic script dates from 1940.

PHONOLOGY

Consonants

Characteristic of Lak is a four-term series, in which the first term is a voiceless surd, the second is a tense, held geminate, the third is the voiceless ejective (notated in this article with subscript dot), and the fourth is the voiced counterpart of the first: e.g. /p, pp, p', b/. The labial, dental, and velar series have all four members, but the voiced member is missing in the uvular series: /q, qq, q'/.

The same series occurs in the affricates, but here again the voiced member is missing: /ts, tsts, ts'/; /tʃ, tʃtʃ, tʃ'/; and the fricatives also fall largely into the same pattern, but lacking the ejective /z, s, ss; ʒ, ʃ, ʃʃ; x, xx; ʁ, χ, χχ/.

Also present in Lak are /v/, two nasals, /m, n/, the alveolar sonants /l, r/, and the semi-vowel /j/; further, a pharyngeal voiced plosive, notated here as *g*, and the glottal stop /ʔ/, each of these having an associated spirant (ʕ, h).

Labialization affects many consonants, e.g. /k'°, ts'°/, but is not always notated in the script.

Vowels

The basic series is:

i, e, a, u, o̦, a̦

784

/ọ/ and /ạ/ are glottalized vowels, marked in the Cyrillic script by use of the soft sign. There are many intermediate values. Vowel length is not marked but is phonemic, and labialization also has phonemic value: thus, *ččan* 'foot'; *čč°an* 'to love'.

Stress

Stress is weak and is connected with vocalic length.

MORPHOLOGY AND SYNTAX

Noun

Lak nouns are divided into four grammatical classes with specific concord markers:

		Concord markers	
Class		*Singular*	*Plural*
1	male humans	v/w, b, u	b, v, m
2	some female humans	d, r, n, l	b, v, m
3	most female humans, animals, many inanimates	b/pp, v, m	b, v, m
4	all other inanimates, abstract nouns, some insects	d, r, n, l	d, r, n

There are several dozen ways of making a plural form. Typical endings are: *-ru, -du, -nu, -ri, -ttu*: e.g. *ččan* 'foot', pl. *ččannu*; *či* 'lamb', pl. *čiru*.

DECLENSION SYSTEM

Cases in Lak fall into two classes:

1. nine basic cases, including ergative/genitive, dative, instrumental;
2. six series of locative cases, each specifying a basic locus: e.g. 'in', 'on', 'under'. Each such series is further sub-divided into four or five modes of motion (or absence thereof) relative to the basic locus: e.g. with *qqata* 'house', series 4, 'under':

qqat.lu.lu 'under the house' (no motion);
qqat.lu.lun 'under the house' (motion into);
qqat.lu.lun.may 'towards the underside of the house';
qqat.lu.lux 'through the space under the house';
qqat.lu.la 'from under the house'.

Adjective

The attributive adjective in Lak precedes the noun. It may end in *-ssa*, which denotes an abstract property, and an adjective so marked takes the class markers but is not inflected: e.g. *učssa adimina* 'stout man'; *dučssa ššarssa* 'stout woman'; *bučssa duš* 'stout girl'.

785

Pronoun

	Singular	Ergative/genitive	Dative	Plural
1	na	ttul	ttun	žu
2	ina	vil	vin	zu

The genitive forms provide the possessive pronouns: e.g. *ttul lu* 'my book'. The third person pronouns are provided by the demonstrative series.

DEMONSTRATIVE PRONOUN/ADJECTIVE
These are coded to denote degree of removal and direction in space: e.g. *wa* 'this' (close to speaker); *mu* 'that' (close to addressee); *ta* 'that' (distance from both first and second persons); *ḳa* 'that up there'; *ga* 'that down there'.

INTERROGATIVE PRONOUN
cu 'who?'; *ci* 'what?'.

Numerals

1–10: *ca, ḳi, šan, muq, χχyu, ryaχ, arul, myay, urç̌, aç̌*. These take class markers: e.g. *ḳiya oṛç̌* 'two boys'; *ḳiva duš* 'two girls'; *ḳira ššarssa* 'two women'.

Verb

The verb is inflected for person, class, and number; the class markers are in concord with the subject of an intransitive verb, or with the object of a transitive: cf. *na uvḳra* 'I (male) came'; *na buvḳra* 'I (girl) came'; *na durḳra* 'I (woman) came'. Plural form for all three: *žu buvḳru* 'we came'.

From the primary base provided by the root (often + infix) are formed the infinitive, the imperative, and the indicative present and past. The indicative present takes the following endings: sing. 1 *-ara*, 2 *-ara*, 3 *-ay*; pl. *-aru*. Examples: *na čičara* 'I write'; *zu čičaru* 'you (pl.) write'. The past-tense endings are: sing. 1 *-av*, 2 *-unni*, 3 *-unnu*; pl. *-ardu*. Examples: *na čičav* 'I wrote'; *žu lasardu* 'we took'.

From a secondary base, identical with the infinitive, a future in *-nu*, and an optative in *-nav* are formed: e.g. *na učanna* 'I'll come'; *žu bučannu* 'we'll come'.

ASPECT
A durative is made with *-l-/-la-*, a recurrent with *-av-*: thus, from *čičin* 'to write': *čičlan* 'to keep on writing'; *čičavan* 'to write at regular intervals'.

The subject of a transitive verb in the past tense is in the ergative case: e.g. *tanal čaʁar čivčunni* 'he wrote a letter'; *tanal* 'by him'. In Lak, however, the subject of a transitive verb in the present tense may be in the nominative.

Relative clauses may be formed by using a participial form of the sense-verb, e.g. in *-ssa*, in attributive position preceding the head noun; e.g. *Musdal arcu dullusa ššarssa largunni* 'the woman to whom Musa gave the money has gone'.

NEGATIVE

The marker is *qqa*, prefix or infix: e.g. *qqa.čičinna* = *či.qqa.činna* 'I shan't write'.

Word order

Rather free. V often final; inversion for emphasis is possible.

Order is important in transitive verbal complexes with pronominal object, if one form denotes both agentive and nominative case: agentive must then precede: cf. *na zu čivčunu buru* 'I enrolled you' (*-v-* is Class I, male, marker), *zu na čivčunu buru* 'you enrolled me', where order is crucial, as *na* can be either agentive or nominative. On the other hand, in *ganal ina čivčuna ura* 'he enrolled you' the order could be changed, as *ganal* can only be agentive.

LAMUT

See **Even**.

LAO

INTRODUCTION

Lao belongs to the South-Western group of Tai languages, which also includes Thai, Shan, Yuan, along with many smaller languages.

After 300 years of subjugation, first to the Kingdom of Siam and then as a French colony, Laos became independent in 1954, and two years later Lao was adopted as the official language of the country. French is still widely used in government and administration, but Lao is used exclusively in the media, press, radio, and television, and is increasingly the language of education. It is the spoken and written language of about 10 million people in Laos, with extensive spread into Thailand. There are three main dialectal groupings – North, Central, and South – with a large number of local variants. The main differences between these dialects lie in the tonal structure, some dialects having only five tones (against the six of standard Lao) while others have seven. As the most developed form of Lao, and the most readily accessible to speakers of other dialects, the Vientiane dialect was the natural choice for 'standard' status, which it duly received in 1962.

SCRIPT

The Lao script, the *tua lao*, dates from about the sixteenth century. Before that, the *tham* (< Pali *dhamma*) script was used for religious texts in Lao. The *tua lao* script bears a very close resemblance to Thai, both apparently deriving from a Proto-Thai original now lost. The *tua lao* shares the etymologically motivated but now redundant duplications found in Thai.

PHONOLOGY

Consonants

The stops /p, t, k/ are non-aspirate, and are sometimes transliterated as *bp*, *dt*, *g*. They have aspirated counterparts: /ph, th, kh/. The stop series is completed by the voiced members /b/ and /d/ and the glottal stop.

    affricate: dʒ
    fricatives: f, v, s, h
    nasals: m, n, ɲ, ŋ
    lateral: l
    semi-vowels: j, w

/th, k, kh, ?, dʒ, s, l, ŋ/ occur labialized: /th°, k°/, etc. /dʒ/ → [dʹ]. In this article, ph, th, kh are used to notate the aspirate series, p, t, k, the non-aspirates. /dʒ/ is notated as *j*.

Vowels

The vowel system is of considerable complexity, and close transcription would involve many symbols. A simplified representation is:

> high: i, ɯ, u
> high-middle: iə, ɯə, uə
> middle: e, ɤ, o
> low-middle: ɛ, ɔ
> low: a

Almost all Lao vowel phonemes have long and short values.
In this article, ɪ is used to denote the spread-lipped, i.e. unrounded central vowel.

Tones

There are six tones in standard Lao: three level (low, middle, and high), two falling (high, low) and one rising. Few Lao syllables can take all six tones. Tone can be predicted for any Lao syllable in the light of the following criteria:

1. class of letter (low, middle, or high);
2. vowel length;
3. nature of final: nasal or stop (*p*, *t*, *k*);
4. presence or absence of tone marker (*mai ek*, *mai toh*).

For more detail on this system of tone representation, *see* **Thai**. Tone in Lao is, of course, phonemic.

MORPHOLOGY AND SYNTAX

Noun

In general, very close to Thai. Basic Lao words are mostly monosyllables: e.g. *paa* 'fish'; *nok* 'bird'; *muu* 'pig'. Sanskrit/Pali loan-words are plentiful: e.g. *pathet* 'country', *pawatsat* 'history'. The Mon-Khmer element is represented by such words as *wat* 'temple', *to* 'table'.

There is on inflection of any kind. Syntactic relationships are expressed by means of prepositions and linking particles: e.g. the genitive relationship marker *khong* (cf. **Thai**): *pɪm khong phai?* 'whose book?'. In the case of inalienable relationship, simple apposition is used: *pho khoai* 'my father'.

NUMBER
Usually ignored, but may be expressed periphastically, e.g. by *lai* 'many', or by classifier plus numeral. (*See* **Numerical classifiers**, below.)

Adjective

As attribute, adjective follows noun: *nam yen* 'cold water'.

COMPARISON
A comparative is made with *kwaa*: e.g. *Laaw paak phaasaa keng kwa khooi* 'He speaks Lao better than I do.'

Pronoun

The personal pronoun system offers a multiple choice of status-graded forms. Certain forms are emerging as generally acceptable in normal polite communication. These are: 1st p. sing. *khooi*, pl. form *phuuakkhaw*; 2nd p. sing. *thaan*, pl. form *phuuak.thaan*; *jaw* is a more familiar form for 2nd p. sing.; 3rd p. sing. *laaw*; pl. form is *khaw.jaw*. These are both subject and object forms: e.g. *laaw maa haa khooi* 'he comes to see me'.

DEMONSTRATIVE PRONOUN
Triple series by relative distance: *nii* 'this', *nan* 'that', *phun* 'that (yonder)'. As attributive adjectives, they follow the noun: e.g. *haan nii* 'this shop'.

INTERROGATIVE PRONOUN
phai 'who?'; *nyang* 'what?'.

RELATIVE PRONOUN/ADJECTIVE
Where the antecedent is indefinite, no relative pronoun is necessary. With a definite antecendent, *thi* may be used: e.g. *khɪang thi jaw toong.gaan* 'the things that you need'.

Numerals

1–10: *nɪng, soong, saam, sii, haa, hok, jet, peet, kaw, sip*; 12 *sip.soong*; 20 *saaw*; 30 *saam sip*; 100 *hooi*.

NUMERICAL CLASSIFIERS
All quantified nouns are accompanied by classifiers. The formula is noun – numeral – classifier: e.g. *saang saam tua* 'elephant three bodies' = 'three elephants'; *noong.saaw saam kon* 'three sisters'; *pathet soong pathet* 'two countries' (*pathet* is both noun and classifier). An exception to the general formula is provided by *nɪng* 'one', which follows the classifier: e.g. *hɪian lang nɪng* 'one house'.

Verb

Many verbs are monosyllabic: e.g. *pai* 'to go', *het* 'to do', *waw* 'to speak'. Compound verbs may be:

(a) verb + verb: e.g. *huu.sɪk* 'to feel' (*huu* 'to know' + *sɪk* 'to feel');
(b) verb + noun: e.g. *aap.nam* 'to bathe' (*aap* 'to wash' + *nam* 'water'); *het.kaan* 'to work' (*het* 'to do' + *kaan* 'work');

(c) adjective + verb: *wai.khɪn* 'to hurry' (*wai* 'quick' + *khɪn* 'to move');
(d) reduplicated verb: *pai.pai.maa.maa* 'to walk here and there'.

The verb itself is invariable. Tense and aspect are generated by various particles:

> perfective aspect: *dai* preceding, or *leew* following verb, e.g. *Noong dai pai het naa* '(My) brother has gone to work (in) the field'; *khooi het.kaan leew* 'I've finished working';
>
> imperfective aspect: a typical marker is *key*, which also suggests indeterminacy, and is used in such negative sentences as *Laaw boo key pai wiang.jan* 'He has never been to Vientiane';
>
> progressive action is indicated by the particle *kamlang*: e.g. *laaw kamlang het.kaan* 'he/she is working now'; or by *yuu*: e.g. *laaw kin.khaw yuuw* 'he is eating now';
>
> future: particle of impending action *sii* or *ja*, e.g. *thaan sii pai haa laaw* 'you will go to see him'.

MODAL VERBS

Examples: *toong.gaan* 'to want to'; *yaak* (*dai*) 'to want to', e.g. *khooi yaak pai som wat* 'I want to visit the temple'.

NEGATIVE

The general marker is *boo*: e.g. *laaw boo het.kaan* 'he/she doesn't work'. *Pai* 'to go' and *maa* 'to come', are used as directional particles.

Prepositions

Lao is rich in spatial and temporal prepositions; e.g. *kai* 'near', *kai hɪɪan* 'near the house'; *theng* 'on', *theng to* 'on the table'; *thi* 'in(to)', *thi wat* 'in(to) the temple'; *tee…hoot* 'from … to', *tee saam moong hoot haa moong* 'from 3 o'clock to 5 o'clock'.

Word order

SVO.

໑ ເມື່ອ ຕົ້ນເດີມ ນັ້ນ ພະທັມ ເປັນ ຢູ່ ແລ້ວ ແລະ ພະທັມ ນັ້ນ
໒ ໄດ້ ຢູ່ ນຳ ພະເຈົ້າ ແລະ ພະທັມ ນັ້ນ ກໍ ເປັນ ພະເຈົ້າ.   ເມື່ອ ຕົ້ນ
໓ ເດີມ ພະອົງ ນັ້ນ ໄດ້ ຢູ່ ນຳ ພະເຈົ້າ.   ສາລະພັດ ທຸກສິ່ງ ໄດ້ ເກີດ
  ມີ ມາ ເພາະດ້ວຍ ພະອົງ.   ແຕ່ ສິ່ງໃດໆ ທີ່ ເກີດ ມີ ມາ ແລ້ວ
໔ ນັ້ນ ບໍ່ ມີ ສິ່ງໃດ ເກີດ ມີ ມາ ໂດຍ ນອກຈາກ ພະອົງ.   ຊີວິດ ກໍ ຢູ່
  ໃນ ພະອົງ ແລະ ຊີວິດ ນັ້ນ ເປັນ ຄວາມສະວ່າງ ຂອງ ມະນຸສໂລກ.
໕ ຄວາມສະວ່າງ ນັ້ນ ກໍ ສ່ອງແສງ ຢູ່ ໃນ ຄວາມມືດ ແລະ ຄວາມມືດ
  ນນ ບໍ່ ໄດ້ ລົບ ຄວາມສະວ່າງ ໃຫ້ ມອດ.

LAPPISH

INTRODUCTION

The Lapps (ethnonym Same/Sabme) are dispersed over a wide arc of territory extending from Dalecarlia in Sweden north-eastwards through Arctic Norway, Sweden, and Finland to the Kola Peninsula in the USSR. There are possibly 30,000 to 35,000 Lapps in around 400,000 km^2, and more than half of them live on Norwegian territory. The great majority of Lapps are bilingual in Lappish and the language of the host country, with actual use of Lappish restricted to the family and village circle. There is a broad dialectal division into Southern, Northern, and Eastern Lapp.

Virtually nothing is known about Lapp before the sixteenth century. The first printed book in Swedish Lappish appeared in 1619, in Norwegian Lappish in 1728. There is no common literary language.

In the 1950s several local Lappish organizations combined to form a Northern Council for Lappish Affairs (*Davviriikkkaid Sámiráđđi*) with representation in Oslo, Stockholm, and Helsinki. One result was the formation in 1971 of a Lapp Language Committee and in 1979 of a Lapp Writers' Union.

Genetically, Lappish is a Finno-Ugrian language, very deeply influenced by the Scandinavian languages and by Finnish: the number of Finnish loan-words is put at 2,000, that of Scandinavian borrowings at slightly more. Traces of vowel harmony are still found in Eastern dialects. It is interesting, however, that many Lapp roots, perhaps as many as 25 per cent, are neither Finno-Ugric nor attributable as borrowings to any known source: e.g. *čallet* 'write', *buktet* 'fetch', *bieggaa* 'wind'.

SCRIPT

Roman, with local additions and adaptations. In both Norwegian and Finnish Lapp, the interdentals /θ/ and /ð/ are written as *ŧ* and *đ*.

PHONOLOGY

Consonants

    stops: p, b, t, d, k, g
    affricates: ts, tʃ
    fricatives: f, v, s, ʃ, θ, ð, h
    nasals: m, n, ŋ
    lateral and flap: l, r

/d, l, n, h/ can be palatalized in Norwegian and Finnish Lapp. Extensive palatalization of consonants is a characteristic feature of the Eastern dialects. Initial /b, d, g/ → unaspirated [p, t, k]: e.g. *baze dearvan* [paːce(t) tearᵃvan], 'goodbye' (Finnish Lapp).

There is pre-aspiration of consonants /t, k/ in certain environments: e.g. (in Finnish Lapp) *guokte* [kuokhte], 'two'.

CONSONANTAL GRADATION

(*See* **Finnish**). The Lappish system is much more elaborate than its Finnish counterpart, extending to such gradations as *rr/r, ll/l, ss/s, bm/m, k't/vt, k's/vs, ddj/j*: e.g. from *buktet* 'fetch', first person singular *buvtem*.

The weak state of long (= emphatic) geminates is identical with the strong state of short geminates; i.e.

Strong grade	Weak grade
kk	g
k'k	kk

The mark ' between consonants in strong geminates and other doubled letters in Norwegian Lappish indicates the presence of a shwa vowel: thus *al'bmi* /alᵊbmi/, 'sky'; in Finnish Lappish the shwa is unmarked: e.g. *olgun* /ol°kuːn/, 'outside'.

Vowels

a, e, i, o, ɔ, u

/a/ may be realized as [a], [ʌ], or [ɔ]. /ɔ/ is notated as *å*.

MORPHOLOGY AND SYNTAX

Noun

The noun has two numbers and eight cases (including an abessive formed with postposition). The dual number found in the pronoun and verb is lost in the nominal declension. Specimen declensions from Norwegian Lapp:

	aed'ni 'mother'		*sabmelaš* 'Lapp'	
	Singular	*Plural*	*Singular*	*Plural*
nominative	aed'ni	aednit	sábmelaš	sábmelažžat
genitive	aedni	edniid	sábmelažža	sábmelažžaid
accusative	aedni	edniid	sábmelažža	sábmelažžaid
illative	aed'nái	edniide	sábmelaž'žii	sábmelažžaide
inessive–elative	aednis	edniin	sábmelažžas	sábmelažžain
comitative	edniin	edniiguin	sábmelažžain	sábmelažžaiguin
essive	aed'nin	aed'nin	sábmelaž'žan	sábmelaž'žan
abessive	aedni haga	edniid haga	—	—

Further examples of plural formation from genitive base: *aena* 'land', gen.

aednama, pl. *aednamat*; *rumaš* 'body', gen. *rubmaša*, pl. *rubmašat*; *suolo* 'island', gen. *sul'lu*, pl. *sul'lut*.

Adjective

The attributive form, which precedes the noun, differs from the predicative form, e.g. from Norwegian Lapp: *bar'go lae låssat* 'the work is hard', *dat lae lås'ses bar'go* 'that is hard work'; *viesso lae viel'gat* 'the house is white'; *dat lae vil'ges viesso* 'that is a white house'. Cf. in Russian Lapp: *el'l'is murr* 'high tree'; *tedd murr l'i el'l'e* 'this tree is high'.

COMPARATIVE

-t added to positive; *-mus* for superlative: e.g. *nuorra* 'young', *nuorat*, *nuoramus*; *buorre* 'good', *buoret*, *buoremus*. Adjectives of type *boaris* 'old', *viel'gat* 'white' make a comparative as follows: *boaris – boarrasaeb'bo*; *viel'gat – viel'gadaeb'bo*.

Pronoun

Norwegian Lapp forms: with possessive enclitic markers:

	Singular		Dual		Plural	
1	mån	-n	moai	-me	mii	-met
2	dån	-t	doai	-de	dii	-det
3	sån	-s	soai	-ska	sii	-set

These are declined in eight cases, e.g. for first person singular: *mån*, *mu*, *mu*, *munnje*, *mus*, *muina*, *munin*, *mu haga*. Nouns ending in a vowel change this vowel before certain enclitic possessives: e.g. *áč'či* 'father', *áč'čán* 'my father', *áč'čámet* 'our father'.

DEMONSTRATIVE PRONOUNS/ADJECTIVES

Three degrees of proximity: *dat* 'this' – *diet* 'that' – *duot* 'that (yonder)'. These are both singular and plural forms: cf. *dat jáv'ri* 'this lake', pl. *dat jávrit*; gen. sing. *dan jávri*, gen. pl. *daid jávriid*.

INTERROGATIVE/RELATIVE PRONOUN

There are three general words for 'who?': *gii*, pl. *gaet*, *gutte*, pl. *guðet*, *mii*, pl. *mat*; *goab'ba* means 'who/which of two?' The plural form of *goab'ba* is *goabbat*. Finally, *guttemuš*, pl. *guðemužžat* means 'who/which of many?'. All of these are declined, both singular and plural, in all cases. Thus, *goabbain* 'with which of two?' (comitative case); *guðemužžaiguin* 'with whom/which of many?'. Cf. *Gii ål'bmuid dat lae*? 'What man is this?' (*ål'bmuid* is plural accusative); *Mat bier'gasiid dat laet*? 'What are these things?'; *sii guðet laet dan dakkan* 'they who have done this'; *Gæsa galgan dan ad'dit*? 'To whom shall I give this?' (where *gæsa* is the allative of *gii*).

Numerals

1–10 (in Finnish spelling): *okta, guokte, golbma, njeallje, vihtta, guhtta, čieža, gavcci, ovcci, logi.* 11–20: *oktanuppelohkai, guoktenuppelohkai, golbman-, njealljen-,* etc., with *-uppelohkai;* 20 *guoktelogi,* 30 *golbmalogi;* 100 *čuoði.*
The Norwegian Lapp form of *-uppelohkai* is *-ubbelåkkai.*

Verb

The verb in Lappish has four moods: indicative, conditional, potential, and imperative; and two voices: active and passive. The indicative mood has four tenses: present, imperfect, perfect, pluperfect, the latter two with the auxiliary *laet.* The present may also be used to express the future, which may also be formed analytically with the verb *gal'gat* 'shall', or *ai'got* 'want to'. Thus: *mån manan* 'I go/I shall go'; *mån aigon mannat* 'I want to go'; *mån galgan mannat* 'I shall go'.

Specimen paradigm: *aellit* 'to live', present tense:

	Singular	Dual	Plural
1	aelán	elle	aellit
2	aelát	aellibaet'ti	aelibettet
3	aellá	aelliba	ellet

Examples for *mannat* 'to go': *mån manan* 'I go'; *mån mannen* 'I went'; *mån laen mannan* 'I have gone'; *mån leddjen mannen* 'I had gone'.

IMPERATIVE
Second person singular *mana*; dual *man'ni*; plural *mannet*; + first/third person forms; *man'ni aedni lusa* 'you two, go to (your) mother' (*lusa* is postposition 'to').

CONDITIONAL
Examples: *mån manašin, dån manašit.*

POTENTIAL
Example: *mån manažan.*

PASSIVE
In *-uvvu(j)*; thus from *gullat* 'to hear': *man gul'lujuvvun* 'I am heard'; *man gul'lujuvvujin* 'I was being heard'.

NEGATIVE
The negative auxiliary verb + uninflected stem (in weak state):

	Singular	Dual	Plural
1	in	aen	aet
2	it	aep'pi	eppet
3	ii	aeba	aei

Examples: *in låga* 'I'm not reading' (*låga* is weak stem of *låkkat* 'to read'); *aeba boaðe* 'they (two) are not coming' (*boattit* 'to come').

GERUNDIVE
-min added to strong stem, e.g. *mån laen låkkamin* 'I am (engaged in) reading'.

PRESENT PARTICIPLE
The emphatic strong stem is used: e.g. *boattit* 'to come', *boat'ti* '(he) who comes'. The form can be used adjectivally: e.g. *boat'ti jakki* 'next year'.

Absence of, or failure to perform, the verbal action is indicated by the affix *-kaet'tái* attached to the weak stem; thus from *låkkat* 'to read': *Lågakaet'tai it oappa* 'Without reading you do not learn.'

Prepositions, postpositions

Lappish has one or two prepositions, many postpositions e.g. *duokkin* 'behind'; *sisa* 'inside'; *lusa* 'up to', 'as far as'. The postpositions take directional/locative markers: e.g. *Bija bårramuša baevdi **ala*** 'Put the food on the table'; *Bårramuš lae juo baevdi **al'de*** 'The food is already on the table'; *baevdi vuollai* 'under the table'.

Word order

SVO.

1. Algost læi sadne, ja sadne læi Ibmel lut, ja sadne læi Ibmel.

2. Dat algost læi´Ibmel lut.

3. Buokrakkan dam boft læ dakkujuvvum; ja alma dam taga i mikkege læk dakkujuvvum dast, mi jå læ dakkujuvvum.

4. Dam sist læi ællem; ja ællem læi olbmu c̆uovgas.

5. Ja c̆uovgas sævdnjadassi baitta, ja sævdnjad i dam arvedam.

6. Ibmelest vuolgatuvui olmus̆, gæn namma Johannes læi.

7. Dat duođas̆tussan bådi, c̆uovgas birra duođas̆tet, vai buokak su boft oskus̆i.

8. I sån læm c̆uovgas, mutto (vuolgatuvvum læi) c̆uovgas birra duođas̆tet.

LATIN

INTRODUCTION

Along with Oscan, Umbrian, and Faliscan, Latin belongs to the Italic branch of Indo-European. From being the local language of a small group (the people of Latium, which stretched from Rome and the Tiber down to the Oscan border), Latin spread in the wake of Roman conquest to become the administrative, literary, and liturgical language of the Roman Empire, and, in all three spheres, one of the world's most important languages. Historically, the following periods may be distinguished:

1. Pre-classical, seventh to second century BC. The earliest known inscription dates from the seventh century. In the third and second centuries, literature, under Greek influence, makes its appearance (Plautus, Terence).
2. Classical: second century BC to second century AD. The Golden and Silver Ages of Latin literature.
3. Vulgar Latin, including the patristic period, second to fifth centuries. Includes for example Jerome's translation of the Bible (the Vulgate) and the works of St Augustine.
4. Mediaeval period, sixth to fourteenth centuries. Literary Latin continues to be used as a sort of *katharevousa* (*see* **Modern Greek**) *vis-à-vis* the emergent and divergent demotics based on its own matrices.
5. Fifteenth century to present day. Classical Latin of the Golden Age was rediscovered at the time of the Renaissance. Literary Vulgar Latin continued to be used by scholars up to the eighteenth century, e.g. by Sir Isaac Newton, Samuel von Pufendorf; and for liturgical purposes in the Roman Catholic Church (obligatory till the late twentieth century).
6. Following its transformation into the daughter Romance languages (including Anglo-Norman and the Romance component in English) Latin continued to provide a repertory of root words for many semantic fields, especially cultural and technical, in a variety of languages.

SCRIPT

The Latin alphabet was derived from Greek via Etruscan. The letter *V* was used for both /u/ and /w/. *K* was occasionally used before /a/. *Y* and *Z* were introduced at a later stage.

PHONOLOGY

Consonants

stops: p, b, t, d, k, g; + labialized k°
fricatives: f, s, h
nasals: m, n
lateral and flap: l, r
semi-vowels: j, w

Vowels

i, e, a, o, u

All have long and short values; length is phonemic: cf. *sagitta* 'an arrow'; *sagittā* 'by an arrow'.

Length of syllable does not necessarily depend on length of vowel; thus, a syllable with a short vowel followed by C_1C_2, where C_2 is not a liquid, counts as long.

Diphthongs: ae, au, eu, oe, ui

These two inventories represent Classical Latin, by which period tonic stress had moved from initial position to the penultimate (usual).

The oldest known Latin inscription appears on a bracelet found near Praeneste. It is in Greek letters and reads: MANIOS MED FHE FKAKED NUMASIOI 'Manius made me for Numerius'; in Classical Latin, *Manius me fecit Numerio*. The nominative ending *-os* = CL *-us*; *-d* is the accusative pronominal ending; the verb form is a reduplicated perfective; cf. Sanskrit *ca.kāra*.

MORPHOLOGY AND SYNTAX

In contrast to Greek, Latin has no definite article. There are three genders, signalled up to a point by nominal endings: thus, *-us*, *-er* are typically masculine, *-a* is typically feminine, and *-um* neuter. These categories are not always consistent, however, e.g. *nauta* 'sailor' is masculine, while *mulier* 'woman' is feminine.

Noun

Nouns are marked for two numbers and six cases. There are five declensions:

1. in *-a*: feminine except where denoting male persons;
2. in *-us*, *-er*, *-um*: masculine and neuter, e.g. *amīcus* 'friend', *puer* 'boy', *dōnum* 'gift';
3. consonant stems and *i*-stems: all three genders; e.g. *rēx – rēgis* 'king' (masc.), *corpus – corporis* 'body' (neut.), *urbs – urbis* 'town' (fem.);
4. *u*-stems: mostly masculine, e.g. *frūctus* 'fruit'; *cornū* 'horn' is neuter;
5. *e*-stems: all feminine except *diēs* 'day' (masc.).

Specimen paradigms for first and third declensions: *mēnsa* 'table', *rēx* 'king':

	Singular	Plural	Singular	Plural
nom.	mēnsa	mēnsae	rēx	rēgēs
voc.	mēnsa	mēnsae	rēx	rēgēs
acc.	mēnsam	mēnsās	rēgem	rēges
gen.	mēnsae	mēnsārum	rēgis	rēgum
dat.	mēnsae	mēnsīs	rēgī	rēgibus
abl.	mēnsā	mēnsīs	rēge	rēgibus

Some examples of case usage:

Accusative: direct object of transitive verb; target of directed motion: e.g. *Rōmam rediit* 'He returned to Rome'; *Imperātor equitēs flūmen trānsiēcit* 'The commander threw his cavalry across the river' (i.e. double accusative);

Dative: indirect object; benefactive sense; dative of possession; dative of purpose: e.g. *Est **mihī** plēnus Albānī cadus* (Horace) 'I have a jar full of Alban wine' ***Nōbis** auxiliō vēnērunt* 'They came to help us';

Ablative: e.g. of association or of manner: e.g. *Villa abundat gallīnā, lacte, cāseō, melle* (Cicero) 'The farm abounds in poultry, milk, cheese and honey'; *tacitō ... pede* (Ovid) 'with silent foot';

Ablative absolute: e.g. ***hīs rēbus audītīs*** 'when/because these things had been heard'. An example from later Latin with subject switch:

impendente diē, quō ex hac vītā erat exitura – quem diem tū noveras **ignorantibus nōbis** (Augustine, 9, X)
'the day now approaching that she was to depart this life – which day thou well knewest, though we were ignorant thereof'

Genitive: may be used with certain verbs of remembering and forgetting: e.g. *nec tamen Epicūrī licet oblīvīscī* (Cicero) 'and yet we must not forget Epicurus'.

Adjective

The adjective agrees with its referent in gender, number, and case. There are two main groups of Latin adjectives:

(a) those with three endings, declined like nouns of first and second declensions: e.g. *bonus, -a, -um*; pl. *boni, -ae, -a*;

(b) adjectives with two endings, one for masculine/feminine, the other for neuter: e.g. *trīstis – trīste*; pl. *trīstēs – trīstia*.

Some (b) class adjectives have a specific ending for masculine singular, e.g. *ācer* 'sharp': *ācer – ācris – ācre*; pl. *ācrēs* (masc. and fem.) *ācria*.

Adjectives may be used as nouns: e.g. *īnferī* 'the dead'; *apud īnferōs* 'among the dead'. Attributively, the adjective may precede or follow the noun, and may indeed be separated from it, especially in verse:

quis fuit **horrendos** primus qui protulit **enses** (Tibullus)
'who was it who first invented dreadful swords?'

COMPARATIVE

Examples: *longus – longior*; with suppletive forms, e.g. *bonus – melior/-ius*; *malus – peior/-ius*. The target comparison may be in the ablative, or introduced by *quam*.

Pronoun

PERSONAL

The first and second personal pronouns are: *ego, tū*; pl. *nōs, vōs*. For the third person the demonstratives *is/ea/id* are used. Pronouns are declined in five cases; e.g. for *ego*: acc. *mē*, gen. *meī*, dat. *mihi*, abl. *mē*.

POSSESSIVE ADJECTIVES

me-us/-a/-um; *tu-us/-a-um*; *nos-ter/-tra/-trum*; *ves-ter/-tra/-trum*. For the third person the genitive case of *is/ea/id* is used for all three genders: *eius*; in the plural, gender is marked: *eōrum, eārum, eōrum*.

DEMONSTRATIVE PRONOUN

In addition to *is/ea/id, hic/haec/hoc* 'this'; *ille/illa/illud* 'that'.

INTERROGATIVE PRONOUN

quis (masc. and fem.) 'who?', *quid* 'what?'. *Quis* has plural forms: *quī, quae, qua*.

RELATIVE PRONOUN

quī, quae, quod, with identical genitive and dative forms for all three: *cuius, cui*: e.g. *Is minimō eget quī minimum cupit* (Publilius Syrus) 'He lacks least who desires least'; *Erant itinera duo, **quibus** ... exire possent* (Cæsar) 'There were two ways by which they might withdraw.'

Numerals

1 *ūn-us/-a/um* is declined in five cases, singular and plural (the plural = 'some'); 2 *duo/duae/duo* is also declined in five cases, as is *tres/tria* 'three'. The numerals from 4 to 100 are indeclinable: *quattuor, quīnque, sex, septum, octō, novem, decem*; 11 *ūndecim*; 12 *duodecim*; 13 *tredecim*; 20 *vīgintī*; 21 *ūnus et vīgintī*, etc; 30 *trīgintā*; 100 *centum*.

The hundreds are declined: *ducentī/ducentae/ducenta*, etc.

Verb

Verbs are transitive or intransitive, and verb forms are finite or non-finite. Finite forms are marked throughout for person and number. There are two voices: active and passive. Deponent verbs are passive in form, active in meaning, e.g. *loquor* 'I speak', *fruor* 'I enjoy', *proficīscor* 'I set out'.

The verb has three moods: indicative, imperative, subjunctive; and six tenses: present, simple future, imperfect, perfect, future perfect, pluperfect. From the point of view of aspect, the first three tenses are imperfective, the other three perfective. The aorist with augment is missing.

Non-finite forms: infinitive, three participles, gerund, gerundive, two supines.

Typical personal endings for the active indicative and subjunctive moods are present in the terminations of the present tense of *sum* 'I am':

sing. *sum, es, est*; pl. *sumus, estis, sunt*

In the passive voice, the corresponding forms are:

sing. *-r, -ris/-re, -tur*; pl. *-mur, -minī, -ntur*

Latin has four conjugational patterns, depending on stem vowel:

1. in *-ā*: e.g. *amāre* 'to love';
2. in *-ē*: e.g. *monēre* 'to advise';
3. consonant and *u*-stems: e.g. *regere* 'to rule';
4. in *-ī*: e.g. *audīre* 'to hear'.

From the following four forms – first person present indicative, infinitive, perfect, supine in *-um* – all other forms of the verb can be constructed: thus, for *amāre*, the four base forms are: *amō, amāre, amāvi, amātum*.

There follows a specimen paradigm: *amāre* 'to love'

ACTIVE VOICE
Indicative:

	Singular			Plural		
present:	1 am-ō	2 -as	3 -at	1 -āmus	2 -ātis	3 -ant
future:	amā-bō	-bis	-bit	-bimus	-bitis	-bunt
imperfect:	amā-bam	-bās	-bat	-bāmus	-bātis	-bant
perfect:	amā-vī	-vistī	-vit	-vimus	-vistis	-vērunt

future present: amāver-o/-is/-it, etc.; pluperfect: amāver-am/-ās/-at, etc.

Subjunctive:

sing. 1 *amen*, 2 *amēs*, 3 *amet*; pl. 1 *amēmus*, 2 *amētis*, 3 *ament*

with imperfect: *amār-em/-ēs/-et*, etc.; perfect: *amāver-im/-īs/-it*, etc.; and pluperfect: *amāviss-em/-ēs/-et*, etc.

PASSIVE VOICE
Indicative:

	Singular			Plural		
present:	1 amor	2 amāris	3 amatur	1 amāmur	2 amāminī	3 amantur
future:	amābor	amāberis	amābātur etc.			
imperfect:	amābar	amābāris	amābātur etc.			

The passive perfective tenses are made with the auxiliary *sum* + past participle: perfect: *amātus sum*, etc.; future perfect: *amātus erō*, etc.; pluperfect: *amātus eram*, etc.

SUBJUNCTIVE

Present sing. 1 *amer*, 2 *amēris*, 3 *amētur*, etc.

perfect: *amatus sim*, *sīs*, *sit*; *sīmus*, *sītis*, *sint*.

IMPERATIVE

Sing. *amā(tō)*; pl. *amāte*, *amātōte*

Non-finite forms: infinitive has present, perfect, and future forms in both voices: e.g. for the active: *amāre*, *amāvisse*, *amāturus esse*.

Participles: active: present: *amans*; future: *amātūrus*; passive: perfect: *amātus*.

Supines: active: *amātum* 'in order to love'; *amātū* 'in loving'.

Gerund: active: *amandum* 'the loving'; gerundive: passive: *amandus* '(fit) to be loved'.

Some examples of the non-finite forms:

> Gerund: this is a verbal noun (neuter) declined in four cases, e.g. *Rōman iit ad bene vivendum* 'He went to Rome to live well'; *ars scribendi* 'the art of writing'.
>
> Gerundive: verbal adjective, marked for gender, e.g. *Carthago delenda est* 'Carthage is to be destroyed'; *Ut tibi ambulandum, sic mihi dormiendum est* (Cicero) 'As you have to walk, so I have to sleep'; *Cæsar pontem faciendum cūrat* 'Cæsar has a bridge made'; *Rōmam vēnit ad lūdōs Rōmānōs videndōs* 'He came to Rome to see the Roman games.'
>
> Supine: used after verbs of motion, e.g. *Lūsum it Maecēnās, dormītum ego* (Horace) 'Maecenas goes to play, I to sleep'
>
> *Oratio obliqua*: the construction involves the accusative + infinitive, e.g.
>
> Imperator dixit suos urbem facile cepisse
> 'The commander said that his men had easily taken the city'
>
> Explorātores ducem certiorem fēcērunt hostes appropinquāre celeriter
> 'The scouts informed the general that the enemy was approaching rapidly'

Prepositions

Most Latin prepositions govern the accusative; four (*in*, *sub*, *super*, and *subter*) govern the accusative when motion towards a target is entailed, the ablative for rest in a place. A few govern the ablative only.

Word order

Free; SOV is basic, the verb tending to be in final position at the end of a period, and indirect object preceding direct. Thanks to the precision of the inflectional system, however, virtually any word order is possible; in particular, any component may be promoted to initial position for emphasis.

N principio erat verbum, 1
& verbum erat apud A
Deum , & Deus erat
verbum. * Hoc erat in 2
principio apud Deum. * 3
Omnia per ipsum facta
sunt : & sine ipso factum
est nihil, quod factum est, * in ipso vita erat, 4
& vita erat lux hominum : * & lux in tene- 5
bris lucet, & tenebræ eam non comprehen-
derunt. * Fuit homo missus à Deo , cui no- 6
men erat Ioannes. * Hic venit in testimo- 7
nium , vt testimonium perhiberet de lumine,
vt omnes crederent per illum. * non erat ille 8
lux , sed vt testimonium perhiberet de lumine. *

LATVIAN

INTRODUCTION

Latvian is a member of the Baltic branch of Indo-European. The group from which Latvian derives comprised several other languages – Latgalian, Zemgalian, Curonian – which are now extinct. Latvian is spoken by about 2½ million people, most of these in the Latvian Soviet Socialist Republic, many in other parts of the Soviet Union, with large communities in Canada, the USA, and elsewhere.

The earliest writing in Latvian, in an orthography based on German, appeared in the sixteenth and seventeenth centuries. The first Bible translation dates from the eighteenth century. By the 1980s a standardized literary language had taken shape, which went on to flourish in the brief period of independence, 1918–40.

SCRIPT

Gothic until early twentieth century. In 1909 a switch was made to the Roman alphabet with diacritics: palatalized letters are marked by sub- or superscript dash, long vowels by the macron. /tʃ, ʃ, ʒ, dʒ/ are notated as *č, š, ž, dž*.

PHONOLOGY

Consonants

    stops: p, b, t, d, k, g; palatalized: k', g'
    affricates: ts, tʃ, dz, dʒ
    fricatives: v, s, ʃ, z, ʒ
    nasals: m, n, ɲ, ŋ
    lateral and flap: l, r
    semi-vowels: j, w

/f, h, x/ occur in loan-words.

ASSIMILATION
Voiced consonants are unvoiced before unvoiced and vice versa: e.g. *galds* 'table' = [gʌlts]; *priecīgs* 'happy' = [priecīks].

807

Vowels

> front: i, ɪ, e, eː, ɛ, ɛː
> mid: a, ā
> back: uo, ɔ, u, ū

/uo/ is notated as *o*; the sound /o/ occurs in loan-words only. /ă/ = [ʌ].

DIPHTHONGS
ai, au, ei, ie + oi in loan-words.

Tones

The Central dialect, on which the literary standard is based, distinguishes three tones not notated in script: even, broken, and falling: e.g. *saule* 'sun' is even; *sir̃ds* 'heart', broken; *kàzas* 'wedding', falling.

Stress

On the first syllable with very few exceptions. This fact, coupled with a tendency to reduce the tonal system to a straight opposition between even and non-even, makes Latvian phonology very much simpler than Lithuanian, where stress is mobile and where tone is a function of the stressed syllable.

MORPHOLOGY AND SYNTAX

Noun

There are no articles. Latvian has two genders, masculine (typical endings: *-s*, *-š*, *-is*, *-us*) and feminine (typical endings: *-s*, *-a*, *-e*). Six declensions are distinguished, depending on stem ending: e.g. 1st declension: *darzs* 'garden'; 4th declension: *meita* 'girl'.

	Singular	*Plural*	*Singular*	*Plural*
nominative	dārzs	dārzi	meita	meitas
genitive	dārza	dārzu	meitas	meitu
dative	dārzam	dārziem	meitai	meitām
accusative	dārzu	dārzus	meitu	meitas
locative	dārzā	dārzos	meitā	meitās

Typical plural formations in the other declensions are: 2nd decl. *brālis* 'brother', pl. *brāļi*; 3rd decl. *tirgus* 'market', pl. *tirgi*; 5th decl. *zeme* 'earth', pl. *zemes*; 6th decl. *sirds* 'heart', pl. *sirdis*.

Some uses of cases in Latvian:

> genitive: used with negative to indicate absence of something: e.g. *tur nav grāmatu* 'there isn't/aren't a book/books there' (*nav* = /nau/ 'not'), *viņa nav mājās* 'he isn't at home' (*viņa* is gen. of *viņš* 'he');
> dative: used to express possession: e.g. *saimniekiem ir zirgi un rati* '(the)

farmers have horses and carts';
dative absolute: dative of logical subject + verb in relative *-ot* form: e.g.
pirmajai nedeļas dienai austot 'as it began to dawn towards the first day of
the week' (Matthew, 28.1).

Adjective

As attribute, the adjective precedes the noun and is in concord with it for
gender, number, and case. The adjective can be declined in indefinite or definite
form, the latter making up in some degree for the lack of definite article. The
definite endings are made by the insertion of *-aj-* or by vowel lengthening; some
oblique forms may be truncated for euphonic reasons: cf.

	Indefinite	*Definite*
	labs tēvs 'a good father'	labais tēvs 'the good father'
dative	labam tēvam	labajam tēvam

COMPARATIVE
The comparative is made with *-āks*: e.g. *jauns* 'young' – *jaunāks* 'younger';
definite form: *jaunākais* 'the younger'.

Pronoun

The nominative and genitive forms for first and second person singular and
plural are: sing. 1 *es – manis*; pl. *mēs – mūsu*; 2 *tu – tevis*; pl. *jūs – jūsu*. The third
person forms are marked for gender: masc. *viņš*; fem. *viņa*: pl. *viņi*, *viņas*.

DEMONSTRATIVE PRONOUNS
These also show gender: masc. *šis*, fem. *šī* 'this'; masc. *tas*, fem. *tā* 'that'; with
pl. forms, *šie – šīs*; *tie – tās*.

POSSESSIVE FORMS
mūsu and *jūsu* are indeclinable. The others, *mans*, *mani*, etc., show gender and
number and are declined.

INTERROGATIVE PRONOUN
kis 'who? what?'; *kurš* 'what ...?' These are declined in singular.

RELATIVE PRONOUN
As interrogative: e.g. *māja, kurā dzīvo studenti* 'the house in which the students
live'; *studenti, kas dzivo ...* 'the students who live ...'.

Numerals

1–9: these have masculine and feminine forms; the masculine forms are: *viens,
divi, trīs, četri, pieci, seši, septiņi, astoņi, deviņi*; fem. *viena, divas, trīs, četras,
piecas, sešas, septiņas, astoņas, deviņas*; 10 *desmit*; 11 *vienpadsmit*; 12
divpadsmit; 20 *divdesmit*; 30 *trīsdesmit*; 100 *simt(s)*.

Verb

Verbs in Latvian are either perfective or imperfective. An imperfective verb can be made perfective by the addition of a prefix:

ņemt 'to take' (imperf.) *iz.ņemt* 'to take out/from' (perf.)
lasīt 'to read' (imperf.) *iz.lasīt* 'to read through and finish' (perf.)

There are three voices: active, reflexive, and passive, use of the latter is rare; and five moods: indicative, imperative, conditional, debitive, relative.

Formally, all verbs belong to three conjugational types:

(a) type *runāt* 'to speak': expansion by *-j-* throughout imperfect tense and, partially, in present: e.g. *es runāju* 'I speak', *jūs runājat* 'you speak'; *viņš runā* 'he speaks';
(b) type *dzirdēt* 'to hear': imperfect forms alone expanded by *-j-*: e.g. *es dzirdu* 'I hear'; *es dzirdēju* 'I heard';
(c) type *nākt* 'to come': monosyllabic infinitive, two syllables in present/imperfect: e.g. *es nāku* 'I come'; *es nācu* 'I came'.

The indicative mood has three simple tenses (present, imperfect, future) and three compound (formed by copula *būt* 'to be', + active participle).

Specimen paradigm: *lasīt* 'to read'.

Present indicative: *es lasu, tu lasi, viņš lasa; mēs lasām, jūs lasāt, viņi lasa*
imperfect: *es lasīju, tu lasīji*, etc.
future: *es lasīšu, tu lasīsi, viņš lasīs*, etc.

Compound tenses: *es esmu lasījis* 'I have been and still am reading'
past: *es biju lasījis* 'I had been reading' (before something else happened)
future: *es būšu lasījis* 'I shall have read'

Negative: *ne* is prefixed to finite verb forms and takes the stress: e.g. *es nélasu*; *es négribu strādāt* 'I don't want to work'.

Debitive mood: here, Latvian has one form for all persons – the third person indicative with the prefix *jā-*. The logical subject is in the dative: e.g. *man jālasa grāmata* 'I have to read a/the book', where *grāmata* is in the nominative case. The accusative might be expected here, and this is indeed the case when the object is a first or second personal pronoun: e.g. *viņai **mani** jāredz* 'he has to see me'.

Relative: here also, there is one form for all persons, *-(š)ot*: e.g. *Jānis esot slims* 'it is said/they say that Janis is ill';

(*Viņš*) *šodien aizbraucot* 'He's supposed to be leaving today'

(*Viņš*) *ritu aizbraukšot* 'He's supposed to be leaving tomorrow'

Reflexive mood: the infinitive has the ending *-ties*: e.g. *mazgāt* 'to wash': *mazgāties* 'to wash oneself'.

Prepositions

In the singular, prepositions follow the genitive, dative, or accusative, these reducing to the dative in the plural: cf. *aiz upes* (gen.) 'across the river'; *caur mežu* (acc.) 'through the forest'; but, *aiz upiem* 'across the rivers'; *caur mežiem* 'through the forests', where both *upiem* and *mežiem* are in the dative.

Word order

SVO.

1 Iesākumā bija Vārds, un Vārds bija pie Dieva, un Vārds bija Dievs.

2 Tas bija iesākumā pie Dieva.

3 Caur viņu viss ir radies, un bez viņa nekas nav radies, kas ir.

4 Viņā bija dzīvība, un dzīvība bija cilvēku gaisma.

5 Gaisma spīd tumsībā, bet tumsība to neuzņēma.

6 Nāca cilvēks, Dieva sūtīts, vārdā Jānis.

7 Viņš nāca liecības dēļ, lai liecinātu par gaismu, lai visi nāktu pie ticības caur viņu.

8 Viņš pats nebija gaisma, bet nāca, lai liecinātu par gaismu.

LAZ

INTRODUCTION

Laz belongs to the Kartvelian (South Caucasian) group of languages. It is sometimes, especially in Soviet linguistic parlance, linked with Mingrelian under the title 'Zan' (*see* **Mingrelian**). There are about 50,000 speakers of Laz on the Black Sea coast between Trabzon and Batumi, plus a few hundred in the Adzhar Autonomous Soviet Socialist Republic. Laz is unwritten.

PHONOLOGY

Like Mingrelian, Laz adds a glottal stop to the Georgian inventory (*see* **Georgian**).

MORPHOLOGY AND SYNTAX

Largely as in Mingrelian. Laz does not possess the destinative and translative cases present in Mingrelian.

As in Mingrelian, use of the ergative marker is found in cases which depart significantly from the Georgian norm. But whereas in Mingrelian the role of the ergative has been diluted by extension to all aorist tenses, whether transitive or intransitive, in Laz the spread is to all tenses of transitive verbs, not only to the aorist series. The position with regard to ergativity in the three languages can be summed up as follows:

> Georgian norm: the subject of aorist tenses of transitive verbs is in the ergative case.
> Mingrelian extension: the ergative marker is used for the subject of any aorist form, whether transitive or intransitive.
> Laz extension: the ergative marker is used as subject marker, not only for the aorist series but for any tense of a transitive verb.

See Hewitt (1981: 224).

LEGZI

INTRODUCTION

Lezgi belongs to the Lezgian group of Dagestani languages, and is spoken by between 300,000 and 400,000 people in the south-east of the Dagestan Autonomous Soviet Socialist Republic, and in northern Azerbaydzhan. From the Mongol occupation to the establishment of Russian rule in 1812, the Lezgis formed part of various Khanates. There are three main dialects: Kiurin – the basis for the standard literary language – Samur, and Kuba. The Lezgi press dates from the 1920s. There is some original writing (Süleyman of Stal, who died in 1937, is the best-known poet), and at present the language is used for local broadcasting and journalism.

SCRIPT

Arabic script was used to some extent before 1928, when romanization was introduced for a trial period of ten years. Since 1939, Cyrillic + *I*.

PHONOLOGY

Consonants

Typical for the labial, dental, and velar series is the sequence voiced stop – unaspirated voiceless stop – aspirated voiceless – ejective: e.g. in the labial series: /b, ph p p'/. The uvular series is similar, except that the voiced stop is missing. There is a glottal stop.

affricates: ts, tsh, ts'; tʃ, tʃh, tʃ'
fricatives: f, v/w, s, z, ʃ, ʒ, j, x, ʁ, χ, h
nasals: m, n
lateral and flap: l, r

Most of the stops and spirants, both aspirates and non-aspirates, can be labialized: e.g. /t°, th°, t'°/. Secondary articulation of this nature brings the Lezgi consonantal inventory to at least 60 phonemes. Voiced consonants alternate with their unvoiced counterparts.

In this article, the ejectives are marked with a subscript dot.

Vowels

The five basic vowels are:

a, i, e, u, y

These occur palatalized: /ya, yu, yo/, etc., and nasalized (final -*n* then tends to zero). /o/ and /ɪ/ are found in Russian loan-words. Vowels tend to be reduced in non-stressed position. /y/ is notated here as *ü*.

VOWEL HARMONY

Occurs in formation of plural and of oblique cases: cf. *tam* 'forest', pl. *tamar*; *qil* 'head', pl. *qiler*; *çut* 'flea', erg. *çutra*; *γed* 'fish', erg. *γetre*.

Stress

Stress tends to second syllable of word; not on certain inflectional endings.

MORPHOLOGY AND SYNTAX

Noun

In striking contrast to many of the Dagestani languages, Lezgi has no nominal class system. At most, *d* appears as a petrified class marker in the numerals.

NUMBER

The plural formant is -*ar/er*, depending on vowel harmony.

CASE

There are 18 cases, four basic: nominative, ergative, genitive, dative. The remaining cases form the spatio-temporal/rest vs motion grid found in many Caucasian languages.

The basic endings are nominative Ø, ergative -*di* (with many variants). The ergative ending is the base for the genitive (adds -*n*) and dative (adds -*z*): e.g. *balҟan* 'horse', erg. *balҟandi*, gen. *balҟandin*, dat. *balҟandiz*. The subject of transitive verbs is in the ergative case.

The Lezgi mapping of spatial relations is very close to that of Avar: five referential frames – which we might label the 'near' (ending in -*v*), the 'behind' (in -*q*), the 'underneath' (in -*k*), the 'inside' (in -*da*), and the 'upon' (in -*dal*) classes – provide five shades of locative, five ablatives, and four aditives. Formally, all of these cases are based on the ergative. The endings given in parentheses above are the locatives; a typical ablative ending is -*ai*, aditive -*di*. For example, the first referential frame applied to the word *dide* 'mother' (cf. **Georgian**) is: locative *did.di.v*; ablative *dide.di.v.ai*; aditive *dide.di.v.di*.

Over and above their basic spatial meanings, several of these forms are used as objects of certain verbs, e.g. affective verbs; e.g. the ablative of the third (-*k*) series: *buba.di.k.ai kiçeda* 'is afraid of father'.

An extension of the use of the dative as subject of affective verbs and verbs of perception: *buba.di.z. mašin akuna* 'father saw the car'. Similarly, the ablative of the first (*-v*) series is used as the subject of potential verbs: *buba.di.v.ai čar ḳeliz xana* 'Father was able to read the letter' (*čar* 'letter'; *ḳelun* 'to read').

POSSESSION
Possessor precedes, e.g. *buba.di.n balḳan* 'father's horse'.

Adjective

Primary or noun stem in genitive case; declined only when used substantively – then in all cases: e.g. *qsan ḳval* 'fine house'; *čexi qvan* 'big stone'; *qülün fu* 'wheaten bread'.

Pronoun

PERSONAL

	Singular	Plural
1	zun	čun
2	vun	kün
3	am	abur

These are declined: e.g. for *zun*: erg. *za*, gen. *zin*, dat. *zaz.* + spatial cases.

DEMONSTRATIVE PRONOUN
i 'this', *a* 'that', *aṭa* 'that further away'; declined. As in Avar, there are forms specifying relative altitude: *vini* 'that up there', *aha* 'that down there'.

INTERROGATIVE PRONOUN
wuž 'who?'; *vuč̆h* 'what?'; declined.

Numerals

1–10: *sad, qved, pud, qud, vad, rugud, irid, müžüd, ḳüd, çud.* 11 *çusad*; 12 *çiqved*; 20 *qad*; 30 *qani çud*; 40 *yaxçur*; 60 *pudqad*; i.e. the decades are vigesimal. 100 *viš.*

Verb

Lezgi has primary, derivative – formed with a large inventory of pre-verbs – and composite verbs, the latter using two auxiliaries: *xun* 'to be', *avun* 'to do'. The root is neutral as to voice. Verbs are marked for mood and tense, not for person or number.
   The main forms are:

> Verbal noun (masdar), e.g. *atun* 'to come', *fin* 'to go'. These are declined as nouns.
> Purposive form: made from the verbal noun by affixing -V*z* to stem minus *-un*, e.g. *acuqun* 'to sit', verbal noun *acuqiz*: e.g. *buba xeb qačuz fena* 'father went to buy a sheep'.

Participle: *-ur/ür/ai* (with variants) added to stem, e.g. *akun* 'to see', *akur*.
Imperative: *-z* of purposive replaced by *-n*, e.g. *açuqin* 'sit down!'. The
negative form of this mood is in *-mir*, e.g. *qüremir* 'don't laugh!'
Basic past tense: *-Vna* is added to stem.

Tenses are formed from two bases – the purposive and the basic past.

(a) From purposive: seven tenses, the most important of which are:

present: purposive form combined with either *ava* 'to be', or *ama* 'continue
to be': e.g. *ayal ksanama* 'the child is still sleeping' (*ksun* 'to sleep');
future: purposive ending *-Vz → -da*: e.g. *Paka čun šeherdiz fida* 'Tomorrow
we shall go to town' (*fin* 'to go');
past imperfect: present in *-ava + -i*, e.g. *Ayalar ḳvale quyvazvai* 'The
children were playing at home' (*quyun* 'to play').

(b) From basic past: e.g. basic past + *ava*: *am školadiz fenva* 'he went to school'.
A perfective form is made from the participle + *-a*: e.g. *ṭür* 'eaten': *ṭüra* 'ate up'.
Gerund: *-la* is added to participle or past tense, e.g. *zun sobraniedai xtaila ...* 'on
my getting back from the meeting ...'.

NEGATION

By prefixed *t-*: for non-finite forms, e.g. *avun* 'to do', *tavun* 'not do'. The auxiliary
may be negated: e.g. *ksun* 'to sleep' – *ksun tavun* 'not to sleep'. For finite forms,
by suffixed *-č/-čir*: e.g. *fizva* 'come(s)' – *fizvač* 'doesn't/don't come'; *fizvai* 'went'
– *fizvačir* 'didn't go'.

Postpositions

These are virtually all nominal derivatives, e.g. from *vil* 'eye' is derived *vilik* 'in
front of': e.g. *stoldin vilik* 'in front of the table'.

Word formation

By suffixation or compounding.

Word order

SOV is normal.

LITHUANIAN

INTRODUCTION

Lithuanian belongs to the Baltic branch of Indo-European. The total number of speakers, including the sizeable emigré communities in Canada, the USA, and elsewhere, is probably over 3 million. Both phonologically and morphologically the language is of extreme complexity and remarkably archaic.

There are two main dialectal divisions: *žemait* or Lower Lithuanian, and *aukštait* or Upper (High) Lithuanian. The sixteenth century saw the beginnings of Lithuanian literature in the shape of religious and devotional writings. The great landmark in the development of the literary language is the publication in 1818 of the rural epic poem *Metai* ('The Seasons') by K. Donelaitis. The modern literary language is based on the aukštait dialect. Writing in all genres flourished during the period of independence between the wars, and continues up to a point in emigré circles.

SCRIPT

Gothic until the twentieth century; thereafter Roman alphabet + *š, ž, č,* and diacritics: cedilla, superscript dot on *ė,* and macron on *ū. Q* and *w* are not used.

PHONOLOGY

Consonants

    stops: p, b, t, d, k, g
    affricates: ts, tʃ, dʒ, dz
    fricatives: f, v, s, z, ʃ, ʒ, x, ɣ, j
    nasals: m, n
    lateral and flap: l, r

All consonantal phonemes except *j* have palatalized (soft) allophones: [p'], [b'], etc., which are used before the front series vowels, /iː, i, eː, æ, ɛ/. Palatalized /l/ is [l], non-palatalized /l/ is [ɫ]. In a cluster C_1C_2 before a soft vowel, both C_1 and C_2 are palatalized, and C_2 determines the quality of C_1: e.g. *vežti* 'to lead' = [v'ɛšt'i]. Alternation of stem consonants is found throughout the inflectional system.

817

Vowels

front: i, iː, eː, æː, ɛ
back: a, aː, ɔ, oː, u, uː

Stress and pitch

In Lithuanian, dynamic stress is morphophonemically coupled with tone (or pitch). There are three kinds of pitch intonation, notated for reference in Lithuanian dictionaries by grave, circumflex, and acute, though not so marked in Lithuanian texts. The grave occurs with short vowels only; the other two intonations are associated with long vowels and diphthongs, the first of two moras being stressed for the acute (falling) intonation, the second for the circumflex (rising) intonation.

MORPHOLOGY AND SYNTAX

Noun

Inflectional endings in Lithuanian can be sub-divided into two classes: (a) those that attract stress, and (b) those that do not, or which deflect stress to the stem. On the basis of these complex factors, four classes of nouns and adjectives are distinguished: one class has fixed stress throughout on stem syllable; in the other three classes, stress/tone is free, shifting from stem to ending and vice versa in certain fixed patterns. An additional complication is the presence of five declensions. Together, pitch/stress class and declension type prescribe the paradigm for any given noun. Thus, *mēdis* 'tree', for example, is a pitch/stress class 2 noun inflected according to the first declension; *akìs* 'eye', is a class 4 noun inflected according to the third declension.

There follow two specimen declensions: *výras* 'man': pitch class 1, first declension and *sesuõ* 'sister': pitch class 3, fifth declension.

	Singular	*Plural*	*Singular*	*Plural*
nominative	výras	vírai	sesuõ	sēserys
genitive	výro	výru	seseĩs	seserų̃
dative	výrui	výrams	sēseriai	seserìms
accusative	výrą	výrus	sēserį	sēseris
instrumental	výru	výrais	sēseria	seserimìs
locative	výre	výruose	seseryjè	seserysè

Dual forms are found following the numeral *du/dvi* '2', and in some dialects. The genitive case is used after negated verb: e.g. *nebuvo knygų* 'there were no books'; and in a partitive sense: e.g. *Žveryne buvo meškų iř kitų žverių* 'In the zoo were bears and other animals'.

Adjective

The attributive adjective precedes its noun and agrees with it in gender, number, and case. The adjective may be indefinite or definite, this latter possibility compensating for the absence of a definite article: e.g.

> *balta knyga* '(a) white book'; *baltoji knyga* 'the (specific) white book'; *didis šuõ* '(a) big dog'; *didỹsis šuo* 'the/that big dog'.

COMPARATIVE

A comparative is made with *-esnis*, fem. *-esne*: e.g. *gēras* [g'aras] 'good': comp. *gerèsnis/gerèsne* (fully declined).

Pronoun

The personal pronouns have singular, dual, and plural forms; they are: 1 *aš – mudu – mēs*; 2 *tu – judu – jūs*; 3 masc. *jis – juõdu – jiẽ*; fem. *ji – jiẽdvi – jõs*. All of these are declined in six cases; the oblique base of first singular is *man-*.

POSSESSIVE PRONOUN/ADJECTIVE

This is indeclinable: sing. *mano – tavo – jõ/jĩs*; pl. *mūsu – jūsu – jŲ*.

DEMONSTRATIVE PRONOUN/ADJECTIVE

Threefold distinction by relative distance: *šis – ši – šiẽ/šiõs* 'this, these'; *tas – ta – tiẽ/tõs* 'that, those'; *anas – ana – aniẽ/anõs* 'that, those yonder'. These are declined in six cases.

INTERROGATIVE PRONOUN

kas 'who, what?', declined for case, not for gender/number. *Kas* is also a relative pronoun, and there are several others which are used in both capacities: *koks*, *kuris*, *katras*, *keliñtas*, etc. Apart from *kas*, these have feminine forms: e.g. *Aš mataũ stãlą, añt kuriõ guli knyga* 'I see a table on which lies a book'; *Mán patiñka tà knygà, kurią̃ tù mán daveĩ* 'I like the book which you gave me.'

Numerals

1–9: these agree with noun in gender, number, and case. The base (masc. nom.) forms are: *vienas, du, trỹs, keturi, penki, šeši, septyni, aštuoni, devyni*; 10 *dēšimt*; 11 *vienuolika*; 12 *dvylika*; 13 *trylika*; 20 *dvidešimt*; 30 *trisdešimt*; 100 *šiṁtas*.

Verb

Lithuanian verbs are perfective or imperfective. In general, perfective verbs have prefixes, but there are exceptions e.g. *gimti* 'to be born', *miřti* 'to die', are perfective; and *suprasti* 'to understand', is an example of an imperfective verb with a prefix.

Three forms are basic: (a) the infinitive minus the *-ti* ending: this is the so-called indefinite form; (b) the third person present indicative stem; (c) the third person past indicative stem. These may be identical (apart from tonal shift) as in e.g. *gyventi* 'to live': (a) *gyvén-*; (b) *gyvēn-*; (c) *gyvēn-*. Or they may vary, as in *eīti* 'to go': (a) *eī-*; (b) *eīn-*; (c) *ēj-*.

There are three conjugations, the criterion being the third person present indicative ending: 1 *-a*, e.g. *dìrba* 'he works'; 2 *-i*, e.g. *mýli* 'he loves'; 3 *-o*, e.g. *móko* 'he teaches'.

The verbal system further comprises: two voices (active and passive), four moods (indicative, imperative, subjunctive, optative), and an array of tenses – 11 in the indicative – both simple and compound. There are also two infinitives, several participles, and a supine. The system will be illustrated here by the following forms: finite forms in first person singular and plural + nominative singular and plural masculine participial forms in the compound tenses. The verb is *dirbti* 'to work', which is a first conjugation verb. The auxiliary forms are from *būti* 'to be':

> simple present: *dìrbu, dìrbame*
> past frequentative: *dìrb**da**vau, dìrb**da**vome*
> simple preterite: *dìrbau, dìrbome*
> perfect: *esù dìrbęs, ēsame dìrbę*
> future: *dìrbsiu, dìrbsime*
> future perfect: *bū́siu dìrbęs, bū́sime dìrbę*
> pluperfect: *buvaũ dìrbęs, bùvome dìrbę*
> progressive past: *buvaũ bedirbą̃s, bùvome bedirbą̃* (+ two other progressive tenses)

subjunctive:

> present: *dìrbčiau, dìrbtume*
> perfect: *bū́čiau dìrbęs, bū́tume dìrbę*
> imperative: *dìrbk* (2nd sing.), *dìrbkite* (2nd pl.)
> optative: *te-* is prefixed to third person form: *te.dirba*.

participles: e.g.

> present active: *dirbą̃s*, pl. *dìrbą*; passive: *dìrbamas, dirbamì*
> past active: *dìrbęs*, pl. *dìrbę*; passive: *dìrbtas, dirbtì*
> future active: *dìrbsiąs*, pl. *dìrbsią*; passive: *dìrbsimas, dirbsimì*

Reflexive verbs: the marker is *-s(i)*: this is inserted in compound verbs between prefix and stem: e.g. *aš sutinku* 'I meet'; *mēs susitinkame* 'I meet with somone, we meet'.

Negation: *ne-* is prefixed to the affirmative form: e.g. *aš nevalgau* 'I don't eat'.

Participles are widely used to express inferential/impersonal/reported speech: e.g. *Traukinỹs išeīnąs septiñtą̃ vãlandą* 'The train is due to leave at 7'; *Mokytojas sāko, kad mokinỹs ḗsąs gabus* 'The teacher said that the pupil was gifted.'

PUSDALYVIS

This participial form expresses concomitant action by the subject of the principal clause: the form is in *-dam-* + *as/a* and is inflected for gender and number, not case: e.g. *Išeĩdamas profesorius pamiřšo ākinius* 'Going out, the professor forgot his glasses'; *Priẽš išeĩdamas paskam̃bink man* 'Before you go out give me a ring.'

PADALYVIS

This participial form expresses action by other than the subject of the principal clause. Its own subject is in the dative. The present form is in *-ant/-int*, the past in *-ius*: e.g. *aũšrai* (or *dienai*) *aũštant* 'as it is dawning' (*aušra* 'dawn'); *Sutēmus oras atšālo* 'As darkness fell, it grew colder' (*sutemti* 'to darken'; *atšalti* 'to turn colder').

Prepositions

Prepositions govern the genitive, the accusative, or the instrumental. Some take more than one case; *põ*, for example, is used with all three: e.g. *vaikščioti põ mišką* 'to go for a walk in the forest' (acc.); *põ žiemõs* 'after the winter' (gen.).

Word order

SVO; in the genitive relationship, possessor precedes possessed: e.g. *brólis knygà* 'the brother's book'; *Lietuvõs sóstine* 'the capital of Lithuania'; *miẽsto centrè* 'in the middle of the town'.

Pradžioje buvo Žodis, ir (tas) Žodis buvo prie Dievo, ir Dievas buvo (tas) Žodis.

2. Tasai buvo pradžioje prie Dievo.

3. Visi daiktai per tą daryti yra, ir be to nieko niera daryta, kas daryta yra.

4. Jame buvo gyvastis, ir gyvastis buvo šviesybė žmonių.

5. Ir šviesybė tam̃sybėje šviečia, bet tamsybė tai ne permanė.

6. Buvo žmogus, Dievo siųstas, Jonas vardu.

7 Tas atėjo liudymui, apie šviesybę liudyti, kad jie visi per jį tikėtų.

8. Jis ne buvo šviesybe, bet jeib liudytų apie šviesybę.

LIV

See **Balto-Finnic Languages**.

LUSATIAN

INTRODUCTION

Lusatian is also known as Sorbian or Wendish; the ethnonym is *Serbja*. The language, which belongs to the Slavonic branch of Indo-European, is spoken in two main dialects, each with a literary standard: Upper and Lower Lusatian (Hornjo- and Dolnoserbski). The Lusatian homeland – Łužica (Lausitz) – lies on the upper reaches of the Spree in Germany, centring on the towns of Budyšin (Bautzen) and Chošebuz (Cottbus), both largely German in population, language, and culture. A hundred years ago, around 180,000 Lusatians spoke their language; today the estimated number of speakers is 75,000, none of whom are monoglot. The German constitution recognizes Lusatian as a minority language, and it is used in primary education, publishing, and local broadcasting. The process of Germanization, completed in the towns, is, however, gradually spreading to the Lusatian countryside.

The oldest records of writing in Lusatian date from the sixteenth century, with Bible translations appearing from the seventeenth century onwards. A considerable literature in prose and verse was produced throughout the nineteenth and early twentieth centuries.

SCRIPT

Roman with diacritics for specifically Lusatian sounds.

PHONOLOGY

Consonants

    stops: p, b, t, d, k, g; p and b occur palatalized: p', b'
    affricates: ts, tʃ, dʒ
    fricatives: f, s, z, ʃ, ʒ, x, h
    nasals: m, n, ɲ
    laterals: l, ł
    roll: r, r'
    semi-vowels: j, w

ř is pronounced as /ʃ/ after *k*, *p*, and as /s/ after *t*. Aspirated *k'* [kh], occurs initially.

Vowels

a, ε, i, ɪ, ɔ, u

Palatalized *e* = /ɪε/; labialized *o* = /ʷɔ/. All short.

Stress

On first syllable; moves to a preposition preceding mono- and disyllables.

MORPHOLOGY AND SYNTAX

Noun

Three genders, three numbers: the dual is preserved in noun, pronoun, verb. The animate/inanimate distinction affecting the accusative of masculine nouns is observed in all three numbers.

DECLENSION

The majority of Lusatian nominals are

(a) *-i* stems, feminine: e.g. *kósć* 'bone', *lubosć* 'love', *nóc* 'night' (*ó* = /u/);
(b) *-a* stems, mostly feminine: e.g. *žona* 'woman', *zemja* 'earth', *duša* 'soul';
(c) *-o* stems, masculine and neuter: e.g. *nan* 'father', *dub* 'oak', *mječ* 'sword'.

A specimen of declension is *nan* 'father':

	Singular	Dual	Plural
nom.	nan	nanaj	nanojo
gen.	nana	nanow	nanow
dat.	nanej	nanomaj	nanam
acc.	nana	nanow	nanow
instr.	nanom	nanomaj	nanami
loc.	nanje	nanomaj	nanach
voc.	nano	nanaj	nanojo

In the inanimate masculine declension, the accusative has the same form as the nominative, not genitive as in the animate specimen given above.

The instrumental requires a preposition, as does the locative (*see* **Prepositions**).

Adjective

Divided into hard stems in *-y*, e.g. *dobry* 'good', and soft stems in *-i*, e.g. *lětni* 'summer-'. As attribute precedes noun; concord throughout.

POSSESSIVE ADJECTIVES

based on masculine stems: *-owy*, *-owa*, *-owe*;
based on feminine stems: *-iny*, *-ina*, *ine*: e.g. *sotřina kniha* 'sister's book'.

COMPARISON

The comparative is formed with -(*i*)*ši*. Palatalization of final stem consonant e.g. *t, d*: *čisty* 'clean': *čisćiši*; *hordy* 'proud': *hordžiši*.

Pronoun

PERSONAL

Full forms (nom.) and base forms for oblique cases:

		Singular		Dual		Plural	
		Full	*Base*	*Full*	*Base*	*Full*	*Base*
nom.	1	ja	mn-	mój	na-	my	na-
	2	ty	te-	wój	wa-	wy	wa-
	3	wón				woni	
		wona	je-, ni-	wonaj	je-, ni-	wone	je-, ni-
		wono					

These are declined in all cases, e.g. for *ja*: *mnje, mi, mnje, mnu, mni*.

DEMONSTRATIVE PRONOUN

tón, ta, to 'this'; dual: *taj, tej, tej*; pl. *ći, te, te*; *wony, wona, wone* 'that'. These have emphatic forms: e.g. for *tón*: *tutón, tónle*.

INTERROGATIVE PRONOUN

štó 'who?'; *što* 'what?'

RELATIVE PRONOUN

kotryž/kotraž/kotrež; *kiž* may be used for all three genders.

Numerals

1 is marked for gender: *jedyn, jedna, jedno*: declined. 2 *dwaj* (masc.), *dwě* (fem., neut.); animate/inanimate distinction in masculine accusative. 3 *tři* (fem., neut.), *třo* (masc.; acc. *třoch*). 4 *štyri* (fem., neut.), *štyrjo* (masc.; acc. *štyrjoch*). 5–10: *pjeć, šesć, sydom, wosom, dźewjeć, dźesać*. These are optionally declined with specific masculine forms. 11 *jědnaće*, 12 *dwanaće*; 20 *dwaceći*; 30 *třiceći*; 100 *sto*.

Verb

As in the nominal and pronominal systems, Lusatian preserves the dual throughout the verbal system. The verbal paradigm is further complicated by the presence of an aorist and an imperfect tense. The verb is marked for aspect, voice, mood, tense, number, person, and, in part, for gender (e.g. in past active and passive participles, and in second and third person dual).

The perfective aspect is formed from the imperfective:

(a) by prefix: *pisać* 'to write', perf. *napisać*; *pić* 'to drink', perf. *wupić*;
(b) by change of ending: e.g. *padać* 'to fall', perf. *padnyć*;
(c) by suppletion: *brać* 'to take', perf. *wzać*.

There are indicative and imperative moods; the tense system includes present, imperfect, aorist, and future forms. The present form of perfective verbs is future in meaning. The infinitive is in -ć.

As in Czech, verbs are usefully classified by the characteristic vowel linking the stem to the personal endings: this criterion gives -(j)e, -nje, -a, and -i classes. For example, the personal endings for the present tense of the -a stem wołać (imperfective) 'to call', are:

	Singular	Dual	Plural
1	wołam	wołamoj	wołamy
2	wołaš	wołataj/wołatej	wołaće
3	woła	Ø	wołaja

The first dual second person form is for masculine, the second for feminine and neuter.

The imperfect tense is formed from imperfective verbs: e.g. wołach 'I was calling'; dual, 1st p. wołachmoj; pl. 1st p. wołachmy.

The aorist has the same endings as the imperfect but is made from perfective verbs: e.g. zawołach 'I called'; napisach 'I wrote'.

The imperfective future is made with the future tense of the auxiliary być 'to be' + the imperfective infinitive: e.g. budu wołać 'I'll call'.

Compound past tense: present tense of być + -ł participle declined for gender and number: e.g. sym wołał/a 'I have called'; smój wołałoj 'we two (masc.) have called'.

Conditional: conditional of być + -ł form: e.g. bych wołał/a 'I would call'.

Imperative: formed for second singular, first and second person dual and plural: e.g. bjer 'take!'; kuptaj '(you two, masc.) buy!'; stańce 'get up!'

Non-finite forms: an invariable present gerund in -(j)o is formed from imperfective verbs, e.g. njeso 'carrying'; the past gerund in -(w)ši is formed from perfective verbs, e.g. nabrawši 'having taken'. A present participle active in -acy, -aca, -ace is marked for gender, number, and case, and acts as a relative phrase: e.g. njesacy '(... who (masc.) is) carrying'.

Negation

Nje is prefixed to verb and takes the stress.

Prepositions

Prepositions govern accusative, dative, genitive, instrumental, and locative cases. As noted above, the latter two cases can only be used with a preposition.

For example:

> *do* + gen.: *Jan chodźi do šule* 'John goes to school/into the school'; *hić do džěła* 'to go to work';
>
> *bjez* + gen.: *budź bjez starosće* 'don't worry';
>
> *pola* + gen.: *pola nas doma* 'chez nous' (i.e. 'at our house');
>
> *w(e)* + loc.: *w stwě* 'in the room'; *čłowjek w přirodźe* 'man in nature';
>
> *z* + instr.: *z nanom na polo hić* 'to go with father into the country'.

Word order

Rather free: SVO is normal.

> We sachopeńu běscho to słowo, a to słowo běscho podlá Boga, a Bog běscho to słowo.
>
> 2. To same běscho we sachopeńu podlá Boga.
>
> 3. Schykne wězy su pshes to same huzyńone, a bzes togo samego ńejo ńiz huzyńone, zož zyńone jo.
>
> 4. We ńom běscho zywene, a to zywene běscho to swětło tych złowekow.
>
> 5. A to swětło swěschi we tej schámnoscźi, a ta schámnoscz ńejo jo hopschiměła.
>
> 6. Złowek běscho wot Boga posłany s'měnom Jan.
>
> 7. Ten pschize k'snankstwu, aby wot togo swětła snańił, aby schykne pshes ńogo wěrili.
>
> 8. Ten samy ńeběscho to swětło, ale aby won snańił wot togo swětła.

LYDIAN

See **Anatolian Languages**.